St. Marys PA
May 6, 2011

ONE CONTINUOUS FIGHT

The Retreat from Gettysburg and the Pursuit of Lee's Army of Northern Virginia, July 4–14, 1863

Eric J. Wittenberg,
J. David Petruzzi, and Michael F. Nugent

SB
Savas Beatie
New York and California

Cataloging-in-Publication Data is available from the Library of Congress.

ISBN 13: 978-1-932714-43-2

05 04 03 02 01 5 4 3 2 1
Second edition, first printing

SB

Published by
Savas Beatie LLC
521 Fifth Avenue, Suite 3400
New York, NY 10175
Phone: 610-853-9131

Editorial Offices:

Savas Beatie LLC
P.O. Box 4527
El Dorado Hills, CA 95762
Phone: 916-941-6896
(E-mail) editorial@savasbeatie.com

This book is dedicated to the soldiers of both North and South whose Gettysburg
legacy was to be laid in an unknown and long-forgotten
grave along the route of retreat. Family and friends often never
knew what became of their loved ones, and lamented
not having the opportunity to say goodbye.

"Known But To God"

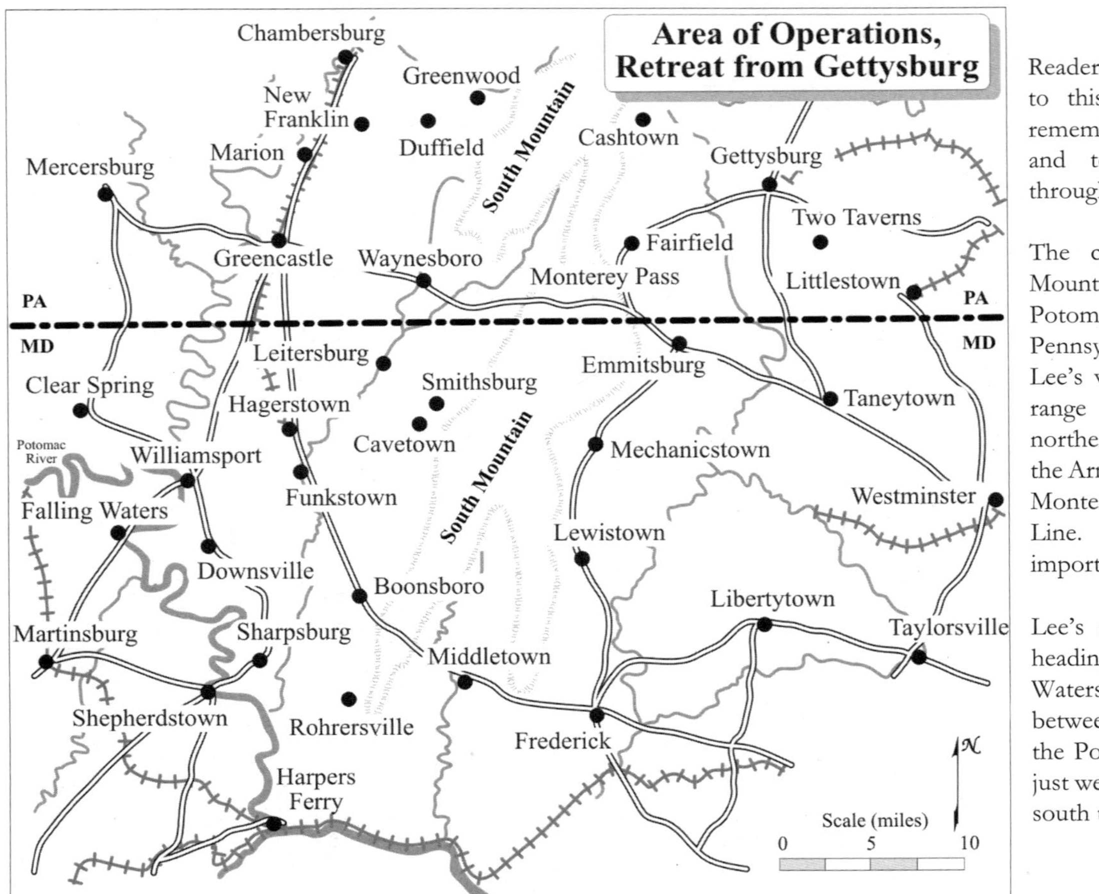

Readers are encouraged to study and refer back to this map in order to understand and remember the relative locations of the towns and terrain features discussed in detail throughout the book.

The critical terrain feature is the South Mountain range, which begins above the Potomac River and runs generally north into Pennsylvania west of Gettysburg. Robert E. Lee's wagon train of wounded traversed the range through the Cashtown Pass near its northern end, while the main components of the Army of Northern Virginia marched via the Monterey Pass just above the Mason-Dixon Line. Control of these passes was vitally important to both sides.

Lee's army and its train of wounded were heading for the Williamsport and Falling Waters crossings to put the Potomac River between them and George G. Meade's Army of the Potomac. Lee's final defensive line began just west of Hagerstown, Maryland, and angled south through Downsville to the river.

Contents

Contents (continued)

Maps

Maps (continued)

Photos and Illustrations

Photos and illustrations have been placed throughout the book for the convenience of the readers.

Foreword

ROBERT E. LEE'S RETREAT from Gettysburg is one of the most misunderstood and least studied events of the Civil War. Much has been written about the prelude to Gettysburg. There have been a number of works on Brandy Station and other cavalry actions that occurred in Virginia before the opposing armies moved north of the Potomac River. The same can be said for Second Winchester and the other actions surrounding that event. One of the best studies of this period remains *Here Come the Rebels!* by Wilbur S. Nye. A seminal work, Nye's book traces in detail the movements of Lee's army from late May to June 30, 1863.

The gold standard for any serious student of the campaign remains Edwin Coddington's *Gettysburg: A Study in Command.* Coddington's work has stood the test of time. It remains the most recommended single volume on the campaign by Gettysburg park rangers and battlefield guides. While Coddington produced a thorough study of the campaign and battle, his coverage of the retreat is thin at best. The reason is that Dr. Coddington was dying of cancer when he wrote the final part of the book. Although it contains much useful data and insights—particularly on Federal commander George G. Meade's generalship during this period—it lacks the depth found in other parts of his book.

Other writers have attempted to address the retreat from Gettysburg. One of the first modern Civil War writers to devote a book to the subject was John W. Schildt. The author of numerous books on Antietam and Gettysburg, Schildt's *Roads from Gettysburg* appeared in 1979 and was reissued in a revised edition in 1999. It is a good read with anecdotal references from diaries and regimental histories. These sources, combined with a stirring narrative, offer readers a good sense of what the retreat was like for the common soldier.

However, Schildt's book is short on analysis and context, which makes it difficult to figure out the "big picture" scenario of what was transpiring on the way back to Virginia.

In 1986, prolific Civil War author Edward G. Longacre published *The Cavalry at Gettysburg: A Tactical Study of Mounted Operations during the Civil War War's Pivotal Campaign, 9 June –14 July, 1863.* This award-winning and solidly researched and detailed study was well received by students of the war, but its weakest coverage was the retreat from the battlefield. Certain accounts of the retreat, particularly dealing with the routes to the Potomac River, appear to have confused Longacre. He is in good company on that score.

I believe that some of the confusion concerning the retreat routes from Gettysburg stems from the maps and text found in *The West Point Atlas of the Civil War.* On one of the maps, the wagon train of wounded protected by Confederate cavalry under John Imboden winds its way to Chambersburg and then south to Hagerstown via Greencastle. Other maps show the train leaving the Chambersburg Pike to head to Waynesboro, and then to Greencastle and Hagerstown. Nearly every historian has continued to use these erroneous routes in their writings. Imboden's own story of the wagon train, published in several postwar magazine articles, as well as numerous eyewitness civilian accounts, confirm the cross-country trek taken through Franklin County, Pennsylvania. I traced the route in my automobile more than two decades ago using old county maps as my guide. Relic hunters at different points along the way have uncovered an array of abandoned artifacts, including bullets, artillery shells, personal items, and more. These finds help confirm the actual path traversed by Imboden's train.

I would be remiss if I did not mention a few other "Retreatistas" out there seeking the "truth" as they see it regarding this neglected subject. In 1999, I had the honor to be the guest editor of a special edition of *North and South Magazine* entitled "The Retreat From Gettysburg." Eric Wittenberg contributed a splendid piece on the Battle of Monterey Pass and two other hardcore "Retreatistas," Steve French and Kent Masterson Brown, also contributed to this issue. Steve, one of the leading gurus on Confederate cavalryman John Imboden and the wagon train of wounded, wrote on that subject. Kent did a solid piece of work on General Lee's defenses at Falling Waters. In 2005, Kent published *Retreat from Gettysburg: Lee, Logistics and the Pennsylvania Campaign*, one of the finest logistical studies ever written.

Now, let me turn to Wittenberg and his company of "Retreatistas," J. David Petruzzi and Michael F. Nugent, and their book *One Continuous Fight: The*

Retreat From Gettysburg and the Pursuit of Lee's Army of Northern Virginia, July 4 - 14, 1863. I have known Eric as a fellow Civil Warrior, colleague, and a good friend for more than a dozen years, and am well aware of the outstanding reputation of both J. D. and Mike. Together, they utilized the scholarship of the people mentioned above and, more importantly, trekked the back roads with me many times to obtain a firm grasp of the terrain over which the armies maneuvered. To their credit, they also went above and beyond the call, rooting out obscure sources others have missed or ignored. Many of them have never been used in any capacity. It is fair to say that this merry band of Retreatistas has combed the countryside more thoroughly than Albert Jenkins' cavalry to bring their readers scores of previously unpublished soldier accounts of the retreat and extensive fighting encompassed within it.

I opened this Foreword by mentioning familiar names associated with the Gettysburg campaign, such as Brandy Station and Second Winchester. There is also a familiar name associated with the retreat from Gettysburg: Falling Waters. What most students of the Civil War in general, and even Gettysburg in particular, don't know is that there were more than twenty separate combats during the retreat to the Potomac River—in addition to the widely mentioned battle at Falling Waters. *One Continuous Fight*—deeply researched, wonderfully written, and perfectly titled—covers each of these nearly two-dozen combats in meticulous detail. In addition to what is probably the best account of Falling Waters written to date, the efforts of Wittenberg, Petruzzi, and Nugent elevate the actions at Hagerstown, Williamsport, Funkstown, Boonsboro, to the status they have long deserved. They prove conclusively that the old saw "who ever saw a dead cavalryman?" was a lie. One of the most interesting segments of *One Continuous Fight* carries readers into Monterey Pass, where a Medal of Honor was earned. Excepting Gettysburg, the heretofore largely ignored fight was likely the largest and bloodiest Civil War action in Pennsylvania.

The long, exhausting, and bloody retreat proved to be a watershed event for the horse soldiers of both sides. Up until that time, the Union cavalry had frequently been misused as an escort for supply trains and for other miscellaneous duties. At Brandy Station on June 9, 1863, the Union troopers proved they could fight spur-to-spur with Jeb Stuart's Confederate horsemen. The blue horse soldiers were relentless in their pursuit of the Confederates following their defeat at Gettysburg. Indeed, the strike forces of Judson Kilpatrick, John Buford, and David Gregg, sent forth by General George Meade, refused to allow Lee's retreating columns any time to rest and reorganize. For example, at Falling Waters, Union cavalry nearly checkmated

Lee's crossing of the Potomac, capturing more than 1,500 Southern infantry and mortally wounding a division commander, Brigadier General J. Johnston Pettigrew.

From June 15 – July 14, Stuart's cavalry rode farther and fought more individual actions than any other command in the Army of Northern Virginia. For more than a week following the battle of Gettysburg, these same horsemen bore the brunt of combat with their Federal counterparts. While casualty figures are inconclusive for this period, Stuart's cavalry probably lost some 1,000 men killed, wounded, and captured. Hundreds more straggled behind on foot because their horses had worn out. The fighting and hard riding whittled down many commands to the bare bone. Brigadier General Beverly Robertson's brigade, for example, began the campaign with some 900 men; fewer than 300 mounted men crossed the Potomac River on July 14.

Like the historic retreat itself, *One Continuous Fight* boasts surprises of its own. Included within these pages is a large amount of vivid firsthand accounts gleaned from letters and diaries. These exciting eyewitness testimonies illuminate and bring to life the momentous events that unfolded along the roads leading away from Gettysburg. Like all Savas Beatie military titles, this one includes good maps and lots of them. They are critical for understanding the tactical details and wide maneuvering of the two armies.

Continuing and improving upon the tour included in the back of their earlier and related book *Plenty of Blame to Go Around: Jeb Stuart's Controversial Ride to Gettysburg* (Savas Beatie, 2006), Wittenberg, Petruzzi, and Nugent offer a detailed driving and walking tour section that includes one for the retreat, and another for the route of the wagon train of wounded. The icing on the cake is the inclusion of GPS coordinates! These tours alone are worth the price of this book. Be prepared to drive off of the beaten path to places most Civil War students have never seen, let alone visited. Ride with George Custer's Wolverines up Monterey Pass and examine at Smithsburg evidence of the accidental damage wrought by Stuart's Horse Artillery on July 5, 1863. Walk the streets of Hagerstown with this tour in hand, and you will immediately be reminded that this was an urban battlefield where combat devolved into small unit firefights (not unlike what we heard about in our own day at places such as Hue City or Fallujah). Discover on the edge of Funkstown a stone barn surrounded by a stone wall. How many people know that elements of Jenkins' cavalry held off Buford's Yankee troopers there? View barns and farmhouses that bear no markers or monuments, but stand today as mute witness to events such as the mortal wounding of General Pettigrew. Stand at Williamsport on the Potomac shore and read how Richard Ewell's Third Corps made the tedious crossing back into Virginia. Follow Imboden's wagon train of misery through the Pennsylvania countryside, much of which remains unchanged since the days of the Civil War. These are but a few of the delightful gems awaiting you.

One Continuous Fight: The Retreat From Gettysburg and the Pursuit of Lee's Army of Northern Virginia, July 4-14, 1863 is one of the most original, most deeply researched, and most scholarly works to come out on the Civil War in many years. With it, Civil Warriors can finally make some sense out of the tangled series of events that occurred during the ten fateful days following the battle of Gettysburg.

Ted Alexander (El Jefe de Retreatistas)
Chief Historian, Antietam National Battlefield
November 2007

Preface

THE CHRONICLES OF CONFEDERATE General Robert E. Lee versus the Army of the Potomac's commander de jour are filled with dramatic encounters that dominate military histories of the Civil War: Lee versus McClellan, Lee versus Burnside, Lee versus Hooker, Lee versus Meade, and Lee versus Grant. For most students of the conflict, even those with more than a passing interest in the subject, Lee versus Meade means Gettysburg, period. Yet Meade faced Lee on his own hook for nearly nine months—much of it involving active campaigning. Perhaps because the end results were unspectacular, or because they fall between the high points of Gettysburg and Ulysses S. Grant's ascension to overall command, the full Lee versus Meade story has not received the attention it deserves.

There is much to recommend a closer inspection of the military actions in the East immediately after Gettysburg to the start of what became known as the Overland Campaign. Both Lee and Meade faced intense political pressure from their respective capitals and both played a wary, careful game, less willing to risk losing than to gamble everything on winning. Both were impotent onlookers as substantial portions of their armies were taken from them and moved across the chessboards of war to operations in the West, where opportunities for major victory seemed greater. Tragically, each suffered personal blows during this period: Lee the death of his daughter-in-law Charlotte, and Meade the news of a turn for the worse in the health of his son John Sergeant.

Interestingly, each man was moved by a mix of personal motives and professional vexations to proffer their resignation, and in each case the request was refused by their respective commander-in-chief. It is my strong suspicion that were each asked to look back at their actions and decisions during this period, the words "lost opportunities" would figure prominently in their individual self-evaluations.

When it came to handling the often touchy relations with the central government, Robert E. Lee was far more practiced than George G. Meade. By this point in the war Lee had become a master at outlining a course of action that was specific enough to obtain the necessary bureaucratic backing but vague enough to allow him maximum flexibility of action once underway. While this provided Lee with great freedom of maneuver, it also led to serious misunderstandings. For example: Lee always claimed than an important part of his pre-Gettysburg strategy included the establishment of a phantom army corps under P. G. T. Beauregard close enough to Washington to draw to it some of the forces that would otherwise be arrayed against him. Jefferson Davis, whose role it was to implement this plan, was equally adamant that it never existed. Lee was also able to remain aloof from any public scrutiny of his performance. When Davis sent him a clipping from the *Charleston Mercury* that was highly critical of Lee's handling of the Gettysburg campaign, the general refused to answer in kind, stating that to "take notice of such attacks would I think do more harm than good and would be just what is desired."[1]

George Meade, on the other hand, was facing the rough and tumble of the political and media spotlight for the first time. He was uncomfortable around correspondents and suspicious of their motives. The mis-reporting of one of them so offended Meade that, at the end of 1864's Overland Campaign, he had the individual publicly ejected from the army's camps. Perhaps the most emblematic image of Meade's political discomfort is that of him in March, 1864, testifying for three hours in a Capital basement hearing room before an unfriendly U.S. Senator (representing the Committee on the Conduct of the War) concerning the combat decisions he had made—starting with Gettysburg. Throughout his testimony one senses the soul of a fighter caught in the headlights of politics and shifting priorities. His comments regarding the ultimately ineffectual sparring with Robert E. Lee that he had directed through the summer and fall of 1863 are peppered with hints at an aggressiveness not translated into actions: "Every disposition was made for the battle . . . which I believed or hoped would take place," "My desire was to give battle to General Lee," "It not being my desire to avoid a battle, except to avoid it on his terms."[2]

The marching and scrapping that Lee and Meade engaged in between August 1 and November 30, 1863, was not a matter of small skirmishes. Mounted brigades backed by infantry clashed on August 1 near Brandy Station in a reconnaissance that cost Hampton's Carolina-Georgia cavalry brigade nearly half its strength. On October 14, an overeager effort by Lieutenant General A. P. Hill to snag the trailing corps of Meade's withdrawal into Washington's defenses resulted in a debacle at Bristoe Station, where waves of valiant Confederates hurled themselves unsuccessfully against an unbending Union entrenched line resulting in thousands of irreplaceable Rebel casualties.

Less than a month later, on November 7, two poorly positioned Southern brigades were pinned against the river at Rappahannock Station, adding another 2,000 to Lee's losses. Lest it seem that Meade was playing the better hand, there followed events in late November when his all-out effort to break up Lee's reduced army came to naught at Mine Run. Capping this period of military activity was Brigadier General Judson Kilpatrick's ill-starred Richmond raid, a badly bungled operation that Meade termed "a pretty ugly piece of business."[3]

The end of the Lee versus Meade period saw both men worn by the travails of their encounters and mentally preparing for a potentially decisive spring campaign. "This time is coming, indeed has come, when everyone must put out their strength," Lee wrote his son Custis in late March, 1864.[4] "Tomorrow we move," Meade told his wife on May 3. "I hope and trust we will be successful, and so decidedly successful as to bring about a termination of this war."[5]

Scrolling back to the top of this little studied but fascinating period, we find Lee and Meade after Gettysburg trying to divine each other's intentions and move their battered pieces of war in the most effective ways possible. War, however, is not a board game. Also in the mix are the effects of bad weather, the vagaries of differing personalities, and the simple limits of flesh and blood. The full story of the opening gambits of Lee versus Meade after Gettysburg is the subject of this book. Authors Eric J. Wittenberg, J. David Petruzzi, and Michael F. Nugent have brought together an impressive array of primary materials, so that much of the action unfolds in the words of those who were there.

The driving tours accompanying the narrative add an important extra dimension. History is not an armchair pastime, and following in the footsteps of the armies provides wonderful opportunities for a personal linking of yesterday with the present. It opens the way to a vicarious appreciation of how everyday people passed through one of the seminal events in the making of the United States. To stand where they stood, to see something of what they saw, adds immeasurable value to the weight of their words and memories. The authors of this book have taken the time and care to get the story right and the tour directions correct; I encourage you to take full advantage of both.

Noah Andre Trudeau
Washington, D. C.

Introduction

"In advancing he cannot be resisted because he bursts through the enemy's weak points; In withdrawing he cannot be pursued because, being so quick, he cannot be caught."

— Sun-Tzu, *The Art of Warfare*[1]

THERE IS NO BATTLE OF the American Civil War that has been more deeply studied, written about, or debated than that which took place in and around the town of Gettysburg, Pennsylvania, during three sultry summer days in July 1863. Each year, nearly two million people visit the fields, ridges, and hills surrounding the town, a veritable sculpture garden of monuments placed lovingly by veterans and state governments to mark this or that portion of earth emblazoned on their individual and collective memories. A dedicated minority of visitors walk the lesser-seen areas of the battlefield, while most elect to stay on the National Park roads and leave their vehicle only long enough to stand at places made famous in Gettysburg lore—Little Round Top, The High Water Mark, Devil's Den.

The guest of the aura of the Gettysburg battlefield, however, sees only one portion of the grand operation known collectively as The Gettysburg Campaign. Dozens of small skirmishes and several all-out brawls erupted between elements of the two armies both during their advance into Pennsylvania and the subsequent withdrawal from its bloody fields. As the "eyes and ears" of the armies, subsisting and maneuvering in that deadly no-man's land between them, the cavalries of both sides bore the brunt of the fighting during the advance and retreat. For many of those troopers, whether they wore blue or gray, the days following the great battle unveiled some of the most arduous contests they had seen since the war began two summers prior.

Until recently, the subject of the Retreat from Gettysburg claimed very little attention compared to the main battle except for some worthy magazine articles here and there. In 2005, Kent Masterson Brown's seminal work *Retreat From*

Gettysburg: Lee, Logistics, & the Pennsylvania Campaign (Chapel Hill: The University of North Carolina Press, 2005) was released to wide acclaim. Finally, the logistical nightmare of the Army of Northern Virginia's withdrawal of its men, equipment, and wounded from the battlefield received its due.

So how does the book you hold in your hands differ from Brown's? Whereas Brown's book masterfully details and highlights the complex logistical aspects of the Retreat, the main subject of this book concerns the fights and skirmishes, both large and small, that erupted as predator chased still-dangerous prey back to and across the Potomac River. With a combined forty-plus years of studying those ten days following the Gettysburg carnage, we had uncovered scores of "new" untapped resources that much more fully told the stories of the men whose fighting was not nearly finished. It is our humble belief that the combination of these two books gives the reader the *full* story of the Retreat, with each providing its own specialty of purpose.

During the retreat, it was the Confederate cavalry's mission to screen the Southern army's routes of march, secure mountain passes, escort the miles-long wagon train of wounded, and fend off attacks from their counterparts. Before the Potomac River and relative safety could be reached, it was the Union cavalry's duty to break them. Both sides were tenacious in their often-detached and deadly work out in the "no-man's land," leading the 13th Virginia Cavalry's surgeon to write from Hagerstown on July 12, "I have seen very little of the cavalry on this trip. They have always been in advance or on the right or left . . . Our men . . . feel confident of giving the Yankees a whipping if they come up to them."[2]

For most of the troopers of either side, many veterans after two full years of bloody struggle in war-ravaged Virginia, a horrid autumn day of massive casualties at Antietam, and finally ponderous assaults that strew their dead upon the broken land and village streets of south-central Pennsylvania, such whippings were expected. "It was one continuous fight," reported an exhausted Private L. T. Dickinson of Company A of the 1st Maryland (C.S.A.) Cavalry, of the long march from Gettysburg, "and even after that, for we had skirmishes every day."[3]

The names of the places of these fights along the routes of retreat are not nearly as famous as those storied landmarks of the Gettysburg battlefield, but they too yearn to be visited and studied. Their names would ring loud in the memories of the soldiers who clashed with their aggressors there – the Monterey Pass, Raven Rock Road, Hagerstown, Funkstown, Boonsboro, Falling Waters, and Williamsport. For Captain John W. Phillips of the 18th

Pennsylvania Cavalry, the scraps leading up to and following the main battle were the defining contests: "While the Battle of Gettysburg ended, as the shadows of night fell on that memorable day [July 3], to the main body of Meade's Army, to the Cavalry Corps, it did not end. As for the days and weeks *preceding*, so for days and weeks *succeeding*, with the cavalry, that which was really the Gettysburg contest went on."[4]

The Gettysburg Campaign began in June 1863 with the Army of the Potomac and the Army of Northern Virginia staring at each other across the Rappahannock River. On June 9, 12,000 Union cavalrymen and 3,000 infantrymen splashed across the Rappahannock and lit into Jeb Stuart's cavalry in the fields around Brandy Station. A fourteen-hour slugging match ensued that still stands as the greatest cavalry battle in the history of North America. However, for all its majesty and glory, Brandy Station only delayed the advance of Robert E. Lee's army by one day. By July 31, the armies had returned to the same positions from which they had commenced the campaign eight weeks earlier. As a book end to the great battle, another day-long cavalry battle raged over the hills and fields at Brandy Station on August 1.

Most studies of the Gettysburg Campaign end with Robert E. Lee's Army of Northern Virginia crossing the Potomac River on July 14. However, it took the armies another two weeks to reach their original starting positions along the Rappahannock, two weeks of hard marching and severe fighting. More telling is that most of the official reports of the campaign extended all the way to the return to the Rappahannock, meaning that the participants did not believe that the campaign ended with the crossing of the Potomac. Although the detailed tactical narrative contained in this book ends with Lee's crossing the Potomac, an Epilogue provides an overview of the fighting that took place between July 14th and the 31st. In that way, the story of the Gettysburg Campaign is completed.

Follow along with us as we recount the exploits of, primarily, the horsemen of North and South, as well as the infantry and artillerymen, down the routes of retreat from Gettysburg. Wherever possible, we have allowed the soldiers themselves to tell you their own story in their own words. Our narration is intended solely to link together their memories of the nearly two-dozen important engagements and skirmishes of the retreat and clarify the strategic value of each major and minor contest along the way. The concluding chapter explores George Meade's decision not to attack Robert E. Lee's fortified positions near Williamsport, as well as the fallout of that resolve. Finally, driving tours of both the main retreat route and the route of the Wagon Train of

Wounded are included, featuring detailed examinations of the landscapes of these engagements, giving the reader the most important ingredient of all to understanding how and why battles took shape as they did: the terrain. One cannot come to a true understanding of these engagements without first examining the ground itself, nor can one begin to question their logic and form an opinion about the merit (or lack thereof) of each without absorbing the invaluable lessons proffered by the landscape itself.

Readers should take note that the retreat encompassed a swirling, and often confusing, series of marches, skirmishing, and larger engagements. Several actions took place in different areas simultaneously—in addition to the constant movements of many different columns from each army through Pennsylvania and Maryland. In an effort to avoid confusion, in a few instances we have devoted complete chapters to distinct battles and major skirmishes. Throughout the narrative we have endeavored to include sufficient commentary to keep readers on track when different events over two or more chapters occur concurrently, and have included the main date under discussion in each chapter title. Even the driving tours in the back of this book could not be laid out entirely chronologically. Hopefully, all of this will serve as a poignant lesson about just how wide-ranging, disconnected, and uncoordinated the movements and fights (however large or small) were during the retreat from Gettysburg.

Whether the ancient Sun-Tzu envisioned the tactical mind embodied in the persona of a Robert E. Lee or Jeb Stuart while penning his lines is impossible to determine; what is abundantly clear, however, is that the "Gray Fox" and the "Beau Sabreur" skillfully earned their monikers as they maneuvered their army out of the Keystone State and onto familiar soil after the martial butchery at Gettysburg. Likewise clear is that those in command of the bluecoats did their utmost to "catch" them.

Upon no one does more praise belong than the common soldier himself, regardless of the color coat he wore. Here for the first time in so many of their own words ringing loud with the horror of battle, the monotony of inactivity, and the anxiety of impending doom, is their story.

Acknowledgments

As with every project of this magnitude, there are many people to thank. To prepare this book for publication, we spent countless hours retracing the steps of the armies along the retreat route and discussing the subject with many folks over the years, and if we omit someone, please know that it is unintentional.

First and foremost, we thank Ted Alexander, the chief historian at the Antietam National Battlefield. Ted grew up and lives along the retreat route, and is one of the leading scholars of the topic. He is always eager and willing to share his knowledge with students. The driving tours herein are based on tours developed by Ted over the years. Ted also accompanied us along the way and shared many of those obscure details and "tidbits" that add so much to such a story. We were constantly amazed and educated as he pointed out those countless points of interest along the way. He also reviewed the manuscript for us, and graciously wrote the Foreword. We are honored to be counted among Ted's Merry Band of Retreatistas, and we can't thank him enough for all he has done to help us.

D. Scott Hartwig, chief historian at the Gettysburg National Military Park and another scholar of the Retreat, reviewed the manuscript for us. Jeffry D. Wert and Noah Andre (Andy) Trudeau, well-known Civil War historians and authors of fine works of their own on the Battle of Gettysburg, also read through our work, and we are grateful to each of these gentlemen. Ed Coleman drew the fine maps for this book that so indispensably complete the story, and we appreciate his diligence in charting the movements of the armies as they headed for their date with destiny along the banks of the Potomac River.

Dave and Carol Moore generously allowed us to use their lovely home on Herr's Ridge in Gettysburg as our base of operations, which we have long appreciated. Their hospitality and support over the years for our various projects is treasured beyond words. Friends and fellow Gettysburg students Steve Basic, Duane Siskey, Stan O'Donnell, Karl Fauser and Ilona Douglas accompanied us as we drove the highways and back roads of the Retreat routes, offering helpful suggestions and ideas that have made this a much better book. Dimitri Rotov gave us some excellent suggestions to tighten up the analysis set forth in this book's conclusion, and we greatly appreciate his input. Bryce A. Suderow assisted with the research, as did Steve L. Zerbe and Tonia J. "Teej" Smith. Henry E. Persons, Jr. provided us with some very useful material on the role of the Georgia infantry at the July 10, 1863 Battle of Funkstown. Jennifer Goellnitz of Cleveland, Ohio, who is the authority on all things related to A. P. Hill, kindly shared her store of material on Hill's role during the retreat with us. We deeply appreciate their assistance in tracking down those obscure and previously unused sources.

Dean Shultz is truly "The Dean" of all things Gettysburg. Dean has forgotten more details than most of us will ever know, and has mapped just about every square inch of soil touched by the Gettysburg Campaign. He accompanied us on drives of the retreat routes and gave us the benefit of his vast store of knowledge about people, places, and events. We thank him for always being there when we need him, for the many conversations throughout the years, and he and his wife Judy for their hospitality at their period home.

Our thanks and appreciation is also extended to several owners of war-time homes along the retreat routes. When approached without prior warning by a group of strangers, they graciously took us in, gave us tours of their properties, and passed on local stories regarding the campaign that simply cannot be found in any book (until now!). Jack and Kristen Holden own the well-preserved Baker Farm near Funkstown, Maryland, which was the headquarters of Federal Brig. Gen. John Buford during the Second Battle of Funkstown. They gave us a tour of their home and period barns, and allowed us to walk the property to get a rare glimpse of that part of the battlefield. Joyce L. Horst, a descendant of Michael Hege, lives next to the Hege Farm home along what was known as the old Pine Stump Road near Marion, Pennsylvania. Joyce is the "family historian" and graciously shared with us her collection of family papers relating to the war. Michael Hege was a victim of Confederate depredations during both the advance and retreat of Lee's army, and left a detailed letter describing his experiences. Joyce gave us copies of the papers, and the letter is quoted herein for the very first time. Joyce's brother Charles Morton owns the Michael Hege home, and we are grateful to both of them for passing on their family's stories and for allowing us to examine the beautiful Hege property.

We also express appreciation to George Franks, owner of the Donnelly farm along Falling Waters Road where Confederate General James J. Pettigrew met the cavalryman's bullet that soon ended his life. George is an avid student of the Retreat, and an untiring and valuable coordinator of efforts to publicize the story of the Retreat and save pertinent sites. George was enthusiastic about this project and gave us very useful information about his property. Our thanks are due to Robert Grandchamp of Warwick, Rhode Island, for pointing us to sources regarding the 1st Rhode Island Light Artillery that proved very useful.

We are likewise grateful to several folks of Chambersburg, Pennsylvania, who passed on valuable local history to us concerning the interesting story of the mortally wounded Lt. Col. Benjamin F. Carter of the 4th Texas Infantry. Carter was taken from a private home along the retreat route to the Zion Reformed Church in Chambersburg for care, as recounted in Chapter 1. Pastor

Jeffrey Diller of the church pointed out to us that Carter had previously cared for the stepson of the pastor at the time, upon the son's mortal wounding in August 1862, and Carter also allowed Capt. Mark Kerns to be buried on the battlefield in Carter's own coat. The story comes full circle when Carter was cared for by the mother at the church in Chambersburg in late July 1863, only days before his own death at the Academy Hospital. We thank Pastor Diller for helping us add this poignant human touch to a story so often full of pain and suffering. F. Joan Bowen, the Historian and Chairperson of Records and History of the First United Methodist Church, did a great deal of digging for us to try to solve the mystery of where Carter's remains were interred. A footnote in Chapter 1 reveals the details known today, and we thank Joan for her assistance. Larry Chalmer of the Franklin County Historical Society copied the Society's file on Carter for us, and we are grateful for his generous assistance.

We owe an enormous debt to Theodore P. Savas, managing director of our publisher Savas Beatie LLC. Ted is every writer's dream, an endlessly patient mentor who stays with a project every step of the way, as he did with the companion volume *Plenty of Blame to Go Around: Jeb Stuart's Controversial Ride to Gettysburg* (2006) by Wittenberg and Petruzzi. Ted allowed us a wide berth in determining the scope of this project and through his masterful editing, helped make a good story a fascinating one. We still owe him an expensive steak dinner. Thank you, Ted, for your friendship and guidance over the years.

Finally, we owe our respective spouses—Susan Wittenberg, Karen Petruzzi, and Diane Nugent—a debt that cannot be repaid. They generously allowed us countless hours of research and writing, as well as many days away from home to visit these sites so that we can fully and properly honor the memories of the men who fought, suffered, and died during these ten crucial days. Then, they tolerated even more hours as we sat in front of our computers and discussed the project endlessly on the phone. This project could not have been begun, worked, or completed without the love and support of these wonderful ladies.

Eric J. Wittenberg
Columbus, Ohio

J. David Petruzzi
Brockway, Pennsylvania

Michael F. Nugent
Wells, Maine

Maj. Gen. George G. Meade, commander, Army of the Potomac.

USAHEC

Gen. Robert E. Lee, commander, Army of Northern Virginia.

LOC

Chapter 1

A Vast Sea of Misery: The Wagon Train of Wounded

"As many of our poor wounded as possible must be taken home."

— Robert E. Lee

THREE DAYS OF COMBAT AT Gettysburg decimated Robert E. Lee's Army of Northern Virginia. Confederate losses were at least 4,637 killed, 12,391 wounded and 5,161 missing.[1] The enormous task of safely evacuating the ambulatory from the field fell upon Brig. Gen. John D. Imboden. Fortunately for the Confederates, Imboden rose to the occasion and turned in his finest performance of the war during the ordeal that followed.

John Daniel Imboden was born forty years earlier near Staunton, Virginia. He attended, but did not graduate from, Washington College in Lexington (today Washington & Lee University). Imboden taught for a time at the Virginia Institute for the Education of the Deaf, Dumb, and Blind in Staunton, studied law, practiced in Staunton, and was twice elected as a representative to the Virginia Legislature.[2] He won acclaim as the commander of the Staunton Artillery at Harpers Ferry, and was wounded at First Manassas in July 1861. The following year, Imboden resigned from the artillery to raise companies of partisan rangers. He fought at Cross Keys and Port Republic during Stonewall Jackson's Valley Campaign.

In January 1863, Imboden received a promotion to brigadier general. His 1st Virginia Partisan Rangers reorganized into two regular cavalry regiments, the 18th Virginia Cavalry and the 62nd Virginia Mounted Infantry, and a battery of horse artillery. However, Maj. Gen. James Ewell Brown "Jeb" Stuart, the Army of Northern Virginia's cavalry division chief, was not fond of Imboden, so his command was not made part of the "regular" mounted forces of the army.

Because of Stuart's animus, Imboden's independent Northwestern Brigade received orders directly from General Lee. Imboden and Brig. Gen. William E.

Brig. Gen. John D. Imboden, Commander, Northwestern Brigade.

USAHEC

"Grumble" Jones led what came to be known as the "Jones-Imboden Raid," a mounted strike into northwestern Virginia during April and May 1863. The raid captured thousands of horses and cattle for the Confederacy and severed the Baltimore & Ohio Railroad.[3] During the Gettysburg campaign, Imboden's command included the 18th Virginia Cavalry, led by his brother Col. George H. Imboden; the 62nd Virginia Mounted Infantry under Col. George H. Smith; the Virginia Partisan Rangers under Capt. John H. "Hanse" McNeill; and the Staunton Horse Artillery, Virginia Battery, under Capt. James H. McClanahan—in all, some 2,245 troopers.[4]

Once it became apparent the battle of Gettysburg had ended, Imboden was summoned to army headquarters at 1:00 a.m. on July 4. A weary General Lee arrived, dismounted, and leaned against his horse, Imboden recalled, "The moon shone full upon his massive features and revealed an expression of sadness that I had never before seen upon his face. Awed by his appearance, I waited for him to speak until the silence became embarrassing."[5] Imboden broke the silence. "General," he exclaimed, "this has been a hard day on you."

"Yes, it has been a sad, sad day to us," replied Lee. He praised the performance of Pickett's Virginians during the infantry assault of the previous day, and then added mournfully, "Too bad! *Too bad!* Oh! Too bad!"[6]

Lee's headquarters tent and those of his staff were staked among the fruit trees of an orchard on the south side of the Chambersburg pike west of Seminary Ridge.[7] Lee motioned Imboden into his tent, where the tired commander seated himself and explained the situation. "We must now return to Virginia," observed Lee. "As many of our poor wounded as possible must be taken home." Lee continued:

> I have sent for you because your men and horses are fresh and in good condition, to guard and conduct our train back to Virginia. The duty will be arduous, responsible and dangerous, for I am afraid you will be harassed by the enemy's cavalry. Nearly all the transportation and care of all the wounded will be entrusted to you. You will cross the mountain by the Chambersburg road, and then proceed to Williamsport by any route you deem best, and without a halt till you reach the river. Rest there long enough to feed your animals; then ford the river, and do not halt again till you reach Winchester, where I will again communicate with you.[8]
>
> I will place in your hands by a staff officer, tomorrow morning, a sealed package for President Davis, which you are to retain in your possession till you are across the Potomac, when you will detail a reliable commissioned officer to take it to Richmond with all possible dispatch and deliver it into the President's own hands. And I impose upon you that whatever happens, this package must not fall into the hands of the enemy. If unfortunately you should be captured, destroy it at the first opportunity.[9]

The next morning, a staff officer delivered Imboden's written orders and a large envelope addressed to Davis.[10] The success of the route of retreat would hinge upon speedy movement and security for the wagon train. Lee impressed upon Imboden that "there should be no halt [along the way] for any cause whatever." Lee's staff prepared a detailed evacuation plan and provided Imboden with specific direction:

> [I]n turning off at Greenwood have your scouts out [to the right] on the Chambersburg road . . . also keep scouts out on your left toward Waynesborough. From Greencastle . . . send a scouting party through Hagerstown, and hold that place until the train shall have crossed the river. At the river . . . [send] out your scouts toward Hagerstown, Boonsborough, etc., . . . I need not caution you as to . . . secrecy of your movements, promptness and energy, and increasing vigilance on the part of yourself and officers.[11]

With his orders in place, Imboden set about preparing for the heavy task that lay ahead of him.

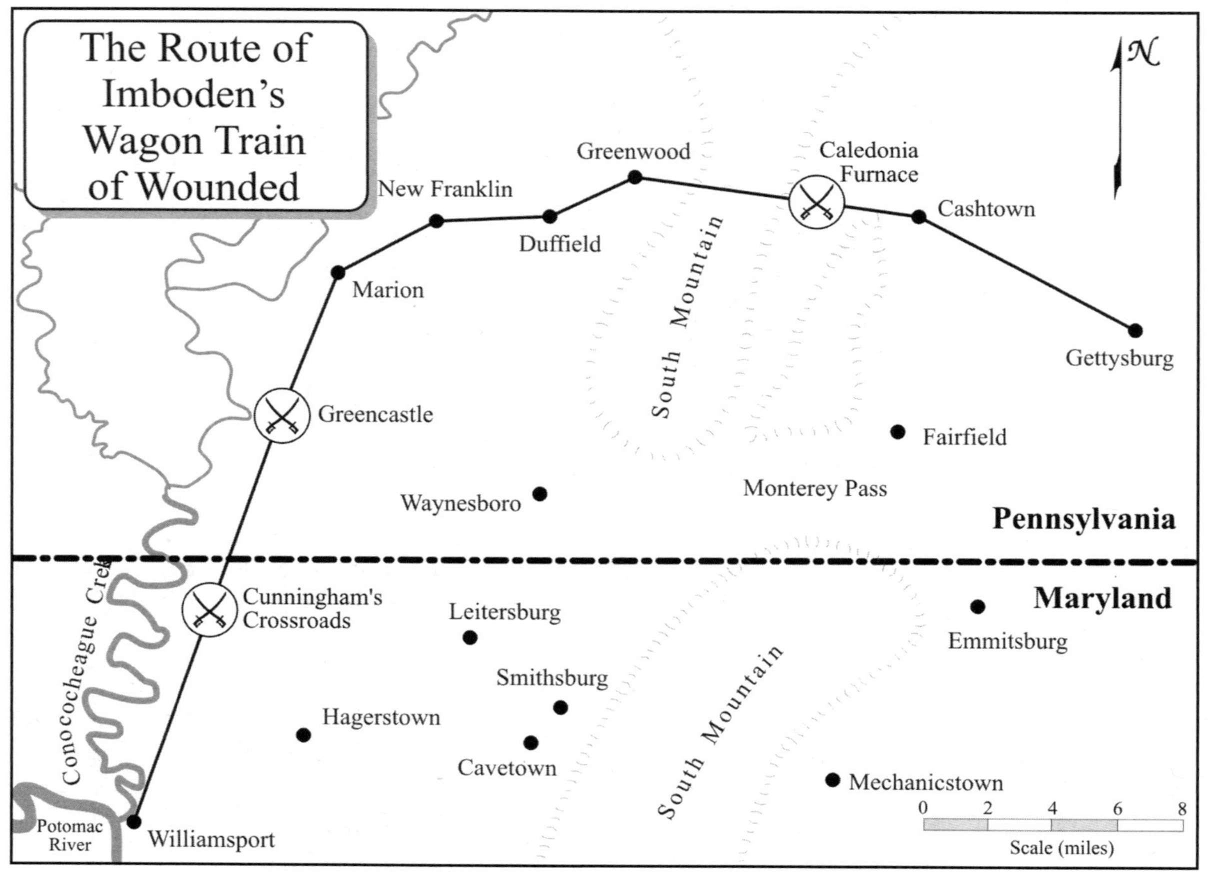
The Route of Imboden's Wagon Train of Wounded
N
New Franklin
Greenwood
Caledonia Furnace
Cashtown
Duffield
Marion
South Mountain
Gettysburg
Greencastle
Fairfield
Waynesboro
Monterey Pass
Pennsylvania
Maryland
Cunningham's Crossroads
Leitersburg
Emmitsburg
Conococheague Cre
Smithsburg
Hagerstown
South Mountain
Cavetown
Mechanicstown
Potomac River
Williamsport
0 2 4 6 8
Scale (miles)

Assembling the Wagon Train

The shortest route to Hagerstown, Maryland, was via Fairfield and the Monterey Pass above it. Unfortunately for Imboden and his already sizeable task, the Monterey Pass was steep, very narrow, and the road wound in a series of sharp turns. Lee knew that Union soldiers were operating in the area. If the enemy cavalry choked off this route, the consequences for the withdrawal would be devastating. Therefore, Lee decided to send the main army by the Fairfield route.

Imboden's wagon train would have to take a cross-country route. It would move west along the Chambersburg Pike through the Cashtown Pass, turn south at Greenwood and proceed on to Marion, pass south through Greencastle and into Williamsport. This route was less likely to be blocked or otherwise impeded, but it too was fraught with peril. The trip would be longer, and there would be more opportunities for Union soldiers to play havoc with the long column.

Confederate preparations for the retreat did not go unnoticed by the town's citizens. On edge after three interminably long days, even the slightest movement grabbed attention. Teenager Daniel A. Skelly and his family had been caught squarely in the middle of the "exciting" scenes in town over the course of the battle. As an old man, Skelly reflected on the night of July 3. He had tried to go to sleep in his West Middle Street home, but was "restless, and was unable to sleep soundly. About midnight I was awakened by a commotion down in the street," he recalled. "Getting up I went to the window and saw Confederate officers passing through the lines of the Confederate soldiers bivouacked on the pavement below, telling them to get up quietly and fall back. Very soon the whole line disappeared." As Skelly remembered it, "we had to remain quietly in our homes for we did not know what it meant. I went back to bed but was unable to sleep.[12]

The task of assembling hundreds of wagons and ambulances and carefully loading the wounded began in the early morning hours. Imboden realized quickly that the train would not get underway until late in the day. Regimental and brigade surgeons and their staffs had to compile lists of the wounded, and physically gathering and loading all those who could be moved into the wagons was a monumental task. Across all units, every able-bodied soul—including band members, black servants, and drummer boys—were conscripted to gather the fallen and load them into the vehicles.[13]

Additional artillery, twenty-three pieces in all, arrived as did Brig. Gen. Fitzhugh Lee's cavalry brigade, which had been ordered to cover the rear of the train. By noon on July 4, a torrential downpour blanketed South Mountain, adding to Imboden's troubles and the agony of the wounded men.[14] Imboden was fully cognizant of the crushing responsibility General Lee had placed on his shoulders. And per Lee's instructions, Imboden resolved that once the train started, it would not halt until it reached its destination—even if that meant that disabled wagons had to be abandoned along the way.[15]

With the rain still pouring in sheets, soaking everything and turning roads into muddy gruel, the wagon train began moving toward Chambersburg at about 4:00 p.m. Luther Hopkins, a trooper of the 6th Virginia Cavalry, was resting on the ground while allowing his horse to graze along the Chambersburg Road when he heard "a low rumbling sound . . . resembling distant thunder, except that it was continuous." Hopkins and a few of his comrades wondered what it was. They soon found out. "A number of us rose to our feet and saw a long line of wagons with their white covers moving . . . along the Chambersburg Road. . . . The wagons going back over the same road that had brought us to Gettysburg told the story, and soon the whole army knew that fact. This was the first time Lee's army had ever met defeat."[16] The wagon train presented quite a sight. "It was the longest wagon train I ever saw," recalled another Southerner, "some said it was 27 to 30 miles long."[17] A band member of J. Johnston Pettigrew's Brigade saw it as "a motley procession of wagons, ambulances, wounded men on foot, straggling soldiers and band boys, splashing along in the mud, weary, sad and discouraged."[18]

Imboden directed the operation from Cashtown. Detachments of guns and troops were inserted into the column at intervals of one-quarter to one-third of a mile.[19] By the time the last wagons had joined the grim procession from Cashtown the following morning, the train stretched more than seventeen miles.[20]

Stuart's cavalry division had hundreds of unserviceable mounts that had broken down at Gettysburg due to the fighting and hard riding. They had been corralled together, and those that could be taken along with the army were placed in an enormous column in the road, constituting, as one of Stuart's troopers recalled, "a grand cortege of limping horses after the wagon train." As the wagon wheels churned up the muddy roads in the monsoonal rains, the poor lame beasts had a progressively harder time keeping up. Those that couldn't were left where they fell.[21]

Most of the wagons were of the "Conestoga" style, so named for the Pennsylvania valley in which they were built and perfected. Typically about eighteen feet long, most of the wagons had been built for rolling stock, and so able to hold six barrels of supplies in two rows of three each. They had no springs to cushion the forty-mile ride ahead. They also offered little or no protection from the downpour.[22] Pvt. Robert James Lowry of Co. G, 3rd Arkansas Infantry, felt compassion for the plight of his comrades—especially since his brother, Sgt. John F. Lowry, was among the wounded. "Scarcely one in a hundred had received adequate medical care and most had not eaten in 36 hours," Lowry explained. "The wagons did not have springs and the wounded lay on the bare boards."[23]

"The rain fell in blinding sheets; the meadows were soon overflowed and fences gave way before the raging streams," wrote Imboden. "During the storm, wagons, ambulances, and artillery carriages by hundreds—nay, by thousands—were assembling in the fields along the road from Gettysburg to Cashtown, in one confused and apparently inextricable mass. As the afternoon wore on there was no abatement in the storm. Canvas was no protection against its fury, and the wounded men lying upon the naked boards of the wagon-bodies were drenched."[24] The sounds of the tempest nearly drowned out the agonized cries of the wounded. "Horses and mules were blinded and maddened by the wind and water, and became almost unmanageable," continued the cavalry leader. "The deafening roar of the mingled sounds of heaven and earth all around us made it almost impossible to communicate orders, and equally difficult to execute them."[25]

Lt. Randolph A. Shotwell of the 8th Virginia Infantry left a vivid description of the journey of the wagon train of wounded:

> Soon the difficulty of the road, which was narrow and rocky, added to the drenching rain, and the bottomless mud, caused the trains to become crowded, and embarrassed, filling the highways and rendering the movements of the footmen, i.e., the prisoners and their guards exceedingly wearisome. Wagons, ambulances, artillery, cavalry, stragglers, wounded soldiers, Yankees, and guards were irretrievably mixed, and the continued succession of momentary halts, to be followed by a rapid trot of a 100 yards, and then another halt, resulting from the breaking down of wagons, or difficulty in passing mud holes, were so inconceivably vexatious, and fatiguing that I have often wondered why all the prisoners did not escape for the guards became almost indifferent, especially in the

> confusion after dark, when the crowded trains were painfully toiling up the winding pass at Cashtown. Doubtless more of the prisoners would have escaped had they not been too near to physical and mental exhaustion.[26]

Signs of the Southern withdrawal provided enormous relief to Gettysburg's citizens. Fannie Buehler lived on Baltimore Street, and had had a trying time since July 1, taking care of the wounded of both sides in her home. Like most civilians, she got little rest on the night of July 3 and heard the same commotion Daniel Skelly had about midnight. "'Our Boys' suspected the enemy was beaten from some little things they heard," she wrote, "and believed they were preparing for retreat from what they saw; consequently they kept a close watch upon them, and soon found they were not mistaken." She continued,

> They were really going away. The enemy retreated cautiously and very quietly, and many of our citizens did not know of their going until seven or eight o'clock in the morning, for they did not withdraw their last pickets until the advance of their now broken army neared the Potomac . . . [W]e could, from our garret window, see the army wagons winding their way among the hills far off in the distance. . . . All we knew certainly was, the Rebels were gone.[27]

According to young Billy Bayly, soldiers, hundreds of wagons, and stragglers began "drifting back in the direction whence they came." Some asked about "the nearest route to Hagerstown." That morning "our host of visitors had, like the Arab, folded their tents and quietly stolen away."[28]

Some Rebels tried to cover the retreat with an ominous threat. Diarist Sallie Broadhead noted that late on the night of July 4, warnings were issued that the town was to be shelled and that all women and children should vacate their homes. Realizing it was a hollow threat and that their unwelcome guests were leaving the field, the next day she exclaimed, "What a beautiful morning!" Her joy was tempered once she took in the sights beyond her doorstep. "It seemed as though nature was smiling on thousands of suffering."[29]

John L. Schick owned a large general store at the corner of Baltimore Street and the town square. The raiding of his stock during the battle, threats of the shelling, and evidence of the Confederate withdrawal, at long last, was more than he could take. On July 4, he reminisced, "I smoked 21 cigars in one day."[30]

An incident along the journey back to Virginia. *Battles and Leaders*

The Wagon Train Rolls South

Imboden left Cashtown about 8:00 p.m. and rode toward the head of the column. For the next four hours he listened to the agonizing cries of the wounded and dying. Recalling the dreadful ride, he wrote, "During this one night I realized more of the horrors of war than I had in all the two preceding years."[31]

From nearly every wagon the wounded cried out. "My God! Will no one have mercy and kill me, and end my misery?"

"Oh God! Why can't I die?"

"Stop! Oh! for God's sake, stop just for one minute; take me out and leave me to die on the roadside."

"I am dying! I am dying! My poor wife, my dear children, what will become of you?" Ever practical, Imboden pointed out, "No help could be given to any of the sufferers. On, on we must move on."[32]

The cries of the suffering men filled the night. Try as they might, no one accompanying the train could ignore them. "Marched all night through rain," Capt. Francis M. Imboden, the general's younger brother, plaintively noted in his diary. "Several thousand wounded suffering awfully."[33]

A wounded Tar Heel found a bale of hay to ride on. It was a luxury compared to the plight of his comrades, but still he endured a cold, wet, and miserable journey. "When we reached the top of the mountain, it got very dark, but there was no halt made, a steady trot being kept up all night. I could never tell how we got along without some accident. During the night we passed Thad Stevens Iron Works, which Ewell's troops had burned as they passed on some days before, and they were still smoking." The next morning, the sun broke through the clouds for a while, warming the countryside. Those wounded men who had been riding through the cold night began to feel the effect of the sun. Although hungry, tired, and sore, they cracked jokes with the natives. The local citizens jeered in return, telling the Confederates that they would never get across the Potomac, and that they would soon be gobbled up.[34]

"When the Confederate army fell back from Gettysburg, I followed our marching column in an ambulance, suffering very much from the wound I received in the arm," recalled Maj. Gen. John Bell Hood, a division leader in James Longstreet's First Corps who had suffered a severe wound on July 2. "In the same vehicle lay Gen. Wade Hampton, so badly wounded that he was unable to sit up, whereas I could not lie down. We journeyed together in this manner to Staunton [Virginia], a distance of some two hundred miles."[35] Arthur Fremantle, an English officer traveling with Lee's army, saw the suffering Hood. "He looked rather bad," he noted, "and has been suffering a good deal; the doctors seem to doubt whether they will be able to save his arm." He also had a chance to visit Hampton, and found the big South Carolinian "in very good spirits" in spite of a bullet in the hip and two saber cuts over his head.[36]

History has left behind no shortage of recollections of the misery of both weather and wounded. "Of all the nights that I spent during the war I think this was the saddest," remarked one of Imboden's men. "We were already sad and disheartened by our misfortune, and this mental condition was made worse by the thunder and lightning, and the great torrents of rain that came down augmented by the horrible groans of the wounded and dying."[37] Pvt. I. Norval Baker of the 18th Virginia Cavalry escorted the train. He remembered that "it rained all night, one thunderstorm after another. The rain fell in sheets and vivid flashes of lightning and so dark we could not see our hands an inch from our eyes when there was no lightning. The roar of the waters and heavy bursting thunder, the cries of the wounded and dying soldiers made it awful."[38]

Imboden intended to cover as much ground as possible during the night, since his experienced warrior's mind expected to see harassment by Federal cavalry at daybreak. The column left the turnpike near Greenwood and rumbled along Pine Stump Road through New Guilford (present day Duffield) and New Franklin before rolling west to Marion.[39] The rain made the very old road, already one of the worst tracks in Franklin County, almost unusable. The road "was in a most deplorable condition, becoming almost impassible," recalled one of the locals.[40] "The retreating army, which kept passing along [Pine Stump Road] for fully forty-eight hours," recalled a resident of Marion, "cut down or opened fences and passed along in the fields, adjacent and parallel to the road. It was a common thing to see some of their horses sticking in the mud nearly body deep. At numerous places wagons and cannon carriages were left on account of the horses not being able to drag them through the mud. The cries and moanings of the wounded rebels could be heard for more than a mile when they were in wagons and crossing over this muddy and rough road."[41]

Many Confederate teamsters, impossibly bogged down by the muddy quagmires, abandoned mired and broken wagons by the roadside. A local recalled, "All along the route by which this train made its way, broken wagons and dead and dying horses were strewed."[42] Another citizen noted in his diary on July 6, "Reports that the Pine Stump Road is filled with broken Rebel wagons and caissons, filled with ammunition much of which is thrown in the mud with a view of destroying it. . . . Also it is said a cannon was found buried by the Rebels near the place on the roadside."[43]

John B. Hege, a young lad living along this road near Marion, fed his curiosity the next day. "At many places along the Pine Stump road, were to be seen cannon balls, bomb shells, muskets and cannons, that were left by the retreating army," he wrote. "There were two cannons left in the timberland of my father near Locust Grove school house, east of Marion. The one was a rifled cannon, and had printed or stenciled on the limber, 'Capt. Armstrong's Battery Washington Artillery.' The wheels of the wagons were somewhat broken and the pivots of the cannons spiked with steel by the rebels before they left them behind. Before leaving their muskets behind, they would either throw them on piles and burn them, or strike them with force against a tree, a post in the fence, or a rock, and turn, or bend the barrel so that they would be useless, if they fell into the hands of the Union soldiers."[44]

Imboden and his men realized that many of their most important cargo simply could go on no longer. Dead and dying soldiers were also left along the road to lighten the wagons and leave the men in the hands of hopefully sympathetic locals. "The enemy are abandoning all their wounded on the retreat. Every house and barn for fifteen miles is a hospital," recounted a newspaper correspondent. "They are leaving all, generals and colonels, as well as privates. All their wounded will fall into our hands. We have taken thus far six thousand prisoners, besides wounded.[45]

New Franklin farmer Jacob Snyder recalled looking out his door late on the night of July 4 when he heard the wagons rumbling past. Soon wounded Confederates overran his farm, begging for water and dressings for their wounds. Famished walking wounded stole some of the cattle from Snyder's barnyard before he managed to shut the gate.[46] According to Snyder's son Milton, "The wagons kept the main road as much as possible, and on either side of the train a continual stream of wounded kept moving. Wounded Confederate soldiers were left along the route of retreat. I shall never forget those ghastly wounds."[47] Across the road from Snyder's farm, Confederates buried an officer—thought to be a colonel by the locals.[48]

Three miles beyond the Snyder place, the wagon train reached the farm of Mennonite Deacon Michael Hege. Ten days earlier, the Confederates had passed Hege's large farm on their way north. Deacon Hege kept a detailed ledger documenting $626 of confiscated livestock and property.[49] Family history relates that Hege, skilled at distilling corn into stronger spirits, buried barrels of whiskey in his fields to hide them from the thirsty Southerners. On June 27, an officer named R. S. Todd issued a certificate to Hege documenting that he had been robbed of his money.[50] Later, when other Rebels demanded Hege's cattle, he produced the certificate and they generally left him and his herd alone.[51] Several soldiers on the retreat, however, took whatever they could and Hege noted the loss of a horse as well as some flour and meat on July 5.[52]

In a letter to a cousin, Hege's nephew, Henry B. Hege, lamented the impact the passing enemy, both on their way to and from Gettysburg, had on his family and neighbors. "I thank God for the rich blessings He has bestowed upon us, that He has taken all the rebels out of our neighborhood," he wrote on July 12. Nearly all the horses in the area had been taken, as well as hogs, poultry, corn, oats, wagons, and tools. "In short, they took everything they could make use of."[53] Henry also reported the murder of a neighbor at the hands of Confederates. "Some of the rebels appear to be nice clever men," he wrote. "Some of them would harm no man or steal anything. But I tell you the greatest portion of them are nothing but thieves and robbers and some murder[er]s. They shot one citizen just about two miles from our house, his name was Isaac Strite, they wanted his money and he gave them part of it. They then wanted to burn his barn, he begged them not to do it, they then shot him dead."[54]

Still, the wounded men bothered Henry: "I was at the road when they retreated, and I saw enough. Their wagon train was about 56 hours passing and nearly all hauling wounded, some would groan at every jerk the wagon made, all those that were just slightly wounded had to walk. I saw some walking that were shot in the arms, some shoulders, some in the face, oh! It looked awful as their wounds were not dressed yet, their wounds looked all black and blue."[55]

Weary men dropped from their saddles, and horses dropped dead from exhaustion. "Over the [Pine Stump Road] some of us had to march barefooted," recalled Pvt. Napier Bartlett of the Washington Artillery, "our shoes having been destroyed by the rough macadamized [Chambersburg Pike], or the heavy mud; and those were especially sufferers whose feet, my own among the numbers, were inconveniently larger than those of the passing Dutchmen whom we could meet on the road." Men sound asleep in the saddle were spotted all along the long column of misery. "The men and officers on horseback would go to sleep without knowing it, and at one time there was a halt occasioned by all of the drivers—or at least those whose business was to attend to it—being asleep in their saddles. In fact the whole of the army was dozing while marching and moved as if under enchantment or spell—were asleep and at the same time walking."[56]

Daniel Mull was asleep in his Marion home, oblivious to the procession of misery passing just outside his doorstep. A pounding at his door shook him out of bed. A dripping, bedraggled Rebel stood outside. He asked Mull if the road was the right one to Hagerstown. Although half asleep, Mull understood the situation and quickly thought of a ruse. "[Y]es," he answered, "but a short distance ahead is a crossroad and there turn to the right." The Southerners, leading a few wagons that had separated from the main column, didn't know the right turn would take them to Chambersburg, where they arrived at daylight and were immediately captured. Luckily for the wounded, they were well taken care of by the doctors and citizens at King Street Hospital and improvised facilities coordinated by Chambersburg physician Abraham H. Senseney. "Sheriff Taylor and a few others continued misdirecting them," recalled a local, "until they were fooled into the lines of the Union soldiers, where they were all captured."[57] Chambersburg citizen Jacob Hoke described the wounded as "filthy, bloody, with wounds undressed and swarming with vermin, and almost

Lt. Col. Benjamin F. Carter, commander, 4th Texas Infantry.

Austin Public Library

famished for food and water, they presented such a sight as I hope I may never see again."[58]

Many stragglers, walking wounded, and the more severely injured left in homes and along the road were also taken to Chambersburg and given medical attention. Lt. Col. Benjamin F. Carter of the 4th Texas Infantry was seriously wounded on July 2 in the fighting near Little Round Top. He was captured during the retreat and brought to Chambersburg. Hearing of the officer's arrival, Rev. Dr. Samuel Reed Fisher and his wife Naomi requested that he be taken to the Zion Reformed Church, where Fisher served as pastor. Carter suffered from a facial wound and others in a hand and leg.[59] Naomi had a connection with Carter dating back to the Second Battle of Manassas of August 1862. There, a Federal battery commanded by Capt. Mark Kerns, Naomi's son from her first marriage, tried to repel an attack by Maj. Gen. John Bell Hood's Texas Brigade. Kerns was mortally wounded during a fight for his guns near Chinn Ridge. Lieutenant Colonel Carter found Kerns, helped as best he could, and permitted Kerns to be buried on the field in Carter's own coat. Naomi never forgot Carter's mercy, and the least she could do for him was to comfort him in his own final hours.[60]

When it became apparent that Carter was mortally wounded, he was removed to the Academy Hospital, which had taken many of the Confederate wounded. With no hope of recovery, Carter asked Dr. Senseney for "some one who would give him the assurance of a Christian burial." Senseney called on prominent Chambersburg resident Alexander K. McClure for assistance, and McClure visited Carter in the hospital. "I called at once and found the sufferer, an unusually bright and handsome man, calmly watching the rapid approach of death," McClure later wrote. "With beseeching eyes that would have melted the sternest enemy, he begged of me to give him the assurance that his body would receive Christian burial." McClure promised Carter he would see to it, and the officer "reached out his trembling hand and gave most grateful acknowledgment." Carter died on July 21, and after much difficulty in finding a local cemetery that would accept the Rebel officer's remains, Carter was finally interred, according to McClure, in the cemetery of the Methodist Church.[61]

Likewise, thirty-four year-old Col. Isaac E. Avery of the 6th North Carolina Infantry, temporarily commanding Brig. Gen. Robert Hoke's veteran brigade in Hoke's absence, was shot through the throat while leading the assault on East Cemetery Hill on the night of July 2. The dying officer was taken to the Henry Culp house, where he expired early on July 3. His faithful slave Elijah was determined the take the body home to Avery's family for burial in North Carolina. He loaded Avery's remains into a wagon for transport, but the body began decomposing rapidly in the heat and humidity, forcing Elijah to reconsider his plan. He had Avery's remains placed in a wooden coffin and buried under a pine tree in a small cemetery on a bluff in Williamsport, overlooking the swollen Potomac River. Avery was just one of hundreds, and perhaps thousands, of Confederate soldiers buried in crude unmarked graves all along the route of the Wagon Train of Wounded.[62]

Chambersburg resident Rachel Cormany heard of the capture of the wagons and recorded her experiences in her diary:

> I was told that 4 or 6 horse wagons filled with wounded from the late battle were captured by citizens & brought to town—the wounded were put into the hospitals and the wagons and drivers were taken on toward Harrisburg. Was also told that a great many more were out toward Greencastle—some went out to capture those but found that it was a train 20 miles long. . . . A report has reached us that the whole rebel army is on the retreat—later that they are driven this way and are expected soon. . . . It is frightful how those poor wounded rebels are left to suffer, they are taken in large 4 horse wagon—wounds undressed—nothing to eat . . . those that are here are as dirty and lousy as they well can be. The condition of those poor rebels all along from Gettysburg to as far as they have come yet is reported dreadful. I am told they just beg the people along the road to help them—many have died by the way.[63]

A Southerner, responding to an inquiry about what the passage of the wagon train meant, admitted, "It means that Uncle Robert has got a hell of a whipping."[64]

Ambush at Greencastle

The rest of the train left Marion and moved to Greencastle, where the head of the column was located at dawn on July 5. Just as Imboden feared, daylight brought more trouble.[65] Greencastle citizens were bitter about their treatment at the hands of the Confederates, remembering the passage of Brig. Gen. Albert G. Jenkins and his men several weeks earlier. "Here came the same men who but eight to ten days before had passed through our town in the prime of health, boasting of the exploits they would do," recalled Rev. J. C. Smith with evident feelings of comeuppance. "A more crestfallen, woe-begone mob may never have been seen. Hurry was the order of the day. They seemed to be pushing themselves forward."[66]

Col. John L. Black, commander of the 1st South Carolina Cavalry, was wounded in the head on the third day at Gettysburg. He and his contingent of 100 troopers joined the wagon train. As he approached Greencastle, an elderly man told Black that he hoped they would never reach safety. "I told him not to be uneasy," recalled Black, "we were even able to turn and fight our way forward." The old man warned that the wagons would never pass Greencastle. Black scoffed in reply, "[I]f we were attacked there we could burn the town to create a diversion and that, as I knew he was a man of wealth, he would be a sufferer & that he had better pray for our safe return." Black was not without a sense of humor. "I think he did pray for us to get away."[67]

With elements of the 18th Virginia Cavalry in the lead, the head of the column moved one mile beyond the town. Without warning, several dozen Greencastle citizens, organized by resident Thomas Pawling, ambushed the wagons with axes. The citizen warriors cut many of the wheel spokes, dropping the beds into the streets. The rude jolts further added to the misery of the men inside as they fell on broken bones and wounds were torn open.[68]

The Greencastle citizens already had a bit of history regarding Rebel wagons. Pawling had been instrumental in freeing blacks captured by the Confederates during the early days of the Pennsylvania invasion. He and some of his band captured wagons loaded with impressed blacks as the Southerners moved down North Carlisle Street on their march north. They freed the captives and made prisoners of four soldiers and a chaplain, who were taken to Waynesboro. The released Confederates returned to Greencastle and threatened to burn the town if $50,000 was not raised to pay for the escaped blacks. Local leaders refused, but Southern officers who learned of the incident ordered the enraged soldiers to leave the town and its citizens alone.[69]

As Pawling's civilians smashed the wagon wheels to the further groans of the wounded, 100 hand-picked troopers of the 6th Pennsylvania Cavalry under Captain Ulric Dahlgren descended on the column. The twenty-one year-old Dahlgren was the son of Rear Adm. John A. Dahlgren, a brilliant naval officer known as the "father of naval ordnance." A close friend of President Abraham Lincoln, the admiral had arranged a staff officer's position for his son, but the dashing man soon grew bored with routine assignments. Craving adventure in the field, he quickly became one of the most daring and accomplished scouts in the entire Army of the Potomac. In November 1862, he had led a bold raid into Fredericksburg. Although young, Ulric had already attracted attention. During Lee's retreat from Gettysburg, he was poised to make one of his greatest contributions to the Union war effort.[70]

Riding out from Gettysburg at 2:00 that morning, the young captain and his squadron of Pennsylvania horsemen arrived in the town just before dawn. They had taken a long and dangerous route to get to Greencastle. They rode to Emmitsburg, on to Fairfield, through Monterey Pass, and on to Greencastle some twenty-one miles away. Dahlgren's force lay in wait until about 300 wagons passed. Sections commanded by Lieutenants Albert P. Morrow and Bernard H. Herkness attacked opposite ends of the train, briefly seizing McClanahan's guns.[71] "The Yankees broke into our lines and captured the battery," recounted Imboden's adjutant, John Hyde Cameron. "Captain [Francis M.] Imboden charged the Yankees and we recaptured the battery. I can now see how my old friends Carter Berkeley, Dr. Willis, and Dr. Ware were delighted at being recaptured."[72]

Confederate staff officer McHenry Howard recalled that when his small party of troopers was about one mile from town, they "heard a shot and then met a mail carrier galloping down the road, who reported that he had been attacked while passing through the town." When Howard and his comrades rode to the outskirts of Greencastle, the town "seemed sullenly quiet, doors and windows closed and nobody on the street." But when they reached the town square, blazing carbines of the Pennsylvania horse soldiers greeted them. "[A]bout fifty of the Southern Cavalry came down South Carlisle Street, demanding to see the town authorities," recalled Howard, "but just before they reached the square, the Federal soldiers made a dash and drove them out in splendid style, capturing a considerable number. Though the shots whistled in close proximity to our ears, the citizens remained on the street to witness the result." He also noted, "So much for my twenty hours in Maryland and Pennsylvania and so much for my only cavalry experience. I had fired but one shot . . . and this was one of the only two shots I fired during the war. I should add that in this little campaign, we had three men captured—at Greencastle—and one wounded, who got off."[73]

Several wounded from Pettigrew's Brigade were captured at Greencastle, but a few managed to escape. Col. John Randolph Lane of the 26th North Carolina, who couldn't speak or eat due to a wound to the throat suffered on July 1, bounded out of his wagon, mounted a horse, and rode out of town for dear life. Eating nearly nothing for the next nine days, he eventually made his way back to his comrades. Federal cavalrymen dashed off with a wagon carrying Sgt. Alexander H. Harris of the 47th North Carolina Infantry and members of his regiment, galloping out of town "at a rapid rate, jostling us almost to death," he later wrote. Some of Imboden's men ran down the speeding party until the Federals cut the wagon loose and rode away with the horses. "Thus we were recaptured," noted the relieved and weary Tar Heel sergeant.[74]

"The enemy's communications completely destroyed," bragged Dahlgren in his diary when the action was over, "remained in the town all day, feeling proud of our work. Citizens very uneasy about our being there."[75] Dahlgren, whose daring knew few bounds, had his horse shot out from under him during this skirmish.[76] The combined force of Union cavalry and civilians destroyed 130 wagons, ran the horses into the woods, and initially captured two guns and 200 prisoners, including Maj. William M. Lock of the 18th Virginia Cavalry.[77] However, a counterattack by Companies F and I of the 18th Virginia Cavalry drove the Federals off, recaptured the guns, and took a number of prisoners including the wounded Lieutenant Herkness.[78] "The Federals had cut the train," noted a Virginian. "My company turned back and Company I came forward; we struck the Yankees in both flanks and drove them away, getting back all they had taken, together with some prisoners."[79]

"The infantry and cavalry escort was entirely too strong for them and they were obliged to beat a retreat, and finally to scatter to avoid the enemy's close pursuit," recalled Capt. Frederic C. Newhall of the 6th Pennsylvania Cavalry. "Lieutenant Herkness of our regiment was severely wounded and captured, with ten or more of the men, and the whole command was badly cut up, while before [Capt. William P. C.] Treichel could get the remnant together again the country about him was swarming with rebels retreating now from their bitter defeat at Gettysburg."[80]

Wounded Confederate Maj. Alfred H. Belo also recalled the attack: "In passing through Greencastle quite a number of citizens came around the wagon, and soon after leaving there a body of Federal cavalry attacked the wagon train. I had on a fatigue jacket with a Major's star. The wreathed star in their army showed the rank of Brigadier General. They asked 'Where's that General?' My servant, who was riding one of my horses and leading the other, hearing this, urged me to try and mount my horse and escape, but before this was done, a body of our cavalry came up and repulsed the Federals."[81]

Greencastle resident David Shook also recalled that citizens boldly snatched horses and cattle from the train. "As cattle passed by I saw many turned into alleys. Horses tied behind wagons had their halters cut, and were led away unobserved. . . . I captured a fine bay horse, hid him in the barn, fed him well and felt proud of my possession."[82]

The Union cavalry remained obstinate and continued harassing the column throughout the day. Imboden himself was nearly captured in a sharp fight south of Greencastle before canister from two of Capt. James H. McClanahan's guns forced the Federals back.[83] Following counterattacks by the Confederates, the Pennsylvania troopers scattered to continue their hit-and-run tactics.[84] "Only by dispersing his men in different directions amid the deep forest" could Dahlgren and his gallant little band escape close pursuit and head off toward Boonsboro, Maryland and safety.[85] On the morning of July 6, the eighty remaining troopers of Dahlgren's task force linked up with Brig. Gen. Judson Kilpatrick's 3rd Cavalry Division near Hagerstown. The 6th Pennsylvania Cavalry's regimental historian proudly recorded that "they had destroyed over two hundred wagons, loaded with valuable supplies that had been stolen from the farmers and merchants of Pennsylvania. At one time they held more than double their number of prisoners."[86] Although many of the Rebel prisoners ultimately escaped, thirty were taken to Waynesboro the following morning.[87]

Of the attacks around Greencastle, Imboden later wrote:

> after the advance . . . had passed perhaps a mile beyond the town, the citizens to the number of thirty or forty attacked the train with axes, cutting the spokes out of ten or a dozen . . . The moment I heard of it I sent back a detachment of cavalry to capture every citizen who had engaged in this work, and treat them as prisoners of war. This stopped the trouble there, but the Union cavalry began to swarm down upon us from the fields and cross-roads, making their attacks in small bodies and striking the column where there were few or no guards, and thus creating great confusion.[88]

* * *

In addition to marauding Federal cavalry and the incessant rain, the downtrodden Confederates had to endure the jeers of civilians who took great pleasure in seeing the enemy in such condition. "Have you been to Philadelphia already?" they asked.[89] Two pretty young girls came out with American flags wrapped around their shoulders, silently taunting the passing Rebs. One butternut soldier halted, leered at them, and declared, "See here, gurls, youens better take off them damned flags; we old Rebs are hell on breastworks!" The blushing girls beat a very hasty retreat.[90]

George H. Mills of the 16th North Carolina was wounded during Pickett's Charge. Riding on a hay bale, he had ample opportunity to interact with local citizens. When the wagons passed through Greencastle, he remembered, "the Dutch women paid us their compliments by abuse and wishing us in a warmer climate than Pennsylvania." Mills could see the effects of Dahlgren's attack on the wagon train: damaged wagons littering the way side, their teams and men captured. "General Imboden had been sent with us as an escort and to protect us, but was a complete failure on that part," complained Mills.[91]

A correspondent for a local paper watched the enemy passage:

> Oh, what a scene! The teamsters with horrid oaths pounded the poor exhausted horses and mules, while the road was strewn with dead horses and broken wagons. Here and there, you could see a team fast in the mud with men prying at it with rails, while by the wayside, against trees, stumps, and in the mud, sat the exhausted wounded unable to go any further. Thousands more fortunate than these poor wretches were endeavoring to make their escape on the worn-out horses which they had stolen, who when requested by some exhausted wretch to leave him ride for a few miles or so, would turn a deaf ear to the supplications of his companions in arms; for in the vortex and confusion all sense of feeling was lost. Misfortune had placed officers and privates on the same level.[92]

Clothing, blankets, knapsacks, guns and empty haversacks littered the route, with the moans of the wounded overarching all. Teamsters left the wounded to their fate as they abandoned broken wagons. "Oh, how they would beg and entreat those around them not to leave them there to die, far from their friends and homes!" wrote the correspondent. "But their supplications and tears were lost upon the men, who, hardened by the misfortunes with which they were surrounded, made the old maxim 'self-preservation is the first law of nature,' their guide." If a horse or mule in a team gave out, the teamsters often lightened their wagons by throwing wounded men out, leaving them behind to fend for themselves.[93]

Cunningham's Crossroads

Some of the fiercest attacks against the Confederates came on the afternoon of July 5 when Capt. Abram Jones, "a fine officer," ambushed the train a few miles into Maryland at Cunningham's Crossroads (present-day Cearfoss).[94] Captain Jones, who led a successful attack on Imboden's command at McConnellsburg on July 1, had a combined force of 200 men consisting of 120 troopers from the 1st New York (Lincoln) Cavalry and eighty from the 12th Pennsylvania Cavalry. Departing Bloody Run (modern-day Everett) and passing through Mercersburg, Jones heard reports from civilians of the huge enemy train retreating to Williamsport. West of the crossroads some 200 yards was a bluff paralleling the turnpike. Concealing his force behind it, Jones saw a train that stretched as far as he could see in both directions.[95] He returned to his troops and ordered, "If you get into close quarters, use your sabers. Don't strike, but *thrust*!"[96]

Jones' charge over the bluff took the Southerners by complete surprise. A contingent under Lt. Franz Passegger raced for the rear of the column to hold back the next section of the train guard. A second contingent under Lt. Charles Woodruff charged into the train, forcing the teamsters to turn towards Mercersburg. Jones'

Capt. Abram Jones,
1st New York (Lincoln) Cavalry.

William H. Beach,
The First New York (Lincoln) Cavalry

reserve, fifty troopers under Capt. David A. Irwin, took charge of the captured wagons, forcing them to keep moving as fast as possible.[97] William Beach of the 1st New York Cavalry remembered that Captain Jones "arranged his men so as to make as large a show as possible facing toward the rear of the train, and waited for the guard to attack, his object being to give as much time as possible for the captured wagons to get away."[98]

North Carolinian George Mills witnessed Jones' attack on the wagon train at the crossroads. As his wagon bounced along toward Williamsport, Mills spotted one of Imboden's troopers dashing by at full speed, run over a man and horse without stopping, and ride on, looking out only for his own safety. Mills looked back to see a small squad of blue-coated cavalry dashing into the road just as the last of Maj. Gen. William Dorsey Pender's train passed. They struck the front of Maj. Gen Henry Heth's train. The Yankee troopers captured several teams, wagons, and ambulances, including one bearing Col. Collett Leventhorp of the 11th North Carolina and Col. John K. Connally of the 55th North Carolina. Maj. Nathaniel E. Scales, Pender's quartermaster, "was the only man I saw that seemed to have a head on him," noted Mills, "and he stopped a few of Imboden's men and gathered a few stragglers together and soon drove the raiders off, but they had done considerable damage in cutting down wagons and running off the teams." A member of Mills' company sharing his wagon decided to save his own bacon. He leaped from the wagon and took off for the woods, electing to walk the rest of the way to Williamsport.[99]

Before the Confederates could mount an effective response to Jones' dash, the New Yorkers made off with 134 wagons, more than 600 horses and mules, 645 prisoners, and two artillery pieces. Jones arrived in Mercersburg about midnight, where his wounded prisoners were given aid. "In the evening we heard of their capture and approach," noted a resident of Mercersburg. "The whole town turned out to see the sight. After dark they began to arrive and pass through the town. A most exciting spectacle never to be forgotten!" The last of the train did not pass through the town until almost 11:00 p.m.[100] With Confederate losses reported as "considerable," Jones lost only three killed and several slightly wounded.[101] "Great gallantry was displayed by Captain Jones and his brave men in this affair," noted a resident of Mercersburg.[102]

Caledonia Furnace

While the 1st New York and 12th Pennsylvania troopers were attacking the wagons at Cunningham's Crossroads, part of Col. J. Irvin Gregg's brigade of

A woodcut depicting the fighting at Cunningham's Crossroads.

James H. Stevenson, Boots and Saddles: A History of the First Volunteer Cavalry of the War, Known as the First New York (Lincoln) Cavalry.

David M. Gregg's 2nd Cavalry Division attacked Fitzhugh Lee's rearguard near Caledonia Furnace. When Lee finally reached Greencastle he tried to requisition supplies, but the citizens refused to identify the town's officials, pretending not to know their names. With Gregg's cavalry close behind, Lee did not linger among the uncooperative locals.[103] Failing to secure supplies or learn anything useful from Greencastle's residents, he quickly plotted a route to Williamsport and moved to rendezvous with Imboden.[104]

Williamsport

When Imboden arrived in Williamsport on July 5, he found that the previous day's storm had flooded the Potomac River, making it impossible to ford the river. Williamsport, founded by a friend of George Washington named Gen. Otho Holland Williams, sat on the north bank of the Potomac at its confluence with Conococheague Creek. The important river town, originally called Conococheague Settlement, was briefly considered as a candidate for the national capital in 1790, but its location on the Potomac rapids, which could not be navigated, ruled out that idea. Williamsport was settled in the late 17th Century and was incorporated in 1823. With the opening of the C & O Canal in the area in 1834, Williamsport grew into a thriving waterfront town.

"At Williamsport, all was crowded and in confusion," recalled a Federal prisoner with the column.[105] While army surgeons and local doctors tended to wounded, Imboden ordered local civilians to feed his disabled charges. Those dead that had not been left by the roadside were removed from the wagons and buried.[106] "The town was taken possession of," wrote Imboden, "all of the churches, schoolhouses, etc. were converted into hospitals, and proving insufficient, many of the private houses were occupied."[107]

Col. John L. Black of the 1st South Carolina Cavalry was shocked by what he saw when he arrived in Williamsport. "As I rode into Williamsport where our entire wagon train was parked, unable to cross the swollen Potomac, [the town was] crowded with thousands of our wounded," he recalled. "All we could bring from the field and we had brought off, all capable of being moved and many whose wounds were of such character they ought not to have been removed."[108] One of Imboden's staff officers recognized their vulnerability: "[W]e found the river not fordable, and immediately prepared for an expected attack."[109]

Trooper Norval Baker of the 18th Virginia Cavalry left behind an especially gripping description of conditions in the beleaguered town. "It was an awful place, the dead horses and offal of the great number of beeves, etc., killed for the army packed around the little town made it very unpleasant for us when we returned to camp after night. The green flies," he continued, "were around us all the time and orders were not to unsaddle or unbridle our horses[,] and be ready for duty all the time. Our blankets were under our saddles and soaked with water[,] and the green flies were working under the rawhide covering of our saddles and ulcerated backs of our horses." Imboden's weary horse soldiers weren't permitted a moment's rest. "It was rush all the time, when we would go to camp for food and sleep, we would very likely be ordered out on the line again by the news of the outposts being attacked and drove in, and then we would very likely spend the rest of the night looking for a fight." The strain of the combination of the weather conditions and the lack of rest caused many to fall ill.[110]

Federal cavalry had destroyed the pontoon bridge at Falling Waters, a little more than four miles downstream, and it would have to be rebuilt for the army to cross there. The continuing rain made fording the swollen river at either Falling Waters or Williamsport unlikely for some time. One small operating ferry at Williamsport, Leman's Ferry, was the only available means of getting the wounded back to Virginia and to safety. "This ferryboat had a wire cable overhead, stretching from bank to bank, on which ran two small wheels, and the stern of the flatboat being loosened so as to make the current strike the side obliquely like the wind on the sails of a vessel, the force of the current drove the boat over, like sailing on the wind."[111]

After the injured soldiers had been fed and the surgeons had done their best, the agonizingly slow process of crossing the river began.[112] According to Imboden, "There were two small ferry boats or 'flats' there, which I immediately put into requisition to carry across those of the wounded who . . . thought they could walk to Winchester. Quite a large number were able to do this, so that the 'flats' were kept running all the time."[113] The ferry carried only wounded men and couriers. Eventually three additional ferries were constructed at Lee's order, but the bulk of the Confederate infantry, artillery, and trains would not be able to complete crossing the Potomac River to Maidstone until July 14. From Maidstone, the wounded were to be conveyed down the Valley Turnpike to depots and hospitals in the Shenandoah that were already being prepared to receive them.[114]

Additional Confederate units streamed into Williamsport throughout the day on July 5. Separated from Stuart's cavalry on July 4, Brig. Gen. William E. "Grumble" Jones, who commanded a veteran brigade of Virginia cavalry hailed as the "Laurel Brigade," had evaded Federal patrols and made his way to Williamsport.[115] Imboden organized his forces and his twenty-four available artillery pieces, placing them in a three-mile arc to the north, east, and south to cover the five major approaches into town.[116] Satisfied with Imboden's preparations, Jones left to find Stuart near Leitersburg and to bring additional forces for the expected Federal attack.[117] All Imboden could do was wait and prepare as best he could. "Our situation was frightful," he wrote. "We had probably ten thousand animals, and nearly all the wagons of General Lee's army under our charge, and all the wounded, to the number of several thousand, that could be brought from Gettysburg. Our supply of provisions consisted of a few wagon-loads of flour in my own brigade train, a small lot of fine fat cattle which I had collected in Pennsylvania on my way to Gettysburg, and some sugar and coffee procured in the same way at Mercersburg."[118]

Although he had few able-bodied men available to him, Imboden had plenty of artillery. On the roads leading northeast to Hagerstown and southeast to Boonsboro, he placed four guns from Maj. Benjamin F. Eshleman's Louisiana battery and four more from Capt. James F. Hart's South Carolina battery of horse artillery. Three of Capt. James H. McClanahan's six guns were placed on each flank of Imboden's defensive line, and another battery was put into position on the Greencastle road. A Virginia battery was placed in the center of the line. Most of the Confederates knew that many of these guns were in poor condition, and that some had little or no ammunition. The Federals, of course, had no way of knowing that the guns were rolled into place purely for visual effect.[119]

Part of Maj. Ridgley Brown's 1st Maryland Cavalry (C.S.A.) went into the line between the Hagerstown and Boonsboro roads. Col. John L. Black of the 1st South Carolina Cavalry and Col. William R. Aylett of Armistead's Brigade assisted with Imboden's preparation of the defense. Aylett was suffering from a wound received during Pickett's Charge. Despite being seriously wounded at a sharp cavalry skirmish at Hunterstown on July 2, Col. William G. Delony of the Cobb Legion Cavalry left his wagon and organized a number of wounded and dismounted men into a fighting unit.[120]

Although these men already had suffered mightily and fended off several brisk enemy assaults, their sternest test was still ahead of them. Federal cavalrymen were preparing to pounce upon Imboden's hasty defenses at Williamsport.

Chapter 2

The Retreat of the Main Confederate Army Begins

"Genl Meade never brought his 'rascally virtue' of caution to a better market than when he let us alone—for we should probably have given a good account of him."

— Maj. Campbell Brown, Confederate Gen. Richard Ewell's staff

July 3: Gettysburg

AFTER THREE DAYS OF SOME of the most brutal fighting the world had ever seen, the doors of Hell slammed shut late on the afternoon of July 3. The heavens opened, and a thunderstorm of biblical proportions drenched the battlefield, soaking dead, wounded, and able-bodied men equally. "The downpour was in proportion to the violence of the preceding cannonade," noted a staff officer of the Federal 2nd Corps. "The soldiers were drenched in an instant; and sudden torrents swept over the hills, as if to wash out the stains of the great battle."[1]

"As the sun went down on the night of July 3, 1863, there was not a man in our regiment who did not realize that the three days' battle in which we had taken so active a part and the closing scenes of which we had witnessed from our excellent vantage point on Little Round Top, had been one of the greatest and most decisive of the war," recalled a member of the 146th New York Infantry of the Federal 5th Corps.[2]

Crazy rumors flew through the ranks. A sergeant of the 12th U. S. Infantry reported hearing that Maj. Gen. George B. McClellan, a former commander of the Army of the Potomac, was approaching in the rear of the Confederates with 40,000 militia. "If this is true I rather think the rebs will find a warm spot somewhere around here," concluded the sergeant.[3]

Robert Edward Lee's Army of Northern Virginia entered Pennsylvania with 70,274 men and lost 32.5% of its strength in the ensuing bloodbath—22,874 casualties over the course of the battle. George Gordon Meade's Army of the Potomac marched across the Mason-Dixon Line with 89,815 men, and lost 22,813 men, or 24.4% of its effective strength. The butcher's bill added up to nearly 45,000 men killed, wounded, or captured in three days of combat. At the end of the final day's fighting, Lee's army, whittled down to some 47,000 men, stood defiantly on Seminary Ridge inviting Meade to cross the open farmland and attack. Meade's army, reduced to 67,000 effectives, stayed put, waiting to see if the bloodshed was really over. And so the two sides stared at each other, each waiting for the other to resume the fighting; neither did.[4]

That evening, to the joy of the weary Union soldiers, Meade disseminated a message to his army announcing that the enemy had been repulsed at all points. That night, they lay on their weapons trying to remain dry as the heavy rains fell. Sporadic skirmish fire and volleys of musketry rang out, preventing the men from sleeping in any fashion but fitfully that long night. The cold rain fell all night, soaking the men to the skin and adding to their misery and detracting from the glory of their magnificent victory over Lee's vaunted army.[5]

As darkness fell, Lee ordered Lt. Gen. Richard S. Ewell to pull his Second Corps back to Seminary Ridge, abandoning the town of Gettysburg. Ewell's men began moving after midnight. They took up a position northwest of the town on the first day's battlefield, where they could cover both the Chambersburg and Fairfield roads. Lee had Ewell fortify his position in anticipation of a Union counterattack.[6]

Lee and his senior subordinate, Lt. Gen. James Longstreet, commander of the Army of Northern Virginia's First Corps, rode along the Confederate lines to get a sense of the condition of the army. As they both knew, it was not in good shape. Losses included seventeen of its fifty-two general officers, including several killed. In addition, the army was low on ammunition and rations. Maintaining the campaign so far from its base of supplies after suffering such heavy losses was problematic. Lee and Longstreet conferred with other generals, including Ewell and Lt. Gen. A. P. Hill, commander of the Third Corps, on Seminary Ridge a bit more than one mile from the Lutheran Seminary. After seeing the condition of his army and after hearing the opinions of his subordinates, Lee ordered his men to prepare for a retreat.[7]

Lee decided that while a retreat was necessary, it could not be an immediate or hasty one. The appearance of flight had to be avoided. Instead, the withdrawal would be orderly and deliberate, much like the one he had conducted after Sharpsburg the previous September. Then, the Union commander, Maj. Gen. McClellan, was content to just let Lee go. Now, however, a different man was at the helm of the Army of the Potomac, and Meade was no McClellan. Lee doubted that "Major Meade," as he called him, would allow the Confederates to slip away unmolested.

The Army of Northern Virginia's supply wagon trains would depart first on the Fairfield Road, followed by Hill's Corps, which would protect the trains. Longstreet's Corps would follow Hill, and be followed in turn by Ewell's men, who would bring up the army's rear. The army would use the Fairfield Pass through Jack's Mountain, the Monterey Pass through South Mountain, and then march to Waynesboro, Hagerstown, and on to Williamsport—about forty miles all told. It was a direct route of march, but the logistics would be a challenge. Moving so many men, wagons, and cannons over a few roads would be difficult, but Lee had few other choices. He set his staff officers to work making the necessary preparations. The night of planning promised to be a long one.[8]

Col. Philippe Regis de Trobriand commanded a brigade in the Army of the Potomac's 3rd Corps. The forty-seven year-old Frenchman was the son of a baron who had served as one of Napoleon's generals. A cultured poet, novelist, and bon vivant, de Trobriand had a way with words. "It always rains on the day after a great battle," he observed.[9]

July 4

As dawn broke on July 4, 1863—The Glorious Fourth, as it was known—the armies watched each other along the main battle lines at Gettysburg, tending to their respective wounds and waiting to see if the other would make the next move. Three residents, David Kendlehart and his two boys, John and William, thought Meade should know that the Army of Northern Virginia had pulled back from the town, and so set out to find him. They made their way to Meade's headquarters and relayed their intelligence, which was the first news Meade received concerning the retreat of the Rebel lines from the town proper.[10]

At 5:00 that morning, Col. Orland Smith's 11th Corps brigade received orders to move through Gettysburg. "We charged through the Town about half mile in length—-double quick," recounted George B. Fox, a member of the 73rd Ohio. "We drove the enemy out of the town and beyond it some three squares. We captured some 300 prisoners—the fact that we surprised them many were sleeping." Smith's men continued their advance and spent about an hour skirmishing with the Confederate rearguard until Brig. Gen. Adolph von Steinwehr's 2nd Division relieved them. "I have had nothing to eat for three days but Coffee and three hard tacks," grumbled Fox. "Now I will indulge in some tack and coffee."[11] Later that morning, a greatly relieved Brig. Gen. Alexander Schimmelfennig, who commanded an 11th Corps brigade, rejoined his unit after spending three long days hiding in a woodpile behind a house along Baltimore Street on the south side of the town.

At 6:35 that morning, General Lee sent a note across the lines under a flag of truce. "In order to promote the comfort and convenience of the officers and men captured by the opposing armies in the recent engagements," he wrote, "I respectfully propose that an exchange be made at once." Meade responded promptly. "I have the honor to acknowledge the receipt of your communication of this date, proposing to make an exchange at once of the captured officers and men in my possession," he wrote, "and have to say, most respectfully, that it is not in my power to accede to the proposed arrangement." Meade's refusal to make the prisoner exchange guaranteed hardship for the prisoners of war held by both sides. It also meant that once Lee began moving, he would do so with the added burden of guarding and feeding the large contingent of Federal prisoners moving with his army.[12]

"Who shall say that on this day the Nation was not born anew?' inquired another member of the 73rd Ohio.[13] "We spend our Fourth with great joy, which is mingled with sadness at the loss of so many of our men who fell and died that our present victory might be achieved," observed Color Sgt. Daniel Crotty of the 3rd Michigan.[14] The skies opened and a heavy rain fell most of the day, adding to the misery of the thousands of wounded men littering the battlefield. The water in the many creeks crisscrossing the area rose rapidly, rushing southward with great force. A New Jersey soldier watched in horror as the flood waters washed over and carried away badly wounded men unable to move to safety. Many of these poor wretches drowned.[15]

The men of the Army of the Potomac received three days' rations the previous night, their first meal in several days. However, the heavy rains so completely drenched them that it reduced the contents of their haversacks to soggy mush. The result was that they spent July 4 with no food and no prospect of getting anything to eat, which only added to their ongoing discomfort.[16]

Neither General Meade nor his staff got rations, either. Lt. Col. Andrew J. Alexander, a member of the 2nd U. S. Cavalry and a West Pointer, regularly served as an assistant adjutant general at Cavalry Corps headquarters. Since July 1, he had been temporarily attached to army headquarters as an assistant to Meade. By the morning of July 4, Alexander was flat out famished. He had not eaten anything for more than thirty-six hours. Local citizens ventured out to see the great battlefield, many of them carrying picnic lunches with them. Alexander decided it was time to levy a "contribution" to the Union war effort, and gathered enough victuals to feed Meade and his entire staff. The surprised

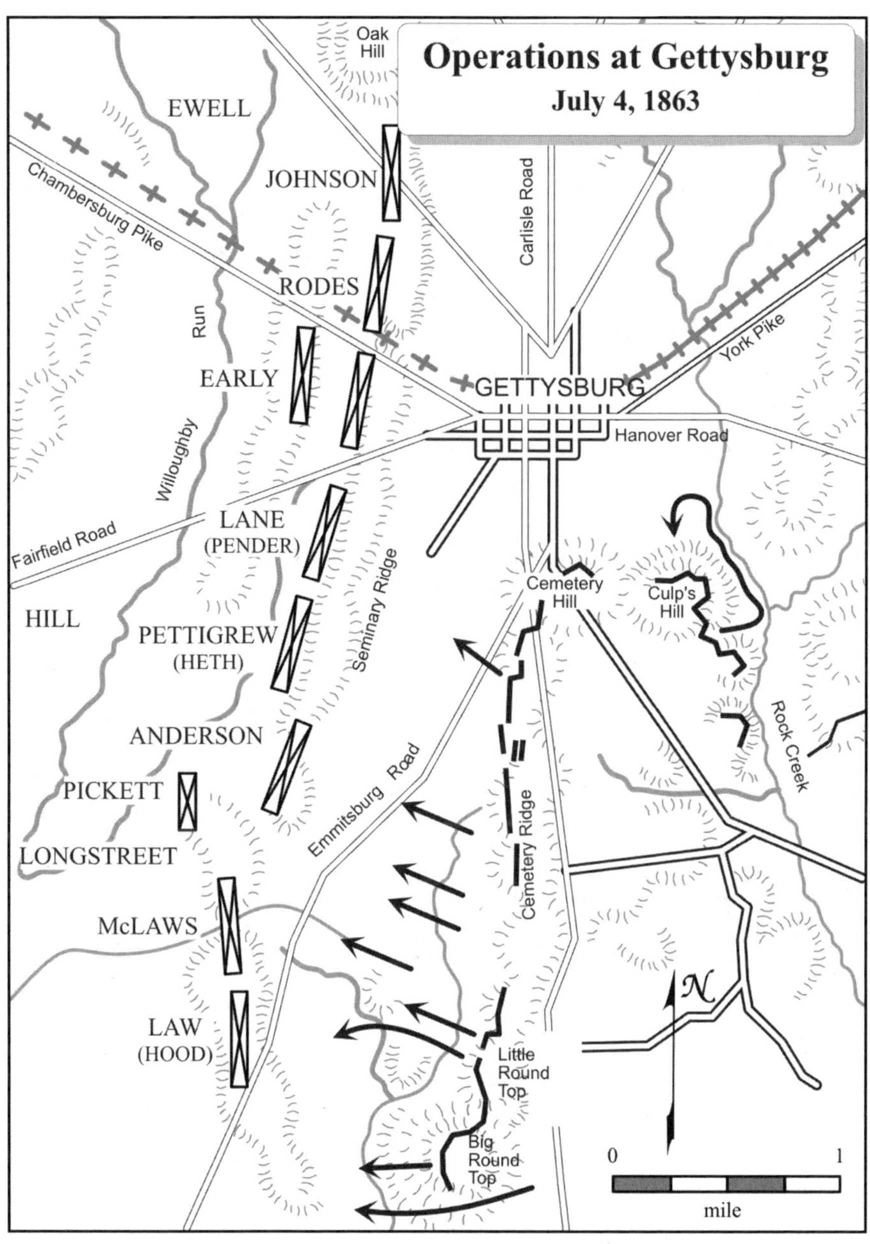

army commander insisted on knowing where the food came from. Alexander modestly avoided claiming credit, telling the general that he had ordered guards placed on the roads and that they had gathered up the food. Realizing that many of the tourists had come to the battlefield in carriages, Meade determined those carriages could be used to convey wounded men back to Washington. The army commander ordered them impressed into service as ambulances.[17]

Both sides launched periodic probes intended to determine whether the enemy's position had changed, but little formal fighting occurred. However, as Brig. Gen. Gouverneur K. Warren, the Army of the Potomac's gifted chief engineer noted, "On the morning of the 4th, General Meade ordered demonstrations in front of our line, but they were very feebly made."[18]

Early that morning, men of Col. Silas Colgrove's brigade of the 12th Corps, together with three regiments from Col. Archibald MacDougall's brigade, escorted by a battery of artillery, sortied southeast along the Baltimore Pike. The force passed north near Wolf's Hill and onto the Hanover Road, where the column headed west toward Gettysburg. The Federals covered nearly six miles without meeting any opposition, moving beyond the shattered remnants of Maj. Joseph Lattimer's artillery battalion on Benner's Hill before returning to their starting point. Other than a few stragglers, no enemy was encountered in their front.[19] "The boys knew then that the enemy had been defeated and had left," recorded a grateful New Yorker.[20]

Meade ordered his army to also probe up and down the enemy's lines in order to try and determine the intentions of Lee's army. Probes by the Army of the Potomac's 5th Corps soon determined that Lee had withdrawn from Seminary Ridge: "Lee had refused his right flank, but was still holding a strong position toward the centre of the line." The 2nd and 6th Pennsylvania Reserve regiments advanced as pickets, and soon after daylight, the Confederate pickets opened on them, "which we returned with much spirit," noted a member of the 2nd Pennsylvania Reserves.[21] Other forays by the 11th Corps and 12th Corps probed Southern positions near Culp's Hill only to discover that Ewell's Second Corps infantry had pulled up stakes and withdrawn for the positions his men held on July 2 and 3.[22]

Pvt. Leander Schooley was a member of the 1st Indiana Cavalry. His squadron served as Maj. Gen. Oliver O. Howard's headquarters escort. Schooley and his comrades escorted Howard when the one-armed general decided to ride into the town to reconnoiter late in the afternoon. The Hoosier private left behind a vivid description of the Gettysburg battlefield and the damage done to the town. "The battle field was the Awfulest sight I ever saw," he wrote. "The woods in front of our men the trees were riddled with Cannon ball and bullets evry limb shot off 20 feet high. Some say the Rebel dead lay six deep in the grave yard where we lay. Nearly every grave stone was shattered by shots and everything torn to pieces. I went through the town on the 4th of July

Maj. Gen. Oliver O. Howard, commander, 11th Corps, Army of the Potomac.

USAHEC

with the General. The streets were covered with dead. Evry frame house were riddled with balls the brick ones dented thick where the shot had hit."[23]

About 10:00 a.m., Col. William Tilton's brigade moved to the left until it arrived at Little Round Top, where it pushed ahead into the Plum Run Valley and beyond to the edge of the Wheatfield. In the distance, hidden Rebel sharpshooters awaited. Their fire drove Tilton's skirmishers back. "About this time large bodies of troops could be seen moving as if to flank us, while a line approached in front with evident intention to engage," recalled Capt. Francis Donaldson of the 118th Pennsylvania. "Our orders being merely to develop the enemy and avoid an engagement, Colonel Tilton . . . gave the signal to retire, which we did, and went into bivouac in the rear of the line of battle." They remained there until 6th Corps troops relieved them. Donaldson added, "shortly after noon it commenced to storm, and the very flood gates of heaven seemed to open upon us. Each moment it increased in fury until every man was drenched by the cold rain."[24]

Col. Hannibal Day's 5th Corps brigade of United States Regulars, joined by Brig. Gen. Joseph Bartlett's 6th Corps brigade, formed into two lines and scoured the woods near the Rose Farm. They advanced a few hundred yards at the double-quick to the edge of the Peach Orchard, where they halted when Confederate skirmishers opened on them. "One of our brigades drove in the enemy's pickets, and the bullets flew around pretty thickly," noted a soldier of the 5th Corps.[25] This skirmish fire, in turn, drew the attention of the main enemy line of battle. Capt. Basil C. Manly's Battery A, 1st North Carolina Artillery opened on them, inflicting casualties on the Regulars.[26] "Their range was so accurate that we were obliged to lay flat for a while the shot & shell just whistling over head & exploding over us," scribbled Sgt. Charles T. Bowen of the 12th U. S. Infantry in his diary. "One huge piece took nearly the whole hand of an officer who lay near me & covered us with earth. When the fire slackened up a little we retired having found the position of the rebs."[27] In spite of Bartlett's encouragement, Day wisely decline to advance farther in the face of this Confederate artillery fire.[28]

Men of the 126th New York, part of the 2nd Corps, spent the day in Zeigler's Grove engaging in heavy skirmishing with troops of Carnot Posey's Mississippi brigade, spread out amongst the burned-out buildings of the William Bliss farm. Many of these Empire Staters considered the heavy skirmishing of the Fourth of July to be the most dangerous service of their time in the Army of the Potomac. The Confederates kept up their murderous fire right up until the moment they withdrew to begin their retreat.[29]

In the fields just to the west of Zeigler's Grove, elements of the 1st Corps were also engaged with the Confederates scattered among the Bliss buildings. A private of the 56th Pennsylvania captured an unlucky Southern major in this "no man's land."[30] The men of the 13th Massachusetts Infantry stayed on the main Union battle line that day, coming under fire from enemy sharpshooters from time to time. On one of those occasions, an officer of the regiment was in the midst of raising a dipper full of coffee to his lips when a bullet zipped right through the dipper, making an unearthly "clink" and spraying coffee everywhere. "A close shot," he declared before proceeding to drink the coffee that hadn't spilled. Another soldier of the 13th Massachusetts was shot in the thigh. The buzzing enemy bullets soon grew to be a major nuisance for the tired Bay Staters.[31]

Most of the men of the 6th Corps spent a quiet day. Many of them could not even see the Confederates across the way. "Aside from the occasional glimmer of their muskets through the foliage, there was nothing to indicate their presence," observed a lieutenant colonel of the 37th Massachusetts. That afternoon, the Bay Staters built rifle pits to protect them in case the Confederates renewed their attack. Using only their bayonets and bare hands, they loosened the earth and piled the dirt in the hope of erecting some shelter. They also gathered fence rails and even used the carcasses of dead horses for protection. The men spent the rest of the day huddling in their soggy rifle pits, trying to escape the heavy rains.[32] "There was a little firing at dark, just to make our Fourth of July fireworks," recorded another Massachusetts man of the 6th Corps.[33]

A soldier of the 49th Pennsylvania recalled that he was only about 100 yards from the enemy lines when a cow wandered over to his position. He milked the cow without any trouble. "Three or four of us got all the milk we wanted," he recalled. Years later, he remembered that the cow was wounded in the right front leg and on the right side of her face, below the horn. Obviously, things were quiet in the 49th Pennsylvania's front if it was calm enough for soldiers to milk the cow while so close to the enemy's lines.[34]

The same could not be said for the 2nd Rhode Island, which spent the day heavily engaged with the 61st Virginia infantry, part of Brig. Gen. William Mahone's Brigade, Hill's Third Corps. "Was ever the Nation's Birthday celebrated in such a way before," grumbled Lt. Elisha Hunt Rhodes of the 2nd Rhode Island.[35] Early that morning, the Rhode Islanders sortied to the south of the Codori farm buildings, where they took up a position behind an earthen bank on the western side of the Emmitsburg Road. They stayed there all day, exchanging a steady and heavy skirmish fire with Mahone's butternuts.[36] "We passed the day in firing upon any Rebels that showed themselves," noted Lieutenant Rhodes. At noon, a national salute was fired from several Union batteries.[37] A detachment of Berdan's Sharpshooters, an elite unit that was heavily engaged on the second day of the battle, arrived to join the Rhode Islanders. The Sharpshooters crossed the Emmitsburg Road near the Sherfy Peach Orchard and joined the heavy skirmishing with the same Rebel pickets.

Orderly Sergeant Josiah Gray of Co. D, 2nd United States Sharpshooters, was killed instantly when a Southern rifleman, hidden behind a breastwork of stones, drilled him in the forehead with a well-aimed shot.[38] "[A]lthough the atmosphere is damp & cool, still the bullets from Johnny rebs make it exceedingly warm for we'ans," a nearby marksman of the green-clad Berdan regiment noted in his diary. "Orderly Sgt. Gray was killed about noon within ten feet of me while sitting behind a tree."[39] Including Gray, three of the Sharpshooters died in the post-battle fighting, and eight more were wounded. The 61st Virginia suffered similar losses of five killed and six wounded.[40]

Others spent a less hectic day. The 15th New Jersey Infantry of the 6th Corps had carried Enfield rifles since the beginning of the war. While the British-made rifle-muskets were by now more than familiar, the Jerseymen knew they were inferior weapons. When no fighting of any consequence broke out on July 4, the 15th's colonel led the regiment down, one company at a time, to the scene of the July 2 fighting. Scattered in every direction were plenty of Springfield rifles to choose from. Each man re-armed himself from the bounty left on the field. When the Jerseymen left Gettysburg, their Enfield rifles remained behind, neatly stacked on the ground.[41] Similarly, the men of the 155th Pennsylvania of the 5th Corps, who had been carrying antiquated buck-and-ball muskets, also fully re-armed themselves from the ample supply of abandoned Springfields scattered around the battlefield.[42] The 29th Ohio of the 12th Corps collected some 5,000 stand of enemy arms from the field in front of their position on Culp's Hill.[43]

Meade's probes determined that Lee had contracted his lines, entrenched, and appeared to be awaiting an attack. The Southerners had apparently gone over to the defensive. The Federal commander continued probing the Army of Northern Virginia's lines, looking for weak spots they never found. Some asked themselves and their friends why more was not done. "Wonder why we don't advance and follow up our victory," asked an officer of the 93rd Pennsylvania Infantry.[44]

Convinced that Lee was about to retreat, Meade acted decisively. He ordered Maj. Gen. William H. French, the commander of the Federal garrison at Harpers Ferry, which had removed to Frederick, Maryland, in the face of the Confederate advance, to return part of his command to Harpers Ferry and to block the passes through South Mountain with the rest. Later that day, Meade changed his mind and countermanded the order. The original order, however, would have consequences the army commander could never have anticipated.[45]

Lee's Army

The Army of Northern Virginia's chief topographical engineer, the talented 34-year-old former schoolteacher Jedediah Hotchkiss, was up early on July 4. He arose at 2:00 that morning to begin drawing a map of the country back to Virginia. Hotchkiss had his work cut out for him: he had to find the shortest and safest route back to the Potomac River crossings in and around Williamsport, and he had only one assistant to help him do so.[46]

As Hotchkiss worked, others in the field waited. "We threw up breastworks on the 4th, with the hope that the enemy would leave his position in the mountains and attack us on the open plain, where we could have routed him and kept him in such confusion that a rally would have been impossible," reported one of Maj. Gen. John Bell Hood's Texans. "And such another fourth I never expect to spend. We had no meat and very little bread for two days. Had not taken off our accouterments during the time, and the rain poured incessantly, so that the water on the level plain was two or three inches deep."[47]

"We are here or near the place we were 1st July," 2nd Lt. James E. Green of Co. I, 53rd North Carolina jotted in his diary that night. "And waited for the Enemy to come on us but they did not. We were willing for them to come on us here, for we had throne up Breastworks, a light work of Cord Wood, Rock & dirt. We had but few Tools to work with, none but the Pioneer Tools but they made good use of them & by 12 Noon we had a lite work throne up."[48]

British officer Lt. Col. Arthur Fremantle served in Her Majesty's Coldstream Guards. He had spent the last three months in the Confederacy observing the war and most recently, Lee's army. Luckily for Fremantle, he arrived in time to join the march into Pennsylvania and observe the battle of Gettysburg. He was particularly close to James Longstreet. "It was hoped that the enemy might attack during the day, as this is the 4th of July, and it was calculated that there was still ammunition for one day's fighting," Fremantle recorded in his now-famous and widely read diary.[49]

"We were roused up about 12 ½ last night and moved back to a first rate position on elevated ground where after day light we built strong breastworks. It rained during the day, & we put on tents & lay under them," recalled Pvt. Samuel Pickens of the 5th Alabama Infantry, Co. D, known as the "Greensboro Guards." Their location west of town, however, was near the first day's battlefield, and much of its wreckage remained. "There were a good many of the enemy's dead & dead horses lying back of our position which produced a most disagreeable smell."[50]

One 6th Louisiana infantryman told his diary on July 4 that his regiment "moved before dawn, with the whole army, and formed line of battle on a ridge one mile to the right of the town, where we remained all day. . . . This being the 'glorious Fourth,' we thought the Yankees would burn great quantities of harmless gunpowder in honor of the day; but they had suffered too much to indulge in any such jubilation, so they spent the day in bringing in their dead. Gen. Lee at this time gave the Federal General a fine opportunity of attacking him, but it was declined."[51]

"Meade knows full well that to whip Lee he will have to charge across an open field and up heights similar to those that Pickett could not overcome," correctly observed a member of the Richmond Howitzer Battalion in his journal, "and he is not to anxious to make the attempt." Although the Army of Northern Virginia was nearly out of ammunition for its rifled guns, it still had plenty for its smoothbore Napoleons, and the men of the Richmond Howitzer Battalion stood ready to repulse any Union attack with their brass pieces.[52]

"All day on the 4th did we await the expected attack," remembered Capt. William W. Blackford, engineering officer to the army's cavalry commander, Maj. Gen. James Ewell Brown (Jeb) Stuart, "but another and greater danger now threatened in the rains which set in that day. We were nearly forty miles from the Potomac, whose fords were deep and wide at their best." Blackford was enough of an engineer to know that the steady downfall might well imperil the army's ability to safely return to Southern soil.[53] "We all expected this to be the heaviest day of fighting of the battle, notwithstanding the terrible work that has already been done," one Virginia artillerist noted in his diary, "but in this we were, I must say pleasingly, disappointed."[54]

"Notwithstanding our great losses of the second and third, we were permitted to hold the field on the fourth by Meade's inactivity," wrote Major G. Moxley Sorrell, Longstreet's top aide. "His army was very strong, had not suffered as had ours, and an enterprising general might seemingly have had us on the run in short order. But no! he had taken a taste of our mettle that day before and wanted no more of it."[55] A. P. Hill did not share this opinion. Sitting by a roaring bivouac fire, Hill turned to the commander of his artillery battalion, John J. Garnett, and declared, "Colonel, we must return to Virginia and prepare to try it again."[56]

Maj. Campbell Brown, the stepson of and staff officer to Lt. Gen. Richard S. Ewell, echoed Sorrell's observations. "It would be ridiculous to say that I did not feel whipped—or that there was a man in that Army who didn't appreciate the position just as plainly. But the 'fight' wasn't out of the troops by any means—they felt that the position & not the enemy had out done us—& Genl Meade never brought his 'rascally virtue' of caution to a better market than when he let us alone—for we should probably have given a good account of him."[57]

Similar comments were spoken and written throughout the army. "[We] lay there all day Saturday, the 4th, waiting for Meade to attack us and give us a chance to pay him back in the same coin which he had dealt to us—to wit, a repulse," recalled an officer of the 4th Alabama Infantry. "He had stood all the while on the defensive in a position well-nigh impregnable and with superior numbers, while all the assaults were made by Confederates. We wished to turn the board around and try the game that way, but Meade ignored our challenge."[58]

"[N]o one thought we were defeated," emphasized Capt. Frank A. Bond of the 1st Maryland Cavalry (C.S.A.). "Just at dark [on July 4] Gen. Ewell summoned me and directed that at 10 P.M. I should stretch my company across the front of his entire corps and remain there until broad daylight, when I was to make a careful observation in the direction of the enemy's position, and then follow the army, which, to my great surprise, he told me he was going to return to Virginia."[59] Bond obediently "threw out his company as videttes and occupied the ground, advancing somewhat to the enemy, who made no effort to move forward until some considerable time after the day opened, when the road having been cleared, we withdrew finally."[60]

Ewell also sent for his pet horsemen, Col. Elijah V. White's 35th Battalion Virginia Cavalry. White's battalion of six companies, under strength with a total of only some 250 men, was divided for differing duties. Three companies were detailed to act as the rearguard for A. P. Hill's Corps, while Ewell kept the remaining three companies under White as his own rearguard. White's ragged but proud horsemen had led Ewell's advance into Pennsylvania two weeks earlier; now, they would be among the very last to leave the battlefield.[61]

As the sun set, Lee finally began moving his Army of Northern Virginia south and west, hoping to escape to safety across the Potomac River. "The retirement was necessary because it became important to re-establish our communications with the government," explained Maj. Gen. Lafayette McLaws in a July 7 letter to his wife.[62] While that was undoubtedly a true statement, it was also dramatically oversimplified. Lee was short on ammunition, his army had been roughly handled, his command structure had been eviscerated, and his lines of communication and supply were in danger of being cut. In short, there was no choice but to return to the safety of the Old Dominion. "The movement was so much impeded by soft roads, darkness, and rains that the rear-guard could not be withdrawn until daylight on the morning of the 5th," recalled one of Lee's staff officers.[63]

Hill's Corps was at the front of the long Confederate column, with Brig. Gen. James H. Lane's brigade leading the way. The Southerners conducted their retreat "splendidly," without demoralization, and with "the greatest deliberation and order," one correspondent to a Richmond newspaper reported.[64] "There was not a rout," reported Capt. Harry Gilmor of the 2nd Maryland Cavalry, "and all that silly stuff we read in the Northern accounts of 'flying rebels' and shattered army are pure fictions prepared for the Northern market."[65]

Generals Lee and Hill, together with their staffs, rode at the head of the Confederate troops as they marched west from Gettysburg. The men were in generally good spirits as they trudged through the rain. "At length the loud laughter of the men, comprising the head of A. P. Hill's column, advancing, banished every indication of sleep," recalled the chaplain of the 14th Louisiana. "They were as cheerful a body of men as I ever saw; and to hear them, you would think they were going to a party of pleasure instead of retreating from a hard fought battle."[66]

Nevertheless, the pitch darkness and the thick mud posed a challenge for the Southerners. "We were up to our knees in mud and water all night," noted a Virginian of Hill's Corps. "It was impossible to preserve the company organization in such darkness and difficult marching. The men would halloo out the names of their companies in order to keep together." Another described it as "a vast moving panorama of misery."[67]

"It was pouring rain and dark as Erebus," recalled Pvt. Anderson W. Reese of the Georgia Troup Artillery, his reference to Greek mythology an apt one. Reese had a long and uncomfortable ride ahead of him. "I sat on my horse all night, getting no sleep, whatever, save a few brief 'nods' now and then, when we halted."[68]

Ewell's veterans acted as the Army of Northern Virginia's rearguard, with Maj. Gen. Jubal A. Early's division bringing up the very end of the Confederate column. Lee stopped to consult with Longstreet and Ewell. According to one witness, the one-legged Ewell desperately wanted to turn on the enemy and attack them again, "crying and begging for a 'fight' just like a schoolboy begging for a bun." Although Lee appreciated his subordinate's fighting spirit, he shook his head. "No, no, General Ewell, we must let those people alone for the present—we will try them again some other time." In the army commander's mind, it was neither the time nor the place to resume the savage battle that had just ended.[69] Ewell and his staff spent the night on some rails by the roadside, four miles from Gettysburg, where they built a large fire and watched the army pass by all night through the pouring rain.[70]

"No defeat to the Confederates was shown in the proud, invincible tread," recounted a Southern officer, "that spirited and bold heart, that grieved but proud and fierce army of freemen. The morale of our army was utterly unaffected," he concluded.[71]

Major Sorrel had seen his share of disagreeable weather, but this night's miserable conditions deserved special mention. "The night of July 4, 1863, was of awful weather—rain in torrents, howling winds, and roads almost impassable."[72] Impassable the roads might be, but no other options were available. "[O]ver this road our large army had to pass," recalled Spencer G. Welch, the surgeon of the 13th South Carolina Infantry. "It rained nearly all night, and such a sight as our troops were the next day! They were all wet and many of them muddy all over from having fallen down during the night."[73]

Pvt. Samuel Pickens of the 5th Alabama, Ewell's Corps, described a wet, stutter-step march in his diary. "The road was perfectly sloppy & so slippery that it was with the greatest difficulty that we could keep our feet. Came not more than 2 or 2 ½ ms. when we stopped on account of the road being blocked up by the wagon trains ahead, I suppose. Here we were drenched by a cold rain, but when it held up we made fires & made ourselves as comfortable as possible under the circumstances. Several hours after day light we continued the march through mud & water ankle deep in places. The wagon trains kept the road & a column of troops marched thro' the fields & woods on each side."[74]

Maj. Gen. George E. Pickett's Division of Longstreet's Second Corps had been decimated on the afternoon of July 3 in the failed grand charge forever memorialized by its commander's name. Pickett's survivors—only enough remained to field a good-sized brigade—were detailed to provost duty. The division left Gettysburg first, ahead of the wagon trains escorting some 4,000 Union prisoners. One of them was Lt. Col. Frederico F. Cavada, the commander of the 114th Pennsylvania, a crack regiment known as "Collis' Zouaves." Cavada had been captured on July 2 in the fighting on the John Sherfy property near the Peach Orchard. "On that 4th of July, so glorious for our arms, our column was once more started, drenched with the torrents of rain which fell without intermission," he later penned. "The Rebel trains and artillery were moving rapidly in the direction of Chambersburg. Before we had proceeded far we were joined by the prisoners captured during the engagement of the 1st. . . . Along with us were long trains of wagons, and a motley assortment of vehicles of all kinds, impressed from the farmers of the neighborhood, loaded with the Rebel wounded."[75]

By mid-afternoon, the column of prisoners and their escorts reached the Black Horse Tavern along the Fairfield Road. They continued through and beyond the village of Fairfield, where they bivouacked that night. "We were marched steadily over the rough mountain roads until after midnight, having proceeded as far as Monterey Springs," Lt. Col. Cavada recalled. "It would be difficult to give a description which could do justice to the trials of that weary night-march; we were pressed forward at the utmost speed of which, we were capable, and many, unable to keep up with the column, fell exhausted by the roadside."[76]

The Federal prisoners had no rations and the men were hungry. "Glorious old fourth but cannot enjoy it much in my present position no rations, no clothes, but what is on my back, and old half of a blanket," complained an officer of the 151st Pennsylvania of the 1st Corps who had been captured on the afternoon of July 1. "Rebs retreating as fast as possible, through drenching rain. Long train of wagons, containing wounded rebels, household furniture, in fact anything everything they could carry off, chairs, bed quilts, covers, lids, mowing machines, scythes, and their horses decorated with sleigh bells."[77] Grumbled a member of the 11th Corps, also captured on July 1, "Rain and with hungry bellies, I shall long remember this Independence Day."[78] Another prisoner of the 11th Corps recalled that the men entertained themselves and celebrated the nation's birthday by "singing patriotic songs and making ourselves jolly generally."[79]

The 39th Battalion of Virginia Cavalry served as General Lee's personal bodyguard. "Arrived at Fairfield at daylight," noted a trooper of the battalion in his diary. "Suffered intensely for a while before day for want of sleep often nodding on my horse and several times coming near falling." After resting a bit, they advanced another two miles and bivouacked until 5:00 p.m. Another advance of eight miles into the mountains followed, where the troopers camped for the night.[80]

"At dark, great was our surprise to see all the troops in motion, and all taking the back track," recalled a Virginia artillerist. "We marched all of that night over one of the worst roads that I ever saw and at five o'clock in the morning, packed at the foot of South Mountain, having passed through the small but rather neat village of Fairfield." Some of the Confederates found some much needed food as they tramped through Fairfield, but most of them would have to remain hungry.[81]

The Confederates "marched very slowly in consequence of the length of the ordnance and artillery train, and the ruggedness and mountainous nature of the road," wrote a Maryland officer in his diary.[82] "We never left a battlefield more leisurely, after defeating the enemy on other fields, than we retreated from this," recalled one of Longstreet's hard-fighting Alabamans.[83]

Now, both the wagon train of wounded and the main army column was on the move. "Old Pete" Longstreet made sure that the column covered as much ground as possible. The First Corps commander was anxious, and he had a right to be. The winding Southern trains and infantry moved slowly at best, offering an aggressive enemy the chance to beat the Army of Northern Virginia to the Potomac River crossings. Whenever he and his staff halted, the burly general "walked ceaselessly backward and forward like a sailor on his quarterdeck," recalled one eyewitness.[84] The question in the minds of many was obvious: which army would reach the river crossings first?

"It rained heavily all night long, and right gladly would I have crawled beneath the sheets of a wagon and found protection from the storm," reported J. B. Polley of Hood's Texas Brigade. "But my steed refused to lead and I was forced to take the rain and be content with such cat-naps as occasional halts permitted." Driven by fear of being caught by Federal cavalry, the column pressed on for as long and as hard as men and animals could bear.[85]

The Army of the Potomac

Lee's withdrawal did not escape notice by the Union soldiers. About 3:00 a.m. on the morning of July 5, a couple of deserters crossed into the 6th Corps line and gave themselves up. They carried with them news that the entire Army of Northern Virginia had slipped away from the front. Lt. Col. J. B. Parsons of the 10th Massachusetts Infantry sent a sergeant and a file of men to verify the report. When they reported back that the enemy was indeed gone, Parsons sent word up the chain of command.[86]

Soon enough, signal officers were regularly reporting on the passage of the long Southern wagon trains. The men in the ranks also knew something was going on across the way. "Six o'clock in the evening. It has been ascertained that the enemy has in reality commenced a retreat," recorded a member of the 14th Vermont Infantry of the 1st Corps. "The engagement of yesterday terminated the battle, and thus, ended another sanguinary contest, and one of the best fought battles of the war."[87] A member of the 13th Massachusetts drew an insightful comparison. "As we reflected on the last three days' terrible work, we could not escape the impression that it was a repetition of Antietam, for in both cases the enemy was granted 'leave to withdraw' at a time when it could have had little expectation of the exercise of so benignant a privilege."[88]

As the long afternoon dragged on, the rains increased in intensity, adding to the misery of the Union soldiers. The men of the 118th Pennsylvania "Corn Exchange" Regiment kept the rainwater from running down the barrels of their rifles by inverting them and pushing their bayonets into the ground.[89] The men also had to keep their powder dry, always a challenge in heavy rains. As the afternoon wore on, the rains grew heavier. Large bolts of lightning lit the sky while thunder shook the air.

The downpour also created a nightmare for the battle-weary Union soldiers as they tried to get some sleep on the saturated earth. "The ground where the regiment lay, or tried to that night was almost flooded with water, and some of the men stood up or sat down on stumps or stone," recalled a member of the 12th New Hampshire, "stretched out at full length in mud and water beneath, and constantly increasing supply of the latter freely bestowed upon them from the heavens above."[90]

A Vermonter of the 6th Corps recalled the same miserable experience. "[O]n the night of the Fourth we were trying our best to keep our ammunition dry, for it did rain in torrents—just seemed to pour right down," he wrote. "My tent mate succeeded in getting a half dozen rails from some quarter, and, laying the ends up on a rock, we put a few boughs on them to take the edge off the corners and spread a rubber blanket over them. Then, taking our second rubber blanket to cover us, we lay down using cartridge boxes for pillows, and putting our rifles between us, and slept as only an old soldier can sleep." The worst thing for the two Vermonters was that three days' worth of hardtack turned to soggy mush and their coffee and salt pork became "one nasty mixture" in the unrelenting rains, leaving them without food. However, these men were the exception and not the rule; few men got so much as a wink of sleep that awful night.[91]

At 7:40 a.m., Meade received a report from some signal officers that the "enemy just relieved their outer pickets. There has been passing for the last twenty-five minutes (and is still passing), along what is called the Fairfield road, a steady stream of heavy wagons, ambulances, cavalry, and what seems to be artillery, or else flying artillery, and no cavalry. They move slowly, and to our left."[92] The report provided irrefutable proof that the Army of Northern Virginia had begun its retreat.

Maj. Gen. Darius Couch, Dept. of the Susquehanna commander.

USAHEC

Maj. Gen. William F. "Baldy" Smith, 1st Division, Dept. of the Susquehanna.

USAHEC

It was time for General Meade to develop a suitable strategy for contending with this new challenge. Meade, noted one eyewitness, "was then tall and slender, gaunt and sad of visage, with iron-gray hair and beard, ensconced behind a pair of spectacles, and with few popular traits about him, but with a keen and well-disciplined intellect, a cool and sound judgment, and by both education and temperament was every inch a soldier."[93] He would need all of these traits and more over the next ten days. Indeed, they would prove to be perhaps the most trying days of his life.

From the beginning, George Meade's subordinates urged caution in pursuing the retreating Confederates. Shortly after noon on July 4, he received a dispatch from his old friend Maj. Gen. Darius N. Couch, the commander of the Department of the Susquehanna in Pennsylvania. Couch maintained his headquarters at Harrisburg. He congratulated Meade on his success at Gettysburg, but warned, "Unquestionably the rebels have fortified the passes in South Mountain—-such information was given me a week ago from Gettysburg."[94]

Meade set about reinforcing his army. "This army has been very much reduced by the casualties of service," he wrote to Maj. Gen. William F. "Baldy" Smith, who commanded a large division of untrained and inexperienced emergency militia troops of Couch's forces from the defenses of the state capital at Harrisburg, "and [I] would be glad to have you join [us]."[95] Couch harbored no illusions about the value of these men. "[Smith] should have 10,000 men, but one-half are very worthless, and 2,000 cavalry, with a battery, can capture the whole party in an open county," he cautioned Meade. "This is why I put them in or near the mountains; there they could do service."[96]

Although these men had no real experience, they could be used to fill gaps in the Union deployments, thereby freeing up veteran troops for other uses.

The Council of War

The night of July 4, Meade convened a council of war to hear the opinions of his subordinates on the best course of action. He reminded his commanders that his primary mission was to protect Washington and Baltimore, and to prevent Lee from moving around the Army of the Potomac's left flank, interposing himself between the Federal army and the nation's capital. With those cautions in mind, Meade posed four questions:

> "Shall this army remain here?"
>
> If so, "Shall we assume the offensive?"
>
> Did his subordinates "deem it expedient to move toward Williamsport through Emmitsburg?"
>
> Finally, he asked, "Shall we pursue the enemy if he is retreating on his direct line of retreat?"[97]

All of Meade's senior officers voted to remain at Gettysburg except 12th Corps commander Maj. Gen. Henry W. Slocum, Cavalry Corps commander Maj. Gen. Alfred Pleasonton, and 1st Corps commander Maj. Gen. John Newton. None wanted to go on the offensive. Most advocated direct pursuit only by cavalry once Lee's retreat could be confirmed, and that the infantry should follow east of South Mountain in order to remain between the enemy and Washington. The Army of the Potomac could try to intercept Lee before he crossed the Potomac River.

Meade deferred to the wisdom of his collective generals, and ordered his chief engineer, Brig. Gen. Gouverneur K. Warren, to use troops from the 6th Corps "to find out the position and movements of the enemy."[98] Later, when called upon to explain the decision not to pursue Lee's army directly, Meade replied that following Lee directly would bring about constant fighting through the mountain passes and continuous engagements with Lee's rearguard. Such activities would slow the Union pursuit more than following along on Lee's flank.[99] Meade's army was also desperately short of ammunition. He could not re-supply until he knew where Lee was going—Lee's destination would determine which rail head would serve as Meade's line of supply. If Lee was only moving his base of operations to the mountains, Meade would use the rail lines at Hanover and Gettysburg for supplies. If Lee was really heading for the Potomac River, Meade could use the railhead at Frederick, Maryland. Logistically, Meade reasoned, it did not make sense to move the army until he knew where to send his supplies.

Regardless of Lee's destination, would the Army of the Potomac be able to catch him north of the river and destroy the Virginia army?

Chapter 3

July 4: The Midnight Fight in the Monterey Pass

"It was one of the most exciting engagements we ever had."

— Capt. James H. Kidd, Custer's Michigan Brigade

LT. GEN. RICHARD S. EWELL WAS worried about getting his wagons across the Potomac River safely. He started most of the Second Corps baggage and captured property back to Virginia on the night of July 3, and instructed his quartermaster, Maj. John A. Harman, "to get that train safely across the Potomac or he wanted to see his face no more." The hard-working and talented Harman, a thirty-nine year-old newspaperman and cattleman from the Shenandoah Valley, faced a daunting trial if he was to fulfill his mission.[1]

One train, the wagons of Ewell's Corps, would leave Gettysburg via the Fairfield Road. Part of it would head through the Cashtown Gap, proceed to the hamlet of New Franklin, continue on to Greencastle, and then roll to Williamsport. A second section would move through the Fairfield Gap, then south to Hagerstown and west to Williamsport. The third column would use the Monterey Pass, head south to Cavetown, roll southwest to Hagerstown, and then move to Williamsport.[2] This last column would follow the route taken by

Lt. Gen. Richard S. Ewell, commander, Ewell's Second Corps.

USAHEC

Maj. Gen. George Pickett, Commander, Pickett's Division.

Valentine Museum

George Pickett's Division, which was escorting the Union prisoners of war.[3] As the column passed through Franklin County, the Confederates took half a dozen local citizens hostage, and brought them along as prisoners.[4]

"Wagons, horses, mules, and cattle captured in Pennsylvania, the solid advantages of this campaign, have been passing slowly along [the Fairfield Road] all day," recorded British officer Lt. Col. Fremantle, "those taken by Ewell are particularly admired. So interminable was this train that it soon became evident that we should not be able to start till late at night." Fremantle and several other officers sat and watched as the column passed by.[5]

The conditions of the roads through Monterey, as prisoner Cavada described that night as they marched ahead of the trains, meant that the third column was in for an especially hard time. "This day's march was also a trying one," he wrote, "worn out, and most of us with torn shoes and bleeding feet, we were urged on with our utmost speed, over slippery, stony roads, and through mud, that in many places was knee deep."[6]

Two main roads led westward from the town of Fairfield, Pennsylvania, six miles west of Gettysburg, to South Mountain. Each road ran on either side of Jack's Mountain, just to the south and west of Fairfield. Both provided direct routes to vital mountain passes and were important roads for Lee's line of march. The southern route intersected the road connecting Emmitsburg and Waynesboro, about six miles north of Emmitsburg, and was the road to the Monterey Pass. Ewell's wagon train was scheduled to take this road. All these roads, and the major mountain passes, were picketed by the cavalry brigades of Brig. Gens. Beverly H. Robertson and William E. "Grumble" Jones. These two commands were

Brig. Gen. Beverly H. Robertson, commander, Robertson's brigade of cavalry.

USAHEC

well-suited to this sort of duty, with Jones in particular being especially adept at this kind of work.

The Federals had previously only made a half-hearted attempt to block the Confederate line of retreat on the afternoon of July 3. A single regiment of horsemen, the 6th U.S. Cavalry, rode to Fairfield unsupported after a small column of wagons was reported to be in the area. The lone Yankee regiment blundered into Jones' brigade and, after a brief but brutal fight, fled in a wild rout.[7] The Army of the Potomac's high command had squandered a great opportunity.

Jeb Stuart knew that securing the mountain passes was paramount to a successful retreat. To that end, he issued orders to Robertson that "it was especially necessary for him to hold the Jack's Mountain passes," including the two major road arteries. Leaving Jones to help picket the gaps, Stuart assigned the brigades of Imboden and Col. Milton Ferguson to guard the other flank, and brought up the rear with the rest of his command.[8] As Stuart and the rest of his cavalry departed Gettysburg, he sent his engineering officer, Capt. William W. Blackford, to inform Robertson that the rest of the cavalry force was leaving, and to remind Robertson of the critical task assigned him.[9] A short distance into his march, Stuart learned that a large force of enemy cavalry was in pursuit. The cavalier sent additional couriers to Robertson to warn him of the threat.[10]

As the army's vast wagon train of wounded rolled and bumped its way through the Cashtown Pass west toward Chambersburg, Ewell's wagons moved toward Hagerstown, Maryland, via the important Monterey Pass in the South Mountain range. Ewell's trains and cattle herd had started much earlier in the day, about 3:00 a.m., and had covered a good bit of ground by the time Imboden commenced his march of the wounded.[11] John O. Casler, a soldier

Brig. Gen. William E. "Grumble" Jones, commander, Jones' brigade of cavalry.

LOC

serving with the 33rd Virginia Infantry of the Stonewall Brigade, part of Ewell's Corps, noted, "We had such an immense wagon train that we traveled very slowly, keeping the wagon train in front."[12] By nightfall, one portion of Ewell's column had passed through the Fairfield Gap and the rest was moving toward the Monterey Pass, several miles farther south. "Much rain fell during the day, making our progress slow," remembered a Virginian. "By night we were ascending the Blue Ridge, and our progress was slower still. It was a weary time."[13]

When Jones recognized that the wagons were threatened by Brig. Gen. Judson Kilpatrick's pursuing Federal cavalry, he asked Stuart for permission to take his entire brigade to support the vulnerable train. Stuart allowed Jones to shift the 6th and 7th Virginia Cavalry regiments and Capt. Roger Preston Chew's battery of horse artillery to bolster the defense of the trains. The 7th Virginia was soon called back, and the 4th North Carolina Cavalry of Robertson's brigade sent to take its place. The immense wagon train blocked the road, however, and it quickly became obvious to Jones that a large force of cavalry and Chew's guns would have a difficult time making it to Monterey Pass in a prompt fashion. Accompanied by only his staff and couriers, Jones rode ahead to hurry on the stragglers from the train and to provide whatever support he could.[14]

Kilpatrick Mounts His Pursuit

Ewell's preparations to leave the battlefield earlier that day had not gone unnoticed by the Federals. Early on the morning of July 4, Lts. Henry Camp and John Wiggins, manning a Union signal station on Cemetery Ridge, spotted

Brig. Gen. Judson Kilpatrick, Commander, 3rd Cavalry Division.

USAHEC

Ewell's train slowly moving out toward the southwest.[15] Maj. Gen. Alfred Pleasonton, commanding the Army of the Potomac's Cavalry Corps, ordered his three division commanders "to gain [the enemy's] rear and line of communication, and harass and annoy him as much as possible in his retreat."[16]

Kilpatrick "spoke words of high commendation to his command" for its performance at Gettysburg on July 3.[17] "It was no studied speech for a 4th of July, but one of a warrior to his victorious men," recalled a member of the 1st West Virginia Cavalry. "He spoke tenderly of the many brave and noble men who had fell while discharging their duties, and down over his cheek stole a tear of sympathy."[18] He then announced that the Union troopers were to "go to the enemy's right and rear," that they would be separated from the main body of the army for some time, and that the men should carry three days' rations with them on the march.[19] "The whole of us felt in excellent spirits when we heard what had been done the day previous, and that Lee's army was in full retreat towards the Potomac," recounted a trooper of the 5th New York Cavalry. "Not even a heavy thunder shower that came up soon after we got on the road, did not dampen the ardor of any in the division."[20] Once his division joined Col. Pennock Huey's brigade at Emmitsburg, Maryland, the combined forces of Kilpatrick and Huey were to locate "a heavy train of wagons" moving on the road to Hagerstown, destroy the train, and operate on the enemy's rear and flanks.[21]

"Little Kil's" cavalry division moved out around 10:00 a.m. The conditions of the march were miserable. "The roads and streets were one conglomerate mass of running water, mud and filth," shuddered a trooper of the 6th Michigan Cavalry.[22] "[T]he rain is falling fast," Louis Boudrye of the 5th New York Cavalry wrote home. "It is a dreadful moment for the poor soldiers who are out. The wind also blows furiously, which makes the rain doubly unpleasant."[23] "I had been out in a good many rain storms, but never before I think had I seen it rain harder," observed Maj. Luther S. Trowbridge of the 5th Michigan Cavalry. "The ditches along the road and the little streams that we crossed were filled to overflowing, and it was evident that before night the Potomac would be bank full with no possibility of fording for some days to come."[24]

Believing that Ewell's wagons actually represented Lee's main supply train, Kilpatrick pushed his men hard after them. When his cavalry division arrived at Emmitsburg, Huey's brigade, consisting of the 8th Pennsylvania, ten companies of the 6th Ohio, the 2nd New York, 4th New York, and two companies of the 1st Rhode Island, joined the column.[25] The combined force headed out on the road to Monterey Pass, where Kilpatrick intended to cross South Mountain, a distance of approximately sixteen miles, from one side to the other.[26] "It was in this pass Gen. Kilpatrick proposed to celebrate the Anniversary of our Independence," wryly observed a New Yorker of his division.[27] Huey's brigade, bringing up the rear of the column, briefly skirmished with a small force of the 1st North Carolina Cavalry of Robertson's command, which was quickly dispatched by a mounted charge by the 6th Ohio Cavalry. The undaunted Yankees pressed on through the heavy rain.[28] "We now and then make long detours to go around the spurs of the mountain," recalled a West Virginian, "but yet we can not see what we are after, and by noon we are many miles away from Gettysburg, but on we go at the same rate all afternoon."[29]

About 9:00 p.m., the head of Ewell's wagon train, led by Major Harman, arrived at Hagerstown.[30] Near the village of Fountaindale, on the Emmitsburg and Waynesboro Turnpike, a local citizen named C. H. Buhrman learned that the rear of Ewell's wagon train was approaching the tollgate at Monterey Springs via the Furnace Road. Buhrman mounted a horse and went looking for the approaching Federal cavalry. He soon found one of Kilpatrick's scouts, whom he knew personally, and was sent on to report his intelligence to Brig. Gen. George A. Custer. The young brigadier, in turn, sent Buhrman directly to Kilpatrick. When he reported his information to Kilpatrick, Little Kil smelled blood and ordered his whole force to advance to Monterey at once. About two miles from the pass, Buhrman and Kilpatrick met a local girl who reported that the Rebels had planted artillery in the road at the pass. The Federals were warned not to go on. Undaunted,

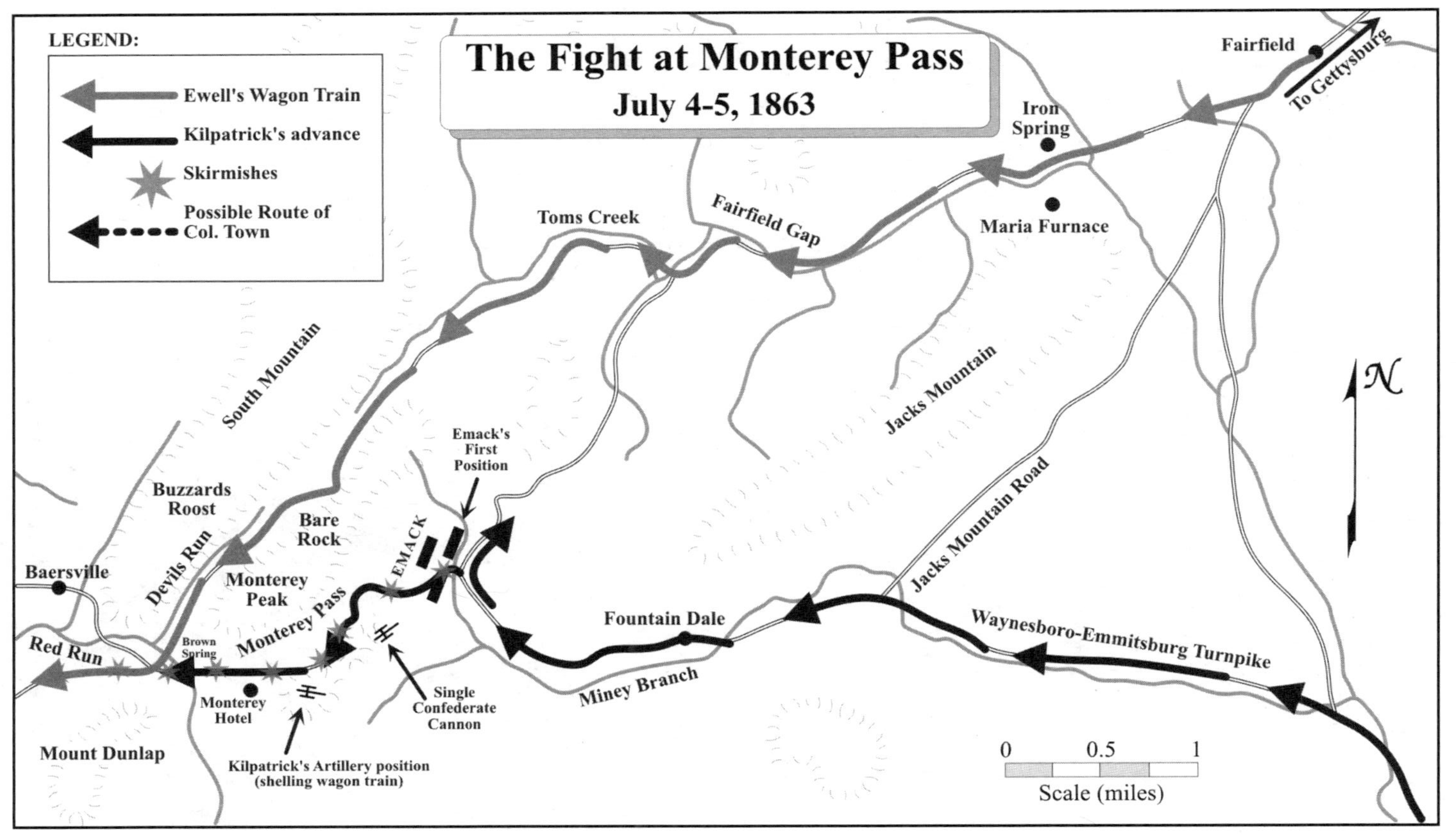
The Fight at Monterey Pass
July 4-5, 1863
LEGEND:
Ewell's Wagon Train
Kilpatrick's advance
Skirmishes
Possible Route of Col. Town
Fairfield
To Gettysburg
Iron Spring
Maria Furnace
Toms Creek
Fairfield Gap
South Mountain
Jacks Mountain
Jacks Mountain Road
N
Emack's First Position
EMACK
Buzzards Roost
Bare Rock
Baersville
Devils Run
Monterey Peak
Monterey Pass
Fountain Dale
Waynesboro-Emmitsburg Turnpike
Red Run
Brown Spring
Monterey Hotel
Single Confederate Cannon
Miney Branch
Mount Dunlap
Kilpatrick's Artillery position (shelling wagon train)
0
0.5
1
Scale (miles)

Kilpatrick may have replied with his trademark snort, declaring that the Federal cavalry kept no account of cannons.

When they reached the gate of Buhrman's farm, the farmer tried to beg off further duty, but Kilpatrick persuaded him to continue on with the Yankee troopers so that Buhrman could "see the fun."[31] "Fun," however, was the last term the troopers would use to describe the march up the mountain. Edward A. Paul, a *New York Times* correspondent accompanying the Michigan Brigade, described the dangerous trek:

> Imagine a long column of cavalry winding its way up the mountain side, on a road dug out of the mountain side, which sloped at an angle of thirty degrees just wide enough for four horses to march abreast—on one side a deep abyss and on the other an impassable barrier, in the shape of a steep embankment; the hour ten o'clock at night, a drizzling rain falling, the sky overcast, and so dark as literally not to be able to see one's own hand if placed within a foot of the organs of vision; the whole command, both men and animals, worn out with fatigue and loss of sleep . . .[32]

As the Yankees rode toward the pass, the Confederate artillery, a Napoleon of Courtney's Battery manned by Capt. William Tanner's gunners, blew a shot at them. The round surprised troopers and horses alike. Buhrman informed Kilpatrick that if he dismounted a regiment and sent it down through the edge of the woods, he could flank the Confederates and capture their guns. Kilpatrick ordered the movement, but Tanner's gunners withdrew before they could be flanked.[33]

Kilpatrick still had his eye on the prize and disregarded what he likely viewed as nothing more than

Brig. Gen. George A. Custer, commander, 2nd Brigade of cavalry.

LOC

Lt. Col. Peter Stagg,
1st Michigan Cavalry.

USAHEC

an artillery diversion. He asked Buhrman where he thought the likely destination of the wagon train might be. Buhrman responded that the probable line of march was from Smithsburg to Boonsboro, then a crossing of the river at Sharpsburg, or to Leitersburg and Hagerstown, with a crossing at Williamsport. Kilpatrick inquired if there was a road that Buhrman could use to take a regiment to cut off the Confederate wagons; Buhrman responded in the affirmative. When the farmer indicated that a Federal regiment could flank the Southern wagons by way of Leitersburg, Kilpatrick set about to do exactly that, making his dispositions accordingly.[34]

The Federals fanned out, heading for the pass. The head of Custer's column collided with the unprotected tail end of the Confederate train in the Monterey Pass. The 1st Michigan Cavalry, commanded by Col. Charles H. Town, was in the van of the advance. Custer sent the 1st Michigan forward, where it encountered troopers from Grumble Jones' Brigade, left behind to guard the gap. When he spotted the Confederate troopers left there, Lt. Col. Peter Stagg led a squadron of Wolverines in a charge on the wagons while the rest of the regiment advanced dismounted as skirmishers in support.

Stagg's charge, a classic mounted attack, drove the Confederates from the mouth of the pass. Several spirited Rebel counterattacks failed to dislodge Stagg's troopers, who stood tall and offered a stubborn defense. During the charge, a Confederate ball killed Stagg's horse, and the colonel and his mount went down in a heap. The poor beast fell on top of the colonel, seriously injuring him. Two officers of the 1st Michigan, Lt. James S. McElhenny, of Company G, and Capt. William R. Elliott, were killed in the fighting.[35] "They died as the Union soldier loves to die, leading in the charge," proudly declared their commanding officer, Colonel Town. Seventeen enlisted men also fell in the charge.[36]

The road leading up South Mountain and into the Monterey Pass was so steep that it prompted one Union infantryman two days after the fight there to dub it "Mount Misery."[37] One of Custer's Wolverines agreed, noting that the summit was high enough that "the clouds and lightning seemed, and in fact were, below us in the valley."[38] The heavy rains had turned the road through the pass into a quagmire. British observer Arthur Fremantle, who was traveling with the Army of Northern Virginia agreed, noting that "the road was knee deep in mud and water."[39] Correspondent Paul remembered, "the howling of the storm, and rushing of water down the mountain-side, and the roaring of the wind, altogether were certainly enough in that wild spot to test the nerves of the strongest."[40]

Atop the pass sat a "large hotel, well lit up, & up in the mountains" called Monterey Springs.[41] A popular summer resort for the well-to-do, the hotel sat on a cleared plateau that commanded the pass.[42] As Kilpatrick's column neared the summit, its commander found "on my left was a deep ravine, on my right a steep, rugged mountain, and a road too narrow to reverse even a gun. To add to this unpleasant position, it was raining in torrents."[43] Bugler John Allen Bigelow of the 5th Michigan Cavalry couldn't believe the conditions around him. "Our course is now up the mountain, the road narrow and crooked, with brush, rocks, and ravines on either side," he recalled, asking rhetorically, "[T]his is a mountain pass?"[44]

Gilbert Chapman of the 5th Michigan might have asked the same question. The gap "was a bad place for us to ride up, a narrow pass in the mountains with artillery planted in front of us and no chance for flanking the enemy."[45] Ewell's wagon train lay just ahead, as did the Confederate rearguard. David Miller, a local boy who lived at Monterey Springs, heard the Yankees approaching. A friend of his told Miller, "I just came down from the observatory on the top of [Monterey Springs] and could hear the Union troops coming up the mountain."[46]

Miller met George Custer near the hotel and was briefly interrogated by the young general. Learning that the boy knew his way around the mountain, Custer sent the lad to Kilpatrick under escort. Kilpatrick asked him to estimate the distance to the foot of the mountain on the western side, and whether troops could successfully march on both sides of the road. When Miller answered that they could only do so as far as the small tollgate house, the general responded by deploying an artillery piece at the tollgate, which immediately dropped trail and opened fire on the retreating Rebels.[47] Around 10:00 p.m. however, realizing that his force was vulnerable to enemy flank movements in the dark, Kilpatrick sent two companies of the 7th Michigan Cavalry, under the command of Capt. Ciro A. Armstrong, to guard the mountain road to the right. Major Trowbridge's battalion of the 5th Michigan Cavalry rode out to guard the flank.[48]

The cannonading in the fighting at the pass was heard by the Federal prisoners Pickett's men were escorting toward Virginia, marching toward Hagerstown at the head of one of Ewell's trains. Lt. Col. Cavada remembered the "rapid firing in our rear, and we flattered ourselves with the hope that we might yet be rescued. The cannonading, we ascertained, was by the artillery of General Kilpatrick, who was harassing the Rebels in their retreat, and endeavoring to cut off their trains. We could distinctly see the shells from the Federal pieces burst in the vicinity of the Monterey House."[49]

The roaring of the guns terrified the civilian hostages carried along with the Confederate column. They were still being "held during the period of heaviest cannonading, very much to their personal discomfort," wrote one eyewitness. The hostages were finally released when the Confederates pulled out after suffering through one of the longest and most unpleasant nights of their lives.[50]

At the sound of the cannon fire, the section of the column that had recently passed over the mountain halted in its tracks. "We were stopped on the Mountain Road about Midnight for fear of being captured by Yankee Cavalry," Charles Moore of the 5th Louisiana Infantry jotted in his diary with his pencil. As if to goad his Northern pursuers, Moore added, "Come & Get Your Cow."[51]

As Kilpatrick's column pushed onward up the soggy road, one piece of Rebel artillery and a handful of dismounted cavalry of Capt. George M. Emack's company of the 1st Maryland Cavalry Battalion were waiting for it. The twenty-man Maryland detachment had been left behind to hold Monterey Pass at all hazards. When Emack learned of the enemy advance, he rode forward and asked the teamsters to pick up the pace of their march. The last thing he wanted was for the Yankees to break through and find vulnerable wagons sitting in the road like ripe fruit waiting to be plucked from a branch. Emack also broke the train up into more than one segment in an effort to try and minimize the exposure of the entire column to the advancing enemy horsemen.

The rubber ponchos Emack and his men wore to shield them from the blowing rain also hid their identity from prying eyes. When the van of Kilpatrick's column arrived with the 5th Michigan in the lead, Emack's videttes cautiously retreated as they prepared a warm reception for the Yankee troopers. When the head of the enemy clumped within sight, the lone artillery piece opened fire and eight of the mounted Marylanders charged with reckless abandon into the head of the column. The loud blast and impetuous charge caught the Northerners by surprise, spread panic through the head of the column, and drove some of the troopers back down the slope nearly one mile. When the artillery and mounted charge hit the Michiganders, wrote correspondent Paul, "the first squadron of the Fifth broke, fell back upon the second and broke that—but there was no such thing as running back a great ways on that road; it was jammed with men and horses."[52]

Emack dismounted the rest of his troopers and deployed them along both sides of the road, waiting for Kilpatrick to resume his advance. The Marylanders waited almost one long and anxious hour before the Yankee troopers began pressing forward again. The Southern wagons, meanwhile, took full advantage of the lull, putting as much real estate as possible between them and their determined pursuers.[53] Emack's men stood patiently until the enemy advanced within a dozen paces, when they opened fire. Their volley, masked by the near total darkness, deceived the Federals into believing that Emack's command was much larger than it really was. The Confederates changed positions, using different trees for shelter, a tactic that only added to the illusion of strength.[54] The lone Confederate gun, while not inflicting much damage upon the Federal column, made "the night hideous with [its] bellowings, the echoes of which reverberated the mountain gorges in a most frightful manner."[55] Unsure of the nature of the resistance in their front, Kilpatrick's men advanced very slowly, firing at every step, sometimes even while nearly a mile away from Emack's defenders.[56]

The men of the 6th Michigan Cavalry marched along in the thick, inky darkness. One of them called up the scene as if he were blind. "We could hear the shoes of our horses rattle against rocks and stones, and the rush and dash of a little, but now swollen mountain torrent as it sped along at our left. Time passed on, and the rain still came, we were getting nearer and nearer the summit," remembered Pvt. Andrew D. Jackson of Co. G. "'Pop,' 'Pop,' in quick succession up in our front, I look up and for the first time in hours, I can <u>see</u> something, it's the flash of a cannon, followed immediately by another, and 'Swish,' 'whizz,' 'Bur-r-r,' over our heads, through the trees and down the mountains goes a half a cart load of iron in some form, but whether is was shot, shell, grape & canister, shrapnel, or the remnants of an old blacksmith shop, I could not tell by the sound."[57]

When Grumble Jones finally arrived on the scene after fighting his way through the wagon-choked road, Emack's small command was still doggedly holding off Kilpatrick's significantly superior force. The Marylanders had had been driven back several hundred yards, almost all the way to the road intersection. More troubling was the fact that less than one-half of the wagon train had passed safely through the Monterey Pass. When Jones and Emack met, the former told the general that he had only a small handful of men to resist Kilpatrick, and urged his superior to keep the road clear so that when the enemy finally broke through the thin defensive screen, they would find nothing on the road. Jones responded that the train must be kept moving, and ordered the wagons to continue doing just that. Jones also promised reinforcements in the form of the 6th Virginia Cavalry. Bolstered by the welcome news, Emack ordered his men to hold their ground while conserving their ammunition.[58]

The Marylanders' nighttime work impressed Jones, who praised Emack's stalwart contingent. "This brave little band of heroes was encouraged with the hope of speedy reinforcement, reminded of the importance of their trust, and exhorted to fight to the bitter end rather than yield."[59] Words were fine, but Jones knew that if Emack was not quickly supported, he would be overwhelmed. The general sent all of his couriers and staff officers forward, instructing them to draw their sidearms and lie on the ground to fire, but cautioned them to husband their ammunition as far as such a thing was possible. The single piece of artillery supporting Emack's troops had already fired its last round and was withdrawing. Only Emack's gallant little band and Jones' staff officers pointing revolvers stood between Kilpatrick's veteran cavalry and the precious Southern wagons. The slow but steady Yankee advance continued largely unabated until one of Kilpatrick's men actually stepped on one of Emack's hidden troopers. When the shocked Federal froze in his tracks, the prone Marylander raised his pistol and killed him on the spot. That fatal bullet was one of the final rounds in the Southerners' arsenal. Luck, however, continued to bless the defenders. The deadly shot caught the troopers by surprise and, unnerved by the weather, exhaustion, and darkness, fell back yet again. "My ammunition was entirely exhausted and some of my men actually fought with rocks," Emack later claimed, and they "did they give back an inch." The rocks, if indeed the Marylanders did hoist them off the muddy ground, were dropped with thanks when troopers from the 4th North Carolina of Robertson's Brigade began to arrive at the intersection to relieve Emack's weary troopers.[60]

As Kilpatrick's men were fumbling their attack, Huey's Federal brigade, bringing up the rear, was struck by elements of Jones' gray cavalry. Thinking the terrain and the Confederate wagon train hemmed him in, Kilpatrick realized he would have to fight his way out. The general sought out the son of a local farmer and inquired about the lay of the land ahead. Armed with the information he gleaned, he ordered two regiments to attack with more aggression.[61]

The Federals thundered forward into the night and rain. "The rebs were trudging on, heads bent to the storm, thinking no doubt of pleasant homes in Dixie, when suddenly out of the darkness and storm, we fell upon them," reported an Ohioan of Huey's brigade.[62] The hard thrust quickly captured the summit of the mountain and a number of Confederates were captured. From the crest, Kilpatrick could hear but not see Ewell's wagons rumbling in the distance as they rolled through the pass below. Emack's company of Marylanders, reinforced by elements of Jones' command and the lone gun, were about one-half mile down the back slope of the mountain near the intersection with the Hagerstown Road. There, they waited for Kilpatrick to attack.[63] The heavy fire laid down by Emack's gallant little band had stymied every Federal advance. "Just imagine yourself . . . not knowing what you was going in to and when you had gone a short distance have the bulits come whiring about your ears like a lot of beas after honey and your horse rearing and pransing half scart to death," was how trooper Allen Rice of the 6th Michigan explained the earlier failures on the steep, dark, and muddy hill.[64]

Kilpatrick called up Lt. Alexander C. M. Pennington's Battery M, 2nd U.S. Artillery, to support his attack, and two guns of the horse artillery quickly unlimbered near a bridge south of the Monterey Hotel to add weight to the coming charge.[65] Pennington asked for support for his guns. Kilpatrick responded, "Here is my escort; they will stand by you." The men of Company A of the 1st Ohio deployed around the unlimbered pieces.[66] When one of the gunnery officers observed that the artillery fire would fall in the midst of the Federal attack, Kilpatrick ordered Pennington to throw his shells high over the Federal troopers.[67] In the meantime, elements of Custer's command dismounted and began skirmishing with the Confederate forces near the bridge.

When the Confederate cavalry escorting the trains learned of the imminent threat behind them, steps were taken to promptly meet it. "The cavalry which was stretched along the wagon train was ordered to the front," recalled Luther Hopkins of the 6th Virginia Cavalry. "It was with great difficulty that we could get past the wagons in the darkness, and hence our progress was slow, but we finally worked our way up to the front and were dismounted and formed in line as best we could on either side of the road among the rocks and trees and then moved forward in an effort to drive [Pennington's] battery away from its position so we could resume our march."[68] The gray cavalrymen crouched while Pennington's salvoes flew over their heads. "[T]he booming of the guns that hour of night, with the roar of the thunder, was terrifying indeed, and beyond description," remembered one trooper. "We would wait for a lightning flash and advance a few steps and halt, and then for a light from the batteries and again advance."[69]

The bridge south of the hotel, recalled Col. Alger of the 5th Michigan Cavalry, "was a very exposed place. The night was very dark, and in order to

Col. Russell A. Alger, commander, 5th Michigan Cavalry, Custer's brigade.

USAHEC

take in the situation I ordered my men to lie down." Alger ordered forward a few hardy souls to reconnoiter the structure. When it was determined that the planking of the bridge had not been burned or torn up by the Confederates, Alger decided to attack. He sent a courier back to Kilpatrick asking for mounted men to make the charge.[70]

The request was music to Kilpatrick's ears. He turned to Custer and ordered him to launch the assault with his Michigan Brigade. "Get ready to charge with sabers!" and other similar commands echoed up and down the line. The men, soaking wet and barely able to see their hands in front of their faces, were perplexed by such an improbable tactic. The 5th Michigan's bugler, John Bigelow, recalled, "Charge! Charge what, and at this midnight hour? Up, up we have come, miles high it seems, and what are we to find up here? 'Tis raining so hard that the water makes it appear lighter."[71]

Darkness or not, the Wolverines prepared to make the attack. As they prepared for what appeared to be a nearly impossible task, remembered one of the men, a noise burst around them: "Pop, pop, popy-te-pop, boom, boom, sh—-, and what sounds like the loose cylinder of a crazy thrashing machine goes through the air over our heads."[72] The ground shook as the lone Confederate field piece opened on the troopers forming for the advance. Luckily for the Yankee horsemen, the angle of descent for the gun was too steep, so the Rebel shells whistled harmlessly over their heads.

Col. Alger knew that, one way or another, the Southern gun would have to be silenced. He gave the order for his own Michiganders to dismount and charge the piece, which was illuminated only by the long tongue of flame

Capt. James H. Kidd, 6th Michigan Cavalry, Custer's brigade.

Bentley Historical Library, University of Michigan

flashing from its muzzle. The men of the 5th dropped to the wet ground, unslung their carbines, and surged forward. Preparations for a mounted charge now all but forgotten, Alger's foot-bound troopers were joined by most of the rest of the Michigan Brigade.

The fight was as difficult as it was memorable. "We were deployed as skirmishers through a thick wood, so dark that we could see nothing, seeing the Rebs only by the flash of their guns," wrote Capt. James H. Kidd of the 6th Michigan. "This was a night never to be forgotten."[73] Hindered by thick vines and dense undergrowth, the advance of the 6th Michigan was painfully slow. More than one trooper went sprawling headlong over an unseen impediment, falling to the ground with a splash of sticky mud. "Had it not been for the noise and flashing of the enemy's fire, we should have wandered away in the darkness and been lost," Kidd added.[74]

Supported only by a handful of troopers from the 4th North Carolina Cavalry of Robertson's Brigade, Emack's little band of Confederates had stymied the Federal advance for nearly five hours. The delay exasperated Kilpatrick, who knew a grand prize awaited a successful assault. General Jones, however, was delighted at Kilpatrick's inability to coordinate the nighttime attack. "[L]ess than 50 men kept many thousands in check," he gloated, "and the wagons continued to pass long after the balls were whistling in their midst."[75]

At around 3:00 a.m., while the men of the Michigan Brigade struggled through the woods, Kilpatrick called for twenty-five year-old Maj. Charles E. Capehart, commanding the 1st West Virginia Cavalry, to bring his regiment forward to his headquarters at the hotel. "Before reaching the gap, the column was called to a halt, and as the regiments had been changed several times in the progress of the march, my regiment (1st West Va.) had been placed in the rear," recalled Joseph Lesage of Co. G, "therefore, we could not well understand the cause of the halt at first, but our ignorance was of short duration for we were soon informed by the sound of musketry and artillery in front of the column that our advance had struck the business end of something."[76]

When Capehart brought his horsemen up, Kilpatrick ordered him to go to Custer's support, who was then heavily engaged with the Confederates about one-half mile in advance of the hotel. "At the time I thought strange of such a move, but all old soldiers learned to obey orders and ask no questions, so on we went at a speedy rate until we reached the head of the column, which was then in the gap," recalled Lesage. "Then for the first time, we fully realized what the trouble was."[77] Capehart later reported that he "immediately informed his officers and men of the duty which devolved upon them. The charge was ordered, and, with a whoop and yell, the regiment dashed down upon the train."[78]

Capehart, with 640 officers and men, charged "against heavy odds, the enemy had the roads guarded with five times the number." Trooper Lesage left a vivid description of the assault. "While we were forming up seconds appeared like hours, but at last the order came. 'Boys, draw sabres and prepare striking at everything that looks like a mane!' We seize the battery, it is tumbled over the embankment down the mountainside," he recounted. "Then we turn our attention to the foremost end of the train, all the while making more noise than a 'pack of wild Indians.' We find it a hot place, as we have it hand-to-hand. Sabres and revolvers are used rather freely."[79] After the war, Capehart was awarded the Medal of Honor for his gallant service in leading the perilous charge against the Confederate wagon train.[80]

Chaos reigned that night. "The road on which we were charging was a good turnpike and down grade. I being mounted on a good horse and being so enthused that when I got fairly underway I could not realize whether I was riding or flying," remembered Lesage. "I knew I was going through the air at a terrible rate. Thus we went til we reached the foot of the mountain. By this time we could see that day was breaking, which enabled us to realize what we had done."[81] And, indeed, they had accomplished a great deal under adverse circumstances.

One of the troopers unable to enjoy the revelations brought about by that morning's sunrise was twenty-year old Lt. Henry W. Clark of Monongahela City, Pennsylvania. A member of Company M, 1st West Virginia Cavalry, Clark was mortally wounded during the charge and died the next day in Monterey, Maryland. His corpse was returned home for burial. Henry Clark was just one of many promising young men whose lives were cut short during that fratricidal and devastating war.[82]

With victory within his grasp, Kilpatrick dispatched his headquarters escort, Company A of the 1st Ohio Cavalry, to support the cheering West Virginians. As the Ohioans formed for the attack, Custer shook hands with the company commander, Captain Noah Jones. "Do your duty and God bless you."[83] With Jones' audacious order—"Use sabers alone, I will cut down the first man that fires a shot"—ringing in their ears, the Ohioans drew their blades and, supported by the men of the 1st West Virginia of Richmond's brigade, rode through Alger's dismounted men. The Buckeyes thundered into the Confederate train, where a heavy volley of musketry from the small Rebel force mixed in among the wagons met them. The precise position of each enemy soldier was revealed by the flash of his muzzle, which allowed the Federal troopers to surge forward with surgical precision. "[A] hand to hand conflict ensued," a Federal captain wrote home to his parents. "The scene was wild and desolating."[84] Pvt. John S. Tucker of the 5th Alabama Infantry confirmed the wild nature of the fighting: "never saw such a running of wagons."[85] No trooper loved a mounted charge more than George Custer. Swept up by the moment, the Boy General went in with the charge. Thrown from his horse during the melee, he was nearly captured for the second time in three days.[86]

Berkeley Minor of the Rockbridge Artillery of Charlottesville, Virginia, was riding in the wagon train nursing a combat wound. His wagon came under fire from Pennington's guns just as it reached the summit of South Mountain. The teamster sitting up front tried to dash through the danger zone, but the wagon in front broke down and stalled the train. Neither driver nor passengers got out or tried to help, as shells whizzed all around them. "We could not have helped them in such a stampede as filled the road from side to side with vehicles of all sorts and flying cavalrymen, for by this time the force of our men who had been holding the enemy back up the road must have given way, and were dashing along the road pell-mell with the wagons and ambulances," was how the artilleryman explained the deteriorating situation. "Minor crawled out of his wagon and, despite a painful wound, scrambled off into the darkness in search of safety. When he found another Confederate soldier who had climbed out of his ambulance looking for protection, the two hobbled cross-country to Leitersburg before they finally felt safe enough to stop.[87]

Lt. Henry E. Shepherd of the 43rd North Carolina was badly wounded in the leg during the assault on Culp's Hill on the morning of July 3. The bullet passed through his calf muscle and grazed the bone, an extremely painful and dangerous wound. "I was captured with our ambulance train on the night of July 4th, in the mountain passes between Monterey, Pennsylvania and Hagerstown, Maryland. My experience was most thrilling and memorable," recounted the North Carolinian. "In its desperate attempt to escape, our train drove through the contending lines of cavalry—the one striving to capture, the other to protect. I was utterly helpless and disabled, and the ghastly recollections of that gloomy, stormy night, when I was driven through the lines of battle—unable to raise my hand, and in momentary peril of my life—can never be dimmed or effaced."[88]

Another member of the Rockbridge Artillery, Edward A. Moore, was riding a large handsome horse as he made his way alongside the train. When he heard the lone bark of Emack's gun he thought little of it—until three cavalry horses with empty saddles galloped past him. A few seconds later the flashes of muzzles erupted nearby, which terrified his mount. When a blast of Union artillery fire struck the horse, one of the frightened beast's legs gave way, nearly dumping Moore in the mud. Somehow the horse rallied and dashed away, carrying its rider to safety. Moore was one of the lucky few.[89]

William "Grumble" Jones narrowly avoided being captured. Jones, along with two regiments of Southern cavalry, got so thoroughly mixed up among the wagons and Yankee cavalry that they were indistinguishable in the darkness and rain. Recognizing the danger, Jones told those around him not to call him by his proper title—general—but to instead "call me Bill." His men wisely complied. "Two days afterwards we got hold of one of the county papers, which, in giving the account of this attack, stated that the rebel, Gen. Wm. E. Jones, was captured. Perhaps but for the shrewdness of Gen. Wm. E. Jones in having his men call him 'Bill' instead of 'General,' it might have been true," observed Luther Hopkins of the 6th Virginia.[90]

The promiscuous mingling of Yankee and Rebel cavalry with the teamsters forced many of the wagons off the road and tumbling down the ravines lining it.[91] "The frightened teamsters attempted to run off their wagons, but wheel locked with wheel and the road was soon impassable," proclaimed a trooper of the 6th Ohio Cavalry. "We captured the entire train and guard."[92] One of Pennington's guns supported the charge and opened on the rear of the train. The shots smashed into and splintered carriages in the rear, hopelessly blocking the line of retreat.[93] The Buckeyes of Company A and the West Virginians saw their opportunity and charged into the massed and tangled wagons, yelling, "Do you surrender?" The question was often answered affirmatively as teamsters threw up their arms in an effort at self-preservation.[94] For many others, self-preservation was little more than a matter of simple luck. The darkness and confusion triggered several friendly fire incidents when Federal troopers accidentally opened on their own lines, killing and wounding their comrades.[95]

The surging Federals rode all the way through the wagon train and into Ewell's infantry beyond, capturing large numbers of Rebels before turning back to repeat their maneuver.[96] When the balance of the Federals available joined in, even more Confederate wagons and prisoners were snared. As the drama played out, the fierce summer storm intensified. The wind and thunder howled, building upon the screams of wounded men, horses, and mules, adding as one soldier put it, "inconceivable terror to the scene."[97] According to Grumble Jones, "ineffectual efforts were made for a rally and resistance, but without avail, until at the foot of the mountain, a few joined" the thin skirmish line held by Capt. W. G. Welsh's company of the Maryland cavalry. Emack's reinforced Marylanders blunted temporarily the Federal charge and briefly drove back the van of the Federal column upon itself, but the small size of defending force was no match for the juggernaut rumbling down the mountain. Separated from his staff and couriers, the Confederate brigadier beat a hasty retreat through fields and by-ways. Jones finally reached safety in the town of Williamsport, Maryland, which was by then held by elements of Imboden's cavalry command.[98] His arrival there was a surprise, since Emack had reported that Jones had been captured in the fighting.

To defend their booty and themselves against any surprise mounted counterattacks along the road, Kilpatrick's troopers hastily threw up a barricade just beyond the front of the wagon train. They piled up anything they could find, including broken wagon parts and fallen trees. A squadron of Lt. Col. William P. Brinton's 18th Pennsylvania Cavalry was placed there as a guard. "No sooner was this done," wrote correspondent Paul, "than cavalry was heard charging down the road." The officer in charge of the squadron raised his revolver, squinted into the darkness toward the beating hoofs, and yelled, "Who comes there?"

"Tenth Virginia Cavalry!" came the reply.

"To — with you, Tenth Virginia Cavalry!"

According to Paul, "the squadron fired a volley into the darkness. That was the last heard of the Tenth Virginia Cavalry that night, until numbers of the regiment came straggling in and gave themselves up as prisoners of war."[99]

Alger, meanwhile, watched as his Wolverines pillaged the Rebel wagon train. A Confederate colonel approached him to ask for the senior Federal officer so that he could surrender. When Alger indicated that he was in command, the colonel dismounted and handed over his sword. The officer was one of more than 1,300 Confederates captured in this sharp and thoroughly confused fight, along with the entire wagon train, which extended from the base of the mountain to the very top.[100] Most of the wagons were later burned or otherwise destroyed, their mules turned over to the Cavalry Corps quartermaster.[101]

The wagons were stuffed with not only sundry items that an army would carry, but also a myriad of booty appropriated from the countryside when Lee's army moved north. "[E]very kind of plunder from a woman's petticoat to a plowing machine," was found inside the wagons remembered one eyewitness. "Many of the boys procured a good suit of clothes from the train."[102]

Correspondent Paul had a good look at the contents of many of the carriages. Besides "ambulances filled with wounded officers and privates from the battlefield of Gettysburg," he wrote, Ewell, Early, and others of the Confederate top brass lost their personal baggage to Kilpatrick's cavalrymen. More wagons were brimming with

> delicacies stolen from stores in Pennsylvania; four and six mule and horse teams; some filled with barrels of molasses, others with flour, hams, meal, clothing, ladies and children's shoes and underclothing mainly obtained from the frightened inhabitants of York County and vicinity; wagons stolen from Uncle Sam with the "U. S." still upon them; wagons stolen from Pennsylvania and loyal Maryland farmers; wagons . . . made for the Confederate gov['t] (a poor imitation of our own); wagons from North Carolina and . . . from Tennessee; a mongrel train all stolen . . . Our men filled their canteens with molasses and replenished their stock of clothing, sugar, salt, and bacon. Some very expensive Confederate uniforms were captured; several gold watches and articles of jewelry were found.[103]

Allen Rice of the 6th Michigan looked upon the vast amount of plunder and mused, "It put me in mind of a fourth of July spree to see the wagons all strung along the road, the wheals choped to pieces, tungs cut off, barels of liqer smashed in and the wagons set afire."[104]

When the fighting ended, Captain Jones led the tired men of Company A of the 1st Ohio back up the hill to the Monterey House, where Kilpatrick established his headquarters. A huge bonfire blazed in the front yard, providing light for the processing of prisoners corralled there.[105] A jubilant Kilpatrick greeted Jones and his company by proclaiming, "I knew you would go through." Custer greeted the same officer with a hearty handshake and the comment that the men who made that charge would charge anywhere.[106] Spotting Capt. Eli K. Simonds of the 5th Michigan, Kilpatrick said, "Captain, as you led the charge on that train, you take your company and set them on fire."[107] Col. Alger was of the opinion that "Too much praise cannot be given to the mounted force that was sent to us."[108] He also observed, "I cannot speak in too high terms of praise of the behavior of my regiment in this engagement. It was the most trying place it had passed through up to that time, if not during its organization."[109]

New York Times writer Paul recalled that after the fighting, one of the "most amusing scenes occurred." Two enemy captains rode up to one of Kilpatrick's reserve commands in the lingering darkness and asked the identify of their regiment. "They discovered their mistake," related Paul, "when Lieutenant Whittaker, of General Kilpatrick's staff, presented a pistol and advised them to surrender their arms. Several other officers who might have easily escaped came in voluntarily and gave themselves up."[110]

Many Southerners blamed their own cavalry for the debacle. "The Yankee cavalry attacked our train of wagons a few days ago and I escaped capture by a hairs breath," Charles J. C. Hudson wrote to his father. "One of our regimental wagons was taken and several of our men but the rest of us escaped having no way of defending ourselves. The Va. Cavalry protecting the train ran and caused the damage. Our cavalry are a poor set!" Hudson's opinion had no foundation of truth. Still, someone had to bear the blame for the disaster at Monterey Pass, and the cavalry was the most convenient target.[111]

Skirmish at Leitersburg

As part of Kilpatrick's command attacked at Monterey Pass, his 1st Vermont Cavalry of Richmond's brigade, along with two of Pennington's guns, all to be guided by civilian C. H. Buhrman, moved to flank the other segment of the wagon train suspected to be near Leitersburg. When no enemy was found at Smithsburg, Lt. Col. Addison W. Preston of the 1st Vermont asked Buhrman where to ride next. When Buhrman told him he would find plenty of Rebels by morning if he rode to Leitersburg, Preston followed his advice and moved out.[112]

The disagreeable weather followed the Vermonters on their ride to Leitersburg. "The night was pitch dark," reminisced one of the troopers, "the rain fell in torrents, and the road was rough: a mere wood road over and amongst the rocks. A great many horses lost their shoes, and soon becoming lame, the riders would have to dismount and lead, and of course fell behind." Some of his comrades took creative measures to ward off the chill. "A few drank too much Maryland whisky, which being taken on an empty stomach, soon rendered them first combatant and then non-combatant."[113]

Lt. Col. Addison W. Preston, 1st Vermont Cavalry, Kilpatrick's 3rd Cavalry Division.

USAHEC

Preston's column reached Smithsburg a few hours later. Descending the hill out of town toward Leitersburg, the men found "a great many stragglers, some wounded and some not," whom Preston paroled.[114] He didn't want anyone to slow his progress.

Near Leitersburg, just before the sun rose on July 5, Preston's contingent came upon the prey they sought: Ewell's other column of carriages—his reserve train. "I never saw such a display of fireworks as I saw through that night," wrote Bugler Joe Allen of the 1st Vermont. "Our men toiled up the mountain, firing as fast as they could, and the Confederates fell back, stubbornly resisting our advance."[115] The brilliant and frequent lightning provided just enough light for the troopers to pick their way along the rocky road in pursuit of the wagons.

The Vermonters cut through the Rebel rearguard and struck at the wagon train. "The mules attached to the wagons were running away down the hill; but we had to go by them, which we did, yelling and firing pistols. The train we were after was two miles long, and I saw many wagons go over the bank into the gulch below," recalled Allen. "Most of the wagons had wounded in them, and as we tore along we could hear the cries of these unfortunate men. Some of them were looking out, and some of them jumped. Many of the drivers were shot by our men; others deserted their teams, and the scene was frightful."[116]

Once past its head, the Federals brought the train to a halt. The Southerners tried to recapture the wagons with numerous sorties, to no avail.[117] When the contest met its fitful end, Preston's troopers lifted the enemy wounded from the wagons and left them by the side of the road. Some of the wagons were put to the torch; the wheel spokes of others were chopped up.[118] The Vermonters gathered up their booty—a drove of cattle and approximately 100 prisoners—and marched them off to be turned over to Kilpatrick the following day.[119]

Despite bad weather and even worse roads that day and night, the Vermonters could look back on an impressive record. They had covered an extraordinary fifty miles since leaving the battlefield twenty-four hours earlier—nearly twice what Army regulations suggested for cavalry in the field.[120]

* * *

George Pickett's Confederate division, which had cleared Monterey Pass ahead of Ewell's wagons, heard the firing in their rear during Kilpatrick's attack. They also heard musketry in their front. "The prisoners appeared to be overjoyed, feeling certain that they would be set free, and our whole army would be captured," recalled a member of the 1st Virginia Infantry, "but the musketry proved to be not the enemy, but our own men resting in the woods, cleaning their guns and shooting the old charges off." Pickett's men marched all night. "The prisoners suffered for want of food. We did all that was in our power to relieve them, but there was not much to be had in the eating line until we reached Williamsport . . . on the 7th."[121]

* * *

Kilpatrick reported that his attack destroyed the entire wagon train save for eight forges, thirty wagons, and a few ambulances loaded with wounded enemy officers. He also claimed "1360 prisoners, one battle-flag, and a large number of horses and mules, several hundred of the enemy's wounded being left upon the field."[122] Kilpatrick's report fails to account for the fact that there were actually multiple Confederate trains involved, and that his command managed to disable only a small portion of one train, and not even the entire train. The wounded Confederate enlisted men were paroled and left behind, while the injured officers were dragged off to their fate in Union prison camps.[123]

Civilian guide C. H. Buhrman played an important role in Kilpatrick's successes against Ewell's wagons at Monterey and Leitersburg. The Federal troopers, he summed up, "had destroyed the wagon train from Monterey to Ringgold, a distance of six miles, and from Ringgold to Leitersburg, a distance of three miles more, making nine miles of wagon train captured or burned or destroyed by cutting off wagon tongues and cutting spokes in wheels."[124] General Lee felt the sting of the loss but downplayed it in his report of the campaign: "In passing through the mountains . . . the great length of the train exposed them to attack by the enemy's cavalry, which captured a number of wagons and ambulances but they succeeded in reaching Williamsport without serious loss."[125]

"I do not believe that we would have lost any of the train had it not been started on the road after I had stopped it," wrote Captain Emack, the Marylander who had held off for hours many times his number at Monterey.[126] Jeb Stuart, in a more honest assessment than Lee's, admitted he was surprised by the magnitude of these losses.[127] So was a mortified Grumble Jones, who tendered to Stuart his resignation, who wisely refused to accept it. The irascible Jones would remain at the head of his brigade.[128] The numerous officers taken prisoner by the Yankees were sent on to Frederick, Maryland, for processing the next morning.[129]

The Federals were justifiably proud of their performance. Maj. Capehart of the 1st West Virginia recalled, "The only assistance [we] had was 40 men of the First Ohio Cavalry, under command of Captain Jones. With but two exceptions, the officers and men acquitted themselves as true and brave soldiers."[130] "It was one of the most exciting engagements we ever had, for while the actual number engaged was small, and the casualties were not that great, the time, the place, the circumstances, the darkness, the uncertainty, all combined to make 'the midnight fight at Monterey' one of unique interest," wrote Captain Kidd. "The force that resisted us did its duty gallantly. . . . Still, they failed of their object, which was to save the train. That we captured after all."[131]

"Citizens along the line from Rouzersville to Leitersburg remember very vividly the pyrotechnic display of July 4 and 5, 1863, made by the burning of rebel wagons thoroughly supplied with the pork and flour of Pennsylvania farmers," recorded an early Pennsylvania historian, "but in the future they prefer to have their celebrations under the direction of men pursuing peaceful callings." For many years, rusting remains of wagon parts could still be found in the underbrush along the road and hillside of South Mountain.[132]

Newspaperman Paul wrote his report one week later. "The road [at Monterey] is more like the bed of a rocky river, the dirt having been washed away by the heavy rains, left large boulders exposed; where there were no boulders, there was mud and water. Over this road the troopers dashed and splashed in the midnight darkness," he continued, "yelling like demons. Is it to be wondered at that the Confederate soldiers unanimously declare that they will never visit Pennsylvania again?[133]

After all their exertions, the weary Yankee troopers finally succumbed to fatigue. Nearly without exception they fell asleep on the backs of their horses as they rode down the mountain toward the nearby hamlet of Smithsburg. "As far as the eye could reach, both front and rear, was a moving mass of horses with motionless riders all wrapped in slumber," recalled Kidd. "The horses were moving along with drooping heads and eyes half closed."[134] The division rode to Ringgold, where Kilpatrick called a welcome halt. The men were "tired, hungry, sleepy, wet, and covered with mud. Men and animals yielded to the demands of exhausted nature," observed a newspaper reporter, "and the column had not been at a halt many minutes before all fell asleep where they stood." Custer, unable to keep his eyes open a minute longer, stretched out under the eaves of a small church and was soon sound asleep in the soft mud.[135]

Before nodding off himself, correspondent Paul glanced over the scene around the little church where Custer's staff and others joined their young leader in blissful slumber. "Under the friendly protection of the dripping eaves of a chapel," he recalled, "a gay and gallant brigadier could have been seen enjoying in the mud one of those sound sleeps only obtained through fatigue, his long golden locks matted with the soil of Pennsylvania." He continued:

> Near him, in the mud, lay a dandyish adjutant, equally oblivious and unmindful of his toilet, upon which he generally bestows so much attention. Under a fence near at hand is reclining a well-got up major, whose stylish appearance and regular features have turned the heads of many fair damsels on Chestnut street; here a chaplain, there a trooper; a Commanding General, aids, orderlies, and servants, here for the once meet on a level. The faithful trooper lies by his horse, between whom there seems to exist an indescribable community of feeling.[136]

The respite lasted but two hours, when the Provost Guard notified the bivouac it was time to move. Captain Llewelyn Estes of Kilpatrick's staff, Paul recorded, "shakes himself and proceeds to shake [Kilpatrick] to let him know that . . . it is time to move. . . . A body of armed men, mailed in mud! What a picture."[137]

Kilpatrick's own casualties at Monterey Pass were negligible: five men killed, including one commissioned officer, ten wounded, and twenty-eight missing, for an aggregate loss of just forty-three.[138]

Thus ended one of the war's most one-sided victories. The men who fought at Monterey Pass recalled the terror of that night for the rest of their lives. Emblazoned in their war memories were the raging tempests of the thunderstorms, the dangerous passage on the side of South Mountain, and most of all, the short, successful, but vicious fight for the wagons. Years after the war ended, Northern veterans vividly recalled the image of the wreckage they left behind as they rode toward Smithsburg the next morning. Those that wore the blue forever remembered the destruction of the wagon trains with pride—a shining badge of honor that burned brighter as the years grew longer.

Chapter 4

Meade's Pursuit Begins

"I wonder if Napoleon or even Robt. Lee were our commander this evening would they pursue a defeated army in this cautious, courteous way?"

— Federal officer

July 5: The Federal Army at Gettysburg

THE APPROACH OF DAYLIGHT ON the morning of July 5 failed to bring about the usual scattering of fire from the opposing picket lines. The silence triggered suspicion among the Union soldiers that the enemy was gone. Investigation confirmed that Lee's Virginia army had withdrawn from its positions on Seminary Ridge.[1] "On the morning of the 5th, we learned that the bird had flown," a New York foot soldier admitted.[2] "I suppose we shall go forward today & find out where they have hid themselves," predicted a sergeant of the 5th Corps.[3] "[T]wo such armies," another Empire Stater observed, "could not remain long in ignorance of each other's intentions."[4]

Pockets of Confederate lookouts remained on the western outskirts of town in case the Federals pushed too close. Teenage citizen Daniel Skelly, who had watched several Southern units begin their evacuation of the town the night before, watched this morning as "several of our officers rode down the street and when about half the length of the square from Baltimore and Washington street, one of them was hit in the fleshy part of his arm by a bullet." Skelly believed the shot must have been especially painful because the officer "yelled at the top of his voice."[5]

Early that morning, General Meade's chief of staff, Maj. Gen. Daniel Butterfield, sent a note to Maj. Gen. William F. "Baldy" Smith, whose division of emergency militia troops from the defenses of Harrisburg was slowly making its way toward Gettysburg. "The general [Meade] directs me to say that he is holding here in a state of uncertainty as to the enemy's movements and intentions," wrote Butterfield. After indicating that the Army of the Potomac would attempt to ascertain the intentions of the enemy, he added, "Your re-enforcement of this army would be a valuable one and appreciated." After the losses of the three days at Gettysburg, even raw and untested militia would be welcome.[6]

Many of Meade's men spent the day burying the dead, tending to wounded, and gathering up tons of weapons and ammunition left on the battlefield. "The stench from the field was dreadful," reported a Vermonter on July 5.[7] Meade's soldiers received their first full rations in nearly five days, and used the opportunity to write letters home to let loved ones know they had safely made it through the conflagration at Gettysburg.[8] Reports filtered in from the army's signal officers, scattered about on nearby hills, that large bodies of Lee's army were moving westward toward Cashtown and Fairfield. "This was one of the days we needed [Gen. Phil] Sheridan," observed an officer of the 6th Corps years after the end of the war.[9]

Brig. Gen. Herman Haupt, like his West Point classmate George Gordon Meade, was a native Philadelphian and gifted civil engineer. The tall and impeccably groomed Pennsylvanian was brilliant and innovative, and made a science of the military railroad. His wife was a native of Gettysburg, and Haupt had spent seven years there as a professor of math and engineering at Gettysburg's Pennsylvania College. He had also laid out the course of the railroad from Hagerstown over South Mountain, and so knew the topography of the area as well as anyone. When he arrived in Gettysburg on July 5, he set out to find his old friend Meade.

Haupt found Meade and his Cavalry Corps commander, Maj.

Maj. Gen. Alfred Pleasonton, commander, Cavalry Corps, Army of the Potomac.

USAHEC

Brig. Gen. Herman Haupt, Chief of Military Railroad Construction.

USAHEC

Gen. Alfred Pleasonton, seated at a small table in the tiny Lydia Leister house. The two generals gave Haupt a quick account of the battle, during which Pleasonton opined that if Confederate commander James Longstreet had concentrated his fire more in the center instead of scattering it over the whole of the left flank and held on a little longer, the Army of the Potomac would have been beaten.

After an hour or so of conversation, Haupt asked Meade what future movements he had in mind, so that Haupt could ensure the availability of adequate supplies. As Haupt later wrote, he anticipated that Meade would march at once for the Potomac River in order to cut off Lee's only line of retreat. If so, Meade's response may have troubled the railroader. According to Haupt, Meade told him he could not start immediately because the men needed rest. Haupt indicated "that the men had been well supplied with rations; that they had been stationary behind the stone walls during the battle; that they could not be footsore; that the enemy before and after the battle had been in motion more than our army; that if it was but little more than a day's march to the river, and that if advantage were not taken of Lee's present condition, he would escape." Lee, countered Meade, had no pontoon train, and that the river was swollen by rains and was not fordable.

Haupt was not convinced. "Do not place confidence in that," he warned Meade. "I have men in my Construction Corps who could construct bridges in forty-eight hours sufficient to pass that army, if they have no other material than such as they could gather from old buildings or from the woods, and it is not safe to assume that the enemy cannot do what we can." Since Meade and Haupt had been friends most of their adult lives, Haupt did not hesitate to state his position clearly and without deference. The pair discussed the situation further, but Haupt "could not, however, remove the idea from General Meade that a period of rest was necessary." He left "much discouraged, and as soon as practicable communicated the situation to [Gen. Henry] Halleck at Washington, in hopes that something could be done to urge General Meade to more prompt action than he appeared to contemplate." Convinced Lee would escape, Haupt caught a train to Washington the next morning to report his findings to Halleck in person.[10]

Meade also had internal political problems to handle. When Maj. Gen. John F. Reynolds was killed on July 1, his senior division commander, Maj. Gen. Abner Doubleday, assumed command of the 1st Corps. Doubleday did a competent job under extraordinarily difficult circumstances, but was relieved of command that night. His replacement was Maj. Gen. John Newton, an officer who was Doubleday's junior in rank and one who did not serve in the 1st Corps. "I declined to obey his orders on the ground that it was illegal to place a junior over a senior officer, that it was a gross injustice and could only be done by authority of the President of the United States," complained Doubleday. Although he claimed he would have yielded on the point had Meade informed him that Lincoln had ordered Newton placed in command of the 1st Corps, nothing in the record suggests that he would have done so. The next day, July 6, Doubleday wrote, "In consequence of my refusal to obey General Newton, I was relieved from duty and ordered to report to the Adjutant-General at Washington." Doubleday was banished to Buffalo, New York, where he assumed command of a draft rendezvous site.[11] With this petty crisis behind him, Meade focused his attention on the task at hand.

A large modern army required good logistical planning

Maj. Gen. John Sedgwick,
6th Corps commander,
Army of the Potomac.

USAHEC

in order to be able to move quickly, and movement depended upon horses. The long and arduous campaign, however, had taken an enormous toll on the Army of the Potomac's draft animals and cavalry mounts. "The loss of horses in these severe battles has been great in killed, wounded, and worn down by excessive work," wrote Brig. Gen. Rufus Ingalls, the army's quartermaster general, on July 4 to Maj. Gen. Montgomery C. Meigs, the Union's quartermaster general. "General Meade and staff, for instance, lost 16 in killed yesterday. I think we shall require 2,000 cavalry and 1,500 artillery horses, as soon as possible to recruit the army."[12] Any pursuit mounted by the Army of the Potomac would begin with a severe shortage of mounts, which would make Meade's task all the more difficult.

Meade's Plan for Pursuing Lee's Army

As described earlier in Chapter 1, General Lee's two columns of retreat marched by way of Cashtown and Fairfield, to converge at the Potomac River. Lee sent cavalry ahead to try and protect his pontoon bridge across the Potomac.[13] The Confederate wagon train of wounded, escorted by John Imboden's troopers, used the Cashtown Pass, while the rest of Lee's army crossed South Mountain through Monterey Pass.

Of all the Union corps at Gettysburg, Maj. Gen. John Sedgwick's 6th Corps (known to its men as "Sedgwick's cavalry") had seen the least fighting. On the morning of July 5, Meade ordered Sedgwick to push his corps (the army's largest) hard toward the enemy's last known positions at Gettysburg to determine their intentions and whether Lee intended to make a stand at South Mountain. Just as so many of the town's citizens had discovered that morning, Sedgwick too learned that the Virginia army had left during the night.[14]

"I directed General Sedgwick, in command of the 6th Corps, which corps had been comparatively unengaged during the battle, and was in full force and strength, to advance on the Fairfield road and pursue the enemy vigorously," reported Meade. "At the same time I dispatched a cavalry force to follow the retreating column on the Cashtown Road, believing that the enemy was retiring into the Cumberland Valley, and not satisfied what his further movements would be, not being satisfied that he was in full retreat for the Potomac, and not aware of what injury I had done him in the battle of Gettysburg, although satisfied that I had punished him very severely."[15]

Like the Army of Northern Virginia, Meade's command had also lost several high-ranking officers. The army's two most senior and most trusted

Brig. Gen Thomas H. Neill, commander, 3rd Brigade, 2nd Division, 6th Corps.

USAHEC

corps commanders had both fallen. Maj. Gen. John Reynolds was killed early during the morning of the first day of battle, and Maj. Gen. Winfield S. Hancock, known as "Hancock the Superb," fell badly wounded on the afternoon of July 3 during Pickett's Charge. Their loss left Sedgwick as the army's senior—and most trusted—subordinate, so it made sense that Meade would depend upon Sedgwick's judgment and experience in deciding enemy intentions and the initial requirements of any pursuit.

Similar to what had been done prior to the battle, Meade divided his army into three wings. Sedgwick took command of the left wing, consisting of the 1st, 3rd, and 6th Corps. Maj. Gen. Henry Slocum commanded the center, consisting of the 2nd and 12th Corps. Maj. Gen. Oliver O. Howard commanded the right, consisting of the 5th and 11th Corps. The army, Meade decided, would concentrate at Middletown, Maryland, on July 7. Pleasonton's cavalry would nip at the heels of the Army of Northern Virginia as it retreated, slowing it down as much as possible while searching for opportunities to strike and gather the critical intelligence Meade needed to conduct a successful pursuit.[16]

Howard rode out to reconnoiter late that morning. His brother, Capt. Charles H. Howard, and his headquarters escort (a company of the 1st Indiana Cavalry) accompanied him. The one-armed general and his band rode rapidly but cautiously west toward Cashtown along the Chambersburg Pike. When they spotted Confederate stragglers, the Hoosier horsemen put spurs to horse and dashed ahead to capture them. The same thing happened at the next ridge. This time, however, the enemy troops were waiting in ambush. As the horsemen approached, the Southerners opened fire, mortally wounding one of Howard's staff officers. Narrowly missing injury, Howard and his little group wisely turned back. A few hours later, he prepared his men for the march ahead.[17]

Sedgwick's Pursuit to Fairfield

General Meade instructed Sedgwick to press his reconnaissance in force, and to determine "how far the enemy has retreated, and also the character of the gap and practicability of carrying the same, in case I should determine to advance on that line." Sedgwick threw out skirmishers, who stood for two hours in the pouring rain. "No enemy was visible," recalled a member of the 15th New Jersey. "All had gone, and the pursuit was now to begin."[18]

Brig. Gen. Thomas H. Neill commanded the 3rd Brigade, 2nd Division of Sedgwick's corps. Neill's men formed in a V-shaped formation, with the 49th Pennsylvania in front as skirmishers and flankers.[19] They marched over the slope of Little Round Top near Devil's Den, cut diagonally across Rose's wheatfield, passed to the right of the Sherfy Peach Orchard, and then across the open fields covered by Pickett's Charge. The probe continued beyond Seminary Ridge, past the site of Lee's headquarters during the battle, and on toward Fairfield along the Fairfield Road. Mere words were inadequate to describe the horrifying sights they and others saw along the way. Every item a soldier could carry was found scattered about. "The battle wreckage included everything belonging to soldiers afoot or on horseback, such as caps, hats, shoes, coats, guns, cartridge and cap boxes, belts, canteens, haversacks, blankets, tin cups, horses, saddles, and swords," recalled a soldier of the 61st Pennsylvania Infantry. "Either in this Wheatfield or nearby we saw where a battery had stood in the midst of a terrific struggle. One gun was dismounted, a caisson had exploded and we noticed one place where three out of four horses belonging to a gun had been killed and lay with their harness on."[20]

The 6th Corps formed line of battle and advanced in the same direction, expecting at any moment to meet some level of resistance. The only enemy they saw were already dead, dying, or grievously wounded. "Dead men, dead horses, guns, equipments, caissons, shot and shell and all the paraphernalia and appurtenances of the battlefield scattered and shattered in painful profusion," remembered a member of the 10th Massachusetts. "Every barn on the line of march was filled to overflowing with the rebel wounded, the dying and the dead." The sight stuck with these soldiers for the rest of their lives.[21]

Brig. Gen. Albion P. Howe, commander, 2nd Division, 6th Corps.

USAHEC

Rumors swirled through the ranks. Just beyond Seminary Ridge, a report arrived that Lee's army was dug in on the next ridge to the west. The 6th Corps halted and hastily threw up rudimentary breastworks of rails and dirt. When it was discovered that the report was untrue, the sweaty and dirty men of the 6th Corps waited for further orders. Mother Nature added to their misery when it began raining hard again during the lull. When Sedgwick resumed the advance on the Fairfield Road about noon, he discovered that the soggy ground made it all but impossible to maintain a line of battle. "[T]he thing was beyond the range of possibilities, for softer mud I never saw," recalled a member of the Vermont Brigade. "The way lay through a cornfield, and to walk across it was like walking in a bed of mortar a hundred feet deep." A frustrated Sedgwick realigned into a column of march with a heavy line of skirmishers in front. The rains had limited his advance to the road.[22] "We have had rain and the roads are bad, so we move slow," observed an officer of the 2nd Rhode Island Infantry.[23]

"About noon we crossed a small stream without opposition, though there were indications of nearness to the retreating enemy," recalled a man in the 15th New Jersey. After a slow march of three miles, the 6th Corps found the expected resistance in force in the form of Lee's rearguard. They could also see the long Confederate wagon train ahead, slowly winding its way to Fairfield. "Here the advance was made in line of battle," explained the same New Jersey soldier. "Our regiment had the extreme left of the first line. Fields of waving grain were trodden perfectly flat by our advance. In encountering fences the first rank crossed and re-formed before the rear rank attempted to do so."

The Skirmish at Granite Hill

When Maj. Gen. Jubal A. Early, a division commander in Ewell's Second Corps, reached Fairfield that afternoon, a scene of utter chaos greeted him. Early was a ball of nervous energy. "General Jubal Early was a small, active nervous man with a curious mixture of force of character and apparent volatileness," wrote one of his soldiers. "His most striking characteristic was unceasing restlessness." His restlessness would serve him well this day.[24]

About 6:00 p.m., Confederate skirmishers watched as Sedgwick's line of battle climbed a prominent rise in the road at Granite Hill, moving toward a farmhouse and barn on the summit. When they reached the top, Lt. Col. Elijah White sent a courier galloping to Early, with the news that Uncle John's bluecoats were closing in.[25] "On arriving in sight of Fairfield, which is situated near the eastern base of South Mountain on a wide low plain or valley surrounded by commanding hills, I found the wagon trains blocked up at the village," Early wrote. "While waiting for the road to be cleared of the wagons in front, Colonel White sent me information that a force of the enemy was advancing in my rear, and being on the plain where I would be exposed to a fire of artillery from the surrounding hills, I sent to hasten forward the trains. . . . When the advance of the enemy appeared on a hill in my rear with a battery of artillery supported by infantry, I opened with shell on it."[26]

Pvt. Wilbur Fisk of the 2nd Vermont recalled Early's greeting. "Just before reaching [Fairfield] . . . we met a couple of rebel shells that informed us that our further progress was disputed very decidedly," he recounted. "Our batteries sent back shells enough

Brig. Gen. Horatio G. Wright, commander, 1st Division, 6th Corps.

USAHEC

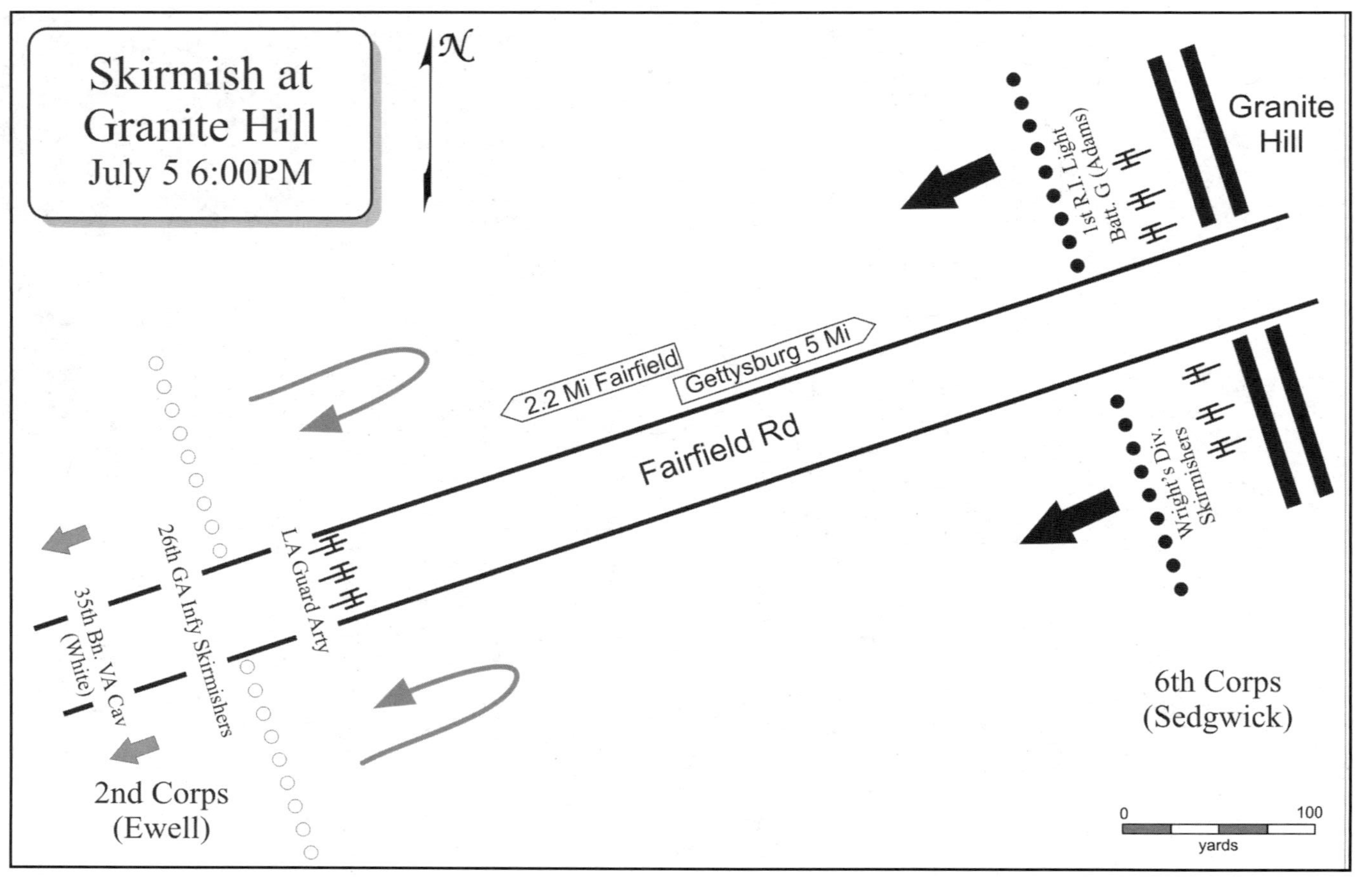
Skirmish at
Granite Hill
July 5 6:00PM
N
Granite
Hill
1st R.I. Light
Batt. G (Adams)
2.2 Mi Fairfield
Gettysburg 5 Mi
Fairfield Rd
Wright's Div.
Skirmishers
LA Guard Arty
26th GA Infy Skirmishers
35th Bn. VA Cav
(White)
2nd Corps
(Ewell)
6th Corps
(Sedgwick)
0
100
yards

to pay them and leave a heavy balance in our favor."[27] The Federal fire was delivered by gunners from Col. Charles H. Tompkins' artillery brigade, which Sedgwick had sent clattering ahead expressly for that purpose.[28]

The 6th Corps advance traded shots for a time with the rearguard composed of troopers from White's 35th Battalion Virginia Cavalry, the 26th and 31st Georgia regiments of John Gordon's Brigade, and Capt. Charles A. Greene's Louisiana Guard Artillery, but few if any casualties resulted. According to the 31st Georgia's colonel, Clement A. Evans, Sedgwick's gunners were perched on "a good position," but "not a man is wounded." "Our advance threw a few shells . . . scattering a body of cavalry," noted a member of the 77th New York, "killing some of the horses attached to their battery." Sedgwick deployed Wright's division into line of battle, and its skirmishers cautiously approached the Southerners. When they came within 100 yards of his line, Georgia Col. Edmund N. Atkinson yelled, "Charge!" Brandishing their bayonets, his Georgians burst into Wright's skirmishers to the glee of White and his cavalrymen. The Federals scampered for safety back toward Granite Hill.[29]

The localized Confederate attack accomplished its goal of delaying Sedgwick's heavy advance. Still, as Ewell's rearguard withdrew toward Fairfield, the Federals followed behind them. "As we moved, a small rearguard of the enemy retreated," testified Brig. Gen. Albion P. Howe when he appeared before the Committee on the Conduct of the War in February 1864. "We followed them, with this small rearguard of the enemy before us, up to Fairfield, in a gorge of the mountains. There we again waited for them to go on. There seemed to be no disposition to push this rearguard when we got up to Fairfield." Howe later claimed that he thought the position at the mouth of the Fairfield Gap could have been easily attacked, but the steep and broken terrain may have made the task more difficult than he thought.[30]

"We pressed the enemy so closely that at one place where they stopped to rest some men who were sent back to fill canteens were captured by our flankers," claimed a soldier of the 121st New York Infantry.[31] A Vermonter of the 6th Corps recalled that not only had their column caught up to Lee's rearguard, they had stopped in an apple orchard. "Some of the apples were as large as a hen's egg," he remembered fondly. "We got together as many as our frying pans would hold and fried them with our pork. This made a palatable supper, but it was our last mouthful of rations, and to aid to our comfort, it was again raining steadily."[32]

The regimental historian of the 5th Maine described this encounter in eloquent terms. "A march of some six miles was made, when the rearguard of the enemy was overtaken, where a slight skirmish was indulged in, a few shell, probably as a parting token, scattering their complimentary fragments round about; but yet neither party specially desirous of giving or bringing on a battle."[33] The Federals made sure to avoid hitting a makeshift Confederate field hospital that they could see in the valley ahead.[34]

No serious effort was launched in the fading twilight to dislodge the Southern infantry.[35] Tompkins' gunners had fired a total of 162 shells in their direction—including parting shots at the enemy wagons as they disappeared from view.[36] Battery G of the 1st Rhode Island Light Artillery's Cpl. Edward Adams reflected, "helped to hasten his journey back to Virginia by a vigorous application of shot and shell."[37]

The men of the 6th Corps bivouacked there in the cold rain, trying to make the best of the terrible weather conditions.[38] Sedgwick's command, which had covered thirty-five miles in a single day just three days earlier, managed only six miles on July 5. The slow advance was the result of a combination of bad weather and a cautious advance, which prudence required when a potentially large and dangerous enemy waited just ahead.[39]

The Confederate Stand at Fairfield

The narrow Fairfield Gap—less than 100 yards wide—was a potential choke point along the Army of Northern Virginia's route to safety. Its commander guided his mount through the pass on the morning of July 5 to get a good look at the terrain. The aggressive leader was always willing to stand and fight if he could find ground of his choosing. It did not take him long to make a decision once he set his eyes on the gap.[40] The narrow pass offered perfect terrain for a stand. General Lee, wrote an unknown officer of the 6th Louisiana in his diary, "halted our corps . . . and told Gen. Ewell to try to induce the enemy to fight. . . . If 'those people' will only come out of their entrenchments and give us an open field fight, we will smash them." Lee was ready again to bloody the enemy. "I never saw Gen. Lee so anxious for a fight." [41] General Ewell, wrote one observer, was "in a state of disgust" over the loss of his train the previous night in Monterey Pass and "refused to be comforted by General Lee." He was more than ready to dole out a measure of revenge, if only the right opportunity presented itself.[42]

One of the Union prisoners caught his first glimpse of Robert E. Lee as the officer made his personal reconnaissance. "Genl. Lee rode past an hour since. He is quite gray, wearing full beard, appears dignified and self-possessed," the POW recorded in his diary. "His salute was very elegant & soldier-like. He certainly has the external appearance of a General. He wore a blue loose coat & a black hat, sits finely on his horse. His face indicates high living."[43]

* * *

Before daybreak the next morning, July 6, Sedgwick sent one of his staff officers and a squadron of cavalry to the 121st New York with orders for the Empire Staters to accompany the staffer further out on the Fairfield Road for a reconnaissance. About 9:00 a.m., the party stepped within sight of the Confederate line of battle and advanced against it. "The balls flew around, over and under me, keeping me winking, dodging and squirming for a full hour," recounted F. W. Morse, an officer with the 121st New York. When Morse reported the skirmish to Col. Emory Upton, the 121st's commander, Upton sent Morse to report to Sedgwick. Morse found the 6th Corps leader sitting on a stump surrounded by his staff. After reporting his morning's adventures, Sedgwick dismissed him, ordering his return to Upton. "By the time I returned to our line, it had ceased firing and was resting," Morse recounted, "the enemy had retired in confusion, and our object was gained."[44]

Meade recognized the perils of fighting for the various mountain gaps, which may help explain why his overall pursuit was so cautiously executed. His caution only increased when Sedgwick reported that the critical passes through South Mountain to the west of Fairfield were already too stoutly defended to assail.[45] "We scarcely pressed them at all, as far as I could judge," was the belief scratched into a diary of one officer in the 93rd Pennsylvania Infantry, "but merely followed and occupied the ground as they evacuated. Thus we slowly advanced all day[,] and night found us six miles from Gettysburg!"[46] William A. Tubbs of the 5th Maine was more simplistic in his assessment: "We came up to their rear . . . and gave them a few shell and shot to hurry them."[47]

Did the Federals miss an opportunity? Some Southern soldiers thought so. According to the diary of the 5th Alabama's Pvt. Samuel Pickens, when their column cleared Fairfield and the rear was slowly moving along the Iron Springs Road, the "troops and wagons [were] crowded together in the little valley on this side & I was somewhat uneasy that the enemy might do us some damage; but some batteries were put in position & a Brigade, I think, formed in line of battle."[48] An officer of the 37th Virginia, part of Maj. Gen. Edward "Allegheny" Johnson's Division of Ewell's Corps, scoffed at the Federal attempts to bring the Confederates to bay, describing their efforts as "feeble."[49]

The appearance of the pursuing Federal infantry spurred the guards to press their prisoners as rapidly as possible. "While marching, and at about 4 P.M., our artillery opened on the rebel rear some three miles behind us, but in full view," recorded one of the Northern captives in his diary. "The firing was brisk and continued some time. After this they hurried us and hurried their train until at about 12 at night we reached Monterey Springs on the top of South Mountain's range. The rebels are making all possible speed for Va."[50] Another recorded, "We passed through the village of Fairfield about noon. The citizens looked on us with pitying look as we passed through and would have given us something to eat but the rebs would not allow us even to buy anything of them. I suppose they wanted to get it themselves." He observed a Confederate captain striking a man with his sword just for reaching for a piece of bread.[51]

After receiving Sedgwick's report of the heavily guarded passes, Meade responded that "All evidence seems to show a movement to Hagerstown and the Potomac. No doubt the principal force is between Fairfield and Hagerstown; but I apprehend they will be likely to let you alone, if you let them alone. Let me know the result of Neill's operations—whether they retire before him, or threaten to push him and you. Send out pickets well on your left flank; reconnoiter in all directions, and let me know the result." Meade concluded, "Whenever I am satisfied that the main body is retiring from the mountains, I shall continue my flank movement."[52]

Given some time to reflect upon Meade's reaction, Maj. Gen. Abner Doubleday disagreed with his decision. "In my opinion Sedgwick should have made an energetic attack, and Meade should have supported it with his whole army, for our cavalry were making great havoc in the enemy's trains in rear," asserted Doubleday, "and if Lee . . . had been forced to form line against Meade, the cavalry, which was between him and his convoys of ammunition, in all probability might have captured the latter and ended the war."[53] While Doubleday's hindsight overstates the case, and perhaps significantly so, an opportunity to at least attack part of the Army of Northern Virginia's scattered infantry commands had been squandered.

When the 6th Corps foot soldiers pulled back from the gap, their frustration was palpable. They had taken only two killed and five wounded, and to a man they were itching for a fight.[54] A New Yorker noted that the skirmish line of the 6th Corps had reached Fairfield in time to watch the Rebels disappear over the hills to the south.[55] "I wonder whether we really whipped the Rebs at Gettysburg so very bad after all?" asked an exasperated officer who had spent the day shadowing the Confederate retreat. "If so, I wonder whether our leaders knew it, or know it yet? If they do, I have one more wonder, I wonder if Napoleon or even Robt. Lee were our commander this evening would they pursue a defeated army in this cautious, courteous way?"[56]

Only sporadic skirmishing took place between the men of the 6th Corps and Lee's rearguard. One 6th Corps advance had moved out with Brig. Gen. Alfred T. A. Torbert's New Jersey brigade in the front, with Torbert riding just behind the skirmishers. A sharpshooter's rifle cracked and the bullet tore a button off the breast of Torbert's coat, narrowly missing the Delawarean's skin.[57]

Later that day, Meade withdrew all of the 6th Corps save one brigade. "You will take every precaution to maintain the position you now hold until dark," he ordered. "You will then withdraw all the Sixth Corps, excepting Neill's brigade and a rifled battery, and proceed with your command (the First and Third Corps included) to execute the order of march of July 5." Neill was to follow the enemy, keeping Meade constantly informed of Lee's movements. Save for Neill's single brigade, Meade's direct pursuit of Lee's army had ended.[58]

The 6th Corps spent the night of July 6 standing a miserable round of picket duty in the rain, watching the Confederates in their front. "We are still laying in the clover field, out of rations and every person hungry," griped a soldier of the 49th Pennsylvania.[59] Pickets with the 123rd Pennsylvania of Brig. Gen. Alexander Shaler's brigade captured 85 prisoners during that long and wet night.[60] "We started out of bivouac at 4 o'clock this morning and are now halted on the march," wrote Lt. Charles S. Brewster of the 10th Massachusetts Infantry. "I suppose to reconnoiter the pass in which the Rebels made a stand last night."[61]

General Meade's Plans for Full Pursuit

Meade faced a major logistical challenge. Having decided upon a flank movement, he had to move seven infantry corps, a cavalry corps, all of the army's artillery, and all of its wagon trains over a limited road network. Heavy rains had turned the unpaved roads into sticky quagmires. The entire army would concentrate in the vicinity of Middletown, Maryland, between Frederick and Hagerstown. The following is the plan Meade and his engineers developed and circulated to the army's corps commanders on the evening of July 5:

> The 1st, 6th, and 3rd Corps would take the direct road to Mechanicstown (Thurmont), Lewistown, cross Catoctin Mountain to Hamburg, and then on to Middletown, Maryland;
>
> The 5th and 11th Corps would take the Taneytown road, passing through Emmitsburg, Creagerstown, Utica, Highknob Pass, and then on to Middletown;
>
> The 2nd and 12th Corps would march via Taneytown, Middleburg, Woodsborough, through Frederick, and then on to Middletown;
>
> The artillery and wagon trains of each corps would accompany their commands as they made their way to Middletown;
>
> Sedgwick would command the army's right wing . . . the 1st, 3rd, and 6th Corps. Maj. Gen. Henry W. Slocum would command the army's left wing, consisting of the 2nd and 12th Corps. Maj. Gen. O. O. Howard would command the army's center, consisting of the 5th and 11th Corps.

This plan maximized the disbursement of the various elements of the Army of the Potomac while avoiding as far as possible too much clogging of the roads. Once concentrated around Middletown, the army could use the macadamized National Road to advance against the Virginia army.[62]

The National Road, sometimes called the Cumberland Road because it originally terminated in Cumberland, Maryland, was the first Federal highway. It was built between 1811 and 1820 for some $7,000,000 to connect Baltimore with Ohio. It followed a route laid out by Gen. James Braddock's pioneers during the French and Indian War and became an important line of commerce. The road was macadamized in the 1830's, meaning that it consisted of three layers of stones put down on a crowned sub-grade with side ditches for drainage. The first two layers consisted of angular hand-broken aggregate. The third was about two inches thick. Each layer was compacted with a heavy roller, which locked the angular stones together. This type of hardened surface was not as susceptible to being turned into a bottomless quagmire of mud, and was the closest thing to a superhighway the 1860s had to offer. Meade's choice to move his army along the National Road was a wise one that would help speed its advance. Although the planned routes were longer and required a flank movement, some of it would be mitigated by using the National Road.[63]

Chapter 5

The Confederates Garrison Williamsport

"The Rebel army is in a bad state & there is no telling how they are going to get out of it."

— Col. John B. McIntosh, 2nd Federal Cavalry Division

July 5: Lee's Main Body

Time was of the essence, and Lee's army had a substantial head start on Meade. As discussed previously, most of the Southern army passed through Fairfield Gap and Monterey Pass. The goal was Williamsport, but whether they would reach it in time—and safely cross the river—remained an open question in the minds of many Confederate soldiers.

"I have seen bad roads, but this was without exception the worst that I have ever seen," grumbled a Virginia artillerist. "One moment we were up to our knees in mud, and the next, lying full length in the mud, having tripped over a rock which we could not shun, owing to the total darkness in which we were enveloped." The cold rain only added to the misery of the marching soldiers.[1]

Capt. James H. Wood commanded Co. D of the 37th Virginia Infantry of Johnson's Division, Ewell's Corps. That afternoon, with a small detail, he was ordered to make a detour to the left of the column and forage for food. Supplied with Confederate currency to pay for the supplies, he and his men marched off with a few available wagons. Wood took a parallel route about a mile from the main column, and he soon had his wagons filled from the well-stocked Maryland farms. Along a country road that eventually converged with the column, Wood was startled by the appearance of a battalion of Federal cavalry bearing down on him from the rear. Wood ordered the teamsters to slap reins and move as quickly as possible. "We quickly reached the outer edge of the open lands," Wood recalled, "and entered the thickly wooded course of the narrow road, so closely pursued that I was compelled to give battle." He only had enough time to deploy his men and ordered them to open fire. "This sudden, and perhaps unexpected attack, threw [the Federals] into confusion, necessitating a reformation further back. They had, however, discovered the inadequacy of my force and were rapidly reforming."

Farther up the road, Wood's wagons curved to the right where the road entered a small valley. His men were spread out thinly quite a distance along the road, with the opposing forces moving on parallel lines only a short distance apart. Wood's men opened fire again, and shot down some of the lead horses of the Union cavalrymen just as they entered a narrow pass in their front. The fallen animals thus blocked the road and threw the rest of the galloping horses into confusion. To Wood's great fortune, some Confederate cavalrymen, hearing the noise of the skirmish, arrived to take on the bluecoats. Wood and his men were able to catch up to their wagons and eventually rejoined the main column. Their foraging mission was thus successful, albeit with no small effort. Wood's comrades desperately needed those provisions, as no one knew how long they might be stranded on the banks of the swelling Potomac River.[2]

Many of the soldiers foraged wherever possible as they slogged along. Most were generally well behaved. However, some were not. As Brig. Gen. Carnot Posey's brigade of Mississippians of A. P. Hill's Corps made their way south, they gathered supplies, food and liquor—perhaps too much of the latter—from the local citizenry. Sgt. James Kirkpatrick of the Army of Northern Virginia's provost guard reminisced, "Had some trouble. Many of the men found whiskey & got drunk. An officer of the 19th Miss was shot by a private of the 12th Miss."[3] These episodes were the exception and not the rule, however. Had they been more common, Lee would have faced more headaches beyond the enormous challenges already staring him in the face.

The Southern soldiers slogged on toward Williamsport, some taking the road but many avoiding the mud by walking through ripe fields. Williamsport and its river crossings were of vital strategic importance to both Lee and Meade. If John Imboden failed to hold it upon his arrival there with the Wagon Train of Wounded, the Federals would cut Lee off from the crossings. That, in turn, would force a trapped Lee into a fight on ground of Meade's choosing. The stakes could not be higher as the two armies marched and maneuvered their way toward the rising water.

Williamsport

Following his harrowing ordeal at Monterey Pass (recounted in the previous chapter), Grumble Jones arrived in Williamsport on the morning of

July 5 to find only chaos in control. Imboden had not yet arrived. The raging, swollen Potomac went "madly rushing by, carrying logs and trees at a terrific rate, and of the color of yellow mud."[4] Jones spotted Confederate soldiers congregating on the bank where a two-raft arrangement called Lemen's Ferry operated. The soldiers were anxious to try to cross the swirling waters of the angry river on one of the rafts, and arguments ensued. Jones immediately took charge of the situation and placed a guard of about twenty men on the ferry. He also ordered riflemen to take positions in the higher buildings should Federal cavalry attack the town.

The flat-boat ferries were pulled along wires anchored to either side of the river, and only two wagons and about forty men could cross during each trip. With things at the ferry calmed down, Jones began allowing wagons of wounded to cross. He also sent across couriers carrying important papers and dispatches.[5] Over the next few days, most of the wounded would make their way across in this manner, but the strain of overuse would cause two of the three ferries to founder before the operation was over. As a result, several wagons were lost and a number of the wounded were drowned.[6]

While the Army of Northern Virginia invaded Pennsylvania, two regiments—the 54th North Carolina and the 58th Virginia—had remained in Williamsport to guard the river crossings. When he arrived on the afternoon of the 5th as Jones directed the early crossings, General Imboden found both regiments still in the town. He ordered the North Carolinians to picket all the roads leaving the town, and dispatched the Virginians nearly four miles away to Huyett's Cross Roads. There, the Virginians were to guard the critical intersection of the Greencastle Pike and the National Road. Company F of the 21st Virginia Infantry, left on the far side of the river to guard that crossing while the rest of the army had moved north to Pennsylvania, was brought across by Imboden to augment his small force. He also was able to gather twenty-three pieces of artillery throughout the day, including the vaunted Washington Artillery of New Orleans, and placed them on high ground to cover the road network.[7]

Jones was well aware of the heavy burden Imboden carried at Williamsport. After consulting with Imboden, Jones and his escort of six horsemen galloped off for Hagerstown to search for the scattered remnants of his own command. Jones planned to bring in all that he could in order to reinforce Imboden's small garrison. Jones found his brigade camped at Leitersburg, still licking their wounds from the debacle at Monterey Pass with Kilpatrick's cavalry. Jones dashed off a dispatch to Jeb Stuart, informing his commander of Imboden's

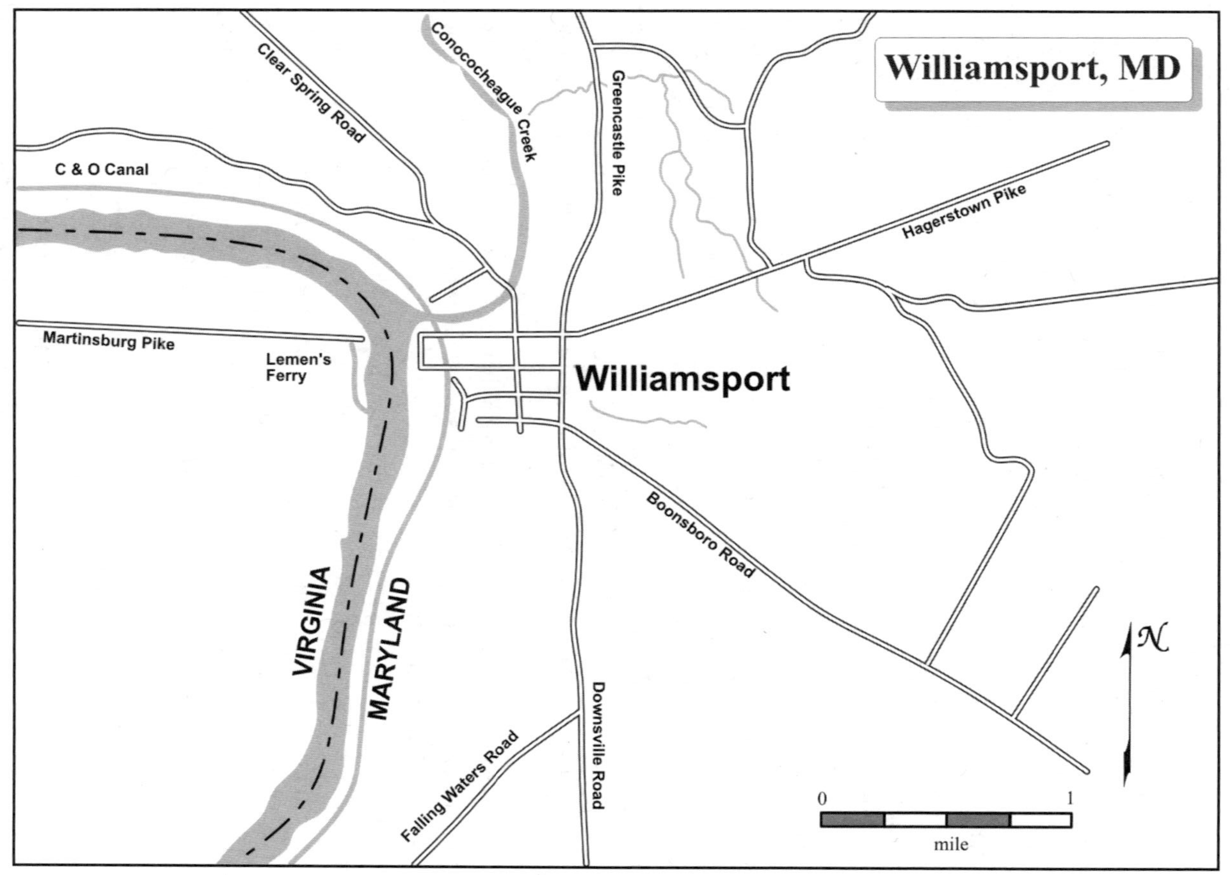
Williamsport, MD
C & O Canal
Clear Spring Road
Conococheague Creek
Greencastle Pike
Hagerstown Pike
Martinsburg Pike
Lemen's Ferry
Williamsport
Boonsboro Road
VIRGINIA
MARYLAND
Falling Waters Road
Downsville Road
N
0
1
mile

predicament at Williamsport. Then, he gathered up his brigade, got them back into the saddle, and led them toward Williamsport.[8] Upon receiving Jones' note, Stuart readied his three brigades to go to Imboden's aid.[9]

If Williamsport was chaotic that morning, by early evening it was hopelessly turned upside down. Nearly 5,000 wagons jammed every single street and most of the open spaces. In the bottomland of the turn basin known as the Cushwa Basin, part of the C & O Canal that ran parallel to the river, many wagons were swamped as they waited for their turn to cross. The pitiful screams of the wounded filled the air, but still unable to drown out the shrill yelps of horses and mules. Imboden sent men to pound on doors and conscript citizens to turn out every morsel of food and refreshment for his men. For the first time since departing Gettysburg, most of the animals were relieved of their wagon entrapments and turned out to graze.[10]

The situation in Williamsport shocked a Confederate surgeon upon his arrival that night. "When I reached Williamsport, I found the streets all barricaded with wagons, and I thought I would never get into town. Had it been light I would have had no trouble, but I had to feel my way, and finally crawled over two or three wagons and reached an open street."[11]

As bad as it was, things would only get worse for Williamsport and Imboden.

Buford's Division

Most of Brig. Gen. John Buford's division spent the Fourth of July at Westminster, Maryland, re-shoeing their horses, refitting, and drawing ammunition. The terrible weather that day made slow work slower and more miserable. All day, long

Brig. Gen. John Buford, commander, 1st Cavalry Division.

NARA

lines of dejected Confederate prisoners tromped their way past them, headed for Union prisoner of war camps. To meet any attack, the unfortunates of the 9th New York Cavalry were ordered to "stand to horse" for more than three hours in a driving rain storm.[12]

After Brig. Gen. Wesley Merritt's brigade of Regulars joined Buford, orders were received early on the morning of July 5 to mount up and head south toward Frederick, Maryland, about twenty-five miles away.[13] The march would be through yet more rain and mud. As one officer of the 1st U.S. Cavalry recalled, "The rain fell in torrents, men and horses hungry and worn out."[14] Corporal Nelson Taylor of the 9th New York knew the march would be hard on their loyal beasts, and told loved ones back home, "our horsses [sic]... have been saddled every day and nearly every night for 4 weeks and not mutch [sic] grain for them to eat."[15]

"Boots and Saddles" rang out in the rising daylight to roust the troopers. Patriotic Maryland girls tried to raise the spirits of Buford's men by lining the road and singing patriotic tunes such as "When This Cruel War is Over."[16] The sweet singing worked as long as it lasted, but as they left the voices behind, the rain dominated the troopers' moods once again.

Along the way to Frederick, Buford's soggy cavalrymen reached a large brick mill. Buford halted his column and summoned its owner, who happened to be a Pennsylvania Dutchman. The general explained that his horses needed hay and corn and that his men could sorely use some flour.

Instead of replying, the citizen simply inquired, "Are you the general commanding these troops?"

"Yes," Buford responded.

"Many of my neighbors are rebels. They say the Union army is whipped and in full retreat. Some of my neighbors are Union men. They say the Rebel army is whipped and in full retreat. Will you tell me the truth?"

Buford shot back, "The Rebel army is whipped and in full retreat. We are trying to get to the Potomac ahead of them."

"Thank God," replied the relieved Dutchman, "I would rather have a country and nothing else, than everything my heart could wish and no country." Gesturing to his property, he concluded, "I have about thirty ton of hay, several thousand bushels of corn not yet shelled, plenty of flour, wheat and buckwheat. Also plenty of corn meal."

The citizen's generosity was music to the cavalrymen's ears. The men hopped out of their saddles and gathered the horses to be fed. For the men, the buckwheat flour was the most popular. "Soon hundreds of fires were kindled in the rain with fence rails and six thousand horses had all of the hay and corn they could eat. A ton of buckwheat cakes baked there that morning would be a small estimate," reminisced Capt. Isaac R. Dunkelberger of the 1st U.S. Cavalry. Buford offered the miller a quartermaster's voucher so the Dutchman could get reimbursement for the large amount of provisions, but it was refused. Buford insisted, however, and had the paper made out. "I wonder if mortal man ever made six thousand men more happy and grateful than that Dutchman did," quipped Dunkelberger. "I regret that I never met him afterwards to personally thank him."[17]

Following the welcome break, Buford's column trudged onward. However, the hard march and the conditions continued to exact a heavy toll. "A horse would give out and its rider would dismount and lead or rather pull it along, for the poor animal had scarcely enough strength left to move its own carcass," noted one trooper. "Horses dropped down in the road from sheer exhaustion, and were left with their saddles, blankets, and bridles, as there was no way to transport them. Men, whose horses were 'played out,' trudged along on foot, in the mud and wet, with nothing to eat and night coming apace, and no spot to lay down upon, except the wet ground. Truly half of what our officers and soldiers endure in this war has never been told, and yet they stand it all cheerfully, and look upon it as a matter of course."[18]

Buford's column made it to within about five miles of Frederick that night. The rain still hadn't let up, so the troopers made yet another soggy camp. The men, too tired to care, simply fell onto the wet ground and went fast to sleep. Even General Merritt slept in the open on the soaked earth.

During the night, an older man about sixty arrived in Buford's camp. He was already a familiar sight to the troopers. During the Maryland Campaign the previous year, he had been a regular visitor in Union camps while peddling a variety of songbooks.[19] He had long been under suspicion, however, for his propensity to ask many questions of a military nature.

The old man found Buford sitting on a log. True to form, he began asking Buford many questions about his camp and the Federal army. After listening silently for a few moments, Buford called out to his provost marshal, Lt. John Mix, and told him simply, "Arrest this man, he is a spy."[20]

The peddler, William Richardson, was grabbed by several staffers and thoroughly searched. Detailed drawings of the Federal troop dispositions, passes from both Lee and Longstreet, and large sums of Confederate and Federal currency were all found sewn into his clothing. For the first time,

Buford looked up from his log and stared Richardson in the eyes. "You have three minutes to pray."

Buford was well within his authority to carry out drumhead courts martial, and perform executions in the field according to a Congressional act passed in March 1863.[21] After the tense three minutes expired while Richardson begged for his life, Buford ordered he be hanged. A heavy line of tent ropes was thrown over the branch of a nearby locust tree, while Richardson watched in horror. Without ceremony, the spy was dangling from the end of the rope within moments. "Buford never got up from the log, nor stopped smoking his pipe, while the man was being executed," observed one of the general's Regulars.[22]

Buford issued strict orders that the body be left hanging to serve as a warning to any like-minded individuals, and a note was pinned to the corpse that it be left swinging for three days. A member of the 1st Vermont Cavalry who passed the dangling Richardson on July 8 noted, "The buttons were all cut off his clothes, and the bark pulled from the tree as high as a man could reach, for relics."[23] Eventually, all of Richardson's clothes would be claimed as souvenirs. The body decayed quickly in the heat and humidity, presenting a disgusting sight and smell to the locals and passersby. When surgeon John Farrington of the 137th New York passed by on the 8th, he noted that the face "was enormously bloated…presenting a horrible appearance."[24] Others remembered that the body was not cut down until it was stark naked, sending an unmistakable message to all who contemplated spying as an avocation.[25]

Following Richardson's execution, Buford and his staff set out for Boonsboro, Maryland, where Judson Kilpatrick's cavalry division was camped. There, the two generals met during the early morning hours to plan their strategy to attack Imboden's wagons, trapped in Williamsport by the rising waters of the Potomac. They agreed that Buford's division would pitch into the Confederates guarding the trains on the banks of the swollen river.[26]

Early on the morning of July 6, after Buford returned to Frederick, word of Kilpatrick's success at Monterey Pass on the night of July 4 filtered through the camp, raising the spirits of the horsemen. They drew rations from the town, and some troopers were able to draw fresh horses.[27] Both man and beast would need all their strength for what lay ahead for them at Williamsport.

Stuart's Cavalry

On the morning of July 5, while Buford's command marched toward Frederick, a column of Robertston's North Carolina cavalry brigade arrived in

Emmitsburg. They quickly captured a Federal signal station atop South Mountain. Signalman Capt. Louis R. Fortesque later wrote in his diary, "We soon learned from these drowsy cavaliers, who had been steadily in the saddle for some days and nights, that Lee had been retreating since early morning of the previous day, July 4." About 7:00 a.m., the little detachment of Fortesque, another officer, and five of his enlisted men was escorted into the streets of Emmitsburg to be personally interrogated by Jeb Stuart.

"Arriving at the intersection of the first street, we were confronted by the cavalry leader of the Army of Virginia, whose headquarters were temporarily established there," Fortesque related. The signalmen-turned-prisoners couldn't help but admire Stuart's gaudy uniform and the dashing, larger-than-life figure he cut. Surrounded by his staff officers, Stuart began questioning his captives. Impressed by him as they were, the Federals nonetheless decided to feed him as much disinformation as they could cook up.

"What command do you belong to?" inquired Stuart.

"Signal Corps," one responded.

"Were you with the cavalry that passed up that pike last night?"

"We were with the troops that moved up there last night."

Stuart cut to the chase. "Who commanded them?"

"A general of the United States Army."

"What infantry regiments were with them?" Stuart shot back.

"We did not observe, nor count them."

"You did not count the cavalry either, I suppose?" Stuart asked, likely with a tone betraying frustration.

"No, sir."

Stuart's questions were getting him nowhere, and he realized he was being asked to believe that these signalmen, of all people, weren't in the business of counting troops. "Were my men fighting Kilpatrick during the night?" Stuart asked, referencing the fight in the Monterey Pass.

"Not having been there, Sir, we are unable to say."

Stuart realized that any further questions would be nothing but an exercise in frustration. "It was our opinion, after the interview, that Stuart was misled into believing that an infantry force was with Kilpatrick, and that, in consequence, his chances of getting through safely were somewhat remote," Fortesque observed. Stuart indeed gave up and directed a staff officer to take charge of the prisoners, "his tone and gesture indicating that while with his column we might look for no favors." The unfortunate signalmen marched off into captivity.[28] For his part, Stuart hardly noted their capture, simply stating,

"In and around Emmitsburg we captured 60 or 70 prisoners of war, and some valuable hospital stores en route from Frederick to the [Federal] army."[29]

Stuart took some time to have breakfast while his column passed through the town and out the road to Hagerstown, where he hoped to link up with Lee' foot soldiers. The brigades of cavalry passed through in a seemingly endless line of four abreast until about noon.[30]

The sight of so many southern cavalrymen in Emmitsburg, so soon after the large battle just to their north at Gettysburg, kept the residents uneasy. Citizens asked the troopers who had won the battle, and the Rebels glibly claimed victory. Some were more curious than others. A few of the townsfolk climbed into the steeple of the Lutheran Church, an edifice almost completely destroyed in a June 15 fire that had swept through the town, to get a good look at the troopers. As they passed, some of Ferguson's horsemen spotted a pair of men in the steeple and thought them to be Federal signalmen or spies. They halted their horses and aimed their rifles up at them. Quick-thinking locals ran up to the cavalrymen, assuring the soldiers that the pair was only curious residents. Ferguson's men lowered their guns and at least two lives were spared.[31]

The gray troopers raided local farms in the surrounding countryside, taking all manner of food, horses, whiskey, and anything else of use. One of Stuart's detachments stopped at a gristmill and began seizing the mill horses. The proprietor soon came running, hands in the air. "You can't take my horses!" cried the miller. "I need them for my work!" Undaunted, the raiders told the miller that the horses were needed to get the troopers back home, and if they could get to Hagerstown and then safely across the river, he could have them back. The troopers kept their word, and a few days later the miller was back home with his beasts, none the worst in spite of his experience.[32]

Jeb Stuart and his staff saddled up and joined the troopers' ride south toward Hagerstown.[33] Stuart paused in the picturesque village of Graceham long enough to frighten the locals. William Cramer and his wife, who operated the local general store, were shocked to see the Confederate troopers trotting into town—they believed they were safe after Union soldiers had passed through on June 29. Their daughter Belva was impressed to operate the water pump for the thirsty butternuts. She had a toothache, however, and the vigorous exercise of pumping only increased her pain. When the little girl began sobbing, one of the rebels tried to comfort her. "Don't cry, little girl. We're dirty and ragged, but we are gentlemen and we will not hurt you."[34]

Leaving Graceham, Stuart's horsemen marched to Creagerstown (which Stuart called "Cooperstown"). From there, he planned to move west along the Westminster-Hagerstown Road.[35] However, when he learned that Union soldiers had blocked Harman's Gap through South Mountain, the cavalier led his column northwest to the small hamlet of Franklinville, where his men stopped to rest a bit. Resuming the march, Stuart headed westward and likely passed through Harbaugh Valley, and then into the Deerfield area. There, he divided his command in order to make the passage of the mountain area more easy and certain. Chambliss' Brigade, under Stuart's immediate command, moved to the right toward Leitersburg, while Ferguson passed to the left toward Smithburg. At some point Stuart returned to the road to Hagerstown, and with his route across South Mountain open, he decided to lead his brigades to Smithburg. There, he suspected Kilpatrick was resting after his engagement at Monterey the previous night. Determined to keep the Federals away from the river crossings at Williamsport, the plumed cavalier decided to cut Kilpatrick off at Smithsburg.[36]

The Engagement at Smithsburg

Thus far, the sleepy hamlet of Smithsburg, Maryland, made up largely of descendants of German immigrants, had avoided the hard hand of war. The only incident of note was that Jubal Early's Division had tramped through the town on June 24 on its way into Pennsylvania. The town's history harkened back to 1813, when its founder, Christopher "Stuffle" Smith, bought a large tract of land and settled it. Incorporated in 1846, farming and orchards played a major role in the town's economy. Situated about halfway between Gettysburg and Sharpsburg, its citizens had heard the booming guns of both sanguinary battles. The horror of war, however, was about to fall into their own lap as both Stuart and Kilpatrick set their sights on the town.

Kilpatrick's 3rd Division arrived at Smithsburg about 2:00 pm on July 5, following the fight at Monterey. The troopers had arrived via Rouserville, with Maj. John Hammond's 5th New York Cavalry in the van.[37] To lighten his responsibility and free as many of his men for possible combat, Kilpatrick sent his large column of prisoners under guard to Frederick. To avoid any surprises, he deployed his command on three different hills facing South Mountain, and dispatched scouts on the road to Emmitsburg. Huey's brigade and a battery of horse artillery held the center on Gardenhour's Hill, while Custer's Wolverines and Pennington's battery held the hill on the left. Col. Nathaniel P. Richmond's

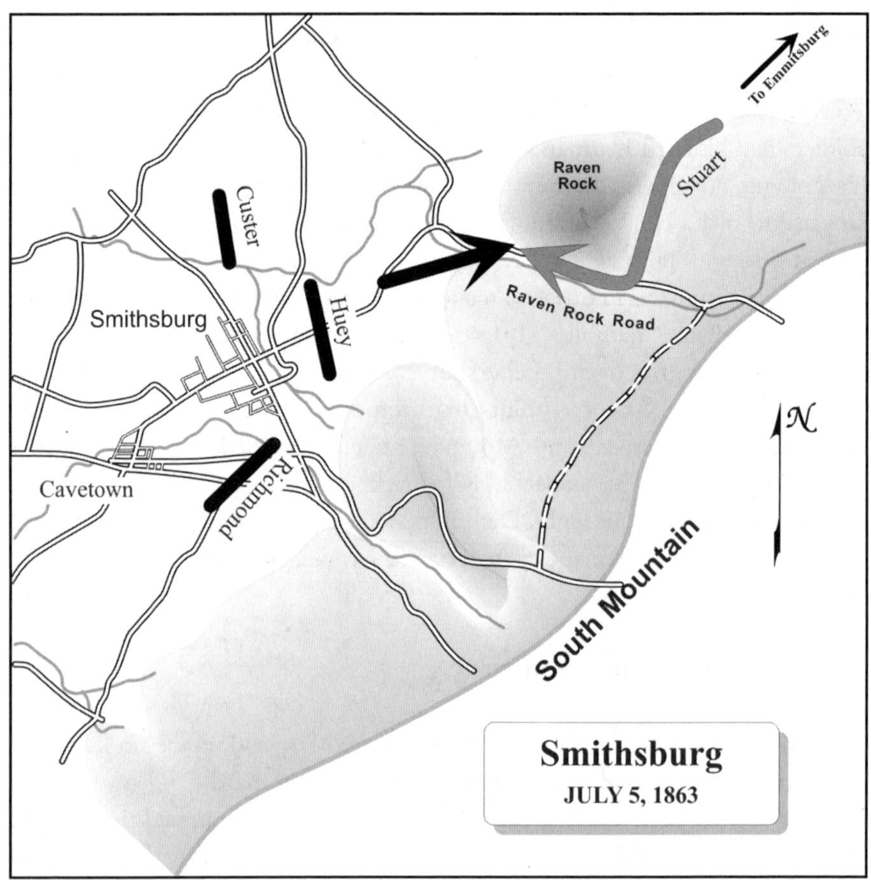

brigade, supported by a third battery, held the Union right on another eminence called Goat Hill, near the foot of South Mountain. To protect his vulnerable left flank, Kilpatrick sent off a squadron of the 6th Michigan Cavalry to watch there. "I am now holding a strong position," he wrote in a quick note to Pleasonton. Perhaps a bit anxious to engage the foe, he continued, "the enemy is in sight, tired and worn out. He shall not have a moment's rest."[38]

Once situated, Kilpatrick's division "lay down to await the approach of the enemy," or as a member of the 5th New York Cavalry jotted simply in his diary, "We rested at Smithsburg."[39] Loyal Unionists were happy the Federals were in and about the town, and opened their homes and pantries to the tired and dirty horsemen. Some of Kilpatrick's troopers butchered a steer and had a large barbeque, while Custer enjoyed a feast of chicken in the home of one friendly local.[40]

The comfort of Kilpatrick's men was soon shattered when Jeb Stuart, leading the brigades of Chambliss and Ferguson, appeared along Raven Rock Road in the distance.[41] The Federals watched the Southern horse soldiers cross the mountain and deploy on the foothills below. Kilpatrick ordered his men to tear down fences and deploy into line of battle. To block Stuart, he advanced a dismounted skirmish line to the foothills of South Mountain, holding both sides of the road.[42] Fuller's battery commenced the fight by firing on Stuart's column, and the fight for the pass overlooking Smithsburg was on.[43]

Stuart's horse artillery dropped trail near an orchard on Nicodemus Hill opposite Kilpatrick's position, and returned fire. The errant shots damaged several homes. "I was in our battery at the time, where I had been watching the maneuvers," recounted a member of the 6th Ohio Cavalry, "and in a few minutes a shell came screaming towards our battery, bursting very near. I concluded it was no place for me, and I returned to the regiment."[44]

Pennington's guns replied, and a stirring artillery duel ensued. "Our batteries exchanged salutes for an hour or so," recalled an Ohioan.[45] "There was a lively exchange of fire between Stuart's troopers on Nicodemus Hill and Kilpatrick's on Gardenhour's Hill lasting about an hour," affirmed Smithsburg civilian Alfred P. Fehl. "One Confederate shell reportedly went through the roof of the Burgesser house, hit a bag of dried fruit and did not explode, another hit the Kimler pottery and did some damage, and another hit the house of Leonard Vogel and caused some slight damage."[46]

A freewheeling artillery battle to little effect was the last thing Stuart could afford. The battles and skirmishes during his troopers' long march to Gettysburg, followed by the large-scale cavalry engagement at East Cavalry Field on July 3, had nearly depleted his store of fixed ammunition. "We had to be very vigilant," noted Pvt. Henry Matthews of Stuart's artillery, "[and] did not use much ammunition during this retrograde movement, as the fight at Gettysburg had almost cleaned us up. We were very closely pressed on several occasions, but whenever the Federal cavalry became too bold and annoyed us as we would let them get close enough for canister and then give them a shot or two, which had the desired effect and caused them to approach us more carefully in the future."[47]

Summoned by Stuart, Col. Ferguson's brigade of Virginians emerged from the hills above Smithsburg and drew immediate fire from both Fuller's guns and Huey's dismounted cavalry. A squadron of the 5th New York cavalry watching Kilpatrick's right detected no movement in that sector.[48]

Despite the advantage of holding an excellent position and terrain that favored him, Kilpatrick decided to draw his men off at dark and head for Boonsboro. In his report, Kilpatrick uncharacteristically admitted that he, and not Stuart, had disengaged, "to save my prisoners, animals, and wagons."[49] As mentioned previously, he had already sent his prisoners to Frederick. In reality, Little Kil had a bigger target in mind—cutting off General Lee's line of retreat.[50] His decision to break off, however, left the critical ground between South Mountain and Hagerstown firmly in Confederate hands, meaning that Lee's army would be able to concentrate there. In this, Kilpatrick inexplicably cost the Army of the Potomac the initiative that it never could regain.

Before leaving Smithsburg, someone in Kilpatrick's division forgot to inform Capt. James H. Kidd and his Company E, 6th Michigan Cavalry, on the far left flank that the division was departing. "My troop…was forgotten when the division moved away after dark," Kidd recalled, "and we lay there for an hour within sight of the Confederate camp until, suspecting something was wrong, I made a reconnaissance and discovered that our command had gone. I therefore mounted the men and followed the trail which led through Boonsboro."[51]

Kilpatrick reached Boonsboro just before midnight and bivouacked his division. As recounted earlier in this chapter, Buford and his staff arrived at Kilpatrick's headquarters about 1:00 a.m. to discuss their plans for the following day.

With Kilpatrick gone, Stuart and his troopers took possession of the town. Late into the evening, Fitz Lee established his headquarters at the home of Dr. and Mrs. Riddlemoser, who were expecting a baby. The baby was born that night, and in honor of their guest the couple named their new little girl Effie Lee.[52]

To picket the area, Stuart spread Lee's brigade out between Smithsburg and Leitersburg, five miles to the west. He hoped to find Lee at or near Leitersburg, and wished to discuss recent troop movements with the army commander. Stuart dispatched Pvt. Robert W. Goode of the 1st Virginia Cavalry, "a trusty and intelligent soldier," to find Lee and to report on Stuart's operations during the last twenty-four hours.[53]

Meade's Intelligence Gathering Efforts

These first couple of days of Lee's retreat were critically important windows for the Army of the Potomac, and General Meade desperately needed good intelligence from his cavalry. As his horsemen battled far to the south of the Gettysburg battlefield, and Sedgwick's Corps nipped at Early's heels near Fairfield, Meade was still unsure whether the Confederates were making for the river, or intending to take a defensive position in the mountains. "The general directs me to say that he is holding here [at Gettysburg] in a state of uncertainty as to the enemy's movements and intentions," confessed his chief of staff Maj. Gen. Daniel Butterfield. "His reconnaissances and scouts will today [July 5], he trusts, furnish it." Butterfield concluded, "Should the enemy be retreating, the general will move rapidly through the Valley toward Frederick."[54] Determining Lee's intentions would enable Meade to set up proper lines of supply for an army on the move. He was also concerned that withdrawing his entire army from Gettysburg would leave Baltimore and Washington vulnerable to attack.

Later that day, after word of Kilpatrick's midnight fight at Monterey and Sedgwick's skirmish near Fairfield filtered in, Pleasonton reported to Maj. Gen. William H. French (who was at Frederick, Maryland), "Major-General Meade desires me to say that, in consequence of a large body of the enemy being concentrated in the road toward Hagerstown, beyond Fairfield, he has suspended his operations for present. Indications go to show that he intends evacuating the Cumberland Valley, but it is not yet positively ascertained." The Federal Cavalry Corps commander concluded, "Until so ascertained, the general does not feel justified in leaving here and moving down toward you."[55]

That evening, French reported in. "Lee is said to be moving to place his right on the river at Williamsport, his left and mass being at Chambersburg. It seems," French postulated, "as if he was taking up the Antietam campaign." He finished by noting that the Confederates had arrived in Hagerstown in force.[56]

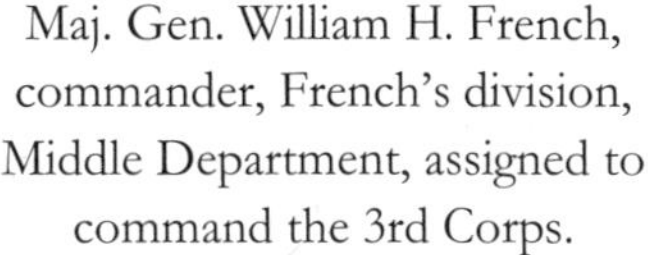

Maj. Gen. William H. French, commander, French's division, Middle Department, assigned to command the 3rd Corps.

USAHEC

Later that night, thanks to the efforts of his scouts and cooperative loyal citizens, French provided more detailed news. "Five hundred wagons (rebel), guarded by about 150 infantry, 150 cavalry, three pieces of inferior-looking artillery, and from 3,000 to 5,000 head of cattle passed through Hagerstown last night after 11 o'clock to about 4 o'clock." French then stated what Meade was endeavoring to confirm beyond all doubt: "[The Confederates] could not cross the ford at Williamsport, the river being too high. Supposed to have gone to Falling Waters, having started from Williamsport in that direction this morning. The wagons were loaded with sick, wounded, and stores."[57]

The important commercial center of Hagerstown, interposed squarely between the river and any movement by Meade, commanded the approaches to both Williamsport and Falling Waters four miles downstream—the river crossings a retreating Lee would have to use. Whoever held Hagerstown, then, had the inside track to the critical fords that would carry Lee and his army to safety.

Chapter 6

July 6: The Battle of Hagerstown

"We've got them now, boys! . . . Charge!"

— Jeb Stuart

JEB STUART KNEW THE CRITICAL sector for the Army of Northern Virginia's retreat lay between South Mountain and Hagerstown. He also knew what he did not know, which was where Kilpatrick's cavalry had gone after it broke off the engagement at Smithsburg. Believing that the Federals would recognize the importance of holding Hagerstown, Stuart sent the small brigades of Chambliss and Robertson there by the shortest route, while he rode with Ferguson and Jones to Cavetown and then on toward Hagerstown. During mid-morning, a courier found Stuart with the news that Kilpatrick had ridden to Boonsboro. With this critical intelligence in hand, Stuart set his plan into motion.[1]

Hagerstown was the county seat of Washington County. Founded in 1762 by German immigrant Jonathan Hager, the town became an important seat of commerce. "The town is situated in a section of beautiful country, on the National Road, sixty-five miles from Baltimore and six miles from the Potomac River," noted a Confederate horse artillerist. Both the National Road and the Boonsboro Pike passed through the town, making it a critical route for commerce moving east to west and north to south. By July 1863, Hagerstown had 6,000 inhabitants, many occupying handsome brick row homes along a well-defined network of straight and well-kept streets. Tidy brick sidewalks lined the streets, which were centered on Henry Hager's large gristmill.[2] On July 6, war clomped along those fine thoroughfares in the form of Chambliss' and Robertson's 1,800 horsemen.

Capt. Frank Bond's Company A of the 1st Maryland Cavalry (C.S.A.), one of the Southern units left behind at Gettysburg to keep an eye on Meade's army, caught up to their comrades outside Hagerstown. "In truth, we were spoiling

A prewar image of Capt. Frank Bond of Company A, 1st Maryland Cavalry (C.S.A.).

Bond Family

for a fight," wrote Bond. "About noon, reached the head of the column—miles upon miles of wagons—which had halted on the outskirts of Hagerstown."[3]

When Kilpatrick learned that the enemy wagons were passing through Hagerstown, he decided to try and add this train to his already impressive tally of booty. To the surprise of the Federal horse soldiers, their initial advance into the town was largely unopposed. They entered from the south along the Baltimore Pike, surprising the Rebel defenders who expected an approach from the opposite direction. Soon enough, however, the Yankees ran up against barricades in the streets and Confederate riflemen shooting at them from church steeples.[4]

The advance guard of Kilpatrick's 3rd Division crashed into Col. J. Lucius Davis' 10th Virginia Cavalry, which was picketing the road to Baltimore, and drove the Rebels back.[5] The men of the 15th Virginia Cavalry were just sitting down at the Washington House Hotel for their first hot meal in days when the sounds of battle interrupted them. Perhaps with heavy sighs and surely with empty stomachs, they mounted their horses and rode to the support of their embattled comrades.

Captain Bond was also enjoying a meal in the center of the town with his 1st Maryland (C.S.A.) comrades when he "was informed that the enemy in force was approaching . . . upon the opposite side to that by which we had entered," he recalled. "As the information seemed reliable, I abandoned my dinner and hastened back."[6] Riding to where his company had agreed to meet in case the alarm bugle blew, Bond rallied forty-six of his 109 troopers and rode to the support of the 10th Virginia. "This regiment was the advance-guard of the army, and the head of its column was just at the edge of the town, and no other troops were between us and the wagons," wrote Bond. "Leaving my small party, I passed to the front, and saw a long column of Federal cavalry approaching by the turnpike and about a mile away. It was very soon apparent that the enemy intended to charge."[7]

Bond hastened back to Davis and urged him to countercharge, but Davis and his troopers seemed paralyzed by their plight and Kilpatrick's superior numbers. Seeing fear in the eyes of the Virginians, Bond realized they would be no help to him. "[Davis] gave no orders at all, and, upon viewing his regiment, I saw that indescribable tremor pervading them which convinced me they would not stand."[8] Bond resolved to do what he could and rode back to prepare his little command for battle.

Kilpatrick formed his troopers on both the Boonsboro Road and Williamsport Pike, readying them for an all-out attack. The Federals galloped into Davis' regiment with revolvers blazing. Davis' horse was shot out from

The Battle of Hagerstown
July 6, 1863

under him, but the colonel continued fencing with passing Yankees until he was captured.[9] The 9th Virginia Cavalry galloped up to offer help. Near the intersection of Baltimore and South Washington Streets, in the center of Hagerstown, Lt. George W. Beale led a charge with part of the regiment and captured a number of men of the 1st West Virginia Cavalry.[10]

The momentum of the surging Federals carried them to the town square, where three batteries of Confederate horse artillery were waiting for them. Shoemaker's, McGregor's, and Breathed's guns opened fire and canister, driving back the charging Northerners.[11] "The Rebel guns bore on us hard," recalled a member of the 5th Michigan Cavalry. "The shells burst all around us. Solid shot like slugs came ploughing through the air descending in a curve making a sharp whizzing noise."[12]

Responding to Chew's accurate and effective gunnery, Kilpatrick's horse artillery (Lts. Pennington's and Samuel Elder's batteries) deployed on high ground at the Female Seminary south of town. "For awhile the artillery fire was severe, the range was short, and their ten-pound shrapnel whizzed fearfully and exploded all around us," recorded one of Chew's gunners. "The artillery duel was hot and lively, yet it was but a prelude to a more severe conflict that raged for several hours along the Williamsport Pike, in which the cavalry and some infantry on both sides took a hand."[13] W. W. Jacobs, a local civilian, sat and watched the battle from atop the Eagle Hotel. "The artillery duel over the eastern end of the city lasted only about a quarter of an hour, yet it shook the city to its very foundation, and terrified its inhabitants," he recalled. Jacobs and his companions could see the shells whizzing across the sky.[14]

James Breathed trained his muzzles on Pennington's familiar guns. These opposing batteries had dueled many times, and several times recently during the ongoing campaign. When he got the opportunity to face his old nemesis, Breathed "was in his element," recalled the battery's Private Matthews after the war. "Nothing gave him more pleasure than to be among bursting shells and the zip of the minie. Artillery duels had no terror for him. He was in his second heaven, especially if the opposing battery was battery M., 2nd U. S. Horse. They were well organized and commanded by Lt. C. M. Pennington," continued the gunner. "If the survivors of Breathed's and Pennington's batteries could get together what a swapping of yarns there would be . . . "[15]

Captain Bond's little company of Marylanders sat on their horses in a column of fours on Potomac Street. "Fleeing cavalrymen" of the Virginia regiments galloped by along both sides of Bond's column, "until we were threatened with being overwhelmed by them in their flight."[16] In response to

Capt. Ulric Dahlgren, Union staff officer, Meade's Headquarters.

NARA

the obvious rout, Bond steadied his men and attempted to retire in an orderly fashion. "But before we reached a side street the [10th Virginia Cavalry] had been routed, and was fleeing in the wildest panic," recalled Bond. "Everyone knows the contagion of such a rout, but . . . each and every one of those forty-six men moved as part of a machine, and the column was solid as if on parade."[17] "We wheeled about and retired," observed a Maryland horse soldier, "hoping to extricate ourselves from the runaway mob."[18]

"The enemy was immediately upon the heels of the flying Confederates," continued Bond, "and as soon as our rear (soon to become the front) was uncovered, my order was 'Fours right about charge!' It was a tremendous struggle for the sections of fours to force their way around, crowded and pressed as they were by largely superior numbers that filled the street from house to house . . . as each man dashed at full speed at the enemy the moment he could face them the charge was made nearly in single file."[19]

The advance of the Maryland troopers convinced Kilpatrick to recall his men to avoid an uneven combat in the town's streets. "Immediately the enemy perceived there was a body of troops who did not intend to run, they checked their pursuit and halted in a confused mass in the street," Bond proudly noted.[20]

Kilpatrick's withdrawal was too late for Ulric Dahlgren. Joined by the remnants of his raiding party, Dahlgren fell in with a squadron of the 18th Pennsylvania Cavalry under command of Capt. William C. Lindsay, which was

Col. John R. Chambliss, Jr., Commander, W. H. F. Lee's cavalry brigade.

USAHEC

already advancing to attack the Confederate positions. Somehow, Dahlgren managed to assume command of Company A of the 18th Pennsylvania. With the Keystone Staters at his side, he made yet another head-long rush down the main street of Hagerstown and crashed into the pickets of the 9th Virginia Cavalry posted there, driving all resistance toward the public square in the middle of the town.

Reinforced by most of Col. John Chambliss' brigade of Confederate cavalry, the gray horse soldiers made a stand. The sharp street brawl erupted into a saber-to-saber, boot-to-boot affair. Civilian W. W. Jacobs watched the action with rapt fascination:

> The cutting and slashing was beyond description; here right before and underneath us the deadly combat was waged in a hand to hand combat, with the steel blades circling, waving, parrying, thrusting, and cutting, some reflecting the bright sunlight, others crimsoned with human gore; while the discharge of pistols and carbines was terrific, and the smoke through which we now gazed down through and on the scene below, the screams and yells of the wounded and dying, mingled with cheers and commands, the crashing together of the horses and fiery flashes of the small arms presented a scene such as words cannot portray.[21]

Col. J. Lucius Davis, commander of the 10th Virginia Cavalry, was captured during the combat. Capt. Lindsay was killed, and his small command took heavy casualties. Dahlgren spotted the Rebel trooper who killed Lindsay, and "immediately cut down the man with his saber.[22]

Capt. Bond's 1st Maryland countercharge was no less spectacular than Dahlgren's mad rush. Leading the way, Sgt. Hammond Dorsey went to work with his saber, cutting down five Yankees in the whirling melee. "[He] was the first man who dashed into the enemy's ranks and began to hew right and left," reported Bond. "Five of them fell under Sergt. Dorsey's sword, and the last of them was a bugler, by this time in full flight. As he leaned over his horse's neck the bugle of brass, as thick as a man's arm, protected his head, and repeated blows were necessary to disable him. I examined this bugle later on, and it was cut nearly through in numerous places as clean as a carrot might be chopped with an axe. Sergt. Dorsey, boiling with wrath, informed me that but for the bugle he would have gotten two or three more."[23] "I shall never forget the magnificent conduct of Sergeant Dorsey Hammond, of our company," recalled an admiring member of the regiment. "With his strong arm he wielded his saber like Hercules, cutting down many of the enemy from their horses."[24] The stubborn resistance of the Southern horsemen stopped the Northern pursuit in its tracks and drove the Federals back.[25] The Confederates made a stand at the stout stone wall surrounding the Zion Reformed Church on North Potomac Street, north of the town square.

Having avenged Lindsay's death, Dahlgren left the remnant of Company A in the alleys on both sides of the town square and rode in search of reinforcements. He found them in the form of Company D. Dahlgren called on twenty men of the regiment to dismount, leave their sabers on the saddle, and proceed on foot. He placed ten troopers on each sidewalk while he rode along in the middle of the street. Dahlgren told the Pennsylvanians not to fire until he gave the order. When was within 300 yards of the town's square, Confederate horse soldiers opened fire, using the mounted captain as a convenient target. Dahlgren rode on, ignoring the danger and the bullets whizzing by his ear.

Once within carbine range of the Southerners, Dahlgren ordered, "Now boys, give it to them!" The Yankees fired a volley from each sidewalk, driving the Rebel cavalry from their position. The Confederates fell back to the Dutch Reformed Church where, supported by artillery, they made a stand. Sheltering behind walls and tombstones, they fired again on the advancing Federals. The bullets tore into the men of the 18th Pennsylvania, inflicting heavy losses "in consequence to having to face, with sabers, in a narrow street, an enemy who was using pistols."[26] An unexpected and heavy flanking fire from a side street caused Dahlgren to wheel to face the new threat. The captain sat his horse on the west side of the street, coolly directing his men to meet the flank attack, when "the rebels behind the church shot him."[27]

A newspaper correspondent traveling with Kilpatrick's division reported this action in the *New York Times*:

> Meanwhile, showers of bullets came on the devoted party from every direction—from streets, alleys, and houses. Several of our men were killed, others were wounded and left behind, and it only remained to get out of town as quickly as possible. Captain Dahlgren was already wounded; the sensation was so slight, that he thought it was nothing more than a glancing ball, and little dreamed that his heavy boot and foot had been pierced. But he must now turn with the remnant of his party and ride for life. His good steed once more bears him from captivity or death, and then he falls from the saddle, exhausted by loss of blood. Friendly hands are near to receive the wounded soldier and bear him to an ambulance.[28]

Maj. Luther Trowbridge of the 5th Michigan Cavalry watched the injured young captain ride up to Kilpatrick and report on his role in the fighting. After hearing the report, Kilpatrick delivered further orders. Dahlgren interrupted him, stating, "General, I am hit," while pointing to his wounded leg. Trowbridge saw the injured captain dismount and lay down on the ground, where he passed out from the shock and loss of blood.[29] Regaining consciousness a short while later, Dahlgren had the strength to pull out his diary and scribble tongue-in-cheek: "Foot not very painful. Slept well."[30] The young captain likely had no idea that his wounded foot was horribly mangled.

The fighting forced Hugh St. Clair of the 18th Pennsylvania Cavalry to dismount, run for a nearby house, and scamper into the cellar. Using a convenient iron bar as a steadying support for his carbine, he rested his gun on it and opened fire across the street. One round drilled a Rebel horse soldier through the body, and he died the next day. Hemmed in, however, the Confederates captured St. Clair. The following day, he had a chance to observe the enemy at close range. "I went out among the Rebs and had all sorts of conversations with them," he recorded in his diary. "They say they are fighting for their homes." He ate breakfast with a captured enemy lieutenant and enjoyed pleasant company and good conversation "without suspicion."[31]

The captured St. Clair was just one of many losses suffered by the 18th Pennsylvania Cavalry in the savage street fighting. Capt. Enos J. Pennypacker was leading a desperate charge by his squadron, Companies L and M, when he was wounded and his horse shot out from under him. Lieutenants Henry C. Potter and William L. Laws were captured in the melee; Laws would die while incarcerated at Libby Prison. All told, the regiment suffered eight killed, twenty-one wounded, and fifty-nine captured or missing, for a total of eighty-eight. As the regimental historian later wrote, "I doubt if a more gallant charge was ever made than that by these four companies in the face of overwhelming numbers and in the teeth of what seemed inevitable death or capture."[32]

Capt. Charles J. Snyder of the 1st Michigan Cavalry was temporarily commanding a squadron of the 18th Pennsylvania Cavalry that day. Snyder had been detailed as an aide to Kilpatrick, who ordered him to lead a charge of the Pennsylvanians. "Fearlessly he went about his duty and as an eyewitness informed me, nobly did he discharge it," reported Col. Charles H. Town, the commander of the 1st Michigan. "Meeting six sturdy Confederates, he engaged them single handedly, cutting three of them out of the saddle and putting the rest to flight, though he received the pistol shot that caused his death and a saber cut upon the head as well, early in the melee."[33]

When Sgt. Horace Ide and others from the 1st Vermont Cavalry came under fire as his regiment advanced through the streets of the town, they took advantage of the urban nature of the battlefield. "We deployed down cross streets as skirmishers, hiding behind the houses and firing around corners," Ide recalled. "I saw a squad of them, and resting beside a telegraph pole, fired my carbine. I didn't know as I hit them, but they dodged mightily sudden. At one time we came on quite a lot of them, three to one, and saved ourselves by running through the house. We found ourselves being gradually forced back, but we went very slow. In fact we had sat down right before Lee's Army and they had to remove us before he could proceed."[34]

Company A, 1st Ohio Cavalry, Kilpatrick's headquarters escort, was also under fire. "We were left for some time drawn up in front of a large church exposed to the aim of the rebels posted in a cupola about three squares away," recalled an Ohioan. "To remain standing in line as the mark of sharpshooters, with their bullets whistling about our ears or going thug into a horse and seeing it tremble and fall or rear and plunge with its rider, and we still remain in line, was even harder than to go on our charge at Monterey." Trooper John Reese's horse was shot, "and many spasmodic recognitions made to passing bullets."[35]

A captain of the 1st Michigan Cavalry cut down three Rebels in less than three minutes before he was himself cut down. The battle spread through much of the city. "The troops were mostly dismounted," noted Jacobs, "and the charging columns fell back into their line, and the streets and alleys were ablaze with fire and smoke from the contending forces." Kilpatrick's aggressive charges nearly drove Chambliss and Robertson from the streets of Hagerstown. The Gods of war seemed to be smiling on the Union troopers.

The fighting swirled in a town that fully reflected the deep schisms that marked Maryland's participation in the Civil War. Demonstrating her Southern leanings, the daughter of a prominent local physician leaned out of a second floor window from a house located on the northeast corner of the town square, took, aim, and killed a sergeant of the 18th Pennsylvania.[36]

A Federal soldier handed citizen W. W. Jacobs a musket and told him to pitch in, which Jacobs did "with a vengeance." Jacobs took up a position near a church, holding his position until the North Carolina infantry of Brig. Gen. Alfred Iverson's Brigade marched into the northern end of town and started forming a line of battle. Jeb Stuart's main body followed closely behind, and a brigade of Texas infantry from James Longstreet's Corps arrived at the double-quick to support the North Carolinians.[37] Civilians also fell in the bloody chaos. John Stemple, a well-known local artist, sat atop a house near the same square and watched the action unfold in the streets below in the hope of painting the scene. The picture was not to be. To the horror of his fellow townspeople, a Confederate sharpshooter shot and killed him.[38]

Realizing that Kilpatrick's forces outnumbered the Southern infantry and horsemen, Jeb Stuart rose in his stirrups and exhorted the men to give their all. His appeal was inspiring. "Our force was very much smaller than the enemy's, and for that reason Gen. Stuart made a personal appeal to his men to do their best," reminisced Pvt. Matthews of Breathed's Battery. "No appeal coming from Stuart was ever disregarded. In this case, as in others, they did not disappoint him."[39]

Iverson's North Carolinians had been both poorly led and roughly handled on the first day at Gettysburg. Adding insult to injury, most of their wagons and baggage had been lost to Kilpatrick's troopers in Monterey Pass. The depleted brigade was leading the Confederate infantry's advance, helping escort the army's vast wagon trains. "We thought that we were miles away from the foe—but the boom of artillery just to our left told that such was not the case," noted a sergeant of the 12th North Carolina. "For a minute there was surprise almost amounting to semi-demoralization—even the teams seemed to sniff impending danger."[40] But the danger also offered a chance to even the score and exact some measure of revenge, and the North Carolinians relished the opportunity.

With steely-eyed determination, the Tar Heels prepared for combat. "When we got there the yankees had possession of the town but we sharpshooters soon had the town and the yankes before us running," claimed a man of the 23rd North Carolina Infantry. "So we whipped them at that place."[41]

Entering the town, Sgt. Edward G. Butler of Co. B, 12th North Carolina Infantry, found himself face to face with one of Custer's Wolverines in a yard. "Standing there in a chimney corner, each with rifle in hand, stood three men," he recalled. "I had entered the yard with so much momentum that I found myself within two or three feet of them—my gun still resting on my shoulder. Not a word was spoken. One of them instantly lowered his rifle—held it low in front of himself the muzzle only a few inches from my stomach—and pulled the trigger." Somehow, the Northerner missed, and the two soldiers grabbed each other and wrestled while holding the other's arms. Just as another of the Federals was about to bash Butler over the head with the butt of his carbine, several other Rebel infantry came to Butler's aid, and the three isolated Northerners, including an officer, surrendered.[42]

Chaois and countercharges filled the streets, joined now by Rebel infantry. Each side gained ground here and lost ground there, the combatants moving back and forth like the ocean waves. A determined charge by Iverson's people finally shattered Kilpatrick's lines and sent his men toward the rear.[43] One member of the 12th North Carolina made the wild claim that Iverson's soldiers captured nearly 500 enemy soldiers during the rout, but Federal casualty returns do not support such a claim. Civil War soldiers often exaggerated opposing casualties, and this is a good example of that tendency.[44] The Tar Heels claimed to have chased the enemy nearly three miles before calling off the pursuit.[45]

"The majority of the casualties in this engagement were occasioned by the fire of the enemy's infantry, who posted in almost every house, poured in a most destructive volley upon our men as the charged through the streets," reported Federal Col. Nathaniel P. Richmond.[46] Iverson agreed. "Sent the train back to the rear, deployed skirmishers, fixed an ambuscade, and I believe killed, wounded, and captured as many of the enemy as I had men," he reported.[47] Iverson's division commander, Maj. Gen. Robert Rodes, complimented his brigadier's performance in his report. "Making a hasty but skillful disposition of his troops, he soon routed them, capturing a considerable number," wrote Rodes approvingly. "Great credit is due Brigadier General Iverson for the handsome and prompt manner in which this affair was managed."[48]

"We were flushed with victory," reported Capt. Bond of the 1st Maryland Cavalry (C.S.A.), who went on to relate an event that nearly canceled out the hard-fought Hagerstown combat:

> [We] retired to our side of the town, where we were soon joined by reinforcements, and two pieces of artillery were added to my command. The enemy dismounted their sharpshooters and skirmished on the left of the town, and we dismounted a few men to meet them, and drove them back. . . . About 4 P.M. there appeared upon our left front a body of mounted men I could not account for, but after what I considered careful investigation I opened fire upon them with the artillery, and I think I never saw shells better placed, but was horrified to find, a few minutes later, that it was the staff and escort of Gen. J.E.B. Stuart. It was a miracle that no lives were lost.[49]

The incident Bond described was one of many "miracles" from which Stuart had emerged unscathed.

Another mini-miracle was the appearance of Iverson and his miraculous conduct. His deadly handling of his infantry turned the tide decisively against Kilpatrick, who prudently broke off the engagement after six long hours of hard fighting. As usual, nearly every participant saw the combat differently. "The cavalry charged and we are firing," recalled Charles McVicar, of Chew's Battery, "It is 8 ½ o'clock. They are on the run. So dark we can't see what shell they are sending back. If we had two more hours of daylight it would have been a Yankee retreat. We have driven them six miles," McVicar exaggerated, "this has been a very heavy division and certainly a hard fight."[50]

"We had a terrible fight . . . with our division against one brigade of infantry and one of rebel cavalry," recalled Maj. John Hammond of the 5th New York Cavalry.[51] Hammond's regimental chaplain credited an enemy corps with the rebuff in Hagerstown, writing, "Had not Gen. Ewell's corps come down upon us, we could have managed the cavalry alone, though they were compelled to fight desperately, as this was their only way of retreat."[52] Kilpatrick ordered his men to withdraw in the direction of Williamsport, where he knew Buford's division was operating.

Men of the 9th and 13th Virginia Cavalry of Chambliss' Brigade pursued the retreating Federals along the Williamsport Road. "We've got them now, boys!" cried Stuart as he put spurs to horse flesh and continued on.[53] Trotting down the macadamized road, the Southerners hoped to bag the retreating Union horsemen. "Before we had gone a mile, shells thrown from guns posted on the crest of a hill in front of us began to burst over and near us," recounted Col. Richard L. T. Beale of the 9th Virginia Cavalry. "As we approached the hill these guns disappeared, but no sooner had we reached the crest and began to descend into the valley beyond than they opened on us from the next elevation with renewed vigor." The undaunted gray horsemen drew up quickly in the middle of the road, surprised by the proximity of the enemy fire.

Beale watched in horror as a cannon from Lt. Samuel K. Elder's veteran horse artillery discharged a round of canister at only twenty paces, throwing riders and mounts "heavily to the ground." Thinking the blast had killed his son, Lt. George Beale, the colonel rode closer to the enemy, drew himself up, and began "quietly discharging his pistol." Stuart rode up and, while waving his saber, declared, "Stop your firing; you are shooting our men. Charge!" One hard thrust by the Federals could have scattered the confused Rebels, but it was an officer of the 9th Virginia who acted first. The regiment broke through the Union center and sent the enemy reeling toward Williamsport. Beale quickly returned to the scene of the canister blast, where he found his son alive and unhurt. His happiness was dashed, however, when he observed the dead body of one of his sergeants being cradled by a weeping brother.[54]

The 1st Vermont Cavalry covered Elder's withdrawal. "These brave Vermont boys would hold the rebel advance in check so the battery could get in position on the next rise behind them, and then fall back on a trot, in perfect order, and form with the battery; then the battery would blaze away at the enemy," recalled an admiring member of the 18th Pennsylvania Cavalry. "The head of the column was moving down the Boonsboro Road when 'Boom!' went a gun and 'Whiz' came a shell from right before us, and these were soon followed by others," noted a Vermont sergeant. "It seems that while they had been amusing us in town, a force had crossed over from Smithsburg to the Boonsboro Road and had cut us off. We were in pretty close quarters now for we had a force of the enemy on three sides, north, east, and south, and the force in front began to press on harder."[55]

The Vermonters forced their way through the road junction for safety. "Twice we were surrounded," recounted regimental commander Lt. Col. Addison W. Preston. Capt. William M. Beeman led the 1st Vermont's third squadron. Preston ordered him to hold a strong position, but the Confederates cut him off and demanded his surrender. "I don't see it," he coolly proclaimed to his would-be captors before leaping a fence and escaping with almost his entire force. Moments later, Capt. John W. Woodward, commanding Co. M, was killed at the head of his men while stubbornly resisting the enemy advance.

Cut off, fourteen Vermonters sought shelter in a house, where the loyal owner hid them for a week until Union troopers rode into town. Pvt. Antipas Curtis, however, quickly grew sick of hiding. Dressed in civilian clothing, Curtis walked out onto the street just in time to see General Lee ride by. Curtis saluted the Confederate commander and walked right out of town and into the fields and hills. He kept walking until he found a Union unit.

As the running rearguard action began to take the shape of a full-blown battle, George Custer rode to the position held by the Vermonters. "General, your horse is shot," one of the Green Mountain boys remarked. Custer looked down, and sure enough, the animal was bleeding profusely from a bullet wound to its side. This was the third horse shot from under him that day. The cavalier cooly called the attention of the Vermonters to a flanking attempt by Southern cavalry before riding off to rejoin his own command.[56]

With the enemy attacking both flanks of Kilpatrick's position, the line bent into the shape of a horseshoe, but it did not break. Capt. Andrew J. Grover, commander of the 1st Vermont's Co. K, led a charge against the main Confederate body to check its progress. With Southern horse artillery firing on the rear of Kilpatrick's column from the direction of Williamsport, Preston decided draw back his hard-pressed Vermonters. "[B]eing thus attacked in the front and rear, we drew off under the cover of night to the Sharpsburg road to the left," he later reported.[57] "Our small brigade against two divisions could not last," noted a lieutenant of the 1st Vermont Cavalry. "The enemy continued to advance and the fighting on our side became more desperate. We were losing numbers fast, the enemy working well out on both of our flanks. It soon became a hand-to-hand conflict; squadrons and companies fighting mounted until the enemy's cavalry were right amongst us, then charging them back, and their infantry again falling back, forming behind each other, and so continued fighting all the afternoon."[58] The Vermonters lost 76 men in the day's fighting.[59]

The Vermonters' stubbornness and the accuracy of Kilpatrick's guns allowed the 3rd Division to fall back toward the sound of the fighting raging at Williamsport.[60] "We fought over every foot of ground between Hagerstown and Williamsport," wrote a member of the 1st West Virginia Cavalry, Richmond's brigade. "The rebels charged our battery six times, but we succeeded in bringing it off each time. Every time they charged they were met with grape and canister, which invariably piled the road so full of dead men and horses as to check them."[61] Rebel guns made life miserable for the Yankees, too. "Batteries in front, batteries in the rear, and the field filled with their infantry, made our position—well, very uncomfortable," admitted a Federal officer.[62]

Elder had fought his guns superbly. "One of the guns must have been lost but for the fierce determination with which Lieutenant Elder and his men

Col. Nathaniel P. Richmond, commander, 1st Brigade, 3rd Cavalry Division, in a previously unpublished image.

Authors' Collection

fought this piece, assisted by a few gallant officers and men of the several regiments who rallied in support of the piece," Colonel Richmond wrote. "Four different times did the enemy charge this piece which was placed upon the pike, and as often they were repulsed with heavy slaughter, Lieutenant Elder pouring his canister into their ranks with most deadly effect. So close was the conflict, that [Gunner] No. 1 of the piece, turning his sponge-staff, knocked one of the enemy from his horse." Richmond concluded, "Too much credit cannot be given to Lieutenant Elder for the splendid manner in which he fought this piece; and the men of his battery are also deserving of special mention for their bravery and good conduct under fire, and their superior discipline both in camp and upon the march."[63]

By this time the Southern horsemen were worn out, having been in the saddle almost non-stop since their big July 3 fight on East Cavalry Field at Gettysburg. "We traveled 3 days and two nights without stopping," noted one of Ferguson's officers, "without scarcely anything to eat." These hardships were taking a toll, and everyone knew the coming days would not be easier.[64]

Kilpatrick blanched when he heard the guns ahead at Williamsport. "It looked as though he had deliberately walked into a trap," wrote a Wolverine. "In a moment I saw him coming, dashing along the flank of the column. He was urging his horse to its utmost speed. In his hand he held a small riding whip with which he was touching the flank of his charger as he rode. His face was pale. His eyes were gazing fixedly to the front and he looked neither to the right nor to the left. The look of anxiety on his countenance was apparent." The 3rd Division leader was facing multiple threats, and he had to respond quickly.[65]

Capt. James Penfield, commander of Co. H of the 5th New York Cavalry, helped defend the artillery as it retreated, and fought for two hours before the dogged Confederates drove them back. While struggling to get out from under his wounded horse, a saber blow struck Penfield in the head. Several others were also sabered and captured, and two men were killed. The dejected New Yorker began his long, lonely trek to Richmond's notorious Libby Prison.[66]

Seeing the Federal rearguard drawn up in the road with the guns deployed on the high ground behind them, Grumble Jones ordered the 11th Virginia Cavalry to attack. Col. Lunsford L. Lomax advanced his men within 200 yards of the enemy and order them to charge "Right down the straight turnpike, swept by the Federal guns, with drawn sabers rode the Eleventh." Bullets and blasts of canister raked their ranks, but the Virginians pressed on. "Nothing could stop the impetuous rush of the grey troopers, as with lifted sabers and battle shouts they plunged through the smoke towards the foe," wrote an eyewitness. The Yankees broke. When the pursuing Lomax spotted two squadrons of enemy cavalry trying to escape through a gap in a stone wall, he headed for them. A sharp saber duel erupted before the the Yankees streamed back toward Williamsport.[67] "Our loss was Write smart, theirs grater," was how one of Ferguson's illiterate Virginians described the action.[68]

Indeed it was. Colonel Richmond reported two Federal officers killed, three wounded, and seven missing, as well as twelve enlisted men killed, forty-one wounded, and 201 missing, for a total of 266.[69]

The following day, when Federal prisoner Lt. Col. Cavada of the 114th Pennsylvania Infantry and his fellow captives marched through Hagerstown to Williamsport, the wreckage of the fight was visible for everyone to see. "All along the road from Hagerstown to Williamsport we noticed indications of General Kilpatrick's cavalry dash into Hagerstown," Cavada later wrote. "Our dead cavalrymen were lying in the road, and on either side of it, completely stripped of their clothing, and dead horses, broken caissons, and other remains of the conflict, were scattered here and there."[70]

Georgia infantrymen from Longstreet's Corps also entered Hagerstown the day after the battle. "There was considerable cavalry fighting in the streets yesterday," reported one soldier. "Everybody seemed scared to death, for no lights were on the streets, and the city appeared like the residence of the dead. There is still some game and defiant residents who dare to maintain repugnance of Yankeeism," continued the Georgian. "They report that after our army left last year no insult which their infamous enemies could heap upon them were spared them and some even arrested. But some are firm to the end."[71]

Chapter 7

July 6: The Battle for Williamsport

"[I] quickly organized a small force of dismounted, sick, and wounded men who were along with the train and who snatched up arms and ammunition as could be found . . . I managed to inspire the men with confidence and led them in."

— Lt. Col. William G. Delony, Cobb's Legion Cavalry

ON JULY 6, WHILE KILPATRICK'S troopers battled in Hagerstown, Buford's division advanced on the river town of Williamsport. Four major roads converged at Williamsport, which was the key to the Confederate retreat movement. The Greencastle Road followed the Conococheague Creek valley, and was the primary route taken by the Wagon Train of Wounded. The Hagerstown Turnpike, which connected Williamsport and Hagerstown to the northeast, and the Boonsboro Road, which angled off to the southeast, also terminated in the town. The Downsville Road, which connected Williamsport and Downsville near Falling Waters four miles downstream, ran southeast. Finally, the critical Valley Pike passed near the Potomac River on the Virginia side.[1] In addition to this important road network, nearby were two major fords on the Potomac River. Light's Ford was only a couple feet deep at certain times of the year, and there was the previously described cable-ferry crossing of Lemen's Ferry.[2] Falling Waters, where the Confederates had built a pontoon bridge to cross the river during the invasion of the North, would be the crossing point of the bulk of Lee's army.[3]

The terrain surrounding Williamsport clearly favored the defenders. Marshy, boggy ground interspersed with rocky ridges, densely wooded lots, swamps and creeks stretched from Downsville north to the Pennsylvania state line. "The town of Williamsport is located in the lower angle formed by the Potomac and the Conococheague Creek," Imboden described. "These streams enclose the town on two sides, and back of it one mile there is a low range of hills that is crossed by four roads converging on the town. The first is the Greencastle road leading down the creek valley; next the Hagerstown road; then the Boonsboro road; and lastly the river road."[4] The range of hills east of Williamsport, in particular, provided an excellent artillery platform that would serve as the backbone of the formidable defensive position Lee's engineers would build in the coming days.

That morning of July 6, when Imboden learned that Buford's and Kilpatrick's cavalry divisions were closing in, he knew he faced a difficult task in spite of the terrain. Imboden and his men scrambled to arm as many of the wounded as were able to get on their feet and fight. He gathered about 700 wounded in all, and arrayed the bandaged and bruised troops on the high ground surrounding the town. Imboden also had access to several batteries of artillery—important firepower he would need to oppose the strong Federal forces bearing down on him.[5] A former artillery officer himself, Imboden made impressive use of those guns by carefully deploying them on the hills along an arc-shaped line around the town. Several slightly wounded officers were tapped to command the artillery. Finally, several hundred wagoners and teamsters were hastily organized into companies of 100 men each and put under the command of wounded officers, commissaries, and quartermasters.[6] Late in the afternoon, Imboden and his scratch "army" of walking wounded and wagon drivers heard the sound of artillery fire out the Hagerstown Road.

Buford and his cavalry division were pushing toward Williamsport via the campus of the College of St. James. Established in 1842, the well-respected and successful Episcopalian boarding school sat along rolling terrain six miles south of Hagerstown and east of Williamsport.[7] St. James' rector and staunch Unionist, Rev. Dr. John Barrett Kerfoot, watched as Buford's cavalry "came pouring along Boonsboro and Williamsport road…"[8] The 1st Brigade under Col. William Gamble drove in Confederate pickets stationed near the college. The 3rd Indiana Cavalry, in the lead, opened the fighting. "About four or five o'clock in the afternoon a pistol shot was heard and a great commotion was seen amongst the teamster farthest from us," recorded Pvt. John Worsham of Co. F, 21st Virginia Infantry. "Soon the field was full of Yankee cavalry, whooping, yelling, and firing pistols . . ." Worsham detailed a trick used by Buford's troopers to destroy Confederate supplies. The cavalrymen were seen "riding up to one of the wagons that had hay or wheat, ordering them to halt, and, instead of injuring or detaining them, quietly pulling out matches and firing the provender, and then letting them go." Many wagons that would have fed the animals of Lee's army upon their arrival were burned in this fashion. "Mules were seen flying across the field with a flame of fire leaping from them," he noted, "which would last only a few seconds before the rider would have it off, and in many instances himself off too, in his effort to remove the burning hay or wheat." Worsham watched helplessly as a large body of enemy horsemen deployed and advanced down the Downsville Road.[9]

Worsham's company was commanded by Captain William Pegram, who observed contingents of the enemy, both mounted and dismounted, advance to within 400 yards of his position. Knowing that he must fight for his ground, Pegram ordered his men to attack. Pegram's men waged a short but sharp engagement among some farm buildings to their front. The Virginians cleared the farm of Union horsemen until they came under artillery fire and were outflanked by a renewed Federal attack. The Virginians lost four men killed during the fight, including the brave Captain Pegram.[10]

A trooper fighting near the college under Buford described the action as "one of the liveliest little skirmishes of the war."[11] Confederate artillery on high ground just west of the campus briefly compelled Buford's troopers to fall back until Lt. John H. Calef's horse battery unlimbered and engaged them in a counter-battery duel the Confederates ultimately won. Calef lost nine killed and wounded in less than ninety minutes and the survivors were briefly driven from their guns, leaving the tubes vulnerable to capture. One of Calef's gunmen, Lt. T. B. Michalowski, was nearly buried by the sand thrown up by a shell that struck the bank behind his section of guns. "We got out of position and returned to the cross-roads, and, going to the left, struck the Johnnies in a narrow road, and I think we were whipped but don't want to own up," concluded another of Buford's men.[12]

To stabilize the front in Calef's threatened sector, Buford ordered Gamble's brigade to support the artillery, a move that

Maj. William H. Medill, 8th Illinois Cavalry.

USAHEC

triggered a sharp fight along the Boonsboro Road. There, Gamble's riders attempted to outflank the enemy defenses in an effort to get between the Confederates and the river at Williamsport, several miles to the west. Gamble dismounted his command and ordered it forward. One who could not wait to participate in the flanking movement was Maj. William H. Medill, the diminutive but pugnacious twenty-eight year old second in command of the 8th Illinois Cavalry. Born in Ohio, he had been a newspaperman in Chicago prior to the war. Medill rode up to his regimental commander, Maj. John Beveridge, and announced, "A field officer should command the battalion, and if you have no objection, I will go." With Beveridge's blessing, Medill caught up to the advancing skirmish line and joined in the attack.[13]

When the Illinois men had advanced halfway across the field to a fenced farmyard, Medill ordered them to throw a volley. As he raised his revolver and fired, he took a Rebel bullet to the abdomen and slumped in the saddle. Pvt. Worsham of the 21st Virginia fixed his gaze for a moment on the plucky little Federal officer. "A mounted officer was in the yard, 'cursing' and flourishing a pistol," Worsham recalled. "As I entered the yard, I told the men to shoot him, but he leveled his pistol at us and fired…My men fired at the officer, who rode off bowed down on his horse." Worsham noted that Medill "was a gallant man." The brave and popular little major was later taken to Frederick, where he died ten days later.[14]

Capt. George A. "Sandy" Forsyth, commander of Co. C of the 8th Illinois Cavalry, ordered his men to dismount. Every fourth man took charge of his own horse and that of his three comrades, "while the rest of us were hustled quickly into single file facing the enemy and ordered to charge," noted an Illini trooper. "Over the fence we went and down into the grain field for about 300 yards, where we found 60 Johnnies on their knees pumping lead at us to beat the band. We captured all of them and brought them in." However, another line of Southerners lay just 300 yards behind them, and a mounted Rebel signal officer, wig-wagging the movements of the Federals, could also be seen. Forsyth rode up to Lt. David H. Fillmore, known as a dead eye in the regiment, and ordered him to take twenty men out and shoot the signalman.[15]

Fillmore promptly obeyed and called for twenty volunteers. The dismounted men bent down and ran across the field as quickly as they could with carbines in hand, using the wheat for some cover. The mission became a running of the gauntlet. "[P]erhaps 500 shots were fired at us during the quarter of a mile run," Fillmore reminisced. While wheat stems, cut by bullets, flew all around them, the men were driven to ground as they reached a fence. There the panting troopers paused for a moment to catch their breath, then slowly began crawling forward. Shortly, they spotted the Rebel signalman on his horse, still about a quarter of a mile distant. Fillmore himself volunteered to go forward and shoot him, and directed the others to follow him afterward. Fillmore then took off at a dead run toward the signal officer for about three minutes. When he thought he was in range of his carbine, Fillmore dropped to a knee, quickly aimed, and cracked off a shot. With pride and satisfaction, Fillmore "saw the horse run down the road riderless."

The shot was the signal for Fillmore's men to follow, and they dashed up behind him. His blood up, Fillmore jumped on a fence post, straddled a rail, and shouted at the Confederates, "Surrender, you white-livered sons of guns!" One Rebel, he later wrote, "with the spirit of revenge and death in his breast, picked up his gun, ran it through the fence, and took deliberate aim, no doubt at my saber belt buckle, and fired. I felt the hot lead penetrate my body, reeled about twice, and fell from them with a musket ball wound through the right side of my abdomen and hip." One of Fillmore's band rushed up, picked up the fallen captain, threw him over his shoulder, and carried him to safety. "The sight I witnessed over my comrade's shoulder will never be erased from my mind," Fillmore wrote over forty years later. "For the moment they thought they had shot me: they jumped over into the wheat field and commenced shooting and commanding us to surrender." His savior was likewise shot, but did not fall, prompting Fillmore to do "some of the finest and most effectual praying that it was ever a mortal's privilege to make." The bleeding pair made it to safety back near the college, and the wounded captain was carried off on a blanket. Like Fillmore, his comrade survived his wound.[16]

There were several conspicuous displays of bravery that day. One involved an Englishman named Winthrop who had served in the British Army, and had enlisted in the Confederacy. Winthrop seized the colors of a Confederate cavalry regiment west of the college, then galloped straight at Buford's line, shouting to the horse soldiers to follow him. He led several such charges until his horse was finally shot out from under him, earning the praise of his comrades.[17]

The Virginians pushed forward in Fillmore's wake and began clearing the field of Gamble's troopers, "but the fight was on in earnest, the enemy having opened with their artillery, some firing at us, others at our guns on the hills." Worsham and his company of Virginians took up a position along a rail fence among the buildings of a farm slightly west of the College of St. James. "We captured, wounded, and killed fifteen of the enemy in the barn yard. We now found that the enemy were advancing on the road in our rear, and we fell back to the road, and were joined there by a company of about thirty, mostly stragglers."[18]

The carbine fire of Buford's three brigades, and Calef's artillery fire, steadily drove many of the Rebels back toward Williamsport. "Our boys stood their ground though the bullets flew like hail stones around us, " proudly recorded a member of the 8th New York Cavalry of Gamble's brigade.[19]

Capt. Charles Blackford of Virginia, a staff officer, and his brother William (who was Jeb Stuart's engineering officer) had a chance to visit that day for the first time in several weeks. The brothers sat chatting in Charles' tent just outside Williamsport, when "we saw some very handsomely dressed cavalry come out of the woods on a hill just opposite us," recalled Charles. "We supposed they were our men, but their handsome dress made us somewhat suspicious and we were getting our glasses out to inspect them when a battery of guns came dashing out of the woods, wheeled into line on top of the hill just opposite, unlimbered and in an instant opened up on the mighty camp in and around town."

The two officers sprang into action, calling for their horses and spurring into town to make themselves useful. "Quite a number of disorganized troops, wounded men and others assembled as soon as the first shot was fired and as soon as they [the Confederates] showed themselves the guns limbered up and the whole party started off at a rapid rate without waiting for our charge."[20]

Likewise, Lt. John Blue, a wounded officer of Grumble Jones' cavalry brigade, was waiting to cross the Potomac at Williamsport. "The lines of blue could be plainly seen on the high grounds not far away," he recalled. "General Imboden's command, reinforced by several hundred teamsters, seemed to be patiently waiting the attack."[21]

As Buford's force pushed its way toward Williamsport, Imboden rushed every available cavalryman to meet the threat. Norval Baker, a member of the 18th Virginia Cavalry of Ferguson's Brigade, dismounted with his comrades and formed a line of battle in the direction of the oncoming noise of fighting. It was evident to the southerners that they were outnumbered some ten to one by the blue wave as it appeared. "The enemy," observed Baker, "had a large force of cannon and they had the air full of flying shells in a very short time and our little brigade, the only organized army to fight them."[22]

Imboden ordered his artillery to open fire. The battle for Williamsport "opened by artillery from both sides," wrote one commentator. "Fortunately for the Confederate force engaged, when it became known that one of the

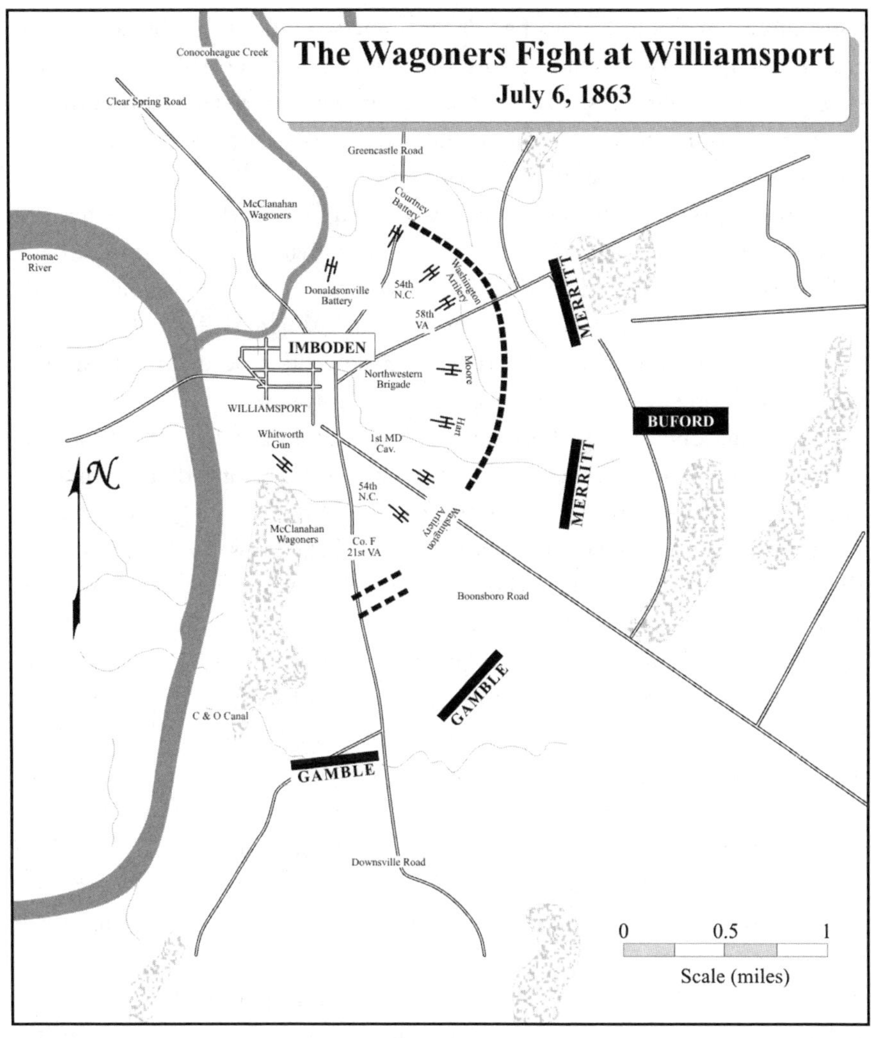

batteries had run out of ammunition [Capt. Joseph D. Moore's Virginia battery], and an ordnance train arrived from Winchester, two wagon loads of ammunition were ferried across the river and run upon the field behind the guns, and the boxes tumbled out to be broken open with axes. With this fresh supply, the Confederate guns were all soon in full play again."[23]

George Mills, a wounded member of the 16th North Carolina, was still resting in Williamsport. About 4:00 p.m., an artillery shell dropped near Mills and his comrades, struck a mule—breaking the poor beast's neck—and plunged into the river. Several other projectiles soon followed, doing little damage but stirring up quite a commotion among the wounded still nursing their battle injuries and who hadn't yet joined Imboden's cobbled defense. Seeing the necessity of action, those that could get up did so, were joined by stragglers and waggoners, and formed themselves into a makeshift company. The motley command marched out, grabbed any weapons they could find, and joined their comrades waiting in line of battle.[24]

A relative of the town's founder, 78 year-old Otho Williams, together with his wife and daughters, were entertaining guests that afternoon at their home called Rose Hill Manor. They had been trying to inject some civility into the misery that befell their town over the past day. When Williams heard shells dropping nearby in fields east of his home, he knew that he and his guests were in for entertainment of a much different and deadly sort.[25]

Grumble Jones galloped up to Imboden and told him to do his best while he would ride off and gather up every last waggoner and form them to fight. "It was not long till we saw General Jones fetching out armed waggoners two and three hundred at a time and in every part of the field," observed Norval Baker. His comrades blessed the arrival of the relatively inexperienced buggy drivers. "The Confederate cavalry there were so palpably insufficient for the defense of the place, that the quartermaster's department was called upon for men," added a South Carolinian of McGowan's Brigade. "About fifty were furnished by our brigade, and placed under the command of Capt. R. E. B. Hewetson, quartermaster of the [1st South Carolina Infantry]."[26]

Hewetson and his men boldly charged the Union cavalry in their front and drove them back, taking ground they would hold until relieved that night. They suffered two men killed and five or six wounded. The southerners were very proud of their little fight. "It was a very creditable affair, and peculiar of its kind," continued the South Carolinian. "Capt. Hewetson was a veteran and stood high for gallantry as a line officer, before being appointed quartermaster, and most of his teamsters had been under fire before. But they deserve none the less praise for showing themselves superior to the demoralizing influences of a bomb-proof department."[27]

When word of the Union advance reached Lt. Col. William Delony, the second in command of the Cobb Legion Cavalry of Georgia, the injured officer lifted himself from his resting place and went into action. The unfortunate recipient of a severe saber wound to the head during the Battle of Hunterstown on July 2, Delony had suffered through the long trip to Williamsport. His head still wrapped in a bloody bandage, Delony sent for his horse. "I was feeling miserably but the booming of their cannon aroused me and I gathered up the stragglers about the wagons and went to the field starting with only thirteen men," he wrote to his wife the following day.[28] He "quickly organized a small force of dismounted, sick, and wounded men who were along with the train and who snatched up arms and ammunition as could be found," and soon had nearly 200 with him.[29] When he spotted one of Imboden's staff officers, he reported his intention to bring his ragtag assembly to the front. "I managed to inspire the men with confidence and led them in."[30] Delony, recorded one eyewitness, had a "commanding presence [and] bull dog courage."[31] Both traits came in handy before the day was over.

Maj. Alfred H. Belo of the 55th North Carolina Infantry also refused to let his wound keep him off the fighting line. Belo had suffered a serious leg injury at Gettysburg, but like Delony, mustered the strength to join the fight. Along with Col. J. M. Stone of the 2nd Mississippi and Maj. R. O. Reynolds of the 11th Mississippi, Belo "went around and got all of the able-bodied men to take places in the trenches in front of us. Besides these, numbers of teamsters and detailed men, soldiers retiring for sick leave, furlough, etc., were drawn up, and checked the Federals and saved the train."[32]

Col. John Logan Black of the 1st South Carolina Cavalry had a high fever and was probably suffering from the early stages of typhoid infection. Imboden pressed Black into service despite the illness, sending him to the Greencastle Pike, where wagons were still coming into town, to "stop and organize all the slightly wounded & stragglers that came in." Black was able to muster up a force of dismounted cavalrymen, approximately 100 wounded infantrymen from John Bell Hood's Texas Brigade, together with some armed teamsters. "Our train was pouring into the town and we soon picked up a number of men," Black recalled. After organizing his conscripts, Black marched them out the Hagerstown Pike and formed them into line of battle. At Imboden's request, Black took command of the left side of the Confederate line. Although the bulk of the fighting this day occurred on the right, Black's sector successfully repulsed a couple of probing attacks by Wesley Merritt's Regulars.[33]

Gamble's attack on the right end of Imboden's outer defense exacted a heavy toll on the Southerners. Maj. Harry Gilmor of the 2nd Maryland Cavalry (C.S.A.) commanded the Rebel troops in the northern sector of Gamble's attack. Seeing his position was vulnerable to Yankee artillery fire, Gilmor sent back to Imboden for reinforcements. There were, however, none to spare. Gilmor ordered his troopers and convalescents into line of battle, then led a small force of 180 men toward a large building occupied by Gamble's people. The attack drove out the Yankees, but Gilmor's command suffered thirty-four casualties.[34]

Gilmor had scarcely taken possession of the building when Calef's artillery opened on him, followed by a dismounted assault. Gilmor's men also repulsed that effort, and then another, before counterattacking with the goal of reaching Calef's guns atop the ridge to their west. The mission was deadly. One of Gamble's troopers recalled, "[O]ur artillery opened on them with grape and canister and mowed them down like grass."[35] Knocked senseless by the concussion of a shell, Gilmor fell into Federal hands, although he later managed to escape.[36]

Maj. Benjamin F. Eshleman, meanwhile, ordered his guns of the Washington Artillery of New Orleans to advance and drive Calef off his perch. Supported by elements of the 54th North Carolina, the Southern batteries advanced to a position about 600 yards in advance of Imboden's main line of battle, unlimbered, and opened fire. "The firing was beautiful and very rapid," declared a Confederate officer. "I never saw such a destructive cannonading; one piece on our side lost thirteen men killed and wounded."[37]

Responding to this new threat of the Rebel guns' sheets of flame, Gamble's soldiers let loose a vigorous carbine fire on the guns and their infantry supports, hoping to drive them back whence they came. An officer of the 54th North Carolina gathered up a squad of stragglers to lend additional support. "I started under the command of a Lieutenant Colonel, with two other companies, under a heavy fire of shell and minie ball," remembered the officer. His task was about to become heavier still. "About 25 of my stragglers, being dismounted Va. Cavalry, were too cowardly to stand fire. They run, leaving me with only 25 men to fight. We advanced in line of battle across a wheat field some 200 yards. Here was the hottest fire that I have ever seen. I lost 12 out of my 25 men, killed and wounded, who stuck with me. But after we reached the fence we gave them such a salute that they will hardly forget it soon."[38]

J. B. Polley of John Bell Hood's Texas Brigade, who accompanied the wagon train to Williamsport, proudly recalled the sight of all the makeshift fighters going into action. "[T]he Yankee cavalry came swooping down on us…and the dire and deplorable misfortunes of capture and captivity stared us broadly and unwinkingly in the face. Still, just as a mouse will fight when cornered," he continued, "so will commissaries, quartermasters and their immediate subordinates, and the small cavalry force escorting the train was at once reinforced by a body of men who, however non-combatant ordinarily, on this occasion faced danger gallantly and, although sadly out of practice, used the few weapons to be had with a deadly skill that soon put the foe to flight."[39]

Brig. Gen. Wesley Merritt, commander, Reserve Brigade, 1st Cavalry Division.

USAHEC

Even for those not wounded, the fighting played on their stamina. "It was an awful hot, sultry day and we had our side arms and sabers and all the straps, etc., a cavalry man has to carry which made it awful hard on us boys and our clothes were soaked with perspiration," noted a member of the 18th Virginia Cavalry.[40]

One of Imboden's staff officers marveled at the general's command of his force, and the fluidity of the defenders. "Our line of battle was nearly three miles long, and the General had to double quick the infantry backwards and forwards so as to offer opposition," he recalled.[41]

Regardless of the gallantry displayed by Imboden's motley collection of wounded, teamsters, and stragglers, his situation quickly grew desperate. A large force of aggressive Union cavalry was now between Robert E. Lee's army and its river crossings. The massive wagon train of wounded filled every inch of Williamsport, and more were arriving each minute. The river was too high and swift to ford, and the wagons offered a terribly tempting target for the Federals. If Buford could take and hold the town, a wedge would be driven between Lee and the critical crossings he needed.

By the time Col. Thomas C. Devin's brigade of Buford's division arrived, Gamble's entire brigade was deployed, and part of Merritt's Reserve brigade was engaged to Gamble's north. Devin massed his brigade in the woods behind the Union position as a reserve, and awaited orders. The Southerners tried to outflank Merritt on his right with a brigade of infantry, which, according to Buford, "was most admirably foiled by General Merritt." While no direct attacks were made in Merritt's direct front, the Confederates posted there "were so obstinate that General Merritt could not dislodge them without too much sacrifice."[42] The 6th Pennsylvania Cavalry held the center of Merritt's line, supported by Capt. William K. Graham's Regular battery. The Pennsylvanians held their position over the next four hours under fire, knowing that "[m]ore than one determined charge of the rebels would have broken our line but for the timely use of canister by Graham's guns."[43]

As Buford's cavalry picked, prodded, and attacked the Rebel line looking for weakness, Imboden received word from Brig. Gen. Fitz Lee that if he could hang on at Williamsport for another thirty minutes, Lee's strong brigade of cavalry would come galloping to his aid. Lee and his troopers had been covering the rear of the Wagon Train of Wounded. Resolved to hold his ground, Imboden gamely resisted, moving pockets of his troops to and fro to meet threats. So did the redoubtable Delony, whose motley command "made a most determined resistance and successfully held [the Federals] at bay until reinforcements arrived, thus avoiding a train stampede and a great disaster to Lee's retreat."[44]

Even though Imboden's men were veterans of two years of the war, and many of the survivors would face two more, the vicious fluid combat at Williamsport was the fiercest they would experience. Reacting to continued threats by Gamble's men, Imboden shifted some of his troops further to the Confederate right, where they took up a position in a wheat field. Only a snake rail fence a short distance to their front protected the Southerners from the Federal cavalry as an intense firefight erupted on that flank. A bullet glanced off the canteen of one soldier of the 62nd Virginia Mounted Infantry and struck a comrade squarely in the forehead, killing the latter instantly. Moments later, a shell fragment struck and killed Lt. John C. Calhoun of the same regiment. As more Rebels dropped, and unable to withstand such a heavy fire, the Virginians charged to the fence, only to be pinned down there by another murderous Federal volley. When one of Imboden's men boldly tried to scale the fence, he was immediately shot down by one of Gamble's troopers.[45]

Judson Kilpatrick, following his drubbing at Hagerstown earlier that day, was making for Williamsport to join Buford. More fighting lay ahead at Williamsport before the sun would set on the beleaguered river town.

* * *

With elements of Stuart's cavalry nipping at his heels, Kilpatrick marched his command toward the sound of the fighting raging at Williamsport. His objective was to link up his command with Buford's large division. The town came into view that evening about 7:00 p.m. as Kilpatrick's column came up behind Buford's lines. "We could see a heavy train, which Kilpatrick took into his head to capture," wrote Sgt. Henry Avery of the 5th Michigan Cavalry of George Custer's brigade. "He formed his division in order for a forward move, and the shot and shells began to fly quickly, passing over our heads, which made some fun for the boys, to see a particular officer on Custer's staff duck and dodge. We could not help but laugh at him."[46] Confederate bullets began to train on the generals and their staffs. One minie ball zipped within inches of Custer's golden locks, nearly finding its mark on the Boy General.[47]

Kilpatrick's troopers were in for more than just "some fun." Indeed, a very rough time awaited the advancing Wolverines. "We found [the Confederates], to all appearances, in a very healthy condition and amply prepared to give us a very warm reception," recalled the 6th Michigan's Pvt. Andrew D. Jackson. "The Virginia banks of the Potomac were well provided with artillery and fully manned while there seems to be no lack of either on our side of the river."[48]

Buford sent a courier to Kilpatrick "to connect with my right for mutual support."[49] Characteristically, Custer was itching to lead a mounted charge. Holding high his Toledo blade his Wolverines knew so well, he ordered them to draw sabers and charge. Kilpatrick, however, immediately countermanded the order. The Wolverines were ordered to draw off and mass on the side of the road in a field. The bugler of the 5th Michigan Cavalry was disappointed. "I have always thought that if the order to charge had been executed as first intended, we would have broken through Imboden's lines and burned up the wagons."[50]

Col. Russell A. Alger formed his 5th Michigan Cavalry in a sheltered place behind some rocks on the left side of the road to Hagerstown. The milling horsemen thus provided a target for the Southern gunners too tempting to pass up. Getting range of the Michiganders' position, the Rebel artillery gave them "a severe shelling."[51] "The Rebs had trained their guns upon this road and solid shot and shell went ricocheting down it as fast as you could count," recalled Private Jackson.[52] Instead of riding off on a mounted attack, the men were told to sheath their blades and prepare to fight on foot.

The 6th Michigan dismounted and advanced in a skirmish line, driving the enemy back until the Rebels reached a stone wall, where they made a determined stand. Knowing it would be dark soon, and fearing that Confederate cavalry in the form of Fitz Lee's brigade could come up behind his position, Custer ordered the 6th Michigan to return to their horses, mount up, and pull back again to the Hagerstown Pike. "The advance crossed it in safety,

Brig. Gen. Fitzhugh Lee, commander, Fitzhugh Lee's cavalry brigade.

USAHEC

and just as my company got fairly into, and cross it at an angle of 45 degrees, the order came to Maj. [George A.] Drew [commanding the battalion]: 'Major, the General says halt.'" Drew responded, "What in God's name does he want us to halt here for?'" More shot and shell rained down on the exposed Wolverines, who stood there waiting for further orders.[53]

Twenty-two year-old Lt. Aaron Jewett of Ann Arbor, Michigan, a member of Co. F of the 6th Michigan, was killed during this shelling. An 1862 graduate of the University of Michigan, Jewett was well liked by his regiment. A shell burst killed him instantly. "He has proved a faithful soldier and good officer, and had he lived would have won a high position," lamented his hometown newspaper. "Our whole community mingle their tears with those of his bereaved parents and sisters.'" Some Confederates later buried Jewett on the field.[54]

The Wolverines could no longer withstand the shelling. "At that moment orders were received to fall back at once, which we did under cover of the twilight, passing along within two hundred yards of the enemy's infantry for more than a quarter of a mile, while they, with stacked arms in the road where we had passed down, saw us march by unmolested, evidently supposing we belonged to their army," recounted Colonel Alger.[55]

To the defenders of Williamsport's great relief, Fitz Lee and his Virginia brigade of horsemen arrived, bearing down on Buford's right flank and upon Kilpatrick's division. "Fitzhugh Lee's division [sic] rolled up in the rear of the enemy's lines and all was saved," reported a relieved Norval Baker of the 18th Virginia Cavalry.[56] Supported by strong artillery fire, Lee's troopers began pushing Kilpatrick back east. "The Rebels began to throw shot & shell thick &

fast," recalled a member of the 6th Michigan Cavalry, "solid shot like long slugs came ploughing through the air."[57] John Gillespie, of the 1st Ohio Cavalry's Company A, a member of Kilpatrick's headquarters guard, remembered a difficult effort to retreat. "The road was swept by their guns as we charged through a deep cut, where we blocked the road as we suddenly came to a halt, so that to escape the iron hail we had to dismount and lead our horses up the steep bank out of the road."[58] Little Kil dashed back and forth trying to rally his troops, but the falling darkness combined with the severe fire of Imboden's guns left Kilpatrick with no choice but to break off from Lee and withdraw. Kilpatrick had been repulsed twice this day, once at Hagerstown and again at Williamsport. Buford called Kilpatrick's efforts on the field as of "no consequence to either one of us."[59]

One of Kilpatrick's troopers opined that "the whole train would have [been burned] had it not been for the rebel infantry and cavalry, which now came up, and furiously attacked, in flank and rear…Long and desperately did [Kilpatrick's troopers] contend with the overwhelming forces opposed to them—in fact, too long, for they were at one time completely enveloped…As it was, however, they successfully extricated themselves from their perilous position…"[60]

According to a frustrated John Buford, "Just before dark, Kilpatrick's troops gave way, passing to my rear by the right, and were closely followed by the enemy."[61] The firing on both sides slowed about 8:00 p.m., which one Pennsylvanian in Merritt's brigade thought was beneficial to his side. "Had the daylight lasted another hour, we would have suffered the most disastrous defeat."[62]

Rebuffed and thoroughly frustrated, the Federals drew off from Williamsport. Devin's brigade maintained its position in the woods east of Williamsport to cover the withdrawal, sporadically skirmishing with Rebels that ventured too close. Devin heavily picketed the roads leading to Williamsport as Buford and Kilpatrick withdrew to the east.[63]

Rev. Kerfoot of the College of St. James, who had watched the approach of Buford's column with high hopes just a few hours earlier, noted sadly in his diary, "At 9 p.m., our cavalry pass back, repulsed."[64] With many of his wounded in tow, Buford retired along the Sharpsburg and Hagerstown Turnpike to Jones' Crossroads about seven miles to the east, at the intersection of the Sharpsburg-Hagerstown and Williamsport-Boonsboro Turnpikes. There he threw out a strong picket line. Buford's division bivouacked for the night amid yet another driving rainstorm. They were cold, wet, and played out.[65]

Shortly before midnight, pickets of Devin's 6th New York Cavalry brought word to him that Confederate infantry and artillery were approaching from Williamsport and making for the Federals' rear. Soon, Rebel skirmishers encountered Devin's picket lines. After a brief fight, the Southerners withdrew, though not before a handful of men, mostly in Devin's 17th Pennsylvania Cavalry, were killed and wounded.[66] "The men passed a wearisome, sleepless night," the regimental historian of Devin's 6th New York Cavalry observed, "mounted, in line, or standing to horse."[67] According to the historian of the 9th New York Cavalry, perhaps a few got moments to snooze, but the brigade "remained saddled all night, the men lying by their horses."[68]

Early the next morning, Devin's brigade "fell back to Boonsboro," wrote Daniel Peck of the 9th New York Cavalry of Devin's brigade. "The enemy pickets are within one mile of us. We expect to have some hot work here soon," Peck opined, predicting that the fighting for this area was far from over.[69]

Utterly flushed with success, Colonel William Delony gathered his makeshift command together in the dark after the fighting, and dismissed them from duty. "They gave me three cheers and said if the Yankees came again…they would all come up if I would command them which I promised to do," the wounded Georgian proudly wrote to his wife. "One of my captains was a chaplain which perhaps accounts for our good fortune." His own duty done, Delony slowly returned to his wagon, lay down—probably with a heavy sigh of relief—and resumed his recuperation.[70]

Many of the dead and wounded from the day's fluid fight were strewn in and around the town, adding to the heavy burden the soldiers and civilians in Williamsport already faced. "Dead Yankees and horses all along the road from Williamsport to Hagerstown," observed a Confederate staff officer.[71]

Like Delony, Imboden's performance against two full divisions of Federal cavalry at Williamsport was little short of masterful. He had selected his defensive ground well, demonstrated strong leadership skills in the face of overwhelming adversity, and maneuvered his motley force to meet every threat. He had repulsed both Buford and Kilpatrick in some of the sharpest fighting to occur along the long retreat to safety. Imboden's brother Frank served in his sibling's command, and was very proud of the day's accomplishments. He scribbled in his diary, "Command attacked by 13 regts. of Stoneman's [sic] Cavalry. & 18 guns at Wmspt. Splendidly repulsed by Genl. Imboden with 2 regts. of Cav., 5 of Infantry, about 2 batteries & many organized stragglers. Even waggoners fought well."[72] An Alabaman serving on Imboden's staff heartily agreed, claiming, "We saved the immense wagon train of our army, and too much credit cannot be given to General Imboden, who organized a mob and whipped the enemy, outnumbering him nearly five to one."[73]

"There had been glory enough won, and neither the wagoners nor Company 'Q' felt any desire to pursue [the enemy] horsemen in search of more," recalled Capt. James F. Hart, commander of a South Carolina battery of horse artillery. "The wagons were safe, and the teamsters went back to feed their mules and talk over the wonderful victory; Company 'Q' sought shelter from the drizzling rain under the grateful cover of a wagon, where his repose was undisturbed for the remainder of the night."[74]

Years after the war, Imboden wrote proudly of the defense of Williamsport. "My whole force engaged, wagoners included, did not exceed three thousand men. The ruse practiced by showing a formidable line on the left, then withdrawing it to the right, together with our numerous artillery…led to the belief that our force was much greater…A bold charge at any time before sunset would have broken our feeble lines, and then we should all have fallen easy prey to the Federals."[75]

Imboden's "ruse," if indeed it was carried out as methodically and purposefully as he claimed, convinced many Federals that the Rebel defenders were substantially stronger than they were. According to one of Gamble's Hoosiers, the Federal horsemen must have attacked an infantry force of nearly 15,000 men.[76] Buford, too, blamed Imboden's perceived strength as an impediment to victory. "The expedition had for its object the destruction of the enemy's trains…This, I regret to say, was not accomplished," he lamented in his report. "The enemy was *too strong* for me, but he was severely punished for his obstinacy. His casualties were more than quadruple mine [emphasis added]."[77]

Imboden dubbed the day's engagement the "teamster's fight" in tribute to the fine service rendered by so many wagon drivers. One Southern newspaper correspondent even played down the role of Fitz Lee's horsemen. "The Confederate cavalry, which, with few exceptions, is regarded with little favor either by the enemy or ourselves, made but slight resistance, and soon fled the field," he wrote, not so correctly. "The teamsters, however, and much of the wounded as could lend a hand, seized the muskets in the wagons belonging to the wounded, formed into line between the train and the cavalry, and with the help of the guards, drove the enemy…and saved the train and the wounded. The affair is known as the 'teamsters battle.' Many of them had been disabled in the infantry service, and fought well, but not without considerable loss, as several of them were killed and wounded."[78]

Imboden had rebuffed both Buford and Kilpatrick. While the environs were safe for the moment, serious work remained to be done. "We slept on the field with our guns that night," remembered one of Imboden's men, "[and] the rain came down like cloud-bursts and drenched us."[79] Trains of wounded continued to filter in to Williamsport, and the bulk of Lee's army was closing in on the Potomac River valley. A flooded river to their backs and having nowhere to go, the Confederates would have no choice but to fight it out if the Army of the Potomac arrived in force and in time to give battle. Col. Edward Porter Alexander, Longstreet's chief of artillery, knew exactly what was at stake. "Here we would be penned up, with a river at our backs, with ammunition greatly reduced, & fresh supplies cut off, & defeat would now be ruin," he wrote. "A chance was offered Meade, as great as [George B.] McClellan had missed the year before at Sharpsburg. We expected him to be on us in forty-eight hours, & vigorous efforts were made to be ready for him."[80]

The critical job of keeping Federal cavalry away from Lee's main body long enough for a stout defensive position to be forged fell upon the able shoulders of Jeb Stuart. Whether he would succeed remained to be seen. In the meantime, his stout defense of Hagerstown on the morning of July 5, and Imboden's successful stand at Williamsport that afternoon, kept Lee's escape route to the latter open. Would the Federal cavalry ever manage to choke it shut?

Lee's Main Body

On the morning of July 6, as the fighting at Hagerstown began, the head of the Army of Northern Virginia emerged from the Monterey Pass and headed toward the crossroads town of Waynesboro, Pennsylvania, two miles north of the Mason-Dixon Line and only twelve miles from Hagerstown. Lee established his temporary headquarters along the banks of the Little Antietam Creek on the Emmitsburg-Waynesboro Turnpike just outside Waynesboro as the army continued to pass. He was studying maps of the area with other officers when Maj. John W. Daniel arrived, sent by Ewell to find the army's headquarters. Daniel was impressed by what he saw. "It was impossible not to be struck with [Lee's] calm, composed and resolute bearing. He seemed to be entirely undisturbed by the trying scenes which he had so lately passed through, and by the still more trying ordeal through which he was now passing," he wrote admiringly. "He had seen the hopes of success blighted in a few hours; he had seen his gallant army twice driven back [at Gettysburg] after hundreds had fallen, and he felt that the responsibility rested on his shoulders. The enemy's cavalry had been in his rear and had destroyed a large portion of his trains [at Monterey], and a broad river was still between him and his country. Yet with all these misfortunes weighing upon him he was as calm as on a peaceful summers day."[81]

Maj. Jedediah Hotchkiss, Ewell's master cartographer, rode up to announce that Ewell had likewise sent him ahead to learn the proposed route of march. Lee told Hotchkiss to ride back to Ewell and inform him that the army had not lost a critical number of wagons along the retreat route, and that Imboden's wagoners "had whipped the Yankee cavalry at Williamsport." Lee continued, "Tell General Ewell if these people keep coming on, turn back and thrash them soundly." Inspired, Hotchkiss spurred off to do just that. When he passed the orders on to Ewell, the corps commander responded, "By the blessing of Providence, I will do it."[82]

"During the afternoon July 6th the rebel train has been passing as fast as they could drive," wrote a Union prisoner in his diary.[83] Such a quick pace was born of necessity. Even as word filtered among the marching Confederates that night of the twin victories at Hagerstown and Williamsport, prudence dictated that they continue to move with alacrity, as there were no guarantees that the route would remain open for long.

The bulk of the Virginia army passed through Waynesboro, turned south, and reached Leitersburg, Maryland, about midnight after an excruciatingly long day of marching. After a brief rest the march continued all night until the men reached outskirts of Hagerstown on the morning of July 7.[84] Had Kilpatrick held the place the previous day, this retreat route would have been blocked.

Robert E. Lee rode along the long column of his army while admiring soldiers saluted him. Lee arrived in Hagerstown about 2:00 p.m., and not long after Brig. Gen. William "Extra Billy" Smith, the governor-elect of Virginia, passed to hearty and prolonged cheering. The locals, however, were happy for a different reason. "[T]he people seem jubilant over what they suppose to be our defeat," observed an artillerist of the Old Dominion. "Now it is true we did not gain a victory [at Gettysburg], but we are far from being defeated. A great part of our want of success is attributed to our falling short of rifle gun ammunition, immense quantities of which were fired by our army."[85]

Lee's vaunted soldiers were indeed far from being defeated. But could they tip the scales back in their favor before it was too late?

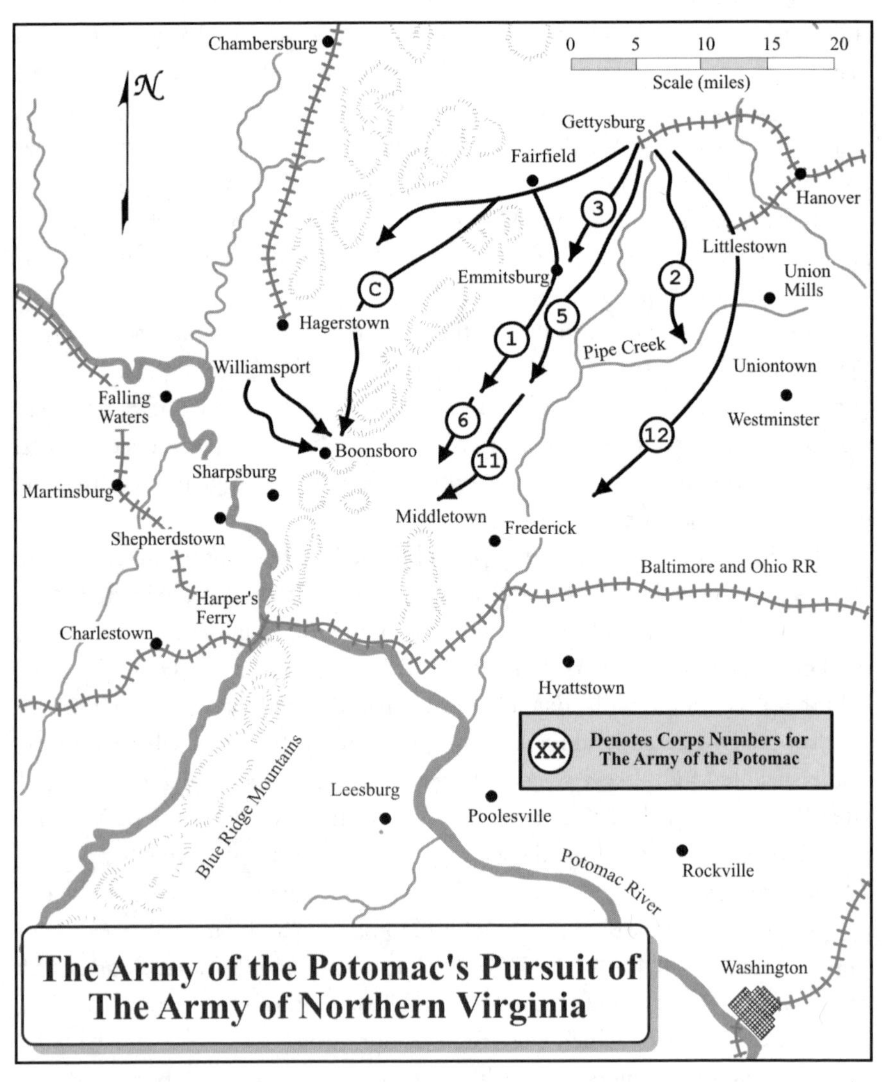
Chambersburg
0
5
10
15
20
Scale (miles)
N
Gettysburg
Fairfield
Hanover
3
Littlestown
Emmitsburg
2
Union
Mills
C
5
Hagerstown
1
Pipe Creek
Uniontown
Williamsport
Falling
Waters
6
12
Westminster
Boonsboro
11
Sharpsburg
Martinsburg
Middletown
Frederick
Shepherdstown
Baltimore and Ohio RR
Harper's
Ferry
Charlestown
Hyattstown
XX
Denotes Corps Numbers for
The Army of the Potomac
Blue Ridge Mountains
Leesburg
Poolesville
Potomac River
Rockville
Washington
The Army of the Potomac's Pursuit of
The Army of Northern Virginia

Chapter 8

July 7: In Full Pursuit

"The boys are confident that we will whip Lee's Army so that he will not be fit to do anything more for some time to come. We have good news all the while from our pursuing forces."

— Sgt. Ellis C. Strouss, 57th Pennsylvania Infantry

THE MORNING OF JULY 6 DAWNED dark and misty in the Fairfield Valley, making it difficult to see more than a handful of yards.[1] John Sedgwick's 6th Corps, still in position northeast of Fairfield following its skirmish with Early's rearguard the previous evening, cautiously advanced through the town toward Fairfield Gap. "The people stare at us as we march past," noted Lt. Elisha Hunt Rhodes of the 2nd Rhode Island.[2] "Many had been the demonstrations of delight along the route by the loyal people, some of whom came from miles away to look upon the valiant veterans who had freed them from the presence of the hateful foe," wrote the historian of the 37th Massachusetts. "There was everywhere the realization of a crushing defeat sustained by the invaders, their own wounded and prisoners frankly admitting for the first time that they had been worsted by the Yankees in fair fight, but charging it all to the mistaken policy of leaving the defensive in Virginia and assuming the offensive on Northern soil."[4]

Facing the mountain defile, Sedgwick halted, formed line of battle, deployed artillery and threw out skirmishers. No enemy was yet visible.[3] Uncle John's soldiers remained in position for several hours, before Sedgwick ordered the corps to advance to the gap. After moving perhaps one mile, Federal skirmishers once again encountered Early's rearguard. "[We] found the enemy in such force in the gap that [we] were nearly all day in dislodging him," observed a member of the 15th New Jersey.[5] The position convinced at least one member of the 6th Corps that the Confederate position still could not be taken without heavy losses. The position at the gap "was very strong and one in which a small force of the enemy could hold in check for a considerable time, a force much larger than its own."[6] After losing six or eight men, Sedgwick called the movement off.

Meade decided to detach Brig. Gen. Thomas H. Neill's brigade, a battery of artillery, and Col. John B. McIntosh's brigade of cavalry to "follow the enemy cautiously as he retires, keeping the commanding general constantly informed."[7] A force that small would be able to keep an eye on Lee's army, but would not be sufficient to stop its withdrawal or damage it in any significant way. "The Yankees played a very cute trick, when they found that Gen. Lee had retired after they commenced it, by following us with one brigade of infantry, to make it appear that they were driving us," was how one of Lee's Alabama soldiers described the anemic pursuit. "They kept at a very respectful distance, and gave us no trouble."[8]

Neill's men crossed South Mountain at Monterey Pass. During the march they admired the handiwork performed by Judson Kilpatrick's Federal cavalry, as evidenced by Lee's demolished wagons. The cheers of the relieved local population only added to their feeling of elation.[9] The challenging climb, however, soon dampened their enthusiasm. South Mountain, dubbed "Mount Misery" by Neill's men, proved a formidable obstacle. "The road lay directly over its summit, rocky and narrow," recalled an officer. "By midnight the head of our column reached the cloudy top in profound darkness and storm. The troops filled the steep highway which was fast becoming a torrent, and their unusual fatigue made a halt necessary." When word filtered back that the weary infantrymen had taken the wrong route, they had to retrace their steps amidst a great deal of grumbling.[10]

Neill's division marched to Waynesboro, where the men camped. "I marched my command from Fairfield to Waynesboro today, and just missed capturing the rear guard of Lee's army, which left at 10 a.m. this morning," reported Neill. "The whole of the rebel army is by this time at least as far as Hagerstown. I cannot overhaul them tonight, but will push them toward Hagerstown tomorrow." Neill also observed that the entire Army of Northern Virginia had taken the road to Hagerstown, and that it was making rapid but orderly progress toward Williamsport.[11] The Confederate rearguard only escaped by burning the bridge across Antietam Creek about two and one-half miles from Waynesboro on the Hagerstown Road.[12]

Colonel McIntosh's troopers rode as far as Zeigler's Mills, near Chewsville, where they engaged Ewell's pickets in skirmish fire. McIntosh formed his dismounted men in line of battle, and the fire of his troopers, supported by artillery, drove some of the Confederate infantry across Antietam Creek in what General Neill described as "gallant style." The attack cost McIntosh four men wounded, including one mortally. This small action, however, anchored Meade's forward elements in a critical spot just a few miles north of the Virginia army's primary crossings of the Potomac River. Unfortunately, nobody exploited this opportunity, and it slipped away.[13]

Because they had just missed catching the rear of Lee's army, the morale of Neill's men sagged. However, as they entered Waynesboro, a pleasant surprise awaited them. The townsfolk lined the sidewalks and handed the weary soldiers bread, sliced and buttered, cooked meats, pies, and lots of other goodies as they marched past. "This was a bright spot to remain fresh in the soldiers' memory through life," fondly recalled a member of the 61st Pennsylvania. The men camped near the town and the citizens sent to Chambersburg for flour and baked bread, selling it to the soldiers for less than the cost of the flour. "All honor to Waynesboro," declared the Keystone Stater.[14] The rest of Sedgwick's 6th Corps set out on a march for Emmitsburg, nine miles distant.

The Federals were eager to pursue Lee's beaten army. Unaccustomed to battlefield victory, they wanted to pitch in again. "We are after the enemy. Our Corps (the 3rd) has not yet started, but we are expecting to go every minute," reported Sgt. Ellis C. Strouss of the 57th Pennsylvania Infantry. "The boys are confident that we will whip Lee's Army so that he will not be fit to do anything more for some time to come. We have good news all the while from our pursuing forces."[15]

A Vermonter of the 1st Corps was not so confident. After marching six miles to the vicinity of Emmitsburg, he wondered why his regiment had stopped after such a short march. "I fear that the efforts to bag Lee will prove a failure for he is already a day and a half the start of us," he lamented, "and unless we have a sufficient force at Williamsport the rebel army will effect an escape."[16]

The Union soldiers found the going difficult. "The roads were in shocking condition from the severe rains, making the march tedious and wearisome, and the men, still being out of rations, were weak with hunger," recalled a member of the 14th Connecticut Infantry. "This becoming more serious," he added, "men were detailed to go into the [Taneytown] and obtain food, the expense of which was to be paid by the government."[17] One Bay Stater colorfully described the roads as being "one immense hogwallow the entire distance."[18] A member of the 9th Massachusetts, of the 5th Corps, recalled that the mud was between ankle and knee deep, meaning that each step was exhausting for the soldiers, who had to drag the extra weight on their heavy, sodden shoes and uniform trousers.[19] [T]he mud," grumbled another, "in some places seems bottomless and ankle deep at best and tenacious as glue."[20]

The 6th Corps artillery bogged down in the thick mud on the road to Emmitsburg, and the guns had to be taken apart in order to pull them free.[21] "It was a wild and picturesque country that we were traversing," recalled an officer of the 37th Massachusetts.[22] "But on we went through mud, mire and water, on and on, till as night approached, we began to anxiously expect a halt," recounted Pvt. Wilbur Fisk of the 2nd Vermont. "Never before had a march seemed to drag so wearily as this." The men were to be disappointed, for Sedgwick had no intention of halting.[23]

Uncle John rode the length of his column, closing up the ranks and inspecting his men. As he trotted past, a veteran from Vermont sang out, "I 'low you want to get to Williamsport tonight, don't you, Uncle John?"

"Yes, my man," replied Sedgwick.

"Well," responded the Vermonter, "in that case you had better put the Vermont brigade in front!" A pleased Sedgwick did just that. The tired soldiers cheered their general and pressed on.[24]

When a local guide offered to conduct the 6th Corps over Catoctin Mountain by a short cut called the Hamburg Pass, Sedgwick ordered his men to use the shortcut, which his soldiers dubbed "Sedgwick's Pass." The local citizenry thought that the Federal soldiers were crazy to take such a road. They suggested that the path would be difficult to traverse during daylight, that the only people who used it were hunters, and that it would be all but impossible to pass along it at night.[25] "Those of his command who followed it will not forget the fatigues of that eventful night," shuddered a veteran. "We were on a rough mountain road, with a single track between the rocks; the roadway, all washed clean of earth, having only a bed of bare stones. The night was pitchy dark, and the rain pouring. We stumbled and fell, and the brigade was in sad confusion."[26]

Others complained just as colorfully about the chosen path of pursuit. "We were obliged to give up the roads to artillery and wagon trains and were led by what some said was a bridle-path, but I don't think that anything that ever wore a bridle could get over it, unless it were a goat," unhappily remembered a Vermonter of the 6th Corps.[27] The narrow road was very rough, and as little traveled as the locals forewarned. It was, confirmed a Federal foot soldier, "literally a bed of mud resting on a foundation of small sharp stones. The soft mud soaked the men's shoes, all of which had seen much wear, and the flinty stones cut them to pieces till many a poor fellow was forced to plod along barefooted or with only his stockings to protect the blistered and bleeding flesh. Unhappy the naturally tender-footed!"[28]

"In some places the mountain was very steep, and we could only crawl along," Lieutenant Rhodes of the 2nd Rhode Island observed.[29] "Up-up-up-the path seemed to have no end," carped a member of the 5th Maine. "To say that there was no growling, and various expressions indicating anger and irritability upon the part of most everybody, would be to state an absolute untruth, and to record an absolute impossibility."[30] B. F. Johns of the 49th Pennsylvania recalled, "It rained nearly all night, and I was so hungry and fatigued that I did not know what to do."[31] Another 6th Corps solider noted, "No supper and no coffee, added to wet clothing, caused great discomfort."[32]

Private Fisk of the 2nd Vermont left a colorful description of the passage over Catoctin Mountain:

> The distance was seven miles. It was four miles to the top of the mountain. The road was narrow, crooked, and rocky, closely hugged on either side by the thicket of trees and bushes. The night was dark as inky blackness, and the rain poured as I have seldom seen it pour before. The road was steep, awful steep, so steep that one fellow, who was perhaps a little inclined to exaggerate, declared it was worse than perpendicular, that the hill rather canted under. Nevertheless, we should have accomplished this march, as we have accomplished a great many other impossibilities, if we could only have marched right along without hindrance. But the road was continually blocked up by some obstructions ahead, so that we had to halt three minutes where we could travel one. It was vexing beyond all control to stand there and hold our aching knapsacks with that gigantic, never-ending hill looking up in front of us, and the long hard journey in prospect. We rarely halted long enough to sit down, but if we did the column would invariably start just as we were fairly seated. Men fell out, whole companies at a time. Some companies took a vote to stop, and fell out, officers and men. One Colonel said he rode on till his men all left him, and he found himself without a command, when he concluded he would stop too. As for your humble servant he trudged on till he got to the top of the mountain, when, with a comrade, he concluded to follow the multitude and camp on his own hook. Heretofore he had kept with the regiment, but he pleads conscientious scruples to justify his course on this occasion. He had seen men whom the Government could ill afford to lose march till they died, and he was exceedingly loath to deprive Uncle Sam of

> another of his valuable soldiers, if by stopping he could prevent it. Perhaps he wanted to live to give somebody an awful "blowing up" for marching us so outrageously that day. If so, no one should complain.

When Fisk stepped off the road, he stumbled over a sleeping soldier who swore and threatened terrible vengeance upon the Vermonter. Fisk regretted waking the man, but there was nothing he could do about it. Jumping away from the first soldier he landed squarely on the stomach of another, who roared with pain. Fisk beat a hasty retreat into the bushes as far as he could, spread his blanket, and lay down for the night in the chilly rain. "There was not a dry thread in our clothes, but for all that we slept, and soundly to," he wrote. "In the morning there was nearly a pail full of water on the rubber blanket under us."[33]

The next morning Fisk and his comrade re-joined their regiment, enjoyed a welcome breakfast, and warmed themselves by a roaring campfire before resuming their march. "Napoleon crossing the Alps will no longer be mentioned as the climax of heroic achievements," Fisk waxed eloquently. "Sedgwick marching over the Catoctin Mountains has entirely eclipsed that. That was undoubtedly bad enough, but it bears a feeble comparison to what we did."[34]

There were a few humorous incidents that miserable night. One mounted officer's personal cook had a bunch of live hens tied to his saddle. In attempting to keep his seat, the officer "pulled his horse from the perpendicular to the horizontal position, and cook, horse, and hens rolled down an embankment together." The exhausted soldiers had a good laugh at that ridiculous (and noisy) display.[35]

When they finally reached the tiny hamlet of Hamburg, atop the mountain, the weary and wet infantry decided that a more appropriate moniker for the place was "Humbug." The name stuck.[36] The conditions confirmed to most of the men that the pursuit would continue to be ponderous at best.

Some of Sedgwick's foot soldiers finally reached Emmitsburg about 1:00 a.m. on July 7, "clattering through the city and making the quiet streets resound with the footsteps of thousands of armed men, horses and cannon bringing night capped heads to windows," recalled an officer of the 10th Massachusetts.[37] According to a member of the 37th Massachusetts, "they staggered rather than walked through Emmitsburg and half a mile beyond, halting in an open field at 2 o'clock and sinking down wherever it might chance to sleep during the few hours that remained before the bugles would again sound the advance."[38] The weary soldiers of the 6th Corps finally got a chance to rest for a few minutes. Some passing soldiers of the 1st Corps handed the resting men of the 6th Corps a hardtack. It was the only food of note Uncle John's soldiers received that day. For many, it was their first food in thirty-six long hours.[39]

The lack of progress disgusted John Sedgwick. "Things had been going wrong," noted one of his staff officers. "The general was walking up and down in the middle of the road, full of unusual wrath."[40] His frustration grew when he learned that his artillery was heading down the wrong road. Sedgwick stood in the road, talking to Maj. Gen. John Newton, the commander of the 1st Corps, when he learned that the 6th Corps guns were thoroughly stuck in the mud. Not long afterward, Col. Charles S. Wainwright, Newton's chief of artillery, rolled by with his guns, later writing, "Newton crowed, and Uncle John was mad."[41]

When morning finally came, ending the frustrating night at last, the soldiers greeted the sunlight with especial delight: the rain had stopped—if only for a little while. When someone discovered a cold mountain stream, the men washed their faces and muddy clothing. It was a welcome change of pace, observed one 6th Corps man, for "We could recognize each other again."[42]

Many of the Federals did not miss the Keystone State. "I am glad to be in Maryland, as the Pennsylvania Dutch are a hard set," observed a soldier of the 5th Corps. "The Marylanders are Americans, live in a land of plenty, and are either friendly or subdued."[43]

The pursuit, hampered by difficult conditions, prompted General Meade to reassess his route of advance. "From information which I had previously received of the character of the passes at Fairfield and Cashtown, having been informed that they had been fortified by the enemy, and that a small force could hold a large body in check for a considerable time, I made up my mind that a more rapid movement of my army could be made by the flank through the Boonsboro Pass [Turner's Gap], than to attempt to follow the enemy on the road which he himself had taken," Meade later testified. "I therefore directed the various corps by way of Middletown and South Mountain towards Hagerstown."[44]

As Meade explained, he still intended to strike Lee a blow north of the Potomac River. "As soon as possible I will cross South Mountain, and proceed in search of the enemy," wired Meade to Halleck on July 6. "If I can get the Army of the Potomac in hand in the Valley, and the enemy have not crossed the river, I shall give him battle, trusting, should misfortune overtake me, that a sufficient number of my force . . . would reach Washington so as to render it secure."[45] He reiterated his intentions on July 8, when the army began concentrating at Middletown. "I most earnestly desire to try the fortunes of war with the enemy on this side of the river," he told Halleck.[46] On July 9, the army commander predicted to Halleck, "the decisive battle of the war will be fought in a few days."[47]

These were words President Lincoln wanted to hear, but the results thus far had been less than encouraging. The frustrated Lincoln vented at Halleck on the night of July 6. "I left the telegraph office a great deal dissatisfied," he announced. "You know I did not like the phrase in Orders, No. 68, I believe, 'Drive the invaders from our soil.' Since that, I see a dispatch from General French, saying the enemy is crossing his wounded over the river in flats, without saying why he does not stop it, or even intimating a thought that it ought to be stopped." The Chief Executive turned his attention to his army commander. "Still later, another dispatch from General Pleasonton, by direction of General Meade, to General French, stating that the main army is halted because it is believed the rebels are concentrating 'on the road toward Hagerstown, beyond Fairfield' and is not to move until it is ascertained that the rebels intend to evacuate Cumberland Valley." Lincoln concluded, "These things all appear to me to be connected with a purpose to cover Baltimore and Washington, and to get the enemy across the river again without a further collision, and they do not appear connected with a purpose to prevent his crossing and to destroy him. I do fear the former purpose is acted up and the latter is rejected."[48] Lincoln's frustration would only increase as more evidence of the lack of aggressive intervention reached him.

Maj. Gen. Samuel P. Heintzelman commanded the troops assigned to the defenses of Washington, D. C. His men were not part of the Army of the Potomac, but they often acted in concert with it. On July 6, noted Heintzelman, "General [Benjamin F.] Kelley has been ordered forward from Cumberland and I hope the troops [have been ordered forward also] . . . General French must be advancing and the cavalry and infantry sent today from here will make him a considerable force. What a pity Maryland Heights have been abandoned. We could not assemble a strong force on the Potomac to intercept Lee."[49] Heintzelman had a valid point, but he expected much from forces already stretched too thin. Kelley moved with his 5,000 troops, arriving near Hancock, Maryland, on the evening of July 7, but no Confederate troops attempted a river crossing there.[50]

By the morning of July 7, with the entire Army of Northern Virginia in full retreat, General Meade planned to keep his army moving southward and rendezvous at Middletown, as he had ordered two days earlier. This disposition would keep his army—exactly as Lincoln so feared—squarely interposed between the Rebels and the Federal capital at Washington, D. C., making the blocking of Lee's escape attempt unlikely. "Meade left all of his superfluous baggage behind, and moved in light marching order," claimed a newspaper correspondent traveling with army headquarters.[51] Some units, however, did not march quickly even if outfitted lightly. The 2nd Division of the 3rd Corps, for example, did not get on the road until July 7, four full days after the battle of Gettysburg ended.[52] Disinformation coursed through Southern ranks, however. "General Meade withdrew his army last night to the direction, it is supposed, of Frederick," a Southern correspondent reported incorrectly on July 5. "It is said that General Lee was aware of the movement, or guessed that it would be made, and commenced to put his own army in motion about the same time."[53]

Regardless of the motivations, the massive multi-pronged race to the Potomac River was on. "We left our position on Little Round Top in pursuit of the Confederates on the afternoon of Sunday, July fifth, with the entire Fifth Corps," noted a member of the 146th New York. "It was an agreeable sensation in some respects to be ordered to pursue. The great majority of us, nevertheless, would have been more satisfied had we been given a few days longer to rest." The men of the 5th Corps were still footsore from too much marching and the heavy fighting of July 2, and many feet were too swollen for even shoes. Consequently, the corps only covered about six miles south on the Emmitsburg Road before going into camp along the banks of a stream that offered the men their first opportunity to bathe and wash out their clothes in days. "We sported about in the water to our hearts' content before turning in for the night," concluded the Empire Stater. They remained at Marsh Creek until the 7th, enjoying the all-too-brief respite.[54]

"The retreat of Lee has caused it necessary for us to do more marching," noted a New Yorker of the 1st Corps a few days later, "which, though hard, is cheerfully done, in the hope that we shall soon have the work accomplished, viz., that of closing this cruel war, with a restoration of our glorious Union."[55] Elements of the 1st Corps marched for seventeen hours to the Catoctin Mountain on July 7, covering thirty-five miles while maintaining an exhausting pace.[56] When they finally got orders to halt for the night, they were not permitted to light fires for fear of giving the Confederates convenient targets. Bullets occasionally whizzed by. "All protects themselves as best they can from those scattering bullets, but occasionally some fellows were hit."[57]

The men of the 83rd New York of the 1st Corps were exhausted after a long day of marching. "The private soldier knows but little of the plans of the commanding general—he is but a mere instrument in the hands of those in authority, and the greater the subordination of the rank and file, the more effective to these instruments become in the hands of brave and skillful generals," explained George A. Hussey. "But the men composing the Union Army had a fashion of doing a good deal of thinking, and also of expressing their thoughts upon their commanding officers and the conduct of the campaigns in which they were engaged. Never before, in the history of the world, did an army contain so many 'thinking bayonets,' and, as the Union troops plodded along in this stern chase after the defeated Confederates, many were the conjectures as to when and where Meade would bring the enemy to bay, and by a bold stroke crush him before he could re-cross into Virginia." The last thing these veterans wanted to see was Lee's army escaping to safety, as it had after Antietam the previous fall.[58]

On July 4, Meade issued a general order congratulating his army for its Gettysburg victory. Regimental commanders read the order to their men. Col. James Gwyn, 118th Pennsylvania Infantry, read the words to his command and called for three cheers for General Meade. Not one man moved in response, nor did any cheers emanate. "That you won't cheer your commander," replied Gwyn, "then I'll do it myself." And he did so, waving his hat and giving three cheers and a tiger. "No more cheering," sniffed Capt. Francis Donaldson of the 118th, "there has been too many changes of commander, besides the army don't like Meade, they don't know much about him. Of all the General officers known to the army, with exception of the 5th Corps, he is least known of any of them." Times had changed. Long gone were the days when the mere presence of George B. McClellan stirred the men to resounding cheer.[59]

The Union infantry, meanwhile, slogged its way along muddy roads, crossing into Maryland with the hope of bringing the enemy to battle on ground of their choosing.[60] By July 7, a division of Oliver Howard's 11th Corps reached the concentration point at Middletown, which one man described as a place that had hoped to become a city, and which might have succeeded had not the steam railway eclipsed the National Road as the country's main route of commerce.[61] The 11th Corps covered twenty-five miles that day, "which is pretty good considering half the men were bare footed and had marched every day for a Month," observed a member of General Howard's headquarters escort.[62]

* * *

Col. Pennock Huey, commander, 2nd Brigade, 2nd Division, Cavalry Corps.

LOC

While Meade planned and the infantry marched, Alfred Pleasonton made a critical error. The cavalry commander knew that the most direct route to the Potomac crossings between Falling Waters and Williamsport was across South Mountain to Cavetown and on through Hagerstown. In other words, the area around Hagerstown was the ideal place for the Federal cavalry to concentrate. If Pleasonton pulled together all three of his divisions between Cavetown and Hagerstown, he could block the Army of Northern Virginia's route to the Williamsport river crossings. This, in turn, would have allowed Meade to bring Lee's Virginia army to battle on ground of his own choosing with his horse soldiers interposed between Lee and the Potomac. Because Lee's plans remained uncertain, however, Pleasonton believed he had to try and ascertain the enemy's intentions.

Instead of concentrating his command, however, Pleasonton scattered his horsemen. He sent J. Irvin Gregg's brigade of David Gregg's division north to Hunterstown, where he was to march west toward Cashtown before turning south. John B. McIntosh's brigade, also of Gregg's division, was to go to Emmitsburg and hold the town in order to prevent Confederate cavalry from attacking the Union rear. Buford's division, which had been in Westminster, Maryland, since the afternoon of July 2, was sent to Frederick, twenty-five miles southeast of Hagerstown, where Merritt's Reserve Brigade would join it. Kilpatrick's division, reinforced by Col. Pennock Huey's 2nd Division brigade, was the only portion of Pleasonton's large and powerful force tasked to make a direct pursuit. Kilpatrick's troopers were the only ones ordered to march southwestward through Emmitsburg toward the crucial Monterey Pass and then on to Hagerstown.[63] By not massing his forces, Pleasonton let a golden opportunity slip through his fingers. The Army of the Potomac would never again enjoy the upper hand while Lee's army remained north of the Potomac.

The wretched condition of Pleasonton's horses compounded the problems of concentration and pursuit. After a long and grueling campaign, the army's cavalry mounts were worn and exhausted. J. Irvin Gregg, whose brigade caught up to the Southern rear at Caledonia Furnace on the evening of the 6th, had to let the enemy slip away because his "horses were much too broken down to push" them. However, reported Gregg, "I think his train is stuck in the mud between [Caledonia Furnace] and Greencastle."[64] Similarly, Buford's ride to Frederick was "necessarily very slow," recalled a man of the Reserve Brigade. "Both men and horses were tired and jaded. For five days we had been without forage for our horses, and in almost constant motion. Hundreds of horses dropped down on this march, and were left on the road with their saddles, blankets, and bridles upon them. Men, whose horses 'played out,' trudged along on foot through muddy roads and swollen streams without food."[65]

Gregg's Division

Brig. Gen. David M. Gregg, a taciturn 31-year-old Pennsylvanian, was a well-respected career cavalryman and a member of the West Point Class of 1856. Tall, spare, and sporting one of the more luxuriant beards in the Federal service, Gregg was quiet, competent, and popular with his men. His weary horse soldiers had defeated Jeb Stuart's vaunted cavaliers on East Cavalry Field at Gettysburg on July 3, beating a much larger enemy force and preventing Stuart from riding into the Army of the Potomac's rear unmolested. The senior

Brig. Gen. David M. Gregg, commander, 2nd Division, Cavalry Corps.

USAHEC

subordinate officer in the Cavalry Corps, Gregg commanded a cavalry division longer than any other soldier.[66] His 2nd Cavalry Division, however, would play almost no role during the retreat.

Late on July 4, General Meade ordered one of Gregg's brigades, commanded by Col. J. Irvin Gregg, the general's first cousin, north and east toward Hunterstown, the scene of a sharp cavalry engagement between Kilpatrick's division and Brig. Gen. Wade Hampton's Confederate cavalry brigade on the afternoon of July 2. Col. Gregg's troopers captured a detachment of the Cobb Legion Cavalry of Hampton's Brigade, which had been left behind by mistake. After ensuring that no other enemy cavalry was lurking in the area, Col. Gregg and his troopers headed west along the Chambersburg Pike in pursuit of the wagon train full of wounded Rebels.[67]

The next day, July 5, most of General Gregg's division rode west from Gettysburg along the Chambersburg Pike, spending the night in the Cashtown Pass after capturing about 2,000 stragglers and nearly 3,000 wounded from the Confederate retreat, many of whom were rounded up by local farmers armed with pitchforks and flails. The farmers were especially enraged because the retreating column had abandoned the road, preferring the open farm fields on either side. Their new route of retreat marched them through the ripe grain fields, where they trampled wide swaths parallel to the road. The 4th Pennsylvania Cavalry alone of Col. Gregg's brigade took possession of about 500 prisoners. "They have nothing to say, and crawl about at our coming with a kind of dazed and stupid stare," noted one officer in this diary.[68]

The head of Gregg's column caught up to the train of wounded near Caledonia Furnace, where a fight with the cavalry acting as the Southern rearguard broke out. "We engaged with the enemy's rear, losing several men killed but capturing many prisoners," recalled an officer of the 4th Pennsylvania Cavalry. "We completely routed them."[69] Gregg's men camped near the Furnace that night and in the morning, "the rebel rear-guard is gone."[70]

They continued riding the next day, following the route of the train of wounded. They found "the road filled with broken-down wagons, abandoned limbers and caissons filled with ammunition, ready for instant use," reported Col. Gregg.[71] At Fayetteville, Gregg ordered Col. William E. Doster, a 26-year-old Harvard- and Yale-trained lawyer from Bethlehem, Pennsylvania, to charge with his 4th Pennsylvania Cavalry into the town of Greencastle. General Gregg's adjutant rode with Doster to ensure that the pace was rapid, and the men rode at the gallop. About 100 stragglers fell in with Doster's column, but Doster could find no signs of the enemy rearguard. At Marion, "the march has made an end of any efficiency in my force," recorded Doster. "I count up out of five hundred men of my regiment with whom I left Potomac Creek, twenty-five with me mounted. The rest are, heaven only knows where, dismounted, killed, wounded, scattered, and not at hand."[72] However, they captured 100 rebels, eight horses, destroyed twenty caissons and gun carriages, and a large quantity of ammunition and wagons.[73]

When Doster arrived in Marion, a local citizen informed him that Fitzhugh Lee's entire Confederate cavalry brigade was leisurely grazing its horses at Brown's Mill, just one mile to the left of the road. Doster sent out scouts, who determined that the intelligence was accurate. "Now is the golden opportunity for surprise," Doster noted in his diary. "If I only had two hundred men it might do, but with twenty-five it is absurd." Instead, Doster sent an orderly back to General Gregg with the news and a request to have men ride up and scatter the enemy horsemen. "Good God!" responded Gregg. "What does the man mean? Let him fall back on me at Fayetteville."[74]

Disappointed, Doster complied. "I'm inclined to believe that Gregg judged his strength insufficient to cope with a whole army, and therefore fell back as he did that night on Goldsboro and Chambersburg," Doster concluded with some bitterness. "Our ammunition was nearly exhausted and the horses sore-backed and exhausted. Still, allowing all that, it seems to me that a vigorous and general charge of Gregg's division on Lee, on the afternoon of the 6th as he lay near Marion, would have routed that demoralized body and driven such consternation throughout the infantry—harassed by a freshet in the rear—as would have given us the Southern army." Instead, J. I. Gregg's brigade enjoyed a leisurely respite in Chambersburg.[75]

"As we passed through this section, the people assembled from all the neighboring districts 'to see the army,'" a member of the 1st Pennsylvania Cavalry observed, "and never did soldiers enjoy the luxuries of richly stored pantries than did the Union troops in passing through this fertile region."[76] The bulk of Gregg's division lingered near the Mason-Dixon Line for several days and did not march into Maryland until July 8. "We tarried at Waynesboro for several days," recalled a member of the 3rd Pennsylvania Cavalry, "taking advantage and making good use of the time by getting our horses reshod, and looking after other matters needing attention."[77] Gregg's horsemen finally arrived in the area of Middletown, Maryland, at the base of South Mountain, on July 9, where they pitched their camp. They did not link up with the rest of the Cavalry Corps until arriving in Boonsboro on July 11.

Col. John B. McIntosh, commander of Gregg's 1st Brigade, received orders to march to Emmitsburg on July 5, the same direction some of the enemy's cavalry had ridden. Pleasonton instructed McIntosh to follow the enemy and prevent them from gaining the rear of the Union army. At Emmitsburg, McIntosh learned that Stuart's main body had passed through the town that morning, heading in the direction of Frederick. Orders were cut to ride to Fairfield, where McIntosh's troopers would join 6th Corps infantry.[78]

Detachments of mounted men moved into the mountains to try and locate the enemy, and a contingent of McIntosh's 1st New Jersey Cavalry clashed sharply but briefly with Stuart's troopers in the terrain towering above Emmitsburg.[79] Some of McIntosh's men chased a contingent of Rebel cavalry, gobbling up their advance guard. When he interrogated his prisoners, McIntosh learned that one of them carried a dispatch setting forth the routes of march of Longstreet's and Ewell's infantry corps. McIntosh quickly forwarded it to Meade. "The Rebel army is in a bad state & there is no telling how they are going to get out of it," observed McIntosh. "It looked as if Lee might be used up."[80] The Jersey men clashed with the Confederate cavalry near Emmitsburg again the next day. Accompanied by Brig. Gen. Thomas Neill's 6th Corps infantry brigade, McIntosh's brigade cautiously followed the Confederate retreat, crossing over South Mountain via Monterey Pass.

Huey's brigade, which had been serving with Kilpatrick's division since July 4, rejoined Gregg's division at Middletown. On July 10, Huey's troopers rode out on patrol in the direction of Williamsport. The Federal horsemen found and skirmished with Confederate cavalry at the important road junction of Jones' Cross Roads between Hagerstown and the old Antietam battlefield, driving the enemy nearly one mile. Huey's command suffered four men killed and six wounded in this sharp running skirmish.[81]

On July 10, the 1st New Jersey of McIntosh's brigade went out on a patrol, charged some enemy pickets, and swept to within four miles of the Confederate stronghold at Hagerstown before withdrawing.[82] "Hot—lay in the field roasting all day," complained a bored trooper of the 16th Pennsylvania Cavalry of J. I. Gregg's brigade on July 10.[83] The near-lethargy continued as the historic days of the first half of July 1863 ticked away. "Not much going on save 'Camp rumors,'" observed the same 16th Pennsylvania trooper.[84]

While some rode and others camped, the horses of every cavalryman suffered. The extensive riding and fighting of the wide-ranging Gettysburg Campaign had taken its toll on both man and beast of the 2nd Cavalry Division. On July 12, while his command was camped at Boonsboro, a large number of the mounts from several of Gregg's regiments were condemned, and the men left dismounted.[85] That same day, the troopers of the 11th New York Cavalry, also known as "Scott's 900," together with detachments of the 13th and 14th Pennsylvania Cavalry regiments, reinforced J. I. Gregg's depleted brigade.[86] On July 14, Pleasonton ordered Gregg to march to Harpers Ferry, where his men skirmished with Southern cavalry south of the Potomac River.

And so Gregg's horsemen played no real role in obstructing the movement of Lee's army to, and fighting it around, Williamsport.[87] Other than the skirmishes with Stuart's cavalry near Emmitsburg and Huey's July 10 skirmish at Jones' Cross Roads, Gregg's division scarcely fired a shot in anger and did not participate in the heavy fighting to come. It was a nearly inexcusable waste of three reliable veteran brigades of horse soldiers. Col. Doster had it right when he noted, "We are going to intercept Lee's passage, but it looks rather late. We should have been at this a week earlier."[88]

General William H. French's Command

It was about nightfall on July 4 when Maj. Gen. William H. French's soldiers learned that Lee's army was retreating from Gettysburg. Expecting Lee to try to use the South Mountain passes as his escape route, Meade wanted to seize them as fast as possible. Hoping to intercept the fleeing enemy, French, who was occupying Frederick, Maryland, with the garrison from Harpers Ferry, was ordered to seize and hold the mountain's lower passes at Crampton's, Fox's, and Turner's Gaps, where the locus of the fighting had unfolded during the 1862 Maryland Campaign. It was imperative for French to hold them before elements of Lee's army occupied them.[89] French was also directed to occupy Harpers Ferry. A forty-eight-year-old native of Baltimore, French was a member of John Sedgwick's West Point Class of 1837. The career Regular Army officer was known for his foul humor and heavy drinking, and was not popular with his men. However, to his credit, French anticipated Meade and had already drafted orders before he was instructed to do so.[90]

French's command consisted of several very large regiments. Most had performed garrison duty for the first two years of the war, were newly formed, and had little if any combat experience. The veterans of the Army of the Potomac held them in contempt. "They looked upon us as new recruits, and remarks were frequently made by them not altogether suiting us," remembered a sergeant with the 14th New Jersey.[91]

Moving out with his rookies, French threw out a strong line of battle with heavy pickets in front. Without fanfare, his men quietly occupied the important mountain passes. No fires were allowed in order to prevent any curious Confederates from realizing that so large a force of Union soldiers held the gaps. Instead, as each regiment arrived, the men formed line, stacked arms, and lay on the wet ground, hoping to grab a few minutes of much-needed sleep. The night was cold, and with nothing more than the ground to lie on and their knapsacks for pillows, French's soldiers spent a thoroughly unpleasant few hours. They remained there for five days, holding the passes and watching the Army of the Potomac march toward Lee's army, now trapped along the banks of the swollen Potomac River. They cheered the veterans of the army as they marched by, hoping to incite them on to greater accomplishments.[92]

French also sent the men of his Maryland Brigade to Monocacy Junction to guard the important bridges across that stream, as well as Nolan's and other ferries on the Potomac. The men of the 10th Massachusetts Battery protected the critical Monocacy Junction on the B & O Railroad just south of Frederick, Maryland. Passing trains brought all sorts of wild rumors, so the Bay State cannoneers had no idea how the true situation was unfolding. When word of the surrender of the Confederate army at Vicksburg tapped across the telegraph wires, the men celebrated twin victories with enthusiasm. Several regiments of infantry reinforced the artillerists, and the whole force stayed in position at Monocacy Junction until marching orders arrived on July 8.[93]

Some of French's troops re-occupied Maryland Heights, above Harpers Ferry, on July 6, but not without a fight. Maryland Unionists led by Brig. Gen. John R. Kenly, of French's command, skirmished with Rebel infantry attempting to repair the bridge burned by the horse soldiers of Cole's Maryland Cavalry. Kenly sent the 1st Maryland to ascend the heights by the way of the eastern slope, while he led the 4th and 8th Maryland regiments by the road along the C & O Canal. The advance guard found the road blocked and came under fire. "The advance immediately dashed forward in gallant style, turned the point of the precipice which abuts on the road, and, taking cover, by their rapid firing soon materially lessened that of their opponents," was how one of Kenly's men later recounted the fighting. The balance of the command took up a position on the road while their battery deployed on the heights. A few well-placed shots by the guns scattered probing enemy cavalry.[94]

After the Federals drove the Rebels from the heights, they established a picket line from the Potomac River to Solomon's Gap. The pickets repulsed a few probes by enemy infantry and squads of cavalry. According to Kenly, he retook the heights after a sharp skirmish of about one hour's duration.[95] The significance of this small action was not lost on French. "The fact that Maryland Heights had been reoccupied, after a forced march, surprising the enemy, and compelling him to abandon the bridge-head and the heights, is a part of the history of the Gettysburg Campaign of which you and your troops may be justly proud," he declared a few months later. Maryland Heights and the critical supply base at Harpers Ferry were now firmly in Union hands once more.[96]

The Maryland Brigade remained in position on Maryland Heights until July 10, when it marched at 9:00 a.m. to join the 1st Corps of the Army of the Potomac on Beaver Creek between Boonsboro and Funkstown.[97]

The Destruction of the Confederate Pontoon Bridges at Falling Waters and Harpers Ferry

When the Confederates captured Winchester, Virginia, in June 1863 on the march north that would eventually carry them to Gettysburg, most of the town's garrison surrendered. However, much of its cavalry escaped and joined General French's Federal garrison at Frederick, Maryland. On July 1, as the fighting at Gettysburg was getting underway, French dispatched a detachment of the 1st New York (Lincoln) Cavalry to scout along the Potomac River to learn how and where the Army of Northern Virginia crossed it on its way into Pennsylvania. The scouts returned the next night to report a large Confederate pontoon bridge across the Potomac at Falling Waters, guarded only by 200 Southern horse soldiers. Of equal import was news that the Williamsport ford was held by a force of similar size.[98]

Col. Andrew T. McReynolds, commander of the 1st New York, led the contingent of horse soldiers assigned to French's garrison at Frederick. On July 3, McReynolds proposed sending a strong striking force of troopers to destroy the pontoon bridge, "which is the only reliance of the rebels for a retreat for their infantry, artillery and wagons in that direction." To French's credit, he promptly approved the request that afternoon.[99]

Departing from Frederick on the night of July 3, Maj. Shadrack Foley of the 14th Pennsylvania Cavalry led 300 men from his own regiment, the 1st New York, 13th Pennsylvania, and a detached squadron of the 6th Michigan Cavalry on the expedition. Making their way through the rain and mud, the troopers proceeded cautiously toward Williamsport and arrived at Falling Waters on the morning of July 4. As a result of a breakdown in Lee's staff work—a problem that had plagued his army for the entire campaign—the river crossing had been left virtually unguarded. With great vigor, the Yankee troopers charged the small Confederate force holding Falling Waters. When they arrived at the river, the Northern horsemen discovered that the pontoon bridge had been cut loose and had swung toward the Virginia shore, where a Rebel guard stood over it. Bugler John Hertz, 6th Michigan Cavalry, offered to swim the river and cut the upper end of the bridge loose. He did so, carrying the end into the swollen river's swift current. Hertz tied the bridge to the Maryland side of the Potomac. Foley and his men crossed, attacked the guard, and captured seventeen of them. After snatching three wagons and more than a dozen mules, the troopers dispersed the rest of the Confederate force guarding the river crossing.[100]

Re-crossing the river, Foley and his men destroyed the bridge. "Three regiments charged it—one fought to the right, another to the left, while the third, supplied with straw and turpentine, set fire to it, cutting it loose from its moorings to let it float down river, a burning wreck," reported a Federal prisoner of war being held in Williamsport. "Our cavalry had cut their way in and destroyed the only bridge that Lee had left in his rear." He concluded jubilantly, "Score another for the cavalry!"[101]

After sending his prisoners back toward headquarters at Frederick, Maj. Foley rode on to Williamsport, where he routed the Southern pickets there. After taking a few more prisoners, Foley safely returned to Frederick, having destroyed Lee's primary passage back to Virginia across what was now a rapidly rising Potomac River.[102] "The destruction of the pontoon bridge and train at Falling Waters was one of the most daring exploits of the war," crowed a *New York Times* correspondent.[103] Foley later received a well-deserved brevet to lieutenant colonel for his valor in leading this daring raid.[104]

"The destruction of our pontoon bridge below Williamsport was owing to carelessness," correctly groused a *Richmond Daily Dispatch* editorial on July 13. "It was guarded by an inadequate body of men, and they without arms. Lee, however, seems to have little use for it at present." In fairness to the Confederate high command, it would have been difficult to predict such a bold and utterly unexpected dash as that conducted by Foley's command.[105]

Elements of the 1st Regiment of Potomac Home Brigade Cavalry, a Union outfit from Maryland also known as "Cole's Cavalry" in honor of the unit's first commander, Henry A. Cole, rode to Harpers Ferry with one piece of artillery. At Knoxville, about four miles from Harpers Ferry, the Marylanders charged and scattered a company of Virginia cavalry, pursuing them to the railroad bridge across the Potomac. Capt. Albert M. Hunter commanded the detachment of Maryland horse soldiers. "I had a pair of red Zouave trousers on and as sitting on our horses, with the high rocks for a background, my red trousers seemed to be an especial mark," he recalled. "The bullets came thick near me striking the rocks with a chuck much like an old chew of tobacco on a board."[106] The Virginians crossed the narrow bridge single file and were protected by friendly troops on the other side of the river, who opened fire on the pursuing Yankee troopers. Stymied, Hunter fell back to await the arrival of his gun. "We then kept up a lively fight across the River until our Engineers set fire to the bridge and burned it down," recalled a lieutenant of Cole's Cavalry.[107] When the gun arrived, its fire drove the Confederates back to Bolivar Heights.

Two Maryland horsemen made their way across the bridge, carrying several buckets of oil they used to soak the wooden stringers. Within moments the entire structure was ablaze. "Cole's Cavalry had destroyed the bridge at Harpers Ferry," proudly claimed the regimental historian, "which Lee would have utilized in crossing the Potomac River, had he been able to force a passage through the gaps in South Mountain."[108] The destruction had other consequences no one seems to have foreseen. Cole's Marylanders cost the Union the opportunity to cross troops at Harpers Ferry and march them behind the Confederates, cutting off their retreat route and forcing Lee to stand and fight even if the river dropped enough to permit him to cross.

French ordered other cavalry out to try to block roads and prevent Stuart from getting the drop on his headquarters at Frederick. Troopers of the 11th New York Cavalry actively patrolled the roads to keep Stuart from reaching the key Maryland city. The New Yorkers doubled their pickets and spent the night sleeping on their weapons in case Stuart's horsemen made an appearance.[109]

In the meantime, the Federals began gathering additional forces to bring to bear against Lee. Brig. Gen. Benjamin F. Kelley commanded a 4,500-man Union garrison at Clarksburg, West Virginia. General-in-Chief Halleck instructed Kelley to gather his command and move it toward Frederick, where it could help confront Lee's army. Kelley's reply—that it would take him several days to concentrate his command, ready it for action, and move out—angered his already tense superiors. "I have seen your dispatch to the Adjutant-General, and regret to hear you talk about 'some days' to concentrate, when minutes are precious," shot back Secretary of War Edwin M. Stanton. "It will be a matter of deep regret if, by tardy movement, you let the chance escape. There should be no rest, night or day. Why are you still at Clarksburg?"[110]

Lee had no choice but to wait for the river to fall before crossing. Thanks to Major Foley's courage and his brave troopers, the Army of the Potomac had been given additional time to trap the enemy. The only question remaining was whether Meade could take advantage of that opportunity.

Chapter 9

July 7: Skirmish at the College of St. James and the First Battle of Funkstown

"[T]he road of slumbering wrath was marked here and there by cleft skulls and pierced bodies . . . "

— Brig. Gen. William E. Jones, Confederate cavalry brigade commander

THE FIRST NEWS OF THE surrender of the Confederate stronghold at Vicksburg, Mississippi, to the Federal Army of the Tennessee under Maj. Gen. Ulysses S. Grant, reached the Navy Department in Washington by telegraph about noon on July 7. Navy Secretary Gideon Welles received Rear Adm. David D. Porter's dispatch bearing the news with elation. "Secretary Welles astonished everybody who knew him by putting on his hat and solemnly proceeding to the White House to tell the news to President Lincoln," recalled Noah Brooks, a close friend of Lincoln and a Washington-based correspondent of the *Sacramento Union*. "It was said at the time that the Secretary, on arriving at the executive chamber, executed a double-shuffle and threw up his hat by way of showing that he was the bearer of glad tidings. This was a mere invention; but Lincoln did say that he never before nor afterward saw Mr. Welles so thoroughly excited as he was then."[1]

Lincoln and Secretary William Seward, together with a senator and a judge, made their way to the War Department, where a telegraph operator was copying the same dispatch. The President and his party, recalled the operator in his diary, were "talking so loudly I can hardly write."[2]

Celebration turned into anticipation in the nation's capital. "Soon, however, Washington was straining its attention toward Maryland," remembered Brooks, where, it was popularly supposed, the Army of the Potomac had at last "corralled" Lee's army, supplies, and guns in an elbow of the Potomac between Williamsport and Falling Waters. "After the battle of Gettysburg," Brooks continued, "railroad communication was again resumed between the Relay House, on the Baltimore and Washington line, and the town of Frederick, Maryland . . . We are in almost hourly expectation of a great battle which should be fought on Maryland soil and result in the annihilation of the army of Virginia and the hastening of the collapse of the rebellion."[3]

Believing that the end of the war was near, Brooks wanted to see it for himself. "President Lincoln sympathized with my natural desire to see the great fight, and he not only furnished me with passes to the front, but gave me letters to General Meade and Adjutant-General Seth Williams of the Army of the Potomac . . . armed with these credentials, I pressed forward to the headquarters of the army by the way of Frederick." Boarding the next train he could find, and with a couple of old friends from California in tow, Brooks was on his way to the seat of war.[4]

George Meade and his staff arrived in Frederick on July 7. The largest town on the National Road between Wheeling and Baltimore, Frederick was an important center of commerce. The army commander established his headquarters there in the United States Hotel, and "was received with much enthusiasm by the people of Frederick and the soldiers."[5] The grateful ladies of the loyal town presented him with bouquets of flowers, and the band of the 7th New York Infantry serenaded him at his hotel that evening. Meade, who did not much enjoy pomp and circumstance, sent his compliments to the ladies and apologized for not being able to grant them an interview, as his time was entirely occupied with very pressing business. He thanked them for their gift and their patriotic expressions of support for the cause.[6]

At that seat of war, conditions remained miserable. Torrential rains fell all day on July 7. The Iron Brigade of the 1st Corps struggled to cross Catoctin Mountain, a route others had found just as miserable. "By a steep, narrow, stony path, practicable only for infantry and pack mules, but dry and shady, the Iron Brigade passed over the Catoctin Mountain and through Hamburg on the summit," recalled a member of the 24th Michigan. "The men were frequently obliged to march in single file, so stretching the line that a halt of several hours was made to get closed up." A better road was found on the western slope of the mountain, where every man enjoyed a spectacular vista of the valley below.[7]

Morning Skirmish at the College of St. James

War was not yet finished with the College of St. James. Buford and his cavalry had thrust across its campus and nearby grounds just one day earlier on July 6. More pounding hooves and gunshots were just hours away.

The college, began in October 1842 at Hagerstown by Rev. William R. Whittingham of Baltimore and Rev. Theodore B. Lyman was founded as an institute for boys called "St. James Hall." When a "fine country estate" called Fountain Rock in Washington County, about six miles from Hagerstown, came on the market, Lyman convinced Bishop Whittingham to purchase the estate for use as their school. Lyman raised the handsome sum of $5,000 from area donors, and the estate was purchased for the new college.[8]

Rev. John Barrett Kerfoot, born in Ireland and Assistant Rector of a school on Long Island, New York, was selected as rector of St. James. Known as an excellent administrator, Kerfoot "entered upon his new duties with zeal and success," and in 1843, the Maryland Legislature passed an act of incorporation by which St. James' Hall became the College of St. James.[9]

The school's handsome brick main building housed only about twelve students, down from the usual few dozen who were present before the Confederates marched north through Maryland. Reverend Kerfoot, a staunch Unionist, arose early on the morning of July 7 and, walking down the entrance lane of the school, "visited [the] 9th N. Y. Cavalry in the woods opposite our gate." Kerfoot had a peaceful visit until the sun began to peek over the horizon, when "skirmishing began, Confederates coming from Williamsport."[10]

At daybreak on the 7th, Col. Thomas Devin ordered a squadron of the 6th New York Cavalry to make a demonstration in the enemy's front northwest of the college. The New Yorkers drove in Rebel pickets, triggering confusion in the enemy's lines.[11] Kerfoot retreated back to the safety of the campus and watched as the reinforced Southerners pushed the Federal horsemen back.

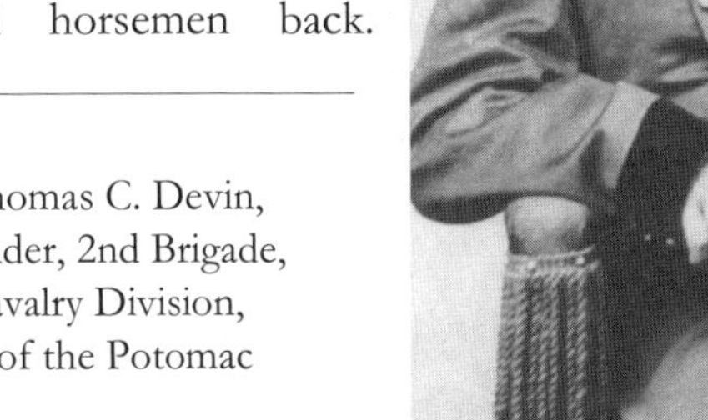

Col. Thomas C. Devin, commander, 2nd Brigade, 1st Cavalry Division, Army of the Potomac

USAHEC

"Their advance, firing as they marched, [was] in full view from the top of the College," he later jotted in his diary, "[it was] right under our eyes, and the slow retreat of our cavalry."[12] Devin withdrew the rest of his command east toward Antietam Creek and established a new line two and one-half miles behind his original position. Resting his men and horses, Devin had orders to hold the position until the rest of Buford's division and all of Kilpatrick's division had crossed Antietam Creek.[13]

At 11:00 a.m., Rebel infantry and artillery appeared in Devin's front. Devin ordered the 9th New York to hold the enemy in check, and sent a messenger to notify Buford. Once Devin learned that the rear of Buford's column was crossing the stone bridge that carried the Boonsboro Road to and over the Antietam, he ordered the New Yorkers to withdraw. Following behind the rest of Buford's column, Devin's men were pressed by pursuing Confederates. The 9th New York fought a stiff rearguard action, occasionally stopping to turn and face their pursuers, making a stand to trade some time for space. "We fell back this morning," Private Daniel Peck of the regiment wrote home. "The enemy followed close up and we were sent back and engaged them between two and three hours, but were ordered to fall back, just as we got at it pretty warm."[14]

When he reached the Antietam bridge, Devin dismounted two squadrons of the 17th Pennsylvania and posted them on the hill overlooking the structure, "intending," in Devin's words, "to give the enemy a warm reception."[15] Recognizing the strength of the 17th's position, the Confederates broke off the engagement and allowed Devin's brigade to cross the bridge unmolested.

Safely out of harm's way, most of Buford's division went into bivouac near the old Antietam battlefield for the rest of the day, looking for some much-deserved rest, despite the blanket of the mud and rain.[16] Once again, the Union horse soldiers had performed admirably. "Our cavalry is doing prodigies of work, and wading through blood to do it," proudly proclaimed a lieutenant of the 1st Pennsylvania Cavalry. "Can be said that it no longer is a useless arm of the service. Has, in this campaign, done even more than equal share."[17]

With the Federal cavalry driven back, the College of St. James fell to the Confederates. The well-kept and quiet campus acreage was about to feel the hard hand of war as never before. "At 1 p.m., called upon by a Confederate surgeon to go out to the road and take up a mortally wounded Union soldier," Rev. Kerfoot noted in his diary that day. Passing a dead trooper and horse of Devin's brigade just outside the gate, Kerfoot "went out in a little wagon . . . Went on to the wounded man, and found him in agony and paralyzed on one side; brought him to the College, and met all his wants. Then had a box made and grave dug in our graveyard, and drove out to bring the dead in and bury him." Kerfoot read the funeral service over the fresh grave and returned to the college buildings, which were quickly becoming targets for hungry Southern soldiers. "Pretty well overrun by Confederate soldiers," he wrote in his diary. That night, "they broke open our spring-house and helped themselves to 100 lbs. of butter. The rest we saved—hid away—as well as good stores of flour, groceries, bacon, etc."[18]

While most of Buford's division rested, the 6th U.S. Cavalry conducted a reconnaissance along the macadamized National Road north toward Funkstown. There, the 6th's troopers encountered the 7th Virginia Cavalry of Jones' Brigade—their opponents in the July 3 fighting at Fairfield. The Virginians had not done well at Fairfield. In fact, they had performed so poorly that Jones noted in his after-action report that, despite outnumbering the small Federal force, the actions of the 7th Virginia that day was "a blemish in the bright history" of the regiment.[19] But today was a another day, Grumble Jones' 7th Virginia Cavalry again outnumbered the Federals, and this time the Virginians were full of fight and eager to redeem their reputation.

The First Battle of Funkstown

The meeting engagement developed quickly as the 6th U.S. Cavalry scouted along the Williamsport Road where, without much warning, it encountered 7th Virginia Cavalry pickets. Anxious to engage the enemy, two companies of the 7th Virginia spurred forward against the Regulars, whose skirmishers fired a volley before falling back. In the initial exchange Capt. Ira Claflin, commanding the Regulars, was wounded and had to retire. As he wheeled his horse, he warned Lt. Louis H. Carpenter, the next ranking officer, that the Confederates were forming for a charge and ordered Carpenter to form two lines to receive it. Claflin wanted to execute a leap-frog type of withdrawal, with successive contingents making a brief stand while the previous line withdrew and established a new line further back. But as trooper Sidney Davis of the 6th U.S. noted sarcastically, "Carpenter obeyed just enough of these instructions to aid in the destruction of his command."[20]

Sensing a quick rout, the 7th Virginia charged the Federals in front and on their right flank. Because of the heavy rain the night before, the 7th's supply of ammunition was both wet and depleted, meaning that the saber was the weapon of choice.[21] After initial resistance, the Virginians drove back the 6th U.S., which withdrew "with deliberation and good order." Despite the good order, the Virginians continued to harass them in a running skirmish. "For a mile or two they persisted in this orderly retreat," noted an officer of the 7th Virginia, "the front appearing to hold the rear back and the rear defending themselves as best they could."[22] A final determined thrust caught the Regulars and finally routed them. "The fallen," recalled one Confederate officer, "lay thick along the road."[23]

A high and narrow bridge over a stream proved an impediment to the flight of the Regulars, as the Confederate horsemen thundered down upon the retreating Federals. "As the afrighted men and horses swarmed upon it numbers were crowded off over the side, and fell headlong into the water below," recalled a horrified Regular.[24] As they approached the environs of Buford's main camp, the Confederates drew up and fired a volley, which was met by a countercharge from the startled Yankee troopers. Lt. Col. Thomas Marshall, the commander of the Virginians, ordered a withdrawal. "[I]t was difficult to call the men off from a fleeing foe and before fairly organized for a fall back, they were upon us, and in the running fight back we suffered considerably in prisoners whose horses gave out," explained an officer of the 7th Virginia. "It was fight and fall back all the way to our starting point."[25]

When the Virginians fell back, they did so at a gallop, with men of the 1st U.S. and 6th Pennsylvania in hot pursuit. As Capt. Isaac Dunkelberger of the 1st U.S. recalled, "As soon as the Confederate cavalry saw us coming they halted and then commenced to retreat, but their horses were so tired and winded that we soon caught up with them . . . a short running fight took place."[26] When the 7th Virginia was joined by reinforcements from the 11th Virginia Cavalry, Buford's troopers gave up the chase.[27]

The running fight pleased Grumble Jones and removed the stain of the earlier humiliation at Fairfield. "Sabers were freely used and soon 66 bloody-headed prisoners were marched to the rear, and the road of slumbering wrath was marked here and there by cleft skulls and pierced bodies," gloated the cavalry general. "Fairfield is fully and nobly avenged. The Sixth Regular Cavalry numbers among the things that were."[28] The 6th U.S. had lost heavily, including all but three or four of its officers since Fairfield but it remained a viable force. After the running fight, the regiment's highest-ranking officer was a lieutenant.[29] "The service of the regiment between the action at Beverly Ford and the last affair at Funkstown was one of incessant marching and fighting, and although nearly decimated by the casualties of the action, the brave little band hung onto Lee's army with a courageous tenacity," claimed the regimental historian of the 6th U.S.[30]

While the opposing cavalry jousted for position, General Lee's engineers began the arduous task of forging a defensive position along the banks of the swollen Potomac River. They scoured the countryside, looking for the best ground for the Army of Northern Virginia to wage what was shaping up to be a grand final stand. Three full days were expended on this arduous task, with Lee himself determining the final selection of the ground where his army would entrench.[31] The general took a moment to send President Davis a dispatch updating him about the army's inability to continue with offensive operations at Gettysburg, and the progress of the retreat. "Finding the position too strong to be carried," he began, "and, being much hindered in collecting necessary supplies for the army, by the numerous bodies of local and other troops which watched the passes, I determined to withdraw to the west side of the mountains. This has safely been accomplished with great labor, and the army is now in the vicinity of this place. One of my reasons for moving in this direction, after crossing the mountains, was to protect our trains with the sick and wounded, which had been sent back to Williamsport, and which were threatened by the enemy's cavalry."[32]

The final extended defensive position had to be ready for the main body of Lee's army, which was rapidly approaching. James Longstreet's and A. P. Hill's commands had already reached the Hagerstown area, and Richard Ewell's Corps reached Hagerstown mid-day on July 7. Ewell's men passed through Leitersburg and went into camp in their positions around the town along Greencastle Road. Lee established his headquarters about two and one-half miles from Hagerstown along the road to Williamsport. The Virginia army remained there the next day, concentrating itself along the banks of the swollen river.[33] It rained hard again that night, making sleeping difficult for the Confederate soldiers, "but all bore it patiently," observed Major Hotchkiss.[34]

The Union Infantry

After their own fitful sleep the preceding night, General Meade's Union infantry roused themselves on the morning of July 7 and tramped along the eastern face of the Catoctin Mountains. The Catoctin range rises 1,400 feet above the Monocacy River Valley on the western boundary of the Piedmont Plateau, two and one-half miles west of Thurmont, Maryland. The Catoctins were a formidable physical barrier on the best days. Under these circumstances, they were nearly impassable.[35]

"To use a Homeric comparison just as a fierce bull will go bellowing along a strong fence seeking, for an opening thro' which he may spring upon his rival who stitch-out," waxed an officer with Sedgwick's 6th Corps. "So with our two armies, and the Catoctin fence between them." The rains continued unabated, inflicting more misery. "It has been raining all day and bids fair to rain all night," he continued, "the men's rations are exhausted and this is the rate at which we are going to cross the mountains, we are going to have a starving time."[36] Another soldier agreed, adding, "Very forlorn indeed was the column which at 7 o'clock next morning [July 7] took up its way toward Middletown, some six or seven miles away."[37] With the roads churned into quagmires and with little food or provisions available, every step was agony for the Northern foot soldiers. In spite of the hardships they endured, "every man is enthusiastic at the hope of overtaking Lee before he crosses the Potomac, and at once and forever finishing up the rebellion," noted William H. Locke, the chaplain of the 11th Pennsylvania.[38]

The condition of the army as it marched toward the river crossings alarmed its commander. "After reaching Middletown, it having been reported to me by my corps commanders that there were many necessary articles of clothing and other supplies that the army were very much in want of, and having myself, as I rode along, seen I may say hundreds of men walking over these broken turnpikes barefooted on these long marches," testified the General before the Committee on the Conduct of the War, "I deemed it my duty to remain at Middletown one day in order to obtain the necessary supplies, and put my army in condition, and give them some rest." As far as Meade was concerned, the sacrifice of losing one day would reap dividends in other ways.[39]

By July 7, the men of the 13th Massachusetts of the 1st Corps "were a dirty, unattractive lot; our equipments battered with the hard usage of many campaigns of marching, digging, and fighting." The men rose with the dawn and marched, reaching Bealsville near Catoctin Mountain. They halted for rest at a crossroads. A group of "pretty bright-eyed girls, all dressed in 'Stars and Stripes,' came from a school nearby, and forming themselves into a group, with the smallest standing on the upper rail of a fence, waving a flag, they sung the 'Battle-Cry of Freedom.'" The sight of these patriotic girls touched the hearts of the veterans of the 13th Massachusetts, "whose eyes moistened as they listened in silence to the words of that noble hymn. It was a graceful thing, which the lapse of time cannot efface from our memory."[40]

The 27th Connecticut of the 2nd Corps slogged its way to Frederick that day. "Frederick City put on its most smiling face," recalled a member of the regiment. "Flags were flung to the breeze and the people gave an enthusiastic welcome to the regiments as they passed through in pursuit of Lee's army." The Nutmeg State men were passing through the town on their way toward Crampton's Gap.[41]

Despite the mud, rain, exhaustion, and hunger, the Union infantry turned in a stellar series of marches that day. The 12th Corps covered thirty-two miles, while the 11th Corps—supposedly demoralized from its whipping on July 1—covered a similar stretch of road. By 11:00 that morning, all but the 2nd and 12th Corps had reached the Catoctin Mountains or the Middletown valley. In spite of the late start, the Army of the Potomac was making eye-popping progress, advancing at an unexpectedly quick pace.

The 14th Vermont Infantry of the 1st Corps arrived at South Mountain about 7:00 that evening. As if to greet them, the heavens opened upon their arrival. "The march was continued until about nine o'clock, and when ascending the mountain it became so dark and rainy—the men and beasts being completely exhausted, having marched about thirty-five miles during the day—we were obliged to halt for the night." The men spent a cheerless and restless night under the drenching downpour, resembling, someone noted, "drowned rats."[42]

On the night of July 7, some twenty hours after being hammered back from the eastern approaches to Williamsport, Buford's division was bivouacked just north of the town of Boonsboro. Because the Union cavalry command feared an attack by Stuart's horse soldiers during the night, most of the men remained awake. As Chaplain Samuel L. Gracey of the 6th Pennsylvania described it, he and the 6th spent most of the night "dismounted in a ploughed field in line of battle, in a heavy storm of rain, without fires and with clothes thoroughly saturated . . . standing in mud to our knees, every horse remaining saddled and in position, and every man at his horse's head. . . . This was one of the most wretched nights of all our experience in the cavalry service."[43] Few of the troopers would argue that July 7 had been the division's worst day of the campaign. More heavy fighting lay ahead in the coming days.

Samuel Gilpin of the 3rd Indiana used the respite to read the *Baltimore Clipper* newspaper. "Today's 'Clipper' represents Lee's retreat a rout and the capture of his army a certainty," he scrawled in his diary. "'I don't see it.' He [Lee] has suffered severely and will lose much still in his retreat perhaps. Our army with Couch and French and Heintzelman and Dix are about his rear and flanks." But would these additional troops arrive in time to make a difference?[44]

Judson Kilpatrick's 3rd Division spent the night in the same fashion, suffering equally in the cold and unrelenting rain that was both their enemy and their ally, for the storming heavens prevented Lee's army from making its escape to Virginia.

About 11:00 that night, a staff officer reported that Maj. Gen. Carl Schurz's 11th Corps division had arrived at Middletown, the first elements of the Army of the Potomac to arrive. Schurz camped on the left side of the National Road one mile beyond the town. The other two divisions of the 11th Corps were still on the far side of South Mountain, with the 5th Corps camped right behind them. The staffer also reported that the advance of the 1st Corps was two or three miles farther back, and that the 3rd and 6th corps were not far behind the 1st. The concentration at Middletown was coming together even faster than Meade likely envisioned.[45]

A dispatch from General Couch reached Meade. After reporting what he knew about the dispositions of Lee's army, Couch added, "If you prefer my troops with your army, only intimate it, as my heart and means are at your disposal. [S]ome think that the New York militia will not march into Maryland," Couch continued. "I don't know how that will be." Although Meade gratefully accepted Couch's offer, the troops comprised nothing more than untrained militia, which might present more of a problem than an advantage.[46]

That day, Meade also received a pleasant and completely unexpected surprise. "It gives me great pleasure to inform you that you have been appointed a brigadier-general in the Regular Army," wrote Henry Halleck, "to rank from July 3, the date of your brilliant victory at Gettysburg."[47] The War Department evidently thought that Meade could be prodded into acting, and that a carrot and stick approach was best. Later that same day, as if to make that point clear, Halleck wrote, "You have given the enemy a stunning blow at Gettysburg. Follow it up, and give him another before he can reach the Potomac."[48]

The Union high command obviously did not appreciate the challenges Meade faced. With each passing hour, Halleck, Stanton, and Lincoln became more heavy-handed in their insistence that the army leader pitch into Lee—whether or not he was ready or even able to do so.

Chapter 10

July 8: Heavy Fighting at Beaver Creek Bridge and Boonsboro

"They are all bully boys, and they don't fear the Rebbs a bit . . . Gen. Buford says . . . the only fault he finds with us is that he can't stop us when we once get the Rebbs to running."

— 8th Illinois cavalryman

A heavy rain fell overnight, soaking men and animals.[1] "It has rained night and day since we have been in Maryland," complained a Hoosier horse soldier in William Gamble's brigade of John Buford's division. "My feet have been wet for two weeks. Our clothes were wet and dirty and all of us tired and worn out."[2] Thankfully, it stopped near sunrise on the morning of July 8. "The sun came out bright and warm this morning," noted a New York horse soldier, "enabling us to in a few moments dry our drenched blankets and garments."[3] The men savored their break from the atrocious weather. It would be short-lived.

That day, Federal signal officers established a signal station atop South Mountain overlooking Boonsboro. A second station was set up a mile beyond Boonsboro. The Northern signalmen would have an excellent view of any action that might take place in or around the town.[4]

Although a small town at the foot of South Mountain, Boonsboro was a lively place. Founded by brothers George and William Boone (relatives of Daniel Boone), it was laid out in 1788 and incorporated in 1831. The place was originally known as Margaretville, in honor of George's wife Margaret, but was later called Boonsborough. In 1841 or 1842, the name was shortened to Boonsboro when a local newspaper editor could not fit the town's whole name on a masthead. The National Road passed through the center of town, whose several taverns made it a favorite stop for wagoners and stage drivers.[5]

Maj. Gen. James Ewell Brown (Jeb) Stuart, cavalry commander, Army of Northern Virginia.

LOC

One visitor to Boonsboro just a few years after the war wasn't impressed with the village. "The traveler's most pleasant experience of Boonsboro is leaving it," John T. Trowbridge dryly observed in 1868. "The town contains about nine hundred inhabitants; and the wonder is how so many human souls can rest content to live in such a mouldy, lonesome place. But once outside of it, you find Nature as busy in making the world beautiful, as man inside has been in making it as ugly as possible. . . . Leave it behind you as soon as convenient, and turn your face to the mountain."[6]

But there was something more important than grog shops and nature on the minds of many in the summer of 1863: Boonsboro commanded the approaches to South Mountain. The opposing armies had their faces to the mountain, but they couldn't leave Boonsboro behind in their plans. It was a strategic spot, which made it a logical place for both armies to hold.

The break in the rain presented Jeb Stuart with an opportunity to locate and engage the Union main body so Lee's infantry could pass unmolested. Stuart concentrated his command at Funkstown and led it eastward toward Boonsboro on the National Road. He did so in force with the brigades of Fitzhugh Lee, Grumble Jones, John Chambliss, and Laurence S. Baker (temporarily commanding the wounded Wade Hampton's brigade).

Unbeknownst to Stuart, Alfred Pleasonton had orders to hold the South Mountain gaps to enable Meade's infantry to cross the range and attack Lee's army before it could bridge the rain-swollen Potomac. The privations of the long campaign were telling on Pleasonton's men and horses. "For five days we

A woodcut depicting the battle of Boonsboro. *Harpers Weekly*

had been without forage for our horses, and in almost constant motion," recalled a member of the 6th Pennsylvania Cavalry. "Hundreds of horses dropped down on this march, and were left on the road with their saddles, blankets, and bridles upon them. Men whose horses were 'played out,' trudged along on foot through muddy roads and swollen streams without food." Many of these Northern horse soldiers had been marching and fighting for more than a month, and they were worn out.[7]

Once they arrived at Boonsboro, Stuart's troopers dismounted and advanced on foot, the "ground being entirely too soft from recent rains to operate successfully with cavalry."[8] The act of dismounting cavalry automatically decreases effective strength by twenty-five percent, as one man out of every four would end up holding his horse and those of three others, so that the horses were available for a rapid re-mounting, and also to protect the horses.

The Rebels presented quite a sight, recalled a newspaper correspondent. "The roads and hollows to the rear of the enemy's line, from favorable positions, could be seen filled with the enemy's forces," he wrote, "and no one doubted but that a desperate attempt would be made to secure the South Mountain Pass just in our rear."[9]

Grumble Jones's brigade led the way, attacking the Federals on the Boonsboro Turnpike at Beaver Creek Bridge, pushing the Yankee videttes back to the edge of the town.[10] Jones took a few prisoners, who informed him that the bulk of the Federal cavalry had massed at Boonsboro. The advance by the Rebel cavalry led Pleasonton to believe Stuart's mission was to seize the South Mountain gaps. If the Southern cavalier could take and hold those gaps, he could bring Meade's pursuit of Lee to a grinding halt.

Stuart, however, was not attacking but feinting, hoping to keep the Federals on the defensive long enough for the rear of Lee's columns to clear Hagerstown and reach their final defensive position along the Potomac. Capt. William R. McGregor's battery of Confederate horse artillery, deployed on commanding high ground, opened the ball in earnest about 10:00 a.m. by enfilading Gamble's position. Lt. John H. Calef's Federal battery responded, and a counterbattery duel broke out. The Southern gunners rained fire on a cemetery where Lt. Alexander C. M. Pennington's Battery M, 2nd U. S. Artillery had set up. "Every shot you fired that missed something in my battery," explained one of Pennington's officers in a letter to his adversary years after the war, "hit a marble tombstone in that graveyard, and the broken fragments of marble came

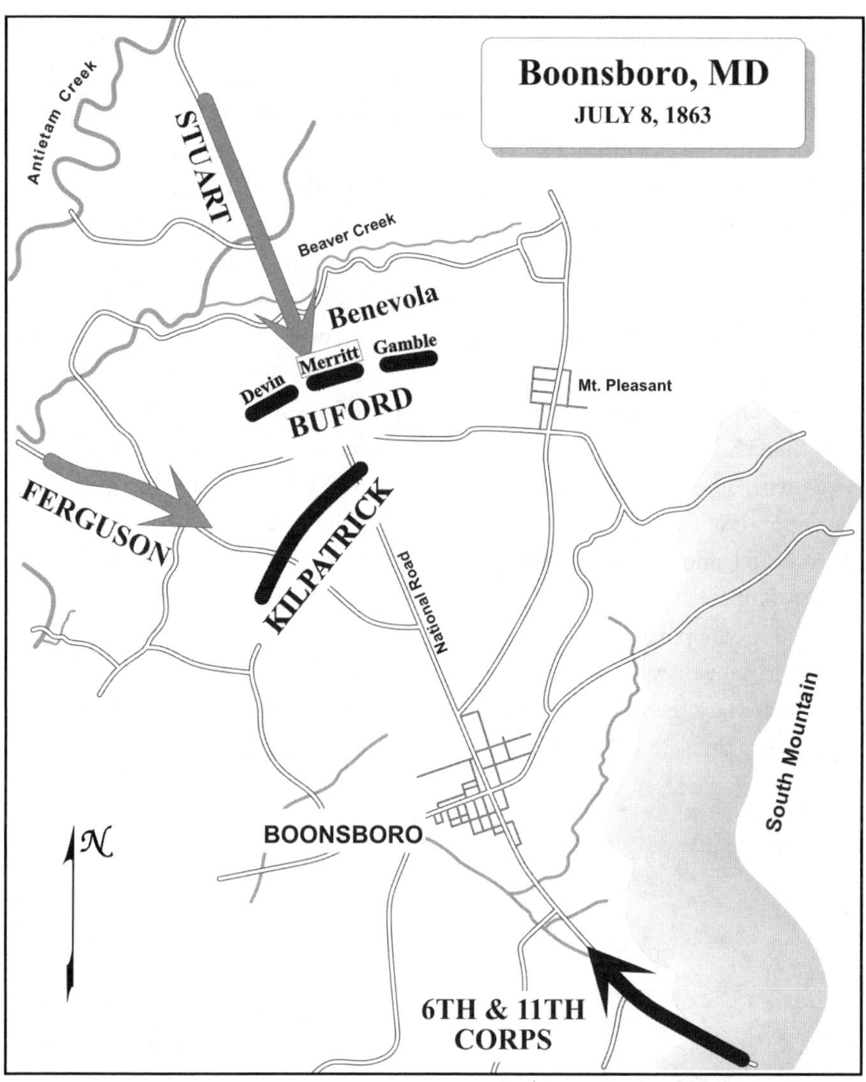

like hail upon my men. You were ruining us. We did not think it fair for you to shoot tombstones at us, and we left."[11]

In addition to flying bits of tombstones, the thick mud made it hard on the artillerists. "We were in a wheatfield with mud six inches deep, which proved too much for our gun carriages," recalled a Northern gunner, "the recoil in such soil strained and broke five out of six axles under the guns, and we were sent to Frederick City for repairs."[12] Southern shells also exploded in the streets of Boonsboro, terrifying the residents of the "pretty little town [where] the houses are nearly all made of brick and kept in good condition all through the town."[13]

Although Calef's men returned the fire, the Confederate artillery enfiladed Gamble's troopers. Along with Calef's battery, they pulled back to the south.

When Gamble retired, Stuart sent his dismounted skirmishers forward toward Buford's position. The sodden ground was too wet and muddy for a mounted charge, and it was raining again.[14] A Southern officer recalled, "There was now a spirited and deafening combat between the artillery of the opposing commands, on ridges facing one another, while in the valley between skirmish lines of dismounted men fought with their long-range guns."[15] So loud was the noise and fierce was the combat that it prompted one of Hampton's troopers to describe the skirmish as having "the fury of a battle."[16]

Responding promptly to Stuart's threat, Buford drew up his division in line of battle. The Kentuckian formed his command in an arc athwart the National Road, with Thomas Devin's brigade on the left, Wesley Merritt's brigade in the center, and William Gamble's brigade on the right. Most of the division was dismounted and still deployed in line from the night before. About noon, Judson Kilpatrick's men heard the booming of the initial guns at Boonsboro and galloped up to meet the challenge. When they reached their assigned positions, they dismounted, as the soggy ground was not conducive to fighting from horseback. Buford held Kilpatrick's two brigades in reserve and threw out skirmishers on both flanks, which quickly triggered a sharp engagement. "It was as heavy a cavalry fight, perhaps, as any during the war," a Wolverine would later write about the battle soon to erupt in full fury.[17] "Over the broad plains, it was a splendid sight to witness the maneuverings of those cavalry chiefs," recalled a member of the 5th New York Cavalry. "The struggle was desperate—Stuart

Col. William Gamble, commander, 1st Brigade, 1st Cavalry Division.

USAHEC

fighting for the safety of the Rebel army, and our boys for the South Mountain pass."[18]

Kilpatrick rode his lines slowly, making sure that his men were ready to go into the fight. When he spotted the men of the 1st Vermont forming a line of battle, Little Kil asked an officer how many cartridges the Vermonters carried. Lt. Col. Addison W. Preston responded that each carried forty rounds. "I said sixty rounds!" an irritated Kilpatrick yelled back. Preston argued that carrying sixty rounds was too heavy, but Kilpatrick insisted. Weighted down with the extra lead, the Vermonters tore down fences and made their final preparations to attack. They could see the heavy fighting raging in front of them and were eager to pitch in.

While Buford's skirmishers were heavily engaged, Stuart launched a flank attack with Jenkins' cavalry brigade, led as it had been since July 2 by Col. Milton Ferguson, a twenty-five year-old lawyer from what is today West Virginia. Ferguson had enlisted in the 16th Virginia Cavalry as a private and was elected captain of his own company. When his regiment was mustered into service, he was promoted to colonel on January 15, 1863. Ferguson was the senior colonel in the brigade, and so assumed command when Jenkins fell wounded at Gettysburg.[19]

Ferguson's troopers stormed down the Williamsport Road from the west, taking up a position along a stone fence, "from which the enemy spent the whole afternoon trying to dislodge us," recalled a member of the 17th Virginia Cavalry.[20] "We went out on a road to the northwest of Williamsport," remembered one of Ferguson's horsemen. "They had a fort on [South Mountain] and it was our duty to look after these Yankees on this part of the line and not let them get too close to Williamsport till our wagons and infantry all passed over to the Virginia side of the river."[21] One of Ferguson's officers bragged, "This was a cavalry fight with some 6 or 8 thousand on a side. We gave them a genteel whipping, killing a great many Horses. Our loss was slight."[22]

The Union signalmen atop South Mountain spotted Ferguson's flanking attempt and informed Buford of the threat. Buford, in turn, passed the critical intelligence on to Devin.[23] Two squadrons of Devin's brigade, along with units of Custer's brigade of Kilpatrick's division, were thrown out to meet the approaching enemy horsemen. As far as Kilpatrick was concerned, the role of the signalmen on South Mountain was crucial to the outcome of the fighting. "The battle of Boonsboro was fought and won by the aid of signals," he penned in his report a few months later. "[E]very movement of the enemy was seen by the signal officers occupying an elevated position, and quickly transmitted."

General Buford at the battle of Boonsboro. *LOC*

This endorsement helped make the Signal Corps a permanent part of the United States Army.[24]

The Confederate thrust was blunted by the fast-firing Spencer rifles carried by some of Custer's troopers. "We had here a good opportunity to test the qualities of the Spencer carbines [sic] and, armed as we were, we proved more than a match for any force that was encountered," recalled an officer of the 6th Michigan Cavalry. "The firing was very sharp at times, and took on the character of skirmishing, the men taking advantage of every cover that presented itself." Many of the Southern men were protected by a stone wall, while a stand of thick woods protected the Wolverines. Several times the Rebels poured over the wall to attack, but each time the heavy fire of the Spencers drove them back. "Once an officer jumped up on the fence and tried to wave his men forward. A shot from a Spencer brought him headlong to the ground, and after that," recalled one of Custer's men, "no one had the temerity to expose himself in that way."[25]

Stuart, however, seems not to have been overly concerned about the Spencers, and kept up a steady pressure against the Union front. By 3:00 p.m., his constant series of thrusts were beginning to tell on Kilpatrick's sagging line west of the National Road. "For half an hour it seemed as though our cavalry were doomed at last to meet with a decisive defeat," noted newspaperman Edward A. Paul of the *New York Times*. "The enemy, moving in expedients, moved in force to the left, and made an attack upon what was then our weakest point, gaining which there would have been little difficulty in securing the mountain pass, the possession of which would have enabled their main force to move about more at leisure, as this flank would be protected and the movements of the Union troops delayed."[26] The moment of crisis was at hand.

"Hold them a little longer boys! The 11th Corps is coming through the Gap!" yelled a staff officer as he dashed along the lines of the Michigan cavalry brigade. Buoyed by this news, the Wolverines redoubled their efforts "with such force that we drove them fully half a mile, then our ammunition began failing, men were dispatched to the rear to bring up cartridges," recalled Pvt. Andrew D. Jackson of Co. G. "Our Batteries played with all their might, but we could not hold them, slowly but surely we were put back to the position of their first line, where we met the boys with Nose-bags full of cartridges. These were quickly passed along the line, our cartridge boxes and pockets filled and again we began to hunt Rebs."[27]

Col. Nathaniel P. Richmond's brigade held the center of Kilpatrick's line. Richmond found the enemy strongly posted behind large rocks sheltered by thick woods. Richmond dismounted the 18th Pennsylvania Cavalry and sent them forward with a section of Elder's guns in support. One of Pennington's guns also rolled forward to support Richmond's troopers. The heavy fire of these three guns drove the Confederates from the woods.[28]

The 1st Vermont Cavalry, part of Richmond's brigade, was in reserve on the extreme right of the Federal line. When Capt. William G. Cummings sent his 6th Squadron forward, the determined Vermonters seized a strong position near a Rebel battery, stabilizing the situation. When Kilpatrick spotted the success Cummings and his men enjoyed, he sent the rest of the 1st Vermont Cavalry forward to assist Buford in repulsing another Confederate probe along the National Road. A battalion of Vermonters under Maj. John Bennett charged into heavy fire, and the assault quickly bogged down. The final battalion of the 1st Vermont under Maj. William Wells, still smarting from the battering it suffered during "Farnsworth's Charge" on the third day at Gettysburg, could only put fifty-five men into the field. Still, Wells led his little battalion forward into combat, taking his men directly into the enemy. The fight at close quarters was intense for several minutes. A saber flashed, cutting Wells across his chest, but he and his men kept to their mounts and repulsed the Confederates on their narrow slice of front.[29]

Lt. Col. Preston reported the action, noting, "At sun-down a spirited charge was made by the 2nd Battalion, under Major Wells, upon the retreating enemy, and the sabers were freely used on both sides."[30] Confederate observers agreed with Preston's assessment. "[H]and to hand they bore up against their pressing assailants in the most gallant style," was how one of Hampton's troopers vividly described the scene as the 1st South Carolina Cavalry met Wells' assault. "They received and returned the well plied steel of the Yankees; horses and riders intermingled recklessly with each other; for ten minutes the red, dripping sabres of each party are unflinchingly parried and thrusted in deadly strife . . . our loss," he admitted, "was pretty severe."[31]

"We fought until six in the evening, when we compelled the enemy to fall back," recounted a member of the 3rd West Virginia Cavalry of Devin's brigade. Sabers and carbines were not the only weapons that killed and maimed that day. As the men were falling back, an artillery shell exploded above the head of Lt. John E. Hoffman. The fragments missed Hoffman, but one struck and morally wounded a member of Company A of the 3rd West Virginia. The hissing iron chunk entered his back below the right shoulder and lodged against his breastbone. It would have passed clean through him if it had not struck his carbine first.[32]

A portion of Maj. William Beardsley's 6th New York Cavalry advanced to an exposed hill to the left of the Williamsport Road, where Stuart had unlimbered a battery to sweep Devin's front. Under heavy fire, the 6th New York withdrew. "Major Beardsley was unable to reach the hill," Tom Devin confessed, "but was forced to retire into the woods under a hot fire." As a consequence, Devin dismounted both the 6th New York and 17th Pennsylvania, which held their position for more than two hours before they ran low on ammunition and had to retire. "Our men behaved splendidly, holding and even driving the enemy with their pistols after their carbine ammunition was expended," recounted the proud Devin.[33]

By 5:30 p.m., Devin's entire line was heavily engaged and nearly out of ammunition. After alerting Kilpatrick of his lack of cartridges, Devin had no choice but to withdraw. His men had spent much of the day in battle. Col. Nathaniel P. Richmond's brigade—Kilpatrick's men—supported by Federal artillery posted near Turner's Gap, rode up to fill the hole Devin's retreat opened in the line.[34]

Supporting Gamble's brigade, Calef's gunners fell back to the right of the town of Boonsboro before receiving orders to turn around and go back to the same position they had just left. While they were gone, enemy artillery worked its way closer to Calef's position, and enemy sharpshooters now occupied a nearby stone barn, from which they laid down a severe and effective fire. Into this maelstrom rode Calef's guns, which unlimbered and immediately came under heavy and accurate fire. Calef deployed the rest of his battery under fire and "by well-directed shots, [the Confederates] were driven, and as our skirmishers advanced, I took up a more advanced position with my battery, and opened again, but being nearly out of ammunition, only a few rounds were fired at their retreating cavalry," reported Calef.[35]

Col. Russell A. Alger, commander of the 5th Michigan Cavalry, held his regiment at the ready and waited for the right moment to strike. "Keep under cover boys till I want you," cried the colonel, "I will watch them!" Alger exposed himself to heavy fire as he watched for the ideal moment. When the time was right, he ordered his troopers to charge. "When the Fifth Michigan was ordered to charge up the Sharpsburg Road," wrote a newspaper correspondent, "the Colonel replied that he had no ammunition, but, nevertheless, would make the charge," which swept the road.[36] Since stout stone walls lined the local farm fields, Alger was forced to dismount his regiment. "We attacked them vigorously, driving [the enemy] out of his lines and far beyond," he recounted.[37] Several were killed and wounded including Alger himself who fell severely injured during his regiment's advance.[38] William L. Rockwell, also of the 5th Michigan, sent a letter to his wife after the battle. "[G]ot my middle finger wounded a little but not to bother me much," he wrote. "This is the eighth fight we have had with the Rebs and have whipped them every time. It was a horridable sight to see the miserable rebs lay mangled and wounded all over the ground. They fight desperately."[39]

As the confused back-and-forth fighting continued, Kilpatrick dashed off a dispatch to Pleasonton indicating that the Confederates had shoved Merritt's brigade back to the northern edge of Boonsboro, and that Buford, worried about being overwhelmed, was planning to withdraw to the safety of the heights of South Mountain. He would hang on in the town as long as he could, Kilpatrick affirmed, but when forced to do so, he would fall back on Buford, fighting as he went. Pleasonton knew the implication of Kilpatrick's missive: the mountain passes were in jeopardy of falling into enemy hands.[40]

George Meade knew it, too. From his headquarters at Middletown, the army commander directed Maj. Gen. Oliver O. Howard's 11th Corps to move rapidly and occupy the crest of South Mountain. Meade next turned to John Sedgwick's 6th Corps, ordering it to move into a position near Boonsboro where it could support Buford and Kilpatrick as they withdrew from the hotly contested valley west of the mountain range. "We came across some mountains," recounted Leander Schooley, a cavalryman attached to Howard's headquarters. "Our cavalry had been fighting the enemy on foot all day and had held them in check from morning till night. It was one of the greatest cavalry fights of the war," he proclaimed.[41]

Elements of the 6th and 11th Corps arrived near Boonsboro just before dark, adding significant weight to the thinned Union line. "I heard the booming of Artillery, and learned that our Cavalry under Kilpatrick and Buford was having a hard fight and were being driven towards the Gap, on the other side of the mountain," recounted a 1st Corps artillerist. "The 1st [sic] and 11th Corps marched up the pike at quick time, side-by-side, and we were soon filing through the Gap." A division of the 11th Corps immediately advanced in the twilight, deploying and driving Stuart's line of troopers back.[42] Other portions of the Army of the Potomac's infantry poured through the gaps in South Mountain and rushed as quickly as exhausted legs could to the sound of the guns. "Late this evening the Yankee cavalry was reinforced by infantry, and then they in turn drove us back about a mile, and to the same position we had when the fight commenced," wrote one of Chew's Southern gunners.[43]

Before the infantry arrived late that day, Gamble's and Merritt's men had been holding off the Confederate attacks for hours and, like Devin's men, were desperately short on cartridges. To allow them to replenish ammunition, Gamble and Merritt were briefly relieved by Kilpatrick's units and then reformed for a counterattack. "As soon as the Union cavalry had cleared our brigade the 1st U. S. gave the rebels the contents of their Sharps rifles," recalled one of the Regulars, "which demoralized them, and they started in the direction in which they came." The arrival of Union infantry and the advance of 11th Corps men hastened Stuart's withdrawal.[44]

As part of Stuart's line was falling back, Buford dismounted Gamble's brigade to repulse another flank movement and, supported by mounted troopers from Kilpatrick's division, counterattacked with the entire brigade, with Buford personally leading the assault. Gamble's men drove the Confederates from the woods under a heavy fire of artillery.[45] Sgt. Samuel Gilpin of the 3rd Indiana Cavalry had his horse knocked down by a stray artillery burst. "I (waiting by his side) was considerably stunned," wrote Gilpin in his diary, "I saw constellations that the astronomy makes no mention of. Neither self nor horse injured." The game Hoosier went back into battle, noting that "[we] fought them hard all day with alternative fortune. At night we were in full possession of the field having driven them back a long distance."[46]

"The artillery fire was heavy for a small fight," recalled a Southern horse artillerist, "for the enemy had ten pieces of artillery engaged and our side had about a like number in the fight."[47] "We succeeded in getting almost in their rear when they discovered us then commenced a grand race for life and liberty, the rebs running for their horses and we to intercept them," remembered one Federal trooper.[48] Though they held the field, Buford's men realized that they had dodged a bullet. "Had the daylight lasted another hour," wrote a member of the Reserve Brigade, "we would have suffered the most disastrous defeat."[49]

"About this time, I was informed that the enemy was heavily reinforced, and that our ammunition, by this protracted engagement, was nearly exhausted," explained Jeb Stuart in his Gettysburg campaign report, "and, despairing of getting possession of the town, which was completely commanded by artillery in the mountain gap, and believing that, in compelling the enemy to act upon the defensive (all that day retreating before us). . . . I began to retire."[50]

The Yankee troopers were ecstatic with their day's success. A member of the 8th Illinois wrote of his comrades in arms, "They are all bully boys, and they don't fear the Rebbs (sic) a bit . . . Gen. Buford says . . . the only fault he finds with us is that he can't stop us when we once get the Rebbs to running."[51]

"Our cavalry dismounted and fought them behind rocks, trees, and fences, and finally routed them, driving them some four miles on foot," proudly declared an Ohio horse soldier. "We were satisfied with our day's work, and felt that we owed the infantry, nothing," noted one Wolverine. "Thus closed one of our hardest fights; we had fought infantry, with more than two to our one, and whipped them clean from the field."[52]

Stuart's command fell back towards Funkstown, a small village of about 600 residents situated on the National Road and along the banks of Antietam

Creek.[53] Gamble's dismounted troopers chased Stuart's command nearly three miles in the dark, with a badly winded John Buford leading the pursuit in person. "The men had run so fast that they were completely tired out, but were pleased to see General Buford shake his fat sides, as he attempted to keep up with them. He said, 'These boys beat anything in the world in a foot skirmish,'" chortled the regimental surgeon of the 8th Illinois Cavalry.[54]

After being driven back across Beaver Creek, the Confederates took up a strong defensive position approximately four miles northwest of the day's battlefield. As pursuing Union troopers approached, the dismounted troopers of the 1st North Carolina Cavalry and Chew's battery opened fire on them and the pursuit ended with the Federals withdrawing to the previous night's campsite near Boonsboro.

After successfully preventing the Federals from reaching General Lee's infantry columns filtering toward the river, Jeb Stuart's weary horsemen camped near Funkstown. They had had little rest since the retrograde began, and this day's fighting, so near the swollen Potomac River, portended that no rest would be forthcoming any time soon. The Confederates' jaded mounts also needed rest and quality forage in order to keep up their diminishing strength. The overall situation looked bleak. A corporal of the Jeff Davis Legion of cavalry in Wade Hampton's Brigade succinctly jotted down his thoughts in the gathering darkness for his diary. "Raining very hard and river rising very fast," he observed.[55] The corporal thought for a moment about how dire the conditions and situation of Lee's army were before adding ominously, "It looks like the Yanks will get us."[56]

Aftermath

Even though the Confederates had gotten the better of them, General Pleasonton's troopers had performed admirably under very adverse circumstances.[57] George Custer was certainly surprised by the day's work. That morning, the alarmed Union officer told his Wolverines that he did not expect to drive the Rebel horsemen, saying that he only hoped to hold them long enough for the infantry to come up and relieve the hard-pressed cavalry. "In the evening he came to us and said we done bully and ordered some regiments close by to give us three cheers," reported a pleased William L. Rockwell of the 5th Michigan. "We returned the compliment by giving three cheers for General Kilpatrick."[58]

"They are trying to force their way through the place," noted another member of the 5th Michigan, "the battle was very sharp. Commenced at 10 o'clock A.M. & lasted till sundown. The Rebels appeared to gain on us till 6 o'clock when we made a charge & drove them 3 miles out of sight & hearing."[59]

Stuart put forward his strongest foot when discussing the outcome of the fight. "The desired object had been fully attained," he wrote in his report of the campaign. Although his men withdrew from the Boonsboro combat, they had kept the aggressive Federal cavalry away from the main body of Lee's army and inflicted sizeable casualties in the process.[60] Both sides suffered about 80 killed and wounded each in the day's fighting.

These accounts provide a fascinating perspective on how every soldier participating in a battle sees it from his personal viewpoint. It is not uncommon for men in the same unit to see the same action very differently. Also, the difference between the way the soldier sees things on the ground, and the true strategic or operational outcome of an operation, often do not agree. These descriptions of the fighting at Boonsboro clearly indicate the different perspectives of the Northerners and Southerners who fought there. One Federal claimed his side "routed" the Rebels, while another from the Reserve Brigade claimed that had daylight lasted another hour, the Union cavalry would have suffered a disastrous defeat. Still other Federals claimed victory because they drove Stuart's men at the end of the day. However, an analysis of the results of the fighting makes it clear that Stuart's men successfully carried out their mission of screening Lee's infantry, and must be considered the victors of Boonsboro. "Here, near Boonsboro, Stuart did some of his hardest fighting [of the campaign], and successfully held his ground," explained Capt. John Esten Cooke, one of Stuart's staff officers.[61] The men, Cooke continued, "spent another night laying in their lines of battle, awaiting another counterattack by the Confederates."[62]

As the Union and Confederate horse soldiers were slugging it out at Boonsboro, Halleck was burning up the telegraph wires. "The President is urgent and anxious that your army should move against [Lee] by forced marches," he wrote to General Meade, whose own patience with Washington meddling was wearing thin. The Army of Northern Virginia, he replied, remained on the north bank of the Potomac between Funkstown and Williamsport. "My army is and has been making forced marches, short of rations and barefooted. I take occasion to repeat that I will use my utmost effort to push forward this army."[63]

Lee Chooses a Defensive Position

While the fighting was raging at Boonsboro, Robert E. Lee and his generals were hard at work selecting the main defensive position for the Virginia army. Accompanied by his three corps commanders, James Longstreet, A. P. Hill, and Richard Ewell, Lee reconnoitered the ground from Hagerstown south to Williamsport. The officers spent the entire day in the saddle trying to identify a formidable defensive position. Their ride consumed the entire day and part of the next morning, July 9, during which Generals Lee, Ewell, Hill, and Jubal Early continued their reconnaissance. When he was satisfied, the Confederate commander ordered his engineers to get to work. The new Confederate line would run along the prominent Salisbury Ridge, which offered clear fields of fire across most of the front. Both flanks would be firmly anchored, one end by the Conococheague Creek at Williamsport and the other at Dam No. 4 along the Potomac River.[64] When it was complete, the position was every bit as formidable as the one held during the Battle of Fredericksburg the previous December.[65]

General Lee established his headquarters at the home of David Atter, located on the National Road about two miles outside Hagerstown. Lee and his staff used Atter's home as their base of operations for the remainder of the Army of Northern Virginia's time in Maryland.[66]

The Federal Infantry

Throughout the day, the remainder of the Federal infantry continued slogging through the heavy rains toward its concentration point at Middletown. As Howard and Sedgwick prepared to take up their assigned positions, the Federal 1st Corps deployed in line of battle at Crampton's Gap.[67] Expecting to go into battle at any moment, they threw up crude stone breastworks and then, with nothing more to do, waited.[68] A dispatch from Meade to Halleck informed the Washington general that enemy horsemen had driven the Federal cavalry to the edge of Boonsboro, and that he was making a forced march with the rest of the army, though short on rations and with many of his soldiers barefoot. The men, Meade added, were under orders to push themselves. "I expect to find the enemy in a strong position, well covered with artillery," he told Halleck, "and I do not desire to imitate his example at Gettysburg and assault a position where the chances were so greatly against success." The army commander concluded with a prophetic pronouncement. "I wish in advance to moderate the expectations of those, who, in ignorance of the difficulties to be encountered, may expect too much. All that I can do under the circumstances I pledge this army to do."[69]

The crossing of South Mountain exacted a heavy toll on the army's men and horses. "It seemed to me the longest day I ever saw," complained an exhausted member of the 11th Corps later that night. "[W]e had to cross a range of mountains. It commenced raining about six o'clock and was so dark we could hardly see anything. Some of the boys would fall down in the mud, but get up again laughing and trudge along."[70]

Plenty of hard work remained. "Few of the batteries had forage and horse after horse would give out and be abandoned," remembered an officer. "The march of the 8th was through muddy roads, while firing in the distance indicated the meeting of pursuers and pursued," recalled a member of the 10th Massachusetts Infantry of the 6th Corps.[71] When they finally arrived near Middletown, the men of the 6th Corps changed their clothes and ate a decent meal for the first time in many days before taking their place in the line of battle.[72]

Middletown sits in a lovely valley bisected by the National Road. "The beautiful green of the meadows and the rich golden yellow of the wheat fields, with orchards here and there, made a scene not altogether strange to us," observed a Vermonter of the 6th Corps, "and I know made many a noble fellow's heart ache for a moment as it carried him home to scenes many of his comrades were never to look upon again." After a short rest, the 6th Corps moved out again. Eventually the soldiers realized that they could move faster by cutting across the fields than by sticking to the roads, "so the head of the column was turned across a splendid wheat field, much to the disgust of the farmer, whose protests did not seem to do much good, more than to create a laugh at his expense. We left him scowling and no doubt swearing as long as there was a Yankee in sight."[73] Sedgwick's corps managed only five miles that afternoon and evening.

The 1st Corps' march was no easier. "We arrived at Hamburg, just on top of the mountain, at dark, wet and weary and the five Batteries were crowded into a little open space not large enough to park one Battery decently," remembered a New York artillerist assigned to the 1st Corps, "but it was the best we can do, as the rain was falling in torrents, the night was pitchy dark and the horses were unable to go down mountains." The gunner left a vivid description of the hardships faced by the Army of the Potomac as it pursued Lee's Virginia army. "The friends at home can hardly conceive the privations and hardships a soldier has to undergo in a campaign like this, he explained. "You may think it strange, but I saw many a poor fellow struggling up the mountain that day, with his heavy knapsack, haversack, gun and canteen, and his bare feet exposed to the sharp, cutting rocks—having worn out his shoes on the long marches. And dozens of others I saw who had sunk down by the road side from fatigue, unable to proceed another step. But all these hardships are forgotten by the soldiers as soon as he gets into camp," he continued, "and he scarcely remembers them as a dream. One good night's rest, and he is ready and willing to go through with them again, if necessary."[74]

When the infantry of Brig. Gen. John Robinson's division, 1st Corps, reached the summit of Catoctin Mountain, he gathered his men together and read the dispatches announcing U.S. Grant's stunning victory at Vicksburg. "Soldiers, the news of your glorious victory at Gettysburg has been telegraphed to the West," Robinson declared. "I propose three cheers for Grant and his army, feeling assured that while we shout their victories from this mountain top, they are shouting our victory along the Mississippi Valley." The men complied, and their cheers echoed from the mountaintop. Re-energized by the great news from Vicksburg, the men trudged on again.[75]

After marching fourteen sloppy miles in a driving rain, the men of the 1st Corps arrived near Boonsboro after dark. With artillery still booming in the distance, the tired soldiers threw up breastworks in case Lee's army attacked. They wouldn't finish building their works until about midnight, when they settled down to try to rest in the cold rain.[76]

"Some portion of the road over which we marched was Macadamized and covered only with a slight coating of thin mud and shallow pools of slush; but in other places the mud was deep, and several of my men who had lost one of their shoes 'away down under ground' and thrown away the other, kept their pants rolled above their knees and declared they would 'wade it through bare-footed, sink or swim,'" recalled an officer of a 3rd Corps regiment.[77]

The 3rd Corps arrived in Frederick that day, and its men were happy to see friendly faces among the populace. They had previously passed through the quaint town on their way to their date with destiny in Pennsylvania. "I do think, without exaggeration, when we that day retraced our steps through Frederick City we were the most unsoldierly, sorry looking victorious Veteran Army it has been the lot of any human being of this country to look upon," recalled a New Yorker. "For two days we had been bespattering each other with mud and slush, and soaked with rain which was then pouring in torrents. Our guns and swords were covered with rust; our pockets were filled with dirt; muddy water oozed from the toes of the footmen's government shoes at every step, ran out of the tops of the horsemen's boots and dropped from the ends of the fingers, noses, and chins of all."[78]

Many of the Federal soldiers were barefooted, having worn out their shoes during weeks of hard marching and harder fighting.[79] Nevertheless, the bedraggled veterans plodded on, buoyed by the prospect of bringing the Confederates to battle with the raging Potomac at their back.

The Federals of the 5th Corps were treated to one of Mother Nature's most impressive spectacles. As they passed the crest of Catoctin Mountain during mid-morning, a violent thunderstorm filled the sky above them. "Upon the summit we were amid the clouds and in the center of the storm," recounted Capt. Francis Donaldson of the 118th Pennsylvania. "The lightning tore and ripped through the clouds which were so dense as to resemble steam, add the rain in maddening torrents poured down the mountain pathways." As they descended the west side of the mountain, the clouds parted, exposing the warm sun, which spread its rays over the beautiful valley below, illuminating the peaceful village of Middletown.[80]

The 2nd Corps arrived at Monocacy Junction on July 8. "Many of the men availed themselves of the opportunity of a good bath in the Monocacy," recorded the historian of the 106th Pennsylvania, "and a wash and a clean up, after that muddy march of about twenty miles was necessary as well as refreshing."[81]

Lt. Col. Greely S. Curtis of the 1st Massachusetts Cavalry of Huey's brigade was in Frederick that day, stricken with symptoms of malaria. In a letter to Maj. Henry L. Higginson of the regiment, who was home in Boston following a serious wound suffered at the June 17 battle at Aldie, Virginia, Curtis recounted the scenes and the sounds:

> The army has been moving through here to-day and yesterday. We hear that the rebs are crossing at Williamsport. I never thought we could overtake them between Gettysburg and W'msport, the map will show you why, but I did hope and fairly believe that Halleck would know enough to try to cut off their retreat with fresh troops either on this side of the river or in the valley of the Shenandoah. Hurrah for Vicksburg! If we only follow these scoundrels up vigorously, we can sit down under our Thanksgiving fig-tree and eat the turkey thereof . . . [82]

By the night of July 8, most of the Army of the Potomac was in the vicinity of Middletown, Maryland. The army was badly in need of shoes and other supplies, and a pause was necessary to accommodate the distribution of these much-needed items. One Federal soldier noted that, while Meade received a great deal of criticism for his perceived lack of aggression in pursuing Lee's army and for delaying at Middletown, "it is readily understood that his stopping was only such a measure as the laws of humanity demanded, and that nothing was lost by this delay, for the men, somewhat rested and refreshed by their short halt, were in a much better condition to resume their work in the morning, which they did with renewed zeal."[83]

A soldier of the 15th New Jersey Infantry of the 6th Corps described the march down the other side of Catoctin Mountain. "Down, down [the mountain] we came, hobbling over rocks and wading through mud and water, into a fertile valley in which Middletown is located, whence we proceeded," he wrote. "Rations being out, the men complained considerably, but we soon received three days' rations of hard tack and salt pork, which we devoured with avidity. During the afternoon we cleaned our pieces, received a mail, and heard of the fall of Vicksburg."[84]

News of Maj. Gen. Ulysses S. Grant's tremendous victory at Vicksburg immediately bolstered the morale of the cheering troops.[85] "This was the occasion of much jubilation on the part of the boys of the Regiment," recalled a member of the 19th Maine Infantry.[86]

Middletown "is where our forces under McClellan attacked the rebels one year ago, resulting in the victory of South Mountain," noted an officer of the 1st Pennsylvania Cavalry. "Our army is advancing on the same road that McClellan did then, and I look for another battle, perhaps on the old Antietam ground. The result is easily foretold, for our army is stronger now from reinforcements than before the Battle of Gettysburg. Meade's army," he continued, "is moving rapidly and I hope will compel Lee to fight again in Maryland. He is not moving at the rate of six miles a day as the young Napoleon did, but twenty, and that, too, after fighting one of the hardest contested battles of the war."[87]

That night, Col. Milton J. Ferguson led a reconnaissance of forty handpicked troopers of the 17th Virginia Cavalry in the direction of the day's battlefield at Boonsboro. Trooper James Hodam accompanied this scouting mission. The Confederates rode to the right of the day's lines and found no sign of the enemy, who had withdrawn to the protection of the Army of the Potomac's guns frowning down from atop South Mountain. "From our observation and what we could learn from citizens the enemy was preparing to advance in force along the Antietam valley." Ferguson sent the 17th Virginia out to picket the Boonsboro road while the balance of the brigade fell back to Jones' Crossroads, just north of the old Antietam battlefield, and only a couple of miles from the College of St. James.[88]

Kilpatrick's and Buford's horse soldiers were without rations that night, and suffered accordingly. They had left their trains behind, and had to live off the land. "This is the third day since our men were out of rations, and as their money is pretty much gone, it leaves them in a hungry condition," observed one of Kilpatrick's officers. "The officers are still worse off than the men, as we draw no rations, having to forage for our grub. For two days I had nothing except two pieces of hard tack, except a breakfast we got at a farm house, which consisted entirely of coffee, lettuce, and radishes."[89]

In an effort to keep Meade fully informed, Buford sent a dispatch to the commander with the intelligence he had obtained that day. "The [Potomac] river is 5 feet higher than before, and rising. I have drawn in close to [Boonsboro], to sleep. My train has been interfered with by the Eleventh Corps. I hope it may arrive in the night. There are no rebs this side of Antietam; none on the old battle-ground, and none at Sharpsburg. Plenty of them, however, can be found between Greencastle and Williamsport and between Hagerstown and Williamsport."[90] News of Grant's Vicksburg victory also triggered happiness in Buford's camp, where his men settled down to a night of well-deserved rest.

"We have been marched night and day since the battle but owing to the fearful condition of the roads could not make much headway," explained a captain of the 118th Pennsylvania, 5th Corps. He also noted that his boots had been worn out for some time, and that he was nearly barefooted. Nevertheless, the spirits of he and the men of his company remained high with the hope that Lee would be trapped and destroyed above the Potomac River.[91] "Our forces are harassing the enemy on every side," wrote an officer of the 10th Massachusetts about the previous day's actions.[92]

The Northern foot soldiers knew how high the stakes were. "I hope we shall be able to destroy Lee and his Army before they get back across the Potomac for I do not want to chase them down through the state of Virginia again," complained an officer of a Massachusetts infantry regiment. The question of whether they would get that opportunity remained open for vigorous debate.[93]

"These night marches unless rendered absolutely necessary by some movements of the enemy never pay," grumbled the commander of the 93rd Pennsylvania, part of the 6th Corps. "The guides lose their way, one regiment loses another, or else hurries its men off their legs to keep in sight of the regt in advance. Men get asleep in the halts and are left behind are able to straggle from the column at any moment, consume more time at difficult crossings in picking their way, etc. etc. and are more worn out anyhow."[94]

Brig. Gen. William F. "Baldy" Smith commanded the militia troops from the Department of the Susquehanna, who were making their way to join Meade. Smith faced a stern task in trying to make these men useful to the war effort, and he knew it. "My command is an incoherent mass, and, if it is to join the Army of the Potomac, I would suggest that the brigades, five in number, be attached to old divisions, and thus disperse the greenness," he wrote candidly. "They cannot be maneuvered, and as a command it is quite helpless, excepting in the kind of duty I have kept them on in the mountains." His advance was hindered by a lack of supplies, and by the rugged terrain. After reporting that he still had approximately 4,000 men after nearly half that number had deserted on the march, he concluded, "I am utterly powerless, without aid and in the short time allotted, to infuse any discipline into these troops, and for the reasons given above make the suggestion as being for the best interests of the service."[95] Most of them were footsore, and most were unaccustomed to the trials and tribulations of arduous service. They had virtually no training, and little discipline.[96]

The prospect of commanding this wretched force amidst the Army of the Potomac's veterans was a humiliating one for Smith. As recently as four months earlier he had been the commander of the 6th Corps, but was relieved when a letter he wrote complaining about Maj. Gen. Ambrose E. Burnside, who was then in command of the army, was discovered.[97] Two days earlier on July 6, Smith had begged Darius Couch, "If you send an order for this command to report to Meade, will you at the same time order me to return to you, leaving [Brig. Gen. Joseph] Knipe in command? You can appreciate how unpleasant it would be for me to serve under existing circumstances with the Army of the Potomac."[98] Couch denied his request. Humiliation would be his to bear.

Although the Union high command seemed willing to believe that these raw, unreliable troops could tip the balance in the effort to bring Lee to battle, Smith's unflinching assessment of the poor quality of his command left little doubt about its lack of usefulness. Obviously, Meade would not be able to rely upon these men.

Major General William French's division arrived from Harpers Ferry and formally became a part of the 3rd Corps that day. The corps' existing three divisions were consolidated into two as a consequence of their heavy losses at

Gettysburg, with French's command becoming the corps' third division. French formally assumed command of the 3rd Corps, replacing the wounded Maj. Gen. Daniel Sickles, who lost a leg to a solid artillery shot on the second day at Gettysburg. "We soon found ourselves in the midst of the great army, cheek by jowl with the men who fought under McDowell, and McClellan, and Pope, and Burnside, and Hooker, as principals," noted a member of the 10th Massachusetts Battery, "and now were fresh from the glory fields of Gettysburg, where Reynolds, of previous memory, and Buford, and Hancock, and Sickles, had immortalized themselves; and we rejoiced at our good fortune in being thus associated."[99]

Not all shared the enthusiasm of the Bay Stater. "His [French's] appointment was a great disappointment to the Third Corps troops, who were anxious that General Birney should be the successor of the gallant Sickles," reported the historian of Battery E, 1st Rhode Island Light Artillery.[100] "From this time the spirit of the Third Corps was broken," observed an early biographer of Maj. Gen. David B. Birney, "and its hallowed associations and strong bond of union could not preserve its identity after the old members were overwhelmed by the tide of new-comers."[101]

Colonel Philippe Regis de Trobriand probably put it best. "While we were fighting in Virginia, they had guarded the railroads, and garrisoned Harpers Ferry, Winchester, and Martinsburg, where they had made but a poor show, when Ewell had presented himself. Amongst us they took the place of those we had left on the field of battle at Chancellorsville and Gettysburg," continued de Trobriand, "but they did not replace those. What the Third Corps gained in numbers it lost in homogeneity. On this account the new-comers were never fully naturalized in the corps. The veterans of Sickles, refractory to the union, maintained their autonomy by the designation universally adopted amongst them: 'The Third Corps, as we understand it.'"[102]

French's Harpers Ferry command had little combat experience. "We are now beginning to see a little service, nothing but hard tack, pork and coffee, which we have to cook ourselves, but I still like it," observed a Massachusetts artillerist of French's command. "In fact I like the whole thing. I think I shall fat up on it. Being tough, will eat, drink, and sleep together."[103]

While the 3rd Corps had been chopped to bits on July 2 and was badly under-strength, its veterans resented the influx of inexperienced new soldiers, who lacked the *esprit d'corps* that marked its ranks.

Even in the terrible weather, the advancing army made quite an impression. "The long lines of ammunition and forage wagons stretching with their white coverings as far as the eye could reach on every road, pressing noisily on in seeming confusion, yet really moving harmoniously under a definite system without any collision; the long, dark blue columns of infantry, their bayonets glistening in the sun, winding down across Middletown Valley and up the opposite slope in advance of the trains," recalled the same Bay State artillerist, "and the bodies of troops temporarily bivouacking by the roadside waiting to take their proper place in column, or perhaps lunching upon hard-tack and coffee after a forced march, combined to give us our first distinct impressions of a large army in motion."[104]

Another one of French's men, a soldier of the 126th Ohio, shared a similar impression. "Of this grand army words seemed meaningless to convey to the reader's mind an idea of its immensity and grandeur—the vast multitude, the martial music, the tramp, tramp, tramp of soldiers; colors flying, horses neighing, cattle lowing, the immense trains of wagons and artillery stretching for miles," admired the Ohio soldier, who was seeing the majesty of the entire Army of the Potomac on the move for the first time.[105]

The 3rd Corps marched another nine miles to South Mountain, bivouacking on the September 1862 battlefield, camping near where Maj. Gen. Jesse Reno fell. The sight of the small stone marking the spot where Reno fell left a sad impression on the men.[106]

The men of the Army of the Potomac remained in wretched condition. Early that morning, Howard sent a note to Brig. Gen. Gouverneur K. Warren, the army's acting chief of staff. "I have not yet gotten shoes and stockings," he wrote. "About one-half of my command are now destitute, or have shoes too poor to march." Although Howard took steps to get supplies to his ragged command, they still needed a lot of supplies in order to be effective.[107]

"I think we shall have another battle before Lee can cross the river, though from all accounts he is making great efforts to do so," wrote Meade to his wife on the night of July 8. "For my part, as I have to follow and fight him I would rather do it at once and in Maryland than to follow into Virginia." After downplaying his role in the victory at Gettysburg, Meade offered great insight into the condition of his army when he described his own plight. "From the time I took command till to-day, now over ten days, I have not changed my clothes, have not had a regular night's rest, and many nights not a wink of sleep, and for several days did not even wash my face and hands, no regular food, and all the time in a great state of mental anxiety. Indeed, I think I have not lived as much in this time as in the last thirty years."[108]

Meade reported to Halleck that Lee's army had entrenched in a line from Falling Waters to Hagerstown. Halleck responded that Meade should "postpone a general battle till you can concentrate all your forces and get up your reserves and reinforcements." The general-in-chief warned Meade against "partial combats," and promised reinforcements from the militia forces gathered in Pennsylvania and from the garrisons at Harpers Ferry and Frederick. Meade obeyed, waiting for his army to concentrate before preparing an all-out assault on the Confederate lines.[109]

That night, Meade circulated a general order directing the movements of his army the next day. The 6th Corps would move to Boonsboro via the National Road, with the 11th Corps marching behind it. The 5th Corps would move along the old Sharpsburg Road to Rohrersville via Turner's Gap, with the 3rd Corps bringing up the rear. The 12th Corps was also ordered to march to Rohrersville, with the 2nd Corps trailing behind it. The 1st Corps was ordered to occupy Turner's Gap near the Mountain House. Meade's army was slowly moving west, advancing toward Lee's positions along the Potomac. Wherever possible, they used the National Road to expedite travel, since the macadamized surface was not as subject to the ravages of the heavy rains as the dirt roads that crisscrossed the Maryland countryside.[110]

Chapter 11

July 9: Sniping Along the Lines

"The game of war went on with determination on one side and desperation on the other."

— Member of the Federal Iron Brigade

AT THE COLLEGE OF ST. JAMES, just south of Hagerstown, Rector Kerfoot had his hands full now that the Federal cavalry had withdrawn from the area. On the morning of July 9, Kerfoot lamented in his diary that the college had been "Overrun by the guerilla cavalry at dawn, and for some hours." The "guerilla cavalry" were the troopers of Col. Milton J. Ferguson's Southern brigade, who camped in the field south of the college the previous night. They were "bad fellows," Kerfoot continued, noting that on July 9 he had to "lock every door; importunate for food for men and horses. Most of them, personally, courteous. Our troops (we discover) hold Boonsboro and the roads west and south of it. . . . But every sign now of this vicinity being a battle-ground."[1]

Just to the west of the campus sits the stately white home of Bai-Yuka plantation, the family home of Capt. James Breathed, commander of the 1st Stuart Horse Artillery. Breathed was a graduate of the College of St. James, and his father, John W. Breathed, sat on the College's board of trustees. Not even these important familial and political connections saved the area from the depredations of Ferguson's ruffians. Eventually, the main Confederate line of battle passed right through the grounds of Bai-Yuka, which Breathed naturally tried to visit. As Breathed rode toward his boyhood home, a member of the St. James faculty who shared Reverend Kerfoot's Unionist sympathies recognized the former student. The instructor reported the gunner's approach to nearby Federal soldiers, who launched themselves in hot pursuit. Breathed escaped, much to the chagrin of the loyal faculty of the College.[2]

Captain James Breathed, commander, Breathed's Battery, Stuart's Horse Artillery.

NARA

While Breathed tried to visit his family, tired Yankee troopers spent most of July 9 resting. Judson Kilpatrick suffered from a painful kidney disorder called Bright's Disease, which was often exacerbated by spending long stints in the saddle. The travails of the past several days triggered a flare-up; pain confined him to a wagon.[3] Resting in camp, one of Custer's men heard about the surrender of the Confederate garrison at Vicksburg. "We think they will soon surrender here, then we will try to take Richmond," he announced. "Then you may look for me home if the good Lord sees fit to still continue to shield me on the field of battle."[4] While most of the weary Yankee troopers wrote letters home or slept, Southern horsemen spent much of the day in the field, searching for intelligence about the dispositions of the Federals.

Federal cavalry from fresh units continued roaming the countryside, grabbing up stragglers and hunting for enemy activity. Troopers of Col. John E. Wynkoop's 20th Pennsylvania Cavalry, an emergency regiment raised to meet the threat of the Confederate invasion of the Keystone State, served with Baldy Smith's command from the defenses of Harrisburg. Some of Wynkoop's men fanned out, searching for stragglers. On July 9, a detachment of forty troopers captured fifty Confederate prisoners and three wagons between Greencastle and Hagerstown. The commander of this detachment estimated that there were nearly 1,000 wagons in the train, but his force was too small to capture so large a prize. The active and pesky Union cavalry continued harassing the enemy, agitating the Southerners and picking them off wherever possible.[5]

Much of Meade's infantry also spent the day resting. The men of the Iron Brigade sat in their camps, listening to the clatter of artillery wheels rolling along the roads. Preparations for a possible attack against Lee's defensive position were being made. "The game of war went on with determination on one side and desperation on the other," keenly observed a member of the Iron Brigade.[6] Few of the infantrymen enjoyed their new surroundings. They carried no baggage and had no tents to shelter them from the driving rain. "I have not slept in a dry blanket or had on dry clothing since crossing the Potomac before the battle," complained Col. Rufus R. Dawes of the 6th Wisconsin, whose regiment had lost heavily in the fighting for the unfinished railroad cut on July 1. "If we can end this war right here, I will cheerfully abide the terrible risk of another battle, and certainly personal discomforts are small comparatively."[7]

The men of the 1st Massachusetts Battery had been on the move for four days, "but this forenoon are compelled to stop for the shoes are about all off of our horses and both they and the men are about played out," observed one of the battery's gunners. "At any rate I know this Army never was put through so before by an Gen[eral] we ever had. The boys bear it like Martyrs saying if we can only get at them again before they get out of Maryland and get as good a Ration of Rebs as we did at Gettysburg that Lee's army will look rather small although our own loss was no trifle but theres was much larger than ours." The men spent the day cleaning and drying their clothes for the first time in almost a week.[8]

General Meade established army headquarters at the South Mountain House, an inn located on the National Road at Turner's Gap. The area had been the focus of most of the hardest fighting during the September 14, 1862 battle of South Mountain. Many in his army remembered how they had fought their way up these deadly slopes just ten months earlier. The men "discussed the possibilities of a renewal of those trying scenes. Such a reflection is not the sweetest, even to the patriot."[9] A soldier in the 1st Corps hoped for a more final result this time, adding, "Over this same mountain, and along this same road, and with much of the same spirit, we were then, as now, in close pursuit of the rebels. Let us hope for a more decisive issue."[10] The men of the 1st Corps remained behind their breastworks all day as rumors flew that a major battle with Lee's army was imminent.[11] "We are near the enemy," Maj. Gen. Oliver O. Howard wrote on July 9. "Lee has not yet crossed the Potomac and we must have one more trial. God grant us success in the next battle. He has preserved us so many times, I begin to feel that He might do so to the end." Time would tell whether the pious one-armed general was correct.[12] That night, the men of the Union infantry slept on their arms and with their accouterments buckled, ready at a moment's warning to march out and meet the enemy. As the hours ticked past, orders to do so never arrived.[13]

That evening, Meade circulated a general order outlining the movements of the army for the following day, July 10. The 12th Corps, followed by the 2nd Corps, was to move at daylight, passing through Keedysville to take up a position near Bakersville. The 5th Corps would wait until the 12th Corps reached Keedysville before marching to the bridge over Antietam Creek, then on the road from Boonsboro to Williamsport to take up a position near the branch road leading to Tilghmanton. The 3rd Corps would follow the 5th Corps and take up a position at the bridge over the Antietam, where it could support either the 5th or 6th corps. The 6th Corps, followed by the 1st Corps, would march along the Hagerstown Pike and take up a position on the north side of Beaver Creek near Funkstown. The 11th Corps, meanwhile, would move to the northwest side of Boonsboro, where it would be held in reserve to provide reinforcements wherever they might be needed.[14] The noose around Lee's lines was slowly but surely tightening.

* * *

When the Army of Northern Virginia reached Hagerstown, John Imboden informed General Lee that reinforcements were on their way to Meade from West Virginia via Hancock, Maryland. Imboden and his 62nd Virginia crossed the river on ferries to guard the Federal prisoners that George Pickett's men had escorted from Gettysburg. The 18th Virginia Cavalry, commanded by Imboden's brother, Col. George W. Imboden, was assigned to picket the roads in that direction. On July 9, Lee admonished Imboden to instruct his brother to "report only such [information] as he has reason to believe to be correct."[15] Lee also demonstrated that, in spite of the setbacks he had faced, he still maintained a sense of humor. "You know this country well enough to tell me whether it ever quits raining about here?" he asked Imboden. "If so, I should like to see a clear day soon."[16] Despite Imboden's successful shepherding of the wagon train of wounded to Williamsport and his brilliant fluid defense of the town on July 6, Lee remained skeptical about both the brigade commander and the horsemen under his command. The army leader confided to Jeb Stuart that he feared they were "unsteady" and "inefficient."[17]

Lt. Thomas L. Norwood of the 37th North Carolina was wounded at Gettysburg and captured. Norwood escaped and made his way back to Lee's lines. He reported that reinforcements were on their way to Meade from General Couch's command. This information deeply troubled Lee, who feared that veteran troops were on their way to reinforce the Army of the Potomac.

On July 10, Lee acknowledged information gathered by Stuart's scouts. "I hope your parties that you have sent out may gain us information of the enemy. It is much needed," he wrote his cavalry commander late that afternoon. Many things weighed heavily on his mind. In addition to his precarious strategic position, the army lacked fixed ammunition, forage, and flour. Worried that a Federal attack was imminent, Lee added, "We must prepare for a vigorous battle, and trust in the mercy of God and the valor of our troops." Lee redoubled his efforts to ascertain the precise dispositions of his enemy. His vigorous Southern probes disconcerted the Federals.[18]

Late on the afternoon of July 9, orders came for the Northern horsemen to mount up. Around 4:00 p.m., Buford ordered Devin to reconnoiter the Confederate positions west of the Beaver Creek bridge between the towns of Boonsboro and Funkstown. While scouting, Devin encountered a detachment of cavalry and artillery left by Stuart on high ground near his main line. About 5:30, Devin deployed a line of mounted skirmishers to sweep the left flank of the Confederates as far as a bend in Antietam Creek. Lt. Albert O. Vincent's combined batteries B and L, 2nd U.S. Artillery, supported the horse soldiers.

Devin dismounted two squadrons and, connecting with elements of Gamble's brigade on the left, advanced against the enemy line. Ferguson's Brigade held a prominent ridge overlooking the Boonsboro Road, and a battery of horse artillery under Capt. Thomas E. Jackson supported him. Grumble Jones rode up with his brigade on the right of Jackson's guns, while Chambliss' Brigade pulled up on the left. Three full brigades of Stuart's horse soldiers now held a strong position on the high ground overlooking Antietam Creek.

One company of the 17th Virginia Cavalry deployed as skirmishers. As their Yankee opposites advanced, both sides dashed for a rail fence about 300 hundred yards in front of each side's main line. The Virginians won the foot race and unleashed a potent volley in the faces of the Federals, who tried to use the protection of waist-high corn to cover their advance. The Southerners swept each row with their rifle fire, inflicting severe casualties.[19]

While the skirmishers dueled, Vincent's Union artillery picked out targets and opened on Ferguson's and Chambliss' positions. "The air above our heads seemed to be full of splinters, bark, and bullets but we were thus far safe and unhurt as the enemies [sic] bullets mostly struck the top of the fence or went over our heads," recalled a member of the 17th Virginia. Their position grew untenable when Chambliss' troopers gave way under Vincent's artillery fire, their withdrawal exposing Ferguson's left flank. When Chambliss' line crumbled, Devin's troopers advanced quickly against it.[20]

After a short and sharp fight, Devin's skirmishers took the crest while the left squadron ran into a large camp of Stuart's cavalry and quickly dispersed it. "The federal cavalry had advanced on the road so far as to nearly cut us off and I distinctly heard loud commands to halt, but in the confusion supposed it was our officers getting their men into line but it was not, it was the enemy, who had nearly overtaken us," wrote Virginia trooper James Hodam, who had advanced with his company and carried off a wounded comrade, all while suffering from a wound of his own. As his comrades fell back in the face of the powerful Union attacks, Hodam stumbled. Covered with his own blood, and feeling weak and sick, he leaned against a fence along the road in an effort to catch his breath.[21]

Pressing their advantage, Devin's and Gamble's brigades drove the Confederates.[22] "[We] drove them about 2 miles like fun," one of Gamble's troopers later recounted.[23] One member of the 8th New York succinctly described the action. "Out again. Found the rebels about 5 p.m. and made them get, up and get."[24] "Sometimes they run us and some times we run them until they brought up their infantry and we had to leave," recalled a member of the 1st Virginia Cavalry.[25] Stuart called upon Chew's Battery of horse artillery to help fend off the enemy attack. With darkness settling on the field, Chew's guns were only able to fire a couple rounds before it was too difficult to find suitable targets.[26]

Devin's men bivouacked on the field. It had been another good day for "Buford's Hard Hitter," as Devin was known to men in Buford's division.[27] "The enemy contested the ground with their usual earnestness," noted one of Gamble's Hoosiers, "but were forced back beyond Beaver Creek. The battle continued until late in evening and we stayed in line of battle."[28] Pleasonton proposed that Devin be promoted to brigadier general and assume the position left vacant by Elon Farnsworth's death at Gettysburg.[29]

A different commander, however, assumed the mantle of leading Farnsworth's former brigade. When Farnsworth fell on July 3, the brigade's senior colonel, Nathaniel P. Richmond of the 1st West Virginia Cavalry, stepped up and assumed command. On July 9, Col. Othneil de Forest, a 37-year-old Yale-educated broker from New York City, reported for duty. The colonel of the 5th New York Cavalry, de Forest had led the brigade prior to Farnsworth's elevation to general. Now, de Forest was returning as that outfit's senior colonel. His assumption of brigade command on July 10 returned Richmond to regimental command.[30]

* * *

During July 9, the 6th Corps advanced another few miles, with the right of the Army of the Potomac (consisting of the 6th Corps and 11th Corps) pivoting on the right, while the left, extending all the way to the Potomac River, closed on the stationary Virginia army. The 6th Corps halted at Boonsboro about noon, where the men pitched tents and passed an uneventful afternoon and evening. Sedgwick's soldiers knew the Union cavalry had driven the enemy horsemen from the town the day before. Most believed a large and decisive battle was in the offing.[31]

As the sun began to fall, the Confederates camped near Hagerstown built fires to settle in for another night of waiting. Maj. Gen. Lafayette McLaws walked his horse among the men of his division. Maj. Robert Stiles rode alongside him to see and hear for himself what he could about the condition of the soldiers. The men, wrote Stiles in his insightful account of the episode, "kept right on with what they happened to be doing when the General arrived—cooking, cleaning their arms and accouterments, or whatever else it might be."

"Well, boys, how are you?" inquired McLaws.

"We are all right, General."

"They say there are lots of those fellows over the way there."

"Well, they can stay there; we ain't offerin' to disturb 'em. We've had all the fighting we want just now; but if they ain't satisfied and want any more, all they've got to do is to come over and get their bellies full."

"Suppose they do come, sure enough, boys. What are you going to do with them?" McLaws asked.

"Why, just make the ground blue with 'em, that's all; just manure this here man's land with 'em. We ain't asking anything of them, but if they want anything of us, why, just let 'em come after it, and they can get all they want; but they'll wish they hadn't come."

"Well, now, I can rely upon that, can I?"

"You just bet your life you can, General. If we're asleep when they come, you just have us waked up, and we'll receive 'em in good style."

"Well, good night, boys. I'm satisfied."[32]

* * *

That evening, part of the Vermont Brigade of Sedgwick's 6th Corps came up in preparation for an attack on Lee's lines guarding the Potomac bridgehead. They were the first of Meade's infantry to reach the scene. Sedgwick could see part of Lee's army arrayed in front of him near Funkstown, and Uncle John was ready to pitch in the next day. He was within easy marching distance of Funkstown, and ready to move out quickly if needed. Buford's cavalry was ordered to drive in Confederate outposts and clear the roads for the advancing infantry. The rest of the Union infantry followed behind, but the thick mud made marching a challenge. "The army is worn out with toil and suffering," reported Col. Rufus R. Dawes of the 6th Wisconsin Infantry. His men had been on the move for nearly a week without a break, and many were without shoes. His regimental surgeons had been left at Gettysburg to care for the thousands of wounded, and Dawes had to share a horse with another man.[33]

Pursuant to Meade's prior orders, all seven Federal infantry corps continued marching along the west side of South Mountain to establish a line of battle opposite the stout defensive line being forged by Lee's Virginia army. If everything fell into place, Meade's corps would be in a position to close the ring around Lee.[34] Meade harbored few illusions about the formidable task facing him. "The army (both men and animals) is very much exhausted," he wrote that same evening to Baldy Smith, "and cannot advance as rapidly as desired."[35]

Meade needed all the reinforcements he could get, and every available man was being sent to the front to join the Army of the Potomac in its efforts to catch and destroy Lee. One of the regiments rustled up for this purpose was the 39th Massachusetts, a regiment that had not seen any action in the field. To date, the men had enjoyed cushy garrison duty in the Washington defenses. Along with another green unit, the 34th Massachusetts, the two regiments received marching orders on July 9.

After doing nothing but provost duty, the Bay Staters were eager to ship out to the front. "Though the Washington tour of duty was free from long marches, the risk of battle and the privations of camp, there was ever the thought that the service was not strictly ideal for real soldiers, hence the willingness with which dress coats and other form of superfluous clothing were packed against their possible need in the following winter," noted a member of the 39th. "Contents for the knapsacks were chosen with considerable more judgment than would have been used nine months before."[36]

To these green and still naive soldiers, nothing could be more exciting than boarding the trains for a rush into the combat zone.

Chapter 12

July 10: The Second Battle of Funkstown

"Our brigade seems to be doing all the fighting. As usual."

— Samuel Gilpin, 3rd Indiana Cavalry, Col. William Gamble's brigade

Funkstown is an old village that rests in a loop of Antietam Creek. It was only four miles south of Hagerstown, and the National Road passed through it. About 1760, two German immigrant brothers, Jacob and Henry Funck, purchased the land and founded the town. Seven years later, there were fifteen log cabins and a gristmill in the town, which was originally known as "Jerusalem." When the town was incorporated in 1840, the name was changed to Funkstown. In addition to the gristmill, the town soon boasted a paper mill, a sawmill, and a woolen mill, as well as several taverns. German immigrants filled the new village, meaning that visitors were just as likely to hear German as they were English.

One of the most prominent structures was an attractive stone building known as South's Hotel, which made the town a popular stop on the National Road. Next to the Shafer gristmill was a handsome 1833 three-arch stone bridge. Built in the fashion of the so-called "Burnside's Bridge" on the Antietam battlefield, the structure carried the National Road 109 feet across Antietam Creek. Another stone bridge across the same creek connected Funkstown with Hagerstown. Funkstown, wrote a member of Battery C of the 1st Rhode Island Artillery, assigned to the 6th Corps, was "one of the principal villages washed by Antietam Creek, and boasts a population of seven or eight hundred."[1] Like Boonsboro, Funkstown had suddenly took on a significant value, for it commanded both the creek and the National Road. It was, then, almost inevitable that the armies would find one another there.[2]

On the morning of July 10, Buford dismounted his brigades along the National Road near Boonsboro under a light rain that would fall all day.

Deploying his line quickly, Buford placed Gamble in the center, Merritt on the right, and Devin on the left. The three brigades pressed across Beaver Creek, where they soon encountered Confederate videttes. The Southern soldiers were expecting the Federals to approach from the north, not from the east.[3]

"[T]he ball opened at once in earnest," Gamble later reported. "They shelled our skirmishers, which our batteries returned with interest." Gamble's dismounted soldiers advanced at "a rappid walk," as one of his Illinoisans described it.[4] When skirmishers of Devin's and Merritt's brigades appeared, and Buford's artillery found the range, Stuart's troopers began retiring toward Funkstown, three miles behind them. A Hoosier of Gamble's brigade noted, "We drove them beyond Antietam on the left and to Funkstown on this road. The fight has been in earnest."[5]

At Funkstown, Stuart deployed his men in a crescent-shaped line running from the J. W. Stonebraker farm on their left, across the western end of Samuel Baker's fields, and through the D. Stockslager farm to the south. The line spread westward across the St. Stauffer farm before ending south of town on the Jacob Hauck farm, which overlooked Antietam Creek. Jones' and Fitz Lee's brigades held the left wing, with Ferguson's, Chambliss', Robertson's, and Baker's brigades holding the right. Southern sharpshooters occupied the Stonebraker farm, using the stone barn there for cover. From this strong position, they exacted a toll on the oncoming Union troopers.[6]

Stuart's defensive position was a strong one, protected by undulations in the rolling farmland, hills, and lots of trees. While his troopers were moving into position, he ordered Chew to deploy his battery on the high ground behind the Hauck barn, where it could cover the entire Confederate line. In addition to his own horse artillery, Stuart also had a battery of Lt. Gen. James Longstreet's artillery in support.[7]

Buford, meanwhile, took up a position in a heavy timber known locally as Stover's Woods. He kept Merritt's Reserve Brigade on the right (in the advance), while Devin's and Gamble's brigades remained hidden by the trees. Buford also held a strong and defensible position, and one well suited as a jumping-off point for attacks all along the line.[8]

When all was ready, Buford sent skirmishers forward from all three brigades while his batteries hammered Stuart's line with remarkable accuracy. Within minutes, the Confederate position began to waver, and then crumble to pieces. "We did not hold our position very long," admitted a Southern artillerist, "as the enemy had too many dismounted sharpshooters crawling up on us, and their long-range rifles rendered our position untenable for artillery, and we retired."[9] Fitz Lee's men skirmished with Merritt's troopers as long as they could, but Buford's artillery made their position too hot to maintain. "[We] commenced a hasty retreat through Funkstown across the two bridges," recounted one of Lee's staff officers. "The enemy shelled the village unmercifully and we sustained some loss."[10]

Luckily for Stuart's men, numerous trees, rocks, and fences offered scattered bits of shelter as they fell back under the barrage of artillery and small arms fire. Chew retired his guns one and one-half miles before they could again be safely unlimbered. As his line cracked and withdrew, Stuart dashed off a note to Longstreet seeking reinforcements. He knew how important it was to the army to hold Funkstown.[11]

Reverend Kerfoot heard the artillery exchange as the enemy troopers and their field pieces drew closer to St. James. "Fearful day, cannonading coming nearer," he wrote in his diary . . .

> Got our main basement ready, with supplies, etc., to retire to, in case of battle. After much consideration, we all decide to stay in the College, through any battle. Where shall we go? The whole vicinity unsafe, and no other house so strong. The Confederates have placed batteries just inside our hedge; we see their guns; the hedge hides them from our army, which is now one mile east of us.[12]

With an enemy force of unknown size, but likely entirely cavalry threatening Stuart and

Lt. Gen. James Longstreet, commander, First Corps, Army of Northern Virginia.

Valentine Museum

Funkstown, and worried about losing valuable wagons, Longstreet decided to move some of his infantry toward Funkstown.[13] "The Union cavalry came severely upon the Army of Northern Virginia's left flank at Hagerstown, forcing General Stuart to call for infantry support," was how Longstreet recalled it.[14] Responding to Stuart's plea for help, Longstreet sent the Georgia brigades of Brig. Gen. Goode Bryan (commanding Semmes' Brigade) and Col. William W. White (commanding Anderson's Brigade) as well as Capt. Basil C. Manly's Battery A of the 1st North Carolina Artillery. Colonel White's 1,150 men were camped north of Funkstown along the Hagerstown Road, and he had no interest in taking orders from a cavalryman. When he arrived at Stuart's headquarters and reported, White protested his new assignment, claiming that he would only take orders from his immediate superior, Brig. Gen. Evander M. Law, who was in command of John B. Hood's Division after that officer fell badly wounded on July 2. Nonplussed, Stuart repeated his order. White was to move his men into the field at once because infantry was needed to shore up the line. White again insisted that he would only take orders from Law.

An irate Stuart rose in his stirrups and in a stronger, but measured tone, repeated the order a final time, noting that he "outranked this General Law, whoever he was," and added, "I know nothing of him anyway." With the sounds of the battle increasing in intensity, Colonel White gave in and led his troops through the streets of Funkstown and reported to Fitz Lee. Lee directed White to halt in a narrow road until his batteries could open on the enemy.[15] He ordered the Georgia veterans forward through a narrow lane to a position within 150 yards of the enemy before deploying into line of battle. Colonel White protested, preferring to shake out into line of battle before drawing enemy fire, but Lee would not permit it.[16] White, however, was right. Lee had poorly positioned the Georgians, who would suffer for Fitz Lee's lack of experience in commanding infantry.[17]

While the rest of White's men moved ahead, Stuart directed the 7th Georgia forward to check the advance of the enemy. Part of the regiment moved out to the south of the town, where they saw only limited action. The rest of the regiment moved out to the east, and soon became engaged in "a lively skirmish" that lasted until their supply of ammunition was exhausted. Although they sent for more, it never came up, so the 7th Georgia was unable to advance with the rest of the brigade when it eventually moved out. Only twelve men from that regiment were left on the skirmish line when the balance of the Georgia brigade marched forward.[18]

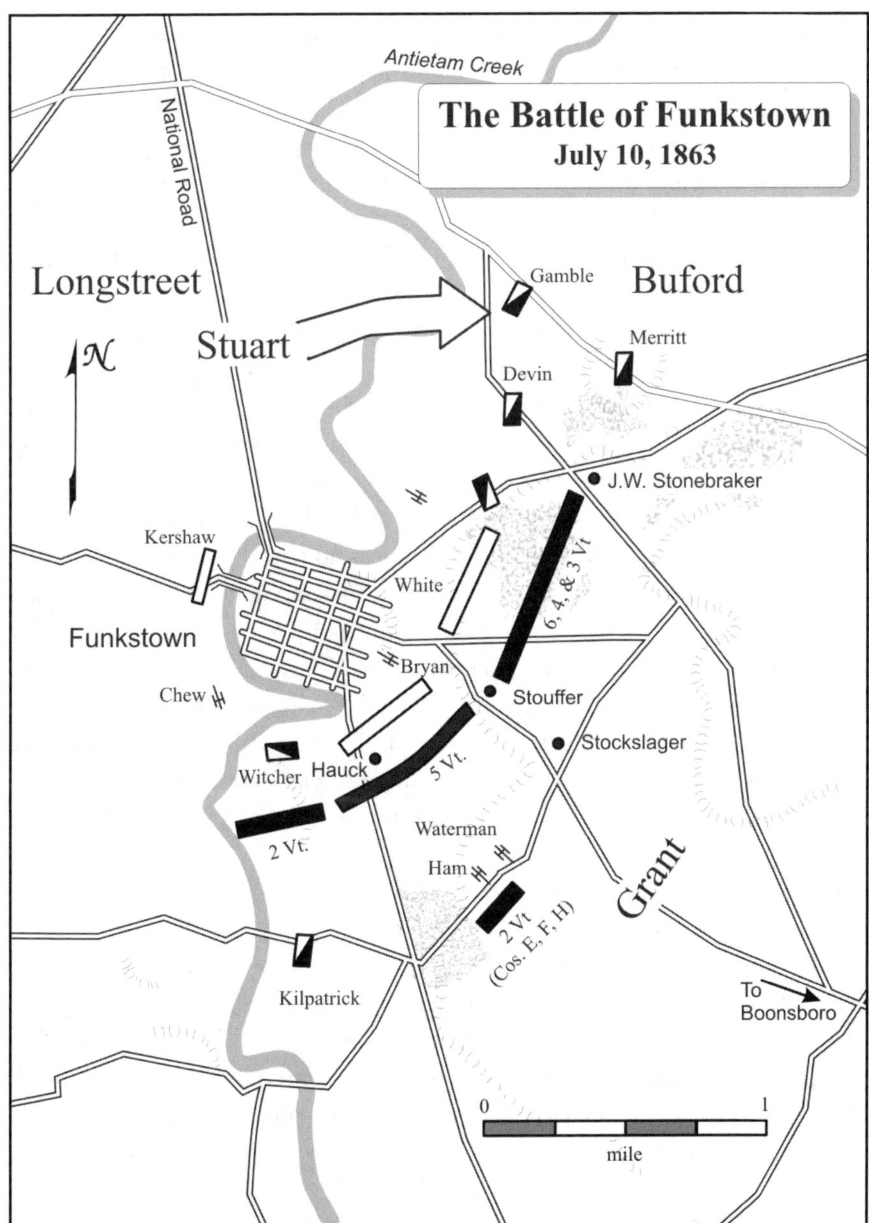

Buford's men, meanwhile pursued the Rebel cavalry back to their gathering infantry support along the banks of Antietam Creek. Jasper Cheney of the 8th New York Cavalry recorded in his diary, "Attacked the enemy about 8 am. and drove them almost to Funkstown, where we found the enemy strongly posted."[19] Cheney's regimental commander, Col. William Markell, was shot in the left hand during the initial assault and had to relinquish command of his horsemen.[20]

Reinforced by infantry, Stuart stood his ground. "We held our ground, there being no alternative; we had to do it," noted a Southern horse artillerist.[21] "Fight commenced very early and lasted through the entire day," noted a Mississippi horse soldier, "We were hotly pursued. . . . The infantry supported us at 12 o'clock."[22]

White had but grudgingly conceded to Lee's earlier deployment request, and within a short while was likely angered with himself that he had done so. Calef's Federal gunners chewed up his lines as the Georgians advanced toward the Beaver Creek Road—just as White predicted they would, inflicting casualties along the entire route. "I was subjected to a raking fire from the enemy," complained the infantry colonel, "and it was with great difficulty that my line was formed, there being several fences and small houses in the way." The Georgians were "caught in a tight place & suffered quite severely on a small scale," recalled a Confederate gunner.[23] "They had dire complaints to make of the way cavalrymen put them in columns of fours against batteries, when they could have advanced more rapidly and effectively in line of battle and saved half of their men lost," Longstreet observed. Despite the effective fire, the courageous Georgians pushed the Northerners back for a time. Just as the situation seemed to be sorting itself out, Fitz Lee ordered the infantry to break off and withdraw, appalling White a second time. "The left and center were advancing in splendid order and would have continued to advance but for orders from General Lee to fall back."[24]

As the Georgians formed, advanced, fought, and prepared for withdrawal while under fire, Chew's Battery fired off all of its available ammunition and was relieved by other batteries before withdrawing itself from a strong defensive position south of the town.[25] During this counter-battery exchange, a stray shell crashed through Jacob Hauck's roof, smashed through the dining room ceiling, and cut a hole in the door separating the living room and the dining room. Somehow, the Haucks managed to avoid injury.[26]

The Funkstown artillery fight was a particularly sharp one. Capt. Manly's battery spent nearly twelve hours fitfully engaged with Federal gunners in the vicinity of Funkstown. The North Carolina gunners arrived at 6:00 a.m., unlimbered on the crest of a hill on the Gilbert farm east of the town, and began firing immediately.[27] They remained engaged in often severe counter-battery fire with their Union opposites until late in the afternoon, their accurate fire forcing the enemy gunners to change positions at least twice.[28]

One of Manly's shells, suffering from the same poor fuses that had plagued Confederate artillery since the beginning of the war, exploded too soon, bursting over the advancing Georgia infantry. "[O]wing to confusion in their ranks by the fire of Stuart's Horse Artillery, who threw and exploded several shells in their ranks, killing and wounding 6 men in one company and several in others," reported White. "It is bad enough to have to face the determined fire of the enemy, without having death lurking in your rear," noted a Confederate cavalryman. The bursting shell "somewhat disconcerted and checked their advance, but they soon rallied, climbed a post and rail fence, and pushed half way across a newly plowed corn field to within two hundred yards of the woods in which [Col. Lewis A.] Grant's and Buford's men were sheltered behind trees and large rocks."[29]

Like Chew's guns, Capt. John Shoemaker's horse artillery also expended all of its ammunition in the exchange, after which its commander ordered the men to lie down in order to minimize their exposure to the Federal fire. As he rode along his lines, Jeb Stuart spotted the prone Confederate gunners and asked why they were not firing. Shoemaker explained that his limber chests were empty, and that they were hugging the ground for protection from the Yankee salvoes until additional ammunition arrived. "Then let them stand up for moral effect," suggested Stuart. The gunners of Shoemaker's Battery, from that point forward, referred to Stuart as "Moral Effect," "but never without respect and admiration because he never failed to go where the battle was raging hottest."[30]

Stuart was not the only cavalryman with supporting infantry. Tramping behind Buford's troopers that morning was Brig. Gen. Albion P. Howe's 2nd Division of Sedgwick's 6th Corps. After a leisurely march of six miles, his infantry crossed Beaver Creek and, under orders from Sedgwick, halted to wait for the rest of the 6th Corps to come up. "We could see the smoke from the enemy's camp fires, and perhaps two miles in our front, could hear the sharp crack of the carbines and see the white puff in the air, showing where a shell had exploded," recalled a member Col. Lewis A. Grant's 6th Corps Vermont brigade. "We understood perfectly that it meant our cavalry were indulging their meddlesome curiosity to the utmost in finding the position of things. They succeeded admirably in stirring up a regular hornets' nest."[31]

At one point during the battle for Funkstown, Buford and his staff dismounted and ascended a rise to observe the fighting. As Buford climbed the hill, a bullet "passed through his blouse, cutting five holes, and narrowly missed the nose of the writer [Surgeon Abner Hard of the 8th Illinois], who was a short distance in the rear."[32]

Judson Kilpatrick's division was also in the neighborhood and joined the fighting for Funkstown. Little Kil personally led several mounted charges. "If I only had my escort here we could take that battery," he proclaimed at one point. Later that day, as he was sitting under a tree penning a dispatch, a Confederate shell landed a few feet away, spraying the diminutive general and his staff with dirt. Kilpatrick did not even flinch, confidently declaring, "A shell never strikes twice in the same place."[33]

As the Funkstown fighting raged, Buford received invaluable intelligence in the form of several dispatches from nearby Signal Corps positions. From their high perches, the Signal officers had a clear view of the movements of the Confederate troops on the sprawling plains below them, and regularly and accurately reported to Buford and his subordinate officers about various enemy threats and movements. This intelligence permitted Buford, Gamble, Devin and Merritt to deploy both their troopers and artillery to meet specific advances by the Southerners. Buford was well served by the men of the U.S. Signal Corps this day, just as he had been at Gettysburg on July 1 and again on the morning of July 2.[34]

Around 1:30 p.m., with the weather hot and sultry, General Pleasonton ordered Buford to move his command to the right to cut off the Confederate line of approach from Hagerstown.[35] At the time, however, Buford's men were pressing Robertson's and Ferguson's troopers hard on the left center of the Federal line. Lt. Col. Vincent A. Witcher's 34th Battalion of Virginia Cavalry, which had been severely handled on East Cavalry Field at Gettysburg on July 3, held a position southeast of town behind a stone wall on the Hauck farm. Witcher's men repulsed several attacks by Buford's dismounted horsemen long enough for Witcher to reinforce his position with the 36th Battalion and the 14th and 16th Virginia cavalry regiments. These additional commands allowed Ferguson to stand his ground in the face of Buford's deadly carbines.[36] As the battle raged, Buford's men began to run out of ammunition. If he was going to carry the position, he would need help doing so.

Like Stuart before him, Buford sent a note back to General Howe for support. "I am pretty hardly engaged here; I have used a great deal of my ammunition; it is a strong place in front; it is an excellent position," he wrote with characteristic brevity.[37]

As Buford's men hoarded their lead and continued the action, Federal infantry poured onto the field. Elements of the 1st Corps deployed and skirmished with the enemy on the outskirts of Funkstown.[38] Worried that the fighting would spread into a potentially large-scale engagement, Sedgwick had ordered his division commanders to advance northward through Boonsboro and along the National Road toward Funkstown, and then to halt and take position in line of battle on the Boonsboro side of Beaver Creek. In an eerie mirror image of July 1, Sedgwick cautioned Howe to avoid bringing on a general engagement. Howe's men could hear the battle raging at Funkstown, but the division commander obeyed his orders and did nothing to come to Buford's aid—even though he wanted to do so.[39] "Guns are booming in front, mingled with the rattling of musketry," the chaplain of the 5th Maine noted in a letter.[40] The lack of infantry support disgusted Colonel Gamble. "Our infantry finally arrived within half a mile in our rear, and although we were hard pressed by the enemy, and nearly all our ammunition expended, the infantry pitched their shelter-tents, and commenced cooking and eating," he complained, "in spite of repeated and urgent requests to the commanding officer of the infantry to occupy our excellent position and relieve us."[41]

General Howe crossed Beaver Creek and found a good defensive position, which he resolved to hold until the rest of the 6th Corps came up. Buford was riding back from the front when he spotted Howe and galloped toward him. The two officers reconnoitered the position. "I ought to go to the right," Buford told Howe, perhaps in response to Pleasonton's earlier orders for him to do exactly that. "Suppose you move up there, or send up a brigade or even a part of one, and hold that position."

"I will do so at once if I can just communicate with General Sedgwick," Howe responded. "I am ordered to take up a position over there and hold it, and the intimation conveyed to me was, that they did not want to get into a general engagement. I will send to General Sedgwick and ask permission to hold that position and relieve you." Howe promptly sent a staff officer to find Sedgwick with a request that he be permitted to come to Buford's immediate aid. Buford waited with Howe for the staff officer's return.

The aide returned quickly with nothing new to report: do not bring on a general engagement. Howe shrugged, turned to Buford, and asked, "Buford, what can I do?" Buford responded, "They expect me to go further to the right; That position is a strong one and we ought not to let it go." Howe agreed, and once again sent a rider to Sedgwick seeking permission to move to the cavalryman's assistance. Both Howe and Buford recognized the position should be held by the infantry. This time, Sedgwick granted permission for

Howe to move—but only if Buford abandoned the position. Howe winked at Buford and said, "If you go away from there, I will have to hold it."

"That's all right," responded a relieved Buford. "I will go away." With that, Buford ordered his division to mount up and ride off. Howe raced his men forward and occupied the position previously held by the dismounted cavalry. Sedgwick's permission had arrived just in time. Soon after deploying, Howe spotted Rebel foot soldiers moving in his direction.

"Soon after relieving Buford, we saw some Rebel infantry advancing," recalled Howe. "They made three dashes, not in heavy force, upon our line to drive us back. The troops that happened to be there on our line were what we considered in the Army of the Potomac unusually good ones." The Vermonters took up a position nearly one and one-half miles in front of the 6th Corps batteries sent to support the dismounted cavalry and infantry. They occupied a portion of Stover's Woods, their line running in a northwesterly direction, with their right resting on the road to the east of the Stonebraker barn. Supported by artillery fire from the 3rd New York Battery and Battery C of the 1st Rhode Island Artillery, the 6th Corps foot soldiers quietly and unspectacularly repulsed two Southern thrusts, driving the Confederates back to Funkstown.[42] An increasingly frustrated Howe concluded, "Yet there was no permission to move on and follow up the enemy."[43]

The arrival of the infantry and supporting artillery invigorated the tired Federal troopers.[44] Their appearance could not have come at a more opportune time for the hard-pressed troopers of Buford's division.

Col. Lewis A. Grant commanded a brigade of five regiments of Vermont infantry

Col. Lewis A. Grant, commander, 2nd Brigade (Old Vermont Brigade), 2nd Division, 6th Corps.

USAHEC

assigned to the 6th Corps. The Vermonters were beyond tired. Pvt. Wilbur Fisk of the 2nd Vermont realized that day that he and his comrades had marched 266 miles in only two weeks. Enervated and footsore they might be, but duty called, and the veteran Green Mountain boys were never ones to shy away from a fight. Their uniforms looked as tired as their bodies. "We drew clothing this morning, boots and shoes. There was not enough for all," complained Fisk. "I waited half an hour for a pair of stockings but after all did not get them and I lost my breakfast waiting into the bargain."[45]

Grant ordered his regimental colonels to hold their positions at all hazards. Unsure what to expect, the colonels set about obeying the grim order. The Vermonters moved to the far right of the extending Union line. As they advanced, a soldier of the 3rd Vermont picked up a notebook that once belonged to the first sergeant of Co. G, 8th Georgia Infantry. The Federal amused himself by calling the roll of Company G and assigning men to extra duty for not answering to their names, and also extending an invitation to the sergeant to come and retrieve his book. Occasionally close enough to yell across to the enemy, one Vermonter sang out, "Look out there, Johnny. I'm agoing to shoot!" A Southerner responded in kind, yelling back, "Look out there, Yank, I'se agwine to shute!"[46]

Lewis' men deployed as follows: the 5th Vermont and two companies of the 2nd Vermont as skirmishers on the left, and the 6th Vermont as skirmishers on the right—the entire skirmish line front stretching some two miles, with the left resting on Antietam Creek. The 3rd and 4th Vermont regiments, meanwhile, supported a 6th Corps artillery battery while the balance of the 2nd Vermont was held in reserve.[47]

Supported by several batteries of artillery, the Vermont infantry stepped off in style, advancing to a little crest along a country road, thereby beating the enemy to the critical higher ground. The Vermonters tore down the rail fences lining the road and carried them to one side, hoping their rudimentary breastworks would buy time until the rest of the 6th Corps came up to reinforce them. The Federal infantry would soon engaged Bryan's Georgians (Semmes' Brigade), who were themselves advancing toward a nearby stand of woods in triple lines of battle in an effort to cut off Lewis' men from the rest of the Federal line. If the Rebels could take the woods, they would drive a wedge into the Union line and isolate Grant's men. Part of Bryan's line struck the artillery-supporting 4th Vermont but made little progress when the 5th and 6th Vermont regiments stubbornly held the stand of trees.[48]

A detachment of Bryan's Georgians angled to the left of the Vermonters, hoping to turn their flank. These Confederates were moving southwest in an effort to cross Antietam Creek and slip into the left rear of Grant's extended skirmish line. Grant, however, sent five companies of the 2nd Vermont and effectively repelled the flanking movement, which also secured the Federal flank on the banks of the creek.[49]

As the 2nd Vermont pushed the Georgians back from the creek, a Rebel minie ball tore into the left knee of Pvt. John Comstock of Company K, leaving a gaping wound. Comstock would survive his wound but be discharged from the army, walking with a cane for the rest of his life. Other men in Company C had just taken position near the creek when a minie ball passed cleanly through the front of the left thigh of Pvt. George M. Colt. Fortunately, the wound did not get infected and healed quickly. Colt returned to duty in a couple of months, only to suffer another combat wound the following year.[50]

Farther north and east, Georgians supported by Manly's artillery drove back the Union cavalry screening the front of the 5th Vermont, which braced to meet the threat. The Georgians advanced almost 500 yards across open meadows, drawing heavy fire much of the way. About 300 yards from Grant's position, a stone wall topped by a board fence stretched across the field. The fence proved to be a formidable obstacle for the Georgians, who had to climb over under a heavy fire. Bryan's foot soldiers gave the Rebel Yell and rushed forward another 200 yards to reach the critical high ground, but the severe fire of the 5th and 6th Vermont regiments stopped them dead in their tracks just 100 yards from the main Union line, where another fence intervened. This new barrier, all boards, collapsed the double line

Col. Thomas O. Seaver, commander, 3rd Vermont Infantry.

USAHEC

Maj. Henry D. McDaniel, commander, 11th Georgia Infantry, in a postwar photo taken while he was serving as the governor of Georgia.

Georgia Department of Archives and History

of battle into a single chaotic rank. The enemy, wrote a Vermont soldier, "got back out of reach as quickly as possible."[51] "The way we made those old Springfield rifles heard was surprising," recalled a member of the 3rd Vermont. "There was not the slightest intention on our part of yielding an inch."[52] The Green Mountain warriors continued to hold the high ground as a storm of shot and shell fell around them. The long, thin Union skirmish line had held once again.

Throughout the engagement, the Federals took advantage of any shelter they could find, including rail fencing and stands of timber. Twenty-nine year-old Col. Thomas O. Seaver of the 3rd Vermont, a graduate of Union College in Schenectady, New York, was a prominent lawyer in Cavendish, Vermont, before the war.[53] He had advanced through the ranks from captain of Co. F to colonel on January 15, 1863. Seaver directed reinforcements "to the weakest points to prevent the rebels from breaking our line, till finally the whole brigade was deployed." He smartly deployed his men in a ditch, which protected his men from the heavy fire of the Georgia Confederates.[54]

The stubborn Vermonters repulsed a third attack by Bryan in a cornfield near the center of their line and continued holding their ground along a line atop a prominent ridge stretching more than two long miles. "It was impossible to concentrate our force, for our whole line was threatened," reported Colonel Grant, "and when repulsed at one point, the enemy would form his line anew and advance upon another."[55]

"By this time the boys were in good fighting humor and this third attempt was mightily close to annihilation for the attacking force," a member of the 3rd

Vermont boasted.[56] Pvt. Wilbur Fisk of the 2nd Vermont remembered how the Confederate officers pressed their men to keep moving. "Their officers tried to urge them on; they shamed and threatened them; they told them that there were but few of us, and we could easily be captured. Some turned on their heels and run, some rallied again to the charge. They came on a few rods further, when their ranks broke, and the whole battalion, officers and all, skedaddled for their very lives. They had discovered that they were blundering on a nest of Vermonters."[57]

The Georgians under Colonel White (Semmes' Brigade) were also being thrown back with loss. Twenty-six year-old Maj. Henry D. McDaniel, a prosperous lawyer and businessman from Monroe, Georgia, commanded the 11th Georgia. A graduate of Mercer University, McDaniel voted for secession during Georgia's 1861 Secession Convention, enlisted in the Confederate Army as a private, and was elected lieutenant in July 1861. After serving as the regimental quartermaster, he was promoted to major in November 1862. In the process, he overcame a terrible stutter that sometimes left him unable to speak at all. McDaniel ended up in command of his regiment when the colonel, Francis H. Little, and the lieutenant colonel, William Luffman, both received serious wounds during the fighting for the Rose Farm on July 2.

As McDaniel led his troops in the attacks on the Vermonters southeast of Funkstown, he received a serious gunshot wound to his abdomen that many thought would be fatal.[58] A Federal minie ball also winged William T. Lasseter, who was standing near McDaniel when he fell gut shot. The lightly wounded Lasseter caught the severely wounded major and prevented him from falling hard to the ground. Under a heavy fire, Lasseter helped carry McDaniel off the battlefield to an ambulance so he could be taken to the rear for treatment.[59] "He bore himself manfully in all the battles and endures his sufferings like a hero," reported a Georgia captain.[60]

Capt. George Hillyer commanded a company of the 9th Georgia, another regiment fighting that day under Colonel White. "My Regiment, the 9th, lost some of its best men killed, and two excellent officers wounded. The regiment behaved as steadily as on dress parade," Hillyer later wrote. "The 59th, from some cause, fell back, which exposed the flank of the 11th, and in succession of the 7th, 8th and finally of the 9th, when I was compelled to give the order to retire, which was slowly and sullenly obeyed. It was reported—I do not know the fact—that the reason the 59th fell back, was that our artillery, by some mismanagement was firing into them."[61]

Col. Charles B. Stoughton, commander, 4th Vermont Infantry.

USAHEC

In truth, the 59th Georgia was driven back. Its position "was on high ground, with not so much as a twig to protect it from the murderous fire in front, and the heavy converging fire from the right," reported a member of the regiment. "In addition to this our artillery fired into them from the rear, with fearful havoc, killing and wounding nearly a score at a single shot." Then, the flank of the 11th Georgia became exposed when it continued advancing after the 8th and 9th Georgia received orders to fall back.[62]

Col. Charles B. Stoughton, an 1861 graduate of Norwich University, Vermont's prestigious military academy, commanded the 4th Vermont at the tender age of 22. Stoughton fell stunned when a Rebel bullet glanced off his forehead. Lauded as "especially distinguished on the field of battle," the young colonel staggered from the blow of the bullet.[63] Weak from loss of blood, he made his way to the rear and eventually lost the use of his right eye as a result of this wound. He never returned to duty and was honorably discharged on February 2, 1864, as a result of his injury.[64]

An officer with the 77th New York, Thomas Neill's brigade, Sedgwick's 6th Corps, recalled the heavy fighting as viewed from behind the embattled skirmish line. "Again, the rebels, disgusted at being repulsed by a skirmish line, came up in several lines of battle and charged upon the Vermonters and they again went to the rear in confusion," he wrote. "A third charge was made against the obstinate skirmish line, and a third time the attack was broken."[65] Grant's long, thin skirmish line not only avoided being pushed back, but began driving the Confederates closer to Funkstown, a gallant effort that earned Sedgwick's admiration. "The remarkable conduct of the brigade on this occasion deserves high praise," he wrote.[66] "That skirmish line," proudly declared a Vermont officer, "was like one of finely tempered steel—it might bend, but it would not break."[67]

A 6th Corps soldier admiringly watched the Vermonters from behind the action. "Our troops were on the alert, and stood waiting to receive the incoming assault," he recalled before reminiscing about the scene with sarcastic praise:

> But the skirmishers would not come in; and when the firing died away, it appeared that the Vermonters thus deployed as a skirmish had repulsed a full line of battle attack. Twice afterward the enemy advanced to carry the position, and were each time again driven back by this perverse skirmish line. The Vermonters, it is true, were strongly posted in a wood, and each man fired from behind a tree. But then everybody knows that the etiquette in such matters is for a skirmish line to come in as soon as they are satisfied that the enemy means business. Those simple-minded patriots of the Green Mountains, however, adopted a rule of their own on this occasion; and the enemy, disgusted with such stupidity, retired across Beaver Creek.[68]

Grant's heroic stand had repulsed the combined thrusts of seven infantry regiments from its front and stopped a flanking maneuver. This brilliant demonstration in field tactics prompted another observer to admiringly write that, while normally "a skirmish-line, upon being confronted by the advance of a line of battle is expected to retire. The Vermonters, however, did not so understand it and, each one holding his position, they delivered such a steady and telling fire that the enemy's line was twice repulsed." The observer concluded that the "history of war furnishes few examples such as this, yet the Vermonters did not think that they had accomplished anything out of the usual line of duty."[69] The Green Mountain warriors expended sixty to eighty rounds each during the skirmish, emptying their cartridge boxes twice in the process.

When the Georgians finally broke and ran, some of the Vermonters "sprang from the fence in front, and tauntingly called on them to come back, as there was nothing there but some 'Yankee militia'."[70] The Vermonters paid dearly for the right to taunt the Georgians. Nine of them lay dead and another 59 fell wounded. White's Georgians suffered suffered substantially more, with 25 killed and 101 wounded.[71]

"As we came near the pretty little village of Funkstown, a familiar rattling skirmish fire made itself apparent, and we could see in the distance a line of rebel infantry charging upon a thin and scattered blue line of ours, and we saw the enemy give back and run, then rally and come forward, only to again break and go to the rear," recalled an officer of Neill's brigade of the fight. "The Vermont brigade in a superb skirmish line were giving their usual good account of themselves."[72]

The obstinacy displayed by the Vermonters garnered a plethora of praise. "The brave mountaineers never dreaming that a 6th Corps skirmish line could not hold a rebel line of battle, resolutely refused to leave and sent the presumptuous rebel line of battle to the rear in confusion," wrote an officer of Sedgwick's corps.[73] A soldier of the 3rd Vermont proudly claimed that the Vermonters "gave the rebs all they wanted" and that they had driven the Georgians all the way "from Boonsboro back to Funkstown." Another claimed "we drove them 2 miles back to Antietam Creek"—both excusable exaggerations.[74]

Jerome Cutler of the 2nd Vermont and several dozen of his comrades spent the fight supporting the artillery until dusk while the rest of the brigade remained out front on picket. The captain of a battery paid the New Englanders a high compliment after their day's work, claiming "he did not need any support while the Vermonters were in front."[75]

The rest of the 6th Corps spent most of the day skirmishing a mile or so east of the turnpike.[76] The 37th Massachusetts passed much of July 10 trading shots with Joseph Kershaw's Confederate infantry, which the Southern general described as "some unimportant skirmishing."[77] Co. I of the 3rd South Carolina Infantry was advanced beyond the bridge over the Antietam, and Pvt. G. L. Beasley was killed during this skirmishing while acting as a sharpshooter.[78]

Lt. Col. Mason W. Tyler of the 37th Massachusetts had a close call that afternoon. Tyler led a reconnaissance of a small hill being used as cover by the enemy. "We were anxious to know whether the hill was occupied by them or had been vacated," he explained. As he led his battalion forward, a rifle ball passed through his hat, and he came very close to being shot at close range along with two other members of his command who were with him on the skirmish line.[79]

The action at Funkstown took place in some of the richest farmland in the state of Maryland. The destruction of grain and crops was immense. "Untold acres of the finest wheat, nearly ripe for the harvest, were trampled by lines of battle, by marching columns or wagon and artillery parks," wrote a member of the 37th Massachusetts, "and well might the unfortunate citizens exclaim,

'From friend and foe alike deliver us.'" The local population would suffer many long months after the armies moved on.[80]

* * *

By late afternoon, the weight of two divisions of Federal cavalry (Buford and Kilpatrick), supported by 6th Corps infantry and artillery, told on the Confederates. "We drove them inch by inch," proudly declared one of Gamble's horsemen, "till finally we got them on the run. We followed them till dark. Just before dark, the last shot I fired I hit a Reb. I saw him fall and went to the place & found him. He was shot in the back. I took his spurs, the other boys took his pistol and gun."

The weight of numbers and metal drove Stuart's troopers and Longstreet's infantry from Funkstown and cleared the roads for the advance of Meade's army all the way to the Potomac River. "Had the Sixth Corps been pushed in on Lee's flank after this transaction, and properly supported, some serious trouble might have been made for the Army of Northern Virginia," correctly observed a Vermont officer. "But the orders to the generals were not to bring on a general engagement; and General Lee was not molested."[81]

"At 5 p.m. Confederate signal corps men come up and announce 'enemy advancing,'" St. James' Reverend Kerfoot recorded in his diary. The college Rector took additional measures to protect his family's belongings against the battle lines that had been seesawing across the school's property for three days. "Stowed our best clothing, house-linen, etc., etc., in a deep cellar, so that, if the house were fired by shells, these might be saved."[82]

General Stuart saw things differently than his Federal opposites. "Owing to the great ease with which the position at Funkstown could be flanked on the right," he claimed in his report of the campaign, "and, by a secret movement at night, the troops there cut off, it was deemed prudent to withdraw at night to the west side of the Antietam which was accordingly done."[83]

Merritt's Regulars came up and relieved Gamble and Devin, sealing the victory.[84] When the firing ceased at dusk, the two sides held approximately the same positions they had occupied that morning.[85] Black powder smoke hung low over the battlefield, trapped by the thick humid air, the acrid stench stinging the nostrils of wounded, able-bodied, and civilians alike.[86] "Our brigade seems to be doing all the fighting," complained one of Gamble's Hoosiers. "As usual."[87] Wounded men of both sides filled most of the town's houses, which were pressed into service as hospitals for both Northerners and Southerners.

"The head-boards of pine, here and there among the trees, showed that the victory had not been gained without a struggle," noted an officer who visited the battlefield the following day.[88]

After being relieved by the infantry, Buford found time to send a dispatch to Pleasonton in which he described the action near Funkstown:

> I have been fighting Fitzhugh Lee's, Hampton's [Baker's], and [Grumble] Jones' brigades; have driven them back upon Longstreet's . . . corps, which occupies the crest beyond the Antietam. My information is that the whole of Lee's army is in the vicinity of Hagerstown, Jones' Cross-Roads, and extending towards Williamsport. His line will be along the Antietam. He has a large force in front of a bridge a mile below Funkstown. I don't care about going farther just now. I will cease firing and try to watch their movements. Staff officers have been all over this section, examining ground and measuring distances.[89]

Buford's performance was cavalry scouting at its best. It provided Meade with the intelligence he needed to close in on Lee's army, which was now trapped along the banks of the swollen Potomac.

* * *

That night, when the Confederates went into camp, Stuart's horse soldiers unsaddled their mounts for the first time in ten days. The travails of their raid prior to Gettysburg, combined with their exhausting labors during the retreat, wore heavily on men and beasts. Both required extensive rest. Other than a few hours of stolen sleep here and there, none would be forthcoming for many days to come.[90]

Stuart himself was "out on his feet" from exhaustion. He had gotten little rest since the beginning of the Gettysburg campaign, and even the indomitable *Beau Sabreur* was at the limits of his endurance.[91] For the first five days of the retreat, the Confederate horsemen had fought only cavalry, but the heavy fight at Funkstown marked the entry of the Army of the Potomac's infantry directly into the retreat combat. Stuart knew full well that his men could not hold off the enemy cavalry and infantry at the same time. At that very hour, three full corps of Federal infantry were concentrating between Boonsboro and Funkstown, massing for what looked to be an all-out assault against Lee's army.

Protected by darkness, Confederate stretcher bearers gathered up as many of their dead and wounded as they could safely reach. When they approached too close to the Vermonters' line, a warning shot or two discouraged them from advancing farther. The next morning, Grant's men claimed they counted nearly 100 Confederate dead that the stewards had been unable to reach. "One touching incident involved the discovery of a Confederate soldier perhaps twenty-five years old clutching "an ambrotype portrait of his young wife and child, and we all felt keenly a small part, perhaps, of the pain the news of this skirmish must carry to the heart of this wife down in Georgia," recalled one of the Vermonters. The order to advance beyond the scattered enemy corpses came as welcome news, and as the Green Mountain men passed through the town, its citizens turned out to congratulate them on their victory.[92]

Mrs. Annie Sharias grew up in Funkstown. By 1913, she was living in Missouri, where she had resided for many years. However, an incident of the July 10 battle still haunted her fifty years later. Her family's farm was caught in the midst of the battlefield, and the barn turned into a hospital. A young soldier of the 153rd Pennsylvania named William Schonebarger had been sick at Gettysburg, but insisted on remaining in the ranks. "No, I will follow my company to the last," he declared. He died at the Sharias homestead on July 14, and was buried in the family orchard near a soldier of the 51st Georgia named David M. Smith, who was killed four days earlier.[93]

The Chaney house, named for the local physician who owned it, also served as a hospital for the wounded of both sides. Operating tables were set up in the yard under the shade of a few trees, and amputations were performed there. Once a surgery was done, the injured soldier was carried inside to recuperate. "It was a horrible sight," remembered a Funkstown resident.[94] One of the assistants was a thirteen-year-old girl named Clara McCoy, who worked as a nurse's aide. Many men died on the Chaney property from their wounds or from the infections that inevitably followed.

The Keller house, across the road from the Chaney home, also served as a field hospital. Badly wounded during the July 10 fighting, Major McDaniel of the 11th Georgia was carried to the Keller house on a mattress and laid on the pavement. "He had an fearful looking wound in his abdomen, the entrails protruding to an alarming extent," observed a Funkstown resident who watched the drama unfold "with a pitying eye." When a surgeon examined the wound, McDaniel asked if he thought the injury a mortal one. The doctor replied that he was unsure, but thought that it was. "Dulce et decorum est, pro patria mori," said McDaniel, resigned to his fate.

The surgeon ordered the wounded major be carried into the house and placed on a table. An army surgeon tried to push his exposed entrails back into the wound with his fingers, but could not do so. The town physician, Dr. George W. Botler, who had been imbibing something stronger than water that day, expounded, "Damn it, Doctor, dilate the wound!" The army surgeon did so, McDaniel's entrails were pushed back into his body, and the wound was dressed.[95]

"He was left in comfortable quarters at a private house in Funkstown, and will, I fear, fall into the hands of the enemy," reported Capt. George Hillyer.[96] The captain was right. McDaniel was captured when the Rebels withdrew from the town. His first destination was Hagerstown. He made the journey on a litter, as did many other wounded Confederates. McDaniel grew weaker with each passing hour, and many worried he would not survive. Those fears were put to rest when McDaniel pulled another officer close and said, "Nesbit, old fellow! Did you ever see such an ungodly pair of ankles as that Dutch woman standing over there on the porch has got?"[97] Laughter sometimes is indeed the best medicine. The lucky major received excellent and compassionate care from a local physician and survived his abdominal wound. He spent the rest of the war as a captive at the prisoner of war camp on Johnson's Island in Lake Erie, and survived that ordeal as well, eventually becoming governor of Georgia in the 1880's.[98]

The Angela Kirkham Davis house, located on the National Road, also served as a field hospital for casualties from the Funkstown battle. As fast as the wounds of the injured could be dressed they were laid in rows. The citizens of the beleaguered town ministered to their needs as best they could, but many men died. Their cries and suffering left a lasting impression on the townsfolk. The screams of the wounded echoed into the night, keeping many awake. Simon Knode, an old Methodist deacon living in Funkstown, "added very much to the confusion as he prayed and sang to the dying." The dead were buried in a nearby cornfield.[99]

After driving the Confederates from the town, the Federals fanned out and explored the positions formerly held by the enemy. The Southerners had fortified one of the bridges over Antietam Creek and dug strong rifle pits surrounding the structure. They had also gouged embrasures for artillery pieces into the sheer stone escarpment overlooking the stream. Luckily for the Yankees, they were not ordered to carry these positions by force.[100]

The Vermonters spent the night holding their extended skirmish line. Many tried to improve their position by digging holes with their bayonets and piling dirt in front of themselves for cover. "We expected as soon as daylight came they would commence to pop away at us," recorded a member of the 2nd Vermont. The Green Mountain men had earned the right to be tired. July 10 had been a truly remarkable day in Vermont history.[101]

The Main Body of the Army of Northern Virginia

As the Funkstown fighting was taking place, Robert E. Lee recognized that the moment of truth had arrived: his Virginia army faced dire peril. After warning of the advance of Smith's men, accompanied by Neill's 6th Corps brigade and McIntosh's cavalry brigade, Lee gave Jeb Stuart specific instructions. "Notify [Brig. Gen. Beverly H.] Robertson to be on the lookout and offer stiff resistance," he ordered early on the morning of July 10. "We must prepare for a vigorous battle, and trust in the mercy of God and the valor of our troops. Get your men in hand, and have everything ready."[102]

"General Lee is acting altogether on the defensive, and seems to desire to be let alone rather than to undertake any offensive operations," correctly noted a correspondent of the *Baltimore American* newspaper that afternoon. Would his army be able to withstand the Federal onslaught that he expected to come at almost any time?[103]

Lee issued a stirring order to his troops, telling them that everything now depended on their fortitude and endurance, and that he required another major effort from them to fend off the Federals. "All eyes saw in this order unmistakable evidence that we were in a critical situation and that fighting was a matter of necessity, not of choice," observed a Virginia cavalryman. "This was, indeed our situation." As the Confederates were steeling themselves for the ordeal ahead, word of the surrender of John Pemberton's army at Vicksburg, Mississippi, began filtering into their camps. The news cast a heavy pall throughout the Southern camps. Still, "under all these adverse influences, the army was comparatively resolute and if not hopeful and cheerful was not despairing and demoralized."[104] As one Maryland officer put it, "The army is in fine spirits and confident of success when they again meet the enemy. This you may rely upon and and so you may comfort yourselves with it. A military blunder was committed, but the men never fought better."[105] They would need to fight well and then some if Meade attacked before Lee could escape across the Potomac.

Federal Reinforcements on the Way

The rookies of the 34th and 39th Massachusetts regiments boarded trains of the Baltimore & Ohio Railroad, riding the cars all the way to Harpers Ferry. Due to delays, the train did not leave the station until almost 11:00 that night. "At length we started; our running was slow," recalled a member of the 34th. "Many of the men had clambered upon the roofs of the box cars, there being no provision made for them to sit down inside." Unfortunately a man named Fitzgerald fell from the roof of one of the cars, which ran over and mangled his body, to the horror of his watching comrades.[106]

The rookie men from the Bay State had orders to assume a position on Maryland Heights. "We came up between two mountains in a narrow road and very steep," reported George Fowle of the 39th Massachusetts. "It was very dark, and muddy in some places where the springs run out. We got up here and laid down for the night. Yesterday the 34th marched a short distance from us, and we pitched our shelter tents again."[107]

"The road was only an apology for one, though its mud was deep and adhesive; following closely one's file leader was necessary, if a man would keep in the procession," noted another member of the 39th. "Finally there came a real climb up a mountains side with every man for himself, until there was a blessed emergence on a plateau where, mud encrusted, the men threw themselves upon the ground and slept the sleep of exhaustion."[108]

Unused to the trials and tribulations of campaigning, the green soldiers faced a significant additional challenge. When Meade assumed command of the Army of the Potomac, he ordered that all mess pans have a hole punched through them, and all tents cut up in order to prevent such useful items from falling into enemy hands and being used against the Federal government. The policy made sense, but it made the plight of the greenhorns all the more difficult, for they also had to overcome this hurdle in their attempt to make themselves comfortable in their new surroundings.[109]

The Bay Staters would not remain long at Harpers Ferry. On July 12, they received orders to join the Army of the Potomac. In less than twenty hours, hindered by rain and mud, they marched nearly thirty miles on bad roads, joining the army's main line of battle. "Up hill and down, so dark that we can scarcely see, all night, right up to 5 o'clock in the morning, when we halt for rest and breakfast in a belt of woods, about two miles from Boonsboro," recalled a member of the 39th Massachusetts.[110]

The new men were formed into a brigade consisting of the 8th, 39th, 46th, and 51st Massachusetts regiments, all commanded by Brig. Gen. Henry S. Briggs. The new brigade, consisting mainly of nine months' regiments on their way home from North Carolina upon the expiration of their term of service, was designated as the Fourth Provisional Brigade, 2nd Division, 1st Corps, arrived too late. The men marched across the old 1862 Antietam battlefield and on to Funkstown, where they joined the 1st Corps. They hoped they would be able to make a contribution to what they anticipated would be a major battle with Lee's army.[111]

The Army of the Potomac's Main Body

The victory at Funkstown cleared the way for General Meade to march most of his army within two miles of Lee's entrenchments. He established his headquarters on the banks of Antietam Creek at a place called The Devil's Backbone, about halfway between Boonsboro and Williamsport, and not far from the Antietam battlefield. Although the origins of the area's name are unknown, there is a rocky ridge along the creek bristling with boulders, which perhaps inspired the colorful moniker. The large and prosperous Booth's Mill overlooked the banks of the creek. In addition, a prestigious private school called Delamere stood there during Revolutionary times, where the two sons of Revolutionary War general Benedict Arnold attended classes.

Henry B. Parsons of the 10th Massachusetts Infantry, another 6th Corps unit, took time to pen a letter to a female friend that night. He described the pursuit of Lee's army, beginning with the departure from Gettysburg. "We have been after them ever since, until yesterday when we got up to here," he wrote. "We have been in line of battle ever since, expecting a fight every moment, but when it will come off, or whether the Rebs will run is more than I can tell you. I hope they will not run, but would rather fight them here than down in Old Virginia, that is a fact."[112]

"During the last two or three days our artillery has been doing considerable 'barking,' wrote another Bay Stater, "but, like a young terrier dog, it was all bark but no bite." He expressed a similar hope that the Army of the Potomac would attack before Lee could escape.[113] An officer of the 5th Corps posited an interesting theory. "I think, as we have been allowed to cross [Antietam Creek] without opposition, that the campaign is over, and the rebels are crossing the Potomac."[114]

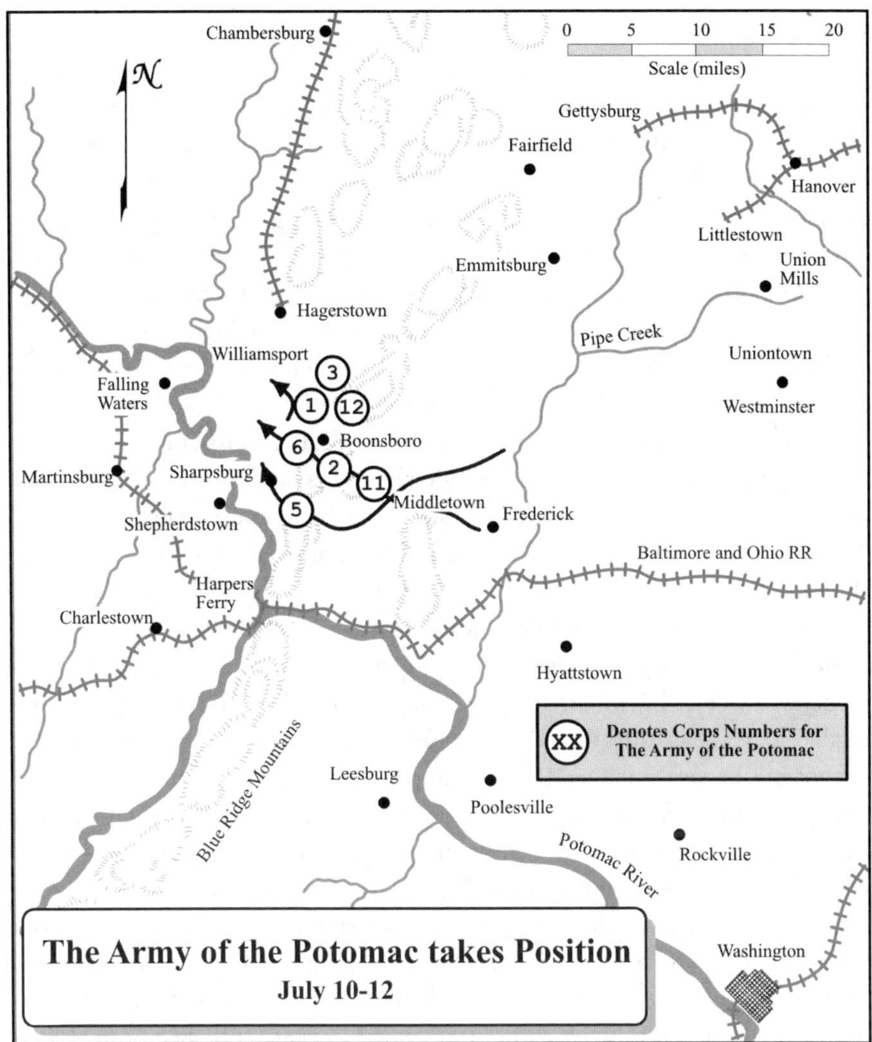

The 20th Connecticut of the 12th Corps passed through Crampton's Gap and headed for Bakerstown. The Connecticut men heard the guns booming at Funkstown, a sign that more stout work might be in store for them.[115] Another 12th Corps unit, the 2nd Massachusetts Infantry, crossed the Antietam battlefield that day. "Every step reminded us of that stubborn fight," an officer of the regiment noted.[116] The Bay Staters moved on toward Williamsport and took up a position near Jones's Crossroads.[117]

As the 12th Corps advanced, the Confederate cavalry pickets retired. The 12th Corps deployed into line of battle, threw up some slight breastworks, and sent forward a strong force of pickets.[118] The 1st Corps also threw up breastworks of logs, rails, and dirt, and spent the night behind them, waiting for the order to attack Lee's lines to arrive. They remained there for two more days.[119] The 63rd Pennsylvania of the 3rd Corps passed through Keedysville, crossed Antietam Creek, and camped by Burnside's Bridge, the site of some of the bloodiest fighting at Antietam.[120] "We are nearing his main force and in a day or two the struggle must commence," predicted a Northern horseman.[121]

Staff officer Charles H. Lynch, who regularly served with the 18th Connecticut, was assisting the Army of the Potomac with logistical issues. "We are either skirmishing or changing our position most of the time so that we are kept on the go about all the time and most of the movements are done at double quick time," he scrawled in his diary on July 10th. "The most important subject under discussion is 'Why doesn't Meade attack Lee?' as we have a number of regiments here who were not at Gettysburg, having come as reinforcements." The same question haunted the thoughts of most of the men of the Army of the Potomac.[122]

"Lee has not crossed and does not intend to cross the river, and I expect in a few days, if not sooner, again to hazard the fortune of war," wrote a concerned General Meade to his wife that night. "I know so well that this is a fortune and that accidents, etc., turn the tide of victory, that, until the question is settled, I cannot but be very anxious. If it should please God again to give success our efforts, then I could be more tranquil. I also see that my success at Gettysburg has deluded the people and the Government with the idea that I must always be victorious, that Lee is demoralized and disorganized, etc., and other delusions which will not only be dissipated by any reverse that I should meet with, but would react in proportion against me." Meade went on to note that Lee's army held a strong position and that the Southern commander seemed determined to fight it out on the north side of the Potomac. "I believe if he had been able to cross when he first fell back, that he would have done so; but his bridges being destroyed, he has been compelled to make a stand, and will of course make a desperate one." Meade ended his missive with a rather ominous conclusion, writing, "The army is in fine spirits, and if I can only manage to keep them together, and not be required to attack a position too strong, I think there is a chance for me. However, all is in God's hands. I make but little account of myself, and think only of the country."[123]

Meade again issued a circular, this time directing the next day's movements. The 5th Corps was to move forward and take position with its right resting on the Antietam and linking up with the 6th Corps. The left of the 6th Corps would be extended toward Jones' Cross Roads while the 2nd Corps moved forward to Jones' Cross Roads, where its right would connect with the left of the 6th Corps. The 12th Corps would move through Fair Play and take up a position between Jones' Cross Roads and Marsh Run, in the general direction taken by the 2nd and 5th Corps. The 3rd Corps would mass in the vicinity of the Antietam Creek bridge on the Boonsboro and Williamsport road, about the center of the Union line, and be held in readiness to move quickly wherever needed.[124] Meade's new line paralleled that held by Lee's army.

The Southern position extended from Hagerstown to Falling Waters Road, and was impressively fortified.[125] Having spent most of his pre-war Regular Army career as an engineer, Lee had a keen eye for terrain and it showed in the position he took up. As one Federal officer observed, Lee's line of works "were by far the strongest I have seen yet, evidently laid out by engineers, and built as if they meant to stand a month's siege."[126] Most of the Confederate entrenchments were sprawled atop a series of ridges along Marsh Run, a tributary of the Potomac, making the position a commanding one. Concerted infantry attacks against such a line might well have resulted in a Union slaughter similar to the debacle at Fredericksburg.

As his troopers rested, Buford took pride in the accomplishments of his command over the past few days. "There was splendid fighting on the part of the division on the 7th, 8th, 9th, and 10th," he lauded. "There was no faltering or hesitation. Each man went to work determined to carry anything in reason."[127] That night, having been relieved by the arrival of the Federal infantry, Buford's troopers were withdrawn from the front. They passed through Boonsboro, over South Mountain, and went into camp along the Catoctin Creek, near Middletown, Maryland. As the regimental historian of the 6th Pennsylvania Cavalry noted, "We here had access to our wagons; put up our tents, and luxuriated in clean linen, and an abundance of commissary supplies, enjoying positive rest for two days."[128] One officer in the 9th New York Cavalry recalled that evening their jaded horses were "unsaddled for the first time in several days."[129]

Col. Pennock Huey's brigade of the Army of the Potomac's 2nd Cavalry Division had been separated from the rest of the division since before the fighting at Gettysburg. During the first days of the pursuit, Huey's troopers were attached to Kilpatrick's command. On July 10, the 1st Rhode Island Cavalry rejoined the brigade. The 1st Rhode Island had been cut to pieces at Middleburg, Virginia, on June 17, and spent the next three weeks recuperating and refitting at Alexandria. The Rhode Islanders left Alexandria on July 6 and reached Frederick the next day with only three officers and 93 men, all looking to join the pursuit of Lee's army.[130] The 1st Massachusetts also rejoined the division that day. Like the Rhode Islanders, the Bay Staters had suffered heavily at the battle of Aldie on June 17, and had been resting and refitting after their frightful losses. However, the cavalry corps needed bodies, and the remnants of these two veteran regiments added able-bodied men to Pleasonton's command.

On July 10, Huey received orders for a different mission. That morning, his command marched to the old Antietam battlefield before turning north toward Jones' Crossroads, where the Sharpsburg Turnpike and Williamsport-Hagerstown Road intersected. There, the Federal horsemen met the enemy. After a sharp skirmish, Huey's men drove the stubborn Confederate horse artillery back a mile or so in the direction of Williamsport. Huey suffered four killed and six wounded in exchange before retiring half a mile and camping for the night.[131]

While the weary horse soldiers rested a bit before resuming their travails, George Meade sent a wire to General Halleck. "In consequence of the very efficient service and the material aid rendered to me by the cavalry during the recent operations, I would esteem it a personal favor if the President would assign Major-General Pleasonton to the command of the Cavalry Corps, the position I found him in when I assumed command."[132] The next day, Halleck wrote Meade that Secretary Stanton had no intention of removing or superseding Pleasonton, but there was "an objection to any formal order at present" making the Knight of Romance's appointment permanent. The War Department preferred that Pleasanton remain a temporary replacement for Maj. Gen. George Stoneman, who had been on medical leave since mid-May.[133]

Halleck also penned a curious note. Since nearly the beginning of Lee's retreat, the general-in-chief had been agitating Meade to attack. And then, without a hint of warning, he sounded a note of caution. "I think it will be best for you to postpone a general battle till you can concentrate all your forces and get up your reserves and reinforcements," Halleck instructed. "Bring up and hurl upon the enemy all your forces, good and bad."[134]

Chapter 13

July 11: The Armies Jockey for Position

"Mr. Yank would have smelt powder & ball before getting us out of the breastworks."

— Confederate infantry officer

MOST OF BUFORD'S DIVISION SPENT the next two days picketing and watching the movements of the Confederates. The Southern soldiers were awaiting both a Federal attack along the river, and an opportunity to cross the still flooded Potomac. Everyone in Lee's army was concerned, and for good reason. "The idea of fighting with a left flank sticking in the air & an unfordable river behind us was unpleasing in the extreme, until indeed we got our works built—& then we were ready & confident," declared one soldier.[1]

Buford's men were confident as well, but they were also bone weary. "We had been fighting almost continuously since July 6th, besides doing picket duty at night, and the men were 'almost used up'," wrote one of the troopers, "but no rest came."[2] In a letter home on July 11, Capt. William C. Hazelton of the 8th Illinois Cavalry acknowledged that the fighting during the retreat thus far had been devastating to the regiment's officer corps, Major William Medill being among the eight officers killed. "We have now but 3 or 4 officers in the regiment that have not been hit," Hazelton lamented, "and I am among the inglorious minority."[3]

A member of Gamble's 3rd Indiana Cavalry found time to scrawl a few lines in his diary. "Traveled to Boonsboro across Antietam Valley Mills and encamped on the Williamsport road. Came up with the enemy pickets but did not attack them," wrote Samuel Gilpin. "Monuments and nice white boards mark the graves of the boys that fell here last year. Our right connects with the infantry line. A little firing down here this afternoon." Like all of his comrades, Gilpin wondered what would happen next.[4]

Lee's Defensive Line Takes Shape

General Lee's engineers performed some of their finest work of the war north of the Potomac River. Working under extreme time constraints, they laid out a formidable defensive line running from the outskirts of Hagerstown to nearly Falling Waters. The line skirted along a range of hills on the left bank of Marsh Run, a tributary of the Potomac that flows through a swampy valley. On the right (northwest) bank of the creek runs a similar range of hills, nearly parallel, but not as high as the first. Lee entrenched his army on the ridge to the right of Marsh Run. The hills gently sloped down to the creek. The distance between the nearly parallel ranges varied from one to two miles, the intervening space comprised of open farm fields. The engineers kept Lee's men "busy all day in fortifying" the line, as a member of Ewell's Second Corps told in his diary that night.[5]

When it was finished, James Longstreet's First Corps held the right flank, anchored on the Potomac River near Downsville. A. P. Hill's Third Corps held the center in the vicinity of the College of St. James. Ewell's Second Corps held the left flank at Hagerstown. The entire Army of Northern Virginia was dug in on a strong defensive line. Federal attackers would have to contend with heavy rifle and artillery fire from a protected and largely concealed enemy. "It was a strong position, deliberately and carefully selected," observed a Federal horse soldier. "It covered the Williamsport crossing of the Potomac, which was directly in rear of its centre, and was a position in which artillery could be used with decisive effect." He concluded, "In such a position the chance of repulsing the enemy was considerably in favor of the defensive; but success was absolutely essential, for if the position could be carried . . . the Confederate army could hardly expect to escape annihilation."[6]

The commanding hill occupied by the College of St. James housed several batteries of artillery and was the linchpin of this stout defensive position—much to the chagrin of the Union-leaning Rector Kerfoot. After a fitful night of sleeping with his family on the hard surface of the north side of the first floor (for fear of the building being shelled), Kerfoot rose early on July 11. "Weary, anxious hours till noon; no battle, though the skirmishers of the two armies were visible—many of them—and closing in on one another, and firing, about three-quarters of a mile south of us."[7]

"The greatest part of it was on top of a range of hills on the left bank of Marsh Run, a small creek which flows through a swampy valley into the

Potomac," was how one of the clergymen assigned to St. James began his description of Lee's defensive position. He continued:

> On the right bank of the creek is a similar range of hills, nearly parallel, but somewhat lower, than the first. There the main army was entrenched. The hills are gently sloping down to the creek, the distance between them varies from one to two miles, and the space between them is almost an entirely open field. The attacking party would have been from the first moment, where they left their entrenchments, exposed to the artillery and musketry fire, of a well-protected and concealed enemy. The key of the rebel position was, according to their own statements, a prominent hill on the farm of John L. Roland, about three-fourths of a mile behind the College of St. James. The rebels had, of course, strong batteries, on top of it and in the neighborhood. The College itself was held as a kind of a out-post and strongly occupied by sharp-shooters.

The clergyman noted that Confederate generals regularly visited the college to reconnoiter Federal positions. He overheard one declare, "Now we have Meade where we want to have him. If he attacks us here we will pay him back for Gettysburg. But the old fox is too cunning. He waits for our attack; but we surely will not make the same blunder twice."[8]

Along the eminence and ridges surrounding St. James, the Southerners erected stout breastworks of fence rails, straw, and dirt. When completed, this defensive line rivaled the defenses erected upon Marye's Heights at Fredericksburg.[9] "As we got things into shape, oh! How we all did wish that the enemy would come out in the open & attack us, as we had done them at Gettysburg," wrote Col. Edward Porter Alexander, Longstreet's acting chief of artillery. The artillerist unlimbered most of his battalion around the village of Downsville. It was there he expected Meade would focus his principal effort to break through the Southern line, for that sector protected the pontoon bridge being constructed at Falling Waters.[10] "Lee picked out this vantage ground as the best to cover the withdrawal of his army, both at Williamsport and Falling Waters is natural and was sound military sense, which he never lacked," declared a Union staff officer.[11] The previous day, July 10, as the sounds of Stuart's battle at Funkstown raged, Longstreet's First Corps infantry continued strengthening their front. "The troops were put to work, and, in twenty-four hours, our line was comfortably intrenched," recalled the corps leader in his after-action report.[12]

"Our troops are drawn up in line of battle on a splendid range of hills," wrote a Virginia artillerist with confidence, "and as we have received a large supply of ammunition, I think we will give the enemy a big whipping, notwithstanding the large superiority of their numbers. Everything seems to indicate a large battle in which it is necessary that we should prove victorious, as our rations are running low with but little chance of getting more, until we take them from the enemy." The Southerners remained full of fight.[13]

"All of our forces are in this neighborhood, and we doubt we will have another heavy battle," decided a Confederate horse artillerist. "We have done the Yanks great damage since we have been here. The Cavalry has had several heavy fights, and have been very successful."[14]

There was another view circulating within the ranks of the Virginia army. Hermann Schuricht, one of Albert Jenkins' officers, recalled that once the news of Maj. Gen. Ulysses S. Grant's dramatic victory at Vicksburg, Mississippi, reached the North, and this combined with rumors of a large Federal concentration near Winchester, panic broke out among some in the Confederate ranks. Schuricht's account does not reflect or line up with the majority of Confederate accounts. Most, in fact, claimed the twin defeats at Gettysburg and Vicksburg did not significantly impact Southern morale, and that Lee's army remained ready to fight, any time and any place.

While it did not lack courage or willpower, the Army of Northern Virginia certainly lacked for bread and flour. For two or three days, no ration of bread was issued at all. The men were forced to broil beef on the coals and to make their meals upon the embers. Beef, however, was also in short supply. The hungry Confederates impressed a flock of sheep into service at one point, since there was no other way for them to get rations.[15]

"We were in a field of wheat, behind rifle-pits made of fence rails," recalled a hungry Southerner. "We rubbed the ears of wheat in our hands, and ate the grains uncooked. The regiment sent out foraging, but with little success. There was great suffering from hunger."[16] A Richmond newspaper reported on the lack of food, noting that "the country in the vicinity of Hagerstown is literally eaten out. The family at whose house Lee and his aides quartered themselves have not so much as a pound of subsistence of any kind left. They were compelled to hand over their flour, bacon, vinegar, and everything else, and though Gen. Lee was himself appealed to, nothing availed against the hunger of the famishing gray-backs."[17] According to another newspaper account, "The rebels have swept everything from the country around Hagerstown. Scarcely a serviceable horse is left within an area of ten miles. The grain crops are trampled down, and the flour and corn and hay carried off."[18]

The weary butternut cavalry waited in line of battle for a day and a half, "ready for action" for an attack that would never materialize. As Lieutenant Schuricht put it, the "enemy [hesitated] to give battle."[19] Another Virginia horse soldier recalled, "We lay behind the breast works for three days expecting an attack for the last two days. We threw shells into them so as to bring on a fight but [they] would not attack us."[20] Energized by Lee's General Order, and confident a great battle was upon them, an officer of the 9th Virginia Cavalry noted, "All of us felt quite certain that Maryland's soil had to be again crimsoned with the blood of one of the most important and desperate battles of the war."[21]

Northern soldiers could do little but watch as the formidable defenses grew stronger by the hour. "Our Government was putting forth Herculean efforts to crush Lee's army before the river fell," observed a New York infantryman, "but in great movements there are always some delays."[22] The Army of the Potomac, saddled with the institutional memory of the Fredericksburg debacle, had little stomach for attacking such a strong position. Still, with the soldiers in the scattered infantry corps concentrating in the vicinity of Boonsboro or taking up positions that faced Lee's army, it looked as though they might be ordered to do exactly that.[23]

"The enemy is cornered, and we shall have another battle," Maj. Gen. Gouverneur K. Warren, Meade's chief engineer, informed his wife on July 9. "May God continue to prosper our cause, and peace will soon smile on the land."[24] As they filed into place opposite the Confederate lines, the Yankee soldiers threw up strong breastworks of their own—just in case Lee decided to turn the tables and attack himself. "We have got Lee in a tight place," recounted a Massachusetts artillerist, "and we all hope we can cut his whole army to pieces in fact we are pretty confident he won't get out of this with a whole skin."[25] A Rhode Islander agreed, noting, "Everybody but the Rebels are in good spirits, and they must feel lonesome after their defeat."[26]

Not every Federal shared in this enthusiasm. The men under French's command, still being integrated into the Army of the Potomac, had little combat experience. The prospects of a major battle with the fate of the war riding on its outcome did not much please them. "We are trying our best to catch Johnny Reb," wrote one. "Don't know as we shall succeed. The boys are feeling well, but have no desire to be in a fight but would like to see one." At least he was honest.[27]

"It is thought that we ought not to risk a battle here as we have not over 50,000 efficient troops and the enemy to be equal that if not more, with advantage of position and troops concentrated," recorded a Northern signalman in his diary on July 10.[28] "The enemy were opposite us on the Williamsport Road and were throwing up earth works using some buildings which they tore down to assist in construction," recalled a sergeant of the 1st Vermont Cavalry with a different take on things. "They were on higher ground than we were and had heavier artillery than our light horse batteries."[29]

The Southern earthworks, strong and well positioned, extended nearly nine miles in length. "These were by far the strongest I have seen yet," observed a Northern gunner, "evidently laid out by engineers and built as if they meant to stand a month's siege." The parapets were nearly six feet wide on top, and the engineers had placed their guns perfectly to create converging fields of fire that could sweep the entire front of the position.[30] Brig. Gen. Andrew A. Humphreys, Meade's newly-appointed chief of staff, had spent more than thirty years as a topographical engineer. He had a sharp eye for terrain. "Wherever seen, the position was naturally strong, and was strongly intrenched," recalled Humphreys. "[I]t presented no vulnerable points, but much of it was concealed from view . . . its flanks were secure and could not be turned."[31]

One Federal, however, offered a dissenting voice. "The Rebel works in their front were built of wheat sheaves covered with earth," he claimed, "so slightly covered that when he jumped upon them they let him through. In the rear of these was a very strong line of gopher holes and rifle pits."[32] The Confederates saw it quite differently. They knew their position was powerfully built. "Mr. Yank would have smelt powder & ball before getting us out of the breastworks," observed a confident Confederate.[33] Another declared, "For two days we offered Meade battle. But he declines. He knew with anything like equal ground, we can whip him."[34]

Lee of course recognized the magnitude of the task that lay before his army. He urged his cavalry commander, Jeb Stuart, to be prepared for anything that Meade and the Federals might throw at them. "Get your men in hand," Lee cautioned, "and have everything ready."[35] Hoping to inspire the men, Lee issued a general order on July 11. "Once more you are called upon to meet the army from which you have won on so many fields a name that will never die," Lee proclaimed. "Once more the eyes of your countrymen are turned upon you, and again do wives and sisters, fathers, mothers, and helpless children lean for defense on your strong arm and brave heart. Let every soldier remember that on his courage and fidelity depends all that makes life worth having—the freedom of his country, the honor of his people, and the security of his home." He concluded, "Soldiers! Your old enemy is before you! Win from him honors worthy of your righteous cause—worthy of your comrades dead on so many illustrious fields."[36]

On top of everything else, General Lee's personal burden increased. His second son, Brig. Gen. William Henry Fitzhugh Lee, known to the family as "Rooney," had been badly wounded at the Battle of Brandy Station on June 9, and was taken to his father-in-law's home in Hanover County, Virginia, near Richmond, to recuperate. A Federal cavalry raid snatched the wounded general and carried him off to captivity at Fortress Monroe. Word of his son's plight had finally reached Lee. "I have heard with great grief that Fitzhugh has been captured by the enemy," he wrote to his wife. "Had not expected that he would have been taken from his bed and carried off; but we must bear this additional affliction with fortitude and resignation, and not repine at the will of God. It will eventuate in some good that we know not of now. We must all bear our labors and hardships manfully. Our noble men are cheerful and confident."[37]

General Lee's order of the previous day, July 10, calling for fortitude and determination from his proud soldiers to fend off the fierce Federal attacks until the Southerners could cross the river to safety, began circulating through the ranks. From the highest officers to the lowliest privates, everyone recognized how critical their situation was, and that it would continue to be so for at least the next twenty-four to forty-eight hours.[38]

On July 11, a Tar Heel recorded in his diary, "Orders read out to-day from our father, R. E. Lee, that we would fight the enemy once more on their own soil, as they were now in our front. That order got to them, and fulfilled its mission, as we were then on our way to the Potomac." Feeling confident, he continued, "They were still thinking we could not cross the river, because the river was very high from the recent rains, and we had but one pontoon bridge. At 10 in the night we formed in line of battle, got to our position, when our regiment was ordered to support a battery. Laid on our arms all night."[39] "We are still in Maryland and expect another large battle," noted a captain of the 2nd South Carolina Cavalry. "Our soldiers believe they worsted the enemy."[40] One of Longstreet's disappointed Georgians noted, "Saturday, the 11th, found us in line of battle . . . and in such a position as to render an attack by the enemy rather desirable than otherwise, but he exhibited greater caution than courage, and the quiet along our line remained unbroken."[41]

Williamsport

While the Federals temporized, the Confederates kept busy trying to build a new pontoon bridge across the Potomac. They tore local houses to pieces, and dismantled many of the warehouses from Williamsport to Falling Waters for wood to construct pontoons.[42] John Casler and some of his comrades from the Stonewall Brigade were temporarily assigned to the pioneers. Using lumber from every available building in Williamsport, they constructed sixteen pontoon boats in just two days. They borrowed kettles from the local women to heat tar for pitch to seal the boats. When the citizens objected to having their homes torn apart and their belongings confiscated, Maj. John Harman, the army's chief quartermaster, chuckled and told them, "Just charge it to Jeff Davis. Our army is worth more than all your lumber in gold."[43]

George Pickett's battered division made its way across the Potomac on the ferries at Williamsport that day. Once across, its members set about performing picket duty on the roads south of the river, keeping them open for the passage of the wagons full of wounded men headed for the massive Confederate hospital at Staunton in the Shenandoah Valley.[44]

"You are right in keeping your cavalry in front of the infantry as long as possible," the Confederate army commander wrote Stuart. "I do not desire you to take position on our left with your whole force, until pushed back on the infantry in front, but if you could station a portion of your cavalry on our left toward the Conococheague it would be desirable. As our limits are reduced by the advantage of the enemy, I think this would be practicable." Lee also instructed Stuart to take charge of Imboden's command and to use these men where he thought they could do the most good.[45] Stuart's active pickets blanketed the front, keeping the weary Northern infantrymen constantly on the alert. Stuart's aggressive picketing meant the Federals got little rest as they prepared to attack.[46]

* * *

By July 11, most of the Army of the Potomac's infantry was in place or about to arrive. The 1st Corps struggled its way over South Mountain. "It was hard traveling," noted one New Yorker. "We are all suffering to some extent for want of shoes and socks—our work causing a necessity for supplies to remain in the rear, and walking is wearing away our shoes and socks very rapidly."[47] Despite the discomfort, a Vermonter of the 1st Corps declared, "Hope Meade will not suffer the rebel army to escape, for his army is abundantly able to pursue and crush Lee's disordered columns."[48]

Hardships of the long and grueling campaign aside, the Federals steeled their hearts as they bustled with activity to launch a grand assault against the trapped Virginia army. "Saturday and Sunday preparations were going on," recalled a Yankee. "Baggage wagons to Frederick, our base of supplies lined the roads day and night, hauling ammunition and supplies for man and beast."[49] Capt. Francis Donaldson of the 118th Pennsylvania Infantry, 5th Corps, reported, "A most splendid sight—the whole army in line of battle offering to fight Lee who so far declines. Troops in splendid spirits. Am well and nice and dirty & ragged . . . Can't write much, expect battle every moment."[50]

The army's morale remained remarkably high as the men anticipated waging an epic battle—even though everyone knew massive combat meant heavy casualties. Anticipating those losses, an additional 50 surgeons and "many volunteer nurses" arrived at Army of the Potomac headquarters, ready to respond when and where they might be needed. Their appearance presented an ominous, even chilling, sight.[51]

With the army largely situated, Meade ordered the 3rd and 5th Corps to advance to flesh out the enemy position to their front. The 5th Corps formed in columns by division, meaning they would advance in three columns, organized by division. "This is the first time I ever saw this formation in our army on an advance but the rebels have often used it," remembered a puzzled Sgt. Charles T. Bowen of the 12th U. S. Infantry. "We sent our skirmishers on first, next the pioneers to level the fences & then we went up." The Federal line stretched nearly two miles. The Union skirmishers ascended a hill where the enemy had been seen earlier, and then went down the back side, with no sign of the enemy in front. The 5th Corps advanced for nearly a mile without seeing any signs of the Confederates. The men spent the night where they stopped, resting on their arms.[52]

Earlier in the day, the 2nd Division of the 2nd Corps marched through Tilghmantown and another mile or so toward Williamsport, when the Southern skirmish line was discovered. Skirmishing broke out quickly. According to a Delaware soldier, the 2nd Corps went into line and assumed a defensive position, readying itself to receive a heavy enemy attack.[53] The 72nd and 106th Pennsylvania formed line of battle on the right of the road and skirmished with the enemy until darkness fell. They remained there until about midnight, when orders arrived for them to form up, march about two miles, and shake out into line of battle again across the road, where they remained for the rest of the night. The fitful march, punctuated with skirmishing, made for another long and miserable night.[54]

The 29th Ohio of the 12th Corps moved to Fair Play, a tiny hamlet located just south of the College of St. James near the center of the Confederate position. There, they advanced as skirmishers to uncover their opposites. In this advanced position, the Buckeyes spent the entire day engaged in exchanging shots with Confederate cavalry. The Ohioans made no bones about how much they disliked the nature of their exposed position.[55]

The men of the 123rd New York Infantry, part of the 1st Division, 12th Corps, spent much of the day building "as splendid a line of breastworks as were ever built by soldiers was to be seen." They had few shovels, and had to use their bayonets to break up and move the hard earth, which they carried off by hand. The farmer who owned the land where they built the breastworks came into the 123rd New York's camp to complain about the taking of his fence rails. He demanded to know who was going to pay him for his loss, and wanted to know how he was going to be able to tell his rails apart from those of his neighbors. "The boys had considerable sport with the old fellow," recalled the regimental historian of the 123rd New York, "and we are sure he did not get satisfactory answers to his inquiries."[56]

Meade ordered 6th Corps commander John Sedgwick to send a division and an additional brigade to advance upon Funkstown and to take possession of the town. Once in possession of Funkstown, Sedgwick had orders to effect a lodgment on the high ground beyond overlooking the town. If the enemy resisted in force, Sedgwick was to bring his entire corps forward to support the troops and hold the town.[57]

The gunners of Battery C of the 1st Rhode Island Artillery, 6th Corps, participated in the fight at Funkstown the day before and held their position over night. On the morning of July 11, they advanced a section of two guns about 1,500 yards and fired four rounds over the village, hoping to draw a response from the Confederates. No response came, however, for the Southerners had already pulled back to their main line.[58]

Some soldiers of Horatio G. Wright's division, part of Sedgwick's 6th Corps, slipped into the village for conversation, drink, and pretty girls. After swimming in Antietam Creek, they caught fish for dinner. A few of the more rambunctious among them executed a raid on a local henhouse. They succeeded despite a rooster's crows that betrayed them to the farmer. When he reached his henhouse, the raiders had already departed, each proudly carrying a fat chicken in each hand.[59]

Maj. Gen. Henry W. Slocum, commander, 12th Corps, Army of the Potomac.

USAHEC

Meade also ordered Thomas Neill's division to rejoin the 6th Corps at Funkstown, together with McIntosh's cavalry brigade and William "Baldy" Smith's militia. These troops had been left languishing in Waynesboro, Pennsylvania, waiting for orders. In other words, the veterans of Neill's division and McIntosh's horse soldiers had played no active role since the engagements at Fairfield on July 5 and 6. Reliable veteran troops had been kept out of the pursuit entirely for reasons that remain dubious, at best.[60]

On the whole, the Confederates liked their defensive position, but many of the Federals could not say the same thing for their own posts. "I have the honor to inform you that my corps is in position, pursuant to orders, the right resting at [Jones' Crossroads] and the left near Marsh Run," wrote Maj. Gen. Henry W. Slocum, commander of the 12th Corps, to General Meade. "I regard the position utterly untenable," proclaimed Slocum. "There are two ranges of hills in my front, the first of which commands my position, and the second commands the first. Both ranges are occupied by the enemy. I have been informed that the enemy have been constructing works on the second range." Although Meade respected Slocum's concerns, no other viable option was available. Regardless of where the Army of the Potomac attacked, a formidable barrier awaited its divisions—and every general and most of its privates knew it.[61]

Strong though Lee's defenses were, Meade ordered his corps commanders to probe them on the 11th. Their orders noted that if these probes found the enemy, the Federal generals were to drive the Confederate pickets until they came up against the main body of Lee's army. Sharp skirmishing broke out as the lines advanced, the light popping of small arms accompanied by intermittent blasts of artillery fire. The cavalry demonstrated constantly, probing the Confederate defenses for weak spots that tenaciously refused to reveal themselves.[62] They also received orders to ride to Funkstown and solidify the Union's hold on the critical junction town.[63]

The situation at the College of St. James grew more dangerous for its inhabitants with each passing hour. Eliza Porter, the mother of Maj. Gen. Fitz-John Porter (who had been cashiered from the Federal Army in January) was a friend of Rector Kerfoot's family and had been staying among the dangerous conditions at the college for several weeks. Lt. Gen. A. P. Hill and Brig. Gen. Cadmus M. Wilcox had been Porter's classmates at West Point. When both officers learned that Fitz-John's mother was on the perilous grounds of the college, they determined to act. Concerned for her safety, "at noon," recorded Kerfoot, the two Southern generals rode to the main college building "to warn Mrs. Porter to leave at once. They kindly urged me to take every lady and child away at once. Men might, ought to stay, to protect property. . . . My wife and daughter did not wish to go. Safer here; and battle just at hand. Cannonading already near us. (Gen. Hill said, 'If it were my wife and daughter, I would make them go.')"[64]

Kerfoot decided to heed Little Powell's wise advice, but leaving was not as simple as just riding away. The fragile party would have to run the gauntlet of two armies to escape to safer ground. The decision, wrote Kerfoot, was "The most harrowing doubt and debate of my life, but decide to go. In haste," he continued,

> packed up a few clothes and stowed away a few more valuables in the cellar, and at 1:30 p.m. drove off the College wagon with wife, two daughters . . . and my little carriage came along, Mrs. Porter in it. The cannon of our United States Army were already throwing shells, visible and audible, against the batteries of our outer gate; and the brigade of cavalry (Confederate) wheeling into position on our lawn as we drove off. Our ride for two miles was right along the Confederate sharpshooters, who were crouching under the fence, ten feet on our left. Our United States sharpshooters three-quarters of a mile on our right. God's mercy took us through safely to Hagerstown. General Hill gave me and my party a pass anywhere, on parole not to give any information to their detriment. Hagerstown in full possession of the Confederates.[65]

On the morning of July 11, Gamble's and Devin's cavalry brigades were ordered to move. They rode through Boonsboro and Keedysville, crossed Antietam Creek, and trotted through the old 1862 battlefield before going into camp that evening around 9:00 p.m. about seven miles from the previous day's bivouac.[66] Given the strategic nature of the opposing armies, however, most of the horses had to remain saddled.[67] During this forty-eight hour period, the troopers reconnoitered the countryside to their front as well as the enemy's position facing Downsville.[68]

"I went on a scout [and] could hear the enemy moving their train," Jasper Cheney of the 8th New York told his diary.[69] Joseph McHenry Adkinson of the 3rd Indiana Cavalry found a little time to write his brother a short letter. "After so long I find myself seated to penn you a few lines and but few, for we expect every moment an engagement. Already this morning we have saddle twice[.] We expect a hard fight here soon. The troops are eager for it. They seem very sertain of what the issue will be. I have no time to write—haven't had for the last two weeks, as we have marched every day. . . . The boys are all right and in good spirits considering the hard duty."[70]

That evening, a Federal signal officer reported that a citizen had told him that only about 6,000 Confederates still occupied Hagerstown, and that the rest had moved on to Williamsport. The signal officer conducted his own reconnaissance and confirmed the civilian intelligence.[71] According to a newspaper correspondent, Lee, Longstreet, and Ewell were the last Confederate officers to leave the town.[72] If the Army of the Potomac could seize the critical crossroads town of Hagerstown, it could control the road network to Williamsport. With only 6,000 Confederates left defending it, the time was right for Meade to attempt exactly that.

Union infantry streamed in behind the cavalry, occupying familiar ground they had fought over during the September 1862 Maryland Campaign. The men of the 12th New Hampshire Infantry found themselves crossing the same portion of the Antietam battlefield they had fought their way across the fall before. The veterans compared Meade to their former commander, Maj. Gen. George B. McClellan, who had been widely criticized for not being aggressive enough in his pursuit of Lee. A sense of déja vu settled over their ranks as they trudged on.[73]

The rest of Gregg's cavalry division, which had been dispersed by General Pleasonton on July 4, finally assembled in the vicinity of Boonsboro, where it stayed for a day. Back in the saddle, Gregg's men rode to Harpers Ferry on July 13, and so would play no role in the actions near Williamsport.[74]

Even the emergency troops from the defenses of Harrisburg joined the battle lines. "Our camp was located in the line of the grand army, with rebel breastworks 1½ miles in front," recounted a member of the 28th Pennsylvania Emergency Infantry. "Our boys are in fair spirits, considering the situation—enduring hard marching in the heavy rains, without tents or blankets, and rations half the time. These things keep up a 'regimental growl' generally."[75]

The men in the ranks were not permitted to build large fires, so they had to make do with whatever they had, both for warmth as well as for cooking. Men huddled around small piles of burning twigs, hoping to generate enough heat to boil their coffee, roast their pork, or make some other crude meal. "For myself, a cup of coffee and a piece of raw pork between two hardtack was a good supper," recalled a Rhode Island artillerist.[76] Lt. Elisha Hunt Rhodes of the 2nd Rhode Island enjoyed a rare treat: fresh bread and butter. "It was very good," he noted in his diary with satisfaction.[77]

Another storm blew in early on the morning of July 12. "At 2 o'clock a most terrific thunder-storm arose, such as had never overtaken our army, even in Virginia," recalled a member of the 6th Corps. "Huge black clouds rose from the north and from the west and south, and meeting overhead poured down great volumes of water, until the road through which we were marching, and which was bordered by high banks on either side, was filled with a mad torrent which reached to the knees, and in places to the waists of the men."[78] To the dismay of the Southern soldiers, the Potomac, which had begun to drop, quickly swelled again.

In Washington, meanwhile, Lincoln "seemed in a specially good humor today, as he had pretty good evidence that the enemy were still on the North side of the Potomac and Meade had announced his intention of attacking them in the morning," Lincoln's secretary John Hay explained to his diary that day. "The Prest. seemed very happy in the prospect of a brilliant success. He had been rather impatient with Gen Meade's slow movements since Gettysburg, but concluded today that Meade would yet show sufficient activity to inflict the coup de grace upon the flying rebels."[79]

Chapter 14

July 12: The Second Battle of Hagerstown

"Call no council of war. It is proverbial that councils of war never fight."

— General-in-Chief Henry Halleck to George Meade

ON JULY 11, COL. PENNOCK HUEY'S BRIGADE of horse soldiers of Gregg's 2nd Division pressed forward along the Williamsport Road from its campsite near Jones' Crossroads and engaged Confederate infantry along the Sharpsburg turnpike near the College of St. James. "Finding they had the advantage in position, we opened on them with artillery, driving them from it, and our dismounted men, pushing forward, captured 5 in a house and killed 3," reported Huey. His horsemen held their position that night until they retired to their campsite. The following morning, July 12, they advanced again to renew the skirmish and drove the enemy into his breastworks along the whole line. "We now held a position about 150 yards from the first line of the enemy's breastworks, which they were busily engaged in extending," observed Huey.[1]

Sgt. James M. Mathews of Berdan's 2nd U.S. Sharpshooters penned a remarkably accurate forecast of events in his diary for the 12th. His regiment moved to the road junction that morning in support of Huey's men. "We are now near Jones Crossroads. One of A. P. Hill's scouts was captured today, so it seems we're fighting as usual against his command," wrote Mathews. "There are two lines of battle in our front and we move as they move. Prisoners are being captured but no general engagement has commenced. Meade is feeling along and the enemy does not seem to be inclined to fight. We have all kinds of reports as regards the enemy's means of crossing the Potomac. It is said they are tearing down houses for the material to construct bridges etc."[2]

The 19th Maine also marched to support the horse soldiers fighting at Jones' Crossroads. "The column came to a halt without orders. The men began to drop in the road just where they stood and soon every man was asleep," recalled a member of the 19th Maine. "The writer recalls awaking at early dawn and as far as he could see north and south the road was full of sleeping men."[3] The College of St. James' Reverend Kerfoot and his little party of women and children arrived in Hagerstown the evening of July 11, where they found the chaotic town in Confederate hands. Although July 12 was a Sunday, Kerfoot noted that there were "no churches open." The arrival of Federal troops shattered whatever silence hung over Hagerstown due to the lack of ringing church bells. "At 8 a.m. our (U.S.) cavalry dashed in," Kerfoot later jotted in his diary, leaving him to wonder if he and his family were "hardly less in peril here than at the College."[4]

Col. Huey's brigade advanced to within a short distance of the college on the right of the road from Boonsboro. Huey reported that he found the enemy in force on his right and a strong line of skirmishers in his front. "I have driven them from their first position on the left of the road," he asserted. "They have a long line of rifle pits just back of the college, covering the ground in that vicinity." Huey concluded that he had advanced as far as possible without infantry support, as his line had grown too extended.[5] As night fell, the Union horsemen withdrew, again resuming their familiar camp at Jones' Crossroads. They had fought long and hard, with little to show for it.[6]

Kilpatrick and his division advanced on Hagerstown on July 12, supporting an 11th Corps infantry brigade commanded by Brig. Gen. Adelbert Ames. The town had become a bastion of annoying Confederate sharpshooters "armed with telescopic rifles, who could pick a man's ear off half-a-mile away," noted Capt. James H. Kidd of the 6th Michigan Cavalry. "The bullets from their guns had a peculiar sound, something like the buzz of a bumble-bee, and the troopers' horses would stop, prick up their ears and gaze in the direction whence the hum of those invisible messengers could be heard."[7]

Kilpatrick's troopers captured nearly the entire Confederate picket line. A handful of dismounted Southerners protected by a stone fence to Kilpatrick's right began popping away at them. Annoyed, Little Kil turned to George Custer and ordered him to send a regiment to capture the enemy holding the stone fence. Custer, who usually itched for a fight, hesitated, pointing out that a battery and cavalry on the other side of the field protected them. Kilpatrick turned to his headquarters escort, Company A of the 1st Ohio Cavalry and ordered, "Go and pick up those men. Use your pistols on them."

The Ohioans drew sabers and dashed across the field and into the barnyard. The quick attack surprised the Southerners and resulted in the capture of an entire company and its lieutenant. "Our artillery fired over our heads on the cavalry, and one of our brigades coming down on the right scattered them, but if our prisoners had been a few rods over the stone wall they would have defended themselves and made us suffer," noted a Buckeye. "But this was another providential escape and added to our General's confidence in our courage." Adelbert Ames and his 11th Corps infantrymen, who moved to the support of the Ohioans, also captured a number of dismounted skirmishers and scattered the rest of the pickets.[8]

The way into Hagerstown now open, Kilpatrick ordered Custer's Wolverines to charge into the town. The Michiganders put spurs to horse and scattered the Confederate infantry, chasing many down in the streets and side yards. Lt. Col. Ebenezer Gould, in front of his 5th Michigan Cavalry, was severely wounded. When their momentum carried them westward through and beyond the town, the Wolverines had a clear view of the bristling defensive position held by Lee's army less than three-quarters of a mile distant.[9] As they were about to cross a small stream, the enemy rose up from behind a stone wall and unleashed a murderous volley. "Returning the fire, and finding them too strong, we returned [to Hagerstown]," recalled one of Custer's troopers.[10] The charge and subsequent heavy fighting freed Hugh St. Clair of the 18th Pennsylvania Cavalry, who had been captured during the savage street brawl in Hagerstown on July 6. St. Clair rejoined his company and took a hand in this day's fight.[11]

"No man could have appeared more cool in battle than did Custer on this occasion," observed a civilian. "He rode by us near the head of his column, his long yellow curls flowing over his shoulders, his hat in his left hand, waving it and bowing to the ladies at the windows, who were waving handkerchiefs, while storms of bullets were sweeping his ranks." "The First Vermont charged their entrenchments at Hagerstown, and put two brigades of infantry in great disorder," reported Major Hammond of the 5th New York, with more than a little exaggeration. "Had Gen. Meade allowed one or two brigades to go to their assistance, we might have captured ten thousand of the ragamuffins."[12]

The victorious Michiganders took possession of the town, noting that the Confederates had constructed barricades on several streets in an effort to stifle (unsuccessfully) the sort of cavalry dashes that occurred on July 6.[13] "We chased the enemy beyond their hastily constructed earthworks beyond Hagerstown, which stretched away beyond the river," recorded a Buckeye of Kilpatrick's headquarters escort. "Several companies were surrounded in our rapid advance and captured entire. We had about 500 prisoners from this day's work."[14]

The Army of the Potomac's 11th Corps advanced simultaneously, marching into the center of the town and occupying it. After suffering depredations at the hands of the occupying Confederates, the "citizens were overjoyed at the appearance of our troops," remembered a Federal.[15] This combined arms attack pushed the Southerners back to their prepared line of defenses around Williamsport, helping to further hem in Lee's army along the banks of the swollen Potomac River.[16]

Pvt. Andrew D. Jackson of the 6th Michigan Cavalry watched Confederate prisoners pass by. The Wolverines halted as the prisoners lay down by a fence or climbed atop it to rest. Jackson spotted a long, lean, ragged man leaning against the fence chewing tobacco and spitting prodigious amounts of juice.

"Well, Johnny, we've caught you too far from 'Canada' this time!" called out Jackson.

"Yas, Yank!, But you-uns couldn't do this in old Virginia," he answered, no doubt feeling more at home there than he did on the soil of Maryland.[17]

Williamsport

Williamsport in July 1863 was a horrid place, and its Southern defenders were subjected to all of its many unpleasantness. Imboden's men still had the job of defending the town and the river crossing. "It was an awful place," noted a member of the 18th Virginia Cavalry, "the dead horses and offal of the great number of beeves, etc., killed for the army packed around the little town made it unpleasant for us when we returned to camp after night. The green flies were around us all the time and orders were not to unsaddle or unbridle our horses and be ready for duty all the time." The horse soldier continued, "Our blankets were under our saddles and soaked with water and the green flies were working under the rawhide covering of our saddles and ulcerated backs of our horses . . . It was rush all the time, when we would go to camp for food and sleep, we would very likely be ordered out on the line again by the news of our outposts being attacked and drove in, and then we would very likely spend the rest of the night looking for a fight." The sleep deprivation only made their plight that much worse.[18]

That morning, July 12, John Buford reconnoitered between Williamsport and Downsville. Heavy fog hindered his ability to see much. "At or near Downsville is a division of Longstreet entrenching themselves," reported Buford. "Their line is on a height just this side of Downsville. It extends south toward the river, in a very rugged country, with many stone walls parallel to their front. The country on my left next to the river is impracticable for any considerable force to advance." An attack against the southern end of Lee's line was, as Buford discovered, impracticable.[19]

Later that day when the fog thinned, Buford forwarded additional intelligence reports to headquarters. "I have information confirming the information that the enemy is not crossing the river," he wrote. "Nothing but sick and wounded go over. At Williamsport there is but one flat-boat, which crosses the river in about seven minutes. It crosses by means of a wire rope. The river is not fordable. This morning several horses with equipments floated down the river in front of my pickets. All quiet in my front," he concluded.[20]

Although trapped, Lee's men were in an exceedingly good defensive position. Full of fight, they waited impatiently for the Federals to assault their lines. "We were drawn up in the line of battle yesterday near Hagerstown and still lie in wait for the enemy to attack us," noted a regimental surgeon of one of Maj. Gen. John B. Hood's brigades. "Our men have thrown up breastworks on a good position, and feel confident of giving the Yankees a whipping if they come up to them." He concluded, "If we had the Yankees in the fix they had had us in for several days, I do not think many of them would escape."[21] Regimental chaplains visited their flocks, praying with and for them as they waited for the Union assault almost everyone expected to occur.[22]

Lee expected the attack would take place on this day, July 12, and that it would likely be delivered against Richard Ewell's front. "Should it be, and there be nothing to occupy you, I wish you to bear down on the enemy's right, endeavoring to select good positions with your horse artillery, to harass and retard him," the commanding general instructed Stuart. Several hours later, Lee elaborated on his instructions to his cavalry chief. "Keep an eye over the field, use your good judgment, and give assistance where necessary," he implored.[23]

When he learned that Meade was massing his troops in front of James Longstreet and A. P. Hill, Lee informed Stuart that he expected the main attack to take place between the Williamsport-Boonsboro Road and the Frederick Road that morning. Trusting Stuart to do what he did best, Lee took some comfort in knowing that his army's flanks would be protected.[24]

That night, General Lee found a few moments to write to his wife. "You will have learned before this reaches you that our success at Gettysburg was not as great as reported. In fact, that we failed to drive the enemy from his position & that our army withdrew to the Potomac," he said. "Had the river not unexpectedly risen, all would have been well with us. But God in His all wise Providence willed otherwise, & our communications have been interrupted &

almost cut off. The waters have subsided to about 4 feet & if they continue, by tomorrow I hope our communications will be open." The pious Southern commander concluded, "I trust that our merciful God, our only help & refuge, will not desert us in this our hour of need, but will deliver us by His almighty hand, that the whole world may recognize His power & all hearts be lifted up in adoration & praise of His unbounded loving kindness."[25]

The Main Body of the Army of the Potomac

As earlier noted, Meade's troops were physically almost completely played out. The endless days of hard marching and harder fighting had stripped away their energy. When fresh troops relieved the 18th Pennsylvania Cavalry along the front skirmish line at Hagerstown, Capt. John W. Phillips remembered that he "dragged myself back to the meadow where, in the falling rain without cover the boys lay sleeping with their saddles for pillows, only to be awakened a few hours later by the bugle call to 'Boots and Saddles' and this, for the purpose of hurrying out to the front in order to give the retreating forces a parting salute."[26]

While Kilpatrick fought for, and took possession of, Hagerstown, Capt. L. B. Kurtz of the 17th Pennsylvania Cavalry volunteered to ascertain the precise dispositions of the Army of Northern Virginia. He swam his horse across the flooded Potomac at Falling Waters and learned the Confederates were building a new pontoon to facilitate their crossing back to Virginia. He also observed wagons, artillery, and limbers crossing the river by flatboats, and dashed back to Col. Thomas C. Devin's headquarters to report his findings. Unless the Army of the Potomac moved quickly, it looked as though Lee and his embattled army would escape to safety.[27] "The boys wonder why Meade has not attacked Lee," observed one of Gamble's men in his diary that night.[28]

The main body of the Union infantry was now in place and expecting to be called upon to assault the Confederates. The advancing infantry cheered as they moved into position facing Lee's main line of battle.[29] "We must have a battle in the morning as Lee cant get over the river today," wrote a Pennsylvanian in his diary on July 12. "Every one is anxious, but determined for it must be a terrific battle with a desperate foe and we must win."[30]

The deployment of the army was as follows: Oliver Howard's 11th Corps held the Union right flank, between Hagerstown and Funkstown; John Newton's 1st Corps was to Howard's left, and to Newton's left was John Sedgwick's 6th Corps; George Sykes's 5th Corps was to the left of Sedgwick, and Alexander Hays' 2nd Corps fell in alongside Sykes, extending down to

Jones' Crossroads; Henry Slocum's 12th Corps formed the left flank, occupying a high ridge along the Williamsport-Boonsboro Road. This line extended from just south of Hagerstown to just north of the old Antietam battlefield. Orders arrived for the Yankee infantry to dig in.

"We arrived here about an hour ago, and about half an hour behind the retreating Rebels," wrote a Massachusetts officer from the 6th Corps from the front lines at Funkstown. "We just passed through the town and have come up with their rear guard and skirmishing is going on while I write. Our Brigade is in the front line today and if we have a fight we shall have our share of it." He continued, "We have been in line expecting a fight momentarily for 3 days and nights but it has not come off yet . . . I do not know what is going on but we expected to have another desperate battle before this, but we get on mighty slow, and I am afraid they will get away from us though I hope something is doing on our left to get between them and the river."[31]

"We marched through Funkstown to a position about a mile beyond that place," Pvt. Wilbur Fisk of the 2nd Vermont Infantry, 6th Corps, wrote in his diary. "I should think the ladies of Funkstown were highly pleased to see Union troops again." Fisk used the opportunity to mail a letter by handing it to one of the local women as he marched by. Passing beyond the town, the Vermonters formed into line of battle and advanced to skirmish with the Confederate troops beyond the town. The 6th Corps veterans spent most of the afternoon engaged with the enemy.[32]

Although the conditions were less than ideal for visitation, a number of Washington politicians made their way into the Union camps. "The Regiment was cheered by the sight of the face and form of United States Senator Henry Wilson, all the way from Washington," noted an officer of the 10th Massachusetts, part of the 6th Corps. "Evidently he wanted to see what active campaigning was like. If he had remained with his 22d Regiment he would have known very well long before this."[33] Wilson, one of the "Radical Republicans," would later use the information gleaned during his visit to the front to torment George Gordon Meade through the Committee on the Conduct of the War.

"There was marching and countermarching along the Hagerstown turnpike, for what purpose the men were ignorant," complained a member of the 14th Connecticut, "finally taking a turn in a wheat field in the midst of a severe rain, where a line was formed with great nicety." The men then began building a line of earthworks. They could not understand why they were not attacking the enemy lines instead.[34]

Maj. Gen. William F. "Baldy" Smith's militia forces from the defenses of Harrisburg had been slowly moving toward a rendezvous with the main body of the Army of the Potomac, hoping to complete the encirclement of Lee's isolated army. Moving out from Carlisle on the morning of July 3, they made for Williamsport. Along the way, these green soldiers experienced quite an ordeal. They had cautiously begun their pursuit on July 5. "Mud more than ankle deep, up hill and down hill, through deep meandering streams, on, on toward Pine Grove," noted a Pennsylvanian that day. "Hundreds gave out and lay in the wayside in the woods."[35] They passed through Waynesboro and headed into Maryland on July 9. "I followed along keeping close to the mountains and with what speed I could, with the impossibility of drawing supplies from the country," recalled General Smith, "and the difficulty of getting them forwarded from Harrisburg—had more or less little skirmishes, and finally joined the Army of the Potomac."

These men were not seasoned soldiers, and so drew the contempt of the Army of the Potomac's veterans. Elements of Neill's division of the 6th Corps met up with them near Waynesboro, Pennsylvania. "The militia was composed mostly of young gentlemen who had left their places behind the counter or at the desk, for the double purpose of lending their aid to their country in its hour of need," wrote one of Sedgwick's veterans, "and enjoying a month of what they hoped would be amateur soldiering." Undisciplined and inexperienced, many of these men were more interested in plundering than in fighting.

"They were all complaining bitterly of the terrible marches they had endured, and swore they would shoot the general if they ever got into a fight," facetiously recalled a member of the 77th New York. He continued his tongue-in-check observations: "They had marched all the way from Harrisburg, to which point they had been brought in cars, at the rate of from eight to fifteen miles a day! In addition to the severe marches, they had been subjected to great privations; many of them had not tasted any butter for more than a week, and nearly all declared that they had absolutely nothing to eat for several days." The quartermasters distributed hardtack to the militia, who turned their noses up at it. The veterans laughed at the greenhorns when they declared, "You don't expect us to eat that hard tack, do you?"[36]

Baldy Smith and some of his unruly command of militiamen finally arrived near Williamsport on July 12, adding their weight to the large Federal force closing in around the Army of Northern Virginia. "While bathing in the afternoon, a terrific thunderstorm came on. Hastily putting on my shirt I skedaddled for the nearest barn more hastily than dignifiedly. The lightning and

Maj. Gen. Henry W. Halleck,
General-In-Chief,
United States Army

USAHEC

thunder was awful," reported a Pennsylvania militiaman. "More of the men were slightly shocked, the lightning playing among the guns."[37] When Smith reported to Meade, he suggested the army commander scatter the inexperienced militia among the Army of the Potomac's veteran units, so that they could go into battle supported by experienced soldiers. Meade, however, rejected the suggestion because he had no intention of using Smith's command in combat.[38]

As Smith's men were joining Meade, tons of critical supplies of ammunition were on their way to Lee's army, heading for the Potomac crossings at Williamsport. The Federals had an opportunity to interdict these wagons and so prevent them from getting through to Lee with their precious cargo. Some 4,500 Union men from the Department of West Virginia, commanded by Brig. Gen. Benjamin F. Kelley, advanced east along the National Road from Cumberland with exactly that task in mind. As early as July 5, Halleck had ordered Kelley to march his command east "by rapid and vigorous motion" from the Clarksburg, western Virginia area to Williamsport, and to "do everything in your power to capture or destroy Lee's trains, which will endeavor to cross at Williamsport or Falling Waters."[39] Although Kelley and his two brigades reached Hancock by the night of July 7, Kelley elected to stop there and wait for reinforcements instead of pressing on to Williamsport, less than twenty miles distant.

Although Halleck's July 5 orders directed Kelley to attack Lee's wagons, seemingly contradictory orders reached Kelley at Hancock on July 9. "If Lee gives battle, do not be absent, but come in and help General Meade gain a victory," wrote the general-in-chief. "A battle is not far off."[40] This second directive left Kelley with the reasonable impression that he was to move to

Meade's support if and when the Army of the Potomac attacked (or Lee attacked it), rather than not take the initiative and attack the enemy wagon train.

Despite reports of the arrival of the Confederate pontoon and ammunition trains, Meade did not take any action to prevent them from reaching Lee's army. He could have requested Kelley to attack the supply point, but for reasons that remain unclear, failed to do so. And so the best opportunity Meade had to prevent Lee's army from being re-supplied slipped away without a shot being fired. Had Kelley been aggressive—had he simply read Halleck's order differently—his men could have damaged or destroyed the Confederate wagon trains with artillery fire alone.[41] Instead, these men skirmished with Confederate cavalry in the vicinity of Clear Spring on July 10 as the wagons rolled unmolested to the river.

As Kelley's opportunity to grasp history fell away, another 6,500 men were underway to join Meade under command of Brig. Gen. Henry M. Naglee. These men made up the Harpers Ferry garrison, and many of them were due to be mustered out. Additional men, some 8,000 from William H. French's command, moved from Frederick to reinforce Naglee. "The march was directly toward the sound of cannon which was heard early in the day," remembered one of French's foot soldiers. "It was necessarily a forced march, and the day becoming excessively hot there was much straggling from sheer exhaustion. Men dragged themselves along until they dropped down in their tracks."[42]

These three commands, nearly 20,000 (largely inexperienced) troops, were about to join Meade's army. The odds already facing Lee's veterans were about to get longer.

The Council of War

"I found Lee in a very strong position, intrenched," wrote General Meade, adding wisely, "I hesitated to attack him without some examination of the mode of approaching him." Meade called a council of war on the night of July 12 in order to determine whether to attack Lee's formidable line of entrenchments.[43] That same night, he cabled Washington that "it is my intention to attack them tomorrow, unless something intervenes to prevent it, for the reason that delay will strengthen the enemy and will not increase my force."[44]

Meade called the council because his options were limited and each decision was portentous. As one staff officer recalled, the army commander "was greatly anxious and troubled over what to do and how to do it. Halleck was urging him to attack every day—almost every hour—'hit or miss.' But

Halleck was safe in the War Department at Washington, eighty miles away, while Meade was in the field at the head of the army, and keenly alive to his duties and responsibilities." Meade had just won a tremendous battle, and he knew that a defeat on the banks of the Potomac would negate that victory. Now, Lee held the interior lines and would be on the defensive and largely entrenched. The last thing Meade wanted to reenact was Fredericksburg. "I well remember that week or so at Williamsport," recalled the same Federal staff officer. "At Army headquarters we were all on the qui vive every day, and eager for action. Each day we expected something big to happen, but nothing came of it."[45]

Meade, his chief of staff General Andrew A. Humphreys, and his corps commanders, attended the conference. The corps commanders included Gens. James Wadsworth (filling in for an ill General John Newton), William Hays (in temporary command of the 2nd Corps), William H. French (commanding the 3rd Corps after Maj. Gen. Sickles fell wounded), George Sykes, John Sedgwick, Oliver O. Howard, Henry W. Slocum, Alfred Pleasonton, and Baldy Smith. Also in attendance was the Army of the Potomac's chief engineer, Brig. Gen. Gouverneur K. Warren. "Meade read us Lee's proclamation, apparently fresh and hearty, wherein ostensibly he courted an opportunity for another trial of strength under more favorable circumstances than those which caused him his reverse at Gettysburg," remembered Howard. "All regarded that proclamation as something to keep up Confederate courage and allowed to come to us for 'strategic' effect."[46]

Despite the odds, Meade favored an attack the next day, July 13. Wadsworth, Howard, Pleasonton, and Warren also favored an attack. Sedgwick (Meade's ranking subordinate), Slocum, Sykes, French, and Hays, however, opposed going over to the offensive. Humphreys, Pleasonton, and Warren were not permitted a vote, meaning that a five-vote to five-vote deadlock ensued. "I do not think I ever saw the principal corps commanders so unanimous in favor of not fighting as on that occasion," recalled Warren.[47]

"Pleasonton, Wadsworth and I voted to attack," remembered Howard, "[the] rest voted to leave well enough alone. Sedgwick said [to me], 'I will support you.' Meade said he was only supported by one corps commander, but he did not give much weight [to my vote because I] always wanted to fight. Meade would not issue the order . . . Pleasonton was very anxious to attack . . . I was in favor of throwing out a strong skirmish line, and then with the main body, attack Lee's left flank."[48]

Sedgwick later explained his rationale for voting against an attack, and why he believed that caution was the best course of action. "Two such armies, having fought each other so often, having known each other so long and intimately, cannot very well afford to play at fast and loose," he wrote in a private letter. "At Hagerstown Lee had a very strong position, which Meade, with his certainly not superior force, could not with safety attack. He could not be morally certain of success, and dared not risk a failure which would entail such serious consequences as a defeat would not have failed to bring about."[49] However, the responsibility ultimately rested on Meade's shoulders. He could have overridden their vote with his authority as the commander of the army. General French summed it up well when he offered, "If you give the order to attack, we will fight just as well under it as if our opinions were not against it."[50]

* * *

With most of his corps commanders voting against an assault, Meade changed his mind and decided against an attack on July 13. The decision allowed his grateful men another day's rest. Still, the inaction frustrated Meade. That same afternoon, July 13, information reached Meade that "Lee has a bridge, composed of thirteen boats, across the center of the river, continued thence on both shores by trestlework, supporting long timbers." Bridge or no bridge, Meade had not been able to find a suitable spot against which he could crack open Lee's defensive line, and his subordinates refused to support an effort to find one with a general attack. As early as July 8, he had written his wife, "I think we shall have another battle before Lee can cross the river, though from all accounts he is making great efforts to do so. For my part, as I have to follow and fight him, I would rather do it at once and in Maryland than to follow into Virginia."[51]

When he learned that Meade had postponed his attack, a frustrated Henry Halleck reacted with predictable anger. "You are strong enough to attack and defeat the enemy before he can effect a crossing," scolded the general-in-chief. "Act upon your own judgment and make your generals execute your orders. Call no council of war. It is proverbial that councils of war never fight."[52]

Meade at least partially obeyed by issuing orders for a reconnaissance in force by at least one division each from the 12th, 2nd, 5th, and 6th Corps. The move was to begin promptly at 7:00 a.m. on the morning of July 14.[53]

General French, the newly appointed leader of the Army of the Potomac's 3rd Corps who is not generally credited with military acumen, offered a lucid assessment of the situation. "There is one of two things which will happen," he wrote Meade on July 12. "(1) Lee has a chosen position in which he awaits our attack; or (2) we will stumble on him in our present advance. Which has the advantage of a previous study of the configuration of the country, water-courses, roads, ridges, extension of roads, &c., with the best order for marching, and the best routes of direction, will have so far the advantage."[54] French was correct. Lee's engineers had combed every inch of ground in that sector, and they had chosen their position with great care.

General Howard ordered a reconnaissance toward Lee's left flank by a regiment of Brig. Gen. Alexander Schimmelfennig's brigade and some of Kilpatrick's cavalry. As soon as the dismounted horsemen approached the enemy line, the butternuts opened a brisk fire with both infantry and artillery. This reconnaissance persuaded Howard that Lee would retreat without giving battle, and he was eager as always to pitch in. The one-armed corps leader sent a note to Meade asking permission to lead a larger reconnaissance in force at 4:00 a.m. on the morning of July 14. Meade ordered the reconnaissance begin three hours later.[55]

"Remained quiet all day and night expecting much but seeing nothing," complained a Massachusetts officer of the 3rd Corps.[56] "It is thought we are delaying the attack waiting for reinforcements," noted a Federal soldier. "The rebs seemed to make a stand and whether compelled to or not being able to cross the river or at their own option, is not fully known."[57] A Pennsylvanian wrote along the same lines noting, "We lay in line all day long. An anxious, expectant day because every moment we looked for the attack that was to be the beginning of the end. But it came not. Meade must either be very confident that Lee cant escape or else, he or his advisors want him to escape."[58] Elements of the 2nd Corps spent the day strengthening their breastworks. They expected Lee to take the fight to them at any minute.[59]

Not every Northerner believed attacking was a good idea. Col. Charles S. Wainwright, chief of artillery for the Army of the Potomac's 1st Corps, conducted a careful examination of the Confederate defenses in front of his position. "I know nothing about the left of our line, but Lee's position in front of us is very strong, and so far as we can see well mounted with artillery," he scrawled in his diary on July 12. "My opinion is most decided that we could not carry it."[60]

The 10th Vermont Infantry was a new regiment and part of French's former division. These inexperienced soldiers had just joined the Army of the Potomac, and the rookies were nervous. "We shuddered at the thought of commencing a battle on Sunday," recalled the regimental chaplain, E. M. Haynes. "Men said that no battle had proved successful to the attacking party when commenced on that day, in the whole experience of this army. Some who ought to know have affirmed that this is universally true, and that the whole history of military records is not sufficient to disprove this observation. At any rate, rough-speaking, irreligious men, who were not afraid to fight at any time, did not want a battle begun in earnest at a time the civilized nation deemed holy."[61]

The Confederates had a different view of the unfolding events. "It looks to me as if the Yanks are afraid to attack General Lee when he is prepared for their reception," observed a Virginia horse artillerist of Chew's Battery.[62] The Southerners had a stout defensive position and they knew it. With the line of battle forged by Lee's engineers finally ready to invite an attack, Jeb Stuart's troopers uncovered the front and moved his horsemen off to cover the Army of Northern Virginia's flanks.

Although no attack took place that day, the residents of Boonsboro enjoyed a martial spectacle of a different variety. That evening, Buford's large division of cavalry clomped through the town, bands playing, flags flying, and the men in a compact solid column. The town itself was overflowing with people, with the inhabitants crowded out of their houses and the hordes of soldiers and refugees occupying the town were like a plague of locusts, eating all in sight.[63]

That night the atmosphere grew so heavy and the humidity so thick that objects could only be discerned at a short distance. It also rained periodically—hardly ideal conditions for an all-out assault.[64] Rain or not, the respective positions and circumstances of the opposing armies had not changed. And Meade still faced the decision whether or not to attack his enemy.

Chapter 15

July 13: A Frustrating Day Spent Waiting

"We hope Lee can't get away but his neck is slippery and we can only count on him when we get him."

— Sgt. Frank Saunders, 6th New York Cavalry

WHEN SKIRMISHING BROKE OUT ALONG the lines on July 13, both sides believed the long-awaited Union attack was finally underway. "At last the fire of the skirmishers became unusually heavy, and the impression general, that another great battle was about to be fought," reported a 1st Corps brigade commander.[1] The lines were so close the Federals could see squads of Confederates moving about preparing for an attack or getting ready to retreat. "We thought it strange that the rebels had made no attack upon us," observed a puzzled Rhode Island artillerist of the 2nd Corps.[2] "The enemy's lines of battle can be plainly seen only about six hundred yards away," observed an officer of the 10th Massachusetts of the 6th Corps.[3] General French, accompanied by his headquarters escort (a company of the 6th Pennsylvania Cavalry) discovered just how close the lines were when enemy soldiers opened fire on French and his little band during a reconnaissance ride, killing two troopers of the 1st New Jersey Cavalry.[4]

Federal morale along some parts of the line remained high. "The Union troops were eager for the anticipated assault. For two hours did they stand in line under a pelting rain, fervently desiring to be led forward in a charge upon the rebels," wrote a member of the 125th New York, part of the 2nd Corps. "They were full of confidence and were nerved by the highest hopes of crushing Lee and ending the war."[5] "Our picket lines were in sight of each other, and everyone looked forward to a battle the next day," recalled an officer of the Irish Brigade.[6]

Robert E. Lee was ready, willing, and able to give battle. However, when the firing petered out, Lee learned the Army of the Potomac was digging in instead of preparing an attack. "This is too long for me," proclaimed Lee. "I cannot wait for that." The army leader concluded, "They have but little courage!" With no obvious assault in the immediate offing, Lee made preparations to retreat across the Potomac, which was slowly but steadily dropping despite occasional thundershowers.[7]

Many of the Union soldiers across the way knew that the opportunity to bag the Virginia army was rapidly slipping through their fingers. "How I wish Meade could be induced to attack the enemy, and not weakly and ignorantly throw away the certainty of capturing or annihilating the entire rebel army," wailed a Vermonter in his diary. "There certainly must be effective and ardent troops enough, if properly managed, to destroy Lee's flying and demoralized army."[8] An officer of the 5th Corps speculated that even though the Confederates were careful about conserving powder and ammunition, they had probably been re-supplied. "I do not think we can injure them much without a siege, which, of course, they will avoid by crossing the river," he correctly observed.[9]

Time, as everyone on both sides of the line realized, was against the Confederates. Much as Lee might want to bring the Federals to battle along the banks of the Potomac, he could no longer remain there. "As further delay would enable the enemy to obtain reinforcements and as it was difficult to procure a sufficient supply of flour for the troops, the working of the mills being interrupted by high water, it was determined to await an attack no longer," wrote Lee's aide, Col. Charles Marshall.[10]

Abraham Lincoln spent the day fretting, waiting by the

Abraham Lincoln,
President of the United States.

LOC

telegraph for word of the battle he fully expected to be fought. "The President begins to grow anxious and impatient about Meade's silence," observed John Hay. "I thought and told him that there was nothing to prevent the enemy from getting away by the Falling Waters, if they were not vigorously attacked . . . Nothing can save them, if Meade does his duty." Hay, however, had his doubts. He knew Meade was an engineer, which made him cautious by nature, and the presidential secretary suspected that he would not attack.[11] Although Hay had no way of knowing it, he had correctly divined the situation unfolding along the Potomac.

On the night of July 12, Jeb Stuart and Maj. Henry B. McClellan, his able adjutant, rode along one of the turnpikes near Hagerstown attended by only a single courier. Stuart was dictating dispatches that McClellan was scribbling down, and the pair dismounted at a tollhouse so the aide could write by lamp light. As McClellan wrote out his dispatches, Stuart leaned forward, resting his head on his arms. Within a few seconds he was sound asleep. McClellan shook the general awake to get his approval once the messages were completed. There was precious little time for rest, and even generals learned to take advantage of every opportunity to grab a few moments' respite.[12]

Judson Kilpatrick wanted the militia to relieve his horse soldiers of duty in order to free them up to operate along the picket lines, but the militia would not advance beyond the protection of Hagerstown's houses. Stuart's cavalry was probing at his defenses, and Kilpatrick needed help from the green militiamen.[13] The Union cavalry leader sent his color bearer out to encourage them, but the Pennsylvanians refused to budge. Frustrated, Kilpatrick ordered his cavalry to charge, and the militia finally advanced to support the horse soldiers. Pvt. Maryam Judy of the 1st Ohio Cavalry was the color bearer sent to bolster the militia. Riding out and dodging the bullets that whizzed by his ears, Judy "remained unhurt until the cavalry charged, when, as he turned about to join the General, a stray bullet hit him in the right knee and passing through lodged against his saddle," wrote one eyewitness. "His brother, Elihu, who was nearby, saw that he was wounded and supported him back to our line, when he was taken to the hospital and attended by some kind Union ladies." Maryam Judy died not long after.[14]

Shortly after Kilpatrick's cavalry advanced, he received a note from General Meade indicating that Little Kil's attack had interfered with his own plans to assault along the lines the following morning. Meade's note only served to increase Kilpatrick's anger, for the cavalryman already was frustrated with the lack of aggressiveness on the part of the Army of the Potomac. Kilpatrick instructed his adjutant to reply that his push was necessary to drive the enemy back so he could hold Hagerstown. "I know that is not quite true," exclaimed Kilpatrick to his staff, "but I did not want the cowardly militia to return home without meeting the enemy."[15] Kilpatrick's frustration notwithstanding, the Union noose was still tightening, and Lee was making one critically important decision after another to save his army.

When elements of the 6th Corps advanced to their left, a heavy fire broke out from the Confederate lines anchored atop commanding high ground. "The ridge held by his skirmishers being vital to us, an attack was made upon it by a strong skirmish force from the three brigades of the division, which carried it handsomely just before dark, and held it," wrote Brig. Gen. Horatio G. Wright, commander of the 1st Division, 6th Corps. "Our casualties were, 4 officers and 4 men wounded."[16] Small unit actions like this raged all along the front the entire day.

As mini-battles were being waged, Buford's pickets fought a brisk skirmish near the College of St. James, advanced another three or four miles, and pushed to within 800 yards of Longstreet's entrenchments at Downsville. The Confederate cavalry resisted stoutly, falling back from hill to hill, holding each piece of high ground as long as possible before withdrawing, the Federal cavalry pursuing closely. A few videttes were wounded or captured, but there were no serious losses on either side.[17]

Through it all, the weather continued taking its toll on the soldiers of both sides. The men suffered through two torrid days, interrupted by heavy thunderstorms, which many welcomed. "In five minutes the water came down the hills, carrying away some tent-flies we had put up, and stood over a foot deep in camp. The artillery of Heaven had supplanted that of man," recalled an Illinois soldier. "Little fighting was done, and only two prisoners brought in, though the pickets exchanged shots, and kept the camp alarmed."[18] "[The rain] dashed down in huge drops. Then how cool it became," noted trooper James Bell of the 8th Illinois. "One could afford to take a good wetting to see such a refreshing storm. It done us lots of good."[19] According to a member of the 11th New York Cavalry, "our position was decidedly uncomfortable, as the only shelter we had was improvised by making shelter-tents of blankets, talmas, and ponchos."[20]

The 1st Vermont Cavalry deployed for skirmish duty on the western side of Williamsport. Companies D and I led the way, supported by some of Smith's rookie militia. When a few of the militiamen were slightly wounded, chaos broke out among their ranks. Kilpatrick laughed. "Hold on, boys, and I will show you some fun with a cavalry charge." About 7:00 p.m., Kilpatrick sent for Col. Edward B. Sawyer of the 1st Vermont. Sawyer brought his troopers up at a trot. "I want you to charge a squadron on those people down there, and I am going to lead the charge," proclaimed Kilpatrick. Sawyer threw out dismounted skirmishers while the squadron of Vermonters prepared to charge. The dismounted men took position behind shocks of wheat and were soon warmly engaged. Kilpatrick led the mounted squadron forward to the skirmish line, turned, and said, "Give 'em hell, boys!"

"On we dashed, squeezing through the skirmish-line, which was blocked in the road by kicking, squirming horses and men, caused by the deadly fire of the enemy," recalled Lt. Stephen A. Clark of the 1st Vermont.[21] Raked by flanking fire, the veteran horse soldiers drove the enemy pickets back through a wheat field onto a knoll, where they came under the protection of a battery. The gunners opened a severe fire, but the Vermonters pressed the attack, forcing the artillerists to pull back. The defenders pressed the Northerners, hoping to surround and capture the lot of them. The Vermonters took a few casualties and withdrew after recognizing they did not have sufficient strength to carry the day. They returned with a number of prisoners, escaping from a trap set for them by the Southerners. "Every man on that charge was deserving of a medal for getting out of the enemy's lines when entirely surrounded," claimed Lieutenant Clark, "instead of surrendering, which so many would have done."[22]

Reverend Kerfoot and his family watched the fighting from the safety of a friend's home in Hagerstown. "General Kilpatrick's 'reconnaissance in force' against enemy's left, just three-fourths of a mile west of Mrs. Kennedy's house, where we were. The Confederate shells flying and bursting in our view in the dark of the evening." He decided an assault against Lee's lines was imminent. He closed his diary that evening with, "Battle to-morrow about us!"[23]

The general inactivity frustrated some of the Federals, who sensed the chance for a decisive engagement slowly slipping away. "There is two army corps on our right, while one division holds the ground to the Potomac distant three miles," complained one Yankee horse soldier. "It seems to me that the whole rebel army must be over the river by this time, tho I suppose the commanding general knows better."[24] Sgt. Thomas W. Smith of the 6th Pennsylvania Cavalry, whose company was attached to army headquarters as its guard, noted, "We are expecting another battle now every hour . . . we are all saddled up and expect the General to go to the front every moment."[25] They watched and waited, as the excruciating minutes stretched into hours and hours into seemingly endless days.

Newspaper correspondent Charles C. Coffin visited Meade's headquarters. Maj. Gen. Seth Williams, the army's adjutant general, greeted him outside Meade's tent. The general, explained Williams, was observing the enemy's lines.

"Do you think that Lee can get across the Potomac?" inquired Coffin.

"Impossible!" declared Williams. "The people resident here say that it cannot be forded at this stage of the water. He has no pontoons. We have got him in a tight place. We shall have reinforcements tomorrow, and a great battle will be fought. Lee is encumbered with his teams, and he is short of ammunition."

Dripping water from the rain, Meade arrived on the scene. "His countenance was unusually animated," recalled Coffin. Meade, usually reticent around reporters, was positively giddy. "We shall have a great battle tomorrow," he declared. "The reinforcements are coming up, and as soon as they come we shall pitch in."

Coffin left Meade's tent and rode the lines with Maj. Gen. Howard, commander of the 11th Corps. Coffin could see the enemy fortifications across the way, and picket fire sounded regularly. He could also see men moving about. "I fear that Lee is getting away," Howard told him. He sent a staff officer to Meade with a request that he be given permission to attack. "I can double him up," he said, indicating that since he was on Lee's flank, he could strike an effective blow. Meade reiterated his instructions that no general engagement was to be brought on until the next day.[26]

A storm blew up once more after Meade climbed back into the saddle to try and get the full measure of Lee's position. The driving rain and low horizon made it impossible to see any great distance. Despite his inability to learn much about the Army of Northern Virginia's position, Meade remained determined to attack all along the lines at dawn the next morning.[27]

According to one source, at least part of Meade's army received orders that evening to prepare for an attack in the morning. After the war, then-Lieutenant William P. Seville of the 1st Delaware Infantry wrote an interesting recollection on the subject. "About ten o'clock at night an order was received directing a general charge on the rebel works at daylight in the morning, in which no other weapon was to be used than the bayonet; the men being required to take out of their cartridge-boxes all the ammunition and turn it in," recalled Seville. "This order was countermanded just before daylight, in all respects excepting that in regard to marching."[28] Seville's assertion cannot be corroborated with any other extant records, and it is unknown how many Federal units, if any, received such an order.

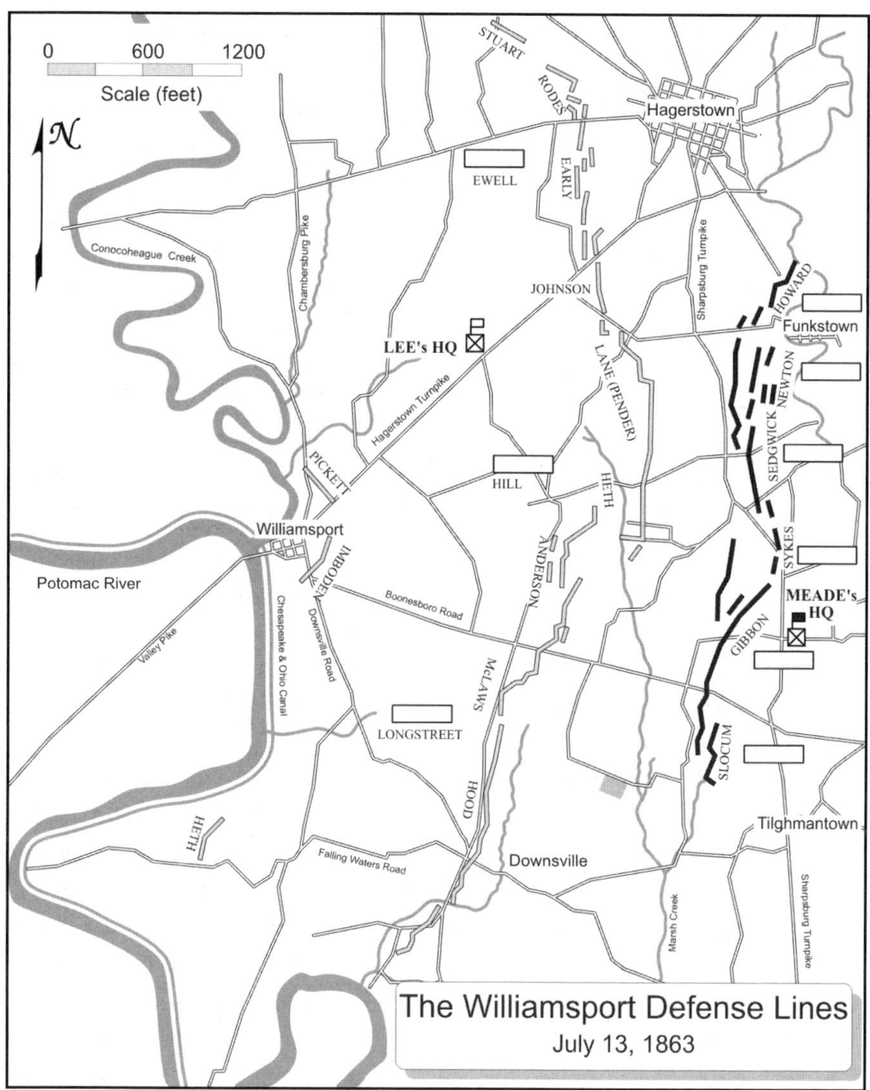

The monotony likewise frustrated the Southerners. "We moved to Downsville on the 10th and took position in line of battle facing the enemy; but they made no attack," reported one of Longstreet's artillerists. "I never saw the army so 'mad' as it was on that Downsville line; and if occasion had called it forth, we would have put up the biggest kind of a fight."[29]

Others welcomed the respite. Sgt. Frank Saunders of the 6th New York Cavalry was one of these men. "We have been hard at work for a long time. We have had tough fighting and hard marches," he reported on July 13. "I had been suffering all the while with diarrhea, which taken together has run me down to a perfect skeleton and I found myself too used up to proceed farther. The doctor advised me to go back to the hospital. There are quite a number of wounded cavalrymen here." He echoed the thoughts of most of the Federal soldiers. "We hope Lee can't get away but his neck is slippery and we can only count on him when we get him."[30]

Stuart's Confederate horse soldiers, who had not had much of an opportunity to rest since the Battle of Brandy Station on June 9, were even more worn down than Pleasonton's Federals. "The cavalry was driven in yesterday, since which time heavy skirmishing has been going on along our lines. The enemy, I have no doubt, are going to make a desperate effort to crush us here," observed Lt. George W. Beale of the 9th Virginia Cavalry. "If we are defeated, indeed the blow will be a terrible one to us and our cause; but we have no reason to fear we will be defeated. If we do our duty, that Divine Being who has so often given victory to this army, will surely not desert us now. The issue is in His holy hands; may He comfort and aid those who put their trust in Him!" Beale continued. "Our Generals think the cavalry will have a heavy part to bear in the coming battle. We are called upon to do our duty bravely. I look to the only true source of safety, for protection, amid the dangers to which we may be exposed."[31]

On July 13, after huddling with an anxious Lee for several hours, Stuart withdrew all of his men from the Army of Northern Virginia's front and massed them on the left of the Confederate position, all the while expecting a general assault by the Army of the Potomac. Stuart dispatched staff officer Lt. Frank Robertson to tell Lee that his picket lines were in place, but his men and horses were exhausted, his mounts badly needed rest and shoeing, and that his horse artillery was in wretched condition, their limbers empty.[32]

Robertson found Lee sitting alone in a piece of woods. "Come, boy, what news of the cavalry?" inquired the Southern commander. Robertson sat on a campstool and related all that he knew. He remembered that Lee "looked worn and tired, but his eyes blazed with energy and he seemed to me as nobly and as splendidly defiant and confident as ever." After about twenty minutes of conversation, Lee concluded by saying, "There will be no rest for man or beast until we whip these people." Robertson rode back to Stuart's headquarters and reported what he had learned. The news sent and received, Stuart dispatched Ferguson and his Virginians into the breastworks so the infantry could begin withdrawing toward the river crossings. The movement to evacuate Maryland was under way in earnest.[33]

The Crossing of the River Begins

The Army of Northern Virginia's infantry began withdrawing during the night of July 13. Stuart's horsemen relieved Ewell's and Longstreet's infantry on the front lines, and the foot soldiers began moving quietly toward the river crossings. Stuart instructed his men to be vigilant and bold, and not to allow the enemy to discover that the withdrawal was underway. At daylight, the Confederate horse soldiers would withdraw from the front and cover the infantry's movement to the river crossings. "I know it to be a difficult, as well as delicate, operation to cover this army and then withdraw your command with safety," wrote General Lee to his cavalry chief, "but I rely upon your good judgment, energy, and boldness to accomplish it, and trust you may be as successful as on former occasions."[34] As they had done throughout the retreat, Stuart and his horsemen did a superb job of covering Lee's withdrawal. "Lee's retreat was skillfully managed and evinced great forecast," reported Brig. Gen. Horatio G. Wright. "My own pickets—not 200 yards from his main line did not discover the retreat till day light."[35]

Maj. John A. Harman, Lee's resourceful chief quartermaster, had stripped every barn and fence in the area of its wood, as well as several homes, in order to cobble together a new pontoon at Falling Waters—"a crazy affair," as Longstreet's chief of staff described it. Two corps, those under Longstreet and Hill, would cross on the new pontoon. Ewell's entire corps, however, was ordered to wade the Potomac at Williamsport.[36]

Pvt. Thomas Bailey of the 47th North Carolina helped build the bridge at Falling Waters. Bailey and his comrades spent July 7 to 12 carrying heavy wood planks on their shoulders half a mile at a time, collecting a stockpile of bridging materials. The Southern engineers erected a dirt causeway across the Chesapeake & Ohio Canal near the riverbank and connected the causeway to the new pontoon. Once they finished the bridge, the pioneers dug earthworks for the Confederate rearguard, including six small artillery emplacements about two miles from the crossing. With their work finished on the morning of July 13, the weary pioneers crossed the pontoon to the safety of Virginia.[37]

The pace of construction of the Falling Waters pontoon troubled Lee. One of his engineers left a telling description of a meeting with the general:

> [T]he engineer companies were ordered to construct a pontoon bridge as soon as possible, as our army was held there with little or no ammunition. Finding suitable lumber for the boats a short distance up stream from the

> site selected for the bridge, it was floated down and the bridge completed in about three days. . . . The company of pontoon bridge builders of the First Regiment of Engineer Troops was . . . delayed greatly in finishing it, when General Lee rode up. . . . I was standing near the end of the bridge, and the General asked me who was in charge of the erection. I said, "Lieutenant Smith," and pointed him out. Turning to him General Lee said: "What is the trouble here? My people have been waiting for hours to cross. . . . The bridge should have been finished long ago." Lieutenant Smith made some excuse that he did not have certain necessary things, especially some guy ropes. The General replied: "Mr. Smith, a person who has everything at hand to accomplish an undertaking should have no credit for doing it. It is only those that surmount obstacles who should have credit for what they do." He then walked out on the part of the bridge which had been finished, and, noticing the end of a rope under a seat in one of the boats, he called to a soldier to pull it out, and this proved to be a coil of just such rope as Lieutenant Smith had said he needed. The General told the soldier to drop it in front of Lieutenant Smith, and without saying a word more, he mounted his horse and rode off.[38]

The retreating Southern infantry faced quite an ordeal. It rained all night, sometimes in blinding sheets, bogging down wagons, horses, and men in the thick mud.[39] "It is said we lost 8,000 pairs of shoes in crossing," recounted Jed Hotchkiss, Stonewall Jackson's former cartographer.[40] "The whole night had been spent in groping & pulling through the mud, a few feet at a time, & then waiting for the vehicle in front of you to move again," recalled Col. E. Porter Alexander, Longstreet's chief of artillery. "And men would go to sleep on their horses, or leaning in fence corners, or standing in the mud."[41]

The 4th Alabama Infantry of Longstreet's Corps spent ten long hours slogging through the rain and gooey mud before reaching the pontoon.[42] A North Carolinian long remembered the terrible conditions. "The retreat from Hagerstown through mud and rain was worse than that from Gettysburg, which was 'awful,'" he recalled. "Some fell by the wayside from exhaustion, and the whole command was fast asleep as soon as halted for a rest about a mile from the pontoon bridge at 'Falling Waters.'"[43] "[S]uch a rain I thought I never before knew to fall," recalled Surgeon Welch of the 13th South Carolina, "and such a road I think troops never before traveled over. It appeared to me that at least half of the road was a quagmire, coming in places nearly to the knees."[44]

The foot soldiers reached the pontoon via Falling Waters Road, but because of the soggy conditions, Longstreet's and Hill's artillery rolled to the river along the somewhat drier canal towpath.[45] The approach proved difficult and several wagons and caissons fell into the river during the night, even though fires had been kindled to light the way. The occupants of those wagons were rescued, although it took Herculean efforts to save them.[46]

"In this movement, necessarily involving much labor, greatly increased difficulty was imposed upon those responsible for artillery operations by the enfeebled condition of the horses drawing through roads saturated with rain, and by the swollen state of the river, which confined the whole army, train and all, to one route across the pontoon bridge at Falling Waters," reported Brig. Gen. William N. Pendleton, Lee's chief of artillery. "Still the task was cheerfully undertaken, and in the main successfully accomplished." All but a few abandoned caissons and lost horses made their way across the river to the safety of Virginia.[47]

"[We] crossed on the bridge of boats that had been thrown over the river at Falling Waters by the engineers," recalled Major Sorrel of Longstreet's staff. "Our corps was all night crossing, and at dawn was able to approach General Lee on the south bank. . . . The General's anxiety was intense. He expected to be attacked at the passage of the river. There was good reason to fear; why Meade failed to do so has yet to be explained. General Lee, like every one," added Sorrel, "had been up the whole night, and his staff officers were stretched in sleep on the ground."[48]

Rev. A. D. Betts served as the regimental chaplain of the 30th North Carolina Infantry. He had spent the last two days keeping the spirits of his charges up, visiting with them and praying with them as they awaited the Union attack that never came. At twilight on July 13, the 30th North Carolina moved out, heading toward the Potomac River. "Ride down through rain and mud to pontoon bridge at Falling Water," he wrote in his diary. "Cross at 10:30 and pass on in rain and mud to within one mile of Martinsburg. Sleep a little on two rails under a wagon. God bring our soldiers over safely!"[49]

As the infantry and artillery withdrew, Stuart and his staff spent the night riding the lines, engaging in loud conversation and singing to deceive the nearby Yankees into believing the Army of Northern Virginia remained in its works. At one point Stuart sent Robertson to Williamsport with a dispatch. Robertson had never been in the town, and was uncertain where he was going. Unable to see in the pitch darkness, and temporarily blinded by the bonfires lighting the river crossing, Robertson and his horse took a painful and embarrassing spill, but he delivered his message.[50]

As his men fell back, Lee ordered regimental bands to play loudly in an attempt to mask the sounds of his withdrawal from the front lines. "The stirring airs of Dixie, Bonnie Blue Flag, and Soldiers Joy sent a thrill of enthusiasm through me," recalled a member of Ferguson's command, "and when they closed with pathetic 'Maryland, My Maryland' and the sweet old 'Home Sweet Home' with all my faculties alert for the deadly foe near by yet my heart went back to my home in the 'West Virginia Hills.'"

Instead of pressing the attack, the Army of the Potomac's bands took up the challenge. Before long, "John Brown's Body," "Hail Columbia," "Yankee Doodle," and "The Star Spangled Banner" rang out.[51] "I saw men around me—strong men, too—cry like children and I was told afterward by one of opposing side, the music had the same effect on their soldiers," recalled a Virginia infantryman.[52]

In order to clear the way for the Confederate army to cross the Potomac River that dark and drizzly night, Brig. Gen. William E. "Grumble" Jones' brigade slipped over and picketed the road to Winchester. The rest of the Southern cavalry remained in place on the opposite side of the river, ready to cover the rear and the main crossing. The final act of the Gettysburg Campaign above the Potomac River was about to play out.[53]

Chapter 16

July 14: The Crossings at Williamsport and Falling Waters

"Old Virginia never looked so sweet and inviting."

— John J. Shoemaker, Stuart's Horse Artillery

The Crossing at Williamsport

AT WILLIAMSPORT, THE CONFEDERATES STRUGGLED across the still-swollen Potomac River. Most realized they had dodged a bullet when Meade did not attack all along their line, and they knew that if the Yankees caught wind of the crossing and assaulted while the Virginia army was in the act of crossing, a disaster of untold proportions could still ensue. "It need scarcely be suggested, the fording of a corps under these circumstances was a very different thing from what it would have been in the haste and demoralization of retreat under fire of an advancing army," opined Capt. Frank E. Moran of the 73rd New York Infantry.[1]

Dim bonfires lit the opposite bank of the river some 250 yards distant. "We went to a ford several hundred yards up the river than where we crossed before—going up through the aqueduct through water that smelt very offensively," Pvt. Samuel Pickens of the 5th Alabama Infantry wrote in his diary the following day. He continued at some length:

> As soon as we got near the river we knew the men were wading, by the yelling & hallooing that we heard. The Potomac being very swollen, was very wide & was over waist deep. The water felt cool when we first entered it, but afterwards very pleasant. We waded two & two side by side, holding on to each other in order to resist the current better & be more steady. There were orders for the men to hang their cartridge-boxes around their necks, but a great many failed to do it & there was a considerable amount

> of ammunition damaged & destroyed by getting wet. Our clothes, blankets (partly) & haversacks all got wet, which increased our load & made it very disagreeable marching after crossing. The banks were muddy & on this side so steep & slippery that it was difficult to scuffle up it. We were very tired & confidently expected to stop directly after getting over the river, but on we went without stopping. Although the distance from Hagerstown was only about six miles, & we were on our feet from 8 or nine O'clock last night, it was day-break when we got across the Potomac. We passed by "Falling Water" where our Pontoon bridge spanned the river, on which Longstreet's & A. P. Hill's Corps were crossing & also the artillery & wagon trains. At 6 or 7 O'clock this morning we came to a halt. After being on our feet the whole night—marching on a sloppy pike, & stopped to rest only once (5 or 10 mins.) during the whole trip. Oh! it was a killing march. It beggars description.[2]

Maj. Gen. Edward Johnson's division, Ewell's Corps, arrived in Williamsport at midnight and immediately began crossing. "We marched one mile to the right of and crossed the Potomac at midnight, after wading through the canal, which we destroyed. The river was up to my chin, and very swift. We crossed in fours, for protection, as otherwise we could not have crossed," recalled Louis Leon of the 1st North Carolina Infantry. "Our cartridge boxes we carried around our necks to keep the powder dry. On the south bank tar was poured so that we would not slip back in the river, as the mud was very slick. J. Engle, of our company, was stuck in it until some of the boys pulled him out," continued Leon. "We went six miles further, and I honestly believe more of us were asleep on our night's march than awake. But, still, all kept up, for the rear was prison. We then halted, made fire to dry ourselves, just as day was breaking on the morning of the 14th."[3]

"We marched at once into the river and forded, the water taking us up to our breasts," recalled John Worsham of the 21st Virginia Infantry. "It was necessary that my comrade and myself should help little [Pvt. W.] Bates, and every time we stumbled on some of the large rocks at the bottom of the stream, his head went under the water." Laughing at the plight of their diminutive friend, Worsham, Bates, and their unidentified comrade made it to safety on the south side of the river.[4] "Forded the river, it being almost to the shoulders of the men—a picturesque but miserable scene," recalled a Marylander.[5]

At 4:00 a.m., an officer of the 6th Louisiana Infantry was lucky enough to be able to cross the river on a crude scow with his brigade commander, Brig.

Gen. Harry T. Hays. "The passage of the Potomac was a very hazardous undertaking," he nonetheless noted. "The water was very high, and the crossing was effected in the face of a watchful and powerful enemy."[6]

The retreat was hard enough without music, but one Mississippian fixed that once he reached the Virginia side. When he passed his regimental band, he called out, "Stewart, by blood, play Dixie!" The bandsmen took up their instruments, and soon the sound of the Southern anthem wafted upon the breeze. It was followed by a keening Rebel yell of defiance, indicating that the men of the Army of Northern Virginia, although defeated in Pennsylvania, remained bold and plenty full of fight.[7]

"The men had to wade through the aqueduct, down the steep bank of soft and slippery mud, in which numbers lost their shoes and down which many fell," reported Maj. Gen. Robert Rodes, one of Ewell's division commanders. "The water was cold, deep, and rising; the lights on either side of the river were dim . . . the cartridge boxes of the men had to be placed around their necks; some small men had to be carried over by their comrades."[8] As noted, Hotchkiss reported that thousands of shoes were lost during the crossing.[9]

One of Jeb Stuart's staff officers, Capt. William W. Blackford, watched as Rodes' soldiers struggled across the still-swollen river. "By the bright, lurid light," he wrote, "the long line of heads and shoulders and the dim sparkling of their musket barrels could be traced." According to Blackford, some of the wagon train could not make it as the bleating mules desperately fought against their harnesses. "As the water rose over their backs they began rearing and springing vertically upward, and they went deep and deeper the less would be seen of them before they made the spring which would bring their bodies half out of the water, until by violent efforts the small brutes would spring aloft; and indeed after the waters had closed over them, occasionally one would appear in one last plunge high above the surface."[10]

Maj. Gen. Jubal A. Early's Division began crossing near the aqueduct at dawn on the 14th. Early watched as his men waded the river, the water up to their armpits, so that they "had to hold their guns and cartridge boxes above their heads." The Virginian's division crossed without incident and proceeded on to Hainesville.[11] Brig. Gen. John B. Gordon, who commanded a brigade in Early's Division of Ewell's Corps, watched proudly as his men forded the river. "To the giants in the army the passage was comparatively easy, but the short-legged soldiers were a source of anxiety to the officers and of constant amusement to their long- legged comrades," he recalled. "With their knapsacks high up on their shoulders, their cartridge-boxes above the knapsacks, and their

Maj. Gen. Jubal A. Early, commander, Early's Division, Ewell's Second Corps.

USAHEC

guns lifted still higher to keep them dry, these little heroes of the army battled with the current from shore to shore. Borne down below the line of march by the swiftly rolling water, slipping and sliding in the mud and slime, stumbling over the boulders at the bottom, the marvel is that none were drowned."[12]

About five that morning, after Early's men had crossed the river safely, the bulk of Stuart's horse soldiers began crossing. They left their campfires burning brightly as a decoy and made their way across the Potomac. "The water took our horses within twelve inches of the top of the shoulders," recalled one of Fitz Lee's staff officers, "and wet our legs thoroughly eight inches above the knees at least."[12] "My horse had to swim some," noted a member of the 4th Virginia Cavalry of Lee's Brigade in his diary that night.[13] Once across, the troopers had to remain in their soggy saddles, which only added to their weariness and saddle soreness. "The wetting received was not uncomfortable, however, to men who had not been dryly clad for fourteen days," recalled a member of the 9th Virginia Cavalry.[14] Stuart's troopers still had to protect the crossing from the heights on the Virginia side of the river, so their misery continued.

Stuart dispatched Lt. Frank Robertson of his staff back toward Williamsport with a message for the rearguard. Robertson was in the act of returning when he spotted Yankee horsemen pursuing the rear. Robertson headed straight for the ford. When he spotted wagons in the water, he dashed out into the river, where his horse, Miranda, plunged under the chilly water and began swimming. Expecting to have to swim to safety, Robertson unhooked his saber and dropped it into the river. As he passed the wagons, he noticed the mules had drowned and the wagons were drifting aimlessly. When he was about halfway across, his Northern pursuers opened fire and bullets splashed in the water all around him.

"After sundry deep plunges we reached the Virginia shore, only to find a line of rocks some two or three feet about the water, making it impossible for Miranda to get out," remembered Robertson. "I got off and led her down the river perhaps fifty yards, bullets getting livelier and closer, when I found a place where the little mare could scuffle out." Still stiff and sore from his earlier spill, Robertson found Stuart and sat with him as the Southern cavalry commander watched the final stages of the action at the crossing. The men cheered when Southern artillery drove Buford's and Kilpatrick's cavalry away from the pontoon site at Falling Waters. With the immediate threat over, Stuart spurred away to begin making arrangements to cover the army's further retreat.[16]

The Federal prisoners taken during the previous weeks crossed the river at Williamsport on two flatboats. Confederate guns perched on the ridge on the far side of the Potomac frowned down upon them as they forlornly made their way across. "As each boat swung from the Maryland shore," explained the 73rd New York's Captain Moran, "they left their hopes behind, and turned their sad faces toward Virginia, many of them to languish and die in Libby, Belle Isle, and Andersonville."[17]

Milton Ferguson's Virginia cavalrymen were the last to cross. "I was in command of the last Confederate troops leaving Maryland," recalled Lt. Hermann Schuricht of the 14th Virginia Cavalry. "General Fitzhugh Lee was awaiting us on the bluffs on the Virginia side . . . and [with] Federal cavalry and artillery appearing on the Maryland side after I had safely crossed the river, we marched on towards Martinsburg."[18] "The water was pretty swift and was up mid sides to our horses," recalled a member of the 17th Virginia Cavalry. "I saw some of the infantry wading across it and it was nearly up to their armpits. The hill opposite Williamsport was black with our men and ammunition wagons when we got to the river but by the time we had gotten over all had disappeared over the hill and in the timber."[19] Jenkins' men were waiting to cross when a Federal artillery shell whistled in, killing Lt. David Shepperson and wounding Capt. Edward Bouldin and three other members of the 14th Virginia Cavalry.[20] "The cavalry and horse artillery were the last to cross, after picketing all night," wrote a Southern horse artillerist, who then succinctly summed up the sentiments of everyone making the crossing: "Old Virginia never looked so sweet and inviting."[21]

As the last of the Southern cavalry made its way to safety, Northern horsemen appeared on the hills above Williamsport. "They seemed to be in no hurry," observed one Virginian. "But when we saw two pieces of artillery getting in position we knew what they were waiting for. They were a mile from us, and never did I see as fair a target for artillery as we presented to those Yankee gunners." The first shot was short and exploded high and harmlessly in the air. The Federal artillerists quickly got the range and "in a minute or two another shell came screaming through the air and exploded" among the ranks of the 14th Virginia Cavalry of Ferguson's Brigade, killing an officer and two enlisted men, and driving off the Confederate cavalry on the other side of the river.[22] The Southern cavalry "crossed just in time," noted a North Carolina horse soldier, "for in a few hours after we got over the River was not fordable. The Yankees came up on the other side and seemed to be very much provoked at our giving them slip."[23]

"The rebels were on the Virginia hills, jubilant at their escape," recalled a newspaper correspondent. "There were wagons in the river, floating down with the current, which had been capsized in the crossing." When Kilpatrick realized he could do nothing more at Williamsport, he rode off for the other crossing point at Falling Waters.[24]

* * *

When he discovered the Confederates had evacuated Hagerstown that morning, and the town in "great tumult," the College of St. James's Reverend Kerfoot decided to try to make his way back to the school. It is not known what he expected to find upon his return, but given the circumstances, he was likely surprised by what he observed. The ride south to St. James was slow going, with the "roads thronged by trains of wagons, artillery, etc., and of refugees; roads blocked by trees cut down."[25]

"Sad, harrowing sight in my own house and the College," were the words he used to begin his description of his home. He continued:

> Outer and inner doors burst open; closets, wardrobes, trunks, broken open; kitchen and dining-room filthy; evidently much stolen. But no furniture broken for mere wantonness. But so, too, in the College and boys' rooms. Dormitory, wardrobes, trunks, rifled; dining-room, store-room, etc., robbed utterly. Food wasted and scattered. All this was done despite a general's orders, who could not prevent it. The Rectory was ransacked from cellar to garret, and articles stolen everywhere. Not a trunk but was broken, etc. The loss has been very serious.[26]

The Southern guards stationed at the buildings had joined in the pillaging of their contents. In addition to a multitude of bullet holes in the outside walls, one of the chapel's windows had been shot out.[27]

The damage to the College shocked those Federal troops marching across its grounds on their way to Williamsport. Members of the 10th Massachusetts Battery camped on the grounds of the College that night. To their disgust, they found the campus "deserted and ravaged" by the Confederates.[28]

It could have been much worse. The battle everyone expected to be fought on the school's grounds never materialized. Disappointed though he surely was, Kerfoot may have breathed a sigh of relief that the buildings were standing at all.[29]

* * *

The night of July 13-14 looked quite different from the opposite side of the lines. About midnight, a soldier of the 1st Maryland Infantry (U.S.) stealthily climbed over the Federal breastworks. When he discovered the enemy's rifle pits empty, he reported the news to the commander of the picket line, who kicked it upstairs to his division commander, who directed him to advance the entire picket line as far as it could go. The Maryland skirmishers advanced to within one mile of Williamsport, scooping up twenty-one Confederate stragglers along the way.[30]

The rain continued to fall throughout the early morning hours of July 14, and the sky was unusually dark.[31] About 3:00 a.m., George Custer sent a staff officer to Maj. Luther S. Trowbridge, now commanding the 5th Michigan Cavalry. "Make no noise about—no bugle calls—but boots and saddles right away," directed the staffer. "The enemy has fallen back, and we are ordered to find out where he has gone." Trowbridge quickly mounted his men. The same staff officer reappeared a few minutes later. "Are you ready?" he inquired. When Major Trowbridge indicated that he was, Custer's aide told him, "Then move out and take the road to Williamsport. I know it is not your turn to take the advance, but the 6th is not ready yet, so move out and push ahead." The advancing Michigan men rode past the deserted camps of the Confederates, noting the smoldering remains of campfires and debris.[32]

The men of the 2nd U.S. Sharpshooters also moved forward in support. "Moved nearer the enemy's picket line," Sgt. James M. Matthews noted in his diary on the 14th. "They are reported retreating. Moved up and camped within the enemy's earthworks at night. The works are poor but would repel a heavy assault."[33]

Custer and Kilpatrick rode along the flank of the marching column. "As we neared Williamsport, Gen. Custer came dashing across the fields, and said to me, 'First two companies advance carbine, balance, draw saber, and charge into the town'," recounted Major Luther S. Trowbridge of the 5th Michigan Cavalry. Trowbridge replied, "General, this regiment is armed with the Spencer rifle, and we can't carry that at the position of advance carbine."

"Well, then," responded Custer, "first two companies draw pistol, balance draw saber and charge." Trowbridge quickly gave the necessary orders, and away went the Michigan men.[34]

The Crossing at Falling Waters

As Buford soon learned, with the exception of a rearguard Lee's army had finally made its escape across the Potomac. Fitz Lee's cavalry brigade crossed over the pontoon bridge at Falling Waters earlier than it should have, and its troopers impeded the movement of some of the Southern infantry. When General Robert E. Lee sought out his nephew to ask why the cavalry was mixed up with the foot soldiers, Fitz responded that he did not know, but immediately set out to untangle the mess. "It was quite a picturesque sight," noted the adjutant of the 2nd Virginia Cavalry of Lee's Brigade, "when we crossed to see men wading the River up to their necks, and then a train of ambulances, and then two or three Regiments of Cavalry one below the other."[35]

One of those last cavalry units was Cobb's Georgia Legion led by Col. Pierce M. B. Young. "On the last night my regiment took up the line of A. P. Hill's corps which crossed the Potomac at 12 o'clock. . . . To my regiment was assigned the honor of covering the rear of the army over the Potomac."[36] The premature crossing of the river by Fitz Lee and the rest of the mounted soldiers meant only Harry Heth's and Dorsey Pender's infantry remained north of the river—and there was no cavalry screen to shield them from Meade's troopers.[37]

Despite the lousy weather, artilleryman Henry Matthews of Breathed's horse battery passed a relatively peaceful night. "I laid that night in a field with my head resting on a stone for a pillow and two fence rails under my body to keep the falling rain from drenching me. No prince of the realm could have slept sounder than I. I was completely exhausted, tired out, worn out, but my spirit was unbroken. . . . I did not wake until daylight the next morning, when I immediately went to the ford where the cavalry was crossing." Joining his

Pontoon bridge crossing at Falling Waters. *NARA*

battery, Matthews—together with the rest of Cobb's Legion, made good his escape.[38]

Buford thought a determined thrust would cut off Heth's division—Lee's rearguard north of the river—from the Potomac crossing. As Buford planned his full-scale attack, Kilpatrick openly and rather recklessly arrived on the scene. Capt. James H. Kidd of the 6th Michigan Cavalry understood Kilpatrick's zeal to catch the Rebel rearguard. "The march from Williamsport to Falling Waters was a wild ride. For the whole distance the horses were spurred to a gallop. Kilpatrick was afraid he would not get there in time to overtake the enemy, so he spared neither man nor beast," wrote Kidd. "The road was soft and miry, and the horses sank almost to their knees in the sticky mud. For this reason the column straggled, and it was not possible to keep a single troop closed up in sets of fours. At such a rapid rate the column plunged through the muddy roads."[39]

The Wolverines could see Lee's artillery massed on the Virginia side of the Potomac, and noticed a large force of infantry drawn up in line of battle on the south bank of the river. Major Trowbridge watched the last of the Confederate cavalry crossing the river on the makeshift pontoon bridge. "I cannot describe my feelings of disappointment and discouragement," he later recalled. "A week before it was expected that the fight would be renewed and the escape of Lee's army impossible.... But it was not to be. Other counsels prevailed, and the end which had seemed so near had been indefinitely postponed."[40] Still, enemy infantry and wagons remained.

"We reached the top of a high hill overlooking the Potomac a mile away. It must have been after ten o'clock," recalled one of Henry Heth's soldiers. "On the Virginia hills we could see a great host of men, and long lines of artillery and wagons—some filing slowly away to the south, others standing in well-ordered ranks. On some prominent hills batteries had been planted. It was a great sight. The sun was shining on this display. Lee's army had effected a crossing." The soldier was witnessing his comrades funneling in large numbers toward the river crossing on the Maryland side. "At the river was a dense mass of wagons, and brigade upon brigade, with stacked arms, the division resting and waiting for its turn to cross; for there was but one bridge, over which a stream of men was yet passing, and it would take hours for all to cross."[41]

Only the Southern divisions of Dorsey Pender and Henry Heth remained on the north side of the Potomac, and some of the latter's men were already beginning to cross. When Heth rode to Pettigrew and ordered the North Carolinian to remain in place, acting as his rearguard, Pettigrew aligned his brigade of North Carolinians, together with the remnants of James J. Archer's

Maj. Gen. Henry Heth, commander, Heth's Division, A. P. Hill's Third Corps.

USAHEC

battered Tennessee brigade, on both sides of the Falling Waters Road. Most of his line was on the J. M. Donnelly farm, about one mile from the river. The rest of Heth's command was behind it waiting to cross. The exhausted Southern infantry had orders to lie down and try to sleep, so were unprepared for battle. While Heth was talking with Pettigrew, the pair spotted a large force of cavalry on high ground nearly a mile away. Neither officer could tell if they were friend or foe.

"They carried the stars-and-stripes of the United States, but the color of their uniforms seemed to be Confederate, and their manner of moving (by the flank, and leisurely) confirmed all in the belief that they were our own cavalry," recalled a South Carolinian. "Suddenly they deployed into line and rushed upon the division."[42] Maj. Charles Marshall, General Lee's aide-de-camp and his personal secretary, recalled that the Union cavalry was "mistaken by our men for our own cavalry retiring, no notice having been given of the withdrawal of the latter, and was suffered to approach our lines."[43] Pettigrew grew irritated that the friendly cavalry would so boldly display a captured Federal flag, and determined to arrest the offending officer commanding the detachment.[44]

Heth, only mildly concerned by the mounted riders, believed that infantry could easily repulse the cavalry if indeed they turned out to be enemy troopers.[45] It only took a few more short moments for the Southerners to figure out that the approaching horsemen were Federals. "As soon as our men realized that an assault had been made, they sprang up [and] opened fire," noted a North Carolinian.[46]

Kilpatrick's eagerness to pitch into the enemy prevented him from coordinating his assault with Buford's division, which was even then approaching to assault the crossing point. Instead of launching a joint assault that may well have bagged an entire Rebel division, Kilpatrick galloped into the first Confederates he spotted. As one Rebel phrased Little Kil's effort, "[It is] difficult to believe that sane men would attack as this small body of cavalry did."[47]

But attack they did, and with a suddenness and severity that surprised many of the recipients. One of the mounted attackers was Maj. Peter A. Weber. Frustrated that his regiment had conducted most of its fighting dismounted throughout the campaign, Weber told Kidd, "I want a chance to make one saber charge."[48] Kidd agreed and Weber's squadron pounded toward the enemy. The horsemen struck the Confederate rearguard near the pontoon bridge.[49]

One of Pettigrew's Tar Heels described the fight as "the funniest affair I have ever been in. The men clubbed their guns and knocked the yankees off their horses. One man knocked one off with a fence rail and another killed a yankee with an ax."[50] According to a newspaper correspondent, "The charge made against the earthworks was one of the most gallant on record—a squadron of fifty-seven men charging upon three or four brigades behind earthworks."[51]

Pvt. John T. McCall of the 7th Tennessee's Company B recalled Weber's assault:

> Early on the night of the 13th the army began to cross the river, although it was very dark and a drenching rain poured down. When day broke our brigade was within a half mile of the river. . . . Some of our artillery had bogged up, and the men were soon asleep. A few of us were up, when one of the boys called the attention of Lieut. Jack Moore to a troop of cavalry advancing with blue uniforms and Yankee flags; but, supposing Stewart's [sic] Cavalry to be behind, Lieut. Moore said not to fire, thinking the flags had been captured. But it was a Michigan battalion of cavalry . . . and when in about thirty yards the major [Weber] gave the command to "Wheel into line and, damn 'em, split their heads." They struck the head of our column yelling, cutting right and left, and riding over our men while asleep, breaking arms and legs and trampling some to death.[52]

Maj. Peter A. Weber's charge, captured in a woodcut. *LOC*

"Of the one hundred men who made this charge," wrote another Union correspondent, "only thirty escaped uninjured. Seven of their horses lay dead within the enemy's works. Twelve hundred prisoners were here captured from the enemy, and the ground was strewn with dead and wounded rebels."[53]

Weber got his wish, but the cost was high. The swirling one-sided fight cost the lives of Weber, his adjutant, and twenty-eight other Wolverines. Weber fell at the head of his command, shot through the head, his hand still gripping his saber.[54] Considered "the best officer in the regiment," his death was viewed as a tragic loss for the 6th. The rash charge at Falling Waters, complained one of the regimental surgeons, "cost us Some of our Bravest & Best men."[55] Lt. Charles E. Bolza, commander of Company B of the 6th Michigan, was also killed in the charge.

The price the Confederates paid for victory in the small skirmish was even higher. As the Wolverines bore down on them, Harry Heth rode off through Donnelly's garden to secure the river crossing, leaving Pettigrew to his own devices. The North Carolinian's panicked horse threw him. "Rising, the General took his position at the corner of the fence upon which our right rested, and with perfect calmness gave directions to our men, who were in some confusion from the suddenness with which the enemy rode into our lines, and the vigor of the attack," recalled one of Pettigrew's staff officers. "Stand your ground, boys," Pettigrew calmly ordered.[56] Because the general had been wounded in the arm at Gettysburg, his hand was splinted and in a sling. The only way he could mount a defense was to raise a small pistol.

As Weber's troopers drew near, Pettigrew attempted to remount his horse, but slipped and fell painfully to the ground.[57] Struggling to his feet as the enemy approached, he lifted his pistol and pulled the trigger, but his weapon misfired.

Brig. Gen. James J. Pettigrew, commander, Pettigrew's Brigade, A. P. Hill's Third Corps.

USAHEC

His enemy's weapon, however, did not malfunction. The well-aimed bullet struck Pettigrew squarely in the abdomen, knocking him down with a wound that would soon prove a mortal one. A hastily organized detail carried him across the pontoon, where surgeons examined the injured general. When he expressed his desire not to be left behind and captured, relays of four men carried him eighteen miles to Bunker Hill, near Martinsburg, western Virginia. There, the injured scholar-general lingered for a few painful final days before expiring on July 17.[58]

A member of the 5th Alabama Infantry recalled the scene that struck down Pettigrew:

> I was looking at him, riding with his arm in a sling . . . trying to arouse his weary soldiers, who were asleep after an all-night tramp in rain and mud on retreat from Hagerstown, Md., just a few minutes before he received his mortal wound . . . my attention was suddenly called to a startling vision on the hill just beyond me. There on that ridge I saw a sight that for a moment paralyzed me. A long line of blue rapidly forming in shape for a charge. It flashed over me in a minute what was going to happen; and I fairly flew toward my comrades . . . yelling at the top of my voice: "Look out! Look out! The Yankees! The Yankees! Look out!" . . . the Yankee cavalry came bursting in among us in full tilt, shouting as they waved their carbines: "Surrender!" . . . and it was in this melee that General Pettigrew, one of North Carolina's great men, was killed.[59]

Seeing their general reel upon being struck, his North Carolinians opened fire on the charging Wolverines. "Simultaneously, a quick volley from the aroused veterans emptied the saddles of the leader and his nearest horsemen," recalled an infantryman from Archer's outfit. "The impetus of the charge could not be checked; the rear pressed forward to the front. It became at once a melee, a fierce, bloody, hand-to-hand struggle, and quickly all was over." The Southerners interviewed a wounded Wolverine left behind when the Michigan men pulled back. "In answer to the inquiry why they rode on us, he said they supposed we were only stragglers, and they sought to take us in. A fatal mistake, for out of the eighty-six only three escaped. This turmoil lasted about three minutes."[60] Weber's impetuous charge led one captain of the 11th Virginia Infantry to call them "a few drunken cavalrymen."[61]

Captain Kidd's company of the 6th Michigan also participated in the attack. His company was the fourth from the rear of the regiment as it galloped off. "When I reached the fence, along the side of the field next to the woods, I found Lieutenant A. E. Tower . . . at the gap giving orders. He directed me to take my command across the field, and form on the right of that next preceding." Kidd rode so fast that he got out in front of his company, while the rest of his men were strung some distance behind. "But taking those that were up, and asking the adjutant to tell the others to follow, I dashed into the field, and soon found that we were targets for the enemy on the hill, who made the air vibrant with the whiz of bullets." Kidd made it across the field without being hit and joined the rest of the regiment as it formed for the attack, suffering all the while under a heavy fire from the infantry atop the hill, which was inflicting losses on the Wolverines.

"Dismount[ing] to fight on foot and, glancing back, saw my men coming in single file, reaching to the fence—probably an eighth of a mile—and the rear had not yet left the woods," Kidd recounted. "The two leading sets of fours which alone were closed up obeyed the order and, dismounting to direct the alignment, I stepped in front of my horse, still holding the bridle rein in my right hand, when a minie bullet from the hill in front with a vicious thud went through my right foot, making what the surgeon in Washington afterwards said was the 'prettiest wound I ever saw'."[62] The injured captain did not return to duty until October. With Weber's little force shattered by the charge, Custer sent the balance of the Wolverines forwarded dismounted and spread out, their rifles and carbines blazing.

Company G of the 6th Michigan Cavalry moved to the support of Weber's embattled squadron. "As we came out of the woods at a gallop, we saw in our front, within range, a long line of rebels, some standing upon their works, blazing away at the shattered remnants of those two glorious companies as they fled down the hill towards us," recalled Pvt. Andrew Jackson. "Our squadron, A and G companies, turned to the left and dismounted, advanced to the crest of a little knoll and began to play away with our Spencers, the rebs soon 'covered' behind their earth-works, and began to make it quite uncomfortable for us. The lead flew around us at a fearful rate. Company A having no commissioned officer present, the command fell on their gallant 1st Serg't. T. A. Eddie, who tried to hold his men in line, but in spite of his urgent commands, some of the boys left the line and sought safety behind a fence in our rear."[63]

"We charged back and forth here for four hours," observed an Ohioan of Kilpatrick's headquarters escort. "Each time the rebels came out we would drive them back. Once they came forward to the crest of the hill upon which our batteries were placed. A lad of no more than twelve summers was carrying their battle flag some distance in advance of their line, his youth and courage protecting him. But when their line retreated he sat on the fence waving his flag in defiance and calling on his men to charge again until some one shot him. It was a most heart-rending sight to see the boy thus mortally wounded and piteously calling on his mother. We carried him under the shade of a tree and left him like a wounded bird to die."[64] "At Falling Waters," one of Little Kil's officers wildly exaggerated, "Kilpatrick's men charged the Rebels in their intrenchments, and with success, although many a trooper and horse bit the dust. We drove them like sheep, and captured near two thousand of them."[65]

Confederate B. K. Benson was waiting for his turn to cross the river when the Federal troopers attacked. The cracking of small arms fire woke him from a fitful sleep. Someone fired a rifle next to his head, and the concussion left him nearly deaf in his right ear for weeks. It only took the dazed soldier a few moments to realize that Yankee horsemen were mixed among the ranks of the Confederate infantry. "A horseman was coming at me straight—twenty yards from me," he recalled. "He was standing in his stirrups and had his sword uplifted. I aimed and fired. He still came on, but for a moment only. He doubled up and went headforemost to the ground."

Benson's company scrambled to form a line of battle to face the next wave of Federal cavalrymen, advancing dismounted against their flank. Benson's company occupied a field of ripe berries, and the hungry soldiers alternated between eating berries and loading their rifles, popping lead in one direction and sticking fruit into their mouths. When a Yankee horseman demanded that a Virginian surrender, the Southerner responded by knocking the cavalryman from his saddle by swinging a fence rail at him. The steady Federal advance drove the butternut infantrymen backward one step at a time down the hill toward the river crossing.

As Benson reached the top of the hill, he could see that the pontoon bridge was clear, and only a few stragglers were rushing across the bridge. "And now came our turn," wrote Benson. "We retreated down the hill. At once the hill was occupied by the Federal skirmishers, and at once they began busily to pop away at us. I ran along, holding my white hat in my hand." When Benson and his comrades reached the bottom of the hill, the Southern batteries on the Virginia side of the river opened fire in an effort to drive back the Federal pursuit. In a dramatic display, Benson and his battalion reached the bridge as Yankee bullets splashed the water around them. Under cover of artillery fire, they made their way to safety.[66]

A member of Samuel McGowan's South Carolinia brigade left a vivid description of the fighting at Falling Waters. "The wildest excitement ensued. There was no time for arrangement, but every man must depend on his own reason, or rather his own instincts. The enemy dashed in, firing pistols and sabreing everything in their way," he recounted. "Some men recovered their arms in time to fire upon them, some ran away, some fought with empty pieces, some even had recourse to stones. One man in Archer's brigade knocked a Federal from his horse with a fence rail. The din was horrible, the confusion inextricable. There was fighting, flying, shouting, robbing of dead men, all at once."[67]

Custer sent a portion of the 7th Michigan Cavalry off to the right, where some of the Wolverines charged a column of the 55th Virginia Infantry. Twenty-five-year-old Sgt. Charles M. Holton of the 7th Michigan's Company A joined one of the attacks. "Seeing the color-sergeant of the Fifty-fifth Virginia fall wounded, I sprang from my horse and seized the colors," recalled Holton. As he remounted, he heard the wounded color-bearer exclaim, "You Yanks have been after that old flag for a long time, but you never got it before." After helping round up prisoners, Holton carried his prize to Kilpatrick. The feisty Celt closely examined the battle honors adorning the flag, admiring the regiment's deeds. That night, the 7th Michigan's adjutant wrote an inscription on the margin of the flag, describing its capture. Holton was awarded the Medal of Honor for his accomplishment.[68]

Maj. Henry W. Granger of the 7th Michigan captured a 10-pound Parrott rifle and turned it on its former owners, firing canister at them with great effect. Lt. Col. Alleyne C. Litchfield of the same regiment dashed into the midst of a large contingent of terrified and confused Southern infantrymen. "Down with your guns, every mother's son of you!" he roared. "All you could see," noted one of his men, "were the hands and hats of the Rebels waving frantically in the air." It was over a few minutes later, and the Wolverines turned their attention to corralling their haul of prisoners.[69]

While Kilpatrick waged his disjointed battle, Buford's division advanced about three miles, slipping around the Confederate flank into the rear. Kilpatrick did not support Gamble's men as Gamble expected he would. As a member of the 8th Illinois recorded, "Our brigade was immediately on foot as we came on them . . . "[70] The Confederates fell back toward the ford, where the approaching Northern troopers came under a severe fire from Southern batteries positioned on the bluffs on the Virginia side of the river.[71] Gamble's men regrouped, dismounted, and attacked Pettigrew's infantry in the flank over rough ground a second time.

Reinforced by Col. Thomas Devin's brigade, Gamble's dismounted Federals advanced "over rifle-pits, breastworks, wheat fields and fences."[72] As one trooper noted, "The rebels were so loaded with their heavy knapsacks that we cavalry boys with nothing but belt and carbine, could easily run them down and take them prisoner."[73] "We . . . were overtaken and surprised by the yankee cavalry . . . about two miles from the river," recalled a North Carolinian. "We formed and repulsed them but their infantry soon came up. Then a regular stampede occurred. Every man ran to save himself. They got a good many of us prisoners. . . . They came very near getting me. I was exhausted having marched all night and mired knee deep."[74] When Col. A. C. Goodwin, who led a brigade of Tar Heel infantry, realized his men had not had time to load their weapons, he ordered them to fix bayonets and form line of battle to receive the charge.[75]

"It is no use for me to attempt to describe those fights on paper," noted a Mountaineer of Devin's brigade, "it was the grandest thing I was ever in. The rebels would get behind fences and we would charge on them and make them skedaddle like fun." This trooper was amazed at the condition of the enemy soldiers. "More than one half of the prisoners we took were barefooted, and they said they had had nothing to eat for two days except some fresh beef boiled without salt. They were a rough looking set."[76]

While most of the Confederates were retreating across the pontoon bridge, Col. John M. Brockenbrough, who commanded a brigade in Heth's Division, made a poor decision. Instead of withdrawing, he sent his brigade forward into the enemy. Some of his men refused to go, which was understandable since Brockenbrough himself retreated with others from the division. He shamefully left behind his aide, Capt. Wayland F. Dunaway, to lead the brigade in its close-quarters fight with the dismounted Illini horsemen.

In spite of the thick mud, the Virginians launched their attack with the color bearer of the 47th Virginia leading the way, crying, "Come on boys it's nothing but cavalry!"[77] The Virginians crashed into the 8th Illinois, triggering a hand-to-hand melee. "For an hour we held the Yankees in check at close quarters," exaggerated one of the Virginia participants. With his men running low on ammunition, Dunaway discovered another cavalry regiment forming in the woods. He knew he could not hold his front much longer, especially since there were no other Confederate forces remaining on the north side of the river. Dunaway attempted a general retreat. "All of a sudden it flashed through my mind that we could neither fight nor run," he later wrote. "Further resistance was vain; escape, impossible." As he and his brave little band tried to make their way to safety, the charging Federal cavalry swept down on them and gobbled them up, taking Dunaway and some 700 other officers and men prisoners. The 40th, 47th, and 55th Virginia lost their battle flags. As the gallant but disgusted Dunaway saw it, he and his men "had been sacrificed."[78]

Noticeably defensive in his official report of the action, Harry Heth tried to explain the fiasco at Falling Waters. "The rear guard of a large army protecting its crossing over a wide river can seldom fail to lose heavily if vigorously pursued by the enemy, especially when in the act of crossing. Under the circumstances, attacked as we were by a large and momentarily increasing force, we have every reason to be thankful that our losses were so small."[79]

The debacle enraged Brig. Gen. Joe Davis, the commander of a mixed brigade of Mississippi and North Carolina troops. Davis, who had engineered his own

Lt. Gen. Ambrose P. Hill, commander, Hill's Third Corps, Army of Northern Virginia.

USAHEC

bloody mischief at the Railroad Cut on the first day of fighting at Gettysburg, refused to accept Heth's version of events. Several weeks later, the brigadier wrote a candid letter to his uncle and President of the Confederacy, Jefferson Davis. "Our Major General I am sorry to say has lost the confidence of the men of this Brigade on account of the Falling Water affair. I doubt if he was to blame, but some one blundered and many more men were lost than is admitted. In my small command the loss was over one hundred and other Brigades suffered much more."[80] The 13th South Carolina's surgeon Welch felt much the same, writing his wife the following month, "The attack was a complete surprise and is disgraceful either to General Hill or General Heth. One is certainly to blame."[81]

As the last few Confederates struggled across the pontoon bridge, Federal horsemen bore down on them, sabers waving. "But before we reached the bridge, when our knees began to tremble and hope was pinning on its wings for a farewell flight, a cannon roared and a shell exploded among the charging columns, another and another, by order of A. P. Hill," recalled a Tennessee foot soldier. "Did you ever hear sweet music when you happened to be very tired, somewhat anxious, and just a little bit scared? Talk about your harp of a thousand strings; there was more melody in the roar of that old gun and the pow of that beautiful shell than all the hand organ and jew's harps in the world put together. It was mesmeric, soothing exhilarating, inspiring, a nerve restorer."[82]

General Lee sat astride his war horse Traveler on the Virginia shore. As his infantry made its way across, he instructed the 4th Alabama to guard the crossing while the rest of Hill's men trekked over the bridge. "The crossing of the brigade had to be done fighting," recalled one of Pettigrew's Tar Heels, "and some loss was sustained, including a few captured, doubtless because they were too exhausted to keep up."[83] Lt. Col. James M. Crowell commanded the 28th North Carolina. His troops were the last to cross. Once they were over, General Lee told the Alabamians that a squadron of cavalry was bringing up the rear, and that they could withdraw once the horsemen crossed. After the troopers clopped over the bridge, the officer commanding the cavalry squadron informed the infantry that there were no others left behind, and the 4th Alabama likewise withdrew.[84]

The thunder of Capt. William P. Carter's King William (Virginia) Artillery, according to Major Sorrell, filled "the gorge of the river with most threatening echoes. 'There,' said the General [Lee], 'I was expecting it, the beginning of the attack.' But he was wrong. The enemy made no further demonstrations and [Heth] came safely across."[85] An Alabama soldier watched in defiance as the guns fired across the river and "shelled the woods on the other side . . . and we marched away peacefully."[86] A group of about two dozen officers and men of the 13th North Carolina Infantry, however, had been left behind to serve as a rearguard and their entire skirmish line, including commander Lt. Nathaniel S. Smith, were captured.[87]

After the last of the Tar Heels and Alabamians made it to the Virginia shore, Lt. Col. Crowell cut the pontoon bridge loose from its moorings on the Maryland side, leaving the Federal cavalry to watch helplessly as the currents of the Potomac swept that end of the bridge away. "As the brigade crossed about 12 o'clock, the pontoon bridge was cut loose, and for the first time for many days the command drew a free breath," recalled one of the North Carolinians with no little relief. Heth's remnants scrambled up the heights on the south side of the Potomac, finding safety under the barrels of Hill's guns.[88]

"The pontoons were being cut loose as I crossed, so I was about the last one to get over," a South Carolina infantryman reminisced. "The Yankees followed us very closely, pushing us to the very banks of the river. . . . We were shot to pieces, worn out, and very hungry."[89]

One Southern cavalryman was almost not as lucky as most of his comrades. "[J]ust as we untied the cable on the Maryland side," recalled an Alabaman, "and the bridge began to swing around, a Confederate trooper came dashing at full speed and barely had time to leap his horse and jump on the bridge. His horse, apparently as anxious to get back into old Virginia as his rider, plunged into the rapid stream and swam over to the Virginia side."[90] The final hair-breadth escape of the trooper and his horse was a fitting final act for the interminably long crossing at Falling Waters.

Seeing the last of Heth's men scramble to safety, Lee heaved an audible sigh of relief. Without a word, Jeb Stuart handed him a cup of coffee. The two men stood there and drank in silence, taking in the sights below as the Confederate troops scrambled up the hill. Exactly what each man was thinking at the time was never recorded.

To John Buford's dismay, his Federal troopers arrived at the river just a few minutes too late. "As our troops neared the bridge," the Kentuckian lamented, "the enemy cut the Maryland side loose, and the bridge swung to the Virginia side." A New York horse soldier probably observed what Buford was thinking: "The rebs are acrossed the river into Va they got badly whipped at Gettysburgh and they would have got another if they had stopped thiss side of the river a few days longer."With the fighting over, the Federal horse soldiers turned their attention to mopping up the battlefield. "Our Brigade picked up many staggering graybacks, minus shoes as well as respect for the Confederate humbug for which they had fought," was how a member of the 5th New York Cavalry summed up the experience.[91]

Defeated in Pennsylvania they were, and soundly so, but there was considerable pluck left within the ranks of the Confederate army. "After crossing the Potomac," wrote an officer with the 11th Mississippi Infantry,

> . . . a roll of the 'rebel yell' of defiance that meant too plainly to the enemy on the other side there was yet remaining strength, determination, and fight in the Army of Northern Virginia. Outgeneraled and outnumbered, but not conquered; defeated, but by no fault of its own; a great loser, yet inflicting a greater loss; it remembered with pride former victories and accepted this reverse as but a "ripple on the stream of its destiny."[92]

Lee's chief of artillery, Brig. Gen. William N. Pendleton, personally conducted the defense of the Confederate crossing at Falling Waters. For ten long hours, the 53-year-old Episcopal preacher turned cannoneer "remained at his important post, unaided by a single member of his staff, all of whom were without horses and some of whom themselves were broken down by their exertions of the past two weeks," wrote a Confederate many years after the war. "For 28 hours the Chief of Artillery was without a morsel of food, and for 40 was unable to gain a moment's rest."[93] The effort along the Potomac was probably Pendleton's most important service to the Confederate cause during the entire war.

If Judson Kilpatrick's attack had been coordinated with Buford's effort, Rebel losses would have been significantly higher. "If [Kilpatrick] had waited twenty minutes, General Buford would have swung his command between the [entrenchments] and the river, thereby capturing all the enemy left behind without the loss of a man," complained one of Buford's officers.[94] "Kilpatrick by his folly lost heavily," correctly noted Sergeant Gilpin of the 3rd Indiana Cavalry.[95]

Buford's 1st Brigade commander, William Gamble, pulled no punches in his report of the action. "While the brigade was moving round to flank and attack the enemy in rear, to cut them off from the ford and capture them all . . . which we could easily have accomplished, I saw two small squadrons of General Kilpatrick's division gallop up the hill to the right of the rebel infantry, in line of battle behind their earthworks, and, as any competent cavalry officer of experience could foretell the result," continued Gamble, "these two squadrons were instantly scattered and destroyed . . . not a single dead enemy could be found when the ground there was examined a few hours afterward."[96] Kilpatrick reported losing an additional thirty-six wounded and forty missing, for total losses of 104—heavy losses indeed for such a small action.[97]

"Gen Kilpatrick is called here Gen "Kill-Cavalry" which is about as appropriate as his real name," observed a captain of the 6th Michigan Cavalry just after the affair at Falling Waters.[98]

Kilpatrick wasn't the only commander who drew his horsemen's ire. When he looked back upon the disjointed cavalry pursuits of the previous week, Col. Greely Curtis of the 1st Massachusetts Cavalry was candid about his feelings. "Our brigade, under the d—dest fool you ever dreamed of, H[uey] by name, was sent down the St. James road to W'msport to feel the enemy. We did nothing. Our regt. was put on the advance 2 days in 3, and if I had obeyed all the orders I rec'd from the sapient H there would have been very little of the regt. left. But he was such an overpowering damned fool of a retired barkeeper that I made no bones at all of doing just what I pleased and he was happy. We fired away lots of carbine ammunition as skirmishers dismounted . . . The aft[ernoon] we crossed came the news that the rebs had crossed the night before . . . I think there was a want of information which should have been procured at any cost, save a general engagement, which seemed and seems to me the only want of generalship on Meade's part."[99]

* * *

In a letter home to his family, W. G. Thompson of the 13th North Carolina Infantry revealed his thoughts once he reached the safe side of the river. "I hope we never will cross the Potomac again," he wrote, "for I don't believe we ever made anything by crossing it yet."[100]

Moxley Sorrel would likely have agreed with the North Carolinian. "Our corps had found camp some ten miles south of the river and there I soon threw myself down for rest and food," wrote Longstreet's staff officer. "After a week of the most exhausting physical and mental trial it was indeed time for some repose."[101]

Chapter 17

The Federal Advance and Aftermath

"It is enough to say that although [Lincoln] was not so profoundly distressed as he was when Hooker's army recrossed the Rappahannock after the battle of Chancellorsville, his grief and anger were something sorrowful to behold."

— Noah Brooks, newspaper correspondent and friend of President Lincoln

THE ENTIRE ARMY OF THE POTOMAC was under orders on July 14 to be "under arms in readiness for a general engagement" that morning. The men were to charge the enemy works using only their bayonets; they were ordered to empty their cartridge boxes and turn in their ammunition in order to ensure that the assault would be made using only the bayonet. The order was countermanded just before daylight, the consequence of the fact that the Confederates had abandoned their works and were crossing the river.[1]

At 6:35 a.m., Maj. Gen. Oliver Howard reported abandoned Confederate works in his front on the Union right, and moved forward immediately to try to exploit the withdrawal of the Army of Northern Virginia. Brig. Gen. Horatio G. Wright, a commander of a division of the 6th Corps, witnessed the same thing. Wright ably summed up the stealthy enemy withdrawal. "Lee's retreat was admirably managed and evinced great forecast," he grudgingly admitted. "My own pickets—not 200 yards from his main line did not discover the retreat till day light."[2]

General Meade ordered his staff officers to eat breakfast at dawn and be in the saddle by 7:00 a.m. As they mounted, Howard's courier arrived at army headquarters carrying the unwelcome news that the trapped enemy was no more.[3] Although news of the Confederate escape spread rapidly, Meade did not order an immediate general pursuit. Rebel guns were clearly visible on the high ground overlooking the Potomac, and Meade decided against attacking the river crossings. "At 7 A.M. ordered forward in line of battle," observed a lieutenant colonel of the 1st Massachusetts Infantry, "marched four miles, found no enemy, and bivouacked."[4]

By the time Meade finally ordered a general advance, the clock showed half past 8:00 a.m. When it finally moved, the army's advance was an impressive sight to behold. "Perhaps the finest thing that the army ever saw was the movement forward in line of battle near Williamsport and Hagerstown," noted a Massachusetts soldier. "As far as the eye could reach on either hand were broad open fields of grain with here and there little woods, the ground being undulating but not broken, and we were formed in close column of division by brigade." The dense lines advanced, cutting a wide swath through farm fields.[5] "Our advance was not interrupted by the enemy," confirmed Brig. Gen. Joseph Bartlett, a commander of a 6th Corps brigade.[6]

"The fields were one sheet of ripe grain and young corn, which were trampled smooth," observed an officer of the 5th Corps. "The Marylanders seemed stunned by the destruction of their property, and came in crowds to know what to do." The passage of the armies wreaked havoc on the civilians of Washington County, Maryland, leaving them in jeopardy of not being able to feed their families.[7]

The advance frustrated some of the soldiers. "We act like a lot of scared monkeys," declared a disgusted Massachusetts man.[8] "There is no picket in our front at all, and so we quietly fall in and march six miles to Williamsport, for what purpose?" complained the commander of the 93rd Pennsylvania Infantry, 6th Corps. "God knows! It's plain we're not going to cross at Williamsport and its plain we'll have to march back again."[9] Many soldiers grumbled that their efforts had gone to naught because the enemy had been allowed to slip out of their grasp.

"No one, who saw the approach of that army to Williamsport can ever forget the sight," wrote the historian of the 5th Corps. "Upon advancing beyond the Antietam, the army moved in battle-array, each corps in line, each brigade in columns of regimental front, and as the ground marched over consisted of open cultivated fields, the whole line could be seen, with its colors proudly floating in the breeze and bayonets by the tens of thousands gleaming in the sunlight." The artillery moved along two parallel roads in the center of the army's massed ranks, while pioneers swept away all obstructions, including fences, stone walls, and outhouses. "The fields were groaning with the yellow ripened grain, and when the army had passed everything bore the appearance of having a tornado pass over it. Hardly a stalk of grain was left standing in the fields."[10]

After reaching the Confederate defensive line, "the Northern infantry halted, and its men took position behind the formidable line of earthworks," recalled an officer with the 124th New York Infantry. "The camp fires, over which Lee's rear guard had boiled the last cups of coffee it was destined any considerable portion of the Army of Northern Virginia should ever drink north of the Potomac, were yet burning and, a fresh supply of brush being added, soon blazing away again, under the tin cups of our always dry—no matter how wet they are—boys in blue." Not long after, the men spotted the welcome sight of commissary wagons bringing rations. The men settled down in the vacated Rebel lines and enjoyed their first real meal in days.[11]

"Another campaign on the Rappahannock, boys," declared a disgusted Union officer, bitter by the escape of the Confederates. "We shall be in our old quarters in a few days," grumbled another.[12] Yet another predicted, "Nothing now remains but to follow the enemy through Virginia, where the advantage of roads, position, and everything else will be in his favor."[13] They were right of course, but it would take another two weeks of hard marching and hard fighting to get there—and then begin the fighting all over again.

The 3rd Wisconsin Infantry of the 12th Corps led the way toward the crossing at Falling Waters. When the head of their column was within sight of the Donnelly house, Kilpatrick's cavalry thundered up, prompting the Wisconsin men to scatter in order to permit the horse soldiers to pass by on their way to the Potomac. "They had scarcely passed out of sight through a patch of woods, when the roar of artillery and the sharp crack of musketry announced that the enemy had been found," recalled an officer with the 3rd Wisconsin. "We moved forward as rapidly as possible, but were not in time to take any part in the conflict."[14]

"Our men have become ragged and shoeless, thousands have marched for days barefooted over the flinty turnpikes," noted Colonel Dawes of the 6th Wisconsin, part of the Iron Brigade. "We may now reasonably hope for rest."[15] An officer of the 5th Corps sounded a similar note. "The campaign is now over, and the army thoroughly worn out, requiring at least six weeks to refit."[16] Events would prove both men wrong.

Confederate prisoners told the Federals that they were too late, that Lee was already pushing his way up the Shenandoah Valley. "A hot, hard, dusty march as we go pushing along," complained staff officer Charles Lynch. "A soldier's life in the field is a severe one."[17]

The commanding officers of the 2nd Corps were not particularly disappointed to find the enemy gone. A stream ran through the front of the 2nd

Corps position, and it would have presented a real obstacle for an all-out assault on Lee's works. The stream would have broken up the Federal line of battle, and it was too close to the enemy line for the troops to cross and reform. A palpable sense of relief permeated 2nd Corps headquarters.[18]

That night, yet another heavy thunderstorm blew in, "drenching out and washing away what little spirit still remained in the tired bodies" of the men of the Army of the Potomac.[19] "The invasion of the North had been providentially brought to an end through the valor of the Army of the Potomac," stated an officer of the Philadelphia Brigade, part of the 2nd Corps.[20] "The enemy has got away from us again and gone back to the Potomac, having left a strongly fortified position," declared General Howard.[21]

The long and difficult pursuit of the Army of Northern Virginia was, for the time being, at an end.

* * *

While the Virginia army was withdrawing and the Federal host was marking time, Abraham Lincoln was waiting impatiently for news from the Potomac front. About noon, "came the dispatch stating that our worst fears were true. The enemy had gotten away unhurt," recalled John Hay. Lincoln was deeply grieved. "We had them within our grasp," he lamented. "We had only to stretch forth our hands & they were ours. And nothing I could say or do could make the Army move." The pacing and profoundly unhappy President Lincoln added, "This is a dreadful reminiscence of McClellan. The same spirit that moved [McClellan] to claim a great victory because Pa & Md

Noah Brooks, newspaper correspondent and a friend of President Lincoln.

Illinois State Historical Library, Springfield

were safe. The hearts of 10 million people sank within them when McClellan raised that shout last fall. Will our Generals never get that idea out of their heads? The whole country is our soil."[22] The next day, the President's son, Robert Todd Lincoln, told Hay that he had heard his father say, "If I had gone up there I could have whipped them myself."[23]

Lincoln's newspaper friend, Noah Brooks, had been hanging around Meade's headquarters all morning. Brooks accepted an offer from Chief Quartermaster Maj. Gen. Rufus Ingalls to take a cavalry horse and orderly and ride to the front toward Falling Waters. Brooks left a lengthy, and probably the most detailed, description we have today on the landscape. His gripping and invaluable word portraits made for compelling reading then, just as they do now. "This was about noon, July 14th," he recalled,

> and all that morning there had been rumors of a retreat of the enemy across the Potomac. General Ingalls was positive that the Confederate army had made good its retreat to Virginia, and some of the younger men at headquarters did not hesitate to say the Meade had been "most egregiously fooled." About twelve o'clock noon, heavy cannonading was heard from the front in the direction of Williamsport, on the Potomac, and opinions differed as to whether this was the beginning of a general engagement or was the firing of Kilpatrick's and Buford's cavalry on the retreating flanks of the rebels.
>
> About two miles from Antietam Creek, we came upon the Federal line of intrenchments (now abandoned), and found the Third Corps drawn up in line of battle; the Second and Fifth having pushed on ahead. We soon overtook those troops, marching in three columns over fields of grain, through thrifty orchards, clover-fields and gardens. The ground was soft and the country roads were in a dreadful state of mire. The movements of the troops, however, were regardless of roads, and in their forward advance they maneuvered precisely as they would through a savage country.
>
> It was rather entertaining, on the whole, to come into the abandoned rebel lines, as we soon did. Here were rifle pits and other hastily constructed earthworks; but not a picket or a sentry was to be seen. All had "skedaddled" incontinently, leaving behind them the refuse of their camps. Here and there I found letters half-written, which the rebel

> soldiers were inditing [sic] to friends at home and had thrown away, apparently, in the sudden haste of their departure. The relic-hunter could have collected a museum of military curios in these deserted camps. Fragments of army equipage and wearing-apparel, abandoned horses, broken artillery-wagons, and other debris, were dropped about in picturesque confusion.[24]

Brooks and his escort turned downstream toward Falling Waters. Along that road, they found the detritus of war:

> disabled caissons, wrecked ambulances and army forges, muskets, knapsacks, and a few country wagons, left by the fleeing enemy. The cannonading we had heard at headquarters ceased, but a few volleys of musketry were fired in the vicinity of Falling Waters, four miles below Williamsport, on the Potomac.

Brooks continued his invaluable observations:

> Striking into the woods near Falling Waters, we came upon squads of rebel prisoners in hundreds or more, lying on the ground and guarded by a few Union cavalry. These poor fellows were ragged, wet, and muddy, many of them having been caught while in the river attempting to ford the stream. The roads were choked with cavalry, and here and there were parks of artillery at rest, brought out on a bootless errand, the drivers sleeping under the caissons.
>
> Now we learned that the rebels had drawn in their lines at about six o'clock that morning, the main body of the army having previously crossed the stream by means of bridges hastily thrown across. The approach to the little village of Falling Waters, Maryland, was over a hill which rose sharply from the grain-fields around it. Having mounted this hill, one saw that the roads passed over gentle undulations gradually sloping down to the river. On the top of the hill, which commanded all these roads leading to the river crossing, and parallel to the stream, were a series of light earthworks which the rebels had occupied with a rear-guard of four thousand men, Early's division of the rebel army. Behind the works were still passing out the last of the rebels when our forces came up at noon that day.

> Lee had finished here, on the previous Saturday, a pontoon-bridge across the Potomac, and the structure, eked out with scows, boats and lumber seized in the vicinity, was standing when we arrived. It was a very good piece of engineering and trestle-work. Here and there on the floor of the bridge lay a dead soldier, and occasionally a gray-coated body could be seen half in and half out of the water that lapped the shore.
>
> The rebels who were protecting the retreat of their army in the breast-work on the hill, had received our cavalry as they charged up the hill with a volley which laid low about twenty of our men and wounded many more; at the same time, a considerable force of rebel infantry was deployed on their right where the hills sloped down into a wheat-field, in which the shocks of grain stood in scattered cocks.
>
> But the onslaught of the Union cavalry was so furious that the Confederates could not stand before it, and began a fighting retreat. The cannonading which we had heard two hours before, when we were on the Sharpsburg pike, was the firing of the Union light artillery, brought to bear upon the enemy as they fought bravely through the flowery lanes and grain-fields of Falling Waters on their way to the temporary bridge.
>
> In the mean time, another cavalry force had surrounded the small squads of rebels who were trying to escape across on the floating scows which had been used at Williamsport, and had been brought down to this point. About three hundred and fifty of them were taken prisoners, and these, with sixteen hundred who were cut off at the end of the bridge, were all that were found here of Lee's army, which was to have been "bagged" while it was securely caged in the elbow formed by the bend of the Potomac at this point.
>
> All, did I say? There were a score or more lying there with the Union soldiers in the wheat-fields among the sheaves which their fight had overturned, their faces toward the sky, gray-backs and blue-backs sleeping the sleep that knows no waking.[25]

Of all the wreckage of war Brooks examined, none left such an impression as that made of flesh and blood. "To one unused to the gory sights of battlefields, the picture presented there was strangely fascinating," Brooks continued:

> The dead soldiers, blue-clad or gray-clad, lay in various positions scattered over the grain-field and in the clover meadow; but most of them had been turned over on their backs since they fell. The expressions on the countenances of these poor fellows were usually peaceful. One rebel soldier attracted my attention by the attitude in which he lay still in death, his head upon his arm, just as I remembered that David Copperfield saw his friend, the drowned Steerforth, lying on the beach, as he had "often seen him lie at school."
>
> In a military hospital that had been hastily improvised in a barn, at the head of a leafy lane, were gathered the wounded of both armies, under the charge of Federal surgeons, of whom I occasionally caught glimpses of their bare hands and arms reddened with the gore of the poor fellows, whose cries and groans sounded lugubriously within. The men captured in this little fight were from the 40th, 47th, and 55th Virginia, and 55th North Carolina regiments. There were commanded by Brigadier-General Pettigrew. They made a courageous stand and a brave fight against the Union cavalry . . . commanded by General George A. Custer. Among those who did not survive their wounds at Falling Waters was the rebel General Pettigrew, who was then lying in a barn at Falling Waters, but was next day taken across the river under a flag of truce from Lee's army. He died at Bunker Hill, [West] Virginia. . .[26]

Leaving the makeshift hospital, Brooks guided his borrowed mount toward the river. "Turning my horse's head in the direction of Meade's headquarters, I looked across the swollen and turbid Potomac where I could see the smoke of rebel camps rising in the thick Virginia woods on the other side of the stream." The sight infuriated the newspaper correspondent:

> It is impossible now to describe—almost impossible to recall—the feeling of bitterness with which we regarded the sight. Lee's army was gone. In spite of warnings, expostulations, doubts, and fears, it had escaped, and further pursuit was not even to be thought of.

> I remembered the anxiety, almost anguish, with which Lincoln had said before I left Washington that he was afraid "something would happen" to prevent that annihilation of Lee's army, which, as he thought, was then certainly within the bounds of possibility. But the last hope of the Confederacy had not failed them yet. The desperate venture of an invasion of Pennsylvania and Maryland had failed, it was true. But the fatal blow which seemed to hang in the air when I left Washington did not fall.
>
> As I rode down the hill and through the undulating fields beyond, the blue-coated soldiers, jolly and insouciant, greeted the solitary civilian horseman with jocose remarks about the "Johnny Rebs" who had so cunningly run away from them. Many of these men had enlisted "for the war," and when I stopped to exchange salutations, they good-naturedly said, "Well, here goes for two years more."

The correspondent could not help but overhear "a curious effect of whispering speech" as he rode through the woods:

> Two or three thousand men waiting for orders were scattered over the ground among the bushes, beguiling their time by eating, drinking, and talking in low tones. The curious fluttering noise of this wide conversation of so large a body of men was something like that undistinguishable chorus of which we have heard in one of Gilbert and Sullivan's operas . . . it was the gabble of two or three thousand men, all talking at once, and producing an undulating volume of sound like the noises of birds seeking their roosts at night.[27]

After riding amongst the idle men, Brooks finally completed the circle of his tour and arrived back at army headquarters. The pall that had fallen over it was palpable:

> Meade's headquarters, on my return, presented a chopfallen appearance; probably the worst was known there before I had left on my own private and special reconnaissance. Here I met Vice-President [Hannibal] Hamlin, who was also a visitor at Meade's headquarters, and who had been taken out to see the fight (which did not come off), at a point nearer Williamsport.

Hannibal Hamlin, Vice President of the United States.

LOC

As we met, he raised his hands and turned away his face with a gesture of despair. Later on, I came across General Wadsworth, who almost shed tears while he talked with us about the escape of the rebel army. He said that it seemed to him that most of those who participated in the council of war had no stomach for the fight. "If they had," he added, "the rebellion, as one might say, might have been ended then and there."[28]

Having seen about all he had set out to see, and more, Brooks took his leave of the general and army headquarters and prepared for the long trip back to Washington. His task was to relay the news to Lincoln, who had requested a detailed report the following day. Brooks was joined by Vice President Hamlin, who had a dual purpose for visiting the army. Besides wishing to witness a war-ending fight that never happened, Hamlin's son Charles was assistant adjutant general on the staff of Brig. Gen. A. A. Humphreys, the army's new chief of staff. Hamlin arrived on the field, where he found "the Union lines impregnable, the enemy in retreat, and his son unharmed and recommended for promotion. His presence on the field created speculation, and some officers appeared to think that it was another case of 'Washington interference.'"[29]

Brooks continued his account:

Vice-President Hamlin and myself were despatched by General Meade in an ambulance under the charge of a young lieutenant of cavalry by the

> turnpike road to Frederick, where we took a train for Washington. Columns upon columns of army wagons and artillery were now in motion toward Frederick, crossing the fields, blocking the roads, and interlacing the face of the whole country with blackened tracks which heavy wheels cut in the rich, dark soil of Maryland, saturated with days of rain.
>
> Here and there one passed a knot of wagons inextricably tangled or hopelessly mired by the roadside. At one point, I was amused by seeing an eight-mule team thus stalled in a marshy piece of ground, every animal being on its back with its four legs motionless in the air. Whenever a teamster essayed to touch any part of the harness, all those thirty-two legs would fly with the speed and regularity of a tremendous machine, and the unfortunate meddler would bounce high in the air and come down again angry and swearing.
>
> It is no exaggeration to say that the Boonsboro pike that day was a blue streak of profanity from Meade's headquarters to Frederick.[30]

Simon Cameron, Lincoln's first Secretary of War, also had made his way to the headquarters of the Army of the Potomac. On the morning of July 14, as the army began its fitful advance against Lee's entrenchments, Cameron sent a wire to Lincoln. "I left the Army of the Potomac yesterday, believing that the decision of General Meade's council of war on Saturday night, not to attack the rebels, would allow them to escape. His army is in fine spirits and eager for battle. They will win if they get a chance." Cameron also expressed the opinion that since the Army of Northern Virginia had pulled back to the Potomac, the Susquehanna no longer needed protection, and that all of Couch's command, which Cameron described as "a fine army," should be ordered to join Meade at Williamsport.[31]

Harpers Ferry

While the final drama was playing out at Williamsport and Federal teamsters assuaged their plight with profanity, Union horse soldiers from the Harpers Ferry garrison commanded by Brig. Gen. Henry M. Naglee moved to picket the roads in the area. Fifty horsemen of the 1st Connecticut Cavalry led by Maj. Charles Farnsworth crossed the Potomac beyond Bolivar Heights to probe the Confederate lines on the south side of the river. Capt. Erastus

Blakeslee led the advance guard of eighteen men. About two miles from Harpers Ferry, Blakeslee's men found thirty pickets of the 12th Virginia Cavalry and charged.

Unbeknownst to Major Farnsworth and his small command, they were advancing headlong into the entire enemy reserve of nearly 200 counter-charging troopers. After a fierce hand-to-hand fight, the superior Confederate force repulsed Farnsworth's Federals, rescuing several prisoners that had been taken earlier, and capturing Major Farnsworth and twenty-four of his Connecticut cavalrymen. "The major's horse was shot under him, and he fought most gallantly on foot with his saber until he was overpowered and taken prisoner," reported Captain Blakeslee, who took command of the defeated survivors. Blakeslee fell back with a Rebel captain, two lieutenants, and two privates as prisoners.

The small but sharp affair demonstrated that the Confederates still controlled the south bank of the Potomac River.[32]

The Aftermath

By July 15 the fighting was just about over. Noah Brooks kept his appointment with Lincoln that day, riding to the President's house to report all he had witnessed and all he had heard. "It is enough to say," Brooks recalled, "that although he was not so profoundly distressed as he was when Hooker's army recrossed the Rappahannock after the battle of Chancellorsville, his grief and anger were something sorrowful to behold."[33]

Back in Gettysburg, wounded prisoner of war David Johnston of the 7th Virginia awaited news of the outcome of the stand-off along the banks of the Potomac River. For a week and a half Johnston had put up with the gloating of his Ohio male nurse, and he was eager to hear the fate of his comrades in arms. His nurse entered that day to read him the news. As the Buckeye approached, Johnston noted a marked change in his demeanor. "He read, when General Meade moved out to attack the rebel army, behold! 'the old fox had gone,' having crossed the river the night before!" This time, Johnston could not resist gloating just a bit.[34]

In Lee's wake was a devastated Williamsport. A correspondent for one of the Baltimore newspapers left a vivid description of the aftermath for the residents of the ravaged river town:

> A more dismal looking place than the town of Williamsport and the neighboring fields present, now converted into commons by the destruction of fences, can hardly be imagined.
>
> In the town itself we found Rebel hospitals, containing those of their badly wounded whom it was not possible to remove, and a more miserable exhibit in this regard it seems impossible to conceive. Through the town the streets were a perfect bed of mire, dotted occasionally with that never-failing feature in the rear of an army, dead horses, whose effluvia burdened the sultry air. Such of the citizens as were visible looked worn, dispirited and miserable; in keeping with the scenes about them—on the high bank of the river a group of signal officers, with their flag, stood out in strong relief against the mountains of the Virginia shore, whilst the muddy river, upon whose depth so much had been staked, rolled peacefully along, the tops of some wrecked and submerged army wagons appearing at different points to mark the critical nature of the Rebel retreat. Of pontoons or trestle work bridge of "flat" or even canoe, there was not a sign, the silence of the scene being almost painful in contrast with the lien of the advance previously left. Back of the town and in the rear of the old Rebel encampments the advance of our army was gathering rapidly, long lines of artillery and infantry coming along the Hagerstown and Boonsboro roads, and heavy bodies of cavalry—the advance of it all—being drawn up in masses, as if to complete the picture.

It would take many months for the citizens of Williamsport to recover and for life to return to normal after the armies finally left.[35]

The tired and hungry troopers of Buford's division rode that day through Sharpsburg, Harpers Ferry, Sandy Hook, and Knoxville before going into camp near Berlin (the present-day town of Brunswick).[36] Wesley Merritt's brigade had ridden, skirmished, and camped for several days without wagons or forage, and rations. Despite these hardships, Merritt proudly noted, his Regulars had destroyed nearly 800 wagons, captured 3,000 horses, and nearly 5,000 prisoners in the ten days since the Gettysburg battle ended.[37] The men needed clothing, shoes, ammunition, and most important, food and sleep. On July 16, the camp moved to Petersville, and Buford's men got two days of well-deserved rest. More rain fell on the 17th. "In the last fifteen days we had engaged the enemy in ten battles, had marched over two hundred miles, with but little sleep and on half rations, and in every engagement fighting against superior numbers of infantry," recalled a Pennsylvanian.[38]

Writing on July 16, Corporal Nelson Taylor of the 9th New York observed, "this is the first time we have had a chance to wash and dry a shirt since we left Stafford."[39] "I think but a day or two will elapse before we shall be again on the move, but alas the golden opportunity for crushing Lee's army has slipped by to the chagrin of everyone," complained an Illinois horse soldier. "Our generals made a sad mistake and I think some changes will take place. . . . Every man feels mortified that the Rebs were allowed to escape so easily." The common soldiers and officers seemed to understand what many of the higher ranking generals did not.[40]

"The procrastination and delays, caused by the talk and then the advice of the corps commanders soon removed whatever of élan the troops possessed," observed an officer of the 5th Corps. "When they discovered that the enemy had gone, they consoled themselves with the fact that they had answered the call which had been made upon them. That call, when Lee crossed the Potomac and threatened Northern cities with fire and sword, had been a cry for protection. In a fortnight's time, by marches so wearying that only the strongest reached the battlefield—by conflicts so desperate that its ranks had been more than doubly decimated—the army had delivered the country from the presence of invaders, the people breathed freely; and then began to be heard the complaints of a large class of war critics who were not satisfied that Lee's army had not been 'bagged'."[41]

The marathon of marching and fighting had also been hard on the Confederate cavalry. "These days will be remembered by the members of General Stuart's staff as days of peculiar hardship. Scanty rations had been issued to the men but nothing was provided for the officers," recalled one of Stuart's staff officers. "The country had been swept bare of provisions, and we could purchase nothing. For four or five days in succession we received our only food, after nightfall."[42] These hardships, combined with the sharp defeat at Gettysburg, took a major toll on the morale of the Confederate troopers.[43] "Our army seem to be very generally pleased at the idea of returning to Va. & seem to think they are at home & on hospitable soil in the 'Old Dominion,'" noted a weary trooper of the 3rd Virginia Cavalry.[44] "Troops glad to return to good old Virginia but have been in good spirits all the time," echoed a captain of the 1ith Virginia Cavalry.[45]

The armies left a desolate wasteland behind them. Elder Daniel P. Saylor, a preacher of the Church of the Brethren, knew Abraham Lincoln from Illinois.

Elder Saylor had started a preaching tour while the Gettysburg Campaign raged. He rode to Frederick and headed west on the National Road until he reached the village of Bolivar on the eastern slopes of South Mountain. The 11th Corps had camped there for two days, so that "the fields were laid waste and all . . . was trampled underfoot." From Bolivar west to Williamsport lay "an unbroken scene of desolation and waste . . . the fences were no more," having been used for firewood or to build the Confederate breastworks. The wheat crops were used to feed hungry horses of both armies. Cattle and hogs had gone to feed hungry soldiers. There was little evidence that "these had once been farms." The local citizenry would not soon forget the visit of the armies. They suffered great privations that winter as a consequence of the loss of their crops and livestock.[46]

* * *

After fifty days of hard marching and fighting, the Gettysburg Campaign ended with the war-weary armies right back where they started, staring at their adversaries across the Rappahannock River. During the course of the campaign, John Buford's division suffered 1,160 casualties.[47] "I think I have not spoken of the dark and rainy nights we have had to crawl out of our tents and saddle up and march until the next day, nor have I mentioned hard tack and pork, and often we are without a paper for over a week at a time," wrote one of Gamble's troopers. "But we do not complain; all we want is our ranks to be filled up."[48]

Even the other branches of the service noticed the fine performance of the Federal cavalry. Col. Charles Wainwright, chief of artillery for the 1st Corps, complimented the branch in his diary, "Our cavalry has done some very good service on this campaign, much more than ever before."[49] The 5th New York Cavalry of Kilpatrick's 3rd Division passed some infantry on the road to Harpers Ferry on the afternoon of July 14. A weary foot soldier called out, "You are finally beginning to do something for your country!" As one New Yorker put it, "In fact, our infantry acknowledges that cavalry is now worth something. In the past three weeks our division has captured more than its number of rebel prisoners. The sarcastic remark attributed to Gen. Hooker, 'Whoever saw a dead cavalryman?' is heard no more," he continued. "At Falling Waters twenty-eight brave men fell on our side. But it was a glorious death to die."[50]

Lee's Confederate wagon train of wounded. *Battles and Leaders*

Conclusion

"Covering the retreat of an army is not a fun thing to do. It was one continuous fight until we reached Hagerstown, Md.; and even after that, for we had skirmishes every day until Gen. Lee recrossed the Potomac."

— Pvt. L. T. Dickinson, 1st Maryland Cavalry (CSA)

AND SO THE GETTYSBURG CAMPAIGN came to a close. The escape of Lee's army left many questions unanswered. The resulting controversy quickly became one of the most virulent arguments of the entire campaign, among both the Federal officer corps and its rank and file, as well as throughout the halls of the United States government. Could Meade have done more? Should he have attacked Robert E. Lee's defensive positions at Williamsport? Could Lee's army have been bagged as it fought for its life against the swollen waters of the Potomac River? Does anyone deserve blame for the failure to bring the Army of Northern Virginia to bay? Finally, was the Army of the Potomac in any condition to launch the sort of attack that would have been required to defeat Lee's army in Maryland? We shall explore these questions in this conclusion. To help us, we have carefully selected quotations from participants that reflect all of the various viewpoints of these questions. Some may be familiar to readers, but many will not be.

First, we'll present some of the most cogent comments by soldiers of both sides regarding the Army of the Potomac's opportunities to have done more before Lee's escape.

The Southern Viewpoint

The rank and file in Lee's army believed Meade was afraid to attack the formidable Southern defensive position at Williamsport. "For three days General Lee held his army in line of battle, and during these three days he resorted to every means in his power to bring on a general engagement, but in vain," sneered a Maryland Confederate. "General Meade had had enough, and contented himself with watching and waiting for Lee to move on, when he, too, would resume the monotonous march to the Potomac and follow the Confederate army into Virginia."[1]

Capt. Charles Blackford, a Virginia staff officer, observed, "General Lee had tendered them battle for a week, and as they did not accept and were reinforced hourly he very wisely, I think, recrossed the river." He continued, "To do so in safety in the presence of so great an army without the loss of a man or of any property was a great military feat," he added, not altogether accurately. "That he should have been permitted to do so shows how hard a blow he struck."[2]

Maj. Edward McDonald of the 11th Virginia Cavalry agreed. "Our whole army lay in sight of the enemy for a week, but he did not dare attack us," wrote McDonald. "We were without ammunition or rations, and the order to the infantry was that when their arms gave out they were to use bayonets, and those who had not bayonets were to use stones. The Yankees boast that they whipped us, yet with many reinforcements and all the rations and ammunition they desired, they did not dare attack us."[3]

A few days after the end of the campaign, a member of the 13th Virginia Cavalry of Chambliss' Brigade observed that, but for "the excitement of the everyday skirmishing and frequently hard fighting we never would have exerted ourselves to such an extent."[4] "Covering the retreat of an army is not a fun thing to do," observed Pvt. L.T. Dickinson of the 2nd Virginia Cavalry. "It was one continuous fight until we reached Hagerstown, Md.; and even after that, for we had skirmishes every day until Gen. Lee recrossed the Potomac."[5]

"Since the 9th of last June our Brigade has been engaged in twelve severe battles and skirmishing every day," noted an officer of the 10th Virginia Cavalry. "It has done more than any other brigade of cavalry. The men are nearly all worn out with loss of sleep and heavy duty. [H]aven't more than four hundred men in the brigade left for duty out of four regiments."[6] An officer of the 4th North Carolina Cavalry of Robertson's Brigade observed that these were "days which will ever be remembered by those present as days of unprecedented hardships and anxiety, as with scant ration, amid country swept bare of provisions, with the enemy hanging 'round in every direction and the swollen waters of the Potomac at our backs."[7]

Part of the reason Meade was stymied and unable to do more was the direct result of the duties performed by Southern horse soldiers under very adverse circumstances. "No man can stand more," explained Captain Wills, "and I never wish to be called on to stand this much again. I had one horse killed under me and rode three others down."[8] These men withstood the travails of an eight-day cavalry ride to Pennsylvania followed by the intense riding and fighting that punctuated the retreat from Gettysburg. Stuart was proud of his cavaliers. "My cavalry has nobly sustained its reputation and done better and harder fighting than it ever has since the war," he boasted to his wife Flora.[9]

The Confederate horse artillery supported the troopers through their joint ordeal. It, too, was in bad shape. Capt. James Breathed's battery had effectively emptied its limber chests by the fight at Boonsboro on July 8. Two of the four guns received a supply of ammunition after they crossed the Potomac early on the morning of July 14, but the limber chests of the other section remained empty. The horse artillerists had also seen steady heavy fighting, and they were just as worn out as their comrades in the cavalry.[10]

The Northern Viewpoint

The Northern soldiers were tired *and* frustrated. Most who left accounts believed a great opportunity had been squandered. "We are worn and jaded down," sighed Maj. John Hammond of the 5th New York Cavalry on July 17. "The cavalry has done all the work and fighting since Gettysburg. We charged into Hagerstown on Sunday last, and held the place for two days against a large body of infantry and cavalry, hoping Gen. Meade would attack them." He concluded derisively, "But no, he waited one week from the time the advance of the rebels came into Hagerstown, which was the Monday we fought them. We felt that we had them and should have annihilated them."[11] A Massachusetts artillerist agreed. "We…formed in line of battle expecting a battle to commence momentarily but none came off, as we all hoped it would for we were confident of whipping Lee there, then, but our Generals knew what was for the best (or at least it was expected that they did) and Lee was allowed to get away, it is said for strategic purposes."[12]

On July 17, Colonel Patrick R. Guiney of the 9th Massachusetts Infantry lamented what he also deemed to be a lost opportunity in a letter to his wife. "Lee, you are aware 'has escaped' etc. It is no silly job to catch him, I assure you. When once he left Gettysburgh it was impossible to give him any <u>fatal</u> blow. Gettysburgh, the evening of July 3rd were the time and place to ruin his Army. We saw his Army flying from the field, broken, beaten, terrified! O! how I felt the significance of that moment. But Meade allowed it to pass—stood still, and gave us—<u>another years work</u>. In common with thousands I was disgusted to see such an opportunity lost."[13]

Another Massachusetts man put it more succinctly. "Allowing Lee to cross the Potomac River without interference had a very demoralizing effect on the army," he declared. "To march all the way from Gettysburg to Williamsport merely to see that Lee got safely across the river seemed an unnecessary expenditure of muscle. The army felt exactly as General Meade described his own feelings to be, and it seemed a pity that his strength of mind was not equal to his judgment. The army was heartily sick of this shilly-shally way of fighting. The growing feeling of discontent that rankled in the hearts of the men found daily utterance as we marched along."[14]

"I will state . . . that men wearing 'stars' on their shoulders, are not always celestial beings, and that there has been a time when a battle line could be formed out of very poor generals," bitterly declared an officer serving with the 19th Maine Infantry. "That quality, however, is rapidly disappearing from the field, to be known in the future only as they display their gay and costly equipages on civic holiday occasions."[15]

The chaplain of the 145th Pennsylvania Infantry, John Stuckenberg, spent the first few days after the Gettysburg battle attending to the wounded of his regiment before riding to catch up to his comrades at Taneytown on July 8. After watching the Rebels escape at Falling Waters, he scribbled in his diary, "Why battle was not given by Meade I could not divine. . . . All seemed to be greatly disappointed at Meade's failure to attack them. . . . Lee and his army were safely in Va and immediate pursuit was in vain. For this we had been hurried from Gettysburg's bloody field—for this we had been marched through deep mud, drenching rain, intense heat to catch a few stragglers while the great body of the army was safe—could laugh at us to scorn," the chaplain continued. "It makes me think of a squirrel—catch it by the tip of the tail and a few hairs remain in your hands whilst the squirrel runs briskly away, none worse for its trifling loss which it scarcely feels. All we, all the whole army had done and suffered since the G[ettysburg] battle was in vain."[16]

Chaplain Stuckenberg recounted a conversation on July 14 with Lt. Robert Walsh Mitchell of the army commander's staff, as the regiment cautiously approached the river crossing. "Just as we started forward again Lt. Mitchell of Gen Meade's staff came up," he recalled. "He had been sent to the front of the 6th Corps to find out the position of the enemy—and had not yet found where they were, after riding about for hours. He felt very indignant that the rebels had been allowed to escape. He attributed it to damnable imbecility. He could find no words to express his disappointment and chagrin. 'Chaplain' he said 'I ought not to talk to you, for I have been swearing all morning.'"[17]

Henry Van Aernam, the surgeon of the 154th New York Infantry, was even more blunt when he wrote to his wife on July 15. "When we were chasing the rebs, the boys, although barefooted and ragged and half fed, were cheerful on their forced marches, but today they feel chagrined and humbugged. They are silent and morose and what little they say is damning the foolishness and shortsightedness of their officers. They are right," concluded Van Aernam, "for they have endured everything, braved everything for the sake of success, and success bountiful and lasting was within their grasp—but lost by the imbecility of commandery. Our army is an anomaly," he finally exclaimed, "it is an army of Lions commanded by jackasses!"[18]

Pvt. John Buchanan of the 105th Pennsylvania Infantry also affirmed what seemed to be the sentiments of many in Meade's army. "We gave them a good whipping in Pa and would have whipped them again if General Lee had not managed to get across the river," observed Buchanan. "Our army in general is very angry at our leading men for allowing Lee to cross the river without attacking them. I have often thought that if our army had attacked them on Sunday or Monday that we would have taken the principal part of Lee's Army prisoners." Buchanan concluded, "I think we are elected to spend another year in Virginia. It was on account of the heavy rains that prevented General Mead from attacking the Rebs. You must not be angry with us for driving the Jonny Rebs back to Va."[19]

The Army of the Potomac's chief engineer, Brig. Gen. Gouverneur K. Warren, was deeply involved in the decisions made by the army's high command. "The 'Invader's Hoof' has left the soil of our Maryland," he informed his wife on the night of July 14. "He retreated in haste during the night, and we captured his rear-guard today. Terrible has been the ruin of the rebels' hopes, as I told you it would be, if they invaded the North," he stated proudly. Warren, however, recognized the opportunity that had slipped away. "But we have not yet destroyed Lee's army; and the campaign must go on. We shall follow their retreat, and you must live without me, and I without you."[20]

There is little doubt that a sizeable number of the men and officers in the ranks, as well as several high placed officers, believed the Virginia army could have been successfully attacked while it was trapped on the Maryland side of the swollen Potomac River, or at the least, the effort should have been made.

Meade certainly had his supporters among his army, however. Col. Charles H. Morgan, who served as Maj. Gen. Winfield S. Hancock's chief of staff, left behind a particularly cogent observation in response to the criticism of Meade's conduct of the pursuit of Lee's army. "It may be said here that a feeling was prevalent and quite freely expressed while we were confronting Lee that we had done all that could be expected in defeating Lee's plan of invasion, and forcing him to retreat," he wrote, "and that to attack him in position would be to risk the loss of what we had gained. The Army of the Potomac had not been so uniformly successful in its encounters with the Army of Northern Virginia as to encourage the belief that victory would necessarily incline again to our side."[21]

"The marches had been hard, but there was no complaining, for the great victory had inspired the men and made them feel that the end of the war was no longer doubtful and nearer at hand," wrote a member of the 20th Massachusetts Infantry, who believed that, given the circumstances, Meade had done a fine job of massing the army so quickly near Hagerstown and Williamsport.[22] At least one 2nd Corps soldier was glad to find Lee's strong defensive positions empty when the Army of the Potomac finally advanced on the morning of July 14.[23]

When asked the inevitable question about why Meade had permitted Lee to escape, Capt. I. P. Powell of the 5th Corps' 146th New York Infantry had a well-reasoned answer. "When Lee retreated to the river he selected a splendid position and fortified it strongly. Soon the two armies were again opposite each other . . . [Lee] had by far the best position," he wrote in August 1863. "To have been defeated would have been to lose more by far, then we had gained. The possibility of such a disaster must not be allowed for a moment. The only course therefore, was to act on the defensive and wait till a portion of the enemy had crossed the river before we attacked him." He concluded, "But it was impossible to tell when this happened. They escaped from us as we had frequently escaped from them. Their retreat was in the night, and during a heavy rain storm, when it would have been absolutely impossible to have followed them had we known they were going. Gen. Meade acted just as any wise General should have done."[24]

A Northern cavalryman stated a similar opinion. "General Meade had concluded, and wisely, that it would be impossible to pursue the enemy with any hope of bringing him to battle. The roads which General Lee had found difficult were now impassable. The mountainous country through which we had passed was full of strong defensive positions, from which no one knew better than he that the Confederate commander would derive the utmost advantage," wrote George B. Davis of the 1st Massachusetts Cavalry. "In such positions, too, the disparity of numbers would disappear, as the positions thus occupied would be such as were susceptible of defense by greatly inferior forces. Trusting, therefore, that the high stage of water in the river would continue, General Meade decided to move along the eastern base of the mountains, cross by the lower South Mountain passes into the Cumberland Valley, and give battle to the enemy under the best conditions which he could obtain in the vicinity of the Potomac."[25]

General John Sedgwick also raised a legitimate point. While the veterans of the Army of the Potomac received large numbers of reinforcements during the pursuit of Lee's army, these men were of dubious value. "You will hear of the immense reinforcements that are being sent to this army, and wonder why we do not crush their army," Sedgwick wrote to his sister. "All the troops sent to us are thirty days' militia and nine months' volunteers, and are perfectly useless. I am tired of risking my corps in such unequal contests."[26] Thus, Meade could not depend on these men to play a significant role in an assault on Lee's lines, and he said as much in his own writings.

Sgt. Charles A. Frey of the 150th Pennsylvania also offered an interesting perspective on the situation. "Meade, no doubt, felt a little like a person often does in pitching quoits. If he makes a 'ringer' the first throw, rather than try to make two, and perhaps spoil both, he will throw a cowardly quoit. Meade had made a 'ringer' at Gettysburg and the country applauded. Had he made another on the banks of the Potomac, he would have been the greatest general of the war. Had he failed in the second attempt, he would have been denounced the world over." Frey's homespun analogy had obvious merit; Meade was damned if he did and damned if he didn't. It was not an enviable position for any general to be in.[27]

Much of the criticism of Meade's actions either came from non-military personnel with no real understanding of the practical realities facing the army commander, or it came from rear echelon personnel who were not present and had the luxury of being a Monday morning quarterback. "Some of the editorial criticisms of those days would have been better if based upon a little actual experience in the presence of the enemy," proclaimed an officer of the Army of the Potomac's 5th Corps. "A great deal of it was pitiable in the utter non-comprehension by the writers of the nature of military operations on a large scale. However, had General Lee remained north of the Potomac on the 14th of July, notwithstanding the opinions of the corps commanders, General Meade would have attacked with a tremendous force; or, in other words, he would have stormed the Confederate position with the concentrated power of his whole army. What the result of that would have been no human being knows." He concluded, "These criticisms, no doubt, represented not so much the opinions of the authors as they did the disgust at having to undergo the necessities of the operation of the law for drafting men for the army, for while the Army of the Potomac was trudging its way back into Virginia, this law was put in force."[28] While this may overstate the case, the point nevertheless remains valid—it is always easy to second-guess the decisions of those carrying the burden and responsibility for making those decisions.

Lt. Col. David Hunter Strother was a career cavalry officer. He was temporarily serving in Washington during the Battle of Gettysburg, and was not present at Williamsport when the critical decisions were made. Referring to the escape of Lee's army, Strother declared, "This is about the meanest and most humiliating incident of the war. Hooker would have done better and no one could have done worse," he vented in his diary on July 15. "Meade is proved—a plain soldier fit to lead a corps but without power or ambition and utterly incompetent at the head of a hundred thousand men."[29] Strother's comments reflect the sorts of attitudes held by rear echelon personnel, and show the type of perceptions that Meade had to endure.

* * *

At least one well-respected Southern officer supported Meade's conduct. Confederate General John B. Gordon defended Meade's decision in his memoirs years after the war. "One of the wisest adages in war is to avoid doing what your antagonist desires, and it is beyond dispute that, from General Lee down through all the ranks, there was a readiness if not a desire to meet General Meade should he advance upon us. Meade's policy after the Confederate repulse at Gettysburg did not differ materially from that of Lee after the Union repulse at Fredericksburg."[30] In other words, Gordon believed that Meade felt that the enemy had suffered enough—so let him go. Gordon, however, was wrong. Meade's own words clearly demonstrate that he would have destroyed Lee's army if he could have, but *not* by making attacks that had a small chance of success. Gordon seems not to have understood this.

* * *

When General Meade reported that Lee's army had escaped, he received a blistering telegram from Henry Halleck. "The escape of Lee's army without another battle has created great dissatisfaction in the mind of the President, and it will require an energetic pursuit on your part to remove the impression that it has been sufficiently active heretofore."[31] Halleck accurately echoed the sentiments of the Lincoln administration. "We had them in our grasp," complained President Lincoln to his secretary, John Hay. "We had only to stretch forth our hands and they were ours. And nothing I could say or do could make the Army move."[32] On July 17, Lincoln proclaimed at a cabinet meeting, "Meade had made a terrible mistake."[33] Secretary of War Edwin Stanton agreed, writing on July 22, "Since the world began no man ever missed so great an opportunity of serving his country as was lost by [Meade's] neglecting to strike his adversary."[34]

Offended by the tone of Halleck's wire, Meade turned to his old friend, Brig. Gen. Rufus Ingalls, the Army of the Potomac's quartermaster general, and asked, "Ingalls, don't you want to take command of this army?"

"No, I thank you," replied Ingalls. "It's too big an elephant for me."

"Well," retorted Meade, "it's too big for me, too."[35] The army commander requested that he be relieved of command of the Army of the Potomac, a request quickly declined by Halleck.[36]

Meade anticipated the War Department's response to Lee's escape, but he still found Halleck's message insulting. "They have refused to relieve me, but insist on my continuing to try to do what I know in advance it is impossible to do," Meade wrote in a letter to his wife on July 16. "My army (men and animals) is exhausted; it wants rest and reorganization; it has been greatly reduced and weakened by recent operations, and no reinforcements of any practical value have been sent." He continued with no little bitterness, "Yet, in the face of all these facts, well known to them, I am urged, pushed and *spurred* to attempting to pursue and destroy an army nearly equal to my own, falling back upon its resources and reinforcements and increasing its morale daily. This has been the history of all my predecessors, and I clearly saw that in time their

Edwin M. Stanton, President Lincoln's Secretary of War.

LOC

fate would be mine. This was the reason I was disinclined to take the command, and it is for this reason I would gladly give it up."[37]

And thus Meade plainly stated his own opinion on the question of whether his army could have driven Lee's troops into the Potomac River. He did not believe he had the manpower or wherewithal to defeat Lee's army. It is also apparent that he believed that his opinion, as commander in the field, should have carried more weight in Washington. His response to Halleck's sharp telegraph was understandable, as was his expressed desire to give up the command that he never asked for or wanted in the first place.

Lincoln vented his frustration in a letter to his army commander; fortunately for both, he never sent it. "I have just seen your dispatch to General Halleck, asking to be relieved of your command, because of some supposed censure of mine. I am very—very—grateful to you for the magnificent success you gave the cause of the country at Gettysburg; and I am sorry now to be the author of the slightest pain to you," wrote Lincoln. Still, he did not try to hide his disappointment. "Again, my dear general, I do not believe you appreciate the magnitude of the misfortune involved in Lee's escape. He was within your easy grasp, and to have closed upon him would, in connection with our late successes, have ended the war. As it is the war will be prolonged indefinitely. If you could not safely attack Lee last Monday, how can you possibly do so South of the river, when you take with you very few more than two thirds of the force you then had in hand? It would be unreasonable to expect, and I do not expect you can now effect much. Your golden opportunity is gone, and I am distressed immeasurably because of it."[38] One can only wonder what effect this letter would have had on Meade if Lincoln had forwarded it to the general.

Two days later, Meade again picked up his pen to complain to his wife. "The Government insists on my pursuing and destroying Lee. The former I can do, but the latter will depend on him as much as on me, for if he keeps out of my way, I can't destroy," he observed, quite correctly. "Neither can I do so if he is reinforced and becomes my superior in numbers, which is by no means improbable, as I see by the papers it is reported a large portion of [General Braxton] Bragg's [Army of Tennessee] has been sent to Virginia."

Meade concluded with an accurate statement of his handling of affairs, given the battered and exhausted condition of his army:

> The proper policy for the Government would have been to be contented with driving Lee out of Maryland, and not to have advanced till this army was largely reinforced and reorganized, and put on such a footing that its

> advance was sure to be successful. As, however, I am bound to obey explicit orders, the responsibility of the consequences must and should rest with those who give them. Another great trouble with me is the want of active and energetic subordinate officers, men upon whom I can depend and rely upon taking care of themselves and commands. The loss of Reynolds and Hancock is most serious; their places are not to be supplied. However, with God's help, I will continue to do the best I can.[39]

Compelled by his strong sense of duty to continue on, Meade vowed to do his best to obey the War Department's orders.

Ever the realist, Lincoln was able to face the bare facts, however. "What can I do with such generals as we have?" complained Lincoln to his Secretary of the Navy, Gideon Welles. "Who among them is any better than Meade? To sweep away the whole of them from the chief command and substitute a new man would cause a shock and be likely to lead to combinations and troubles greater than we now have," he concluded, undoubtedly remembering what happened when John Pope came east in the summer of 1862.[40] While Lincoln believed a great opportunity had been lost, he realized that there were no good alternatives.

On July 18, Maj. Gen. Oliver Howard wrote to the president in defense of Meade. "As to not attacking the enemy prior to leaving his stronghold beyond the Antietam it is by no means certain that the repulse at Gettysburg might not have been turned against us," explained the one-armed corps commander. "At any rate the Commanding General was in favor of an immediate attack but with the evident difficulties in our way the uncertainty of a success and the strong conviction of our best military minds against the risk, I must say, that I think the general acted wisely."[41] A week after Lee's army crossed to safety, Lincoln gave his final assessment. "I am now profoundly grateful for what was done, without criticism for what was not done," wrote the president. "General Meade has my confidence as a brave and skillful officer, and a true man."[42]

* * *

Officers inside and outside the Federal Army did not have to read Meade's public or private correspondence to believe he had fumbled a golden opportunity. A New York officer fiercely loyal to Maj. Gen. Daniel E. Sickles (accused by many of being insubordinate at Gettysburg), proclaimed, "Meade was not the commander that the army needed at Gettysburg, nor during the ten days which followed Lee's repulse, and not all the sermons his hasty partisans have pronounced, nor the resurrection of his old letters by indiscreet friends, can give him rank as a successful commander of the Army of the Potomac." He continued, "While his timid failure to pursue, attack, and disastrously rout, Lee's army that, with a train nearly twenty miles long, without ammunition and almost without shoes, and food, went limping for ten days, through muddy and encumbered roads, towards the swollen and bridgeless Potomac, can never be satisfactorily explained to the country, nor successfully defended, upon any sound principal of military science."[43] "We are tired of scientific leaders and regard strategy as it is called—a humbug. Next thing to cowardice," wrote Brig. Gen. Alexander Hays, the fiery 2nd Corps division commander. "What we want is a leader who will go ahead."[44]

In February 1864, Meade revealed that he had not wanted to attack at Williamsport without having had an opportunity to examine the Confederate position fully, and that his subordinate commanders fully agreed with him on this issue. The Army of the Potomac spent much of July 13 probing the Southern defenses in order to gain the desired intelligence, but "not much information was obtained." Meade also stated that he firmly believed that Lee had already been re-supplied with ammunition, and that he did not believe that the Confederates were demoralized or had been rendered combat ineffective—a fact amply borne out by the contemporary correspondence of Southern soldiers.

Maj. Gen. Henry J. Hunt, Chief of Artillery, Army of the Potomac.

USAHEC

"I doubt whether it was any more demoralized than we were when we fell back to Washington in 1862, after the second battle of [Bull Run]," he stated. He said, quite clearly, "An examination of the enemy's lines, and of the defenses which he made—of which I now have a map from an accurate survey, which can be laid before your committee—brings me clearly to the opinion that an attack, under the circumstances in which I had proposed to make it, would have resulted disastrously to our arms."[45] Finally, the Army of the Potomac was also short on ammunition, and Meade was worried about whether he had the resources to mount a full-scale assault on Lee's line.

"Whose fault that we did not attack them or whether it was our policy to let them recross, is the query of all," lamented a Union signalman. "They had a very strong position but we would have better been repulsed than to let them get away as they did."[46] Col. Charles S. Wainwright, artillery chief of the First Corps, disagreed. "My own opinion," he explained after inspecting the powerful enemy position, "is that under the circumstances and with the knowledge General Meade then had he was justified in putting off his attack."[47] The Army of the Potomac's chief of artillery, Brig. Gen. Henry Hunt, echoed that sentiment. "A careful survey of the enemy's intrenched line after it was abandoned justified the opinion of the corps commanders against an attack, as it showed that an assault would have been disastrous to us. It proved also that Meade in overriding that opinion did not shrink from a great responsibility, notwithstanding his own recent experience at Gettysburg, where all the enemy's attacks on even partially intrenched lines had failed. If he erred on this occasion it was on the side of temerity."[48]

Meade's new and able chief of staff, fifty-three year-old Brig. Gen. Andrew A. Humphreys, had spent more than thirty years as a topographical engineer. He agreed with Meade, Wainwright, and Hunt. "A careful survey of the intrenched position of the

Brig. Gen. Andrew A. Humphreys, Gen. George Meade's Chief of Staff.

USAHEC

enemy was made," recounted Humphreys, "and showed that an assault upon it would have resulted disastrously to us." He also raised a salient comparison. "On the other hand, General Burnside was severely criticized for attacking at Marye's Heights, Fredericksburg, where the intrenchments were not more formidable than those of Williamsport."[49] Meade was likewise a career engineer, and he fully recognized these same qualities in Lee's position, which helps explain why he hesitated to attack without having had the benefit of reconnoitering the line in its entirety.

In a similar vein, a soldier of the Irish Brigade offered an interesting analysis. "To the unbiased mind it is food for thought, if not for argument, when one remembers the fact, that it took one year and nine months afterwards, with all the resources of an immense army, under Grant, and his lieutenants, Sheridan and Meade, to 'bag' the same General Lee and his fighting veterans," wrote Sgt. Daniel G. McNamara of the 9th Massachusetts Infantry. "Even then, if it had not been for Sheridan's ceaseless activity, Lee and his army would have escaped and gone to North Carolina and joined Johnston's forces."[50]

Another member of the Iron Brigade agreed an attack would have been unwise. "A glance showed what a slaughter an assault, upon Lee's naturally defensive line, doubly strengthened by skill, [would have been]."[51] "It has always been clear to my mind that the council [of war] was right," wrote a 6th Corps officer years later. "I had the presentiment often told that I was going to be killed that day, and I respected the decision of the council. It was a question of attacking intrenched works with no special advantage on our side. Such a thing was dangerous then; in these later days of war, simply impossible."[52]

A Pennsylvanian gave a similar but equally prescient opinion. "Certainly 50,000 veteran soldiers are not easily captured when prepared for an attack," he observed quite correctly, "as that army was at [Williamsport], especially under such a leader as Gen. Lee, and the line of retreat well secured." He pointed out that a successful blow "can only be supposition; and that supposition, may be, that Meade's army would have been hurled back to Baltimore or Washington by the recoil of the blow."[53]

As early as July 7, an especially astute newspaper correspondent had apparently figured all this out:

> Can the enemy retreat safely? I fear this question must be answered mainly in the affirmative. Sanguine people may dream of "bagging" or "annihilating" a great army, and sensation correspondents ornament hyperbolical paragraphs with such predictions. But the doing of the thing

is next to impossible. In this case there are geographical facts that increase the difficulties. The Potomac, above Harpers Ferry, makes a considerable bend northward, and Lee's line of retreat from Gettysburg to the river at Williamsport is shorter than any other route that we can pursue. His own knowledge of an intention to retreat before it could become known to General Meade, and the consequent preparations made for it, is equal to at least twelve hours in the start.[54]

If it was that obvious to a newspaperman in the middle of the retreat, it should come as no surprise that many felt the same.

* * *

Regardless, Meade withstood a storm of criticism from his high-ranked subordinates. On July 16, Maj. Gen. James Wadsworth, the veteran commander of a 1st Corps division, visited the Executive Mansion. Lt. Col. Andrew J. Alexander, a West Point-trained staff officer, bluntly asked him, "Why did Lee escape?" Wadsworth gruffly, and just as bluntly, responded, "Because nobody stopped him." After describing the council of war on July 12 and spelling out Meade's plan of attack, he then addressed Maj. Gen. David Hunter, who was present and taking part in the conversation. "General, there are a good many officers of the Regular Army who have not yet entirely lost the West Point [notion] of Southern superiority," he declared. "That sometimes accounts for an otherwise slowness of attack." While Wadsworth certainly had a point about nobody stopping Lee, the rest of his criticism was probably unfair.[55]

Maj. Gen. Abner Doubleday, who had been relieved of command of the 1st Corps on the night of the first day of the Battle of Gettysburg, had every reason to be bitter about his treatment at the hands of Meade. In 1882, when he wrote a history of the Gettysburg campaign, Doubleday used the opportunity to lash out at the army commander and perhaps obtain a measure of revenge. "The moment it was ascertained that Lee was cut off from Richmond and short of ammunition the whole North would have turned out and made a second Saratoga of it," Doubleday railed. "As it was, he had but few rounds for his cannon, and our artillery could have opened a destructive fire on him from a distance without exposing our infantry. It was worth the effort and there was little or no danger in attempting it." He concluded that Meade "delayed moving at all until Lee had reached Hagerstown and then took a route that was almost twice as long as that adopted by the enemy. Lee marched day and night to avoid pursuit, and when the river rose and his bridge was gone, so that he was unable to cross, he gained six days in which to choose a position, fortify it, and renew his supply of ammunition before Meade made his appearance."[56] It is worth noting that Lee had had ammunition ferried across the Potomac while he occupied the defensive lines at Williamsport, and while his army was not flush with an abundant supply of it, his stocks were not as low as many believed.

Col. Philippe Regis de Trobriand, who felt Meade should have attacked, offered an interesting perspective on its risks that is worth repeating. "I think it would have been better to have attacked. Our men were full of ardor, and asked only to make a finish of it. That fact made it worth the trouble to make a strong effort, and to take a new risk," he wrote. "In any event, there was everything to gain and nothing to lose. If we succeeded, the road to Richmond was opened before us; if we failed, the road to Washington was still closed to them. Even putting the worst face on matters, we could have fallen back to South Mountain, and they never could have forced the defiles, should they make the effort, which would be very doubtful. The most probable result would have been that, content with having repulsed our last attack, the advantage they would have from being able to cross the river in entire security would have satisfied them." Meade evidently came around to this way of thinking by the night of July 13, or he would not have ordered the general assault along the lines on the following morning.[57]

Years after the war and years after Meade's death, his old friend, fellow Philadelphian, and West Point classmate Brig. Gen. Herman Haupt, ripped the former commander of the Army of the Potomac for his performance during the retreat from Gettysburg. "Meade's army could have reached the Potomac certainly in less than two days; it was less fatigued than its enemy; it would be marching towards its base of supplies via the Baltimore & Ohio Railroad; no large supply of rations was required and, as General [Rufus] Ingalls reported, they had an abundance; they had, I understood, two pontoon trains for bridges, and there was no large, if any, force of the enemy on the south side of the Potomac, for Lee had carried with him into Pennsylvania all his available forces," wrote Haupt. Given all of these factors, Haupt did not believe that there was any viable reason for Meade not to have attacked Lee's army.

Instead, "Meade could have taken position below Lee on the river, covering Washington and his base of supplies at the same time. He could have chosen a spot readily defensible against attack, and thrown a part of his force, by means of his bridges, across the river, keeping them within supporting distance. This force could safely have been spared and, if necessary in case of attack, could have been recalled. A force on the south side with a small amount of artillery would have effectually cut off all reinforcements and supplies, and the construction of bridges under fire would never have been attempted. Lee would never have renewed the attack if Meade had occupied a defensible position; he would have sent in a flag of truce and capitulated then and there," concluded Haupt.[58]

Theoretically, Haupt had a valid point. Despite his reasons for his opinion, however, reality was something altogether different. First, finding the proper spot south of the river would have been an enormous challenge, and would have required advance planning on the part of Meade's engineers. Second, it was impossible for Meade to keep his army between Lee and Washington unless it was sitting directly in front of Lee's army. Third, Haupt's plan, if implemented, would have left Lee free to operate in Maryland almost as he saw fit. While qualities of Haupt's plan certainly had merit, it rested upon too many assumptions that weakened its feasibility.

* * *

Lee's Army of Northern Virginia enjoyed an often overlooked but very real advantage during the retreat from Gettysburg. Initially, Meade had only been in command of the Army of the Potomac for less than a week. He had also lost John Reynolds and Winfield S. Hancock, the two corps leaders he relied on the most. In their place were untried corps commanders. Maj. Gen. George Sykes, the commander of the 5th Corps, had only been in corps command since June 28. Oliver Howard had assumed command of the 11th Corps in April. John Sedgwick became commander of the 6th Corps in February. The longest serving corps commander in Meade's army was Henry W. Slocum, who had assumed command of the 12th Corps only nine months earlier. Thus, three of Meade's seven infantry corps commanders had less than one week's experience in corps command, and only one had served more than six months. It is, therefore, no surprise that Meade lacked confidence in his subordinates, as he had confessed to his wife. And it should not be overlooked that his army had been roughly handled at Gettysburg despite its victory.

"When on July 12th the question of attacking its enemy in position was considered, five of the seven corps commanders, including the four senior officers, voted against it," observed a Northern infantry officer. "This shows conclusively the crippled condition of the Federal army. There is no reason to think that such an attack would have proved successful." In conclusion, this particular officer noted, "Meade, yielding to his corps commanders, refrained from doing the thing his adversary desired, and deserves no less praise for his prudence and good judgment at Hagerstown than for his tenacity at Gettysburg."[59]

Considering that Meade had unexpectedly received orders to take command of the Army of the Potomac just three full days prior to the fighting at Gettysburg, he had not even had the opportunity to select his own staff officers. He was still using Joseph Hooker's staff, including his oft-scheming chief of staff, Maj. Gen. Daniel Butterfield, whom Meade had long despised. After the war, General Howard sensed that Meade's short time in command had something to do with his not ordering an attack at Williamsport following the council of war. When asked the reason, Howard replied, "Well, he [Meade] had just been put in command, and did not feel sure. He had prepared an order to attack, but had not issued it. . . . Meade finally did give the order to advance, but it was too late, Lee had crossed the river."[60]

Another issue worthy of discussion is that Meade was almost entirely unknown to the Lincoln Administration. He was not a political general, and he had not spent any time in the personal presence of Lincoln or Stanton. He was not a Joe Hooker, who understood Lincoln's expectations, and he likewise was not a George McClellan, who had been removed from command of the army for not acting consistently with Lincoln's wishes. Meade did not know his superiors and had not had the opportunity to hear their expectations of him directly from them as his predecessors had. This situation is rarely recognized or discussed in most studies of the Gettysburg Campaign.

Could Meade Have Done More?

The Army of the Potomac faced many significant handicaps, and Meade may well have decided that his army had done enough—it had defeated Lee on the field of battle, and it had repulsed the great invasion and saved the Federal capital. Meade believed that his army was about equal in strength to Lee's. If he attacked, he reasoned, it would be at more or less equal terms instead of by the three-to-one ratio of attackers to defenders that conventional military wisdom said was required for successful offensive operations. Further, nearly all of Meade's officers opposed an aggressive pursuit coupled with a premature attack. The Army of the Potomac needed to be re-supplied at Frederick, which greatly hindered its ability to pursue.

It is an old cliché that "councils of war never fight." Meade, still new to army command, later admitted that he probably relied on councils of war during his tenure more than he should have. He denied that they were formal councils of war however, and instead called them *consultations*. "They were probably more numerous and more constant in my case," he admitted, "from the fact that I had just assumed command of the army, and felt that it was due to myself to have the opinions of high officers before I took action on matters which involved momentous issues." Although that was an entirely reasonable approach for someone so new to army command, Meade was perhaps too cautious in his decision making because of his reliance on these consultations.[61]

Meade's army was exhausted and short of ammunition. Its men had marched and fought the war's critical campaign and his men needed rest and a refitting. "Our troops require rest, shoes, and clothing," observed Brig. Gen. Alpheus S. Williams, who commanded a 12th Corps division, on July 16. "They have been some five weeks on the march. None but veteran troops could stand it, especially as we have not had a dry day for nearly three weeks. It is pouring down in torrents today, but I think the Army of the Potomac is simmered down to the very sublimation of human strength and endurance."[62] By July 14, as a little-known example, over half of the men of the 37th Massachusetts Infantry of the 6th Corps were without shoes, meaning that further marching would take a toll on them. The 37th Massachusetts was far from the only regiment in this fix, and some were in even worse condition.[63] In short, the Army of the Potomac simply was not able to mount an attack of any real consequence much before July 13, and by then the Confederates were making their escape before any such attack could be launched.

When Meade was ordered to assume command of the Army of the Potomac on June 28, he was given an extremely difficult assignment. In addition to assuming command of a large army smack in the middle of a campaign with an expected battle looming over everyone's heads, Meade had to operate under the same orders and restrictions as had all of his predecessors in command of the army. At all times, he was to keep his army between the enemy and the national capital at Washington. The only way that Meade could keep the Army of the Potomac between Lee and Washington was to move his army along the spine of the South Mountain range. Had he used any other route of transit, Meade would have disobeyed his direct orders, and he would have exposed the capital to attack. While we have the benefit of hindsight and knowing that Lee's army was likely in no condition to undertake such an ambitious attack, and was instead eager to return to the safety of Virginia,

George Meade did not have that luxury. He knew he had to move his army into a position where it could attack Lee but still cover Washington and Baltimore. This left him with no choice but to select the longer route for his army to move south, which added time to the march and also added to the fatigue of the men and animals of the Army of the Potomac. While it is easy enough to criticize Meade for these choices with the luxury of nearly 150 years of hindsight, Meade not only did not have that benefit, he had difficult choices to make under difficult circumstances that were restricted by his standing orders.

Meade's abrupt and unwanted appointment to army command also presented unique challenges unlike those faced by any other army commander in the East. Ordered to take command of the army while a campaign was already under way, just three days before a major battle was fought, was all but unique. Only Gen. Pierre G. T. Beauregard, who had to take command of Gen. Albert Sidney Johnston's army on the field after Johnston suffered a mortal wound at Shiloh, faced an equally difficult situation. To expect Meade to assume the offensive under such circumstances probably was not a reasonable expectation on anyone's part. As a contrast, when Lee assumed command of the Army of Northern Virginia from Gustavus W. Smith, Lee had nearly a month to get his army in hand and bring it to bear against Maj. Gen. George B. McClellan's army on the Peninsula of Virginia. We are unaware of any army taking the offensive with a new commander and being expected to do so immediately after fighting (and winning) a major battle. The logistics are simply against it.

The Impact of the Routes of Retreat

For his retrograde, Lee took the direct routes to Williamsport, meaning that the left of his lines was only thirty miles from Gettysburg, and the right only thirty-five miles away. Meade's route, which required him to cross over South Mountain, was much longer. His route to his right was over fifty miles, and his route to his left was nearly fifty-five miles. Lee had the advantage of having gotten an earlier start than Meade, and he also had the interior route of march. The head start, combined with the shorter route and Stuart's fierce defense, meant that Lee had ample opportunity to dig into one of the most formidable defensive positions of the war. It should come as no surprise, then, that Meade and several of his corps commanders elected to not attack.

Journalist William Swinton covered the Army of the Potomac for the *New York Times*. Just after the end of the war, he wrote a book of his observations while with the army, and he mercilessly criticized Meade's decision not to follow Lee's direct route to the Potomac. He noted that Baldy Smith's militia had seized the next pass through South Mountain north of the Cashtown Pass. "By this the whole army might readily have defiled through the South Mountains to fall on Lee's flank and rear," he wrote in 1866. "If nothing had been accomplished by this means, the retreat of Lee would still have been followed so closely, that coming to the Potomac, and having an impassable river in his rear, the situation would have been one of the very greatest peril."[64]

Accepting this theory requires a quantum leap of faith. It assumes that Smith's untried and untrained militia could have seized and held the mountain pass in the face of Lee's veterans; it is impossible to conceive of Lee not reacting to the threat of the entire Army of the Potomac passing around his flank and into his rear unmolested. And, as pointed out previously, had Meade followed Lee's direct route of march, he would have uncovered Washington in direct violation of his orders and against the wishes of the Lincoln Administration. Swinton's argument smacks of armchair quarterbacking of the worst kind, but the popularity of his book only reinforced the public perception that Meade had bungled the opportunity presented him at Williamsport.

At the same time, Meade's chosen route of march—the flanking route, as opposed to the direct route taken by Lee—had some real advantages. Once the main body of the Army of the Potomac reached Frederick, Maryland, nearly all of its elements took advantage of the macadamized National Road. This march, albeit longer, utilized the best possible roads and definitely helped to speed the Army of the Potomac's march. This certainly assisted with its logistics; the army's wagons traveled on roads less muddy than those that took their toll on Lee's army as it retreated. Thus had Meade started earlier—instead of waiting for proof that Lee had evacuated the South Mountain range near the Monterey Pass—his army could have been in position to launch an all-out assault on Lee's army before its formidable defensive position along the Potomac River was completed. The problem, therefore, lay more with the delays in commencing the march of the Army of the Potomac than it did with the choice of route of travel.

In that vein, it must be remembered that Meade had actual knowledge that Lee would receive no reinforcements during the Gettysburg battle, and that Lee would have to make do with what he had. On July 2, the intrepid Capt. Ulric Dahlgren, leading a squad of men from the Army of the Potomac's Bureau of Military Information, captured a Confederate courier in Greencastle. The courier bore dispatches to Robert E. Lee from Pres. Jefferson Davis and Gen.

Samuel Cooper, the Southern adjutant general, informing him that there were no reinforcements available to send to Lee's support. Dahlgren galloped the thirty-five miles back to Gettysburg and personally delivered this intelligence coup to Meade not long after that night's council of war adjourned.[65] Freed from having to watch his rear, Meade possibly could have been more aggressive in his pursuit of Lee's army, and likewise might have been more aggressive about pitching into Lee once he arrived on the banks of the Potomac River.

Who Is To Blame?

If there is blame to be cast for the Army of the Potomac's failure to destroy Lee's Army of Northern Virginia on the north side of the Potomac River, much of that blame should be cast on Alfred Pleasonton. Pleasonton's ill-advised order to disperse his cavalry on July 4 meant that the opportunity to interdict Lee's route of retreat between South Mountain and Hagerstown was frittered away. The pursuit of Lee's vaunted soldiers after Gettysburg was a time for surgical coordination and a massing of the power of the Union horsemen, a feat never accomplished during Pleasonton's ten-month tenure as Cavalry commander.

Pleasonton's first mistake was his failure to barricade the Jack's Mountain passes, both of which are narrow and have steep sides. Federal cavalry, supported by artillery, would have bottled up Lee's army there. One of two things would have happened. Either Lee would have had to fight his way through the Federal blocking forces, or he would have had to take a longer retreat route with his entire army, probably through the Cashtown Pass (the route taken by Imboden and the Wagon Train of Wounded). Either way, a better use of the Union horse by Pleasonton would have given Meade an opportunity to either interdict Lee's route of march through Maryland, or beat Lee's army to the banks of the Potomac River.

Instead of quickly massing his cavalry near Hagerstown to block the retreat routes Lee was known to be taking toward the river, Pleasonton parsed out his riders, each portion too small to bring a substantial part of Lee's army to bear. All the while, Pleasonton characteristically stuck close to army headquarters rather than actively commanding in the field of operations—quite in contrast to Jeb Stuart's *modus operandi*. Despite having his cavalry scattered on nearly all points of the compass, Meade complained as early as the morning of July 6 that "I cannot get very reliable intelligence of the enemy's movements."[66]

"Reliable information of the enemy's position or movements, which is absolutely necessary to the commander of an army to successfully conduct a campaign, must be largely furnished by the cavalry," wrote Brig. Gen. William Woods Averell, a West Point graduate, in defining the traditional role of cavalry in the conventional doctrine taught at the Military Academy and as practiced at the beginning of the war. "The duty of the cavalry when an engagement is imminent is specially imperative—to keep in touch with the enemy and observe and carefully note, with time of day or night, every slightest indication and report it promptly to the commander of the army. On the march, cavalry forms in advance, flank and rear guards and supplies escorts, couriers and guides. Cavalry should extend well away from the main body on the march like antennae to mask its movements and to discover any movement of the enemy." Averell concluded, appropriately, "In defeat [cavalry] screens the withdrawal of the army and by its fortitude and activity baffles the enemy."[67] Stuart performed this duty magnificently during the retreat to the Potomac River.

As discussed in the narrative, Gregg's division never had an impact on the retreat, and the efforts of Buford and Kilpatrick were disjointed and uncoordinated. Had Pleasonton had the foresight to mass his forces in combination with French's garrison from Frederick, he would have found adequate forces available to prevent Lee from reaching the Potomac River without the Federals having to fight their way through. If Cole's cavalry had not burned the bridge over the Potomac at Harper's Ferry, Federal troops could have used it to get in behind Lee's army, forcing Lee to give battle on the north bank of the river, irrespective of whether it was flooded. The burning of the bridge, combined with Pleasonton's failure to concentrate all three of his divisions of cavalry between the Monterey Pass and Williamsport meant that by the time the Army of the Potomac had concentrated around Williamsport and Hagerstown, Lee's position was just too strong to assault. In addition, those Confederates acting as a rear guard at Falling Waters were effectively able to blunt uncoordinated Federal assaults, using dozens of steep ridges and hills perpendicular to the road leading to that crossing. By the time Longstreet and Hill reached that ground, it was too late for the Federals to close the door. Thus, the lion's share of the blame lies with the Cavalry Corps commander and not with George Meade.

Fifteen years after the battle, Pleasonton wrote a lengthy article about his role in the Gettysburg Campaign for the *Philadelphia Weekly Times*. It was no less than a diatribe of blatant lies, designed to cover for his own failures and shortcomings beginning with the day-long cavalry battle at Brandy Station on

June 9. His audacity, in light of the facts, is remarkable. Regarding Meade's handling of the situation from July 3 onward, Pleasonton wrote: "The Battle of Gettysburg was over, and in speaking of the subsequent events of the campaign, I do so with reluctance. I was in the position to form a correct opinion of the failure of the army to follow General Lee. . . . General Meade had not that grasp of mind, when thrown into a new and responsible position, to quickly comprehend and decide upon important events as they occurred." Pleasonton was not finished pontificating, however: "From the time he assumed command of the army until after the battle of Gettysburg, the most important events were occurring with such rapidity, and with such resistless force, that his decisions were the consequences of these events rather than the operations of his individual intelligence."[68]

Pleasonton, after personally attacking the intelligence of the now-deceased Meade, went so far as to claim that he had proffered a challenge to his army commander at the close of the final day's battle. "I rode up to him, and, after congratulating him on the splendid conduct of the army, I said: 'General, I will give you half an hour to show yourself a great general,'" Pleasonton wrote. "Order the army to advance, while I will take the cavalry, get in Lee's rear, and we will finish the campaign in a week." Pleasonton claimed that after he and Meade looked over Lee's lines in the waning daylight, "we rode along the ridge for nearly a mile, [and] the troops cheered him in a manner that plainly showed they expected the advance . . . I was so impressed with the idea that Lee was retreating that I again earnestly urged General Meade to advance the army; but instead of doing so, he ordered me to send some cavalry to ascertain the fact."[69]

The cavalry chieftain noted that it took all night to get information from Brig. Gen. David Gregg's scouts, and then, the following morning, "the two other divisions of cavalry [Buford and Kilpatrick] were sent to intercept and harass Lee in crossing the Potomac; but the Army of the Potomac did not leave Gettysburg for four or five days after," Pleasonton lied. "General Meade declined to attack, and Lee's army escaped. The cavalry rendered important service after the battle of Gettysburg, in pursuit... and were in such position that, had General Meade followed Lee on the 4th of July, the surrender of Lee would have been unavoidable."[70]

Although grossly failed by Pleasonton, some blame must also fall on Meade's shoulders. Meade had seven infantry corps and a corps of cavalry at his disposal during the pursuit of Lee's army. Only two of those corps—the 6th Corps and the Cavalry Corps—saw any real action during the pursuit of the Army of Northern Virginia. Two divisions of the Cavalry Corps engaged in one heavy fight after another, while the third division saw almost no action. The 6th Corps, which had taken the fewest casualties at Gettysburg, was the logical candidate to serve as the tip of the Union spear, but it ended up carrying the brunt of the infantry fighting for the entire ten days of the pursuit. Other than some insignificant skirmishing, the other five infantry corps of the Army of the Potomac saw no action to speak of over the course of the pursuit. Meade alone is responsible for this failure to commit all of his available troops, and he deserves criticism for that failure.

Likewise, Meade erred in not ordering French's command to take and hold Williamsport before Imboden could garrison the town. Had he done so, French would have forced the Army of Northern Virginia to *fight* its way to the Potomac. Instead, Meade sent French's infantry to seize and hold South Mountain passes which Lee had no intention of using. While doing so properly covered Washington, it wasted a valuable resource in the form of French's infantry. Those foot soldiers could have been used to try to prevent the Army of Northern Virginia from comfortably assuming a position of its choice on the northern bank of the Potomac River.

Meade also might have attempted to flank Lee's position at Williamsport. He might have thrown his right forward to the banks of the Conococheague onto more favorable ground for offensive operations, overlapping the Confederate left. Then he might have attacked Lee's position from a more favorable position. This approach might not have worked, but at least it would have given Meade an opportunity to attack on more favorable terms while still covering Washington.

Another golden opportunity slipped through Meade's fingers on July 11. As Meade stated to Halleck late that day, "Upon advancing my right flank across the Antietam this morning, the enemy abandoned Funkstown and Hagerstown."[71] He was referring to Ewell's Second Corps. However, that opportunity was only good for a few fleeting minutes, for Ewell later reported that his corps soon "began fortifying, and, in a short time my men were well protected. Their spirit was never better than at this time, and the wish was universal that the enemy should attack."[72]

If Meade had been aggressive that day and had he followed up on the opportunity presented by driving Ewell's men from Funkstown instead of staying in position, he could have exploited that gap and driven a significant portion of his army through it like a bull. As Lt. Col. William Terpeluk, a modern commentator, put it, "A Union movement at that time would *not* have been premature and would have entailed entirely *acceptable risk* based on

Meade's knowledge of enemy positions and intentions. Should Lee sortie from his prepared positions near Downsville, a weakened Union left or center could still effectively use the series of north-south ridges and creeks to defend or delay. With a river to restrict Lee's movement to his right and the Union-held South Mountain to his eventual front, the Confederate commander would put his army at great risk with very little chance to gain by such a maneuver." However, that opportunity—the only one that presented itself—slipped away unexploited because the Army of the Potomac did not have aggressive corps commanders capable of independent action and also because the Army was unable to respond quickly enough to exploit the opportunity.[73]

In addition, the army commander allowed an opportunity to interdict Lee's lines of re-supply and retreat to slip away when he failed to take control of the south bank of the Potomac at Lee's anticipated crossing points, as Haupt had suggested and was earlier discussed. But instead of having to use any elements of his main army, more than 10,000 veteran soldiers from French's and Kelley's commands were available for this duty, but Meade failed to employ them.[74] However, it also bears noting that Kelley was not under Meade's direct command, and it would have taken an order from Halleck to make this happen. Halleck failed to give the necessary orders, and the opportunity quickly evaporated. Had Kelley marched expeditiously from Hancock to Williamsport, he might have destroyed Lee's lightly-guarded ordnance trains, prevented construction of the new pontoon bridge at Falling Waters, and he also could have hindered Lee's crossing on July 13 and 14. The presence of a strong Union force on the south side of the Potomac most certainly would have forced Lee to find alternative river crossings in the direction of Hancock, which would have given Meade an opportunity to attack Lee's army on ground of his choosing.

Performance of the Cavalry

Despite Pleasonton's shortcomings, his troopers had performed magnificently throughout the pursuit, earning the respect of their comrades in the infantry and artillery. "Honor to our cavalry," marveled an infantry officer of the Sixth Corps. "They used to be despised. Now they are splendid. Once a certain General said that amongst the Union dead on many battlefields, he never saw a dead cavalryman. I <u>have</u> seen them often on this march, poor fellows! Lying by the roadside in the wheatfield, behind the stone wall."[75] A member of the 3rd Wisconsin of the 12th Corps agreed. "Our cavalry had made it exceedingly uncomfortable for the rebels on their retreat," he said.[76] The

Confederates realized that the Northern cavalry had matched them blow for blow on the field of battle. "Our cavalry had a number of engagements with theirs on the right of our army near Boonsboro," recalled a sergeant of the 1st Virginia Cavalry. "In these fights the enemy got the better of us, as they managed so as to have infantry always close at hand to assist them when it was necessary."[77]

They had faced a heavy test. "There is no fighting so hard to do as covering the rear and flanks of a retreating army," observed a Southern horse artillerist, "and none so easy and inspiring as pursuing one, and we have tried both kinds."[78] In fact, one Federal horse soldier inquired, "Is it too much to claim that the cavalry of the Army of the Potomac made the victory at Gettysburg possible?"[79] While that undoubtedly overstates the case, the importance of the role played by the Union horsemen during the entire campaign, and especially during the retreat, cannot be overstated.

On the Southern side, Stuart's vigilant and active horsemen had held off the entire Army of the Potomac for more than a week. "The cavalry under General Stuart performed most valuable service in guarding the flanks of our army during the retrograde movement," commented Col. Walter H. Taylor, Robert E. Lee's military secretary and a vociferous critic of Stuart's conduct during the cavalier's ride to Pennsylvania preceding the battle. "It materially aided in the repulse of the enemy in his attack upon our wagon-trains at Williamsport, and, by a bold movement on the 8th in the direction of Boonsboro, checked the advance of the enemy, drove him back to Boonsboro, and so gained more time for General Lee in which to perfect his line of defense."[80]

Most of the Rebel horsemen spent essentially eighteen straight days in the saddle, and suffered heavily in the process. By assuming the initiative, Stuart kept the Army of the Potomac's Cavalry Corps off balance and prevented the Northern horsemen from finding the main body of the Army of Northern Virginia. If Jeb Stuart had somehow disappointed Lee before the Battle of Gettysburg, the Plumed Cavalier had more than redeemed himself during the retreat. But for Stuart's superb performance and stout resistance, Buford's and Kilpatrick's horsemen might well have wreaked havoc on the Confederate wagons and by capturing and holding the Potomac River crossings.

Also, John Imboden and his untried Northwest Brigade had more than risen to the challenge that General Lee gave them. Imboden did a masterful job of fulfilling the sacred trust of the Wagon Train of Wounded given him by Robert E. Lee, and his desperate defense of Williamsport not only protected those wounded men, it also preserved the critical river crossings for Lee's army.

Had Imboden failed on July 6, and had Buford taken and held Williamsport, the balance of the campaign would have taken on a very different tone and, perhaps, had a different outcome. Imboden's role has been largely unappreciated by many students of the Gettysburg Campaign, largely because his real contribution did not begin until after the end of the great battle. However, he deserves praise for his performance during the retreat, both in shepherding the vast wagon train of misery to safety at Williamsport, and then in defending the town and the river crossing.

The Joint Committee on the Conduct of the War

The Committee, an *ad hoc* commission made up of Radical Republicans from both the House of Representatives and Senate, convened a series of hearings during the winter of 1863-64, bent on finding reasons to remove Meade from command for his failure to destroy Lee's army following Gettysburg. The hearings dragged on into early spring, and members of the Committee trotted out any general officer of the Army of the Potomac most likely to be unfriendly to Meade, and elicited their opinions on the general's conduct of the campaign. Sen. Benjamin Wade of Ohio, one of the most prominent of the Radical Republicans, led the cabal against Meade. Finally, in February 1864, the Committee abandoned its efforts, clearly having failed. However, the experience left a bitter taste in Meade's mouth when the Committee managed to portray him as a mediocre and uncommitted general who permitted Lee's army to escape largely unmolested. That, perhaps, was the greatest tragedy of all—George Gordon Meade had conducted a nearly flawless campaign, had won the Civil War's pivotal battle, and had made the apparent correct choice in not attacking the nearly impregnable defensive position occupied at Williamsport by Robert E. Lee's Army of Northern Virginia.[81]

A Washington newspaper probably described the political climate best, as early as July 8, before Lee's army had even made it across the Potomac. "General Meade has the misfortune of not being a raving radical politician," correctly observed the editorial. "He is therefore belittled and traduced by that description of persons. Senator Wilson, of Mass., had already begun to brawl and carp. It was Sickles' military genius which saved the day, he says. It was Hooker who got the army into condition and discipline. Meade had nothing to do with the success." While there is an element of truth in Wilson's statements, they nevertheless reflect a biased and unknowledgeable view of the nature of commanding a large army in the field. Meade, an honest and steady soldier who never sought the command of the army, had to suffer such slings and arrows fired from many directions.[82]

George Meade Jr.'s Defense of his Father

Meade's son and aide-de-camp, Capt. George Meade, Jr., watched his father bear such slings and arrows for the rest of the elder Meade's life. George Jr. published a long and detailed dissertation about his father's performance during the campaign in 1883, eleven years after the general's death. The paper was largely a refutation of Abner Doubleday's outlandish claims that Meade wished to retreat from Lee's front on the evening of July 2. The younger Meade eloquently defended his father's roles in both command of the Army of the Potomac and the annals of the Civil War. "It is high time that dispute should cease as to the award due him who won the greatest battle of the war, upon which it turned, saving the nation's capital and giving to the Rebellion a blow from which it never recovered," argued the son. "It must cease, under penalty of the malcontents making themselves and the nation ridiculous. It will cease, for all battles, save for a time in Gettysburg, have been universally recognized and acknowledged as won by the general in command; and despite all its escaped heroes, it remains for history to record that, from the beginning to the end of the Rebellion, it was only when Meade was chief that Lee was ever met in pitched battle and defeated on equal terms."[83]

* * *

Contrary to popular belief, the retreat from Gettysburg was indeed "one continuous fight." Twenty-two engagements, skirmishes, and battles filled the ten-day retreat phase of the campaign. During this time, the Army of the Potomac suffered more than 1,000 casualties, almost entirely in the cavalry corps. The costliest single day was July 6, when Kilpatrick's division lost 263 men at Hagerstown, and Buford's division took another 120 at Williamsport. Robert E. Lee's Army of Northern Virginia lost at least 5,000 men from all causes during the retreat, including more than 1,000 captured at Monterey Pass, another 1,000 stragglers bagged by Gregg's division (which pursued the wagon train of wounded), another 500 at Cunningham's Crossroads, and yet another 1,000 or so snagged at Falling Waters on July 14. Stuart's cavalry lost 460 in its various fights during the retreat, and the Confederate infantry and artillery added an additional 300 killed, wounded, and missing at Hagerstown,

Funkstown, Williamsport, and Falling Waters. All told, the armies lost about 6,000 men during the ten days of the retreat.[84]

While these losses pale in comparison to the savage butchery at Gettysburg, they testify to the nature of the retreat in the race back to the Potomac River. We have discussed a variety of reasons why George Meade did not pitch recklessly into Lee at Williamsport, and these casualty figures help clarify them. An assault there would have necessarily led to heavy losses that may have offset the hard-won Union victory at Gettysburg. Lee's retreat from Gettysburg was skillfully executed. By not providing Meade a clear opening to strike a serious blow, he preserved his army for future combats. Still, the Gettysburg Campaign was little short of a disaster for the South. Lee's army suffered immense losses with very little to show for them besides the supplies it seized. Whatever gains accrued by the move north were offset by the loss of men, particularly in the officer corps.

The retreat from Gettysburg provides a plethora of "what-if's" for any armchair general, but the reality on the ground and in the ranks indicate that both army commanders made correct decisions during the withdrawal. Readers of the *Richmond Dispatch* were hungry for a silver lining in the dark Gettysburg cloud. They got one on July 17, 1863, when the paper offered them the following:

> Lincoln, Seward, Halleck, and the whole Yankee press, are hugging themselves in the delusion that they already see the end of the war, and that [that] end is, to us, the death of our liberty, and the beginning of an interminable servitude. To their taunts and sneers we reply, in the defiant language of Paul Jones, "We have not yet begun to fight." . . . This people has never yet put forth its strength to half its extent, furious as has been the war in which it has been engaged, mighty as have been its struggles, glorious as have been its victories. . . . What we have done is scarcely a type of what we can do.[85]

Bias and forced rhetoric aside, for those who had lived through Gettysburg and slogged through its retreat—those who would see more bloody earth at the Wilderness, Spotsylvania, Cold Harbor, Petersburg, and Appomattox—these words rang true with a dark portent that none could have ever anticipated.

Epilogue

ON JULY 14, BRIG. GEN. DAVID M. GREGG'S 2nd Cavalry Division of the Army of the Potomac crossed the Potomac at Harpers Ferry on a reconnaissance and moved to Shepherdstown the next day.[1] On the 16th, Fitz Lee's, Chambliss', and Ferguson's Confederate cavalry brigades attacked Gregg there in what Meade described as a "spirited contest."[2] The Pennsylvanian held his position in spite of the determined attack by the enemy troopers and withdrew unmolested to Harpers Ferry at daylight on July 17.

Following his successful crossing of the Potomac, on July 14 Lee moved the Army of Northern Virginia to Bunker Hill, a handful of miles from Falling Waters, where his men rested for a few days. His weary foot soldiers enjoyed their first decent meals since the better part of two weeks, and his depleted army was re-supplied. Lee was in the same position he had assumed in September 1862, and so knew the ground well. He intended to move into the more lush Loudoun Valley and avail himself of the bounty it contained.

While the Army of Northern Virginia rested, General George Meade continued trying to flank Lee. "Meade's plan of advance into Virginia was confessedly modeled on that of McClellan in November 1862," observed a newspaper correspondent. "And it was probably the best that could have been adopted."[3] Meade had to stay close to his principal lines of supply and, as always, he had to keep his army interposed between the enemy and the Federal capital at Washington. By continuing his campaign of maneuver, the Pennsylvanian hoped to bring Lee to battle on ground of his choosing.

The attempt to flank Lee began when the Army of the Potomac crossed the Potomac River at Harpers Ferry and Berlin on July 17 and 18 and advanced up the Loudoun Valley, where his men seized and held the Blue Ridge passes with cavalry and infantry. "The movement of Meade was made with such vigor—

indeed with so much vigor that, on reaching Union, on the 20th of July he was compelled to halt a day, lest by further advance he should dangerously uncover his right."[4] On July 21, Pleasonton sent John Buford's 1st Cavalry Division to occupy Manassas Gap and to watch Chester Gap. The 3rd, 5th, and 2nd Corps followed the troopers, entering Manassas Gap on July 23 in the hope of intercepting a portion of Lee's army.[5] These Federal movements kept Washington covered, blocked Lee's intended entry into the Loudoun Valley, and caused him to worry about being cut off from his main line of supply from Richmond.

Lee ordered James Longstreet to move his First Corps to Culpeper Court House by way of Front Royal on July 19. Old Pete's veterans marched the next day, passing through Chester Gap on the 22nd. A. P. Hill's Third Corps followed, arriving at Culpeper on the 24th. Ewell's Second Corps had marched on Martinsburg, hoping to capture Brig. Gen. Benjamin F. Kelley's force there, but the Federals evaded Ewell. Lee ordered Ewell to rendezvous with the rest of the Army of Northern Virginia. Two of Ewell's divisions passed through Front Royal on July 23 and entered Chester Gap.

A rude surprise was waiting for Ewell's men. As the head of his column arrived, the 3rd, 5th, and 2nd Corps of the Army of the Potomac advanced through the mouth of Chester Gap. "The insignia of two corps could be seen in the Gap," reported Ewell, "and a third was marching up; over 10,000 men were in sight."[6] As Maj. Gen. Andrew A. Humphreys, Meade's able chief of staff, described it, "a brief, spirited encounter between the advanced forces of the opposing columns ensued, the Excelsior Brigade [of the 3rd Corps], General [Francis B.] Spinola commanding, charging and driving its opponent back upon its main force, inflicting a severe loss in killed, wounded, and prisoners."[7] The Excelsior Brigade, personally selected by 3rd Corps leader Maj. Gen. William H. French to make this attack, "rushed upon the enemy with the bayonet, giving cheer after cheer, and driving him back in confusion out of the Gap."[8] This little-known action, known as the battle of Wapping Heights, was the Union army's best chance to defeat Lee's army in detail. French, however, was cautious by nature, and allowed Ewell to disengage without vigorously pursuing him.

Thwarted by finding such a strong force in his front, Ewell fell back to Front Royal the next morning, moved up the South Fork of the Shenandoah River to Luray, crossed the Blue Ridge at Thornton's Gap, and headed to Madison Court House. "I had reason to believe that Meade's whole army was in our front, and having but two divisions to oppose him, I decided to send Early up the Valley, by Strasburg and New Market, while I marched the other two divisions up the Page Valley to Luray, the route pursued by Jackson, in 1862," recounted Ewell.[9] Jubal Early, once again covering the rear of Ewell's column, moved up the North Fork of the Shenandoah to re-join the main body of the Second Corps. Ewell then joined the rest of the Army of Northern Virginia, which was camped in the vicinity of Culpeper Court House, in the triangle of land between the Rappahannock and Rapidan Rivers. In short, Lee had returned to the place where his army had massed to invade Pennsylvania two months earlier.

Unforeseen circumstances complicated things for George Meade. For the first time in American history, the Federal government had instituted conscription, and violent, bloody riots broke out in New York City in protest of this policy. The first draft lottery was held on July 11, and two days later, as the armies faced off along the banks of the Potomac, five days of chaos and mayhem broke out. With the city in danger of tearing itself apart, the War Department declared martial law and ordered Meade to send troops to New York to help put down the riots, further depleting his available forces, which were already worn down by months of endless marching and fighting.[10] Brig. Gen. Judson Kilpatrick, commander of the Army of the Potomac's 3rd Cavalry Division, answered the call, volunteering to go to New York to help, depriving Meade of one of the highest-ranking officers in his Cavalry Corps.[11] By July 16, several thousand Federal troops occupied New York City, meaning that these men were not available to join the pursuit of Lee's army. Within a few weeks, the 5th Corps division of United States Regulars, a brigade of Vermonters, and another nine regiments followed. Most of these units did not return to the Army of the Potomac until September.[12]

In addition, beginning in late July, nine two-year and nine-month regiments left the army upon the expiration of their terms of service. The combination of the detachments for service in New York City and the discharges of the men whose terms of service had ended depleted the strength of the Army of the Potomac by nearly 15,000 men. Add in the casualties from the Battle of Gettysburg, and more than 35,000 men were missing from the ranks of Meade's army. Although new recruits and conscripts were joining the army, these were all veteran troops whose loss was keenly felt. The depletion of the ranks of the Army of the Potomac left it unable to assume offensive operations again.[13]

With his army depleted by the combination of the crisis in New York and the discharge of the men whose terms had expired, and under orders from a worried Washington to take up a threatening position but not to advance against Lee, Meade headed for the north bank of the Rappahannock River. His army took up position on those familiar grounds at the end of July, meaning that the Army of the Potomac had returned to the place where the Gettysburg Campaign began in early June. As the historian of the 2nd Massachusetts Infantry put it, his regiment, which had also participated in the Battle of Brandy Station, "had come back to the old river, after fighting two battles, and marching four hundred and four miles."[14] Two months after it began, the Gettysburg Campaign had well and truly ended.

General Meade had the last word on August 3. "The Government, for some reason best known to itself, has ordered me to cease the pursuit of Lee, though I strongly recommended an advance. This is confidential, though the newspapers for some days have been announcing that I would have to assume for the defensive," he wrote to his wife. "Halleck in one despatch said it was because a considerable part of my army would be required to enforce the draft, but afterwards said he would only require sixteen hundred men, which I have sent. I don't know what this all means, but I suppose in time it will all come right."[15]

More than 50,000 casualties later, the two armies found themselves separated by the narrow, meandering Rappahannock River once more, occupying the same positions they had held prior to the bloodletting north of the Mason-Dixon Line.

In some ways, it seemed like nothing had changed. In many ways, however, things would never be the same again.

Appendix A

Driving Tour: The Retreat from Gettysburg

A NOTE OF EXPLANATION IS NECESSARY before beginning this driving tour. The first half of the tour covers events chronologically; the second half of the tour does not. Covering that part of the tour in the correct chronological order would require a great deal of doubling back and nearly twice as much driving. Accordingly, the second half proceeds geographically instead. For instance, the July 7 fight at Boonsboro comes after the July 10 fight at Funkstown, and the July 6 fight at Williamsport appears at the end of the tour. The tour of the route of the Confederate Wagon Train of Wounded that follows, however, does proceed chronologically. We suggest that you try to allow a full day for each tour to fully enjoy the sites of interest.

Beginning at the Taneytown Road entrance to the National Cemetery in Gettysburg, this driving tour of the route of the main retreat column covers 64.8 miles. The optional side trips to Bunker Hill and the West Virginia side of Falling Waters add another 49.1 miles to the trip. **Set your odometer's mileage to 0.0 when at the Cemetery Entrance.** Eleven times along the tour you will reset your mileage to 0.0 before continuing, to help keep you on track. This will allow for differences in odometers and different parking locations at rest stops and the suggested stops enroute

Please watch for road signs and historical landmarks along the route, and be very aware of traffic. Respect private property and please do not trespass. To assist you with both tours and add to your enjoyment, we have also recorded the Global Positioning System (GPS) coordinates for the key points along the routes. These are listed in the driving directions as Retreat Waypoint (RW) 1 through 74 in this tour, and as Wagon Train Waypoint (WTW) 1 through 35 in the second tour. In addition to being included with each stop, the coordinates

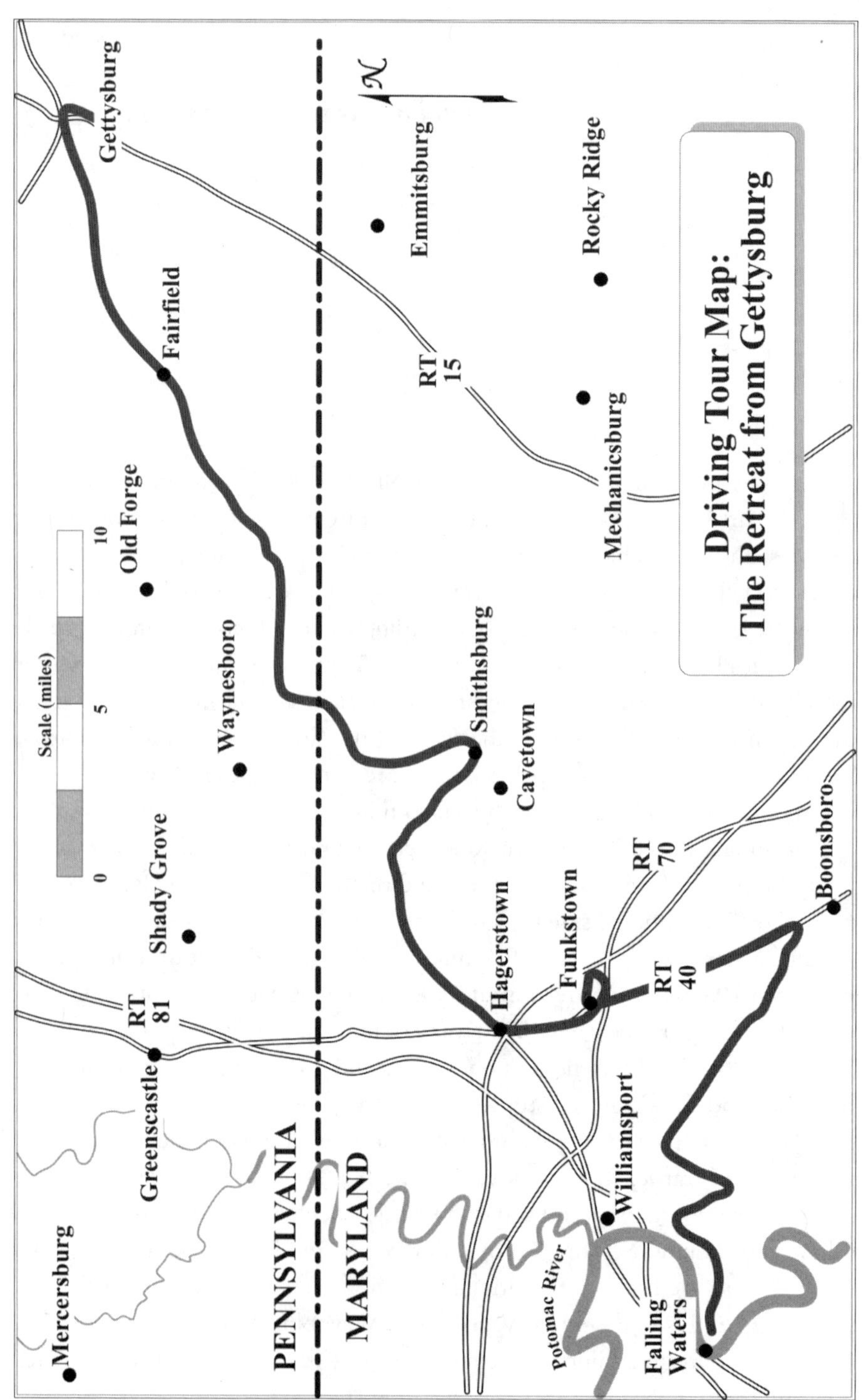
Driving Tour Map:
The Retreat from Gettysburg
N
Scale (miles)
0
5
10
Gettysburg
Fairfield
Old Forge
Waynesboro
Shady Grove
Emmitsburg
Rocky Ridge
RT 15
Mechanicsburg
Smithsburg
Cavetown
Hagerstown
Funkstown
RT 70
RT 40
Boonsboro
Williamsport
Falling Waters
Potomac River
Greenscastle
RT 81
Mercersburg
PENNSYLVANIA
MARYLAND

for the waypoints are also listed at the end of each tour should you wish to program them into your GPS unit ahead of time.

* * *

Begin the tour in Gettysburg, Pennsylvania at the Taneytown Road entrance to the National Cemetery, facing north toward town (the Cemetery entrance will be on your right). **Set your odometer to 0.0.**

RW 1 – (N 39° 49.057' W 077° 13.949') – **Proceed north on the Taneytown Road toward town.**

RW 2 – (N 39° 49.273' W 077° 13.997') – **After .2 miles, you will reach the traffic light at Steinwehr Avenue. Continue straight through the traffic light and proceed onto Washington Street**.

RW 3 – (N 39° 49.784' W 077° 14.007') – **After .6 miles, turn left at the traffic light onto Middle Street**.

RW 4 – (N 39° 49.786' W 077° 14.643') – **After .6 miles at the traffic light, note West Confederate Avenue to your left, and Seminary Road to your right.** This is Seminary Ridge, the Confederate line of battle. The retreat of the Army of Northern Virginia began from this point. **Continue straight through the traffic light**. Middle Street now becomes the Fairfield Road (Route 116), and you will pass by a portion of the first day's battlefield. (Do not follow the National Park Service "Auto Tour" sign onto Reynolds Avenue.)

RW 5 – (N 39° 49.112' W 077° 17.037') – **In 2.2 miles, you will come to Black Horse Tavern Road** (there are roadside tablets on the right, in front of the war-time building). The Black Horse Tavern served as a Confederate Field Hospital. It also served as a huge wagon park for the Confederate trains, and many of them began their retreat journey here. During the retreat, General Robert E. Lee stopped here to watch his troops begin their arduous journey home. The property is privately owned, so please do not trespass. To your rear you will see Breams Hill Road. This is the original road trace of the Fairfield Road.

RW 6 – (N 39° 48.628' W 077° 19.276') – **After another 2.2 miles, you will see the Lower Marsh Creek Church on the right.** Confederate Lieutenant General Richard S. Ewell's Second Corps trains extended from here back to the Black Horse Tavern. Many of the period buildings along this route were used as temporary field hospitals. Badly wounded men were removed

Black Horse Tavern. *Authors' Photo*

from the wagons as needed, and left to recuperate at local homes. Many dead were buried alongside the road. **Continuing .6 miles beyond the church you will see the "Granite Hill Campground" which marks the vicinity of the first skirmish during the retreat between the Confederate rear guard and pursuing elements of the Union 6th Corps.**

RW 7 – (N 39° 47.500' W 077° 21.825') – **After 2.6 miles from the church, you will see Caroll's Tract Road on your right** (known during the war as the Fairfield-Ortanna Road). On the afternoon of July 3rd, 1863, the 6th US Cavalry fought a pitched battle against Confederate Brigadier General William E. "Grumble" Jones' cavalry brigade along the Fairfield-Ortanna Road, 2.5 miles north of this intersection. During the retreat, Confederate trains moving south from Cashtown along joined the main retreat route here. The resulting traffic jam caused Confederate General Jubal Early's troops to unlimber an artillery piece nearby and fire (firing powder only with no projectiles) toward their own trains to spur them along. **Do not turn, but continue straight and you will enter the town of Fairfield, Pennsylvania.**

RW 8 – (N 39° 46.866' W 077° 22.694') – **After 1.25 miles, turn right onto Iron Springs Road.** The hill ahead on your left is Jack's Mountain. The narrow Fairfield Gap is immediately to its right. The fields to the left were the location of Heth's Division's camps on June 30th. The June 30th skirmish between elements of the 8th Illinois Cavalry and two regiments of Southern infantry occurred near here at the base of the Fairfield Gap. You will pass through the Fairfield Gap as you proceed. The stream flowing along either side of the road here is Tom's Creek. The "Tapeworm Railroad," dating from 1834, will be visible on your right. The railroad will cross the route several times as you travel through the pass. You will note that the pass is very narrow as the road winds to the summit (please drive with caution). Lee barricaded the Gap until July 7 in an attempt to prevent the Federals from pursuing his army into the mountains.

RW 9 – (N 39° 46.017' W 077° 25.998') – **3.35 miles along Iron Springs Road, you will see Gum Springs Road on your right**. While the Infantry continued along Iron Springs Road, the Confederate trains turned onto Gum Springs Road in the driving rainstorm and then traveled down Mariah Furnace Road (only a trace of which remains in thick woods today). From here you are beginning to ascend South Mountain. **Do not turn, but continue on Iron Springs Road through the hamlet of Greenstone.**

RW 10 – (N 39° 44.708' W 077° 27.209') – **After 2.1 miles, turn right onto Old Waynesboro Road**. Across from the intersection is a roadside marker addressing the Battle of Fountain Dale. Brigadier General Judson Kilpatrick's Federal cavalry division, plus the brigade of Colonel Pennock Huey, had come up from Emmitsburg, Maryland during the evening of July 4, 1863. The troopers used the Waynesboro Turnpike (as it was known) as their route of march, and you are now following in their steps. As Kilpatrick's division proceeded, Colonel Peter Stagg's 1st Michigan Cavalry charged up Iron Springs Road before being repulsed by Confederate cavalry of the brigades of Brigadier Generals William E. "Grumble" Jones and Beverly H. Robertson. Captain George M. Emack of the 1st Maryland Cavalry (CSA) held off Kilpatrick's cavalry with a single company of about 50 men and one artillery piece. Initially this gun was positioned where the road intersects with the current-day entrance to the Greenstone plant. In 1863, this was a narrow one-lane road with sheer drop offs on the left side.

RW 11 – (N 39° 44.398' W 077° 27.934') – **1.1 miles along Old Waynesboro Road, you reach the second position of the Confederate artillery piece which was deployed here on the left of the road facing toward Fountain Dale**. Captain William Tanner of Courtney's Artillery Battery ordered this lone Napoleon gun to occupy this position should the enemy appear in the road. The caisson carried only five rounds of ammunition.

Original location of the Monterey Springs Hotel. *Authors' Photo*

In the gathering darkness and pounding rain on the night of July 4, the cannon fired three of its rounds at the 5th Michigan Cavalry as they approached. After repulsing the Federals, Emack ordered that the cannon be redeployed about 100 yards further up the road. For the next several hours, confused and deadly fighting due to the rain and darkness raged in this area. In 1863 this was the popular Monterey Springs resort area, and on both sides of the road you will see a number of ornate homes from the period.

RW 12 – (N 39° 44.277' W 077° 28.282') – **After another .3 miles, note the home on the left at the intersection of Monterey Lane.** The original location of the grand Monterey Springs Hotel is to the rear of the existing house. The hotel was long thought to stand across the lane where the small golf course is, however its foundation has been discovered more recently. Following the fighting the hotel briefly served as Kilpatrick's headquarters. His troopers processed the prisoners captured here by the light of a large bonfire. First Lieutenant Alexander C. M. Pennington Jr. posted his battery of the 2nd US Artillery in front of the hotel here.

RW 13 – (N 39° 44.303' W 077° 28.738') – **At .4 miles from the site of the Monterey Hotel, turn right into the Lion's Club "Rolando Woods Park"** and park near the pavilion. The stream here is "Brown's Run" and "Brown's Spring" is just to the left of the Lion's Club monument. The slightly visible trail to the rear of the monument was thought be the original trace of the Mariah Furnace Road, however the actual road trace is a gated, gravel service road that

Road trace of the Mariah Furnace Road near the Rolando Woods Park. *Authors' Photo*

lies to the left, beyond park's restrooms. After crossing a wooden bridge over Brown's Run, Mariah Furnace Road joined the Waynesboro Road at the Toll House (noted at the next waypoint). This area was very flooded from the extremely heavy rains at the time of the battle. The 5th Michigan Cavalry fought an engagement here at midnight on July 4th. A mounted charge by Company A of the 1st Ohio Cavalry (Kilpatrick's Headquarters guard) was finally able to break through Captain Emack's defenses near this spot, permitting the Federal cavalry to slam into the trail elements of Ewell's trains.

Exit the park from the same road you entered on and RESET your odometer mileage to 0.0 as you turn right from the Park back onto the Waynesboro Road. Use caution crossing Route 16 and continue straight through the intersection.

RW 14 – (N 39° 44.303' W 077° 28.943') – **After .2 miles, note the small, red and brick (with some white siding) building on your right.** This is the old Waynesboro Road Toll House. The actual breakthrough by the 1st Ohio Cavalry occurred in this vicinity.

RW 15 – (N 39° 44.173' W 077° 29.791') – **After .7 miles from the Toll House, note the steep drop off to the right of the road.** Hundreds of Confederate wagons ended up in the bottom of this ravine.

The Waynesboro Road Toll House, now a private home. *Authors' Photo*

RW 16 – (N 39° 44.082 W 077° 31.231') – **After 1.5 miles, you will pass through the town of Rouserville.**

RW 17 – (N 39° 44.254' W 077° 31.758') – **In .6 miles, the Waynesboro Road merges into Route 16. Turn right at the stop sign here, then turn left onto Route 16 West.**

RW 18 – (N 39° 44.311' W 077° 31.913') – **Proceed .2 miles on Route 16 West.** The Stephy Tavern formerly stood on the left side of the road here. During the retreat Robert E. Lee is said to have stopped here for some refreshment while en route to Waynesboro.

RW 19 – (N 39° 44.332' W 077° 32.000') – **Continue .1 miles and turn left onto Midvale Road.** (This is one of only a few areas along the tour where there are convenience stores and public rest facilities readily available.) Here the route of the Confederate retreat continued ahead to Waynesboro and then turned south to Greencastle and Hagerstown. **RESET your odometer mileage to 0.0 as you turn onto Midvale Road or upon leaving the convenience facility**. Proceeding along Midvale Road, you are following the route that Union General Judson Kilpatrick's cavalry's took to Smithsburg on the morning of July 5, 1863.

RW 20 – (N 39° 43.203' W 077° 32.609') – **1.5 miles along Midvale Road, you will cross the Mason Dixon Line from Pennsylvania into Maryland.**

The Confederate artillery position (center distance) at Smithsburg, Maryland, as seen from the Federal position. *Authors' Photo*

RW 21 – (N 39° 42.472' W 077° 34.373') – **1.8 miles from the Mason Dixon Line, turn left onto Route 64 toward Smithsburg.**

RW 22 – (N 39° 39.551' W 077° 33.736') – **3.6 miles along Route 64, turn right onto Water Street**.

RW 23 – (N 39° 39.518' W 077° 33.889') - **.1 mile along Water Street, as you start to go up the hill, stop near the condominiums.** This elevation was called Gardenhour Hill in 1863. The Federal position here on July 5, 1863 faced back towards Route 64 and South Mountain. As you face toward South Mountain, Brigadier General George A. Custer's brigade occupied the hill to your left, where the Smithsburg Middle School now stands. Colonel Pennock Huey's cavalry brigade was on the hill where you are currently and Colonel Nathaniel P. Richmond's brigade manned positions on the high ground to your right, which is now known as Federal Hill.

Lieutenant William D. Fuller's Battery C, 3rd US Artillery was located directly to your right. As the Confederate cavalry approached from Raven Rock Road at the base of South Mountain, Major General James Ewell Brown (J.E.B.) Stuart was in personal command. If you look straight ahead, you will probably be able to see traffic moving on Raven Rock Road, and see its intersection with modern Route 64. Stuart's artillery deployed along the ridge adjacent to the road, which was known as Goat Hill.

The Vogel House at Smithsburg, Maryland. *Authors' Photo*

RESET your odometer mileage to 0.0 at this point and continue on Water Street into Smithsburg.

RW 24 – (N 39° 39.340' W 077° 34.266') – **After .3 mile, note the second red brick house on the left at 25 Water Street.** This was known as the Vogel Home. It retains visible battle damage from the fighting here. If you look carefully, you will see a Confederate artillery shell stuck in the side of the house. The Vogel house and the Bell house (the latter's address is 13 and 15 Water Street) were both pressed into use as field hospitals after the end of the fighting at Smithsburg.

RW 25 – (N 39° 39.285' W 077° 34.368') – **After .1 mile from the Vogel home, turn right onto Main Street.**

[OPTIONAL] Here you have a choice of making an optional side trip to see a Maryland Civil War Trails marker. To see it, continue straight through the intersection of Main and Water Streets, and after .2 mile (RW 26 – N 39° 39.189' W 077° 34.686'**) you will see the Smithburg Veterans Park on your right.** The Trails marker is located here, and parking is available. Note that the Federal withdrawal from Smithsburg followed the

Home at 13-15 Water Street, Smithsburg, Maryland. *Authors' Photo*

Boonsboro Road to the right as you exit the park. After you are finished viewing the marker, **return to the intersection of Main and Water Streets, turn left onto Main Street, and RESET your odometer mileage to 0.0.**

RW 27 – (N 39° 39.534' W 077° 34.579') - **As you proceed along Main Street for .3 mile, note the brick circa 1820 townhouse at 42 Main South Main Street.** Brigadier Generals George Custer and Judson Kilpatrick supposedly enjoyed a chicken lunch here on the afternoon of July 5, 1863.

Continue on along Main Street. The red brick school on the right is the Smithsburg Middle School. This was the location of Custer's brigade on the left of the Union position.

Continue straight on Main Street and it becomes the Leitersburg Smithsburg Road.

RW 28 – (N 39° 41.068' W 077° 36.708') – **2.6 miles from the home at 42 South Main, you will cross Antietam Creek on the Old Forge Bridge, and begin heading into Leitersburg.** The 1st Vermont Cavalry attacked part of General Ewell's train in this vicinity on the morning of July 5.

RW 29 – (N 39° 41.628' W 077° 37.423') – **After another .9 mile, turn left onto Route 60.**

RW 30 – (N 39° 39.703' W 077° 42.084') – **After 5.2 miles along Route 60, you will enter the Hagerstown city limits.** Route 60 becomes Potomac Avenue, the main street through Hagerstown.

RW 31 – (N 39° 38.826' W 077° 42.984') – **After 1.7 miles, you enter the Potomac Avenue Historic District.** This was the site of heavy mounted street fighting during the July 6 battle between Brigadier General Judson Kilpatrick and Confederate cavalry and infantry. Also note that the Federal forces approached from the south and the Confederates from the north. Various points of interest and details of the fighting will be described over the next several stops.

RW 32 – (N 39° 38.697' W 077° 43.085') – **After .4 mile, stop at the Zion Evangelical and Reformed Church at Potomac and Church Streets.** The church was founded in 1770, and the churchyard here is the final resting place of veterans from the French and Indian War, the American Revolution, the War of 1812, the Mexican War, the Civil War (Union and Confederate) and World War I. Hagerstown's founder, Captain Jonathan Hager Sr. (1719-1775) is also buried here. After Hagerstown was taken, George Custer used the church's bell tower as an observation post.

The 10th Virginia Cavalry barricaded the street two blocks beyond here at Washington Street in the town square during the July 6 fight. Brigadier General

Zion Evangelical and Reformed Church in Hagerstown, Maryland. *Authors' Photo*

Kilpatrick broke through and found the Confederates in strong positions behind stone walls and in the church cemetery. Federal Captain Ulric Dahlgren was gravely wounded in the leg at the bottom of the hill, in the town square. The Union troops received fire from windows and rooftops occupied by both Confederate soldiers and civilian spectators. Confederate infantry from Iverson's brigade arrived and forced Kilpatrick to fall back, out of the town. The Hagerstown battle was the scene of an exceedingly rare event - an urban, mounted cavalry fight.

RESET your odometer mileage to 0.0 and continue on Potomac Street. The Hagerstown Visitor's Center is located in the town square at the intersection with Washington Street. When open, they can provide a visitor's guide and information about the Hager House, Rose Hill Cemetery and a number of area attractions.

RW 33 – (N 39° 38.344' W 077° 43.333') – **After .5 miles, turn left onto Alternate 40 (Baltimore Street).**

RW 34 – (N 39° 38.233' W 077° 43.111') – **After another .2 mile, bear right onto Frederick Street (Alternate 40).** On the morning of July 6, Kilpatrick came into Hagerstown along this route from Boonsboro to the south. During the July 6 battle, Federal artillery was positioned on the high ground at the site of the present day hospital, just beyond the intersection.

RW 35 – (N 39° 36.737' W 077° 42.603') – **After 1.8 miles, you will cross the Antietam Creek at the Funkstown line.**

RW 36 – (N 39° 36.623' W 077° 42.637') – **In .2 mile, turn right at the traffic light onto Baltimore Street. Stop in the parking area before the bridge.** On July 7th, the 6th U.S. Cavalry fought the Battle of Funkstown here against Confederate cavalry under Brigadier General William E. "Grumble" Jones. After being nearly decimated by Jones' cavalry during the fighting at Fairfield, Pennsylvania on July 3rd, the 6th U.S. lost heavily here as well. Afterwards, Jones said "The 6th US Regular Cavalry numbers among the things that were."

On July 10th, the high ground across the creek was held by Brigadier General Albert Jenkins' cavalry, and elements of James Longstreet's First Corps. Union troops advanced from the direction of Boonsboro (which is behind you as you face the bridge). The fighting here, which involved both

Bridge over Antietam Creek in Funkstown, Maryland. *Authors' Photo*

infantry and cavalry forces, was the largest battle during the retreat in terms of numbers engaged. Most of the battle took place toward Boonsboro.

Turn back the way you came, RESET your odometer mileage to 0.0 at the intersection with Baltimore Street and continue east on Baltimore Street.

RW 37 – (N 39° 36.555' W 077° 42.375') – **After .3 mile, you will come to two period homes on opposite sides of Baltimore Street.** The Keller Home on the left and the Hudson House on the right both served as Confederate field hospitals for the battle. A marker in front of the Keller Home notes that wounded including Major H. D. McDaniel of the 11th Georgia were cared for here. **As you continue on, Baltimore Street will become Beaver Creek Road**.

RW 38 – (N 39° 36.365' W 077° 41.835') – **After .5 miles, watch for low ground to your right.** This was the site of infantry fighting involving Georgians from Longstreet's Corps on July 10th. The Confederate infantry attacked toward the high ground directly to your front, trying to drive off the Federals.

RW 39 – (N 39° 36.175' W 077° 41.591') – **In .3 mile, turn left onto Emmert Road**. This was the position of Colonel Lewis A. Grant's brigade from the 2nd Division of the Union 6th Corps. Federal artillery lined this road and ridgeline since it is the highest ground in the vicinity. Note that in 1863 this was open area and none of the trees to your left would have been here.

The J. W. Baker Farm, Brig. Gen. John Buford's Headquarters. *Authors' Photo*

RW 40 – (N 39° 36.547' W 077° 41.320') – **After .5 mile along Emmert Road, turn left onto Hebb Road** (before the intersection with Route 40).

RW 41 – (N 39° 36.529' W 077° 41.596') – **After .2 mile along Hebb Road, note the circa 1820 fieldstone farmhouse on the right (102 Hebb Road).** This was the Baker Farm and was Brigadier General John Buford's headquarters for his Federal cavalry division. The Union line of battle ran along

Stuart's position at Funkstown, including the Hauck barn. *Authors' Photo*

the high ground in front of you on the right, behind the home. While observing the heavy fighting here, Buford's uniform jacket was hit by minie balls - later he discovered his coat to have five holes in it. Luckily for him, none hit flesh.

RW 42 – (N 39° 36.498' W 077° 42.020') – **In .5 mile, bear to the right back onto Beaver Creek Road.**

RW 43 – (N 39° 36.524' W 077° 42.293') - **.2 mile along Beaver Creek Road, turn left onto Alternate 40 (Frederick Road) at the World War I monument.**

RW 44 – (N 39° 36.406' W 077° 42.311') – **After .2 mile, you will see a historical marker on the right noting the "Battle of Funkstown."**

RW 45 – (N 39° 36.218' W 077° 42.264') - **.2 mile beyond the historical marker, note the period Hauck barn that marks the location of J.E.B. Stuart's position on July 10.** Interstate 70 is in front of you. Captain Roger P. Chew's Confederate horse artillery battery was positioned on the high ground just behind the Hauk barn during the battle of Funkstown.

RW 46 – (N 39° 36.038' W 077° 42.177') – **After .3 mile, just before the Interstate 70 overpass is a Maryland Civil War Trails marker on the right.**

RW 47 – (N 39° 33.062' W 077° 40.788') – **At 3.7 miles, this area was the site of the July 7, 1863 "Battle of Benevola," which consisted of dismounted cavalry fighting at Beaver Creek Bridge.** The very heavy rains had turned the roads into impassable quagmires, meaning that mounted operations were impossible. Colonel William Gamble's brigade of Federal

The bridge over Beaver Creek, scene of the battle of Benevola. *Authors' Photo*

cavalry on the ridge to the left attempted to move to Funkstown but was repulsed by "Grumble" Jones' cavalry supported by Chew's artillery. Gamble's brigade then returned to Boonsboro.

RW 48 – (N 39° 31.792' W 077° 39.953') – **In 1.1 miles, you will see that Turner's Gap is directly in front of you.** Federal 11th Corps artillery was in position along South Mountain in this vicinity, and supported the fighting at Boonsboro.

RW 49 – (N 39° 31.604' W 077° 39.848') – **In .7 mile, turn right into the parking area of "Auction Square" on the right, just before the Maryland Civil War Trails marker.** You may wish to exit your vehicle to get a good view of this area. The July 8th Battle of Boonsboro occurred in the fields to the left of the road. Buford's division with Colonel Thomas Devin's brigade on the left, Brigadier General Wesley Merritt's brigade in the center, and Colonel William Gamble's brigade on the right advanced through this area toward Funkstown. They were engaged by Stuart's entire force in these fields in dismounted action and were repulsed.

RW 50 – (N 39° 31.212' W 077° 39.609') – **Exit the parking lot by turning right. After .7 mile, RESET your odometer mileage to 0.0 and turn right onto Route 68**. (There is a convenience store with public facilities just beyond the intersection with Route 68.)

[OPTIONAL] - The Boonsborough Museum of History (containing the old spelling of the town's name) at 113 N. Main Street in Boonsboro has an extensive collection of Civil War items from the local battlefields of Boonsboro, South Mountain, Antietam and Harpers Ferry, including firearms, edged weapons and a large display of uniquely carved bullets. The museum is open seasonally and by appointment.

There is also a Maryland Civil War Trails marker on Main Street at the entrance to Shafer Park (**RW 51** – N 39° 30.529' W 077° 39.217') noting Boonsboro's role in the Antietam and Gettysburg campaigns. From the intersection of Main Street and Shafer Park Drive, look across towards South Mountain. At the crest you can see the Washington Monument in Washington Monument State Park.

Return to Route 68, turn left and RESET your odometer mileage to 0.0.

Devil's Backbone State Park, site of Maj. Gen. George Meade's HQ. *Authors' Photo*

RW 52 – (N 39° 32.239' W 077° 42.604') **After 3.3 miles along Route 68 you will come to Booth's Mill Bridge.** Just across the bridge (which was built in 1833) is the "Devil's Backbone Park" along the banks of the Antietam Creek. This was the site of the Delamere School, established in 1776, and attended by Richard Henry Lee and sons of Robert Morris and Benedict Arnold. During the retreat on July 10th, Meade made his headquarters in the area. (The park has seasonal public rest rooms, picnic benches and outdoor grills.) A Maryland Civil War Trails marker in the parking area notes that General Meade held a council of war here on July 12th to discuss whether to attack the strong Confederate defenses at Williamsport.

RW 53 – (N 39° 33.212' W 077° 44.255') – **1.9 miles beyond the bridge and Park, you will come to the intersection of Routes 68 and 65, which is the location of "Jones' Crossroads."** The Antietam (Sharpsburg) Battlefield is six miles to the south. Brigadier Generals John Buford and Judson Kilpatrick met here on the night of July 6th after they were repulsed at Williamsport in the "Wagoner's Fight." On July 11, elements of Huey's Cavalry and 12th Corps infantry engaged Confederate infantry and cavalry forces here in an after-dark skirmish.

An optional side trip follows – if you wish to continue on with the standard tour, however, then RESET your odometer mileage to 0.0 and

Historical marker at Jones's Crossroads. *Authors' Photo*

continue straight through the intersection on Route 68 which is also called Lappans Road here.

[OPTIONAL] – Instead of going straight onto Route 68, turn left onto Route 65 South. After .7 miles you will see a white frame farmhouse on the left (RW 54 – N 39° 32.588' W 077° 44.305'). This home served as the headquarters of Major General Henry W. Slocum's Federal 12th Corps.

Return to the intersection of Routes 68 and 65, turn left on Route 68 (Lappans Road) and RESET your odometer mileage to 0.0.

RW 55 – (N 39° 34.108' W 077° 45.922') – **After 1.8 miles, turn right onto College Road towards the College of Saint James (now St. James School).**

RW 56 – (N 39° 34.384' W 077° 45.752') – **In .4 miles, stop near the end of the green fence on your right.** In 1863 this was a mostly open area of working farms. The center of Robert E. Lee's defenses around Williamsport is to your left, near the handsome, large white house called "Bai Yuka." Natural breaks in this ridgeline were augmented by rifle pits and artillery lunettes that provided interlocking fields of fire. These positions were constructed on July 9th and 10th. The ground to your right is the location where the 3rd Indiana and 8th Illinois Cavalry regiments of Colonel William Gamble's brigade fought a dismounted action during the "Wagoner's Fight" on July 6th. The farm

This farm was the site of much of the fighting during the Battle of Williamsport on July 6, 1863. Also, Lee's main line of defense extended along the ridge line that you can see in the distance. *Authors' Photo*

buildings on the left mark the site where Captain William Pegram of Company F, 21st Virginia Infantry lost his life leading his men in an attack on the dismounted Federal troopers. It also marks the spot where Major William H. Medill of the 8th Illinois Cavalry was mortally wounded.

Turn around and go back to the Route 68 and College Road intersection. RESET your odometer mileage to 0.0 and turn right onto Route 68. Lee's main defensive line ran along the high ridge immediately to your front.

The J. M. Donnelly house along Falling Waters Road, where Brig. Gen. James J. Pettigrew suffered his mortal wound. *Authors' Photo*

RW 57 – (N 39° 34.586' W 077° 46.918') – **After 1.0 mile, turn left onto Maryland Route 632 toward Downsville.** Continuous skirmishing occurred throughout this area from July 10 to 12, while each side probed the other's positions.

RW 58 – (N 39° 32.921' W 077° 48.152') – **In 2.2 miles, turn right onto Route 63 North (Spielman Road) in Downsville.**

RW 59 – (N 39° 34.409' W 077° 48.859') – **1.9 miles along Route 63 North, turn left onto Falling Waters Road.** Note the successive series of small ridges along this road as you drive it. By July 10, Robert E. Lee's engineers had fortified these ridges with rifle pits and gun emplacements. As the Confederates began to cross the river on July 14, this terrain channeled attacking Federal troops who encountered Confederate rear guard defenders at each ridgeline in turn. These natural defensive positions were nearly impregnable.

RW 60 – (N 39° 33.162' W 077° 51.267') – **At 3.0 miles, note the high ground in front of you.** On the morning of July 14, much of Major General Henry Heth's Division of the Confederate Third Corps was positioned along the high ground here, serving as a rear guard to protect the withdrawal of the rest of the Corps. There is a large bend in the Potomac River (which is about 1.5 miles ahead). Both flanks of the Confederate position were anchored on the riverbanks. Obeying Brigadier General Judson Kilpatrick's orders, Major Peter Weber led a squadron of the 6th Michigan Cavalry in a mounted charge (from the treeline to your left rear) against Heth's defenders. Confederate Brigadier General James J. Pettigrew was mortally wounded in the fighting here, and Weber was killed. The nature of the terrain funneled Weber's mounted charge to the left of the J.M. Donnelly House, the handsome red brick house on your right.

RW 61 – (N 39° 33.348' W 077° 52.593') – **Another 1.3 miles ahead, you will see a sign for the Potomac Fish and Game Club on the left.** The gated unimproved road on the right leads to Falling Waters, and is an excellent example of how most of these roads appeared during the Civil War. The area at Falling Waters is part of the C&O Canal National Park, operated by the National Park Service. The locked gate prohibits vehicle access without prior approval.

Park your vehicle in a safe area that will not block traffic or official access through the gate. Walk around the gate to continue on the dirt road. Please note that it is .5 mile to the river along a steep, unimproved path. Proceed

Historical marker near the Falling Waters crossing. *Authors' Photo*

with caution. The road here looks very much as it did in 1863. As you near the river, you will easily see the dry bed of the old C&O Canal as well as the towpath. There are remnants of the old bridge abutments over the canal, a Maryland Civil War Trail marker as well as a historical marker for Falling Waters. Carefully approach the steep bank to the river, and you have come to the site of the Confederate pontoon bridge (**RW 62** – N 39° 33.418' W 077° 53.160') Confederate General James Longstreet's First Corps and General A.P. Hill's Third Corps crossed the Potomac here, completing the crossing on July 14th. In the fields behind you on both sides of the road, Federal cavalry made their final attacks upon the Confederate rear guard, then watched helplessly as the pontoon bridge was cut from the opposite side.

Once you have finished examining the Falling Waters crossing, retrace your steps along the old road and return to your vehicle. **Turn around, return 4.2 miles on Falling Waters Road, turn left onto Route 63 and RESET your odometer mileage to 0.0.**

RW 63 – (N 39° 35.097' W 077° 48.804') – **After .9 mile, turn left at the traffic light onto Route 68 West toward Williamsport.** Established in 1787, Williamsport was an important commercial center on the Potomac, with the C&O Canal turn basin on the river and the Valley Pike running through the center of town. From July 5 through 14, these streets were packed with soldiers, wagons, ambulances, and thousands of animals waiting to cross the river.

RW 64 – (N 39° 36.019' W 077° 49.276') – **In 1.2 miles, turn left onto Route 11, also known as Potomac Street** (Route 11 was known as the "Valley Pike").

RW 65 – N 39° 36.023' W 077° 49.557') – **In .3 mile, turn right and stop in the National Park Service's parking area at "Cushwa's Basin," the C&O Canal Visitor's Center.** One of the fords across the Potomac was located where the present-day bridge abutments cross the river. A second ford was located about 200 yards to the right (upstream), on the other side of the Conococheague Creek aqueduct. Confederate General Richard Ewell's Second Corps crossed at these fords on July 14.

The National Park Service museum and Visitor's Center here documents the history of the C&O Canal and has much to see, including a small bookstore. You may wish to take additional time here.

This marks the end of the tour of the retreat route. However, two optional side trips follow. If you do not wish to visit them, and to return to Gettysburg via a shorter route, bear left when leaving the C&O Canal Basin parking area to turn onto Potomac Street. After .2 mile, turn right onto Conococheague Street. Follow the signs to Interstate 81 North. Take Interstate 81 North to Exit – (Old Exit 16) into Chambersburg, and then follow Route 30 East to Gettysburg.

* * *

Optional side trips to Bunker Hill (location of General James J. Pettigrew's death) and the West Virginia side of Falling Waters:

RESET your odometer mileage to 0.0, and turn left from the parking lot of the C&O Canal Basin onto Potomac Street.

RW 66 – (N 39° 36.024' W 077° 49.292') – **After .2 mile, turn right onto Conococheague Street.**

RW 67 – (N 39° 35.354' W 077° 49.082') – **After .8 mile, take Interstate 81 South.**

RW 68 – (N 39° 21.881' W 078° 02.862') – **After traveling 21.9 miles along 81 South, take Exit 5 for Inwood, then turn left off the exit onto Eastbound West Virginia Route 51.**

RW 69 – (N 39° 21.648' W 078° 02.267') – **In .5 mile, turn right at the traffic light onto Route 11, the Valley Turnpike.**

RW 70 – (N 39° 19.791' W 078° 03.301') – **In 2.3 miles, you will come to Bunker Hill, West Virginia.** Monument Lane is on the left, the Pettigrew monument is on the right. Confederate Brigadier General James J. Pettigrew was brought here to the Boyd House, known as "Edgewood," after being mortally wounded at Falling Waters on July 14. Relays of four men carried the General the eighteen miles to this location (this was part of West Virginia still loyal to the Confederacy). He died in the stately red brick house to the right of the Pike on the morning of July 17 after dividing his horses and equipment among his officers. Pettigrew is buried in the family cemetery in Tyrrell County, North Carolina.

Erected in 1918 by the North Carolina Historical Commission and the North Carolina Division of the United Daughters of the Confederacy, the monument here notes that Pettigrew commanded Heth's Division during Longstreet's attack (the Pickett-Pettigrew-Trimble Charge) on Cemetery Ridge at Gettysburg on July 3. It includes a quote from Robert E. Lee that *"He was a brave and accomplished Officer and gentleman and his loss will be deeply felt by the Country and the Army."* The home is private property, so please do not trespass.

"Edgewood," the Boyd family home where General Pettigrew died. *Authors' Photo*

A monument to General Pettigrew in front of the Boyd home. *Authors' Photo*

Turn around and RESET your odometer mileage to 0.0. Return along the way you came on Route 11, the Valley Turnpike.

RW 71 – (N 39° 21.648' W 078° 02.267') **In 2.4 miles, turn left onto Westbound West Virginia Route 51.**

RW 72 – (N 39° 21.777' W 078° 02.818') – **After .4 mile, turn RIGHT to take Interstate 81 North.**

RW 73 – (N 39° 34.682' W 077° 52.804') – **After 18 miles, take Exit 23 and turn right onto Route 11 South.**

RW 74 – (N 39° 33.615' W 077° 53.265') – **In 1.6 miles, turn left onto Encampment Road.** "Lees Landing" on the left marks the West Virginia side of the Confederate pontoon bridge crossing. "Falling Waters" refers to the little stream running underneath the bridge and into the river. In 1863 this area was much more open with far less foliage. Confederate artillery positions lined the high ground on this side of the river to protect the crossing.

Return on Route 11 North, which will take you directly to the C&O Canal Visitor's Center.

The site of the Falling Waters pontoon bridge crossing from the west.

Authors' Photo

GPS Waypoints for *The Retreat from Gettysburg* Driving Tour:

RW 1:	N 39° 49.057'	W 077° 13.949'
RW 2:	N 39° 49.273'	W 077° 13.997'
RW 3:	N 39° 49.784'	W 077° 14.007'
RW 4:	N 39° 49.786'	W 077° 14.643'
RW 5:	N 39° 49.112'	W 077° 17.037'
RW 6:	N 39° 48.628'	W 077° 19.276'
RW 7:	N 39° 47.500'	W 077° 21.825'
RW 8:	N 39° 46.866'	W 077° 22.694'
RW 9:	N 39° 46.071'	W 077° 25.998'
RW 10:	N 39° 44.708'	W 077° 27.209'
RW 11:	N 39° 44.398'	W 077° 27.934'
RW 12:	N 39° 44.277'	W 077° 28.282'
RW 13:	N 39° 44.303'	W 077° 28.738'
RW 14:	N 39° 44.303'	W 077° 28.943'
RW 15:	N 39° 44.173'	W 077° 29.791'
RW 16:	N 39° 44.082'	W 077° 31.231'
RW 17:	N 39° 44.254'	W 077° 31.758'
RW 18:	N 39° 44.311'	W 077° 31.913'

RW 19:	N 39° 44.332'	W 077° 32.000'
RW 20:	N 39° 43.203'	W 077° 32.609'
RW 21:	N 39° 42.472'	W 077° 34.373'
RW 22:	N 39° 39.551'	W 077° 33.736'
RW 23:	N 39° 39.518'	W 077° 33.889'
RW 24:	N 39° 39.340'	W 077° 34.266'
RW 25:	N 39° 39.285'	W 077° 34.368'
RW 26:	N 39° 39.189'	W 077° 34.686'
RW 27:	N 39° 39.534'	W 077° 34.579'
RW 28:	N 39° 41.068'	W 077° 36.708'
RW 29:	N 39° 41.628'	W 077° 37.423'
RW 30:	N 39° 39.703'	W 077° 42.084'
RW 31:	N 39° 38.826'	W 077° 42.984'
RW 32:	N 39° 38.697'	W 077° 43.085'
RW 33:	N 39° 38.344'	W 077° 43.333'
RW 34:	N 39° 38.233'	W 077° 43.111'
RW 35:	N 39° 36.737'	W 077° 42.603'
RW 36:	N 39° 36.623'	W 077° 42.637'
RW 37:	N 39° 36.555'	W 077° 42.375'
RW 38:	N 39° 36.365'	W 077° 41.835'
RW 39:	N 39° 36.175'	W 077° 41.591'
RW 40:	N 39° 36.547'	W 077° 41.320'
RW 41:	N 39° 36.529'	W 077° 41.596'
RW 42:	N 39° 36.498'	W 077° 42.020'
RW 43:	N 39° 36.542'	W 077° 42.293'
RW 44:	N 39° 36.406'	W 077° 42.311'
RW 45:	N 39° 36.218'	W 077° 42.264'
RW 46:	N 39° 36.038'	W 077° 42.177'
RW 47:	N 39° 33.062'	W 077° 40.788'
RW 48:	N 39° 31.792'	W 077° 39.953'
RW 49:	N 39° 31.604'	W 077° 39.848'
RW 50:	N 39° 31.212'	W 077° 39.609'
RW 51:	N 39° 30.529'	W 077° 39.217'
RW 52:	N 39° 32.239'	W 077° 42.604'
RW 53:	N 39° 33.212'	W 077° 44.255'
RW 54:	N 39° 32.588'	W 077° 44.305'
RW 55:	N 39° 34.108'	W 077° 45.922'
RW 56:	N 39° 34.384'	W 077° 45.752'

RW 57:	N 39° 34.586'	W 077° 46.918'
RW 58:	N 39° 32.921'	W 077° 48.152'
RW 59:	N 39° 34.409'	W 077° 48.859'
RW 60:	N 39° 33.162'	W 077° 51.267'
RW 61:	N 39° 33.348'	W 077° 52.593'
RW 62:	N 39° 33.481'	W 077° 53.160'
RW 63:	N 39° 35.097'	W 077° 48.804'
RW 64:	N 39° 36.019'	W 077° 49.276'
RW 65:	N 39° 36.023'	W 077° 49.557'
RW 66:	N 39° 36.024'	W 077° 49.292'
RW 67:	N 39° 35.354'	W 077° 49.082'
RW 68:	N 39° 21.881'	W 078° 02.862'
RW 69:	N 39° 21.648'	W 078° 02.267'
RW 70:	N 39° 19.791'	W 078° 03.301'
RW 71:	N 39° 21.648'	W 078° 02.267'
RW 72	N 39° 21.777'	W 078° 02.818'
RW 73:	N 39° 34.682'	W 077° 52.804'
RW 74:	N 39° 33.615'	W 077° 53.265'

Appendix B

Driving Tour: "The Wagon Train of the Wounded"

Beginning at the Taneytown Road entrance to the National Cemetery in Gettysburg, the driving tour of the route of the Wagon Train of the Wounded covers 49.5 miles. **Set your odometer's mileage to 0.0 when at the Cemetery Entrance.** Three times along the tour you will reset your mileage to 0.0 before continuing, to help keep you on track. This will allow for differences in odometers and different parking locations at rest stops and the suggested stops enroute. We suggest that you try to allow a full day for each tour to fully enjoy the sites of interest.

Please watch for road signs and historical landmarks along the route, and be very aware of traffic. Respect private property and please do not trespass. To assist you with both tours and add to your enjoyment, we have also recorded the Global Positioning System (GPS) coordinates for the key points along the routes. These are listed in the driving directions as Wagon Train Waypoint (WTW) 1 through 35. In addition to being listed with each stop, the coordinates for the waypoints are also listed at the end of the tour should you wish to program them into your GPS unit ahead of time.

Begin the tour in Gettysburg, Pennsylvania at the Taneytown Road entrance to the National Cemetery, facing north toward town (the Cemetery entrance will be on your right). **Set your odometer to 0.0.**

WTW 1 - (N 39° 49.057' W 077° 13.949') – **Proceed north on the Taneytown Road toward town.**

WTW 2 – (N 39° 49.273' W 077° 13.997') – **After .2 miles, you will reach the traffic light at Steinwehr Avenue. Continue straight through the traffic light and proceed onto Washington Street.**

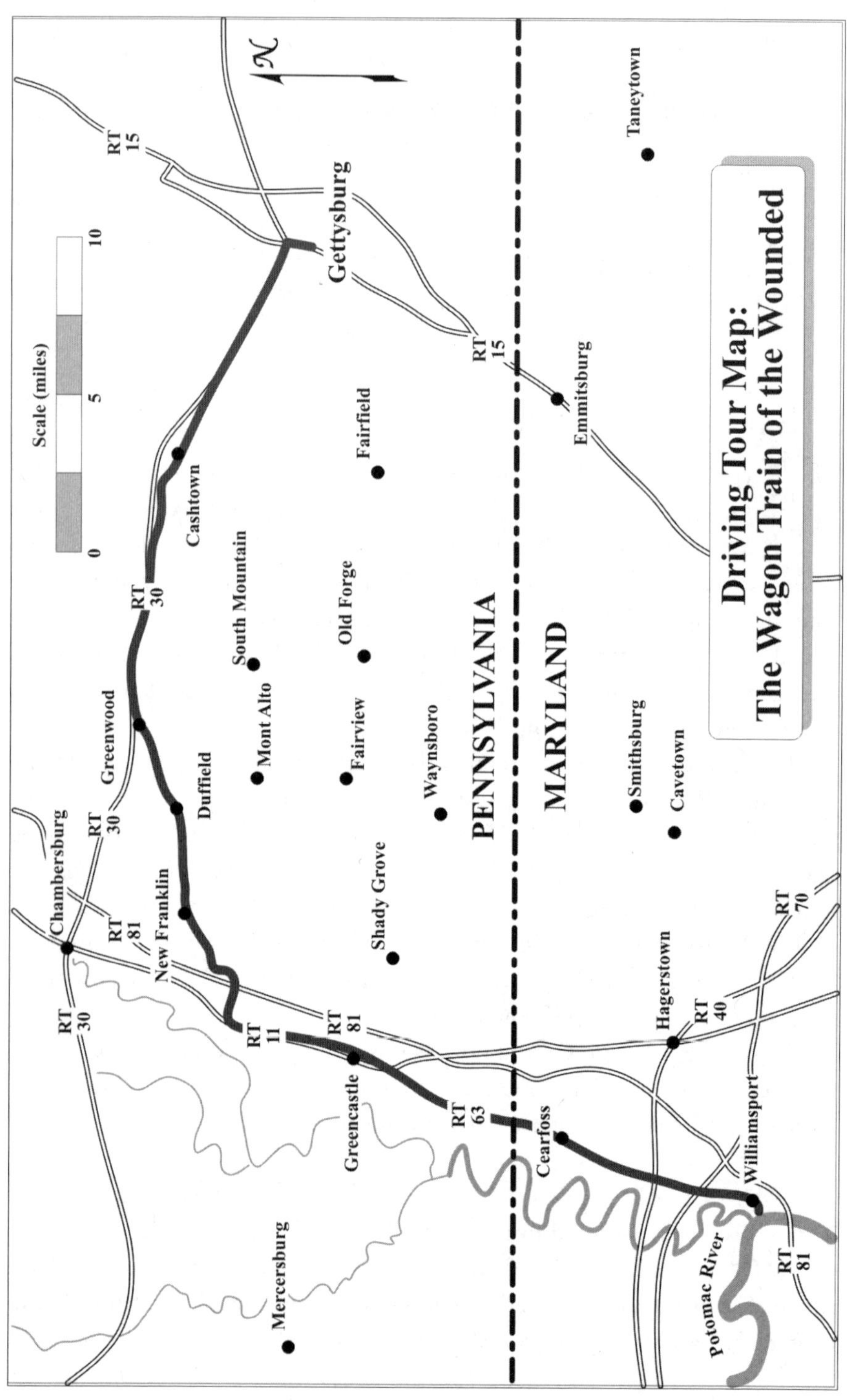
Driving Tour Map:
The Wagon Train of the Wounded
Scale (miles)
0
5
10
N
PENNSYLVANIA
MARYLAND
Gettysburg
Cashtown
South Mountain
Fairfield
Old Forge
Mont Alto
Fairview
Greenwood
Duffield
Waynsboro
Chambersburg
New Franklin
Shady Grove
Greencastle
Mercersburg
Cearfoss
Williamsport
Hagerstown
Smithsburg
Cavetown
Emmitsburg
Taneytown
Potomac River
RT 15
RT 30
RT 81
RT 11
RT 63
RT 40
RT 70

WTW 3 – (N 39° 49.862' W 077° 14.006') – **After .6 miles turn left at the traffic light onto Chambersburg Street.**

WTW 4 – (N 39° 49.883' W 077° 14.224') - **After .2 miles bear to the right at the intersection, staying on modern Route 30 (The Chambersburg Pike).** Continuing .5 miles you will pass Seminary Ridge and .2 miles further, McPherson Ridge and you will leave the boundaries of the Gettysburg National Military Park. In a blinding rainstorm on July 4, 1863 the Wagon Train formed along this route. This road was jammed with wagons, ambulances, animals and more than 12,000 wounded Confederate soldiers.

WTW 5 – (N 39° 50.513' W 077° 15.721') - **.9 miles beyond McPherson Ridge you reach the crest of Herr's Ridge**. Note Herr's Tavern on the left. Established in 1815, the tavern has a colorful history. Local lore relates that in the tavern's early days the basement housed a banknote counterfeiting operation and the upstairs served as a brothel. Later the tavern was used as a stop along the "Underground Railroad" assisting escaping slaves on their way to freedom. During the Battle of Gettysburg the tavern was used as a Confederate hospital. If you look across the fields to the right you can see the Eternal Peace Light Memorial which was dedicated by President Franklin D. Roosevelt during the 75th Anniversary of the battle in 1938.

Herr's Tavern on the Chambersburg Pike. *Authors' Photo*

The Cashtown Inn. *Authors' Photo*

WTW 6- (N 39° 52.008' W 077° 19.089') – **Continue 3.6 miles and bear left onto Old Route 30 (the old Gettysburg - Chambersburg Pike).**

WTW 7- (N 39° 53.077' W 077° 21.622') – After 2.6 miles stop in the parking area of the Cashtown Inn. Established in 1797, the Cashtown Inn is likely the location of Confederate Lt. Gen. Ambrose Powell Hill's Third Army Corps headquarters in the opening phases of the Gettysburg battle. General Robert E. Lee and a number of Confederate officers stopped here en route to Gettysburg. On July 5, 1863 the "Wagon Train of the Wounded," led by Confederate Brig. Gen. John Imboden started from here on its journey across the mountain pass. Imboden organized the train between here and the area of Herr's Ridge. By the time the last wagons had passed the Cashtown Inn, the train stretched out over 17 miles.

Continue on Old Route 30 as it ascends through the Cashtown Pass. Note that the large orchards along this route were not here in 1863. Individual farmers had smaller orchards but the large commercial orchards were established later. The terrain through this area was much more open with far less foliage in 1863. Many of the trees that were here were cut down for building materials, fencing and to fuel the area's iron industry.

WTW 8 – (N 39° 53.847' W 077° 25.543') – **Continue for 4 miles and bear left onto modern Route 30 West.** Note that the original road trace of the

1863 route varies off to either side of the modern road. In places you will be able to see where the old route deviated from the modern, straighter route.

WTW 9 – (N 39° 54.359' W 077° 31.265') – **After 2.8 miles, stop in the parking area of Caledonia State Park.** This was the site of Sen. Thaddeus Stevens' Caledonia Furnace and Iron Works, erected in 1837. This was a wide open industrial area in 1863 and was completely cleared of trees and foliage. A radical abolitionist, Stevens was despised by the Confederates. Troops under Maj. Gen. Jubal A. Early burned the Iron Works on June 26, and they were probably still smoldering on the afternoon of July 5, 1863. That afternoon, Union Col. J. Irvin Gregg's 3rd Brigade of the 2nd Cavalry Division fought a rear guard action here with Confederate Brig. Gen. Fitzhugh Lee's Cavalry Brigade, which was serving as the Wagon Train's rear guard. **(RESET your odometer mileage to 0.0 and turn right from the parking area of the State Park back onto Route 30 West.)**

WTW 10 – (N 39° 54.359' W 077° 31.265') – **Continue 2.3 miles and turn left at the traffic light onto Route 997 South.** Note that this is not the precise location where the Wagon Train turned off the main road. The trace of the original route, "Pine Stump Road," lies largely to the right along the tree line. Note, however, that the terrain here is largely unchanged and the original route is within yards of the modern road. These were narrow dirt roads in 1863. Thousands of wagon wheels and the torrential rains combined to make this

Thaddeus Stevens' Caledonia Iron Works. *Authors' Photo*

route a quagmire. Many of the "walking wounded" took to the fields on either side to avoid the road.

WTW 11-(N 39° 53.960' W 077° 31.729') - **After .6 miles, turn right onto Bikle Road.** Again, note that the modern roads generally follow the actual route but the original road trace varies to both sides of the current road.

WTW 12 – (N 39° 53.566' W 077° 33.544') – **Continue 1.7 miles and bear left at the Stop Sign onto SR 2031, Mont Alto Road.** (The modern town of Duffield was known as New Guilford in 1863.) To your left you can see the South Mountain range.

WTW 13 – (N 39° 53.018' W 077° 34.586') – **After 1.2 miles turn right onto SR 2020, "New Franklin Road" towards the town of New Franklin.** Exercise caution as this is a potentially confusing five-way intersection. Do **not** continue onto Falling Spring Road.

Continuing 2.3 miles you pass the location of the Jeremiah George Farm. None of the farm's original buildings still exist. Wounded soldiers including Lt. Col. Benjamin F. Carter of the 4th Texas Infantry were temporarily cared for here. He had wounds in his face, a hand, and a leg. Carter was later taken to the Zion Reformed Church in Chambersburg, then to the Academy Hospital, where he died of his wounds on July 21. He was buried in an unmarked grave in the United Methodist Cemetery (the graves were exhumed and removed to the Cedar Grove Cemetery in 1896). Since there is no record that any family members claimed his remains at any point, Carter likely still reposes in the Unknown section of Cedar Grove.

WTW 14 – (N 39° 52.758' W 077° 37.526') - **.5 miles past the site of the Jeremiah George Farm, bear right onto Guilford Station Road.**

WTW 15 – (N 39° 52.874' W 077° 37.889') – **Continue .3 miles and on the right you will see the Jacob Snyder Farm**. The original barn was to the left, near where a modern outbuilding now stands. Confederate soldiers from the Wagon Train took several of Snyder's cattle before he managed to close the barnyard gate. Wounded Confederates got water and dressed their wounds in Snyder's springhouse, visible to the left and rear of the main farm house. Snyder and his son Milton left accounts of the Wagon Train passing their farm. Milton told of Confederate dead from the Train being buried alongside the route near here, and of dying men being left by the roadside. To the immediate left of the main house you can see an original outdoor "bake oven" accessible from inside the kitchen.

The Jacob Snyder farm. *Authors' Photo*

Note that the nearby railroad was not here in 1863. **Continuing on Guilford Station Road, it becomes New Franklin Road.**

WTW 16 – (N 39° 52.855' W 077° 38.134') – **Continue .2 miles on New Franklin Road through the town of New Franklin. Proceed through the traffic light.**

WTW 17 – (N 39° 51.911' W 077° 40.449') – **After 2.4 miles turn left.** Again the modern route here varies somewhat from the original road trace.

WTW 18 – (N 39° 51.499' W 077° 40.528') – **Continue .5 miles**. The large stone farmhouse on the right is the Hege (pronounced 'Hagey') Farm. The fieldstone barn dates from 1818 and the main farmhouse was built in 1822. There are accounts of the Mennonite Deacon Michael Hege's family baking bread for Confederate soldiers enroute to Gettysburg prior to the battle. Mr. Hege kept detailed records of the livestock and property the Confederates had confiscated from his farm while enroute to Gettysburg and noted the loss of a horse, flour and meat taken on July 5 during the retreat. He managed to keep several barrels of whiskey from falling into Confederate hands by burying them in his fields. **Continue into the town of Marion** (named for Revolutionary War hero Francis Marion).

WTW 19 – (N 39° 51.286' W 077° 40.800') - **.4 miles beyond the Hege Farm, turn right onto Route 914 West, Swamp Fox Road.** The original

The Michael Hege farm. *Authors' Photo*

route of the wagon train was off to the right in this vicinity. Traces are visible near the Swamp Fox Farm.

WTW 20 – (N 39° 51.905' W 077° 41.912') – **Proceed 1.3 miles and turn left onto Route 11, The Valley Pike.** Local lore states that this is the vicinity where 4 or 5 wagons from the Train were purposely misdirected to Chambersburg where the Confederate teamsters and wounded men were captured. The original route of the Train is likely to the left, through the town of Marion. Current day Route 11 remains relatively close to the original trace of The Valley Pike. Note there are still a number of period buildings along the route in this area.

WTW 21 – (N 39° 48.227' W 077° 43.363') - **4.7 miles further note the Fleming Farm on the right.** Not related to the retreat of the Wagon Train, but worth noting is the stone obelisk monument at the roadside. This marks the place where 21 year-old Corporal William F. Rihl, of Company C, 1st New York Cavalry, was killed in a skirmish with elements of the 14th Virginia Cavalry on June 22, 1863. Corporal Rihl has the dubious distinction of being the first Union soldier killed north of the Mason Dixon line during Lee's invasion of Pennsylvania. The inscription on the monument reads: *"To the memory of Corporal William F. Rihl, Co. C, First N.Y. Lincoln Cavalry, who was killed on this spot, June 22, 1863. A humble but brave defender of the Union."*

Monument to Cpl. William F. Rihl,
1st New York (Lincoln) Cavalry. *Authors' Photo*

WTW 22 – (N 39° 47.845' W 077° 43.592') - **.3 miles beyond the Fleming Farm, turn left onto Walter Avenue.**

WTW 23 – (N 39° 47.773' W 077° 43.513') – **After .2 miles turn right onto North Carlisle Street** through the historic district of Greencastle. Lee followed this route on his way to Gettysburg and the Wagon Train traveled directly down this street during the retreat.

WTW 24 – (N 39° 47.405' W 077° 43.672') - Stop in the town square (or "diamond" as it was known) where Carlisle Street intersects Baltimore Street. At the southeast corner of the square is a marker noting the July 2, 1863, action here between Confederate cavalry and Union cavalry under Captain Ulric Dahlgren. Dahlgren captured documents informing General Lee that no additional Confederate reinforcements were available. East of the square on Baltimore Street on the rise beyond the Antrim House, citizens barricaded the street. Their July 5 attack against the retreating wagon train originated from here. (**RESET your odometer mileage to 0.0 and continue from the square onto South Carlisle Street.**) Note the number of Civil War era buildings along the route here.

WTW 25 – (N 39° 46.893' W 077° 44.026') – **After .7 miles, turn right onto Route 11**. Here the modern route diverts momentarily from the original route.

Historical marker in the city square at Greencastle, Pennsylvania. *Authors' Photo*

WTW 26 – (N 39° 47.016' W 077° 44.102') – **After .1 mile turn left towards Williamsport on the Williamsport Pike**. In 1863 this was known as Greencastle Road.

WTW 27 – (N 39° 46.627' W 077° 44.275') – **Proceed .5 miles.** This is the vicinity where the Wagon Train was attacked at dawn on July 5, 1863 by Captain Ulric Dahlgren and 100 troopers of the 6th Pennsylvania Cavalry, as well as by a band of 30 to 40 Greencastle civilians organized by local resident Tom Pawling.

WTW 28 – (N 39° 45.525' W 077° 45.293') – **Continuing 1.6 miles you will notice a large, red brick building off to the right.** This is the Johnston Distillery. Local lore tells of a number of Confederate soldiers stopping here enroute to Gettysburg. Dead from the Wagon Train were buried along the route in this vicinity and there are accounts of Southern families coming here after the war to retrieve the bodies and return them home.

WTW 29 – (N 39° 43.281' W 077° 46.107') – **2.7 miles past the Johnston Distillery you will cross the "Mason Dixon Line" from Pennsylvania into Maryland.** Visible in the yard to the left is one of the original stone benchmarks from the 1763-1767 survey of the Mason Dixon Line.

WTW 30 – (N 39° 42.017' W 077° 46.564') – **Continue for 1.5 miles**. The traffic circle in the modern town of Cearfoss is the location of Cunningham's Crossroads. **Take Route 63 South from the circle and stop in the parking**

Traffic circle in Cearfross, Maryland. This was the location of Cunningham's Crossroads, where the Confederate wagon train was attacked. *Authors' Photo*

lot of the convenience store on the right, near the Maryland Civil War Trails marker, WTW 31 – (N 39° 42.000' W 077° 46.623'). This is the vicinity where the Wagon Train was attacked on the afternoon of July 5, 1863, by Captain Abram Jones and elements of the 1st New York and 12th Pennsylvania Cavalry regiments. About 200 yards to the west of Route 63 you can see a white farmhouse on a low bluff (the farm existed at the time of the battle). Jones hid his men behind this bluff prior to charging the Wagon Train.

The store here has public rest stop facilities. **RESET your odometer mileage to 0.0 and turn right, continuing on Route 63 South.**

WTW 32 – (N 39° 39.101' W 077° 48.014') – **Proceed for 3.6 miles, cross the National Pike and continue on Route 63 South.** The ridgeline visible to the left is part of the main Confederate defensive line surrounding Williamsport.

WTW 33 - (N 39° 36.166' W 077° 49.105') – **After 3.7 miles you will enter the town of Williamsport.** The high ground on the left is the location where Imboden anchored the left flank of his defenses.

Cushwa's Basin on the Chesapeake & Ohio Canal
in Williamsport, Maryland. *Authors' Photo*

WTW 34 – (N 39° 36.040' W 077° 49.135') – **Continue .1 mile and turn right onto Potomac Street.**

WTW 35 – (N 39° 36.023' W 077° 49.557')- **After .4 miles, turn right into the parking lot of the C&O Canal Basin.** The National Park Service museum here documents the history of the C&O Canal.

This marks the end of the route of the "Wagon Train of the Wounded." To return to Gettysburg, bear left when leaving the C&O Canal Basin parking area to turn onto Potomac Street. After .2 mile, turn right onto Conococheague Street. Follow the signs to Interstate 81 North. Take Interstate 81 North to Exit – (Old Exit 16) into Chambersburg, and then follow Route 30 East to Gettysburg.

* * *

GPS Waypoints, "The Wagon Train of the Wounded" Driving Tour:

WTW 1:	N 39° 49.057'	W 077° 13.949'
WTW 2:	N 39° 49.273'	W 077° 13.997'
WTW 3:	N 39° 49.862'	W 077° 14.006'

WTW 4:	N 39° 49.883'	W 077° 14.224'
WTW 5:	N 39° 50.513'	W 077° 15.721'
WTW 6:	N 39° 52.008'	W 077° 19.089'
WTW 7:	N 39° 53.077'	W 077° 21.622'
WTW 8:	N 39° 53.847'	W 077° 25.543'
WTW 9:	N 39° 54.413'	W 077° 28.678'
WTW 10:	N 39° 54.359'	W 077° 31.265'
WTW 11:	N 39° 53.960'	W 077° 31.729'
WTW 12:	N 39° 53.566'	W 077° 33.544'
WTW 13:	N 39° 53.018'	W 077° 34.586'
WTW 14:	N 39° 52.758'	W 077° 37.526'
WTW 15:	N 39° 52.874'	W 077° 37.889'
WTW 16:	N 39° 52.855'	W 077° 38.134'
WTW 17:	N 39° 51.911'	W 077° 40.449'
WTW 18:	N 39° 51.499'	W 077° 40.528'
WTW 19:	N 39° 51.286'	W 077° 40.800'
WTW 20:	N 39° 51.905'	W 077° 41.912'
WTW 21:	N 39° 48.227'	W 077° 43.363'
WTW 22:	N 39° 47.845'	W 077° 43.592'
WTW 23:	N 39° 47.773'	W 077° 43.513'
WTW 24:	N 39° 47.405'	W 077° 43.672'
WTW 25:	N 39° 46.893'	W 077° 44.026'
WTW 26:	N 39° 47.016'	W 077° 44.102'
WTW 27:	N 39° 46.627'	W 077° 44.275'
WTW 28:	N 39° 45.525'	W 077° 45.293'
WTW 29:	N 39° 43.281'	W 077° 46.107'
WTW 30:	N 39° 42.017'	W 077° 46.564'
WTW 31:	N 39° 42.000'	W 077° 46.623'
WTW 32:	N 39° 39.101'	W 077° 48.014'
WTW 33:	N 39° 36.166'	W 077° 49.105'
WTW 34:	N 39° 36.040'	W 077° 49.135'
WTW 35:	N 39° 36.023'	W 077° 49.557'

Appendix C

Order of Battle

ARMY OF THE POTOMAC
Maj. Gen. George G. Meade

First Army Corps
Maj. Gen. John Newton

First Division
Brig. Gen. James S. Wadsworth

First Brigade
Col. William W. Robinson
19th Indiana (Col. Samuel J. Williams)
24th Michigan (Capt. Albert M. Edwards)
2nd Wisconsin (Capt. George H. Otis)
6th Wisconsin (Lt. Col. Rufus R. Dawes)
7th Wisconsin (Maj. Mark Finnicum)

Second Brigade
Brig. Gen. Lysander Cutler
7th Indiana (Col. Ira G. Grover)
76th New York (Capt. John E. Cook)
84th New York (14th Brooklyn)
(Col. Edward B. Fowler)
95th New York (Maj. Edward Pye)
147th New York (Maj. George Harney)
56th Pennsylvania (9 cos.)
(Col. J. William Hoffman)

Second Division
Brig. Gen. John C. Robinson

First Brigade
Col. Richard Coulter
16th Maine (Maj. Archibald D. Leavitt)
13th Massachusetts
(Lt. Col. N. Walter Batchelder)
94th New York (Maj. Samuel A. Moffett)
104th New York (Col. Gilbert G. Prey)
107th Pennsylvania
(Capt. Emanuel D. Roath)

Second Brigade
Brig. Gen. Henry Baxter
12th Massachusetts (Lt. Col. David Allen, Jr.)
83rd New York (9th Militia)
(Lt. Col. Joseph A. Moesch)
97th New York (Maj. Charles Northrup)
11th Pennsylvania (Capt. John B. Overmyer)
88th Pennsylvania (Capt. Henry Whiteside)
90th Pennsylvania (Col. Peter Lyle)

Third Division
Brig. Gen. Thomas A. Rowley

First Brigade
Col. Chapman Biddle
80th New York (20th Militia)
(Col. Theodore B. Gates)
121st Pennsylvania (Maj. Alexander Biddle)
142nd Pennsylvania
(Lt. Col. A. B. McCalmont)
151st Pennsylvania (Col. Harrison Allen)

Second Brigade
Col. Edmund L. Dana
143rd Pennsylvania (Lt. Col. John D.
Musser) 149th Pennsylvania
(Capt. James Glenn)
150th Pennsylvania
(Capt. Cornelius C. Widdis)

Third Brigade
Col. Francis V. Randall
13th Vermont (Lt. Col. William D. Munson)
14th Vermont (Col. William T. Nichols)
16th Vermont (Col. Wheelock G. Veazey)

Artillery Brigade
Col. Charles S. Wainwright
Maine Light, 2nd Battery (B)
(Capt. James A. Hall)
Maine Light, 5th Battery (E)
(Capt. Greenleaf T. Stevens)

1st New York Light, Batteries L & E
(Lt. George Breck)
1st Pennsylvania Light, Battery (B)
(Capt. James H. Cooper)
4th United States, Battery (B)
(Lt. James Stewart)

Second Army Corps
Brig. Gen. William Hays

First Division
Brig. Gen. John. C. Caldwell

First Brigade
Col. H. Boyd McKeen
5th New Hampshire
(Lt. Col. Charles E. Hapgood)
61st New York (Col. K. Oscar Broady)
81st Pennsylvania (Lt. Col. Amos Stroh)
148th Pennsylvania
(Lt. Col. Robert McFarlane)

Second Brigade
Col. Patrick Kelly
28th Massachusetts (Col. Richard Byrnes)
63rd New York (2 cos.)
(Capt. Thomas Touhy)
69th New York (2 cos.) (Lt. James J. Smith)
88th New York (2 cos.)
(Capt. Denis F. Burke)
116th Pennsylvania (4 cos.)
(Maj. St. Clair A. Mulholland)

Third Brigade
Lt. Col. John Fraser
52nd New York (Capt. William Scherrer)
57th New York (Lt. Col. Alford B. Chapman)
66th New York (Maj. Peter Nelson)
140th Pennsylvania (Lt. Col. John Fraser)

Fourth Brigade
Col. John R. Brooke
27th Connecticut (2 cos.)
(Maj. James H. Coburn)
2nd Delaware (Capt. Charles H. Christman)
64th New York (Maj. Leman W. Bradley)
53rd Pennsylvania
(Lt. Col. Richard McMichael)

145th Pennsylvania (7 cos.)
(Capt. Moses W. Oliver)

Second Division
Brig. Gen. William Harrow

First Brigade
Col. Francis E. Heath
19th Maine (Lt. Col. Henry W. Cunningham)
15th Massachusetts
(Lt. Col. George C. Joslin)
1st Minnesota and 2nd Co. Minnesota
Sharpshooters (Capt. Henry C. Coates)
82nd New York (2nd Militia)
(Capt. John Darrow)

Second Brigade
Brig. Gen. Alexander S. Webb
69th Pennsylvania (Capt. William Davis)
71st Pennsylvania (Col. Richard Penn Smith)
72nd Pennsylvania
(Lt. Col. Theodore Hesser)
106th Pennsylvania
(Lt. Col. William L. Curry)

Third Brigade
Col. Norman J. Hall
59th New York (Col. Norman J. Hall)
19th Massachusetts
(Col. Arthur F. Devereaux)
20th Massachusetts (Capt. Henry L. Abbott)
7th Michigan (Maj. Sylvanus W. Curtis)
42nd New York (Col. James E. Mallon)
59th New York (4 cos.)
(Capt. William McFadden)

Unattached
Massachusetts Sharpshooters 1st Co.
(Lt. Emerson L. Bicknell)

Third Division
Brig. Gen. Alexander Hays

First Brigade
Col. Samuel S. Carroll
14th Indiana (Col. John Coons)
4th Ohio (Lt. Col. Leonard W. Carpenter)
8th Ohio (Lt. Col. Franklin Sawyer)

7th West Virginia
(Lt. Col. Jonathan H. Lockwood)

Second Brigade
Lt. Col. Francis E. Pierce
14th Connecticut (Maj. Theodore G. Ellis)
1st Delaware (Lt. John D. Dent)
12th New Jersey (Maj. John T. Hill)
10th New York Battalion
(Maj. George F. Hopper)
108th New York (Lt. Col. Francis E. Pierce)

Third Brigade
Lt. Col. James L. Bull
39th New York (4 cos.)
(Maj. Hugo Hildebrandt)
111th New York (Capt. Aaron B. Seeley)
125th New York (Lt. Col. Levin Crandell)
126th New York (Lt. Col. James L. Bull)

Artillery Brigade
Capt. John G. Hazard
1st New York Light, Battery (G) and 14th New York Battery (Lt. Robert E. Rogers)
1st Rhode Island, Battery (A)
(Capt. William A. Arnold)
1st Rhode Island, Battery (B)
(Lt. T. Fred Brown)
1st United States, Battery (I)
(Lt. Tully McCrea)
4th United States, Battery (A)
(Sgt. Frederick Fuger)

Third Army Corps
Maj. Gen. William H. French

First Division
Maj. Gen. David B. Birney

First Brigade
Col. Andrew H. Tippin
57th Pennsylvania (8 cos.)
(Capt. Alanson H. Nelson)
63rd Pennsylvania (Maj. John A. Danks)
68th Pennsylvania (Capt. Milton S. Davis)
105th Pennsylvania (Col. Calvin A. Craig)
114th Pennsylvania (Capt. Edward R. Bowen)
141st Pennsylvania (Col. Henry J. Madill)

Second Brigade
Brig. Gen. J. H. Hobart Ward
20th Indiana (Lt. Col. William C. L. Taylor)
3rd Maine (Col. Moses B. Lakeman)
4th Maine (Capt. Edward Libby)
86th New York
(Lt. Col. Benjamin L. Higgins)
124th New York
(Lt. Col. Francis L. Cummins)
99th Pennsylvania (Maj. John W. Moore)
1st United States Sharpshooters
(Col. Hiram Berdan)
2nd United States Sharpshooters (8 cos.)
(Maj. Homer R. Stoughton)

Third Brigade
Col. P. Regis de Trobriand
17th Maine (Lt. Col. Charles B. Merrill)
3rd Michigan (Lt. Col. Edward S. Pierce)
5th Michigan (Lt. Col. John Pulford)
40th New York (Col. Thomas W. Egan)
110th Pennsylvania (6 cos.)
(Maj. Isaac Rogers)

Second Division
Brig. Gen. Andrew A. Humphreys
Brig. Gen. Joseph B Carr

First Brigade
Brig. Gen. Joseph B. Carr
Lt. Col. Clark B. Baldwin
1st Massachusetts (Lt. Col. Clark B. Baldwin)
11th Massachusetts (Lt. Col. Porter D. Tripp)
16th Massachusetts
(Capt. Matthew Donovan)
12th New Hampshire (Capt. John F. Langley)
11th New Jersey (Lt. John Schoonover)
26th Pennsylvania (Maj. Robert L. Bodine)

Second Brigade
Col. William R. Brewster
70th New York (Col. J. Egbert Farnum)
71st New York (Col. Henry L. Potter)
72nd New York (Lt. Col. John Leonard)
73rd New York (Maj. Michael W. Burns)
74th New York (Lt. Col. Thomas Holt)
120th New York (Maj. John R. Tappen)

Third Brigade
Col. George C. Burling
2nd New Hampshire (Col. Edward L. Bailey)
5th New Jersey (Capt. Henry H. Woolsey)
6th New Jersey (Lt. Col. Stephen R. Gilkyson)
7th New Jersey (Maj. Fred Cooper)
8th New Jersey (Capt. John G. Langston)
115th Pennsylvania (Maj. John P. Dunne)

Artillery Brigade
Capt. A. Judson Clark
1st New Jersey Light, 2nd Battery (B)
(Lt. Robert Sims)
1st New York, Battery (D)
(Capt. George B. Winslow)
New York Light, 4th Battery
(Capt. James E. Smith)
1st Rhode Island Light, Battery (E)
(Lt. Benjamin Freeborn)
4th United States, Battery (K)
(Lt. Robert James)

Fifth Army Corps
Maj. Gen. George Sykes

First Division
Brig. Gen. James Barnes

First Brigade
Col. William S. Tilton
18th Massachusetts (Col. Joseph Hayes)
22nd Massachusetts
(Lt. Col. Thomas Sherwin, Jr.)
1st Michigan (Lt. Col. William A. Throop)
118th Pennsylvania (Lt. Col. James Gwyn)

Second Brigade
Col. Jacob B. Sweitzer
9th Massachusetts (Col. Patrick R. Guiney)
32nd Massachusetts (Col. George L. Prescott)
4th Michigan (Lt. Col. George W. Lumbard)
62nd Pennsylvania (Lt. Col. James C. Hull)

Third Brigade
Col. James C. Rice
20th Maine (Col. Joshua L. Chamberlain)
16th Michigan (Lt. Col. Norval E. Welch)
44th New York (Lt. Col. Freeman Conner)
83rd Pennsylvania
(Capt. Orpeus S. Woodward)

Second Division
Brig. Gen. Romeyn B. Ayres

First Brigade
Col. Hannibal Day
3rd United States (6 cos.)
(Capt. Richard G. Lay)
4th United States (4 cos.)
(Capt. Julius W. Adams, Jr.)
6th United States (5 cos.)
(Capt. Levi C. Bootes)
12th United States (8 cos.)
(Capt. Thomas S. Dunn)
14th United States (8 cos.)
(Maj. Grotius R. Giddings)

Second Brigade
Col. Sidney Burbank
2nd United States (6 cos.)
(Capt. Samuel A. McKee)
7th United States (4 cos.)
(Capt. David P. Hancock)
10th United States (3 cos.)
(Capt. William Clinton)
11th United States (6 cos.)
(Maj. DeLancey Floyd-Jones)
17th United States (7 cos.)
(Lt. Col. J. Durell Greene)

Third Brigade
Col. Kenner Garrard
140th New York (Lt. Col. Louis Ernst)
146th New York (Lt. Col. David T. Jenkins)
91st Pennsylvania (Lt. Col. Joseph H. Sinex)
155th Pennsylvania (Lt. Col. John H. Cain)

Third Division
Brig. Gen. Samuel W. Crawford

First Brigade
Col. William McCandless
1st Pennsylvania Reserves (9 cos.)
(Col. William C. Talley)
2nd Pennsylvania Reserves
(Lt. Col. George A. Woodward)
6th Pennsylvania Reserves

(Lt. Col. Wellington H. Ent)
13th Pennsylvania Reserves
(Maj. William R. Hartshorne)

Third Brigade
Col. Joseph W. Fisher
5th Pennsylvania Reserves
(Lt. Col. George Dare)
9th Pennsylvania Reserves
(Lt. James McK. Snodgrass)
10th Pennsylvania Reserves
(Col. Adoniram J. Warner)
11th Pennsylvania Reserves
(Col. Samuel M. Jackson)
12th Pennsylvania Reserves (9 cos.)
(Col. Martin D. Hardin)

Artillery Brigade
Capt. Augustus P. Martin
Massachusetts Light, 3rd Battery (C)
(Lt. Aaron F. Walcott)
1st New York Light, Battery C)
(Capt. Almont Barnes)
1st Ohio Light, Battery (L)
(Capt. Frank C. Gibbs)
5th United States, Battery (D)
(Lt. Benjamin F. Rittenhouse)
5th United States, Battery (I)
(Lt. Charles C. MacConnell)

Sixth Army Corps
Maj. Gen. John Sedgwick

First Division
Brig. Gen. Horatio G. Wright

First Brigade
Brig. Gen. Alfred T. A. Torbert
1st New Jersey (Lt. Col. William Henry, Jr.)
2nd New Jersey (Lt. Col. Charles Wiebecke)
3rd New Jersey (Col. Henry W. Brown)
15th New Jersey (Col. William H. Penrose)

Second Brigade
Brig. Gen. Joseph J. Bartlett
5th Maine (Col. Clark S. Edwards)
121st New York (Col. Emory Upton)
95th Pennsylvania (Lt. Col. Edward Carroll)
96th Pennsylvania (Maj. William H. Lessig)

Third Brigade
Brig. Gen. David A. Russell
6th Maine (Col. Hiram Burnham)
49th Pennsylvania (4 cos.)
(Lt. Col. Thomas L. Hulings)
119th Pennsylvania (Col. Peter S. Ellmaker)
5th Wisconsin (Col. Thomas S. Allen)

Second Division
Brig. Gen. Albion P. Howe

Second Brigade
Col. Lewis A. Grant
2nd Vermont (Col. James H. Walbridge)
3rd Vermont (Col. Thomas O. Seaver)
4th Vermont (Col. Charles B. Stoughton)
5th Vermont (Lt. Col. John R. Lewis)
6th Vermont (Col. Elisha L. Barney)

Third Brigade
Brig. Gen. Thomas H. Neill
7th Maine (6 cos.) (Lt. Col. Selden Connor)
33rd New York (detach.)
(Capt. Henry J. Gifford)
43rd New York (Lt. Col. John Wilson)
49th New York (Col. Daniel D. Bidwell)
77th New York (Lt. Col. Winsor B. French)
61st Pennsylvania (Lt. Col. George F. Smith)

Third Division
Brig. Gen. Frank Wheaton

First Brigade
Brig. Gen. Alexander Shaler
65th New York (Col. Joseph E. Hamblin)
67th New York (Col. Nelson Cross)
122nd New York (Col. Silas Titus)
23rd Pennsylvania (Lt. Col. John F. Glenn)
82nd Pennsylvania (Col. Isaac C. Bassett)

Second Brigade
Col. Henry L. Eustis
7th Massachusetts
(Lt. Col. Franklin P. Harrow)
10th Massachusetts
(Lt. Col. Joseph B. Parsons)
37th Massachusetts (Col. Oliver Edwards)
2nd Rhode Island (Col. Horatio Rogers, Jr.)

Third Brigade
Col. David J. Nevin
62nd New York (Col. David J. Nevin)
93rd Pennsylvania (Maj. John I. Nevin)
98th Pennsylvania (Maj. John B. Kohler)
139th Pennsylvania (Col. Fredrick H. Collier)

Artillery Brigade
Col. Charles H. Tompkins
Massachusetts Light, 1st Battery (A)
(Capt. William H. McCartney)
New York Light, 1st Battery
(Capt. Andrew Cowan)
New York Light, 3rd Battery
(Capt. William A. Harn)
1st Rhode Island Light, Battery (C)
(Capt. Richard Waterman)
1st Rhode Island Light, Battery (G)
(Capt. George A. Adams)
2nd United States, Battery (D)
(Lt. Edward B. Williston)
2nd United States, Battery (G)
(Lt. John H. Butler)
5th United States, Battery (F)
(Lt. Leonard Martin)

Eleventh Army Corps
Maj. Gen. Oliver O. Howard

First Division
Brig. Gen. Adelbert Ames

First Brigade
Col. Leopold von Gilsa
41st New York (9 cos.)
(Lt. Col. Detleo Von Einsiedal)
54th New York (Lt. Ernst Both)
68th New York (Col. Gotthilf Bourry)
153rd Pennsylvania (Maj. John F. Frueauff)

Second Brigade
Col. Andrew L. Harris
17th Connecticut (Maj. Allen G. Brady)
25th Ohio (Lt. Isreal White)
75th Ohio (Capt. George B. Fox)
107th Ohio (Capt. John M. Lutz)

Second Division
Brig. Gen. Adolph von Steinwehr

First Brigade
Col. Charles R. Coster
134th New York (Lt. Col. Allan H. Jackson)
154th New York (Lt. Col. Daniel B. Allen)
27th Pennsylvania (Lt. Col. Lorenz Cantador)
73rd Pennsylvania (Capt. Daniel F. Kelly)

Second Brigade
Col. Orland Smith
33rd Massachusetts
(Col. Adin B. Underwood)
136th New York (Col. James Wood, Jr.)
55th Ohio (Col. Charles B. Gambee)
73rd Ohio (Lt. Col. Richard Long)

Third Division
Maj. Gen. Carl Schurz

First Brigade
Brig. Gen. Alexander Schimmelfennig
82nd Illinois (Col. Edward S. Salomon)
45th New York (Lt. Col. Adophus Dobke)
157th New York (Col. Philip P. Brown, Jr.)
61st Ohio (Col. Stephen J. McGroarty)
74th Pennsylvania (Capt. Henry Krauseneck)

Second Brigade
Col. Wladimir Krzyanowski
58th New York (Capt. Emil Koenig)
119th New York (Lt. Col. Edward F. Lloyd)
82nd Ohio (Lt. Col. David Thomson)
75th Pennsylvania (Major August Ledig)
26th Wisconsin (Capt. John W. Fuchs)

Artillery Brigade
Maj. Thomas W. Osborn
1st New York Light, Battery (I)
(Capt. Michael Weidrich)
New York Light, 13th Battery
(Lt. William Wheeler)
1st Ohio Light, Battery (I)
(Capt. Hubert Dilger)
1st Ohio Light, Battery (K)
(Capt. Lewis Heckman)
United States, Battery (G)
(Lt. Eugene A. Bancroft)

Twelfth Army Corps
Maj. Gen. Henry W. Slocum

First Division
Brig. Gen. Alpheus S. Williams

First Brigade
Col. Archibald L. McDougall
5th Connecticut (Col. Warren W. Packer)
20th Connecticut
(Lt. Col. William B. Wooster)
3rd Maryland (Col. Joseph M. Sudsburg)
123rd New York (Capt. Adolphus H. Tanner)
145th New York (Col. Edward J. Price)
46th Pennsylvania (Col. James L. Selfridge)

Second Brigade
Brig. Gen. Henry H. Lockwood
1st Maryland Potomac Home Brigade
(Col. William P. Maulsby)
1st Maryland Eastern Shore
(Col. James Wallace)
150th New York (Col. John H. Ketcham)

Third Brigade
Brig. Gen. Thomas H. Ruger
27th Indiana (Lt. Col. John R. Fesler)
2nd Massachusetts (Maj. Charles F. Morse)
13th New Jersey (Col. Ezra A. Carman)
107th New York (Col. Nirom M. Crane)
3rd Wisconsin (Col. William Hawley)

Second Division
Brig. Gen. John W. Geary

First Brigade
Col. Charles Candy
5th Ohio (Col. John H. Patrick)
7th Ohio (Col. William R. Creighton)
29th Ohio (Capt. Edward Hayes)
66th Ohio (Lt. Col. Eugene Powell)
28th Pennsylvania (Capt. John H. Flynn)
147th Pennsylvania (8 cos.)
(Lt. Col. Ario Pardee, Jr.)

Second Brigade
Brig. Gen. Thomas L. Kane
29th Pennsylvania (Col. William Rickards, Jr.)
109th Pennsylvania
(Capt. Frederick L. Gimber)
111th Pennsylvania
(Col. George A. Cobham, Jr.)

Third Brigade
Brig. Gen. George S. Greene
60th New York (Col. Abel Godard)
78th New York
(Lt. Col. Herbert Von Hammerstein)
102nd New York (Capt. Lewis R. Stegman)
137th New York (Col. David Ireland)
149th New York (Lt. Col. Charles B. Randall)

Artillery Brigade
Lt. Edward D. Muhlenberg
1st New York Light, Battery (M)
(Lt. Charles E. Winegar)
Pennsylvania Light, Battery (E)
(Lt. Charles A. Atwell)
4th United States, Battery (F)
(Lt. Sylvanus T. Rugg)
5th United States, Battery (K)
(Lt. David H. Kinzie)

Cavalry Corps
Maj. Gen. Alfred Pleasonton

First Division
Brig. Gen. John Buford

First Brigade
Col. William Gamble
8th Illinois (Maj. John L. Beveridge)
12th Illinois (6 cos.)
(Lt. Col. Hasbrouck Davis)
3rd Indiana (6 cos.)
(Col. George H. Chapman)
8th New York (Lt. Col. William L. Markell)

Second Brigade
Col. Thomas C. Devin
6th New York (Maj. William E. Beardsley)
9th New York (Col. William Sackett)
17th Pennsylvania (Col. Josiah H. Kellogg)
3rd West Virginia (2 cos.)
(Capt. Seymour B. Conger)

Reserve Brigade
Brig. Gen. Wesley Merritt
6th Pennsylvania (Maj. James H. Hazeltine)
1st United States (Capt. Richard S. C. Lord)
2nd United States
(Capt. Theophilus F. Rodenbough)

5th United States (Capt. Julius W. Mason)
6th United States (Capt. Ira W. Claflin)

Second Division
Brig. Gen. David McM. Gregg

First Brigade
Col. John B. McIntosh
1st Maryland (11 cos.)
(Lt. Col. James M. Deems)
Purnell (Maryland) Legion Co. (A)
(Capt. Robert E. Duvall)
1st Massachusetts (Lt. Col. Greely S. Curtis)
1st New Jersey (Maj. Myron H. Beaumont)
1st Pennsylvania (Col. John P. Taylor)
3rd Pennsylvania (Lt. Col. Edward S. Jones)
3rd Pennsylvania Artillery, Battery H
(Capt. William D. Rank)

Second Brigade
Col. Pennock Huey
2d New York (Lt. Col. Otto Harhaus)
4th New York (Lt. Col. Augustus Pruyn)
6th Ohio (10 companies)
(Maj. William Stedman)
8th Pennsylvania (Capt. William A. Corrie)

Third Brigade
Col. J. Irvin Gregg
1st Maine (10 cos.)
(Lt. Col. Charles H. Smith)
10th New York (Maj. M. Henry Avery)
4th Pennsylvania (Lt. Col. William E. Doster)
16th Pennsylvania (Lt. Col. John K. Robison)

Third Division
Brig. Gen. Judson Kilpatrick

First Brigade
Col. Nathaniel P. Richmond
Col. Othneil DeForest
5th New York (Maj. John Hammond)
18th Pennsylvania
(Lt. Col. William P. Brinton)
1st Vermont (Lt. Col. Addison W. Preston)
1st West Virginia (10 cos.)
(Maj. Charles E. Capehart)

Second Brigade
Brig. Gen. George A. Custer
1st Michigan (Col. Charles H. Town)
5th Michigan (Col. Russell A. Alger)
6th Michigan (Col. George Gray)
7th Michigan (10 cos.)
(Col. William D. Mann)

Horse Artillery

1st Brigade
Capt. James M. Robertson
9th Michigan Battery (Capt. Jabez. J. Daniels)
6th New York Battery
(Capt. Joseph W. Martin)
2nd United States, Batteries (B & L)
(Lt. Edward Heaton)
2nd United States, Battery (M)
(Lt. A. C. M. Pennington, Jr.)
4th United States, Battery (E)
(Lt. Samuel S. Elder)

2nd Brigade
Capt. John C. Tidball
1st United States, Batteries (E & G)
(Capt. Alanson M. Randol)
1st United States, Battery (K)
(Capt. William M. Graham)
2nd United States, Battery (A)
(Lt. John H. Calef)

Artillery Reserve
Brig. Gen. Robert O. Tyler

1st Brigade (Regular)
Capt. Dunbar R. Ransom
1st United States, Battery (H)
(Lt. Chandler P. Eakin)
3rd United States, Batteries (F & K)
(Lt. John G. Turnbull)
4th United States, Battery (C)
(Lt. Evan Thomas)
5th United States, Battery (C)
(Lt. Gulian V. Weir)

1st Volunteer Brigade
Lt. Col. Freeman McGilvery
Massachusetts Light, 5th Battery (E)
(Capt. Charles A. Phillips)

Massachusetts Light, 9th Battery
(Capt. John Bigelow)
New York Light, 15th Battery
(Capt. Patrick Hart)
Pennsylvania Light, Batteries (C & F)
(Capt. James Thompson)

2nd Volunteer Brigade
Capt. Elijah D. Taft
Connecticut Light, 2nd Battery
(Capt. John W. Sterling)
New York Light, 5th Battery
(Capt. Elijah D. Taft)

3rd Volunteer Brigade
Capt. James F. Huntington
New Hampshire Light, 1st Battery
(Capt. Frederick M. Edgell)
1st Ohio Light, Battery (H)
(Lt. George W. Norton)
1st Pennsylvania Light, Batteries (F & G)
(Capt. R. Bruce Ricketts)
West Virginia Light, Battery (C)
(Capt. Wallace Hill)

4th Volunteer Brigade
Capt. Robert H. Fitzhugh
Maine Light, 6th Battery (F)
(Lt. Edwin B. Dow)
Maryland Light, Battery (A)
(Capt. James H. Rigby)
1st New Jersey Light, Battery (A)
(Lt. Agustin N. Parsons)
1st New York Light, Battery (G)
(Capt. Nelson Ames)
1st New York Light, Battery (K)
(Capt. Robert H. Fitzhugh)
11th New York Battery
(Capt. Robert H. Fitzhugh)

Train Guard

4th New Jersey (4 cos.) (Maj. Charles Ewing)

DEPARTMENT OF THE SUSQUEHANNA
Maj. Gen. Darius N. Couch

Pennsylvania Home Guard
Maj. Granville O. Haller
26th Pennsylvania Militia:
(Col William W. Jennings)
First Troop Philadelphia City Cavalry (1 co.)
(Capt. Samuel J. Randall)
Bell's Adams County Cavalry (1 co.)
(Capt. Robert Bell)
Pa. Home Guard Scouts
(Capt. David McConaughy)
20th Pennsylvania Militia
(Col. William B. Thomas)
27th Pennsylvania Militia
(Col. Jacob G. Frick)

First Division
Brig. Gen. William F. Smith

First Brigade
Maj. Gen. N.Y. Militia: Charles W. Sandford
20th Pennsylvania Cavalry
(Col. John E. Wynkoop)
21st Pennsylvania Infantry
(Col. James A. Beaver)
67th New York Militia
(Col. Chauncey Abbott)
68th New York Militia (Col. David S. Forbes)
31st Pennsylvania Militia
(Col. John Newcomer)

Second Brigade
N.Y. Militia Brig. Gen. Charles Yates
5th New York Militia
12th New York Militia

Third Brigade
Brig. Gen. Orris S. Ferry
Pennsylvania Militia
(Col. Alexander K. McClure)
65th New York Militia (Col Jacob Krettner)
74th New York Militia (Col. Watson A. Fox)
29th Pennsylvania Militia
(Col. Joseph W. Hawley)
12th Pennsylvania Cavalry
(Col. Lewis B. Pierce)

1st New York Cavalry
(Capt. William H. Boyd)
Artillery Battery
(Lt. Comdr. Pendelton C. Watmough, USN)

Fourth Brigade
Brig. Gen. Joseph F. Knipe
8th New York Militia (Col. Joshua Varian)
71st New York Militia
(Col. Benjamin Traffold)

Fifth Brigade
Brig. Gen. N.Y. Militia: Philip S. Crooke
13th New York Militia
(Col. John B. Woodward)
28th New York Militia (Col. Michael Bennett)

Sixth Brigade
Brig. Gen. N.Y. Militia: Jesse C. Smith
23rd New York Militia
(Col. William Everdell, Jr.)
52nd New York Militia
(Col. Matthias W. Cole)
56th New York Militia (Col. John Q. Adams)

Seventh Brigade
Brig. Gen. N.Y. Militia: John Ewen
11th New York Militia
(Col. Joachim Maidhof)
22nd New York Militia
(Col. Lloyd Aspinwall)
37th New York Militia (Col. C. Roome)
28th Pennsylvania Militia
(Col. James Chamberlin)
32nd Pennsylvania Militia
(Col. Charles S. Smith)
33rd Pennsylvania Militia
(Col. William W. Taylor)
27th Pennsylvania Militia
(Lt. Col. David Green)

Landis' Battery Philadelphia Militia
(Capt. Henry Landis)

Second Division
Maj. Gen. Napoleon J. Dana

First Brigade
Brig. Gen. N.Y. Militia: Charles Yates
5th New York Militia (Col. Burger)
12th New York Militia
(Col. William O. Ward)
20th Pennsylvania Militia
(Col. William B. Thomas)
26th Pennsylvania Militia
(Col. William W. Jennings)
35th Pennsylvania Militia
(Col. Henry McKean)
45th Pennsylvania Militia
(Col. James T. Clancy)

Second Brigade
Brig. Gen. James Nagle
30th Pennsylvania Militia
(Col. William N. Monies)
37th Pennsylvania Militia (Col. John Troup)
38th Pennsylvania Militia
(Col. Melchior H. Hom)
39th Pennsylvania Militia
(Lt. Col. James H. Campbell)
41st Pennsylvania Militia
(Col. Edward R. Mayer)

Third Brigade
Col. Emlen Franklin
40th Pennsylvania Militia (Col. Alfred Dale)
42nd Pennsylvania Militia
(Col. Charles H. Hunter)
43rd Pennsylvania Militia
(Col. William W. Stott)
44th Pennsylvania Militia
(Col. Enos Woodward)
47th Pennsylvania Militia
(Col. James B. Wickersham)
50th Pennsylvania Militia
(Lt. Col. Thaddeus Stevens, Jr.)

Cavalry: Capt. James S. Brisbin

MIDDLE DEPARTMENT (8th CORPS)
Maj. Gen. Robert C. Schenck

First Division
Brig. Gen. Benjamin F. Kelley

First Brigade
Brig. Gen. Erasmus B. Tyler
47th New York Militia
(Col. Jeremiah V. Meserole)

84th New York Militia
(Col. Frederick A. Conkling)
1st Delaware Cavalry
(Maj. Napoleon B. Knight)
Purnell Legion Cavalry (1 co.)
(Capt. Thomas H. Watkins)
Baltimore Light Artillery
(Lt. H. Eugene Alexander)
5th New York Heavy Artillery
(Maj. Caspar Urban)
3rd Pennsylvania Heavy Artillery, Battery H
(Capt. William D. Rank)
Maryland Junior Battery
(Capt. John M. Bruce)

Second Brigade
Brig. Gen. William H. Morris
5th Maryland Infantry (Col. W. L. Schley)
50th New York Engineers
Gaskill's Pennsylvania Engineer Company
1st Massachusetts Heavy Artillery (4 cos.)
(Col. Thomas R. Tannatt)
6th New York Heavy Artillery
(Col. John H. Kitching)
4th Maine Battery

Third Brigade
Col. Benjamin F. Smith
126th Ohio Infantry (Col. Benjamin F. Smith)
106th New York Infantry
(Col. Edward C. James)
15th West Virginia Infantry
1st Maryland Potomac Home
Guard Cavalry Battalion
2nd Maryland Potomac Home
Guard Cavalry Battalion
1st West Virginia Artillery, Battery F
(Capt. Thomas A. Maulsey)

Fourth Brigade
Col. Jacob M. Campbell
54th Pennsylvania Infantry
(Col. Jacob M. Campbell)
1st West Virginia Infantry
(Col. Joseph Thoburn)
Lafayette Cavalry
Washington County Cavalry
Ringgold Cavalry

1st West Virginia Artillery, Battery E
(Capt. Alexander C. Moore)

Fifth Brigade
Col. James A. Mulligan
2nd Maryland Potomac Home Guard
(Col. Robert Bruce)
23rd Illinois Infantry (Col. James A. Mulligan)
14th West Virginia Infantry
(Maj. Daniel D. Johnson)
1st Illinois Artillery, Battery L
(Capt. John Rourke)

Sixth Brigade
Col. N. Wilkinson
6th West Virginia Infantry (Col N. Wilkinson)
11th West Virginia Infantry
(Maj. Van H. Bukey)

Second Division
Maj. Gen. Robert H. Milroy

First Brigade
Brig. Gen. Washington L. Elliott
110th Ohio Infantry (Col. Joseph W. Keifer)
116th Ohio Infantry (Maj. W. T. Morris)
122nd Ohio Infantry (Col. William H. Ball)
123rd Ohio Infantry (Col. William T. Wilson)
12th Pennsylvania Cavalry
(Col. Joseph L. Moss)
13th Pennsylvania Cavalry
(Maj. Michael Kerwin)
1st West Virginia Artillery, Battery D
(Capt. John Carlin)
5th U. S. Artillery, Battery L
(Edmund Dana Spooner)

Third Division
Brig. Gen. Eliakim P. Scammon

First Brigade
Col. Rutherford B. Hayes
23rd Ohio Infantry
(Col. Rutherford B. Hayes)
5th West Virginia Infantry
(Lt. Col. Abia A. Tomlinson)
13th West Virginia Infantry
(Col. William Rufus Brown)
1st West Virginia Cavalry (2 cos.)

3rd West Virginia Cavalry, Co. G
(Capt. John S. Witcher)
Simmonds' Kentucky Battery
(Capt. Seta J. Simmonds)

Second Brigade
Col. Carr B. White
12th Ohio Infantry (Col. Carr Bailey White)
34th Ohio Infantry (Maj. John W. Shaw)
91st Ohio Infantry (Col. John A. Turley)
2nd West Virginia Cavalry, Cos. G & K
(Capt. Edward S. Morgan)
1st Ohio Independent Battery
(Capt. James R. McMullin)

1st Separate Brigade
Brig. Gen. Henry Hayes Lockwood
1st Maryland Eastern Shore Infantry
(Col. James Wallace)
1st Maryland Potomac Home Guard Battalion
(Col. William F. Maulsby)
1st Delaware Cavalry (4 cos.)
(Maj. Napoleon B. Knight)
Smith's Maryland Cavalry
Purnell Legion Cavalry, Cos. A & C
11th New York Cavalry (3 cos.)
(Lt. Henry C. Bates)

2nd Separate Brigade
Bvt. Brig. Gen. William H. Morris
5th Delaware Infantry
7th New York Militia
17th New York Militia
(Lt. Col. John P. Jenkins)
18th New York Militia (Col. James Rider)
55th New York Militia
(Lt. Col. Samuel Graham)
69th New York Militia (Col. Mathew Murphy)
179th Pennsylvania Infantry
Patapsco (Md.) Guards
2nd U. S. Artillery, Battery I
(Lt. James E. Wilson)
5th New York Heavy Artillery
(Col. Samuel Graham)
8th New York Heavy Artillery
(Col. Peter A, Porter)

**FRENCH'S COMMAND,
HARPERS FERRY**

Maj. Gen. William H. French (became part of Army of the Potomac, July 1863)

1st Maryland Infantry
4th Maryland Infantry
7th Maryland Infantry
8th Maryland Infantry
14th New Jersey Infantry
(Col. William Snyder Truex)
151st New York Infantry
10th Vermont Infantry (Col. A. B. Jewett)
4th Maine Artillery Battery
17th Indiana Artillery Battery
Baltimore Light Artillery Battery
10th Massachusetts Battery
1st Massachusetts Heavy Artillery (4 cos.)
(Col. Thomas R. Tannett)
6th New York Heavy Artillery
(Col. John Howard Kitching)
1st West Virginia Artillery Battery F
(Capt. Thomas A. Maulsey)

First Division (organized at Harpers Ferry, July 8)
Brig. Gen. Henry M. Naglee

First Brigade
Col. George D. Wells
34th Massachusetts Infantry
(Lt. Col. William S. Lincoln)
43rd Massachusetts Infantry
175th Pennsylvania Infantry
1st Connecticut Cavalry Battalion
(Capt. Erastus Blakeslee)

Second Brigade
Col. P. A. Porter
9th Maryland Infantry
10th Maryland Infantry
8th New York Heavy Artillery

ARMY OF NORTHERN VIRGINIA
General Robert E. Lee

First Army Corps
Lt. Gen. James Longstreet

McLaws' Division
Maj. Gen. Lafayette McLaws

Kershaw's Brigade
Brig. Gen. Joseph B. Kershaw
2nd South Carolina (Lt. Col. F. Gaillard)
3rd South Carolina (Col. J. D. Nance)
7th South Carolina (Col. D. Wyatt Aiken)
8th South Carolina (Col. John W. Henagan)
15th South Carolina (Maj. William M. Gist)
3rd South Carolina Battalion
(Lt. Col. William G. Rice)

Semmes's Brigade
Col. Goode Bryan
10th Georgia (Col. John B. Weems)
50th Georgia (Col. William R. Manning)
51st Georgia (Col. Edward Ball)
53rd Georgia (Col. James P. Simms)

Barksdale's Brigade
Col. Benjamin G. Humphreys
13th Mississippi (Col. John W. Carter)
17th Mississippi (Lt. Col. John C. Fiser)
18th Mississippi (Lt. Col. W. H. Luse)
21st Mississippi
(Col. Benjamin G. Humphreys)

Wofford's Brigade
Brig. Gen. William T. Wofford
16th Georgia (Col. Goode Bryan)
18th Georgia (Lt. Col. Solon Z. Ruff)
24th Georgia (Col. Robert McMillin)
Cobb's (Georgia) Legion
(Lt. Col. Luther J. Glenn)
Phillips' (Georgia) Legion
(Lt. Col. Elihu S. Barclay)

Artillery
Col. Henry Coalter Cabell
1st North Carolina Artillery Battery (A)
(Capt. Basil C. Manly)
Pulaski (Georgia) Artillery (Lt. W. J. Furlong)
1st Richmond Howitzers
(Capt. Edward S. McCarthy)
Troup (Georgia) Artillery (Lt. C. W. Motes)

Pickett's Division
Maj. Gen. George E. Pickett

Garnett's Brigade
Col. Eppa Hunton
8th Virginia (Col. Eppa Hunton)
18th Virginia (Lt. Col. Henry A. Carrington)
19th Virginia (Lt. Col. John T. Ellis)
28th Virginia (Lt. Col. William Watts)
56th Virginia (Lt. Col. P. P. Slaughter)

Kemper's Brigade
Col. Joseph Mayo, Jr.
1st Virginia (Lt. Col. F. G. Skinner)
3rd Virginia (Lt. Col. A. D. Callcote)
7th Virginia (Lt. Col. C. C. Flowerree)
11th Virginia (Maj. Kirkwood Otey)
24th Virginia (Col. William R. Terry)

Armistead's Brigade
Col. William R. Aylett
9th Virginia (Maj. John C. Owens)
14th Virginia (Lt. Col. William White)
38th Virginia (Lt. Col. P. B. Whittle)
53rd Virginia (Col. William R. Aylett)
57th Virginia (Col. John Bowie Magruder)

Artillery
Maj. James Dearing
Fauquier (Virginia) Artillery
(Capt. Robert M. Stribling)
Hampden (Virginia) Artillery
(Capt. William H. Caskie)
Richmond Fayette Artillery
(Capt. Miles C. Macon)
Lynchburg (Virginia) Artillery
(Capt. Joseph G. Blount)

Hood's Division
Brig. Gen. Evander M. Law

Law's Brigade
Col. James L. Sheffield
4th Alabama (Col. Lawrence H. Scruggs)
15th Alabama (Col. William C. Oates)
44th Alabama (Col. William F. Perry)
47th Alabama (Maj. J. M. Campbell)
48th Alabama (Capt. T. J. Eubanks)

Robertson's Brigade
Brig. Gen. Jerome B. Robertson

3rd Arkansas (Lt. Col. R. S. Taylor)
1st Texas (Col. Phillip A. Work)
4th Texas (Maj. J. P. Bane)
5th Texas (Maj. J. C. Rogers)

Anderson's Brigade
Col. William W. White
7th Georgia (Col. William W. White)
8th Georgia (Col. John R. Towers)
9th Georgia (Capt. George Hillyer)
11th Georgia (Capt. William H. Mitchell)
59th Georgia (Capt. M. G. Bass)

Benning's Brigade
Brig. Gen. Henry L. Benning
2nd Georgia (Maj. W. S. Shepherd)
15th Georgia (Col. M. Dudley DuBose)
17th Georgia (Col. Wesley C. Hodges)
20th Georgia (Lt. Col. J. D. Waddell)

Artillery
Maj. Mathis W. Henry
Branch (North Carolina) Artillery
(Capt. Alexander C. Latham)
German (South Carolina) Artillery
(Capt. William K. Bachman)
Palmetto (South Carolina) Light Artillery
(Capt. Hugh R. Garden)
Rowan (North Carolina) Artillery
(Capt. James Reilly)

Artillery Reserve
Col. James B. Walton

Alexander's Battalion
Col. Edward P. Alexander
Ashland (Virginia) Artillery
(Lt. James Woolfolk)
Bedford (Virginia) Artillery
(Capt. Tyler C. Jordan)
Brooks (South Carolina) Artillery
(Lt. S. C. Gilbert)
Madison (Louisiana) Artillery
(Capt. George V. Moody)
Virginia (Richmond) Battery
(Capt. William W. Parker)
Virginia (Bath) Battery
(Capt. Osmond B. Taylor)

Washington (Louisiana) Artillery
Maj. Benjamin F. Eshleman
1st Company (Capt. Charles W. Squires)
2nd Company (Capt. John B. Richardson)
3rd Company (Capt. Merritt B. Miller)
4th Company (Lt. H. A. Battles)

Second Army Corps
Lt. Gen. Richard S. Ewell

Early's Division
Maj. Gen. Jubal A. Early

Hays' Brigade
Brig. Gen. Harry T. Hays
5th Louisiana (Capt. T. H. Biscoe)
6th Louisiana (Lt. Col. Joseph Hanlon)
7th Louisiana (Col. Davidson B. Penn)
8th Louisiana (Maj. G. A. Lester)
9th Louisiana (Col. Leroy A. Stafford)

Smith's Brigade
Brig. Gen. William Smith
31st Virginia (Col. John S. Hoffman)
49th Virginia (Lt. Col. J. Catlett Gibson)
52nd Virginia (Lt. Col. James H. Skinner)

Hoke's Brigade
Col. A. C. Godwin
6th North Carolina
(Maj. Samuel D. McD. Tate)
21st North Carolina
(Col. William W. Kirkland)
57th North Carolina
(Col. Archibald C. Godwin)

Gordon's Brigade
Brig. Gen. John B. Gordon
13th Georgia (Col. James L. Smith)
26th Georgia (Col. Edmund N. Atkinson)
31st Georgia (Col. Clement A. Evans)
38th Georgia (Capt. William L. McLeod)
60th Georgia (Capt. Waters B. Jones)
61st Georgia (Col. John H. Lamar)

Artillery
Lt. Col. Hilary P. Jones
Charlottesville (Virginia) Artillery (Capt.
James McD. Carrington)

Courtney (Virginia) Artillery
(Capt. William A. Tanner)
Louisiana Guard Artillery
(Capt. Charles A. Green)
Staunton (Virginia) Artillery
(Capt. Asher W. Garber)

Rodes' Division
Maj. Gen. Robert E. Rodes

Daniel's Brigade
Brig. Gen. Junius Daniel
32nd North Carolina
(Col. Edmund C. Brabble)
43rd North Carolina (Lt. Col. W. G. Lewis)
45th North Carolina (Capt. J. A. Hopkins)
53rd North Carolina (Col. William A. Owens)
2nd North Carolina Battalion
(Capt. Van Brown)

Iverson's Brigade
Brig. Gen. Alfred Iverson
5th North Carolina
(Capt. Benjamin Robinson)
12th North Carolina
(Lt. Col. William S. Davis)
20th North Carolina (Capt. Lewis T. Hicks)
23rd North Carolina
(Capt. William H. Johnston)

Doles' Brigade
Brig. Gen. George Doles
4th Georgia (Maj. M. H. Willis)
12th Georgia (Col. Edward Willis)
21st Georgia (Col. John T. Mercer)
44th Georgia (Maj. W. H. Peebles)

Ramseur's Brigade
Brig. Gen. Stephen D. Ramseur
2nd North Carolina (Capt. James T. Scales)
4th North Carolina (Col. Bryan Grimes)
14th North Carolina
(Maj. Joseph H. Lambeth)
30th North Carolina (Maj. W. W. Sillers)

O'Neal's Brigade
Col. Edward A. O'Neal
3rd Alabama (Col. Cullen A. Battle)
5th Alabama (Col. Josephus M. Hall)
6th Alabama (Capt. M. L. Bowie)
12th Alabama (Col. Samuel B. Pickens)
26th Alabama (Lt. Col. John C. Goodgame)

Artillery
Lt. Col. Thomas H. Carter
Jeff Davis (Alabama) Artillery
(Capt. William J. Reese)
King William (Virginia) Artillery
(Capt. William P. Carter)
Morris (Virginia) Artillery
(Capt. Richard C. M. Page)
Orange (Virginia) Artillery
(Capt. Charles W. Fry)

Johnson's Division
Maj. Gen. Edward Johnson

Steuart's Brigade
Brig. Gen. George H. Steuart
1st Maryland Battalion Infantry
(Capt. J. P. Crane)
1st North Carolina
(Lt. Col. Hamilton Allen Brown)
3rd North Carolina (Maj. William M. Parsley)
10th Virginia (Col. Edward T. H. Warren)
23rd Virginia (Lt. Col. Simeon T. Walton)
37th Virginia (Maj. Henry C. Wood)

Nicholls' Brigade
Col. Jesse M. Williams
1st Louisiana (Col. Michael Nolan)
2nd Louisiana (Lt. Col. Ross E. Burke)
10th Louisiana (Maj. Thomas N. Powell)
14th Louisiana (Lt. Col. David Zable)
15th Louisiana (Maj. Andrew Bradey)

Stonewall Brigade
Brig. Gen. James Walker
2nd Virginia (Col. John Q.A. Nadenbousch)
4th Virginia (Maj. William Terry)
5th Virginia (Col. John H. S. Funk)
27th Virginia (Lt. Col. Daniel M. Shriver)
33rd Virginia (Capt. James B. Golladay)

Jones's Brigade
Brig. Gen. John M. Jones
21st Virginia (Capt. William P. Moseley)
25th Virginia (Lt. Col. J. A. Robinson)

42nd Virginia (Capt. S. H. Saunders)
44th Virginia (Capt. T. R. Buckner)
48th Virginia (Maj. Oscar White)
50th Virginia (Lt. Col. Logan H. N. Salyer)

Artillery
Capt. John C. Carpenter
1st Maryland Battery
(Capt. William F. Dement)
Alleghany (Virginia) Artillery
(Capt. John C. Carpenter)
Chesapeake (Maryland) Artillery
(Capt. William D. Brown)
Lee (Virginia) Battery
(Lt. William M. Hardwicke)

Artillery Reserve
Col. J. Thompson Brown

First Virginia Artillery
Capt. Willis J. Dance
2nd Richmond (Virginia) Howitzers
(Capt. David Watson)
3rd Richmond (Virginia) Howitzers
(Capt. Benjamin H. Smith, Jr.)
Powhatan (Virginia) Artillery
(Lt. John M. Cunningham)
Rockbridge (Virginia) Artillery
(Capt. Archibald Graham)
Salem (Virginia) Artillery
(Lt. Charles B. Griffin)

Nelson's Battalion
Lt. Col. William Nelson
Amherst (Virginia) Artillery
(Capt. Thomas J. Kirkpatrick)
Fluvanna (Virginia) Artillery
(Capt. John L. Massie)
Georgia Battery (Capt. John Milledge, Jr.)

Third Army Corps
Lt. Gen. Ambrose P. Hill

Anderson's Division
Maj. Gen. Richard H. Anderson

Wilcox's Brigade
Brig. Gen. Cadmus M. Wilcox
8th Alabama (Lt. Col. Hilary A. Herbert)
9th Alabama (Capt. J. Horace King)
10th Alabama (Lt. Col. James E. Shelley)
11th Alabama (Lt. Col. George E. Tayloe)
14th Alabama (Lt. Col. James A. Broome)

Wright's Brigade
Col. William Gibson
3rd Georgia (Col. Edward J. Walker)
22nd Georgia (Capt. B. C. McCurry)
48th Georgia (Col. William Gibson)
2nd Georgia Battalion
(Capt. Charles J. Muffett)

Mahone's Brigade
Brig. Gen. William Mahone
6th Virginia (Col. George T. Rogers)
12th Virginia (Col. David A. Weisiger)
16th Virginia (Col. Joseph H. Ham)
41st Virginia (Col. William A. Parham)
61st Virginia (Col. Virginius D. Groner)

Perry's Brigade
Col. David Lang
2nd Florida (Maj. Walter R. Moore)
5th Florida (Capt. Richmond N. Gardner)
8th Florida (Lt. Col. William Baya)

Posey's Brigade
Brig. Gen. Carnot Posey
12th Mississippi (Col. Walter H. Taylor)
16th Mississippi (Col. Samuel E. Baker)
19th Mississippi (Col. Nathaniel H. Harris)
48th Mississippi (Col. Joseph M. Jayne)

Artillery (Sumter Battalion)
Maj. John Lane
Company A (Capt. Hugh M. Ross)
Company B (Capt. George M. Patterson)
Company C (Capt. John T. Wingfield)

Heth's Division
Maj. Gen. Henry Heth

Pettigrew's Brigade
Brig. Gen. James J. Pettigrew (mortally
wounded, July 14, 1863)
11th North Carolina
(Col. Collett Leventhorpe)
26th North Carolina (Maj. John T. Jones)
47th North Carolina
(Col. George H. Faribault)

52nd North Carolina (Col. James K. Marshall)

Brockenbrough's Brigade
Col. John M. Brockenbrough
40th Virginia (Capt. R. B. Davis)
47th Virginia (Col. Robert M. Mayo)
55th Virginia (Col. William S. Christian)
22nd Virginia Battalion (Maj. John S. Bowles)

Archer's Brigade
Col. Birkett D. Fry
5th Alabama Battalion
(Maj. Albert S. Van De Graaf)
13th Alabama (Col. Birkett D. Fry)
1st Tennessee (Provisional Army)
(Maj. Felix G. Buchanan)
7th Tennessee (Lt. Col. Samuel G. Shepherd)
14th Tennessee (Capt. Bruce L. Phillips)

Davis's Brigade
Brig. Gen. Joseph R. Davis
2nd Mississippi (Col. John M. Stone)
11th Mississippi (Col. Francis M. Green)
42nd Mississippi (Col. Hugh R. Miller)
55th North Carolina
(Col. John Kerr Connally)

Artillery
Lt. Col. John Garnett
Donaldsville (Louisiana) Artillery
(Capt. Victor Maurin)
Huger (Virginia) Artillery
(Capt. Joseph D. Moore)
Lewis (Virginia) Artillery
(Capt. John W. Lewis)
Norfolk Light Artillery Blues
(Capt. Charles R. Grandy)

Pender's Division
Brig. Gen. James H. Lane

Perrin's Brigade
Col. Abner Perrin
1st South Carolina (Provisional Army)
(Maj. Charles W. McCreary)
1st South Carolina Rifles
(Capt. William M. Hadden)
12th South Carolina (Col. John L. Miller)
13th South Carolina
(Lt. Col. Benjamin T. Brockman)
14th South Carolina
(Lt. Col. Joseph N. Brown)

Lane's Brigade
Col. Clark M. Avery
7th North Carolina (Capt. James G. Harris)
18th North Carolina (Col. John D. Barry)
28th North Carolina (Lt. Col. W. H. A. Speer)
33rd North Carolina (Col. Clark M. Avery)
37th North Carolina
(Col. William M. Barbour)

Thomas's Brigade
Brig. Gen. Edward L. Thomas
14th Georgia (Col. Robert W. Folsom)
35th Georgia (Col. Bolling H. Holt)
45th Georgia (Col. Thomas J. Simmons)
49th Georgia (Col. Samuel T. Player)

Scales's Brigade
Col. W. Lee J. Lowrance
13th North Carolina (Lt. Col. H. A. Rogers)
16th North Carolina (Capt. Leroy W. Stowe)
22nd North Carolina (Col. James Conner)
34th North Carolina (Lt. Col. G. T. Gordon)
38th North Carolina (Lt. Col. John Ashford)

Artillery
Maj. William T. Poague
Albemarle (Virginia) Artillery
(Capt. James W. Wyatt)
Charlotte (North Carolina) Artillery
(Capt. Joseph Graham)
Madison (Mississippi) Light Artillery
(Capt. George Ward)
Virginia (Warrington) Battery
(Capt. James V. Brooke)

Artillery Reserve
Col. R. Lindsay Walker

Mcintosh's Battalion
Maj. D. G. McIntosh
Danville (Virginia) Artillery
(Capt. R. Sidney Rice)
Hardaway (Alabama) Artillery
(Capt. William B. Hurt)
2nd Rockbridge (Virginia) Artillery

(Lt. Samuel Wallace)
Virginia (Richmond) Battery
(Capt. Marmaduke Johnson)

Pegram's Battalion
Maj. William J. Pegram
Crenshaw (Virginia) Battery
(Capt. William G. Crenshaw)
Fredericksburg (Virginia) Artillery
(Capt. Edward A. Marye)
Letcher (Virginia) Artillery
(Capt. Thomas A. Brander)
Pee Dee (South Carolina) Artillery
(Lt. William E. Zimmerman)
Purcell (Virginia) Artillery
(Capt. Joseph McGraw)

Cavalry Division
Maj. Gen. James E. B. Stuart

Hampton's Brigade
Col. Laurence S. Baker
1st North Carolina (Col. Laurence S. Baker)
1st South Carolina (Col. John L. Black)
2nd South Carolina
(Maj. Thomas P. Lipscomb)
Cobb's (Georgia) Legion
(Col. Pierce B. M. Young)
Jeff Davis (Mississippi) Legion
(Col. Joseph F. Waring)
Phillips' (Georgia) Legion
(Lt. Col. Jefferson C. Phillips)

Fitz Lee's Brigade
Brig. Gen. Fitzhugh Lee
1st Maryland Battalion (Maj. Harry Gilmor)
(Maj. Ridgely Brown)
1st Virginia (Col. James H. Drake)
2nd Virginia (Col. Thomas T. Munford)
3rd Virginia (Col. Thomas H. Owen)
4th Virginia (Col. William Carter Wickham)
5th Virginia (Col. Thomas L. Rosser)

Robertson's Brigade
Brig. Gen. Beverly H. Robertson
4th North Carolina (Col. Dennis D. Ferebee)
5th North Carolina (Col. Peter G. Evans)

Jenkins's Brigade
Col. Milton J. Ferguson
14th Virginia (Maj. Benjamin F. Eakle)
16th Virginia (Col. Milton J. Ferguson)
17th Virginia (Col. William H. French)
34th Virginia Battalion
(Lt. Col. Vincent A. Witcher)
36th Virginia Battalion
(Capt. Cornelius T. Smith)
Jackson's (Virginia) Battery
(Capt. Thomas E. Jackson)

Jones's Brigade
Brig. Gen. William E. "Grumble" Jones
6th Virginia (Maj. Cabel E. Flourney)
7th Virginia (Lt. Col. Thomas Marshall)
11th Virginia (Col. Lunsford L. Lomax)

W. H. F. Lee's Brigade
Col. John R. Chambliss, Jr.
2nd North Carolina
9th Virginia (Col. Richard L. T. Beale)
10th Virginia (Col. J. Lucius Davis)
13th Virginia (Capt. Benjamin F. Winfield)

Stuart Horse Artillery
Maj. Robert F. Beckham
Breathed's (Virginia) Battery
(Capt. James Breathed)
Chew's (Virginia) Battery
(Capt. R. Preston Chew)
Griffin's (Maryland) Battery
(Capt. William H. Griffin)
Hart's (South Carolina) Battery
(Capt. James F. Hart)
McGregor's (Virginia) Battery
(Capt. William M. McGregor)
Moorman's (Virginia) Battery
(Capt. Marcellus M. Moorman)

Imboden's (Northwest) Brigade
Brig. Gen. John D. Imboden
18th Virginia (Col. George W. Imboden)
62nd Virginia Infantry, Mounted (Col. George H. Smith)
Virginia Partisan Rangers
(Capt. John H. McNeill)
Virginia (Staunton) Battery
(Capt. John H. McClanahan)

Notes

Introduction

1. Sun-Tzu, *The Art of Warfare,* Roger T. Ames, trans. (New York, NY: Ballantine Books, 1993), p. 125.

2. Dr. Caspar C. Henkle, "Letter Delivered After Many Years," *Confederate Veteran*, 16 *(1908)*, 407-08.

3. L.T. Dickinson, "Services of a Maryland Command," *Confederate Veteran*, 2 *(1894)*, 165.

4. Theophilus F. Rodenbough, comp., *History of the Eighteenth Regiment of Cavalry Pennsylvania Volunteers 1862-1865* (New York: Regimental Publication Committee, 1909), 84.

Chapter 1

1. Carl Smith, *Gettysburg 1863* (Sterling Heights, Mich.: Osprey, 1999), 113; John W. Busey and David G. Martin, *Regimental Strengths and Losses at Gettysburg, Fourth Edition* (Hightstown, N.J.: Longstreet House, 2005), 169. Due to missing and incomplete Confederate records, exact strength and loss numbers are impossible to determine, but Busey and Martin's revised study is a well-documented reference tool.

2. Harold J. Woodward, Jr., *Defender of the Valley: Brigadier General John Daniel Imboden C.S.A.* (Berryville, Va.: Rockbridge Publishing, 1996), 10-17.

3. *Ibid.*, 50-1.

4. Smith, *Gettysburg 1863*, 39.

5. John D. Imboden, "The Confederate Retreat from Gettysburg," included in Robert U. Johnson and Clarence C. Buel, eds., *Battles and Leaders of the Civil War,* 4 vols. (New York: Century Printing Co., 1884-1904), 3:420-1 (hereinafter referred to as "B&L").

6. *Ibid.*

7. Timothy H. Smith, *The Story of Lee's Headquarters, Gettysburg, Pennsylvania* (Gettysburg: Thomas Publications, 1995), 41.

8. Imboden, "The Confederate Retreat from Gettysburg," *B&L,* 422

9. *Ibid.*

10. *Ibid.*

11. *Ibid.*, 424; United States War Department, *The War of the Rebellion: A Compilation of the Official Records of the Union and Confederate Armies,* 70 vols. in 128 parts (Washington: Government Printing Office, 1880-1901), series 1, vol. 27, pt. 3, 966-67. Hereafter cited as *OR*. All references are from series 1 unless otherwise noted.

12. Daniel Alexander Skelly, *A Boy's Experiences During the Battle of Gettysburg* (Gettysburg: privately published, 1932), 18.

13. Earl J. Hess, *Lee's Tar Heels: The Pettigrew-Kirkland-MacRae Brigade* (Chapel Hill, N. C.: The University of North Carolina Press, 2002), 159.

14. W. P. Conrad and Ted Alexander, *When War Passed This Way* (Greencastle, Pa.: Beidel Printing House, 1982), 190.

15. Roger U. Delauter, Jr., *62nd Virginia Infantry* (Lynchburg, Va.: H. E. Howard Co., 1988), 18.

16. Luther W. Hopkins, *From Bull Run to Appomattox: A Boy's View* (Baltimore: Press of Fleet-McGinley Co., 1908), 160.

17. Spencer C. Tucker, *Brigadier General John D. Imboden: Confederate Commander in the Shenandoah* (Lexington: University of Kentucky Press, 2003), 154.

18. Julius Lineback diary, 125-27, quoted in Hess, *Lee's Tar Heels,* 159.

19. *Ibid.*

20. Conrad and Alexander, *When War Passed This Way*, 191.

21. D.B. Rea, *Sketches From Hampton's Cavalry, Embracing the Principal Exploits of the Cavalry in the Campaigns of 1862 and 1863* (Columbia, S.C.: South Carolinian Steam Press, 1864), 120.

22. Quentin Ludgin, *Williamsport, Maryland: Grace Under Fire Project* (Kensington, Md.: Forest Glen Commonwealth, n.d.), 28-9.

23. Diary of Robert James Lowry, entry for July 14, 1863. Robert L. Brake Collection, Box 8, U. S. Army Heritage and Education Center, Carlisle, Pennsylvania (hereafter referred to as USAHEC).

24. Imboden, "The Confederate Retreat," *B&L,* 3:423.

25. *Ibid.*

26. Woodward, *Defender of the Valley*, 81-82.

27. Fannie J. Buehler, *Recollections of the Rebel Invasion and One Woman's Experience During the Battle of Gettysburg* (Gettysburg: privately published, 1896), 24.

28. William H. Bayly, "Memoirs of a Thirteen-Year Old Boy Relating to the Battle of Gettysburg," *The Compiler* (October 30, 1939).

29. Sallie M. Broadhead, *The Diary of a Lady of Gettysburg, Pennsylvania, from June 15 to July 15, 1863* (Privately published, n.d.), 3.

30. Robert L. Bloom, *We Never Expected a Battle: The Civilians at Gettysburg, 1863,* (Gettysburg: The Adams County Historical Society, 1988), 181.

31. Imboden, "The Confederate Retreat," *B&L,* 3:424.

32. *Ibid.*

33. Roger U. Delauter, Jr., *18th Virginia Cavalry* (Lynchburg, Va.: H. E. Howard Co., 1985), 8.

34. George Henry Mills, *History of the 16th North Carolina Regiment (Originally 6th N.C. Regiment) in the Civil War* (reprint edition, Hamilton, N.Y.: Edmonston Publishing, Inc., 19920, 39; Walter Clark, ed., *Histories of Several Regiments and Battalions from North Carolina in the Great War, 1861-1865*, 5 vols. (Raleigh: E. M. Uzzell, 1901), 1:181. Stevens, a

famously avowed abolitionist and state representative, endured the destruction of his Caledonia Iron Works at the hands of Maj. Gen. Jubal Early's troops on June 26. At various times, Stevens owned an enormous amount of real estate in and around Gettysburg. See Bradley R. Hoch, *Thaddeus Stevens in Gettysburg: The Making of an Abolitionist* (Gettysburg: The Adams County Historical Society, 2005).

35. John Bell Hood, *Advance and Retreat: Experiences in the United States and Confederate States Armies* (New Orleans: Hood Orphan Memorial Fund, 1880), 60.

36. Arthur J. L. Fremantle, *Three Months in the Confederate States: April-June, 1863* (New York: John Bradburn, 1864), 282.

37. W. A. Popkins, "Imboden's Brigade at Gettysburg," *Confederate Veteran*, 22 (1914), 552.

38. I. Norval Baker diary, entry for July 5, 1863, I. Norval Baker Papers, Archives, Virginia Military Institute, Lexington, Virginia.

39. Conrad and Alexander, *When War Passed This Way*, 192.

40. "Gen. Lee's Retreat," *The Compiler* (Gettysburg, Pa), January 1, 1901.

41. *Ibid.*

42. Jacob Hoke, *The Great Invasion of 1863 or General Lee in Pennsylvania* (Dayton, Ohio: W. J. Shuey, 1887), 477.

43. Diary of William Heyser (July 6, 1863 entry), Valley of the Shadow Project, Special Collections Depertment, Alderman Library, University of Virginia, Charlottesville, Virginia.

44. "Gen. Lee's Retreat," *The Compiler,* January 1, 1901. Much of the castaway ordnance became "highly prized, as war relics" by citizens living along the Pine Stump Road. Many boys collected the scattered artillery shells, with many being wounded (and a few killed) trying to detonate them. Farmers repaired abandoned wagons and used them for years, and many of the lame horses were nursed back to health and saw service behind the plow. *Ibid.*

45. *Baltimore Daily Gazette*, July 8, 1863.

46. Conrad and Alexander, *When War Passed This Way*, 192.

47. Hoke, *The Great Invasion of 1863*, 493.

48. Both local lore, and nearly all of the prior published accounts of the Wagon Train of Wounded, has identified this individual as Lt. Col. Benjamin F. Carter of the 4th Texas Infantry, including the present-day landowners of the farm in question. However, recent research confirms that Carter died in Chambersburg and that he was not buried in an unmarked, roadside resting place. See the discussion accompanying note 59 below for more information. The authors have been unable to identify the officer allegedly buried by the roadside, and likewise have not been able to corroborate the claims that a high-ranking Confederate officer was actually buried in a crude roadside grave after the passage of the Wagon Train of Wounded. Consequently, it is not possible to identify this individual in the main text.

49. Michael Hege, "Rebel Losses and Damages," dated July 5, 1863, Joyce L. Horst collection, Chambersburg, Pennsylvania.

50. Certificate issued and signed by "R. S. Todd, C. S. Army," dated June 27, 1863, Horst Collection.

51. Undated notes of Michael Hege, Horst Collection.

52. Letter from Henry B. Hege to Henry G. Hege, July 12, 1863, Horst Collection.

53. *Ibid.*

54. *Ibid.* Local lore adds that Strite's assailants did him a further injustice by burying him in his own manure pile. Strite's killing is also recorded in George O. Seilhamer, ed., *Biographical Annals of Franklin County, Pennsylvania* (Chicago: Genealogical Pub. Co., 1905), 641.

55. Henry B. Hege letter.

56. Quoted in Kent Masterson Brown, *Retreat from Gettysburg: Lee, Logistics, and the Pennsylvania Campaign* (Chapel Hill: University of North Carolina Press, 2005), 151.

57. "Gen. Lee's Retreat," *The Compiler,* January 1, 1901; Conrad and Alexander, *When War Passed This Way,* 195.

58. Hoke, *The Great Invasion*, 504.

59. "Death of a Rebel Colonel," *Franklin Repository,* July 24, 1863.

60. Rossiter Johnson, ed., *The Twentieth Century Biographical Dictionary of Notable Americans* (Boston, Mass.: The Biographical Society, 1904), 4:83; John J. Hennessy, *Return to Bull Run: The Campaign and Battle of Second Manassas* (New York: Simon & Schuster, 1993), 375-79. The authors are grateful to Pastor Jeffrey Diller of Chambersburg's Zion Reformed Church for providing details of the interesting and ironic connection between Carter and the Fishers.

61. Alexander K. McClure, *Old Time Notes of Pennsylvania: A Connected and Chronological Record of the Commercial, Industrial and Educational Advancement of Pennsylvania* (Philadelphia: The John C. Winston Company, 1905), 105-07. Born about 1831 and a native of Maury County, Tennessee, Carter was a Texas lawyer and the mayor of Austin prior to the war. Carter raised the "Tom Green Rifles," which later became Co. B of the 4th Texas Infantry. Regarding the disposition of Carter's remains, he was initially buried in the cemetery of the United Methodist Church in an (apparently) unmarked grave. In 1906, all the graves were exhumed and the remains relocated to Chambersburg's Cedar Grove Cemetery on Franklin Street, where a separate section holds the relocated graves. Any records of his initial burial were destroyed when the Confederates burned Chambersburg in July 1864, and there is no way to reconstruct those records. There is also no record that anyone claimed Carter's remains to take them south at any time, so he likely still reposes beneath a stone inscribed "Unknown Dead" in the northwest corner of Cedar Grove, in the section containing the remains moved from the old Methodist cemetery. The authors are grateful to F. Joan Bowen, Historian of the First United Methodist Church of Chambersburg, for details regarding these cemeteries and Carter's two interments.

62. Gregory A. Coco, *Wasted Valor: The Confederate Dead at Gettysburg* (Gettysburg: Thomas Publications, 1990), 30 and Arnold S. Platou, "Civil War Mystery Solved," *The Herald-Mail,* November 3, 2007. The Avery family made numerous trips to the Williamsport area in an attempt to find Colonel Avery's remains so that they could be brought home and interred at the family home in Morganton, North Carolina. In the years just after the end of the Civil War, the governor of Maryland arranged for the appropriation of $5,000 to find and rebury the thousands of Confederate soldiers buried near Sharpsburg, Williamsport, and Hagerstown. Several acres within Hagerstown's Rose Hill Cemetery were purchased, and are now known as Washington Confederate Cemetery. Unbeknownst to his family, Avery's remains were disinterred from Williamsport and re-interred in Washington Confederate Cemetery in an

unmarked grave. A local Hagerstown historian did some detective work and re-located Avery's grave in 2006. Consequently, family members had arranged for the grave to be properly marked at last. The stone was dedicated on November 3, 2007. See Alicia Notarianni, "Family Dedicates Tombstone of Civil War Ancestor," *The Herald-Mail,* November 3, 2007. However, there are still thousands of unmarked and unknown Confederate graves scattered about Washington County, Maryland, including many men who died during the retreat from Gettysburg.

63. James C. Mohr, ed., *The Cormany Diaries: A Northern Family in the Civil War,* (Pittsburgh: University of Pittsburgh Press, 1982), 328-341.

64. Hoke, *The Great Invasion*, 504.

65. Imboden, "The Confederate Retreat," *B&L,* 3:425.

66. Hoke, *The Great Invasion*, 501.

67. Eleanor D. McSwain, ed., *Crumbling Defenses; or Memoirs and Reminiscences of John Logan Black, C. S. A.* (Macon, Ga.: The J. W. Burke Co., 1960), 45-6.

68. *Ibid.*

69. William P. Conrad, *Gloryland: A History of Blacks in Greencastle, Pennsylvania,* (Greencastle, Pa.: Beidel Printing House, 1989), 7-13.

70. On July 2, Dahlgren had led a small band of Union scouts to Greencastle, where they captured a courier carrying important letters to Lee, including one from President Jefferson Davis and another from Confederate Adjutant General Samuel Cooper. Both letters indicated that Lee's army would not receive reinforcements in Pennsylvania. Although Dahlgren did not make it back to Gettysburg in time to influence the outcome of the great council of war on the night of July 2, his intelligence provided unprecedented insight into the state of the Confederate army. Maj. Gen. George G. Meade, the Army of the Potomac's commander, would be able to continue the campaign against Lee without fear of his foe receiving substantial reinforcements. Impressed by the young man's dash, the army commander had given Dahlgren permission to return to Greencastle with a more substantial force. For more on Ulric Dahlgren's important role in the Gettysburg Campaign, see, Eric J. Wittenberg, "Ulric Dahlgren in the Gettysburg Campaign," *Gettysburg Magazine* 22 (January 2000): 96-111.

71. Samuel L. Gracey, *Annals of the Sixth Pennsylvania Cavalry*, (Philadelphia: E. H. Butler & Co., 1868), 190. Morrow, a handsome and brave young man, had already been wounded twice in combat and had been captured once. His fearlessness and dashing good looks had caught the attention of Brig. Gen. John Buford, who commanded the Army of the Potomac's First Cavalry Division. Shortly after the conclusion of the Gettysburg Campaign, young Morrow joined Buford's staff.

72. John Hyde Cameron memoirs, Archives, Virginia Military Institute, Lexington, Virginia.

73. McHenry Howard, *Recollections of a Maryland Confederate Soldier and Staff Officer Under Johnston, Jackson, and Lee* (Baltimore: Williams & Wilkins Co., 1914), 210-211.

74. Hess, *Lee's Tar Heels*, 160.

75. John A. Dahlgren, *Memoir of Ulric Dahlgren* (Philadelphia: J. B. Lippincott & Co., 1872), 165.

76. *Ibid.*, 167.

77. *Wheeling Daily Intelligencer*, July 14, 1863.

78. Gracey, *Annals of the Sixth Pennsylvania Cavalry*, 190.

79. Popkins, "Imboden's Brigade at Gettysburg," 552.

80. Frederick C. Newhall, *Dedication of the Monument of the Sixth Pennsylvania Cavalry on the Battlefield of Gettysburg, October 14, 1888* (Philadelphia: privately published, 1889), 19.

81. Stuart Wright, ed., *Memoirs of Alfred Horatio Belo: Reminiscences of a North Carolina Volunteer* (Gaithersburg, Md.: Olde Soldier Books, n.d.), 22.

82. Conrad and Alexander, *When War Passed This Way*, 193.

83. *Ibid.*, 196.

84. Gracey, *Annals of the Sixth Pennsylvania Cavalry*, 190-191.

85. Dahlgren, *Memoir*, 167.

86. *Ibid.*

87. Conrad and Alexander, *When War Passed This Way*, 196.

88. Imboden, "The Confederate Retreat," *B&L*, 3:425.

89. Conrad and Alexander, *When War Passed This Way*, 193.

90. William A. Love, "Mississippi at Gettysburg," *Publications of the Mississippi Historical Society* 9 (1906), 24-25.

91. Mills, *History of the 16th North Carolina Regiment*, 39.

92. *Lancaster Daily Express*, July 11, 1863.

93. *Ibid.*

94. Women's Club of Mercersburg, *Old Mercersburg* (New York: Frank Allaben Genealogical Co., 1912), 168.

95. William H. Beach, *The First New York (Lincoln) Cavalry*, (New York: Lincoln Cavalry Assoc., 1902), 264.

96. *Ibid.*

97. *Ibid.*, 265.

98. *Ibid.*

99. Mills, *History of the 16th North Carolina Regiment*, 39-40.

100. Women's Club of Mercersburg, *Old Mercersburg*, 168.

101. Beach, *The First New York (Lincoln) Cavalry*, 266.

102. Women's Club of Mercersburg, *Old Mercersburg*, 159.

103. Conrad and Alexander, *When War Passed This Way*, 198.

104. *Ibid.*

105. John L. Collins, "A Prisoner's March from Gettysburg to Staunton," included in *B&L*, 3:432.

106. Conrad and Alexander, *When War Passed This Way*, 198.

107. John D. Imboden, "Lee At Gettysburg," *Galaxy Magazine* (April, 1871), 511.

108. McSwain, *Crumbling Defenses*, 46.

109. *Huntsville Confederate*, July 25, 1863.

110. Baker diary, entry for July 8, 1863.

111. Howard, *Recollections of a Confederate Soldier*, 217.

112. Conrad and Alexander, *When War Passed This Way*, 199.

113. Imboden, "The Confederate Retreat," *B&L*, 3:425.

114. Conrad and Alexander, *When War Passed This Way*, 202; Ludgen, *Williamsport, Maryland,* 38.

115. S. Roger Keller, *Events of the Civil War in Washington County Maryland* (Shippensburg, Pa.: White Mane, 1995), 192.

116. *Ibid.*, 195.

117. *Ibid.*, 192.
118. Imboden, "The Confederate Retreat," *B&L*, 3:426.
119. Keller, *Events of the Civil War*, 195-196.
120. *Ibid.*, 196-197.

Chapter 2

1. Francis A. Walker, *History of the Second Army Corps in the Army of the Potomac* (New York: Charles Scribner's Sons, 1886), 306.

2. Mary Genevie Green Brainard, *Campaigns of the 146th Regiment New York State Volunteers* (New York: G. P. Putnam's Sons, 1915), 127.

3. Edward K. Cassedy, ed., *Dear Friends at Home: The Civil War Letters and Diaries of Sergeant Charles T. Bowen, Twelfth United States Infantry 1861-1864* (Baltimore: Butternut & Blue, 2001), 289.

4. Busey and Martin, *Regimental Strengths and Losses at Gettysburg, Fourth Edition*, 312. Obviously, the specifics of the three days of the Battle of Gettysburg are beyond the scope of this study. For a good overview of the battle, see Edwin B. Coddington, *The Gettysburg Campaign: A Study in Command* (New York: Charles Scribner's Sons, 1968), Noah Andre Trudeau, *Gettysburg: A Testing of Courage* (New York: Harper Collins, 2002), or Stephen W. Sears, *Gettysburg* (New York: Houghton-Mifflin, 2003).

5. Alonzo H. Quint, *The Record of the Second Massachusetts Infantry, 1861-65* (Boston: James P. Walker, 1867), 183.

6. Armistead L. Long, *Memoirs of Robert E. Lee: His Military and Personal History Embracing a Large Amount of Information Hitherto Unpublished* (New York: J. M. Stoddard & Co., 1886), 295.

7. Jeffry D. Wert, *General James Longstreet: The Confederacy's Most Controversial Soldier* (New York: Simon & Schuster, 1993), 293.

8. Long, *Memoirs of Robert E. Lee*, 297.

9. Regis de Trobriand, *Four Years with the Army of the Potomac*, George K. Dauchy, translator (Boston: Ticknor and Co., 1889), 512; see also, Ezra J. Warner, *Generals in Blue: Lives of the Union Commanders* (Baton Rouge: Louisiana State University Press, 1964), 121-122.

10. John W. Schildt, *Roads from Gettysburg* (Shippensburg, Pa.: Burd Street Press, 1998), 3.

11. George B. Fox to his father, July 4, 1863, George B. Fox letters, Cincinnati Historical Society, Cincinnati, Ohio.

12. *OR* 27, pt. 3, 514.

13. Samuel H. Hurst, *Journal-History of the Seventy-Third Ohio Volunteer Infantry* (Chillicothe, Ohio: n.p., 1866), 75.

14. D. G. Crotty, *Four Years Campaigning in the Army of the Potomac* (Grand Rapids: Dygert Bros. & Co., 1874), 95.

15. Samuel Toombs, *New Jersey Troops in the Gettysburg Campaign from June 5 to July 31, 1863* (Orange, N J.: The Evening Mail Publishing House, 1888), 327-28.

16. Charles H. Banes, *History of the Philadelphia Brigade* (Philadelphia: J. B. Lippincott, 1876), 196.

17. James Harrison Wilson, *The Life and Services of Brevet Brigadier General Andrew Jonathan Alexander, United States Army* (New York: n.p., 1887), 43. On July 8, Alexander participated in the Battle of Boonsboro, and then followed Stuart's cavalry to Williamsport, skirmishing the whole way, with Alexander under fire nearly the entire time. On July 10, Judson Kilpatrick sent Alfred Pleasonton a letter praising Alexander's service during the Campaign, and requesting his promotion to brigadier general to replace the fallen Elon J. Farnsworth. Although both Pleasonton and Meade endorsed the suggestion enthusiastically, the promotion never came.

18. Gouverneur K. Warren in *Report of the Joint Committee on the Conduct of the War at the Second Session, Thirty-Eighth Congress*, 2 vols. (Washington, D. C.: U. S. Government Printing Office, 1865-66), 1:387 (hereafter referred to as *JCCS*).

19. *OR* 27, pt. 1, 781-782, 786, 789, and 798.

20. Henry C. Morhous, *Reminiscences of the 123d Regiment, N.Y.S.V., Giving a Complete History of Its Three Years Service in the War* (Greenwich, N.Y.: People's Journal Book and Job Office, 1879), 52.

21. E. M. Woodward, *Our Campaigns; The Second Regiment Pennsylvania Reserve Volunteers or, The Marches Bivouacs, Battles, Incidents of Camp Life and History of Our Regiment During Its Three Years of Service* (Philadelphia: John E. Porter, 1865), 217.

22. William H. Powell, *The Fifth Army Corps (Army of the Potomac): A Record of Operations During the Civil War in the United States of America, 1861-1865* (London: G. P. Putnam's Sons, 1896): 562-63.

23. Leander Schooley to his mother, July 9, 1863, Leander Schooley Civil War Letters, Archives, Northern Illinois University, DeKalb, Illinois.

24. J. Gregory Acken, ed., *Inside the Army of the Potomac: The Civil War Experiences of Captain Francis Adams Donaldson* (Mechanicsburg, Pa.: Stackpole, 1998), 312.

25. Ellen Schermerhorn Auchmuty, ed, *Letters of Richard Tylden Auchmuty, Fifth Corps, Army of the Potomac* (Privately published, n.d.), 95.

26. *OR* 27, pt. 1, 638-9, 641, 643, and 671; George W. Bicknell, *History of the Fifth Regiment Maine Volunteers* (Portland, Maine: Hall L. Davis, 1871), 247.

27. Cassedy, *Dear Friends at Home*, 290.

28. *OR* 27, pt. 1, 638-9, 641, 643, and 671; George W. Bicknell, *History of the Fifth Regiment Maine Volunteers* (Portland, Maine: Hall L. Davis, 1871), 247.

29. Arabella M. Willson, *Disaster, Struggle, Triumph: The Adventures of 1000 "Boys in Blue" from August, 1862 to June, 1865* (Albany, N. Y.: The Argus Company Printers, 1870), 199.

30. *OR* 27, pt. 1, 289.

31. Charles E. Davis, Jr., *Three Years in the Army: The Story of the Thirteenth Massachusetts Volunteers from July 16, 1861 to August 1, 1864* (Boston: Estes and Lauriat, 1894), 243.

32. Mason Whiting Tyler, *Recollections of the Civil War* (New York: G. P. Putnam's Sons, 1912), 109; James L. Bowen, *History of the Thirty-Seventh Regiment Mass. Volunteers in the Civil War of 1861-1865* (Holyoke, Mass.: Clark W. Bryan & Co., 1884), 191.

33. Alfred S. Roe, *The Tenth Regiment Massachusetts Volunteer Infantry 1861-1864* (Springfield, Mass.: Tenth Regiment Veteran Assoc., 1909), 211.

34. B. F. Johns, "Pursuit of Lee: Events Following the Battle of Gettysburg," *The National Tribune*, April 18, 1901.

35. Robert Hunt Rhodes, ed., *All for the Union: The Civil War Diary of Elisha Hunt Rhodes* (Lincoln, R. I.: Andrew Mowbray, Inc., 1985), 117.

36. Augustus Woodbury, *The Second Rhode Island Regiment: A Narrative of Military Operations* (Providence: Valpey, Angell, & Co., 1875), 201

37. Rhodes, *All for the Union*, 117.

38. Homer R. Stoughton to John B. Bachelder, December 21, 1881, included in David L. and Audrey J. Ladd, eds., *The Bachelder Papers: Gettysburg in Their Own Words*, 3 vols. (Dayton, Ohio: Morningside, 1995), 2:769.

39. James Mero Matthews, *Soldiers in Green: Civil War Diaries of James Mero Matthews, 2nd U.S. Sharpshooters*, Peter Dalton, ed. (Sandy Point, ME: Richard's Civil War Roundtable, 2002), 162-63. According to Matthews' diary, Gray's body was buried on the field the following day.

40. *OR* 27, pt. 1, 519.

41. Alanson A. Haines, *History of the Fifteenth New Jersey Volunteers* (New York: Jenkins & Thomas, 1883), 94.

42. D. Porter Marshall, *Company "K" 155th Pennsylvania Volunteer Zouaves* (n.p., 1888), 114.

43. J. Hamp SeCheverell, *Journal History of the Twenty-Ninth Ohio Veteran Volunteers, 1861-1865. Its Victories and Its Reverses* (Cleveland: n.p., 1883), 72.

44. Dana B. Shoaf, ed., "'On the March Again at Daybreak': Major John I. Nevin and the 93rd Pennsylvania Infantry," *Civil War Regiments* Vol. 6, No. 3 (1999), 127.

45. *OR* 27, pt. 3, 517-518.

46. Jedediah Hotchkiss, *Make Me a Map of the Valley: The Civil War Journal of Stonewall Jackson's Topographer*, ed. Archie P. McDonald (Dallas: Southern Methodist University Press, 1973), 158.

47. John C. West, *A Texan in Search of a Fight: Being the Diary and Letters of a Private Soldier in Hood's Texas Brigade* (Waco: J. S. Hill & Co., 1901), 96 and 99.

48. Diary of James E. Green, entry for July 4, 1863. Robert L. Brake Collection, Box 9, USAHEC.

49. Fremantle, *Three Months in the Confederate States*, 273.

50. G. Ward Hubbs, ed., *Voices from Company D: Diaries by the Greensboro Guards, Fifth Alabama Infantry Regiment, Army of Northern Virginia* (Athens, Ga: The University of Georgia Press, 2003), 185.

51. Diary of unknown 6th Louisiana Infantry soldier, entry for July 4, 1863. Robert L. Brake Collection, Box 8, USAHEC.

52. William S. White, *A Diary of the War, or What I saw of It* (Richmond: Carlton McCarthy & Co., 1883), 210.

53. William W. Blackford, *War Years With Jeb Stuart* (Baton Rouge: Louisiana State University Press, 1945), 234.

54. Ken Wiley, ed., *Norfolk Blues: The Civil War Diary of the Norfolk Light Artillery Blues* (Shippensburg, Pa.: Burd Street Press, 1997), 77.

55. G. Moxley Sorrel, *Recollections of a Confederate Staff Officer* (New York: Neal Pub. Co., 1905), 174.

56. John J. Garnett, *Gettysburg: A Complete Historical Narrative of the Battle of Gettysburg and the Campaign Preceding It* (New York: J. M. Hill, 1888), 45.

57. Terry L. Jones, ed., *Campbell Brown's Civil War: With Ewell and the Army of Northern Virginia* (Baton Rouge: Louisiana State University Press, 2001), 225.

58. W. M. Robbins, "The Battle of Gettysburg," *Confederate Veteran*, 8 (1900), 165-68.

59. Frank A. Bond, "Company A, First Maryland Cavalry," *Confederate Veteran*, 6 (1898), 78-80.

60. George Wilson Booth, *Personal Reminiscences of a Maryland Soldier in the War Between the States 1861-1865* (Baltimore: Privately published, 1898), 93.

61. David E. Johnston, *The Story of a Confederate Boy in the Civil War* (Portland, OR.: Glass & Prudhomme, 1914), 223.

62. Frank M. Myers, *The Comanches: A History of White's Battalion, Virginia Cavalry* (Baltimore: Kelly, Piet & Co., 1871), 204. For a modern treatment of White's troopers' service during the war, particularly during the Gettysburg Campaign, and their close relationship with Ewell, see J. David Petruzzi, "He Rides Over Everything In Sight," *America's Civil War* (March 2006), 24-30.

63. John C. Oeffinger, ed., *A Soldier's General: The Civil War Letters of Major General Lafayette McLaws* (Chapel Hill: University of North Carolina Press, 2004), 197.

64. Long, *Memoir of Robert E. Lee*, 297.

65. *Richmond Daily Dispatch*, July 10, 1863.

66. Harry Gilmor, *Four Years in the Saddle* (New York: Harper & Bros., 1866), 233-34.

67. James I. Robertson, Jr., *General A. P. Hill* (New York: Random House, 1987), 227.

68. *Ibid.*, 226.

69. *Southern Banner* (Athens, Ga.), August 26, 1863.

70. White, *A Diary of the War*, 212; Donald C. Pfanz, *Richard S. Ewell: A Soldier's Life* (Chapel Hill: University of North Carolina Press, 1998), 327.

71. Hotchkiss, *Make Me a Map of the Valley*, 158.

72. *Charleston Mercury*, July 20, 1863.

73. Sorrel, *Recollections of a Confederate Staff Officer,* 174.

74. Spencer Glasgow Welch, *A Confederate Surgeon's Letters to His Wife* (New York: The Neale Publishing Company, 1911), 69.

75. Hubbs, *Voices from Company D,* 185.

76. F. F. Cavada, *Libby Life: Experiences of a Prisoner of War in Richmond, Va., 1863-64* (Philadelphia: J. B. Lippincott & Co., 1865), 14. Col. Charles H. T. Collis, after whom the regiment was nicknamed, had been wounded at Chancellorsville in May. At Gettysburg, the regiment still wore the showy Zouave uniform of red pantaloons and blue jackets. John P. Nicholson, ed., *Pennsylvania at Gettysburg* (Harrisburg: E. K. Meyers, State Printer, 1893), 2:600.

77. Cavada, *Libby Life,* 14.

78. Charles P. Potts diary, entry for July 4, 1863, Stu Richards Collection, included in "Pennsylvania Volunteers of the Civil War" web site,www.pacivilwar.com.

79. Horace Smith diary, entry for July 4, 1863, Mazomance Historical Society, Mazomance, Wisconsin.

80. Nathaniel Rollins diary, entry for July 4, 1863, www.soldierstudies.org/index.php?action=view_letter&Letter=564

81. Robert J. Driver, Jr. and Kevin C. Ruffner, *1st Battalion Virginia Infantry, 39th Battalion Virginia Cavalry, 24th Battalion Virginia Partisan Rangers* (Lynchburg, Va.: H. E. Howard Co., 1996), 57-58.

82. Wiley, *Norfolk Blues*, 77-78.

83. Randolph H. McKim, *A Soldier's Recollections: Leaves from the Diary of a Confederate* (New York: Longmans & Green, 1910), 180.

84. Jeffrey D. Stocker, ed., *From Huntsville to Appomattox: R. T. Coles's History of the 4th Regiment, Alabama Volunteer Infantry, C.S.A., Army of Northern Virginia* (Knoxville: University of Tennessee Press, 1996), 113.

85. Wert, *General James Longstreet*, 293.

86. J. B. Polley, *A Soldier's Letters to Charming Nellie* (New York: Neale Publishing Co., 1908), 134-135.

87. *Supplement to the Official Records of the Union and Confederate Armies* in 100 vols. (Wilmington, N. C.: Broadfoot, 1995), 5:208.

88. J. C. Williams, *Life in Camp: A History of the Nine Months' Service of the Fourteenth Vermont Regiment, From October 21, 1862, When It was Mustered into the U. S. Service, to July 21, 1863, Including the Battle of Gettysburg* (Claremont, N.H.: Claremont Manufacturing Co., 1864), 147-48.

89. Davis, *Three Years in the Army*, 242-43.

90. John L. Smith, *History of the Corn Exchange Regiment 118th Pennsylvania Volunteers, From Their First Engagement at Antietam to Appomattox* (Philadelphia: J. L. Smith, 1886), 262.

91. A. W. Bartlett, *History of the Twelfth Regiment New Hampshire Volunteers in the War of the Rebellion* (Concord, N. H.: Ira C. Evans, Printer, 1897), 136.

92. "After Gettysburg. Pursuing Lee to the Potomac. Experiences of a Vermont Victim. A Brilliant Skirmish." *New York Tribune*, July 1, 1888.

93. *OR* 27, pt. 3, 516.

94. James F. Rusling, *Men and Things I Saw in Civil War Days* (New York: Eaton & Mains, 1899), 67.

95. Darius N. Couch to George G. Meade, July 4, 1863, RG 393, Department of the Susquehanna and Pennsylvania, 1862-1866, Letters Sent, June 1863-January 1866, Collection 4606, The National Archives, Washington, D. C.

96. *OR* 27, pt. 3, 517.

97. *Ibid.*, 577.

98. *Ibid.*, 516.

99. *Ibid.*, 517.

100. George Meade, *The Life and Letters of George Gordon Meade*, 2 vols. (New York: Charles Scribner's Sons, 1913), 2:361.

Chapter 3

1. Pfanz, *Richard S. Ewell*, 327. The burly Harman, who had engineered Lee's retreat across the Potomac following the Battle of Antietam, invariably used one of his most famous talents to entice wagon mules to move—profanity. See Stephen W. Sears, *Landscape Turned Red: The Battle of Antietam* (New Haven, CT: Ticknor & Fields, 1983), 73.

2. Beach, *The First New York Lincoln Cavalry*, 270.

3. Charles T. Loehr, *War History of the Old First Virginia Infantry Regiment, Army of Northern Virginia* (Richmond: Wm. Ellis Jones, 1884), 39.

4. Scott L. Mingus, Sr., *Human Interest Stories of the Gettysburg Campaign, Vol. 2* (Orrtanna, Pa.: Colecraft Industries, 2007), 85.

5. Fremantle, *Three Months in the Southern States*, 275.

6. Cavada, *Libby Life,* 15.

7. For more on the Battle of Fairfield, see Eric J. Wittenberg, *Gettysburg's Forgotten Cavalry Actions* (Gettysburg, Pa: Thomas Publications, 1998), and J. David Petruzzi, "Annihilation of a Regiment," *America's Civil War* (July 2007), 26-33.

8. Ferguson was commanding the brigade of Brig. Gen. Albert G. Jenkins, who had been wounded during the first day's fight at Gettysburg.

9. *OR* 27, pt. 2, 699.

10. *Ibid.*, 700.

11. Ludgin, *Williamsport, Maryland*, 31.

12. John O. Casler, *Four Years in the Stonewall Brigade* (Guthrie, OK: n.p., 1893), 177.

13. Berkeley Minor, "The Night After Gettysburg," *Confederate Veteran*, 33 (1925), 140.

14. *OR* 27, pt. 2, 753; William N. McDonald, *A History of the Laurel Brigade* (Baltimore: Sun Job Printing Office, 1907), 158.

15. Edwin C. Fishel, *The Secret War for the Union* (New York: Houghton-Mifflin Co., 1996), 538.

16. *OR* 27, pt. 1, 916.

17. Louis N. Boudrye to Mrs. John Hammond, July 4, 1863, included in *In Memoriam: John Hammond* (Chicago: P.F. Pettibone & Co., 1890), 59.

18. *Wheeling Daily Intelligencer*, July 15, 1863.

19. James H. Kidd to Dear Father and Mother, July 9, 1863, James H. Kidd Papers, Bentley Historical Library, University of Michigan, Ann Arbor, Michigan.

20. R. L. Murray, ed., *Letters From Gettysburg: New York Soldiers' Correspondences from the Battlefield* (Wolcott, N.Y.: Benedum Books, 2005), 144.

21. *OR* 27, pt. 1, 993.

22. Andrew D. Jackson, "Reminiscences of a Private," unpublished manuscript, Walter D. Pomeroy Collection, Mechanicsburg, Pennsylvania.

23. Boudrye to Mrs. John Hammond, July 4, 1863, 59.

24. Luther S. Trowbridge to J. Allen Bigelow, undated letter, copy in files, Gettysburg National Military Park.

25. The 1st Rhode Island Cavalry had been a full regiment just two weeks earlier. However, Pleasonton had sent it, alone and unsupported, on a suicidal reconnaissance into Middleburg, Virginia in late June. There, it ran into Stuart's entire command, and was cut to pieces in a running fight in the streets of the town.

26. *OR* 27, pt. 1, 993; Henry Capehart, "Fighting His Way: The Night Passage of Kilpatrick Through Monterey Pass," *The National Tribune*, January 3, 1895.

27. Murray, *Letters From Gettysburg*, 144.

28. William Brooke-Rawle, ed., *History of the Third Pennsylvania Cavalry* (Philadelphia: Franklin Printing Co., 1905), 283.

29. *Ironton Register*, December 22, 1887.

30. Ludgin, *Williamsport, Maryland*, 31.

31. C.H. Buhrman to J. Fraise Richard, October 12, 1888, included in Conrad and Alexander, *When War Passed This Way*, 394.

32. Frank Moore, ed., *The Rebellion Record: A Diary of American Events 1861-1863* (New York: D. Van Nostrand, 1864), 187.

33. C.H. Buhrman to J. Fraise Richard, October 12, 1888, included in Conrad and Alexander, *When War Passed This Way*, 394-95.

34. *Ibid.*, 395.

35. *The New York Times*, August 6, 1863. Interestingly, Col. Town's report specifically refers to this encounter occurring in the Fairfield Gap and not the Monterey Pass. However, none of the other Federal reports refer to any action occurring in the Gap. The authors believe it likely that Town, who was from Michigan and unfamiliar with the area, simply confused the two, which are in close proximity.

36. Robertson, *Michigan in the War*, 577.

37. Hyde, *Following the Greek Cross*, 158.

38. Asa B. Isham, *An Historical Sketch of the Seventh Regiment Michigan Volunteer Cavalry, From its Organization in 1862, to its Muster Out in 1865* (New York: Town Topics Publishing Co., 1893), 30.

39. Arthur J. L. Fremantle, *The Fremantle Diary* (Boston: Little, Brown & Co., 1960), 221.

40. *New York Times*, July 21, 1863.

41. Edward Porter Alexander, unpublished manuscript on the Gettysburg Campaign, Southern Historical Collection, University of North Carolina Library, Chapel Hill, North Carolina.

42. John Allen Bigelow, "Flashing Sabers: Chasing Lee's Columns After Gettysburg," *The National Tribune*, November 10, 1887.

43. *OR* 27, pt. 1, 994.

44. Bigelow, "Flashing Sabers."

45. Gilbert W. Chapman to Jenny, July 29, 1863, Burton Historical Collection, Detroit Public Library, Detroit, Michigan.

46. David Miller to J. Fraise Richard, November 23, 1886, included in Conrad and Alexander, *When War Passed This Way*, 397.

47. *Ibid.*

48. James Moore, M.D., *Kilpatrick and Our* Cavalry (New York: J. Widdleton, 1865), 99; The *New York Times*, August 6, 1863.

49. Cavada, *Libby Life,* 15.

50. Mingus, *Human Interest Stories, Vol. 2*, 86.

51. Diary of Charles Moore, entry for July 4, 1863. Robert L. Brake Collection, Box 8, USAHEC.

52. Moore, *The Rebellion Record,* 187.

53. McClellan, *Life and Campaigns*, 353-54.

54. Jackson, "Reminiscences of a Private."

55. Willard Glazier, *Three Years in the Federal Cavalry* (New York: R.H. Ferguson & Co., 1873), 268.

56. McClellan, *Life and Campaigns*, 354.

57. Jackson, "Reminiscences of a Private."

58. McClellan, *Life and Campaigns*, 354.
59. *OR* 27, pt. 2, 753.
60. McClellan, *Life and Campaigns*, 355.
61. *OR* 27, pt. 1, 994.
62. Richard J. Staats, ed., *The Life and Times of Colonel William Stedman of the 6th Ohio Cavalry* (Laurel, Md.: Heritage Books, 2003), 164.
63. George W. Booth, *Personal Reminiscences of a Maryland Soldier in the War Between the States, 1861-1865* (Baltimore: privately published, 1898), 93.
64. Nancy Ronemus, ed., "A letter from a young Michigan cavalryman gives a vivid—if ungrammatical—account of Gettysburg and its aftermath," *America's Civil War* (March 1997), 79.
65. *OR* 27, pt. 1, 994.
66. Samuel L. Gillespie, *A History of Company A, First Ohio Cavalry, 1861-1865: A Memorial Volume Compiled from Personal Records and Living Witnesses* (Washington, Ohio: Ohio State Register, l898), 155.
67. Conrad and Alexander, *When War Passed This Way*, 397.
68. Luther W. Hopkins, *From Bull Run to Appomattox: A Boy's View* (Baltimore: Fleet-McGinley Co., 1908), 105.
69. *Ibid.*, 106.
70. Russell A. Alger to L.O. Estes, February 12, 1897, copy in files, Gettysburg National Military Park.
71. Bigelow, "Flashing Sabers."
72. *Ibid.*
73. Kidd to his parents, July 9, 1863.
74. James H. Kidd, *Personal Recollections of a Cavalryman* (Ionia, MI: Sentinel Printing Co., 1908), 170.
75. *OR* 27, pt. 2, 753.
76. *Ironton Register*, December 22, 1887.
77. *Ibid.*
78. *OR* 27, pt. 1, 1019.
79. *Ironton Register*, December 22, 1887.
80. James T. Hunter to Russell A. Alger, October 21, 1897, Charles E. Capehart Medal of Honor file, NARA. Kilpatrick wrote, "Your gallant charge down the mountain side at midnight on July 4th, 1863, in which you cut from Lee's retreating column Gen. Beverly Robertson's entire brigade with 4 pieces of artillery resulting in the capture of [Ewell's] entire wagon train, stretching from Monterey Mountain to Hagerstown, a distance of 13 miles, will long live in history and entitled you and your gallant regiment to the gratitude of this Government and the American people." Judson Kilpatrick to Charles E. Capehart, June 21, 1880, Capehart Medal of Honor file, NARA.
81. *Ironton Register*, December 22, 1887.
82. Henry W. Clark pension file, RG 93, NARA.
83. Gillespie, *History of Company A*, 155.
84. Kidd to his parents, July 9, 1863; *OR* 27, pt. 1, 1019.
85. Hubbs, *Voices from Company D*, 185.

86. Edward G. Longacre, *Custer and His Wolverines: The Michigan Cavalry Brigade 1861-1865* (Conshohocken, PA: Combined Books, 1997), 157.

87. Minor, "The Night After Gettysburg," 140-1.

88. Henry E. Shepherd, "Wounded at Gettysburg," http://www.soldierstudies.org/index.php?action=view_letter&Letter=606

89. Edward A. Moore, *The Story of a Cannoneer Under Stonewall Jackson* (Lynchburg, Va.: J. P. Bell Co., Inc., 1910), 200-205.

90. Hopkins, *From Bull Run to Appomattox*, 107.

91. Ed S. Hastings, "Monterey Pass: A Claim that the 5th Mich. Led the Charge There," *The National Tribune*, March 21, 1895.

92. Staats, *The Life and Times of William Stedman*, 164.

93. Report of Lt. Alexander C. M. Pennington, August 2, 1863, included in *Supplement to the Official Records of the Union and Confederate Armies*, 5:286.

94. Boon, "The Charge at Monterey."

95. *Ibid.*

96. Gillespie, *History of Company A*, 159.

97. Boon, "The Charge at Monterey."

98. *OR* 27, pt. 2, 753.

99. Moore, *The Rebellion Record,* 186-87.

100. Diary of Charles H. Blinn, 1st Vermont Cavalry, Entry for July 5, 1863, copy in files, Gettysburg National Military Park.

101. Report of Col. Russell A. Alger, July 1, 1880, The National Archives, RG 94, War Records Office, Union Battle Reports, Vol. 27, Boxes 48-52.

102. Blinn diary, Entry for July 5, 1863.

103. Moore, *The Rebellion Record,* 188.

104. Longacre, *Custer*, 158.

105. Moore, *The Rebellion Record,* 187-88.

106. Kidd, *Personal Recollections*, 171; Alger report, July 1, 1880.

107. Hastings, "Monterey Pass."

108. Alger to Estes, February 12, 1897. Interestingly, controversy broke out after the war as to which unit had made the charge. Men of the 5th Michigan claimed credit for the successful charge, to the indignation of their comrades in the 1st Ohio. See, for instance, J. L. Millikan, "The Charge at Monterey," *The National Tribune*, February 16, 1888.

109. Report of Alger, July 1, 1880.

110. Moore, *The Rebellion Record,* 187.

111. Charles J. C. Hutson to his father, July 9, 1863, http://www.soldierstudies.org/index.php?action=view_letter&Letter=513

112. Conrad and Alexander, *When War Passed,* 395.

113. Horace K. Ide, *History of the First Vermont Cavalry Volunteers in the War of the Great Rebellion,* Elliott W. Hoffman, ed. (Baltimore: Butternut & Blue, 2000), 119.

114. *Ibid.*

115. Joe Allen, *The Anthology of Another Town*, excerpt in files, Gettysburg National Military Park (GNMP), 178.

116. Allen, 178-79.

117. *OR* 27, pt. 1, 994.

118. Ide, *History of the First Vermont Cavalry*, 119.
119. Moore, *The Rebellion Record,* 188.
120. Péladeau, *Burnished Rows of Steel*, 191.
121. Loehr, *War History of the Old First Virginia*, 39.
122. *Ibid.*
123. Purifoy, "The Horror of War," 224.
124. Conrad and Alexander, *When War Passed This Way*, 395.
125. *OR* 27, pt. 2, 309.
126. McClellan, *Life and Campaigns*, 355.
127. *OR* 27, pt. 2, 701.
128. Millard K. Bushong and Dean M. Bushong, *Fightin' Tom Rosser, C.S.A.* (Shippensburg, Pa.: Beidel Printing House, Inc., 1983), 59. This was perhaps the only instance in which Stuart and Jones managed to put aside their many differences for the betterment of the cause. Less than three months later, their long-standing fight simmered over into open conflict, and Stuart preferred charges against Jones for conduct unbecoming an officer. Jones was convicted and relieved of command. He was sent to assume command in the Shenandoah Valley, where he would die leading a mounted charge at the Battle of Piedmont, June 5, 1864, less than a month after Stuart received his own mortal wound at the Battle of Yellow Tavern. Both protagonists in this tragedy died doing what they did best—leading cavalry in battle.
129. Brooke-Rawle, *History of the Third Pennsylvania Cavalry*, 283.
130. *OR* 27, pt. 1, 1019. Capehart never identified the two culprits, and never specified what act they committed to draw the ire of their commander. The nature of their sin remains a mystery today.
131. Kidd, *Personal Recollections*, 171.
132. Quoted in Mingus, *Personal Interest Stories, Vol. 2*, 86.
133. Moore, *The Rebellion Record,* 188.
134. *Ibid.*
135. *New York Times*, July 21, 1863.
136. Moore, *The Rebellion Record,* 188.
137. *Ibid.*
138. *OR* 27, pt. 1, 994.

Chapter 4

1. Bowen, *History of the Thirty-Seventh Regiment*, 191. As early as 5:40 a.m., Union signal officers reported that the enemy had evacuated the positions they had held on July 4. *OR* 27, pt. 3, 532.
2. William B. Styple, ed., *Writing and Fighting the Civil War: Soldier Correspondence to the New York Sunday Mercury* (Kearny, N. J.: Belle Grove Publishing, 2000), 207.
3. Cassedy, *Dear Friends at Home*, 290.
4. A. P. Smith, *History of the Seventy-Sixth Regiment New York Volunteers* (Cortland, N. Y.: Truair, Smith & Miles, 1867), 252.
5. Skelly, *A Boy's Experiences During the Battle of Gettysburg,* 19.
6. *OR* 27, pt. 3, 531.

7. Péladeau, *Burnished Rows of Steel*, 391.

8. *History of the 121st Regiment Pennsylvania Volunteers* (Philadelphia: Press of Burk & McFetridge Co., 1893), 35. Much of the specifics of these probing operations by the Federals is outside the scope of this book. For a detailed study of Meade's operations on July 4, see Thomas L. Elmore, "Independence Day: Military Operations at Gettysburg," *Gettysburg Magazine* 25 (July 2001), 116-28.

9. Thomas W. Hyde, *Following the Greek Cross; Or Memories of the Sixth Army Corps* (Boston: Houghton, Mifflin & Co., 1894), 158.

10. Herman Haupt, *Reminiscences of General Herman Haupt* (Milwaukee: Wright & Joys Co., 1901), 223-224.

11. Abner Doubleday diary, entries for July 6 and 7, 1863, Abner Doubleday papers, National Archives and Records Administration (NARA).

12. *OR* 27, pt. 3, 524. Meade and his staff lost some of their horses during the cannonade preceding Pickett's Charge. Overshoots by the Confederate artillery fell among the mounts of Meade and his staff at his headquarters at the Widow Leister house, located on the eastern side of Cemetery Ridge.

13. Peck, *Reminiscences*, 36-7.

14. George T. Stevens, *Three Years in the Sixth Corps* (Albany, N. Y.: S. R. Gray, Publisher, 1866), 253.

15. Hyde, *The Union Generals Speak*, 112.

16. *OR* 27, pt. 3, 532-33.

17. Oliver Otis Howard, *Autobiography of Oliver Otis Howard, Major General United States Army*, 2 vols. (New York: The Baker & Taylor Co., 1907), 1:442-43.

18. Haines, *Fifteenth New Jersey*, 96.

19. Robert S. Westbrook, *History of the 49th Pennsylvania Volunteers* (Altoona, Pa.: Altoona Times Print, 1898), 154.

20. A. T. Brewer, *History Sixty-first Regiment Pennsylvania Volunteers 1861-1865* (Pittsburgh: Art Engraving & Printing Co., 1911), 68.

21. Joseph Keith Newell, *"Ours." Annals of the 10th Regiment, Massachusetts Volunteers in the Rebellion* (Springfield, Mass., C. A. Nichols & Co., 1875), 223-224.

22. Emil and Ruth Rosenblatt, eds., *Hard Marching Every Day: The Civil War Letters of Private Wilbur Fisk* (Lawrence, Kan.: University Press of Kansas, 1992), 115.

23. Rhodes, *All for the Union*, 117.

24. Haines, *Fifteenth New Jersey*, 97.

25. Stevens, *Three Years in the Sixth Corps,* 255.

26. Bill Hyde, ed., *The Union Generals Speak: The Meade Hearings on the Battle of Gettysburg* (Baton Rouge: Louisiana State University Press, 2003), 87.

27. Albert N. Jennings, "Pursuit of Lee's Army," *The National Tribune*, June 27, 1901.

28. "After Gettysburg."

29. Thomas Hughes, *A Boy's Experience in the Civil War 1860-1865* (Privately published, 1904), 17.

30. Jubal A. Early, *Autobiographical Sketch and Narrative of the War Between the States* (Philadelphia: J. B. Lippincott, 1912), 280.

31. Rosenblatt and Rosenblatt, *Hard Marching Every Day,* 117.

32. *OR* 27, pt. 1, 695.

33. George W. Bicknell, *History of the Fifth Regiment Maine Volunteers, Comprising Brief Descriptions of Its Marches, Engagements, and General Services from the Date of Its Muster In, June 24, 1861 to the Time of Its Muster Out, July 27, 1864* (Portland: Hall L. Davis, 1871), 247.

34. Edward P. Adams, "Battery G, First Rhode Island Light Artillery," *Revised Register of Rhode Island Volunteers* (1893), 63.

35. Rosenblatt and Rosenblatt, *Hard Marching Every Day*, 116.

36. *OR* 27, pt. 1, 695.

37. Adams, "Battery G," 64.

38. Johns, "Pursuit of Lee."

39. Nelson V. Hutchinson, *History of the Seventh Massachusetts Volunteer Infantry in the War of the Rebellion of the Southern States Against Constitutional Authority, 1861-1865* (Taunton, Mass.: The Regimental Assoc., 1890), 157.

40. Hotchkiss, *Make Me a Map of the Valley*, 158.

41. Diary of unknown member of the 6th Louisiana Infantry, entry for July 5, 1863. Robert L. Brake Collection, Box 8, USAHEC.

42. Fremantle, *Three Months in the Southern States*, 277-78

43. Rollins diary, entry for July 5, 1863.

44. F. W. Morse, *Personal Experiences in the War of the Great Rebellion, from December 1862 to July 1865* (Albany, N.Y.: privately published, 1866), 41.

45. *OR* 27, pt. 3, 554-55.

46. Shoaf, "On the March Again at Daybreak," 127.

47. William A. Tubbs to his parents, July 6, 1863, copy in files, GNMP.

48. Hubbs, *Voices from Company D,* 185.

49. James H. Woods, *The War; "Stonewall" Jackson, His Campaigns, and Battles, the Regiment as I Saw Them* (Cumberland, Md.: Eddy Press Corporation, 1910), 154.

50. Rollins diary, entry for July 5, 1863.

51. Horace Smith diary, entry for July 5, 1863.

52. *OR* 27, pt. 3, 558.

53. Abner Doubleday, *Chancellorsville and Gettysburg* (New York: Charles Scribner's Sons, 1882), 208-9. Doubleday had his own agenda. He was angry that Meade had relieved him of command of the First Corps at the end of the first day of the Battle of Gettysburg, and was determined to do all he could to make Meade look bad. Doubleday took every opportunity to denigrate Meade and Meade's performance during the campaign, so his writings must be considered with a certain degree of caution.

54. Peter C. Vermilyea, "Maj. Gen. John Sedgwick and the Pursuit of Lee's Army after Gettysburg," *Gettysburg Magazine* 22 (2001), 117.

55. Jennings, "Pursuit of Lee's Army."

56. Shoaf, "On the March Again at Daybreak," 127.

57. Haines, *Fifteenth New Jersey*, 98; A. D. Slade, *A. T. A. Torbert: Southern Gentleman in Union Blue* (Dayton, Ohio: Morningside House, 1992), 74.

58. *OR* 27, pt. 3, 561.

59. Westbrook, *History of the 49th Pennsylvania*, 155.

60. William R. Wray, *History of the Twenty Third Pennsylvania Volunteer Infantry Birney's Zouaves: Three Months and Three Years Service Civil War 1861-1865* (Philadelphia: Survivors Assoc. Twenty Third Regiment Pennsylvania Volunteers 1904), 102.

61. David W. Blight, ed., *When This Cruel War is Over: The Civil War Letters of Charles Harvey Brewster* (Amherst: University of Massachusetts Press, 1992), 239.

62. *OR* 27, pt. 3, 532-33.

63. For a history of the National Road, see Archer Butler Hulbert, *The Cumberland Road* (Cleveland: Arthur H. Clark, 1904).

Chapter 5

1. Wiley, *Norfolk Blues*, 79.

2. Wood, *The War,* 154-156.

3. Edward G. Longacre, *Lee's Horsemen: A History of the Mounted Forces of the Army of Northern Virginia* (Mechanicsburg, Pa.: Stackpole, 2002), 229.

4. *OR* 27, pt. 2, 753; *New York Times,* July 11, 1863.

5. *Baltimore American,* July 9, 1863.

6. *OR* 27, pt. 2, 437, 488-90.

7. *Ibid.,* 754.

8. *Ibid,* 701 and 750.

9. Caldwell, *The History of a Brigade of South Carolinians,* 105.

10. Wise, *The Long Arm of Lee,* 2:699.

11. Diary of Samuel J. B. V. Gilpin, entry for July 4, 1863.

12. Cheney, *History of the Ninth New York,* 117.

13. George H. Chapman diary, entry for July 4, 1863, George H. Chapman Papers, Indiana Historical Society, Indianapolis, Indiana.

14. Isaac Rothermel Dunkelberger, "Reminiscences," Michael Winey Collection, USAHEC.

15. Nelson Taylor to Dear Father, July 4, 1863, included in Dr. Gray Nelson Taylor, ed., *Saddle and Saber: The Letters of Civil War Cavalryman Corporal Nelson Taylor* (Bowie, Md.: Heritage Books, 1993), 96.

16. Abner N. Hard, *History of the Eighth Cavalry Regiment, Illinois Volunteers, During the Great Rebellion* (Aurora, Ill.: privately published, 1868), 261.

17. Dunkelberger, "Reminiscences."

18. *Ibid.*

19. *The National Tribune,* March 6, 1884; John Farrington, "137th Regiment Volunteer Infantry," included in New York State Monument Commission for the Battlefields of Gettysburg and Chattanooga, *Final Report at Gettysburg,* 3 vols. (Albany: J. B. Lyon Co., 1900), 3:943.

20. Dunkelberger, "Reminiscences."

21. General Order 73, March 24, 1863, which included Public Law 54 (12 Stat. 735), Section 21. United States law had recognized an officer's right to conduct such courts martial and to hang spies since the time of the Revolutionary War. For a detailed discussion of this subject, including the definition of a spy, what must be demonstrated in order to prove that a person is a spy, and the various forms of punishment prescribed, the reader may wish to see William Woolsey Winthrop, *Military Law,* 2 vols. (Washington, D. C.: W. H. Morrison, 1888), 1:1098-1106.

22. Sidney Morris Davis, *Common Soldier, Uncommon War: Life as a Civil War Cavalryman,* Charles F. Cooney, ed. (Bethesda, Md.: SMD Group, 1994), 450; Dunkelberger, "Reminiscenses"; *The National Tribune,* April 4, 1884.

23. *The National Tribune,* March 6, 1884.

24. Farrington, "137th Regiment," 943.

25. Hard, *History of the Eighth Cavalry Regiment, Illinois Volunteers,* 261.

26. Keller, *Events of the Civil War in Washington County, Maryland,* 153.

27. Diary of Charles S. Hammond, entry for July 6, 1863, Hammond Papers, Clarke Historical Library, Central Michigan University, Mt. Pleasant, Michigan.

28. Diary of Louis R. Fortesque, entry for July 5, 1863, copy in files, GNMP. Louis Fortesque remained a prisoner of war until nearly the end of the war. He was finally exchanged on March 1, 1865, just a few weeks before Richmond fell and Lee's army surrendered.

29. *OR* 27, pt. 2, 700.

30. Schildt, *Roads from Gettysburg,* 18.

31. *Richmond Daily Dispatch,* July 13, 1863.

32. Schildt, *Roads from Gettysburg,* 18.

33. Henry Haw Matthews, "Pelham-Breathed Battery," *St. Mary's Beacon,* April 27, 1905. Matthews, a private in the battery, wrote a fabulously detailed series of articles on the horse artillery's movements, battles, and personalities covering the spring of 1862 (when he enlisted) to late in 1864, at which time he transferred to the 1st Maryland Cavalry (CSA) for the *Beacon.* The articles ran for eight months beginning in November 1904.

34. Schildt, *Roads from Gettysburg,* 17.

35. *Ibid.*

36. *OR* 27, pt. 2, 700.

37. Louis N. Boudrye, *Historic Records of the Fifth New York Cavalry, First Ira Harris Guard* (Albany: J. Munsell, 1868), 68.

38. *OR* 27, pt. 3, 700.

39. *Ibid,* pt. 1, 1014; James Penfield, *The 1863-1864 Civil War Diary of Captain James Penfield, 5th New York Volunteer Cavalry, Company H* (Crown Point, N.Y.: Penfield Foundation, 1999), 71.

40. Schildt, *Roads from Gettysburg,* 38.

41. Chambliss had been commanding Brig. Gen. William Henry Fitzhugh (W. H. F.) Lee's Brigade since Lee was wounded at the Battle of Brandy Station on June 9, 1863.

42. Gillespie, *A History of Company A,* 160.

43. Murray, *Letters From Gettysburg,* 144.

44. Wells Bushnell diary, entry for July 5, 1863, Wells Bushnell Papers, Western Reserve Historical Society, Cleveland, Ohio.

45. Gillespie, *History of Company A,* 160.

46. Charles S. Adams, *The Civil War in Washington County, Maryland: A Guide to 66 Points of Interest* (Dagsboro, Delaware: privately published, 2001), 56. To this day, that artillery shell remains firmly lodged in the side of the Vogel house, where hundreds of people each year seek it out as a lingering curiosity. See our driving tour section of this book, where a photograph of the home can be seen.

47. Matthews, "Pelham-Breathed Battery," *St. Mary's Beacon,* April 27, 1905. For detailed narratives of the complex and often misunderstood events that made up Jeb Stuart's long hard ride to Gettysburg, see Eric J. Wittenberg and J. David Petruzzi, *Plenty of Blame to Go Around: Jeb Stuart's Controversial Ride to Gettysburg* (New York: Savas Beatie LLC, 2006).

48. *OR* 27, pt. 1, 1009.

49. *Ibid,* pt. 1, 1014.

50. Penfield, *The 1863-1864 Civil War Diary,* 71.

51. Kidd, *Personal Reminiscences,* 172-73.

52. Schildt, *Roads From Gettysburg,* 38.

53. *OR* 27, pt. 2, 701.

54. *Ibid,* pt. 3, 531.

55. *Ibid,* 534.

56. *Ibid,* 538.

57. *Ibid,* 546..

Chapter 6

1. *OR* 27, pt. 2, 701.

2. Neese, *Three Years in the Confederate Horse Artillery*, 198.

3. Frank A. Bond, "Company A, First Maryland Cavalry," *Confederate Veteran*, 6 (1898), 78-80.

4. Gillespie, *A History of Company A*, 161.

5. Booth, *Personal Reminiscences,* 93.

6. Bond, "Company A, First Maryland Cavalry," 79.

7. *Ibid.*

8. *Ibid.*

9. Richard L. T. Beale, *History of the Ninth Virginia Cavalry in the War Between the States* (Richmond: B. F. Johnson Printing Co., 1899), 92.

10. *Ibid.*, 93.

11. John J. Shoemaker, *Shoemaker's Battery, Stuart Horse Artillery, Pelham's Battalion, Army of Northern Virginia* (Memphis, Tennessee: Privately published, n. d.), 46. This slender but fascinating volume includes some interesting observations and opinions not found elsewhere. It was made more widely available when it was reprinted under the same title in 1983 by Butternut Press.

12. John B. Kay to his parents, July 9, 1863, copy in files GNMP.

13. Neese, *Three Years in the Confederate Horse Artillery*, 194.

14. W. W. Jacobs, "Custer's Charge: Little Hagerstown the Scene of Bloody Strife in 1863," *The National Tribune*, August 27, 1896.

15. Matthews, "The Pelham-Breathed Battery," *St. Mary's Beacon,* April 27, 1905.

16. Booth, *Personal Reminiscences,* 93.

17. Bond, "Company A, First Maryland Cavalry," 79.

18. Booth, *Personal Reminiscences,* 93.

19. Bond, "Company A, First Maryland Cavalry," 79.

20. *Ibid.*

21. Jacobs, "Custer's Charge."

22. Dahlgren, *Memoir of Ulric Dahlgren*, 169.

23. Bond, "Company A, First Maryland Cavalry," 80.

24. John Gall, *Reminiscences of Four Years as a Private Soldier in the Confederate Army, 1861-1865* (Baltimore: Sun Job Printing Co., 1904), 91.

25. Booth, *Personal Reminiscences of a Maryland Soldier*, 94.

26. Samuel P. Bates, *History of the Pennsylvania Volunteers,* 5 vols. (Harrisburg, Pa.: B. Singerly, 1869-71), 4:1044.

27. Samuel St. Clair, "The Fight at Hagerstown," included in Theophilus F. Rodenbough, comp., *History of the Eighteenth Regiment of Cavalry Pennsylvania Volunteers 1862-1865* (New York: Regimental Publication Committee, 1909), 94-5.

28. Dahlgren, *Memoir of Ulric Dahlgren*, 169-70.

29. Luther Trowbridge to J. Allen Bigelow, undated, copy in files GNMP.

30. Ulric Dahlgren diary, entry for July 6, 1863.

31. Diary of Hugh St. Clair, entry for July 6, 1863, *Hugh St. Clair Civil War Diary, 1 Jan. to 31 Dec. 1863* (Hygiene, Co.: Sunshine Press Publications, 2001), 35.

32. Rodenbough, *History of the Eighteenth Pennsylvania Cavalry*, 85.

33. *New York Times*, August 6, 1863.

34. Ide, *History of the First Vermont Cavalry*, 120.

35. Gillespie, *History of Company A*, 161.

36. Samuel St. Clair, "Col. Dahlgren's Wound," *The National Tribune*, March 12, 1896.

37. Jacobs, "Custer's Charge"; Matthews, "The Pelham-Breathed Battery," *St. Mary's Beacon,* April 27, 1905.

38. St. Clair, "Col. Dahlgren's Wound"; Jacobs, "Custer's Charge."

39. Matthews, "The Pelham-Breathed Battery," *St. Mary's Beacon,* April 27, 1905.

40. Edward G. Butler to Jessica R. Smith, September 11, 1863, Civil War Files, Military Collections, North Carolina State Archives, Raleigh, North Carolina.

41. John F. Coghill to his parents, July 17, 1863, John F. Coghill Papers, University of North Carolina.

42. Butler to Smith, September 11, 1863.

43. *Ibid.*

44. William W. Marston diary, entry for July 6, 1863, Robert W. Woodruff Library, Emory University, Atlanta, Georgia.

45. John F. Coghill letter, undated, James O. Coghill Papers.

46. *OR* 27, pt. 1, 1006.

47. *Ibid.*, pt. 2, 581.

48. *Ibid.*, pt. 1, 998-1000.

49. Bond, "Company A, First Maryland Cavalry," *Confederate Veteran*, 6 (1898), 80.

50. Diary of Charles McVicar, entry for July 6, 1863, Charles McVicar papers, Manuscripts Division, LOC.

51. *In Memoriam: John Hammond*, 61.

52. Boudrye, *Historic Records of the Fifth New York Cavalry*, 68-9.

53. Chris J. Hartley, *Stuart's Tarheels: James B. Gordon and His North Carolina Cavalry* (Baltimore: Butternut & Blue, 1996), 244.

54. Beale, *History of the Ninth Virginia Cavalry*, 94-5.

55. Ide, *History of the First Vermont Cavalry Volunteers*, 121.

56. S. A. Clark, "Did Not Capture It: Buford and Kilpatrick Fought for Lee's Wagon Train at Hagerstown," *The National Tribune*, April 11, 1895.

57. A. W. Preston to P. T. Washburn, Adjutant General, State of Vermont, July 10, 1863, included in Péladeau, *Burnished Rows of Steel*, 191.

58. *Ibid.*

59. Howard Coffin, *Full Duty: Vermonters in the Civil War* (Woodstock, Vt.: The Countryman Press, 1993), 214.

60. St. Clair, "Col. Dahlgren's Wound."

61. James Dean, "Letter to the Editor," *Wheeling Intelligencer*, July 15, 1863.

62. *OR* 27, pt. 1, 1006.

63. *Ibid.*

64. Robert J. Driver, Jr., *14th Virginia Cavalry* (Lynchburg, Va.: H. E. Howard Co., 1988), 24.

65. Kidd, *Personal Recollections*, 174.

66. Penfield, *1863-1864 Diary*, 71; Boudrye, *History of the Fifth New York Cavalry*, 69.

67. McDonald, *A History of the Laurel Brigade*, 161-62.

68. Delauter, *18th Virginia Cavalry*, 9.

69. *OR* 27, pt. 1, 1007.

70. Cavada, *Libby Life,* 16.

71. Styple, *Writing and Fighting the Confederate War*, 170.

Chapter 7

1. Imboden, "The Confederate Retreat from Gettysburg, 3:426.

2. Steve French, "The Rebels at Williamsport," *Gettysburg Magazine* No. 27 (July 2002), 85.

3. J. Watts dePeyster, *The Decisive Conflicts of the Late Civil War* (New York: MacDonald & Co., 1867), 97.

4. Imboden, "The Confederate Retreat from Gettysburg, 3:426.

5. *Ibid.,* 426-27.

6. John Purifoy, "A Unique Battle," *Confederate Veteran* 33 (1925), 132-35; Wise, *The Long Arm of Lee,* 2:699.

7. Richard R. Duncan, "The College of St. James and the Civil War: A Casualty of War," *Historical Magazine of the Protestant Episcopal Church* Vol. 39, No. 3 (September 1970), 265.

8. Hall Harrison, *Life of the Right Reverend John Barrett Kerfoot* (New York: James Pott & Co., 1886), 261. Known today as St. James School, the college is the oldest Episcopalian boarding school founded on the English model in the country. On the eve of the Civil War, most of its students came from the south and many left to join the Confederate army. The campus saw its share of fighting and the passage of the armies over its ground during the war. The school was closed in August of 1864 at the order of Gen. Jubal Early, and reopened following the war as a college preparatory boarding school. *Ibid.,* 190, 870 and Duncan, "The College of St. James," 285-86.

9. John H. Worsham, *One of Jackson's Foot Cavalry: His Experience and What He Saw During the War, 1861-1865* (New York: The Neale Publishing Co., 1912), 170-71.

10. *Ibid.*

11. Dan Goodwin, "Williamsport and Boonsboro," *National Tribune,* October 11, 1883.

12. *Ibid.*

13. T. M. Eddy, *The Patriotism of Illinois,* 2 vols. (Chicago: Clarke & Co., 1865), 1:558.

14. Worsham, *One of Jackson's Foot Cavalry,* 170-71; Eddy, *The Patriotism of Illinois,* 1:560.

15. David Fillmore, "Not at All Quiet Along the Potomac: A Little Unwritten History of Co. A, 8th Ill. Cav.," *National Tribune,* March 28, 1907.

16. *Ibid.*

17. Fremantle, *Three Months in the Southern States,* 284-85.

18. Worsham, *One of Jackson's Foot Cavalry,* 172.

19. Hammond diary, entry for July 6, 1863.

20. Susan Leigh Blackford, ed., *Letters From Lee's Army: Memoirs of Life In and Out of the Army in Virginia During the War Between the States* (New York: Charles Scribner's Sons, 1947), 189.

21. John Blue, *Hanging Rock Rebel: Lt. John Blue's War in West Virginia and the Shenandoah Valley,* Dan Oates, ed. (Shippensburg, Pa.: Burd Street Press, 1994, 210.

22. Baker diary, entry for July 6, 1863.

23. Purifoy, "A Unique Battle," 132-35; Wise, *The Long Arm of Lee,* 2:700.

24. Mills, *History of the 16th North Carolina Regiment,* 40.

25. Ludgen, *Williamsport, Maryland,* 35.

26. I. Norval Baker memoirs, Archives, Virginia Military Institute, Lexington, Virginia; Caldwell, *The History of a Brigade of South Carolinians,* 105-06.

27. Caldwell, *History of a Brigade of South Carolinians,* 106.

28. William Delony to his wife, July 7, 1863, copy in GNMP files.

29. Frances Letcher Mitchell, "A Georgia Henry of Navarre," *Confederate Veteran* 33 (1915), 363.

30. Delony to his wife, July 7, 1863.

31. Wiley C. Howard, *Sketch of Cobb Legion Cavalry and Some Incidents and Scenes Remembered* (Atlanta: Camp 159 U. C. V., 1901), 9-10.

32. Wright, *Memoirs of Alfred Horatio Belo,* 22.

33. McSwain, *Crumbling Defenses,* 46-7.

34. Harry Gilmor, *Four Years in the Saddle* (New York: Harper & Bros., 1866), 100-03.

35. Hammond diary, entry for July 6, 1863.

36. Gilmor, *Four Years in the Saddle,* 103.

37. *Huntsville Confederate,* July 25, 1863.

38. French, "The Rebels at Williamsport," 100.

39. Polley, "Gettysburg and Sharpsburg."

40. Baker memoirs.

41. *Huntsville Confederate,* July 25, 1863.

42. *OR* 27, pt. 1, 928.

43. Gracey, *Annals of the Sixth Pennsylvania Cavalry,* 185.

44. Delony to his wife, July 7, 1863.

45. Delauter, *62nd Virginia Mounted Infantry,* 19.

46. Karla J. Husby and Eric J. Wittenberg, eds., *Under Custer's Command: The Civil War Journal of James Henry Avery* (Dulles, Va.: Brassey's, 2000), 40-41.

47. Ludgen, *Williamsport, Maryland,* 47.

48. Jackson, "Reminiscences of a Private."

49. *OR* 27, pt. 1, 928.

50. Trowbridge to Bigelow, undated letter.

51. *Ibid.*

52. Jackson, "Reminiscences of a Private."

53. *Ibid.*

54. *Michigan Argus,* July 31, 1863. Jewett's father was afterward given directions by troopers participating in the fight, and located his son's remains. He brought the body home for interment, and the lieutenant was buried with full military honors, including the escort of a full contingent of sharpshooters. The flags in his hometown were lowered to half staff out of respect for the fallen horse soldier.

55. Robertson, *Michigan in the War,* 579.

56. Baker memoirs.

57. John B. Kay to his parents, July 9, 1863, copy in GNMP files.

58. Gillespie, *History of Company A,* 161.

59. *OR* 27, pt. 1, 928.

60. Moore, *Kilpatrick and Our Cavalry,* 102-03.

61. *OR* 27, pt. 1, 928.

62. Gracey, *Annals of the Sixth Pennsylvania Cavalry,* 184.

63. *OR* 27, pt. 1, 940.

64. Harrison, *Life of the Right Reverend John Barrett Kerfoot,* 261.

65. Gracey, *Annals of the Sixth Pennsylvania Cavalry,* 185.

66. Henry P. Moyer, *History of the Seventeenth Regiment Pennsylvania Volunteer Cavalry* (Lebanon, Pa.: Sowers Printing Co., 1911), 67.

67. Hillman A. Hall, ed., *History of the Sixth New York Cavalry (Second Ira Harris Guard), Second Brigade, First Division, Cavalry Corps, Army of the Potomac, 1861-1865* (Worcester, Mass.: Blanchard Press, 1908), 146.

68. Newell Cheney, comp., *History of the Ninth Regiment, New York Volunteer Cavalry, War of 1861 to 1865* (Poland Center, N.Y.: Martin Mertz & Son, 1901), 118.

69. Stanford and Erskin, *Dear Rachel,* 50.

70. Delony to his wife, July 7, 1863.

71. Howard, *Recollections of a Confederate Soldier,* 214.

72. Tucker, *Brigadier General John D. Imboden,* 163. Maj. Gen. George Stoneman had commanded the Army of the Potomac Cavalry Corps prior to Pleasonton.

73. *Huntsville Confederate,* July 25, 1863.

74. Quoted in Brown, *Retreat from Gettysburg,* 254.

75. Imboden, "The Confederate Retreat From Gettysburg," 3:428.

76. Gilpin diary, entry for July 6, 1863.

77. *OR* 27, pt. 1, 928.

78. Styple, *Writing and Fighting the Confederate War,* 176.

79. Baker memoirs.

80. Alexander, *Fighting for the Confederacy,* 269.

81. John W. Daniel, "The Rear Guard," Daniel Papers, Alderman Library, University of Virginia, Charlottesville, Virginia.

82. Jedediah Hotchkiss, *Make Me a Map of the Valley: The Civil War Journal of Stonewall Jackson's Topographer,* Archie P. McDonald, ed. (Dallas: Southern Methodist University Press, 1973), 159.

83. Rollins diary, entry for July 6, 1863.

84. Driver and Ruffner, *1st Battalion,* 58.

85. Wiley, *Norfolk Blues,* 79-80.

Chapter 8

1. *OR* 27, pt. 1, 672.

2. Newell, *Annals of the Tenth Regiment*, 224.

3. Rhodes, *All for the Union*, 117.

4. Bowen, *History of the Thirty-Seventh Regiment*, 192.

5. Haines, *Fifteenth New Jersey*, 98.

6. George T. Stevens, *Three Years in the Sixth Corps* (Albany: S. R. Gray, 1876), 255.

7. *OR* 27, pt. 3, 561.

8. William B. Styple, ed., *Writing and Fighting from the Army of Northern Virginia: A Collection of Confederate Soldier Correspondence* (Kearny, N. J.: Belle Grove Publishing Co., 2003), 250.

9. Stewart, *Three Years in the Sixth Corps*, 257.

10. Hyde, *Following the Greek Cross*, 160.

11. *OR* 27, pt. 3, 595-596.

12. *Ibid.*, pt. 1, 679.

13. *Ibid.*

14. Brewer, *History Sixty-first Pennsylvania*, 69.

15. Alan Sessarego, comp., *Letters Home V: Original Civil War Soldiers &Photographs* (Hanover, Pa.: Americana Souvenirs and Gifts, 2003), 7.

16. Williams, *Life in Camp*, 153.

17. Charles D. Page, *History of the Fourteenth Regiment, Connecticut Vol. Infantry* (Meriden, Conn.: The Horton Printing Co., 1906), 168.

18. Robert Goldthwaite Carter, *Four Brothers in Blue; or, Sunshine and Shadows of the War of the Rebellion, A Story of the Great Civil War from Bull Run to Appomattox* (Washington, Press of Gibson Bros., 1913), 329.

19. Daniel George McNamara, *The History of the Ninth Regiment Massachusetts Volunteer Infantry Second Brigade, First Division, Fifth Army Corps, Army of the Potomac June, 1861-June, 1864* (Boston: E. B. Stallings & Co., 1899), 332.

20. Peter Tomasek, ed., *Avery Harris Civil War Journal* (Luzerne, Pa.: Luzerne National Bank, 2000), 80.

21. Wray, *History of the Twenty Third Regiment*, 103.

22. Tyler, *Recollections of the Civil War*, 110.

23. Rosenblatt and Rosenblatt, *Hard Marching Every Day*, 119.

24. James Harrison Wilson, *Life and Services of William Farrar Smith, Major General United States Volunteers in the Civil War* (Wilmington, Del.: John M. Rogers Press, 1904), 36-37.

25. Westbrook, *History of the 49th Pennsylvania*, 155.

26. Haines, *Fifteenth New Jersey*, 99.

27. "After Gettysburg."

28. Bowen, *History of the Thirty-Seveth Regiment*, 193.

29. Rhodes, *All for the Union*, 117.

30. Bicknell, *History of the Fifth Maine Volunteers*, 248.

31. Johns, "Pursuit of Lee."

32. Camille Baquet, *History of the First Brigade, New Jersey Volunteers from 1861 to 1865* (Trenton, N. J.: MacCrellish & Quigley, 1910), 98.

33. Rosenblatt and Rosenblatt, *Hard Marching Every Day*, 118-119.

34. *Ibid.*, 120.

35. Bicknell, *History of the Fifth Regiment Maine Volunteers*, 249.

36. *Ibid.*

37. Blight, *When This Cruel War is Over*, 242.

38. Bowen, *History of the Thirty-Seventh Regiment*, 193.

39. Johns, "Pursuit of Lee."

40. Hyde, *Following the Greek Cross*, 112.

41. Allan S. Nevins, ed., *A Diary of Battle: The Personal Journals of Colonel Charles S. Wainwright, 1861-1865* (New York: Harcourt, Brace & World, 1962), 256.

42. Schildt, *Roads from Gettysburg*, 71.

43. Auchmuty, *Letters*, 101-02.

44. Hyde, *The Union Generals Speak*, 113.

45. *OR* 27, pt. 3, 578.

46. *Ibid.*, pt. 1, 84.

47. *Ibid.*, 86.

48. *Ibid.*, pt. 3, 567.

49. Samuel P. Heintzelman diary, entry for July 6, 1863, Samuel P. Heintzelman papers, Manuscripts Division, LOC.

50. T. M. Eddy, *The Patriotism of Illinois* 2 vols. (Chicago: Clarke & Co., 1865), 1:571.

51. Charles Carleton Coffin, *Four Years of Fighting: A Volume of Personal Observation with the Army and Navy, from the First Battle of Bull Run to the Fall of Richmond* (Boston: Ticknor & Fields, 1866), 302.

52. Clark B. Baldwin to John B. Bachelder, May 20, 1865, *The Bachelder Papers*, 1:194-95.

53. William B. Styple, ed., *Writing and Fighting the Confederate War: The Letters of Peter Wellington Alexander, Confederate War Correspondent* (Kearny, N. J.: Belle Grove Publishing Co., 2002), 165.

54. Brainard, *Campaigns of the 146th Regiment*, 129.

55. Styple, *Writing and Fighting the Civil War*, 204.

56. Péladeau, *Burnished Rows of Steel*, 391.

57. Tomasek, *Avery Harris Civil War Journal*, 80.

58. George A. Hussey, *History of the Ninth Regiment N.Y.S.M.—N.G.S.N.Y. (Eighty-Third Volunteers) 1845-1999* (New York Veterans of the Regiment, 1889), 289-290.

59. Acken, *Inside the Army of the Potomac*, 313.

60. *OR* 27, pt. 3, 554.

61. *Ibid.*, 586; Thomas B. Searight, *The Old Pike. A History of the National Road, with Incidents, Accidents, and Anecdotes Thereon* (Uniontown, Pa.: Privately published, 1894), 195.

62. Schooley to his mother, July 9, 1863.

63. *OR* 27, pt. 1, 1016-17.

64. *Ibid.*, pt. 3, 584.

65. Gracey, *Annals of the Sixth Pennsylvania Cavalry*, 182.

66. Warner, *Generals in Blue*, 187-88. Gregg was also a first cousin of Pennsylvania's war-time governor, Andrew Gregg Curtin. Another first cousin, Col. J. Irvin "Long John" Gregg, commanded a brigade of cavalry in the Second Division. There is only one full-length biography of David M. Gregg. See Milton V. Burgess, *David Gregg: Pennsylvania Cavalryman* (Privately published, 1984).

67. *OR* 27, pt. 3, 517 and pt. 1, 977.

68. William E. Doster, *Lincoln and Episodes of the Civil War* (New York: G. P. Putnam's Sons, 1915), 220.

69. William Hyndman, *History of a Cavalry Company: A Complete Record of Company "A," 4th Penn'a Cavalry* (Philadelphia: J. B. Rodgers, 1870), 69.

70. Doster, *Lincoln*, 222.

71. *OR* 27, pt. 1, 977.

72. Doster, *Lincoln*, 223; Roger D. Hunt and Jack R. Brown, *Brevet Brigadier Generals in Blue* (Gaithersburg, Md.: Olde Soldier Books, 1990), 169. Doster received a brevet to brigadier general of volunteers on March 13, 1865 for meritorious service during the war. He also served as defense counsel for Lincoln assassination conspirators Lewis Payne and George Atzerodt.

73. William E. Doster, *A Brief History of the Fourth Pennsylvania Cavalry Embracing Organization, Reunions, Dedication of Monument at Gettysburg and Address of General W. E. Doster, Venango County Battalion, Reminiscences, Etc.* (Hightstown, N. J.: Longstreet House, 1997), 37.

74. Doster, *Lincoln*, 223.

75. *Ibid.*, 223.

76. William P. Lloyd, *History of the First Reg't. Pennsylvania Reserve Cavalry, From Its Organization, August, 1861, to September, 1864, With a List of Names of All Officers and Enlisted Men Who Have Ever Belonged to the Regiment* (Philadelphia, King & Baird, 1864), 63.

77. Brooke-Rawle, *History of the Third Pennsylvania Cavalry*, 324.

78. *OR* 27, pt. 1, 967.

79. Henry R. Pyne, *Ride to War: The History of the First New Jersey Cavalry* (New Brunswick, N. J.: Rutgers University Press, 1961), 134.

80. John B. McIntosh to his wife, July 6, 1863, copy in files GNMP.

81. *OR* 27, pt. 1, 958 and 971.

82. Pyne, *Ride to War*, 134.

83. James C. Mohr, ed., *The Cormany Diaries: A Northern Family in the Civil War* (Pittsburgh: University of Pittsburgh Press, 1982), 343.

84. Mohr, *The Cormany Diaries*, 343.

85. Noble D. Preston, *History of the Tenth Regiment of Cavalry New York State Volunteers, August, 1861, to August, 1865* (New York: D. Appleton & Co., 1892), 131.

86. Doster, *Lincoln*, 225.

87. *OR* 27, pt. 1, 959.

88. Doster, *Lincoln*, 225-226.

89. *OR* 27, pt. 3, 517-518.

90. *Ibid.*, pt. 1, 489.

91. J. Newton Terrill, *Campaign of the Fourteenth Regiment New Jersey Volunteers* (New Brunswick: Daily Home News Press, 1884), 19.

92. *Ibid.*

93. John D. Billings, *The History of the Tenth Massachusetts Battery of Light Artillery in the War of the Rebellion 1862-1865* (Boston: The Arakelyan Press, 1909), 99-101.

94. Joseph W. Kirkley, "Gen. Lee's Retreat," *The National Tribune*, June 7, 1883.

95. *OR* 27, pt. 3, 585.

96. *Ibid.*, pt. 1, 489.

97. Charles Campter and J. W. Kirkley, *Historical Record of the First Regiment Maryland Infantry, with an Appendix Containing a Register of the Officers and Enlisted Men, Biographies of Deceased Officers, Etc., War of the Rebellion, 1861-65* (Washington, D.C.: Gibson Brothers, 1871), 105.

98. Beach, *The First New York (Lincoln) Cavalry*, 268.

99. *Ibid.*, 268-69.

100. *Ibid.*, 269; *Richmond Dispatch*, July 10, 1863; and James H. Stevenson, "*Boots and Saddles": A History of the First Volunteer Cavalry of the War, Known as the First New York (Lincoln) Cavalry, and also as The Sabre Regiment, Its Organization, Campaigns and Battles* (Harrisburg, Pa.: Patriot Publishing Co., 1879) at 202. See, also, Harold Hand, *One Good Regiment: The 13th Pennsylvania Cavalry in the Civil War, 1861-1865* (Victoria, B. C.: Trafford Publishing, 2000), 68. Bugler Hertz was a tough customer. He continued to serve with the 6th Michigan Cavalry until his capture at the Battle of Trevilian Station on June 11, 1864. Hertz survived a stint as a prisoner of war at Andersonville prison in Georgia, and also survived the explosion of the *Sultana* as it carried liberated Union prisoners of war north at the end of the Civil War. Hertz lived to the ripe old age of eighty-six. For more on Hertz and his capture at Trevilian Station, see Eric J. Wittenberg, *Glory Enough for All: The Battle of Trevilian Station and Sheridan's Second Raid* (Dulles, Va.: Brassey's, 2001), 103-4.

101. Collins, "A Prisoner's March from Gettysburg to Staunton," 3:432.

102. Beach, *First New York*, 269-70.

103. *New York Times*, July 12, 1863.

104. Stevenson, *Boots and Saddles*, 203.

105. *Richmond Daily Dispatch*, July 13, 1863.

106. Albert M. Hunter memoir, Emmitsburg Area Historical Society, Emmitsburg, Maryland.

107. William A. McIlhenny diary, Emmitsburg Area Historical Society, Emmitsburg, Maryland.

108. C. Armour Newcomer, *Cole's Cavalry; or Three Years in the Saddle in the Shenandoah Valley* (Freeport, N. Y.: Books for Libraries Press, 1970), 54-55.

109. Thomas West Smith, *The Story of a Cavalry Regiment: "Scott's 900", Eleventh New York Cavalry from the St. Lawrence River to the Gulf of Mexico 1861-1865* (New York: Published by the Veteran Association of the Regiment, 1897), 108.

110. *OR* 27, pt. 3, 550.

Chapter 9

1. Noah Brooks, *Washington in Lincoln's Time* (New York: The Century Co., 1895), 82.

2. David Homer Bates, *Lincoln in the Telegraph Office: Recollections of the United States Military Telegraph Corps During the Civil War* (New York: The Century Co., 1907), 154.

3. Brooks, *Washington in Lincoln's Time*, 82.

4. *Ibid.,* 83.

5. *Baltimore American*, July 9, 1863.

6. *New York Times*, July 10, 1863.

7. O. B. Curtis, *History of the Twenty-Fourth Michigan of the Iron Brigade, Known as the Detroit and Wayne County Regiment* (Detroit: Winn & Hammond, 1891), 193.

8. Marshall DeLancey Haywood, *Lives of the Bishops of North Carolina From the Establishment of the Episcopate in that State Down to the Division of the Diocese* (Raleigh: Alfred Williams & Company, 1910), 209-10.

9. *Ibid.,* 210.

10. Harrison, *Life of the Right Reverend John Barrett Kerfoot,* 261.

11. *OR* 27, pt. 1, 935.

12. Harrison, *Life of the Right Reverend John Barrett Kerfoot,* 261.

13. *OR* 27, pt. 1, 935.

14. Peck, *Dear Rachel*, 50.

15. *OR* 27, pt. 1, 940.

16. *Aurora, Illinois, Beacon*, August 20, 1863.

17. Dona Bayard Sauerburger and Thomas Lucas Bayard, eds., *"I Seat Myself to Write You a Few Lines": Civil War and Homestead Letters from Thomas Lucas and Family* (Laurel, Md.: Heritage Books, 2002), 160.

18. Harrison, *Life of the Right Reverend John Barrett Kerfoot,* 261.

19. *OR* 27, pt. 2, 752. For background on the pending rematch between the Virginia horsemen and the 6th U.S. Cavalry, see two modern treatments of the July 3 battle at Fairfield: Eric J. Wittenberg, *Gettysburg's Forgotten Cavalry Actions* (Gettysburg: Thomas Publications, 1998), and J. David Petruzzi, "Annihilation of a Regiment," *America's Civil War* (July 2007), 26-33.

20. Davis, *Common Soldier, Uncommon War*, p. 447.

21. Report of Lt. Charles H. Vandiver, William T. Leavell and Edward A.H. McDonald Papers, Perkins Library, Duke University, Durham, North Carolina; Richard L. Armstrong, *Seventh Virginia Cavalry* (Lynchburg, Va.: H.E. Howard Co., 1992), 57.

22. *Ibid.*

23. *Ibid.*

24. Davis, *Common Soldier, Uncommon War*, 447.

25. Vandiver report.

26. Dunkelberger, "Reminiscences."

27. *OR* 27, pt. 2, 761; Armstrong, *Seventh Virginia*, 57.

28. *Ibid.*, 754.

29. *New York Times*, July 12, 1863.

30. Lt. Col. William H. Carter, "The Sixth Regiment of Cavalry," *The First Maine Bugle* (October, 1896), 300-01. Even the Confederates recognized that the 6th had not been completely destroyed. Maj. Henry B. McClellan of Stuart's staff pointed out that this claim was a piece of monumental overstatement by Jones. The 6th U.S. Cavalry returned to fight in a number of subsequent actions and remained an effective fighting force. See McClellan, *The Life and Campaigns of Major General J. E. B. Stuart*, 348.

31. Alexander, *Fighting for the Confederacy*, 270.

32. *OR* 27, pt. 2, 299.

33. Wise, *A Diary of the War*, 213.

34. Hotchkiss, *Make Me a Map of the Valley*, 159.

35. The Presidential retreat of Camp David sits atop Catoctin Mountain, in Catoctin Mountain National Park.

36. Shoaf, "On the March Again at Daybreak," 128.

37. Bowen, *History of the Thirty-Seventh Regiment*, 194.

38. William Henry Locke, *The Story of the Regiment* (Philadelphia: J. B. Lippincott, 1868), 248.

39. Hyde, *The Union Generals Speak*, 115.

40. Davis, *Three Years in the Army*, 250-51.

41. Winthrop D. Sheldon, *The "Twenty-Seventh": A Regimental History* (New Haven, Conn.: Morris & Benham, 1866), 82.

42. Williams, *Life in Camp*, 154-55.

43. Gracey, *Annals of the Sixth Pennsylvania Cavalry*, 186.

44. Gilpin diary, entry for July 7, 1863.

45. *OR* 27, pt. 3, 587.

46. *Ibid.*, 593.

47. *Ibid.*, pt. 2, 82.

48. *Ibid.*

Chapter 10

1. Hammond diary, entry for July 8, 1863.

2. Schooley to his mother, July 9, 1863.

3. Glazier, *Three Years in the Federal Cavalry*, 280.

4. J. Willard Brown, *The Signal Corps, U.S.A. in the War of the Rebellion* (Boston: U.S. Veteran Signal Corps Association, 1896), 373.

5. Searight, *The Old Pike*, 107.

6. John T. Trowbridge, *A Picture of the Desolated States; and the Work of Restoration, 1865-1868* (Hartford, CT: L. Stebbins, 1868), 40-41.

7. Gracey, *Annals of the Sixth Pennsylvania Cavalry*, 182.

8. *OR* 27, pt. 2, 703. Dismounting cavalry was an exact and often-drilled technique. All four troopers would dismount, with three handing their reins down the line to the fourth, who would turn the horses to the rear to safety, where they would be made immediately available should the cavalrymen have to remount quickly.

9. *New York Times*, July 12, 1863.

10. McDonald, *A History of the Laurel Brigade*, 163.

11. Robert J. Trout, *Galloping Thunder: The Stuart Horse Artillery Battalion* (Mechanicsburg, Pa.: Stackpole Books, 2002), 309.

12. *OR* 27, pt. 1, 1026.

13. Gracey, *Annals of the Sixth Pennsylvania Cavalry*, 187; George M. Neese, *Three Years in the Confederate Horse Artillery* (New York: Neale Publishing Co., 1911), 123.

14. Henry Norton, *Deeds of Daring, or, History of the Eighth N.Y. Volunteer Cavalry* (Norwich, N.Y.: Chenango Telegraph Printing House, 1889), 70-1.

15. McDonald, *A History of the Laurel Brigade*, 163.

16. Rea, *Sketches from Hampton's Cavalry,* 121.

17. Husby and Wittenberg, *Under Custer's Command*, 40.

18. Boudrye, *History of the Fifth New York Cavalry*, 69.

19. John Harper Dawson, *Wildcat Cavalry: A Synoptic History of the Seventeenth Virginia Cavalry Regiment of the Jenkins-McCausland Brigade in the War Between the States* (Dayton, Ohio: Morningside House, 1982), 81.

20. James H. Hodam, *Sketches and Personal Reminiscences of the Civil War as Experienced by a Confederate Soldier Together With Incidents of Boyhood Life of Fifty Years Ago* (Eugene, Ore.: Robert P. Hodam, 1995), 81.

21. Baker memoir.

22. Driver, *14th Virginia Cavalry*, 24.

23. Brown, *The Signal Corps in the Rebellion*, 374. In fact, Merritt gave an order that read, "To the Commander on the Right: Cease firing in your front. Capt. McCreary, signal officer, reports three squadrons of cavalry passing to your right. Throw out skirmishers, and keep a sharp lookout to prevent being flanked."

24. *Ibid.*, 199.

25. Kidd, *Personal Recollections*, 179.

26. *New York Times*, July 12, 1863.

27. Jackson, "Reminiscences of a Private."

28. *OR* 27, pt. 1, 1007.

29. G. G. Benedict, *Vermont in the Civil War*, 2 vols. (Burlington, Vt.: Free Press Assoc., 1888), 2:607.

30. A. W. Preston to P. T. Washburn, Adjutant General, State of Vermont, July 10, 1863, included in Péladeau, *Burnished Rows of Steel*, 191.

31. Rea, *Sketches from Hampton's Cavalry,* 122.

32. *Wheeling Daily Intelligencer*, July 27, 1863.

33. *OR* 27, pt. 1, 941.

34. *Ibid.*

35. *Ibid.*, 1033.

36. *New York Times*, July 12, 1863.

37. Robertson, *Michigan in the War*, 579.

38. Husby and Wittenberg, *Under Custer's Command*, 40.

39. Rockwell to his wife, July 9, 1863.

40. *OR* 27, pt. 3, 602.

41. Schooley to his mother, July 9, 1863.

42. Péladeau, *Burnished Rows of Steel*, 191.

43. A. R. Small, *The Sixteenth Maine Regiment in the War of the Rebellion 1861-1865* (Portland, Maine: B. Thurston & Co., 1886), 134.

44. *OR* 27, pt. 3, 604.

45. Murray, *Letters From Gettysburg* 123.

46. Roe, *The Tenth Regiment*, 212.

47. Shoaf, "On the March Again at Daybreak," 129.

48. "After Gettysburg."

49. Murray, *Letters From Gettysburg*, 55.

50. Locke, *The Story of the Regiment*, 249.

51. Murray, *Letters From Gettysburg*, 56.

52. Neese, *Three Years in the Confederate Horse Artillery*, 197.

53. Davis, *Three Years in the Army*, 251.

54. Dr. S. B. Judkins, "A Cavalry Encounter," *The National Tribune*, September 15, 1898.

55. Gilpin diary, entry for July 8, 1863

56. *Ibid.*

57. Neese, *Three Years in the Confederate Horse Artillery*, 197.

58. Hammond diary, entry for July 8, 1863.

59. Gracey, *Annals of the Sixth Pennsylvania Cavalry*, 184.

60. *OR* 27, pt. 2, 703.

61. Neese, *Three Years in the Confederate Horse Artillery*, 196.

62. Hard, *History of the Eighth Cavalry Regiment*, 263.63. Neese, *Three Years in the Confederate Horse Artillery*, 196.

63. Edward G. Longacre, *The Cavalry at Gettysburg: A Tactical Study of Mounted Operations During the Civil War's Pivotal Campaign, 9 June-14 July 1863* (Rutherford, N.J.: Fairleigh Dickinson University Press, 1986), 261.

64. Jackson, "Reminiscences of a Private."

65. Staats, *The Life and Letters of Colonel William Stedman*, 164.

66. Rockwell to his wife, July 9, 1863.

67. Kay to his parents, July 9, 1863.

68. *OR* 27, pt. 2, 398.

69. John Esten Cooke, *Wearing of the Gray: Being Personal Portraits, Scenes, and Adventures of the War* (New York: E. B. Treat & Co., 1867), 249.

70. Hall, *History of the Sixth New York Cavalry*, 148.

71. *OR* 27, pt. 3, 605-6.

72. Ludgen, *Williamsport, Maryland*, 36.

73. Hotchkiss, *Make Me a Map of the Valley*, 159.

74. *The Richmond Daily Dispatch*, July 18, 1863.

75. Weygant, *History of the 124th Regiment of New York State Volunteers*, 196.

76. *Ibid.*, 197.

77. Small, *The Sixteenth Maine Regiment*, 154.

78. Acken, *Inside the Army of the Potomac*, 313.

79. Joseph R. C. Ward, *History of the One Hundred and Sixth Regiment Pennsylvania Volunteers, 2d Brigade, 2d Division, 2d Corps, 1861-1865* (Philadelphia: Grant, Faires & Rodgers, 1883), 176.

80. Bliss Perry, *The Life and Letters of Henry Lee Higginson* (Boston: The Atlantic Monthly Press, 1921), 204. Curtis remained with the regiment for another week, but the

intermittent bouts of malaria, and this latest flare-up, forced him to resign from the army before the end of July.

81. John W. Urban, *Battlefield and Prison Pen, or Through the War and Thrice a Prisoner in Rebel Dungeons* (Philadelphia: Hubbard Brothers, 1882), 229.

82. Luscar Voorhees file, Civil War Miscellaneous Collection, USAHEC.

83. Thomas M. Aldreich, *The History of Battery A, First Regiment Rhode Island Light Artillery in the War to Preserve the Union 1861-1865* (Providence: Snow & Farnham, 1904), 224.

84. John Day Smith, *The History of the Nineteenth Regiment of Maine Volunteer Infantry 1862-1865* (Minneapolis: The Great Western Printing Co., 1909), 94.

85. Sauerburger and Bayard, *"I Seat Myself to Write a Few Lines,"* 161.

86. Hodam, *Sketches and Personal Reminiscences*, 81.

87. *In Memoriam: John Hammond*, 62.

88. *OR* 27, pt. 1, 925.

89. Baker memoir.

90. Donald A. Hopkins, *The Little Jeff: The Jeff Davis Legion, Cavalry, Army of Northern Virginia* (Shippensburg, Pa.: White Mane, 1999), 158.

91. Acken, *Inside the Army of the Potomac*, 292.

92. Blight, *When This Cruel War is Over*, 242.

93. *Ibid.*, 241.

94. Shoaf, "On the March Again at Daybreak," 128.

95. *OR* 27, pt. 3, 611.

96. Elijah R. Kennedy, *John B. Woodward: A Biographical Memoir* (New York: The De Vinne Press, 1897), 113.

97. For a good biographical sketch of "Baldy" Smith, see James Harrison Wilson, *Life and Services of William Farrar Smith, Major General United States Volunteers in the Civil War* (Wilmington, Del.: John M. Rogers Press, 1904).

98. *OR* 27, pt. 3, 580.

99. Billings, *The Tenth Massachusetts Battery*, 101.

100. George Lewis, *History of Battery E, First Regiment Rhode Island Light Artillery, in the War of 1861 and 1865, to Preserve the Union* (Providence: Snow & Farnham, 1892), 226.

101. Oliver Wilson Davis, *Life of David Bell Birney, Major-General United States Volunteers* (Philadelphia: King & Baird, 1867), 193.

102. de Trobriand, *Four Years in the Army of the Potomac*, 517.

103. Susan Hinckle Bradley, ed., *Leverett Bradley: A Soldier Boy's Letters, 1862-1865; A Man's Work in the Ministry* (Boston: Privately published, 1905), 28.

104. Billings, *The Tenth Massachusetts Battery*, 101-102.

105. J. H. Gilson, *Concise History of the One Hundred and Twenty-sixth Regiment, Ohio Volunteer Infantry, from the Date of Organization to the End of the Rebellion; With a complete Roster of Each Company, From Date of Muster* (Salem, Ohio: Walton, Steam Job and Label Printer, 1883), 12.

106. *Ibid.*

107. *OR* 27, pt. 3, 601.

108. Meade, *Life and Letters*, 2:132.

109. *OR* 27, pt. 3, 517.

110. *Ibid.*, 601.

Chapter 11

1. Harrison, *Life of The Right Reverend John Barrett Kerfoot,* 262.
2. David P. Bridges, *Fighting with Jeb Stuart: Major James Breathed and the Confederate Horse Artillery* (Arlington, Va.: Breathed Bridges Best, Inc., 2006), 181.
3. *Baltimore Daily Gazette,* July 11, 1863.
4. Rockwell to his wife, July 9, 1863.
5. *Baltimore Daily Gazette,* July 11, 1863.
6. Curtis, *History of the Twenty-Fourth Michigan,* 194.
7. Rufus R. Dawes, *Service with the Sixth Wisconsin Volunteers* (Marietta, Ohio: E. R. Alderman & Sons, 1890), 185.
8. John S. Collier and Bonnie B. Collier, eds., *Yours for the Union: The Civil War Letters of John W. Chase, First Massachusetts Battery* (New York: Fordham University Press, 2004), 256-257.
9. Smith, *History of the Seventy-Sixth Regiment,* 253.
10. Locke, *The Story of the Regiment,* 249.
11. Hussey, *History of the Ninth Regiment,* 290.
12. Howard, *Autobiography,* 1:444.
13. Smith, *History of the Seventy-Sixth Regiment,* 253.
14. *OR* 27, pt. 3, 617.
15. *Ibid.*, 985, 987-88.
16. Delauter, *18th Virginia Cavalry,* 9.
17. *OR* 27, pt. 3, 985, 987-88.
18. *Ibid.*, 985.
19. Hodam, *Sketches and Personal Reminiscences,* 82.
20. *Ibid.*
21. *Ibid.*, 83-4. Hodam also claimed that Lt. Gen. James Longstreet had ridden by and that the general spotted Hodam leaning against the fence. Longstreet asked whether the young man had been wounded and if he needed help getting an ambulance. When told he had not received a scratch, but had carried off a wounded comrade, Longstreet responded, "Well, young man, you had better get a clean suit of clothes the first opportunity."
22. *OR* 27, pt. 1, 941.
23. Longacre, *The Cavalry at Gettysburg,* 262.
24. Norton, *Deeds of Daring,* 71.
25. Robert J. Driver, Jr., *1st Virginia Cavalry* (Lynchburg, Va.: H. E. Howard Co., 1991), 68.
26. Neese, *Three Years in the Confederate Horse Artillery,* 197.
27. *OR* 27, pt. 1, 941.
28. Gilpin diary, entry for July 9, 1863.
29. Longacre, *The Cavalry at Gettysburg,* 262.
30. Boudrye, *Historic Records,* 70; Roger D. Hunt, *Colonels in Blue: Union Army Colonels of the Civil War: New York* (Atglen, Pa.: Schiffer Military History, 2003), 102.
31. Bowen, *History of the Thirty-Seventh Regiment,* 195.
32. Robert Stiles, *Four Years Under Marse Robert* (New York: The Neale Publishing Company, 1903), 222-24.

33. Dawes, *Service with the Sixth Wisconsin Volunteers*, 186.
34. *OR* 27, pt. 3, 616-17.
35. *Ibid.*, 621.
36. Alfred S. Roe, *The Thirty-Ninth Regiment Massachusetts Volunteers 1861-1865* (Worcester, Mass.: Regimental Veteran Assoc., 1914), 80.

Chapter 12

1. Edwin W. Stone, *Rhode Island in the War of the Rebellion* (Providence, George H. Whitney, 1864), 277.
2. Searight, *The Old Pike*, 197-198.
3. *Baltimore American*, July 13, 1863.
4. Stonebraker, *A Rebel of '61*, 53.
5. Keller, *Events of the Civil War in Washington County, Maryland*, 241.
6. Longacre, *The Cavalry at Gettysburg*, 264.
7. Gilpin diary, entry for July 10, 1863.
8. Lt. Robert T. Hubard, *The Civil War Memoirs of a Virginia Cavalryman*, Thomas P. Nanzig, ed. (Tuscaloosa: University of Alabama Press, 2007), 102.
9. Stonebraker, *A Rebel of '61*, 53
10. Neese, *Three Years in the Confederate Horse Artillery*, 197.
11. *Ibid.*, 197-8.
12. Harrison, *The Life of Right Reverend John Barrett Kerfoot*, 262.
13. *OR* 27, pt. 2, 361.
14. James Longstreet, *From Manassas to Appomattox: Memoirs of the Civil War in America* (Philadelphia: J. B. Lippincott Co., 1896), 428.
15. *OR* 27, pt. 2, 398.
16. *Ibid.*, 398.
17. *Ibid.*
18. *Atlanta Daily Intelligencer*, August 21, 1863.
19. Jasper Cheney diary, entry for July 10, 1863, Civil War Miscellaneous Collection, USAHEC.
20. Roger D. Hunt, *Colonels in Blue: Union Army Colonels of the Civil War: New York* (Atglen, Pa.: Schiffer Military History, 2003), 184.
21. Shoemaker, *Shoemaker's Battery*, 47.
22. Hopkins, *The Little Jeff*, 158.
23. Alexander, *Fighting for the Confederacy*, 271.
24. Longstreet, *From Manassas to Appomattox*, 428.
25. Neese, *Three Years in the Confederate Horse Artillery*, 198
26. Adams, *The Civil War in Washington County*, 52.
27. Stonebraker, *A Rebel of '61*, 53.
28. *OR* 27, pt. 2, 376.
29. Stonebraker, *A Rebel of '61*, 54.
30. Shoemaker, *Shoemaker's Battery*, 47.
31. "After Gettysburg."
32. Hard, *History of the Eighth Regiment*, 264
33. Gillespie, *History of Company A*, 163.

34. Brown, *The Signal Corps*, 373-75 and 199.

35. A.J. Alexander to John Buford, July 10, 1863, C. Ross Smith Papers, Civil War Miscellaneous Collection, USAHEC.

36. *OR* 27, pt. 2, 404.

37. *Report of the Joint Committee*, 315.

38. *OR* 27, pt. 1, 337.

39. *Ibid.*, 929, 936 and 942.

40. John McGregor Adams and Albert Egerton Adams, eds., *Memorial and Letters of Rev. John R. Adams, D. D., Chaplain of the Fifth Maine and the One Hundred and Twenty-First New York Regiment During the War of the Rebellion, Serving from the Beginning to Its Close* (Privately published, 1890), 116.

41. *OR* 27, pt. 1, 936.

42. Stonebraker, *A Rebel of '61*, 54.

43. DePeyster, *The Decisive Conflicts of the Late Civil War*, 118-20 (emphasis in original).

44. Gracey, *Annals of the Sixth Pennsylvania Cavalry*, 188.

45. Diary of Wilbur Fisk, entry for July 10, 1863, Wilbur Fisk Papers, Manuscripts Division, LOC.

46. "After Gettysburg."

47. Lewis A. Grant to Adjutant General of Vermont, July 11, 1863, included in *Report of the Adjutant & Inspector General of the State of Vermont for the Year Ending November 1, 1863* (Montpelier: Walton's Steam Printing Establishment, 1863), 83.

48. "After Gettysburg."

49. *Report of the Adjutant*, 83.

50. Paul G. Zeller, *The Second Vermont Volunteer Infantry Regiment, 1861-1865* (Jefferson, N.C.: McFarland & Co., 2002), 150-151.

51. "After Gettysburg."

52. Roger D. Hunt, *Colonels in Blue: Union Army Colonels of the Civil War. The New England States: Connecticut, Maine, Massachusetts, New Hampshire, Rhode Island, Vermont* (Atglen, Pa.: Schiffer Military History, 2001), 214. Seaver, a gifted officer, commanded the 2nd Brigade, 2nd Division, 6th Corps from December 1863 until January 1864. He then resumed command of the 3rd Vermont, and earned the Medal of Honor for his valor in leading his regiment at the Battle of Spotsylvania on May 10, 1864, when "at the head of three regiments and under a most galling fire, attacked and occupied the enemy's works." After taking his discharge, Seaver returned to Vermont and resumed his legal career. He served as probate judge and also as Vermont railroad commissioner in the years following the war.

53. Robert G. Poirier, *They Could Not Have Done Better: Thomas O. Seaver and the 3rd Vermont Infantry* (Newport, Vt.: Vermont Civil War Enterprises, 2005), 111.

54. "After Gettysburg."

55. Krick, *Lee's Colonels*, 249.

56. William T. Lasseter, "Reminiscences of the Civil War," *The Shreveport Journal*, October 31, 1929.

57. *Athens Southern Banner*, July 29, 1863.

58. *Report of the Adjutant*, 83-84..

59. Poirier, *They Could Not Have Done Better*, 111.

60. Rosenblatt and Rosenblatt, *Hard Marching Every Day*, 123.

61. *Athens Southern Banner*, July 29, 1863.

62. *Atlanta Daily Intelligencer*, August 12, 1863.

63. Lyman Simpson Hayes, *History of the Town of Rockingham, Vermont, Including the Villages of Bellows Falls, Saxtons River, Rockingham, Cambridgeport, and Bartonville, 1753-1907, With Family Genealogies* (Bellows Falls, Vt.: Town of Bellows Falls, 1907), 764. On March 13, 1865, Stoughton received a brevet to brigadier general of volunteers in recognition of his "gallantry on the field." Roger D. Hunt and Jack R. Brown, *Brevet Brigadier Generals in Blue* (Gaithersburg, Md.: Olde Soldier Books, 1990), 593.

64. Benedict, *Vermont in the Civil War*, 2: 166, 194, and 220.

65. Stevens, *Three Years in the Sixth Corps*, 263.

66. *OR* 27, pt. 1, 664.

67. *Proceedings of the Reunion Society of Vermont Officers, 1864-1884, with Addresses Delivered at Its Meetings*, 2 vols. (Burlington: Free Press Assoc., 1885.), 1:417.

68. Quoted in Coffin, *Full Duty*, 212.

69. Poirier, *They Could Not Have Done Better*, 112.

70. G. G. Benedict, *Vermont in the Civil War* (Burlington: Free Press Association, 1886), 390-393.

71. *Ibid.*

72. Hyde, *Following the Greek Cross*, 161.

73. Stevens, *Three Years in the Sixth Corps*, 263.

74. Poirier, *They Could Not Have Done Better*, 111.

75. Jerome Cutler letter of July 17, 1863 in H. Klynstra, ed. *Letters of Jerome Cutler, Waterville, Vermont, During his Enlistment in the Union Army, 2nd Regiment, Vermont Volunteers, 1861-1864* (Privately published, 1990).

76. Newell, *Annals of the Tenth Regiment*, 225.

77. *OR* 27, pt. 2, 370.

78. *Ibid.*, 374.

79. Tyler, *Recollections of the Civil War*, 111.

80. Bowen, *History of the Thirty-Seventh Regiment*, 195.

81. Benedict, *Vermont in the Civil War*, 393.

82. Harrison, *Life of Right Reverend John Barrett Kerfoot*, 262.

83. *OR* 27, pt. 2, 705.

84. Hammond diary, entry for July 9, 1863.

85. Neese, *Three Years in the Confederate Horse Artillery*, 198.

86. Fisk diary, entry for July 10, 1863.

87. Gilpin diary, entry for July 10, 1863.

88. Stevens, *Three Years in the Sixth Corps*, 262.

89. *OR* 27, pt. 1, 925-6.

90. Woodford B. Hackley, *The Little Fork Rangers: A Sketch of Company "D" Fourth Virginia Cavalry* (Richmond: Press of the Dietz Printing Co., 1927), 86.

91. John W. Thomason, *Jeb Stuart* (New York: Charles Scribner's Sons, 1930), 451.

92. "After Gettysburg."

93. Mrs. Annie Sharias, "Buried at Funkstown," *The National Tribune*, August 21, 1913. Schonebarger was later disinterred and taken home for burial.

94. Stonebraker, *A Rebel of '61*, 55.

95. *Ibid.* *"Dulce et decorum est, pro patria mori"* means "it is sweet to die for one's country."

96. *Athens Southern Banner*, July 29, 1863.

97. Stiles, *Four Years Under Marse Robert*, 220-221.

98. James F. Cook, *The Governors of Georgia, 1754-2004*, 3d ed. (Macon, Ga.: Mercer University Press, 2005), 174-177. The lasting legacy of his term as governor included the construction of the state capitol building in Atlanta and his establishment of the Georgia College of Technology (today known as the Georgia Institute of Technology, or Georgia Tech). In spite of the severe wound received at Funkstown and the ordeal of his captivity at Johnson's Island, McDaniel lived until 1926, when he died at the age of 90. Interestingly, Brig. Gen. John B. Gordon, who commanded a brigade of Georgians assigned to Jubal A. Early's division, also served as post-war governor of Georgia.

99. Stonebraker, *A Rebel of '61*, 55.

100. *Baltimore American*, July 14, 1863.

101. Zeller, *The Second Vermont*, 151.

102. *OR* 27, pt. 2, 991.

103. *Baltimore American*, July 11, 1863.

104. Hubard, *Civil War Memoirs*, 103.

105. McKim, *A Soldier's Recollections*, 181.

106. William S. Lincoln, *Life with the Thirty-Fourth Mass. Infantry in the War of the Rebellion* (Worcester: Press of Noyes, Snow & Co., 1879), 114.

107. Margery J. Greenleaf, ed., *Letters to Eliza from a Union Soldier, 1862-1865* (Chicago: Follett Publishing Co., 1970), 25-26.

108. Roe, *The Thirty-Ninth Regiment*, 81.

109. Greenleaf, *Letters to Eliza*, 26.

110. Roe, *The Thirty-Ninth Regiment*, 84.

111. *Ibid.*, 85.

112. Sessarego, *Letters Home V*, 16.

113. Davis, *Three Years in the Army*, 251-52.

114. Auchmuty, *Letters*, 104-105.

115. John W. Storrs, *The "Twentieth Connecticut" A Regimental History* (Ansonia, Conn.: Press of the Naugatuck Valley Sentinel, 1886), 108.

116. Quint, *Second Massachusetts Infantry*, 183.

117. *OR* Supplement, vol. 5, 224.

118. *In Memoriam Henry Warner Slocum 1826-1894* (Albany: J. B. Lyon Co., 1904), 187.

119. Hussey, *History of the Ninth Regiment*, 291.

120. Gilbert Adams Hays, comp., *Under the Red Patch: The Story of the Sixty-Third Regiment Pennsylvania Volunteers 1861-1864* (Pittsburgh: Sixty-third Pennsylvania Volunteers Regimental Assoc., 1908), 204.

121. Gilpin diary, entry for July 10, 1863.

122. Charles H. Lynch, *The Civil War Diary 1862-1865 of Charles H. Lynch, 18th Conn. Vol's.* (Hartford: The Case, Lockwood & Evannard Co., 1915), 25.

123. Meade, *Life and Letters*, 2:133-34.

124. *OR* 27, pt. 3, 627.

125. Jones, *Campbell Brown's Civil War*, 388.

126. DePeyster, *The Decisive Conflicts*, 96.

127. *OR* 27, pt. 1, 929.

128. Gracey, *Annals of the Sixth Pennsylvania Cavalry*, 189.

129. Cheney, *History of the Ninth Regiment, New York Volunteer Cavalry,* 120.

130. Fredric Denison, *Sabres and Spurs: The First Regiment Rhode Island Cavalry in the Civil War, 1861-1865* (Providence: First Rhode Island Cavalry Veteran Assoc., 1876), 275.

131. *OR* 27, pt. 1, 971.

132. *Ibid.*, 90.

133. *Ibid.*

134. *Ibid.*, 89.

Chapter 13

1. Jones, *Campbell Brown's Civil War*, 225.

2. Hard, *History of the Eighth Regiment*, 264.

3. Winfield Scott Hall, *The Captain: An Eighth Illinois Trooper* (Riverside, Ill.: Privately published, 1994), 45.

4. Gilpin diary, entry for July 11, 1863.

5. Diary of unknown member of the 6th Louisiana Infantry, entry for July 11, 1863.

6. George B. Davis, "From Gettysburg to Williamsport," *Campaigns of Virginia, Maryland and Pennsylvania*, Papers of the Historical Society of Massachusetts 3 (Boston: Griffith, Stillings Press, 1903): 461-62.

7. Harrison, *Life of Right Reverend John Barrett Kerfoot,* 262.

8. Urban, *Battlefield and Prison Pen*, 231.

9. Howard, *Recollections of a Confederate Soldier*, 216; DePeyster, *Decisive Conflicts*, 125-26.

10. Alexander, *Fighting for the Confederacy*, 271.

11. Moran to Sickles, January 24, 1882, *The Bachelder Papers,* 2:784.

12. *OR* 27, pt. 2, 361.

13. Wiley, *Norfolk Blues*, 80.

14. Trout, *Galloping Thunder*, 313.

15. Caldwell, *The History of a Brigade of South Carolinians*, 106.

16. B. K. Benson, *Who Goes There? The Story of a Spy in the Civil War* (New York: The MacMillan Co., 1902), 423.

17. *The Richmond Daily Dispatch*, July 18, 1863.

18. *Baltimore American*, July 14, 1863.

19. Hermann Schuricht, "Jenkins' Brigade in the Gettysburg Campaign," *Richmond Dispatch*, April 5, 1896.

20. Driver, *1st Virginia Cavalry*, 68.

21. Beale, *A Lieutenant of Cavalry*, 118.

22. D. N. McClintock, "Driving Lee Out of Maryland," *The National Tribune*, November 10, 1910.

23. Baldwin to Bachelder, May 20, 1865, *The Bachelder Papers*, 1:195.

24. Emerson Gifford Taylor, ed., *Gouverneur K. Warren: The Life and Letters of an American Soldier 1830-1882* (Boston: Houghton-Mifflin Co., 1932), 133.

25. Eric A. Campbell, ed., "'The Severest Fought Battle of the War': Charles Wellington Reed and the Medal of Honor," *Civil War Regiments* Vol. 6, No. 3 (1999): 42.

26. Rhodes, *All for the Union*, 118.

27. Bradley, *Leverett Bradley*, 28.

28. Furst diary, entry for July 10, 1863.

29. Ide, *History of the First Vermont Cavalry Volunteers*, 123.

30. Nevins, *A Diary of Battle*, 261.

31. Andrew A. Humphreys, *Gettysburg to the Rapidan: The Army of the Potomac, July 1863 to April 1864* (New York: Charles Scribner's Sons, 1883), 6.

32. DePeyster, *Decisive Conflicts*, 96.

33. Edwin B. Coddington, *The Gettysburg Campaign: A Study in Command* (New York: Charles Scribner's Sons, 1968), 567.

34. *Milledgeville Southern Recorder*, September 15, 1863.

35. *OR* 27, pt. 3, 991.

36. Lee's General Order of July 11, 1863, copy in files, GNMP.

37. Fitzhugh Lee, *General Lee* (New York: D. Appleton & Co., 1894), 305.

38. Hubard memoir.

39. Louis, Leon, *Diary of a Tar Heel Confederate Soldier* (Charlotte, N. C.: Stone Publishing Co., 1913), 39-40.

40. Leonard Williams to his wife, July 11, 1863, Leonard Williams Letters, David G. Douglas Collection, Ridley Park, Pennsylvania.

41. Styple, *Writing & Fighting from the Army of Northern Virginia*, 257.

42. *Baltimore American*, July 13, 1863; Gary M. Petrichick, *Pocket Guide to the Civil War on the Chesapeake & Ohio Canal* (Belmont, N.Y.: Dave's Printing, 2003), 35.

43. Casler, *Four Years in the Stonewall Brigade*, 180-181.

44. Loehr, *War History of the Old First Virginia*, 39.

45. *OR* 27, pt. 3, 994.

46. *Ibid.*, pt. 1, 834.

47. Styple, *Writing and Fighting the Civil War*, 204.

48. Williams, *Life in Camp*, 157.

49. McClintock, "Driving Lee Out of Maryland".

50. Acken, *Inside the Army of the Potomac*, 293.

51. *New York Sun*, July 13, 1863.

52. Cassedy, *Dear Friends at Home*, 295.

53. William P. Seville, *History of the First Regiment Delaware Volunteers, from the Commencement of the "Three Months' Service" to the Final Muster-Out at the Close of the Rebellion* (Wilmington: Historical Society of Delaware, 1884), 91.

54. Ward, *History of the One Hundred and Sixth Regiment*, 177.

55. SeCheverell, *29th Ohio*, 75.

56. Morhous, *Reminiscences*, 56.

57. *OR* 27, pt. 3, 649.

58. Wood, *Rhode Island in the Rebellion*, 276.

59. Thomas Marbaker, *History of the Eleventh New Jersey Volunteers* (Trenton: MacCrellish & Quigley, 1898), 113.

60. *OR* 27, pt. 3, 653.

61. *Ibid.*, 646-47.

62. Aldrich, *The History of Battery A*, 225.

63. *OR* 27, pt. 3, 648-49.

64. Harrison, *Life of Right Reverend John Barrett Kerfoot,* 263. Fitz John Porter, descended from an impressive American naval family and cousin of Admirals David Dixon Porter and David Glasgow Farragut, was cashiered from the Federal army in January 1863 after charges of disobedience in the Second Battle of Bull Run. Porter was vindicated by President Chester A. Arthur in 1886 and was retired a full colonel in the army, his rank previous to his arrest. For more on this unfortunate incident, see Curt Anders, *Injustice on Trial: Second Bull Run, General Fitz-John Porter's Court Martial and the Schofield Board Investigation that Cleared His Good Name* (Cincinnati: Emmis Books, 2002).

65. Harrison, *Life of Right Reverend John Barrett Kerfoot*, 262.

66. Diary of Abner B. Frank, entry for July 11, 1863, Civil War Miscellaneous Collection, USAHEC.

67. Cheney, *History of the Ninth Regiment, New York Volunteer Cavalry,* 120. The regimental historian noted, "On the way here a small burying ground was passed near the battlefield where some soldiers were buried from a field hospital after the battle of Antietam. White headboards marked the graves and the ground was inclosed with a white board fence." It is assumed these victims were subsequently removed to the National Cemetery, dedicated in 1867.

68. *New York Sun*, July 13, 1863.

69. Cheney diary, entry for July 12, 1863.

70. Joseph McHenry Adkinson to Dear Brother, July 12, 1863, Ruth Adkinson Collection, New Castle, Colorado.

71. *OR* 27, pt. 3, 649.

72. *Baltimore American*, July 13, 1863.

73. Bartlett, *History of the Twelfth Regiment*, 138.

74. *OR* 27, pt. 1, 982.

75. *The Independent Republican*, July 21, 1863.

76. Aldrich, *History of Battery A*, 226.

77. Rhodes, *All for the Union*, 118.

78. Stevens, *Three Years in the Sixth Corps*, 262.

79. Michael Burlingame and John R. Turner, eds., *Inside Lincoln's White House: The Complete Diary of John Hay* (Carbondale: Southern Illinois University Press, 1997), 61.

Chapter 14

1. *OR* 27, pt. 3, 971.

2. Richardson's Civil War Roundtable, *Soldiers in Green,* 167.

3. Smith, *The History of the Nineteenth Regiment*, 94.

4. Harrison, *Life of Right Reverend John Barrett Kerfoot,* 263.

5. *OR* 27, pt. 3, 660.

6. *Ibid.*, 971.

7. Kidd, *Personal Recollections*, 191.

8. Gillespie, *History of Company A*, 164.

9. Trowbridge to Bigelow, undated letter.

10. Husby and Wittenberg, *Under Custer's Command*, 43.

11. *Hugh St. Clair*, 35.

12. *In Memoriam: John Hammond*, 64.

13. Harrison, *Life of Right Reverend John Barrett Kerfoot,* 263.

14. Gillespie, *History of Company A*, 164.

15. *Baltimore Daily Gazette*, July 14, 1863.

16. Jacobs, "Custer's Charge."

17. Jackson, "Reminiscences of a Private."

18. Baker memoirs.

19. *OR* 27, pt. 3, 656-57.

20. *Ibid.*, 657-58.

21. Casper C. Henkel to Fannie Coiner, July 12, 1863, copy in files, GNMP.

22. A. D. Betts, *Experiences of a Confederate Chaplain 1861-1864* (Greenville, S. C.: Privately published, n.d.), 41.

23. *OR* 27, pt. 3, 998.

24. *Ibid.*

25. Clifford Dowdey and Louis R. Manarin, eds., *The Wartime Papers of Robert E. Lee*, 2 vols. (Richmond: Commonwealth of Virginia, 1961): 2:348-49.

26. *History of the 18th Pennsylvania*, 85-6.

27. Moyer, *History of the 17th Regiment*, 67.

28. Gilpin diary, entry for July 12, 1863.

29. *New York Sun*, July 13, 1863.

30. Shoaf, "On the March at Daybreak," 130.

31. Blight, *When This Cruel War is Over*, 243-44.

32. Fisk diary, entry for July 12, 1863.

33. Roe, *The Tenth Regiment*, 212. Wilson, the 18th Vice President of the United States, was the chairman of the Military Affairs Committee prior to the shelling of Fort Sumter. With the coming of war, Wilson went back to Massachusetts to try to raise an entire brigade at the beginning of the war. Instead, he was only able to raise a single regiment, the 22nd Massachusetts Volunteer Infantry, which was also known as the Henry Wilson Regiment. Wilson was aligned with the Radical Republicans, who later targeted George Meade for persecution.

34. Page, *History of the Fourteenth Regiment*, 169.

35. *Pottsville Miner's Journal*, July 17, 1913.

36. Stevens, *Three Years in the Sixth Corps*, 260-61.

37. *Pottsville Journal*, July 19, 1913.

38. William F. Smith, *Autobiography of Major General William F. Smith 1861-1864*, Herbert M. Schiller, ed. (Dayton, Ohio: Morningside, 1990), 69-70.

39. *OR* 27, pt. 3, 550.

40. *Ibid.*, 625.

41. *Ibid.*, 574, 624-25.

42. Kirkley, "Lee's Retreat."

43. Meade, *Life and Letters*, 2:134.

44. *OR* 27, pt. 1, 91-92.

45. James F. Rusling, *Men and Things I Saw in Civil War Days* (New York: Eaton & Mains, 1899), 70-71.

46. Howard, *Autobiograhy*, 1:445.

47. Gouverneur K. Warren in *JCCS*, 1:381.

48. William B. Styple, ed., *Generals in Bronze: Interviewing the Commanders of the Civil War* (Kearny, N.J.: Belle Grove Publishing Co., 2005), 178.

49. Carl and Ellen Batelle Stoeckel, eds., *Correspondence of John Sedgwick, Major General*, 2 vols. (Privately published, 1903), 2:134-35.

50. French, as quoted by Pleasonton in *JCCW*, 1:361.

51. *New York Daily News*, July 14, 1863; Meade, *Life and Letters*, 2:132.0

52. *OR* 27, pt. 1, 92.

53. *Ibid.*, pt. 3, 675.

54. *OR* 27, pt. 3, 667-68.

55. Howard, *Autobiography*, 1:445.

56. Baldwin to Bachelder, May 20, 1865, *The Bachelder Papers*, 1:195.

57. Furst diary, entry for July 13, 1863.

58. Shoaf, "On the March at Daybreak," 130.

59. *OR* 27, pt. 1, 404.

60. Nevins, *A Diary of Battle*, 260.

61. E. M. Haynes, *A History of the Tenth Regiment, Vermont Volunteers, With Biographical Sketches of the Officers Who Fell in Battle and a Complete Roster of all the Officers and Men Connected With It—Showing All Changes by Promotion, Death or Resignation, During the Military Existence of the Regiment* (Lewiston, Maine: Tenth Vermont Regimental Assoc., 1870), 37.

62. Neese, *Three Years in the Confederate Horse Artillery*, 198.

63. *Baltimore American*, July 14, 1863.

64. *Brooklyn Daily Eagle*, July 14, 1863.

Chapter 15

1. *History of the 121st Regiment Pennsylvania Volunteers*, 57.

2. Aldrich, *The History of Battery A*, 226.

3. Newell, *Annals of the Tenth Regiment*, 225.

4. *Baltimore Daily Gazette*, July 16, 1863.

5. Ezra D. Simons, *A Regimental History. The One Hundred Twenty-Fifth New York State Volunteers* (New York: Privately published, 1888), 148.

6. McNamara, *The History of the Ninth Regiment*, 333.

7. Justus Schiebert, *Seven Months in the Rebel States During the North American War, 1863*, trans. Joseph C. Hayes, ed. William Stanley Hoole (Tuscaloosa, Ala.: Confederate Publishing Co., 1958), 121-22.

8. Williams, *Life in Camp*, 158.

9. Auchmuty, *Letters*, 105-106.

10. Charles Marshall, *An Aide-de-Camp of Lee* (Boston: Little, Brown, 1927), 244.

11. Burlingame and Turner, *Inside Lincoln's White House*, 62.

12. McClellan, *Life and Campaigns*, 365.

13. *OR* 27, pt. 1, 996.

14. Gillespie, *History of Company A*, 164-66.

15. *Ibid.*, 166.

16. *OR* 27, pt. 1, 667.

17. Beale, *History of the Ninth Virginia Cavalry*, 96-7.

18. Hard, *History of the Eighth Regiment*, 264.

19. James Bell to Gusta Ann Hallock, July 11, 1863 James Bell Papers, Albert Huntington Library, San Marino, California.

20. Smith, *The Story of a Cavalry Regiment*, 109.

21. S. A. Clark, "A Little Fracas: How Some of the 1st Vt. Got In and Got Out Again," *National Tribune*, May 2, 1895.

22. *Ibid.*; Ide, *History of the First Vermont Cavalry Volunteers*, 124.

23. Harrison, *The Life of Right Reverend John Barrett Kerfoot,* 263.

24. Bell to Hallock, July 11, 1863.

25. Eric J. Wittenberg, ed., *"We Have It Damn Hard Out Here": The Civil War Letters of Sergeant Thomas W. Smith, Sixth Pennsylvania Cavalry* (Kent, Ohio: Kent State University Press, 1999), 99.

26. Coffin, *Four Years of Fighting*, 303.

27. Ethan S. Rafuse, *George Gordon Meade and the War in the East* (Abiline, Texas: McWhiney Foundation Press, 2003), 92-93.

28. William P. Seville, "History of the First Regiment, Delaware Volunteers, From the Commencement of the 'Three Months Service' to the Final Muster-Out at the Close of the Rebellion," included in *Papers of the Historical Society of Delaware* 5 (Wilmington DE: Privately published, 1884), 92. During the Gettysburg Campaign, Seville was Acting Assistant Adjutant General of his regiment, which was in the 2nd Corps. See *OR* 27, pt. 1, 466.

29. F. M. Colston, "Gettysburg As I Saw It," *Confederate Veteran*, 5 (1897), 551-53.

30. Frank Saunders to George Saunders, July 13, 1863, Frank Saunders letters, Sue Martin collection, Fairport, New York.

31. George W. Beale, "Soldier's Account of the Gettysburg Campaign: Letter from George W. Beale (Son of General R. L. T. Beale)," *Southern Historical Society Papers* XI (July 1883), 326.

32. Robert H. Moore, II, *The 1st and 2nd Stuart Horse Artillery* (Lynchburg, Va.: H. E. Howard Co., 1985), 71.

33. Robert J. Trout, ed., *In the Saddle With Stuart: The Story of Frank Smith Robertson of Jeb Stuart's Staff* (Gettysburg, Pa.: Thomas Publications, 1998), 85-6.

34. *OR* 27, pt. 3, 1001.

35. Horatio G. Wright to his wife, July 18, 1863, Robert Brake Collection, USAHEC.

36. Stephen Z. Starr, *The Union Cavalry in the Civil War*, 3 vols. (Baton Rouge: Louisiana State University Press, 1975), 1:458. Harman, described as having "keen grey eyes, long heavy beard" had previously served in the Mexican War. Robert E.L. Krick, *Staff Officers in Gray: A Biographical Register of the Staff Officers in the Army of Northern Virginia* (Chapel Hill: University of North Carolina Press, 2003), 149.

37. Hess, *Lee's Tar Heels*, 162.

38. Channing M. Bolton, "With General Lee's Engineers," *Confederate Veteran*, 30 (1922), 298-302.

39. Longstreet, *From Manassas to Appomattox*, 430.

40. Diary of Jedediah Hotchkiss, entry for July 14, 2002, Hotchkiss Papers, Manuscripts Division, LOC.

41. Alexander, *Fighting for the Confederacy*, 272.

42. Stocker, *From Huntsville to Appomattox*, 114.

43. James H. Lane, "Twenty-Eighth North Carolina Infantry," *Charlotte Observer*, February 17, 1895.

44. Welch, *A Confederate Surgeon's Letters,* 70.

45. Ludgen, *Williamsport, Maryland,* 39.

46. Alexander, *Fighting for the Confederacy*, 272.

47. *OR* 27, pt. 2, 353.

48. Sorrel, *Recollections of a Confederate Staff Officer,* 175.

49. Betts, *Experience of a Confederate Chaplain*, 41.

50. Trout, *In the Saddle With Stuart*, 85.

51. Hodam, *Sketches and Personal Reminiscences*, 85.

52. Oliver Taylor, "The War Story of a Confederate Soldier Boy," copy in files, GNMP.

53. McDonald, *A History of the Laurel Brigade*, 164.

Chapter 16

1. Moran to Sickles, January 24, 1882, *The Bachelder Papers*, 2:784.

2. Hubbs, *Voices from Company D,* 187.

3. Leon, *Diary of a Tar Heel*, 40.

4. Worsham, *One of Jackson's Foot Cavalry*, 174-75.

5. Howard, *Recollections of a Confederate Soldier*, 217.

6. Diary of an unidentified member of the 6th Louisiana Infantry, entry for July 14, 1863.

7. Love, "Mississippi at Gettysburg," 25.

8. *OR* 27, pt. 2, 558-59.

9. Hotchkiss, *Make Me a Map of the Valley*, 161.

10. Blackford, *War Years With Jeb Stuart*, 234-35.

11. John B. Gordon, *Reminiscences of the Civil War* (New York: Charles Scribner's Sons, 1903), 173.

12. Hubard memoir.

13. Hackley, *The Little Fork Rangers*, 86.

14. Beale, *History of the Ninth Virginia Cavalry*, 97.

15. Jubal A. Early, *Autobiographical Sketch and Narrative of the War Between the States* (Philadelphia: J. B. Lippincott, 1912), 284.

16. Trout, *In the Saddle With Stuart*, 86.

17. Moran to Sickles, January 24, 1882, *The Bachelder Papers*, 2:785.

18. Schuricht, "Jenkins Brigade in the Gettysburg Campaign."

19. Hodam, *Sketches and Personal Reminiscences*, 86.

20. Driver, *14th Virginia Cavalry*, 25.

21. Shoemaker, *Shoemaker's Battery*, 49.

22. Hodam, *Sketches and Personal Reminscences*, 86.

23. J. W. Biddle to his father, July 16, 1863, Biddle Papers, Perkins Library, Duke University, Durham, North Carolina.

24. Coffin, *Four Years of Fighting*, 304.

25. Harrison, *Life of Right Reverend John Barrett Kerfoot,* 264.

26. *Ibid.*

27. Duncan, "The College of St. James," 281.

28. Billings, *Tenth Massachusetts Battery*, 105.

29. Kerfoot and his dedicated staff were able to continue to operate the college on a shoestring until his arrest by General Early in August 1864. Kerfoot was told that his detention was in retaliation for the arrest by Northern authorities of Rev. Dr. Andrew H. Boyd of Winchester, Virginia. Early closed the school, but released Kerfoot to Baltimore on parole. St. James remained closed for five years, at which time the college was eliminated and its operations reduced to a private high school for boys. It still operates to the present day as a prestigious secondary school. *Ibid.,* 302-10.

30. Kirkley, "Gen. Lee's Retreat;" Horatio G. Wright to his wife, July 18, 1863, GNMP.

31. Matthews, "The Pelham-Breathed Battery," *St. Mary's Beacon,* April 27, 1905.

32. Trowbridge to Bigelow, undated letter.

33. Richardson's Civil War Roundtable, *Soldiers in Green,* 167-68.

34. *Ibid.*

35. Robert J. Driver, Jr. and Harold E. Howard, *2nd Virginia Cavalry* (Lynchburg, Va.: H. E. Howard Co., 1995), 94.

36. Lynwood M. Holland, *Pierce M. B. Young: The Warwick of the South* (Athens Ga.: University of Georgia Press, 1964), 73-74.

37. Haden, *Reminiscences of J. E. B. Stuart's Cavalry*, 26.

38. Matthews, "The Pelham-Breathed Battery," April 27, 1905.

39. Kidd, *Personal Recollections*, 110-11.

40. Trowbridge to Bigelow, undated letter.

41. Benson, *Who Goes There?*, 424.

42. Caldwell, *History of a Brigade of South Carolinians*, 107.

43. Charles Marshall, *An Aide-de-Camp of Lee* (Boston: Little, Brown, 1927), 245.

44. Hess, *Lee's Tar Heels,* 164.

45. Louis G. Young to Joseph A. Engelhard, August 13, 1874, included in S. D. Pool, ed., *Our Living and Dead: Devoted to North Carolina—Her Past, Her Present, and Her Future*, 2 vols. (Raleigh, N. C.: North Carolina Branch, Southern Historical Society, 1897), 1:29-30.

46. Mills, *History of the 16th North Carolina Regiment*, 41.

47. Hess, *Lee's Tar Heels*, 164.

48. Kidd, *Personal Recollections*, 185.

49. *OR* 27, pt. 1, 990.

50. Hess, *Lee's Tar Heels*, 164.

51. *New York Times*, July 29, 1863.

52. John T. McCall, "7th Tennessee – Battle of Falling Waters," *Confederate Veteran*, 6 (1898), 406.

53. John S. Schenck, *Index of Persons in Ionia County Mentioned in History of Ionia and Montcalm Counties* (Lansing, Mich.: W.P.A. Project, 1940), 94.

54. *New York Times*, July 29, 1863.

55. Jeffry D. Wert, *Custer: The Controversial Life of George Armstrong Custer* (New York: Simon & Schuster, 1996), 100.

56. John Kimble, "Tennesseans at Gettysburg—The Retreat," *Confederate Veteran*, 18 (1910), 462.

57. Clyde N. Wilson, *The Most Promising Young Man of the South: James Johnston Pettigrew and His Men at Gettysburg* (Abilene, Texas: McWhiney Foundation Press, 1998), 74.

58. Young to Engelhard, August 18, 1874, *Our Living and Our Dead*, 1:31. Interestingly, Pvt. John T. McCall of the 7th Tennessee claimed that Major Weber of the 6th Michigan shot Pettigrew after demanding his surrender. "The major, seeing Gen. Pettigrew and staff in a group, dashed up to them and demanded their surrender; and, when they refused to do so, he shot Gen. Pettigrew with his pistol, mortally wounding him," wrote McCall. "In two or three seconds the major was shot from his horse by one of Gen. Pettigrew's staff officers." McCall, "7th Tennessee – Battle of Falling Waters," 406; Wilson, *The Most Promising Young Man of the South,* 76. Pettigrew was taken to the Boyd home at Bunker Hill in West Virginia (this area was still loyal to the Confederacy). The Boyds were cousins of the famous southern spy Belle Boyd. The estate had long been a safe house for Confederates. Pettigrew, who died on the morning of July 17, reposes in the family cemetery near Pettigrew State Park in Tyrrell County, North Carolina. See Richard Owen and James Owen, *Generals at Rest: The Grave Sites of the 425 Official Confederate Generals* (Shippensburg, PA: White Mane Publishing Company, Inc., 1997), 185.

59. Capt. W.F. Fulton, "The Fifth Alabama Battalion at Gettysburg," *Confederate Veteran*, 31 (1923), 379-80.

60. Kimble, "Tennesseans at Gettysburg," 462.

61. Capt. Robert William Douthat, 'Service With the Virginia Army," *Confederate Veteran*, 36 (1928), 61-63. Douthat, a veteran of Pickett's Division who served the entire war, was nationally known in his later years for his lectures on the Battle of Gettysburg.

62. Kidd, *Personal Recollections*, 187-88.

63. Jackson, "Reminiscences of a Private."

64. Gillespie, *History of Company A*, 169-70.

65. John Hammond to his wife, July 18, 1863, included in *In Memoriam: John Hammond*, 64.

66. Benson, *Who Goes There?*, 425-426.

67. Caldwell, *The History of a Brigade of South Carolinians*, 107.

68. Charles H. Holton Medal of Honor file, NARA; Walter F. Beyer, *Deeds of Valor: How America's Heroes Won the Medal of Honor*, 2 vols. (Detroit, Mich.: The Perrien- Keydel Co., 1905), 1:255. Holton was awarded the medal on March 21, 1889.

69. Gregory J. W. Urwin, *Custer Victorious: The Civil War Battles of George Armstrong Custer* (East Brunswick, N. J.: Associated University Presses, 1983), 92.

70. *Aurora Beacon*, August 20, 1863.

71. Gracey, *Annals of the Sixth Pennsylvania Cavalry*, 192.

72. Hall, *Sixth New York*, 150.

73. *Aurora Beacon*, August 20, 1863.

74. Michael W. Taylor, ed., *The Cry is War, War, War: The Civil War Correspondence of Lts. Burwell Thomas Cotton and George Job Huntley, 34th Regiment North Carolina Troops* (Dayton, OH: Morningside, 1994), 148.

75. *OR* 27, pt. 2, 667.

76. *Wheeling Daily Intelligencer*, July 27, 1863.

77. Wayland Fuller Dunaway, *Reminiscences of a Rebel* (New York: Neale Publishing co., 1913), 98; Homer D. Musselman, *47th Virginia Infantry* (Lynchburg, Va.: H. E. Howard, 1991), 56.

78. Robert E. L. Krick, *40th Virginia Infantry* (Lynchburg, Va.: H. E. Howard, 1985), 32; Richard O'Sullivan, *55th Virginia Infantry* (Lynchburg, Va.: H. E. Howard, 1989), 57.

79. *OR* 27, pt. 2, 642.

80. Joseph R. Davis to Jefferson Davis, September 2, 1863, Museum of the Confederacy Library, Richmond, Virginia.

81. Welch, *A Confederate Surgeon's Letters,* 71.

82. W. J. Martin, "The Successor of the First N. C. Volunteers," *Charlotte Observer*, October 13, 1895.

83. Clark, *Histories of the Several Regiments and Battalions from North Carolina*, 1:699.

84. Sorrel, *Recollections of a Confederate Staff Officer*, 176.

85. Bradwell, "From Gettysburg to the Potomac," 428-29/437.

86. Clark, *Histories of the Several Regiments and Battalions from North Carolina*, 1:699.

87. *OR* 27, pt. 2, 667.

88. Capt. Cadwallader Jones, "A Young Soldier of South Carolina," *Confederate Veteran* 34 (1926), 208-9.

89. Stocker, *From Huntsville to Appomattox*, 114-15.

90. *OR* 27, pt. 1, 929; Nelson Taylor to Dear Sister, July 16, 1863, included in *Saddle and Saber*, 97-8.

91. W. A. Love, "Forward and Back," *Confederate Veteran* 32 (1925), 9-10.

92. *Ibid.*

93. Wise, *The Long Arm of Lee,* 2:703.

94. DePeyster, *The Decisive Conflicts of the Civil War*, 149.

95. Gilpin diary, entry for July 14, 1863.

96. *OR* 27, pt. 1, 936. Colonel Gamble watched Kilpatrick's charge from a ridge overlooking Falling Waters, probably not more than 500 yards distant, and so had an outstanding view of the unfolding action.

97. *Ibid.,* 990.

98. Wittenberg, *One of Custer's Wolverines*, 54.

99. Perry, *Life and Letters of Henry Lee Higginson,* 205.

100. W. G. Thompson to "Dear Mother and Sister," July 20, 1863, Robert L. Brake Collection, Box 8, USAHEC.

101. Sorrel, *Recollections of a Confederate Staff Officer,* 176.

Chapter 17

1. Seville, *History of the First Regiment Delaware Volunteers*, 91.

2. *OR* 27, pt. 3, 683.

3. Rusling, *Men and Things I Saw in Civil War Days*, 71-72.

4. Baldwin to Bachelder, May 20, 1865, *The Bachelder Papers*, 1:195.

5. Francis J. Parker, *The Story of the Thirty-Second Massachusetts Infantry* (Boston: C. W. Calkins & Co., 1880), 175.

6. *OR* 27, pt. 1, 672.

7. Auchmuty, *Letters*, 106.

8. Davis, *Three Years in the Army*, 254.

9. Shoaf, "We March at Daybreak," 130.

10. William H. Powell, *The Fifth Army Corps (Army of the Potomac): A Record of Operations During the Civil War in the United States of America, 1861-1865* (London: G. P. Putnam's Sons, 1896), 566-67.

11. Weygant, *History of the 124th New York*, 201.

12. Coffin, *Four Years of Fighting*, 305.

13. Locke, *The Story of the Regiment*, 255.

14. Julian Wisner Hinkley, *A Narrative of Service with the Third Wisconsin Infantry* (Madison: Wisconsin History Commission, 1912), 90.

15. Dawes, *Service with the Sixth Wisconsin*, 187.

16. Auchmuty, *Letters*, 107.

17. Lynch, *Diary*, 25.

18. Walker, *History of the Second Army Corps*, 309.

19. Bowen, *History of the Thirty-Seventh Regiment*, 196.

20. Banes, *History of the Philadelphia Brigade*, 197.

21. Howard, *Autobiography*, 1:446.

22. Burlingame and Turner, *Inside Lincoln's White House*, 62.

23. *Ibid.*, 63.

24. Brooks, *Washington in Lincoln's Time,* 89-90.

25. *Ibid.,* 90-92.

26. *Ibid.,* 92-93.

27. *Ibid.,* 93-94.

28. *Ibid.,* 95.

29. Charles Eugene Hamlin, *The Life and Times of Hannibal Hamlin* (Cambridge: The Riverside Press, 1899), 455. Charles Eugene was Charles' son.

30. Brooks, *Washington in Lincoln's Time,* 95-96.

31. *OR* 27, pt. 3, 700.

32. *Ibid.*, pt. 2, 205.

33. Brooks, *Washington in Lincoln's Time,* 96.

34. Johnston, *The Story of a Confederate Boy*, 224.

35. *Baltimore American*, July 16, 1863.

36. *OR* 27, pt. 1, 929.

37. *Ibid.*, 944; Wesley Merritt, "Personal Reminiscences of the Civil War," included in Theophilus F. Rodenbough, ed. *From Everglade to Canyon With the Second Dragoons* (New York: D. Van Nostrand, 1875), 296.

38. Gracey, *Annals of the Sixth Pennsylvania Cavalry*, 188.

39. Taylor, *Saddle and Saber*, 98.

40. John Sargent to Brother Dan, July 17, 1863, John Sargent letters, Illinois Historical Society, Springfield, Illinois. Sargent further reported to his brother, "Halleck was here yesterday and I hear that high words passed between him and Meade which nearly ended in a fist fight."

41. Powell, *The Fifth Army Corps*, 567-68.

42. McClellan, *The Campaigns of Major-General J.E.B. Stuart*, 364.

43. George W. Beale, *A Lieutenant of Cavalry in Lee's Army* (Boston: The Gorham Press, 1918), 118-20.

44. Thomas P. Nanzig, *3rd Virginia Cavalry* (Lynchburg, Va.: H. E. Howard Co., 1989), 39.

45. Delauter, *18th Virginia Cavalry*, 10.

46. Schildt, *Roads from Gettysburg*, 116.

47. Recapitulation of Divisional Losses, included in Theodore C. Bacon Papers, Connecticut Historical Society, Hartford, Connecticut.

48. Michael Donlon to Patrick Donlon, July 27, 1863, Michael Donlon letters, Civil War Miscellaneous Collection, USAHEC.

49. Nevins, *A Diary of Battle*, 265.

50. Murray, *Letters From Gettysburg*, 146.

Chapter 18

1. Goldsborough, *The Maryland Line in the Confederate Army*, 118.

2. Blackford, *Letters from Lee's Army*, 193.

3. Julia Davis, *Mount Up: A True Story of the Civil War* (New York: Harcourt, Brace & World, 1967), 109.

4. Daniel T. Balfour, *13th Virginia Cavalry* (Lynchburg, Va.: H. E. Howard Co., 1986), 25.

5. L.T. Dickinson, "Services of A Maryland Command," *Confederate Veteran*, 2 (1894), 165.

6. Robert J. Driver, Jr., *10th Virginia Cavalry* (Lynchburg, Va.: H. E. Howard Co., 1992), 44.

7. Quoted in Neil Hunter Raiford, *The 4th North Carolina Cavalry in the Civil War* (Jefferson, N.C.: McFarland, 2003), 56.

8. Halsey Wigfall to his sister, July 18, 1863, included in Mrs. D. Giraud Wright, *A Southern Girl in '61: The War-Time Memories of a Confederate Senator's Daughter* (New York: Doubleday, Page & Co., 1905), 144.

9. Balfour, *13th Virginia Cavalry*, 25.

10. Adele H. Mitchell, ed., *The Letters of Major General James E. B. Stuart* (Richmond: Stuart-Mosby Historical Society, 1990), 326.

11. *In Memoriam: John Hammond*, 63.

12. Campbell, "Charles W. Reed," 44.

13. Christian G. Samito, ed., *Commanding Boston's Irish Ninth: The Civil War Letters of Colonel Patrick R. Guiney, Ninth Massachusetts Volunteer Infantry* (New York: Fordham University Press, 1998), 203.

14. Davis, *Three Years in the Army*, 255.

15. Smith, *The History of the Nineteenth Regiment*, 97.

16. David T. Hedrick and Gordon Barry Davis Jr., *I'm Surrounded by Methodists: Diary of John H. W. Stuckenberg, Chaplain of the 145th Pennsylvania Volunteer Infantry* (Gettysburg, Pa.: Thomas Publications, 1995), 89-91.

17. *Ibid.,* 90. Mitchell, of the 6th Pennsylvania Cavalry (known as Rush's Lancers), had served on Maj. Gen. John F. Reynolds' staff since April 1863, until the latter's mortal wounding on July 1 at Gettysburg. Mitchell then joined Meade's staff, serving there until February 1864. See Gracey, *Annals of the Sixth Pennsylvania Cavalry,* 303.

18. Letter of Henry Van Aernam to Melissa Van Aernam, July 15, 1863, quoted in Mark H. Dunkelman, *Brothers One and All: Esprit de Corps in a Civil War Regiment* (Baton Rouge: Louisiana State University Press, 2004), 231.

19. John Buchanan to Dear Friend, July 19, 1863, John Buchanan Letters, James Sterrett Collection, Brockway, Pennsylvania.

20. Taylor, *Gouverneur Kemble Warren*, 133-34.

21. *OR* 27, pt. 3, 687.

22. Tyler Dennett, ed., *Lincoln and the Civil War in the Diaries and Letters of John Hay* (New York: Dodd, Mead & Co., 1939), 67.

23. *Ibid.*, 69.

24. Benjamin P. Thomas and Harold M. Hyman, *Stanton: The Life and Times of Lincoln's Secretary of War* (New York: Alfred Knopf, 1962), 275.

25. A. Wilson Greene, "Meade's Pursuit of Lee: From Gettysburg to Falling Waters," included in Gary W. Gallagher, ed., *The Third Day at Gettysburg & Beyond* (Chapel Hill: University of North Carolina Press, 1994), 173.

26. *OR* 27, pt. 1, 93.

27. Meade, *Life and Letters*, 2:135.

28. Roy P. Basler, ed., *The Collected Works of Abraham Lincoln*, 8 vols. with index. (New Brunswick: Rutgers University Press, 1953), 6:327-28.

29. Meade, *Life and Letters*, 2:136. Meade was correct, in that Longstreet's Corps was sent to Bragg's army in September. Longstreet's men delivered the decisive attack that led to Bragg's victory at Chickamauga.

30. Moran to Sickles, January 24, 1882, *The Bachelder Papers*, 2:786-87. Interestingly, the same thing happened after the Battle of Antietam, where Lee's army was permitted to escape across the Potomac River largely unmolested.

31. Alexander Hays to John B. McFadden, July 18, 1863, included in George T. Fleming, *Life and Letters of Alexander Hays* (Pittsburgh: n.p., 1919), 418.

32. *Committee on the Conduct of the War*, 334-347.

33. Furst diary, entry for July 14, 1863.

34. Nevins, *A Diary of Battle*, 261.

35. Henry J. Hunt, "The Third Day at Gettysburg," included in *B&L*, 3:282.

36. Humphreys, *Gettysburg to the Rapidan*, 7.

37. McNamara, *The History of the Ninth Regiment*, 334.

38. R. Sharpe, "Gen. Meade, A Word to Those Who Criticized His Caution After Gettysburg." *The National Tribune*, December 30, 1886.

39. Orson B. Curtis, *History of the Twenty-Fourth Michigan of the Iron Brigade, Known as the Detroit and Wayne County Regiment* (Detroit, Mich., Winn & Hammond, 1891), 194.

40. Hyde, *Following the Greek Cross*, 162-63.

41. *Baltimore American*, July 8, 1863.

42. Burlingame and Turner, *Inside Lincoln's White House*, 63-64.

43. Doubleday, *Chancellorsville and Gettysburg*, 209-10.

44. de Trobriand, *Four Years with the Army of the Potomac*, 520.

45. Haupt, *Reminiscences*, 228-229.

46. William Allan, "The Strategy of the Gettysburg Campaign," *Military Historical Society of Massachusetts*, Vol. III (May 9, 1887): 446.

47. Edward K. Eckert and Nicholas J. Amato, eds., *Ten Years in the Saddle: The Memoir of William Woods Averell, 1851-1862* (San Rafael, Ca.: Presidio Press, 1978), 328-29.

48. Walter H. Taylor, *General Lee: His Campaigns in Virginia 1861-1865,with Personal Reminiscences* (Norfolk, Va.: Nusbaum Book and News Co., 1906), 212.

49. Styple, *Generals in Bronze,* 178.

50. Meade in *JCCW*, 1:350-351.

51. Milo M. Quaife, ed., *From the Cannon's Mouth: The Civil War Letters of General Alpheus S. Williams* (Detroit: Wayne State University Press, 1959), 231.

52. *OR* Supplement, vol. 5, 207.

53. Henry J. Hunt, "Meade's Intentions. A Defense of the Hero of Gettysburg by His Chief of Artillery," *The National Tribune*, November 5, 1891.

54. Swinton, *Campaigns of the Army of the Potomac*, 368.

55. *OR* 27, pt. 1, 75-7; Wittenberg, "Ulric Dahlgren in the Gettysburg Campaign," 101-105.

56. Report of Lt. Col. Charles H. Morgan, *The Bachelder Papers*, 3:1368-69.

57. George A. Bruce, *The Twentieth Regiment of Massachusetts Volunteer Infantry, 1861-1865* (Boston: Houghton, Mifflin and Co., 1906), 300.

58. Robert L. Stewart, *History of the One Hundred and Fortieth Regiment Pennsylvania Volunteers* (Philadelphia: Published by the authority of the Regimental Association, 1912), 147.

59. Murray, *Letters from Gettysburg*, 105.

60. Davis, "From Gettysburg to Williamsport," 458.

61. Gordon, *Reminiscences of the Civil War*, 174.

62. Powell, *The Fifth Army Corps*, 568.

63. Stoeckel, *Correspondence of John Sedgwick*, 2:132.

64. Thomas Chamberlin, *History of the One Hundred Fiftieth Regiment Pennsylvania Volunteers, Second Regiment, Bucktail Brigade* (Philadelphia: F. McManus, Jr. & Co., 1905), 168.

65. Carl D. Eby, Jr., *A Virginia Yankee in the Civil War: The Diaries of David Hunter Strother* (Chapel Hill: University of North Carolina Press, 1961), 192.

66. *OR* 27, pt. 3, 559.

67. Alexander K. McClure, ed., *The Annals of the War* (Philadelphia: The Times Publishing Company, 1878), 455.

68. *Ibid.,* 456.

69. *Ibid.*

70. *OR* 27, pt. 3, 559.

71. See *ibid,* 514-689.

72. Shoaf, "On the March Again at Daybreak," 129.

73. Edwin E. Bryant, *History of the Third Regiment of Wisconsin Veteran Volunteer infantry 1861-1865* (Madison, Wis.: The Veteran Association of the Regiment, 1891), 209.

74. Haden, *Reminiscences*, 26.

75. Shoemaker, *Shoemaker's Battery*, 46.

76. Edward P. Tobie, *Service of the Cavalry in the Army of the Potomac* (Providence: N. B. Williams, 1882), 27.

77. J. W. Muffly, ed., *The Story of Our Regiment: A History of the 148th Pennsylvania Vols.* (Des Moines, Iowa: The Kenyon Printing and Mfg. Co., 1904), 471.

78. *OR* 27, pt. 1, 91.

79. *Ibid.*, pt. 2, 448.

80. William Terpeluk. "A Lesson in Battle Tempo: The Union Pursuit After Gettysburg," *Parameters* (Autumn 1995), 79-80.

81. On the night of July 13, while Lee's forces were crossing the river, Halleck instructed Kelley (who was sitting idle at Fairview, Maryland) to "Move up upon the enemy's flank and rear, and attack and harass him wherever you can. If you can reach his crossing, annoy him as much as possible." *OR* 27, pt. 3, 681.

82. John T. Morse, ed., *The Diary of Gideon Welles, Secretary of the Navy Under Lincoln and Johnson*, 3 vols. (New York: Houghton-Mifflin, 1911), 1:440.

83. Basler, *The Collected Works*, 6:341.

84. *Ibid.*

85. George Meade, Jr., *Did General Meade Desire to Retreat at the Battle of Gettysburg?* (Philadelphia: Porter & Coates, 1883), 26-27.

86. For a detailed evaluation of the Joint Committee on the Conduct of the War's efforts to undermine George Gordon Meade, see Bruce Tap, "Bad Faith Somewhere: George Gordon Meade and the Committee on the Conduct of the War," *North & South* 2 (August 1999): 74-81.

87. *The Brooklyn Eagle*, July 10, 1863.

88. Ted Alexander, "Ten Days in July: The Pursuit to the Potomac," *North & South*, Vol. 2, No. 6 (August 1999), 20-21.

89. *Richmond Dispatch,* July 17, 1863.

Epilogue

1. Because the descriptions set forth in this Epilogue are quite general, we have not footnoted them extensively. Unless otherwise noted, the information set forth in this Epilogue primarily comes from volume 27 of the Official Records of the Civil War.

2. *OR* 27, pt. 1, 118.

3. Swinton, *Campaigns of the Army of the Potomac*, 373.

4. *Ibid.*, 374.

5. *OR* 27, pt. 1, 118.

6. *Ibid.*, pt. 2, 449.

7. Humphreys, *Gettysburg to the Rapidan*, 10.

8. *OR* 27, pt. 1, 490.

9. *Ibid.*, pt. 2, 449-450.

10. Regiments sent to New York from the Army of the Potomac included the 152nd New York, the 26th Michigan, 27th Indiana, and the 7th New York State Militia, all of which made a forced march from Frederick, Maryland. For more on the New York City Draft Riots, see David M. Barnes, *The Draft Riots in New York. July 1863. The Metropolitan Police: Their Services During Riot Week. Their Honorable Record.* (New York: Baker & Godwin, 1863) or, for a more modern treatment of the subject, see Iver Bernstein, *The New York City Draft Riots: Their Significance for American Society and Politics in the Age of the Civil War* (London: Oxford University Press, 1990) or Barnet Schecter, *The Devil's Own Work: The Civil War Draft Riots and the Fight to Reconstruct America* (New York: Walker & Co., 2005).

11. Martin, *"Kill-Cavalry,"* 126-127. Kilpatrick somehow managed to get leave in the middle of the campaign to go to New York City to see his wife and newborn son. While there, he offered his services to Maj. Gen. John E. Wool, the commander of the Federal forces in New York, who gladly accepted the offer.

12. Jeffry D. Wert, *The Sword of Lincoln: The Army of the Potomac* (New York: Simon & Schuster, 2005), 311.

13. *Ibid.*

14. Quint, *Second Massachusetts*, 184.

15. Meade, *Life and Letters*, 2:141.

Bibliography

NEWSPAPERS

Adams Sentinel
Army and Navy Journal
Athens Messenger (Athens, Ohio)
Athens Southern Banner (Athens, Georgia)
Atlanta Daily Intelligencer
Atlanta Journal
Aurora Beacon
Baltimore American
Baltimore Daily Gazette
Baltimore Sun
Brooklyn Daily Eagle
Centennial Observer and C & O Canal Chronicle (Williamsport, Maryland)
The Charleston Mercury
Charlotte Observer
Chicago Tribune
Cincinnati Daily Commercial
The Columbia Spy (Columbia, Pennsylvania)
The Compiler (Gettysburg, Pennsylvania)
Daily Richmond Enquirer
Daily Constitutionalist (Augusta, Georgia)
Franklin Repository (Chambersburg, Pennsylvania)
The Free Lance-Star (Fredericksburg, Virginia)
Harper's Weekly
The Herald-Mail (Hagerstown, Maryland)
Huntsville Confederate
The Independent Republican
Ironton Register
Jamestown Journal
Lancaster Daily Express
Michigan Argus
Milledgeville Southern Recorder
Pottsville Miner's Journal
National Intelligencer
The National Tribune
New York Daily News
New York Herald
New York Sun

The New York Times
New York Tribune
Philadelphia Inquirer
Philadelphia Press
The Philadelphia Weekly Times
Pottsville Miner's Journal
The Xenia Sentinel
Richmond Dispatch
Richmond Examiner
Richmond Times-Dispatch
Richmond Whig
Rochester Daily Union and Advertiser
St. Mary's Beacon (St. Mary's County, Maryland)
The Shreveport Journal
Southern Banner (Athens, Georgia)
The Spectator (Staunton, Virginia)
Washington Evening Star
Washington Post
Weekly Jeffersonian (Richmond, Indiana)
Wheeling Daily Intelligencer

MANUSCRIPT SOURCES

Ruth Adkinson Collection, New Castle, Colorado:
Joseph McHenry Adkinson Letters

Eugene C. Baker Texas History Center, Austin, Texas:
James J. Kirkpatrick Diary for 1863

Archives, Cincinnati Historical Society, Cincinnati, Ohio:
George Benson Fox Letters

Emmitsburg Area Historical Society, Emmitsburg, Maryland:
Albert M. Hunter Memoir
William L. McIlhenny Diary
John A. Miller Papers

Franklin County Historical Society, Chambersburg, Pennsylvania:
Benjamin F. Carter File

Archives, Gettysburg National Military Park, Gettysburg, Pennsylvania:
Russell A. Alger to L.O. Estes, February 12, 1897

Joe Allen, *The Anthology of Another Town*, excerpt
Jacob L. Bechtel to Miss Connie, July 6, 1863
J. C. Biddle to his wife, July 4, 1863
Diary of Charles H. Blinn
Henry Clare to William Clare, July 17, 1863
William Delony to Dear Rosa, July 7, 1863
Casper C. Henkel to Dear Cousin, July 12, 1863
John B. Kay to his parents, July 9, 1863
Robert E. Lee to Jefferson Davis, July 7, 1863
Robert E. Lee's General Order of July 11, 1863
John B. McIntosh to his wife, July 6, 1863
Oliver Taylor Account
Undated letter of Luther S. Trowbridge to J. Allen Bigelow
William A. Tubbs to his parents
Junius Wilbur Diary
John Willoughby to James Randolph Simpson, July 21, 1863
Horatio G. Wright to his wife, July 18, 1863

Clarke Historical Library, Central Michigan University, Mt. Pleasant, Michigan:
Charles S. Hampton Diary for 1863

Detroit Public Library, Detroit, Michigan:
Burton Historical Collection

David Douglas Collection, Ridley Park, Pennsylvania:
Leonard Williams Letters

Olive Johnson Dunnett Collection, Hanover, Pennsylvania:
John Wilder Johnson Letters

Georgia State Archives, Atlanta, Georgia:
William W. Hewell Letters

Historical Society of Pennsylvania, Philadelphia, Pennsylvania:
Louis H. Carpenter Letters from the Field
Simon Gratz Collection
Walter S. Newhall Papers
Samuel Penniman Bates Papers

Joyce L. Horst Collection, Chambersburg, Pennsylvania:
George D. Hege Letter
Michael Hege Papers

J. Wistar Huey Collection, Ellicott's Mills, Maryland:
Pennock Huey Papers

Albert Huntington Library, San Marino, California:
James Bell Papers
James E. B. Stuart Papers

Illinois Historical Society, Springfield, Illinois:
John Sargent Letters

Indiana Historical Society, Indianapolis, Indiana:
George H. Chapman Papers

New Jersey Historical Society, Newark, New Jersey:
Sebastian Duncan Jr. Letter

Library of Congress, Manuscripts Division, Washington, D. C.:
Ulric Dahlgren Diary
Wilbur Fisk Diary for 1863
Samuel J. B. V. Gilpin Diary
David McMurtrie Gregg Papers
Samuel P. Heintzelman Papers
Jedediah Hotchkiss Diary and Papers
Henry J. Hunt Papers
George B. McClellan Papers
Charles McVicar Diary

Sue Martin Collection, Fairport, New York:
Frank Saunders Letters

Archives, Mazomance Historical Society, Mazomance, Wisconsin:
Horace Smith Diary, 154th New York Regiment

Military Collections, North Carolina Archives, Raleigh, North Carolina:
Edward G. Butler Letters
Record of Events, 12th Regiment North Carolina Infantry, for July and August, 1863

Eleanor S. Brockenbrough Library, Museum of the Confederacy, Richmond, Virginia:
Military Diary Collection
G. Moxley Sorrel Diary for 1863

The National Archives, Washington, D. C.:
Abner Doubleday Papers
RG 93, Pension Files
RG 94, War Records Office, Union Battle Reports, Vol. 27, Boxes 48-52
RG 94, War Records Office, Manuscripts Division, Alfred Pleasonton Papers
RG 393, Department of the Susquehanna and Pennsylvania, 1862-1866, Letters Sent, June 1863-January 1866, Collection 4606
Medal of Honor files for Charles E. Capehart and Charles M. Holton
"Military History of Major-General Alfred Pleasonton," (January 12, 1864), U.S. Army General's Reports of Civil War Service, M1098.

Archives, Northern Illinois University, DeKalb, Illinois:
Leander Schooley Civil War Letters

Archives, Notre Dame University, South Bend, Indiana:
Read Family Correspondence

Pennsylvania Historical and Museum Commission, Harrisburg, Pennsylvania:
Charles B. Coxe Papers

Perkins Library, Duke University, Durham, North Carolina:
J. W. Biddle Letters
James O. Coghill Papers
Edward A. H. McDonald Papers

Walter L. Pomeroy Collection, Mechanicsburg, Pennsylvania:
Andrew D. Jackson, "Reminiscences of a Private," unpub. manuscript

T. Alan Russell Collection, Paris, Illinois:
James E. Armstrong Diary

James Sterrett Collection, Brockway, Pennsylvania:
John Buchanan Letters

United States Army Heritage and Education Center, Carlisle, Pennsylvania:
Robert L. Brake Collection
Louis R. Fortesque Diary
James E. Green Diary
Hillary Abner Herbert Memoir
William H. Hill Diary

James J. Kirkpatrick Diary
Robert James Lowry Diary
Charles Moore Diary
W.G. Thompson letter of July 20, 1863
Horatio G. Wright letter of July 18, 1863
David Zable Papers
Diary of Unidentified Member of 6th Louisiana Infantry
Civil War Miscellaneous Collection
Eugene Blackford Memoir
Jasper Cheney Diary
Michael Donlon Letters
Abner B. Frank Diary
C. Ross Smith Papers
Gregory A. Coco Collection
Harrisburg Civil War Roundtable Collection
Diary of Jacob W. Haas
Lewis Leigh Collection
William N. Noble Letters
Michael P. Musick Collection
James T. Binion Letters
Luscar Voorhees Papers
Michael Winey Collection
Isaac R. Dunkelberger Memoir

Archives, Virginia Military Institute, Lexington, Virginia:
I. Norval Baker Papers
John Hyde Cameron Memoirs
John Garibaldi Letters

Special Collections Department, University Libraries, Virginia Polytechnic University, Blacksburg, Virginia:
Archibald Atkinson, Jr. Memoir

Western Reserve Historical Society, Cleveland, Ohio:
Wells Bushnell Diary

Wilson Library, Southern Historical Collections, University of North Carolina, Chapel Hill, North Carolina:
Edward Porter Alexander Papers
John F. Coghill Papers

Special Collections Department, Alderman Library, University of Virginia, Charlottesville, Virginia:
John W. Daniel Papers
Robert T. Hubard Memoir
Valley of the Shadow Project

Regional Archives and History Center, Western Michigan University, Kalamazoo, Michigan:
William Rockwell Letters

Eric J. Wittenberg Collection, Columbus, Ohio:
Luther C. Furst Diary

Robert W. Woodruff Library, Emory University, Atlanta, Georgia:
Confederate Miscellany
Robert F. Davis Diary for 1863
William W. Marston Diary
R. H. F. Roerfel Diary for 1863

PUBLISHED PRIMARY SOURCES

Articles

"After Gettysburg. Pursing Lee to the Potomac. Experiences of a Vermont Victim. A Brilliant Skirmish." *New York Tribune*, July 1, 1888.

Alexander, Edward Porter. "Pickett's Charge and Artillery Fighting at Gettysburg," *The Century* (January 1887), 464-71.

Allan, William. "The Strategy of the Gettysburg Campaign," *Military Historical Society of Massachusetts*, Vol. III (May 9, 1887): 414-448.

Barden, W. C. "The Custer Cannon. A Dashing Exploit by Michigan Cavalrymen," *National Tribune*, December 23, 1915.

Bayly, William H. "Memoirs of a Thirteen-Year Old Boy Relating to the Battle of Gettysburg," *The Compiler,* October 30, 1939.

Beale, George W. "Soldier's Account of the Gettysburg Campaign: Letter from George W. Beale (Son of General R. L. T. Beale)," *Southern Historical Society Papers* XI (July 1883), 320-27.

Bigelow, John Allen. "Flashing Sabers: Chasing Lee's Columns After Gettysburg," *The National Tribune*, November 10, 1887.

Bolton, Channing M. "With General Lee's Engineers," *Confederate Veteran* 30 (1922): 298-302.

Bond, Frank A. "Company A, First Maryland Cavalry," *Confederate Veteran* 6 (1898): 78-80.

Bradwell, J. G. "From Gettysburg to the Potomac," *Confederate Veteran* 30 (1922): 428-430.

Bushey, F. A. "That Heroic Dispatch. How it was Captured by Dahlgren and His Little Band," *The National Tribune*, May 14, 1896.

Campbell, Eric A., ed. "'The Severest Fought Battle of the War': Charles Wellington Reed and the Medal of Honor," *Civil War Regiments* Vol. 6, No. 3 (1999): 31-58.

Capehart, Henry. "Fighting His Way: The Night Passage of Kilpatrick Through Monterey Pass," *The National Tribune*, January 3, 1895.

Clark, S. A. "A Little Fracas", *The National Tribune*, May 2, 1895.

——. "Did Not Capture It: Buford and Kilpatrick Fought for Lee's Wagon Train at Hagerstown," *The National Tribune*, April 11, 1895.

Clark, Walter. "Gen. James Johnston Pettigrew, C.S.A.," *Confederate Veteran* 28 (1920): 413-414.

Clarke, Augustus P. "The Sixth New York Cavalry: Its Movements and Service at the Battle of Gettysburg", *United Service* (November 1896): 411-415.

Clemens, John. "The 1st New York Lincoln Cavalry," *The National Tribune*, January 12, 1911.

Cochran, L. L. "The Tenth Georgia Regiment at Gettysburg: Graphic Description of America's Grandest Tragedy," *Atlanta Journal*, February 23, 1901.

Collins, John L. "A Prisoner's March from Gettysburg to Staunton," included in Robert U. Johnson and Clarence C. Buel, *Battles and Leaders of the Civil War*. 4 vols. New York: Century Printing Co., 1884-1904. 3:429-33.

Colston, F. M. "Gettysburg As I Saw It," *Confederate Veteran* 5 (1897): 551-53.

Conway, W. B. "With the Cavalry: General Lee's Course After the Battle of Gettysburg," *Richmond Times-Dispatch*, October 12, 1902.

Davis, George B. "From Gettysburg to Williamsport," *Campaigns of Virginia, Maryland and Pennsylvania*, Papers of the Historical Society of Massachusetts 3 (Boston: Griffith, Stillings Press, 1903): 449-69.

Dean, John. "Letter to the Editor," *Wheeling Intelligencer*, July 15, 1863.

"Diary of Robert E. Park," *Southern Historical Society Papers* 1 (May 1876): 370-87.

Dickinson, L. T. "Services of a Maryland Command", *Confederate Veteran* 2 (1894): 165.

Douthat, Robert William. "Service with the Virginia Army," *Confederate Veteran* 36 (1928): 61-63.

Farrington, John. "137th Regiment Volunteer Infantry," included in New York State Monuments Commission for the Battlefields of Gettysburg and Chattanooga, *Final Report on the Battlefield at Gettysburg*. 3 vols. Albany: J. B. Lyon Co., 1900. 3:942-45.

Fillmore, David H. "Not All Quiet Along the Potomac: A Little Unwritten History of Co. A, 8th Ill. Cav.," *The National Tribune*, March 28, 1907.

Firey, Frank. "Boy's Story of Gettysburg Retreat," *The National Tribune*, November 7, 1929.

Fulton, W. F. "The Fifth Alabama Battalion at Gettysburg", *Confederate Veteran* 31 (1923): 379-380.

Gallaway, Felix. "Gettysburg—The Battle and Retreat", *Confederate Veteran* 21 (1913): 388-89.

Goodwin, Daniel. "Williamsport and Boonsboro", *The National* Tribune, October 11, 1883.

Graham, Ziba B. "On to Gettysburg: Ten Days from My Diary of 1863". *Michigan War Papers*, Vol. 1, Military Order of the Loyal Legion of the United States (March 2, 1889): 1-16.

Griffin, Isaac H. "Crossing the Potomac", *The National Tribune*, July 24, 1913.

Harrison, William H. "Personal Experiences of a Cavalry Officer," *War Papers, Pennsylvania Commandery, Military Order of the Loyal Legion of the United States*, vol. 1 (1895): 225-254.

Hastings, Ed S. "Monterey Pass: A Claim that the 5th Mich. Led the Charge There", *The National Tribune*, March 21, 1895.

Henkle, Dr. Caspar C. "Letter Delivered After Many Years," *Confederate Veteran* 16 (1908): 407-08

Hubbard, J. N. "Praise of Gen. Meade." *National Tribune*, May 10, 1917.

Humphreys, Andrew A. "The Pursuit of Lee. The Army of the Potomac's March from Gettysburg to the Rapidan." *National Tribune*, July 12, 1883.

Hunt, Henry J. "Meade's Intentions. A Defense of the Hero of Gettysburg, By His Chief of Artillery." *National Tribune*, November 5, 1891.

——. "The Third Day at Gettysburg", included in Robert U. Johnson and Clarence C. Buel, *Battles and Leaders of the Civil War*. 4 vols. New York: Century Printing Co., 1884-1904. 3:369-385.

Huntington, James F. "The Artillery at Hazel Grove," included in Robert U. Johnson and Clarence C. Buel, *Battles and Leaders of the Civil War,* 4 vols. New York: Century Printing Co., 1888-1904. 3:188.

Imboden, John D. "Fire, Sword and the Halter", included in *The Annals of the War*. Alexander K. McClure, ed. Philadelphia: The Times Publishing Company, 1878: 173-75.

——. "Lee at Gettysburg", *Galaxy Magazine* (April, 1871): 511-513.

——. "The Confederate Retreat from Gettysburg", included in Robert U. Johnson and Clarence C. Buel, *Battles and Leaders of the Civil War*. 4 vols. New York: Century Printing Co., 1884-1904. 3:420-29.

Jacobs, W. W. "Battle Seen from a Housetop. Hand-to-Hand Combat in the Streets of Hagerstown. Exciting Incidents Attending the Confederate Retreat from Gettysburg—July 1863," *New York Times*, March 15, 1896.

——. "Custer's Charge. Little Hagerstown and the Scene of Bloody Strife in 1863", *The National Tribune*, August 27, 1896.

Jennings, Albert R. "Pursuit of Lee's Army." *National Tribune*, June 27, 1901.

Johns, B. F. "Pursuit of Lee. Events Following the Battle of Gettysburg." *National Tribune*, April 18, 1901.

Jones, B. F. "No Terrors There", *The National Tribune*, June 6, 1895.

Judkins, S. B. "A Cavalry Encounter", *The National Tribune*, September 15, 1898.

Kimble, June. "Tennesseans at Gettysburg—The Retreat", *Confederate Veteran* 18 (1910): 460-63.

Kirkley, Joseph W. "Gen. Lee's Retreat: Leisurely Pursuit by the Army of the Potomac", *The National Tribune*, June 7, 1883.

Klement, Frank L., ed. "Edwin B. Bigelow: A Michigan Sergeant in the Civil War", *Michigan History* 38 (September 1954): 193-252.

Lane, James H. "Twenty-Eighth North Carolina Infantry", *Charlotte Observer*, February 17, 1895.

Lasseter, William T. "Reminiscences of the Civil War", *The Shreveport Journal*, October 31, 1929.

"Letter from Captain George Hillyer." *Athens Southern Banner*, July 29, 1863.

Levy, Aaron. "Meade's Opportunity. It Came at Williamsport, and He Let It Slip." *National Tribune*, August 11, 1904.

Love, W.A. "Forward and Back", *Confederate Veteran* 32 (1925): 9-10.

Love, William A. "Mississippi at Gettysburg", *Publications of the Mississippi Historical Society* 9 (1906).

Martin, Elwood. "Kilpatrick's Cavalry. The Much-Disputed Question and Its Operations After the Battle", *The National Tribune*, January 20, 1916.

Martin, W. J. "The Successor of the First N. C. Volunteers", *Charlotte Observer*, October 13, 1895.

McCall, John T. "7th Tennessee – Battle of Falling Waters", *Confederate Veteran* 6 (1898): 406.

McClintock, D. N. "Driving Lee Out of Maryland", *The National Tribune*, November 10, 1910.

Merritt, Wesley. "Personal Reminiscences of the Civil War", included in Theophilus F. Rodenbough, ed. *From Everglade to Canyon With the Second Dragoons*. New York: D. Van Nostrand, 1875.

Millikan, J. L. "The Charge at Monterey", *The National Tribune*, February 16, 1888.

Minor, Berkeley. "The Night After Gettysburg", *Confederate Veteran* 33 (1925): 140-141.

Mitchell, Frances Letcher. "A Georgia Henry of Navarre," *Confederate Veteran* 33 (1915): 363.

Pleasonton, Alfred. "The Campaign of Gettysburg," included in Alexander K. McClure, ed. *The Annals of the War*. Philadelphia: The Times Publishing Company, 1878: 447-459.

——. "The Successes and Failures of Chancellorsville," included in Robert U. Johnson and Clarence C. Buell, eds., *Battles and Leaders of the Civil War,* 4 vols. New York: Century Printing Co., 1888-1904, 3:179.

Polley, J.B. "Gettysburg and Sharpsburg," *Confederate Veteran 8* (1896): 425-27.

Popkins, W. A. "Imboden's Brigade at Gettysburg", *Confederate Veteran* 22 (1914): 552-554.

Purifoy, John. "A Unique Battle", *Confederate Veteran* 33 (1925): 132-35.

——. "The Horror of War", *Confederate Veteran* 33 (1925): 224-225 and 237-238.

Reynolds, P. M. "Experiences of a Cavalryman", *The National Tribune*, March 23, 1899.

Robbins, W. M. "The Battle of Gettysburg", *Confederate Veteran* 18 (1900): 165-68.

Ronemus, Nancy, ed. "A letter from a young Michigan cavalryman gives a vivid—if ungrammatical—account of Gettysburg and its aftermath", *America's Civil War* (March 1997): 79.

Rose, James A. "Famous Custer Cavalry of Civil War", *The National Tribune*, September 26, 1929.

St. Clair, Samuel. "Col. Dahlgren's Wound", *The National Tribune*, March 12, 1896.

Schuricht, Hermann. "Jenkins' Brigade in the Gettysburg Campaign", *Richmond Dispatch*, April 5, 1896.

Sharias, Mrs. Annie. "Buried at Funkstown", *The National Tribune*, August 23, 1913.

Sharpe, R. "General Meade. A Word to Those Who Criticized His Caution After Gettysburg." *National Tribune*, December 30, 1886.

Shoaf, Dana B., ed. "'On the March Again at Daybreak': Major John I. Nevin and the 93rd Pennsylvania Infantry", *Civil War Regiments* Vol. 6, No. 3 (1999): 107-138.

Stevenson, James H. "The Gettysburg Campaign. Destruction of Lee's Pontoon Bridge at Falling Waters, on the Potomac." *Philadelphia Weekly Times*, September 29, 1877.

"That Greencastle Girl", *Philadelphia Weekly Times*, October 22, 1887.

"Unwritten History: Squad of the 17th Connecticut First Learned of Lee's Retreat at Gettysburg", *The National Tribune*, October 8, 1896.

Walden, D. I. "The 10th Georgia at Funkstown", *Atlanta Journal*, March 29, 1902.

Woodward, Daniel H., ed. "The Civil War of a Pennsylvania Trooper," *The Pennsylvania Magazine of History and Biography*. Vol. 87, No. 1 (January, 1963): 39-62.

Books and Pamphlets

Acken, J. Gregory, ed. *Inside the Army of the Potomac: The Civil War Experiences of Captain Francis Adams Donaldson*. Mechanicsburg, Pa.: Stackpole, 1998.

Adams, John McGregor and Albert Egerton Adams, eds. *Memorial and Letters of Rev. John R. Adams, D. D., Chaplain of the Fifth Maine and the One Hundred and Twenty-First New York Regiment During the War of the Rebellion, Serving from the Beginning to Its Close.* Privately published, 1890.

Aldrich, Thomas M. *The History of Battery A First Regiment Rhode Island Light Artillery In the War to Preserve the Union 1861-1865.* Providence: Snow & Farnham, 1904.

Alexander, Edward Porter. *Fighting for the Confederacy: The Personal Recollections of General Edward Porter Alexander.* Edited by Gary W. Gallagher. Chapel Hill: University of North Carolina Press, 1989.

Auchmuty, Ellen Schermerhorn, ed. *Letters of Richard Tylden Auchmuty, Fifth Corps, Army of the Potomac.* Privately published, n.d.

Balzer, John, ed. *Buck's Book: A View of the 3rd Vermont Infantry Regiment.* Bolingbrook, Ill.: Balzer, 1993.

Bancroft, Frederic and William A. Dunning, eds. *The Reminiscences of Carl Schurz.* 5 vols. New York: The McClure Company, 1908.

Baquet, Camille. *History of Kearny's New Jersey Brigade.* Trenton: MacCrellish & Quigley, 1910.

Baines, Charles H. *History of the Philadelphia Brigade.* Philadelphia: J. B. Lippincott & Co., 1876.

Barnes, David M. *The Draft Riots in New York. July 1863. The Metropolitan Police: Their Services During Riot Week. Their Honorable Record.* New York: Baker & Godwin, 1863.

Bartlett, A. W. *History of the Twelfth Regiment New Hampshire Volunteers in the War of the Rebellion.* Concord, N.H.: Ira C. Evans, 1897.

Basler, Roy P., ed. *The Collected Works of Abraham Lincoln.* 8 vols. with index. New Brunswick: Rutgers University Press, 1953.

Bates, David Homer. *Lincoln in the Telegraph Office: Recollections of the United States Military Telegraph Corps During the Civil War.* New York: The Century Company, 1907.

Baylor, George. *Bull Run to Bull Run; or, Four Years in the Army of Northern Virginia.* Privately published, 1900.

Beach, William H. *The First New York (Lincoln) Cavalry, From April 19, 1861 to July 7, 1865.* New York: Lincoln Cavalry Assn., 1902.

Beale, George W. *A Lieutenant of Cavalry in Lee's Army.* Boston: The Gorham Press, 1918.

Beale, Richard L. T. *History of the Ninth Virginia Cavalry in the War Between the States.* Richmond: B. F. Johnson Publishing Co., 1899.

Bean, W. G., ed. *The Liberty Hall Volunteers: Stonewall's College Boys.* Charlottesville: University Press of Virginia, 1964.

Benedict, George Grenville. *Army Life in Virginia: Letters from the Twelfth Vermont Regiment and Personal Experiences of Volunteer Service in the War for the Union, 1862-63.* Burlington: Free Press Assoc., 1895.

Bennett, Andrew J. *The Story of the First Massachusetts Light Battery, Attached to the Sixth Army Corps: A Glance at Events in the Armies of the Potomac and Shenandoah, from the Summer of 1861 to the Autumn of 1864.* Boston: Press of Deland and Barta, 1886.

Bennett, Edwin C. *Musket and Sword, or the Camp, March, and Firing Line in the Army of the Potomac.* Boston: Coburn Publishing, 1900.

Benson, B. K. *Who Goes There? The Story of a Spy in the Civil War.* New York: The MacMillan Co., 1902.

Best, Isaac O. *History of the 121st New York Infantry.* Chicago: Jason H. Smith, 1921.

Betts, A. D. *Experiences of a Confederate Chaplain 1861-1864.* Greenville, S. C.: privately published, n.d.

Bicknell, George W. *History of the Fifth Regiment Maine Volunteers, Comprising Brief Descriptions of Its Marches, Engagements, and General Services from the Date of Its Muster In, June 24, 1861, to the Time of Its Muster out, July 27, 1864.* Portland: Hall L. Davis, 1871.

Bidwell, Frederick David. *History of the Forty-Ninth New York Volunteers.* Albany: J. B. Lyon Co., 1916.

Billings, John D. *The History of the Tenth Massachusetts Battery of Light Artillery in the War of the Rebellion 1862-1865.* Boston: The Arakelyan Press, 1909.

Blackford, Susan Leigh, ed. *Letters from Lee's Army: Memoirs of Life In and Out of the Army in Virginia During the War Between the States.* New York: Charles Scribner's Sons, 1947.

Blackford, William W. *War Years With Jeb Stuart.* Baton Rouge: Louisiana State University Press, 1993.

Blight, David W., ed. *When this Cruel War is Over: The Civil War Letters of Charles Harvey Brewster.* Amherst: University of Massachusetts Press, 1992.

Bliss, George. *The First Rhode Island Cavalry at Middleburg.* Providence, R.I.: privately published, 1889.

Bloom, Robert L. *We Never Expected a Battle: The Civilians at Gettysburg, 1863.* Gettysburg, Pa.: The Adams County Historical Society, 1988.

Blue, John. *Hanging Rock Rebel: Lt. John Blue's War in West Virginia and the Shenandoah Valley.* Dan Oates, ed. Shippensburg, Pa.: Burd Street Press, 1994.

Bodge, Rev. George M., ed. *Memoir of John Farwell Anderson.* Boston: privately published, 1889.

Boies, Andrew J. *Record of the Thirty-Third Massachusetts Volunteer Infantry, from Aug. 1862 to Aug. 1865.* Fitchburg: Sentinel Printing Co., 1880.

Booth, George W. *Personal Reminiscences of a Maryland Soldier in the War Between the States, 1861-1865.* Baltimore: privately published, 1898.

Boudrye, Louis N. *Historic Records of the Fifth New York Cavalry, First Ira Harris Guard.* Albany: J. Munsell, 1868.

Boudrye, Richard E., ed. *War Journal of Louis N. Boudrye, Fifth New York Cavalry: The Diary of a Union Chaplain Commencing February 16, 1863.* Jefferson, N. C.: McFarland & Co., 1996.

Bowen, James L. *History of the Thirty-Seventh Regiment Mass. Volunteers in the Civil War of 1861-1865.* Holyoke, Mass.: Clark W. Bryan & Co., 1884.

Bradley, Leverett. *A Soldier-Boy's Letters, 1862-1865; A Man's Work in the Ministry.* Ed. Susan Hinckley Bradley. Boston: Privately published, 1905.

Brainard, Mary Genevie Green. *Campaigns of the 146th Regiment New York State Volunteers, Also Known as Halleck's Infantry, the Fifth Oneida, and Garrard's Tigers.* New York: G. P. Putnam's Sons, 1915.

Brewer, A. T. *History of the Sixty-first Regiment Pennsylvania Volunteers 1861-1865.* Pittsburgh: Art Engraving & Printing Co., 1911.

Brooke-Rawle, William, ed. *History of the Third Pennsylvania Cavalry.* Philadelphia: Franklin Printing Co., 1905.

Brooks, Noah. *Washington in Lincoln's Time.* New York: The Century Co., 1895.

Brown, Edmund Randolph. *The Twenty-Seventh Indiana Volunteer Infantry in the War of the Rebellion 1861-1865.* Monticello, Ind.: n.p., 1899.

Bruce, George A. *The Twentieth Regiment of Massachusetts Volunteer Infantry, 1861-1865.* Boston: Houghton, Mifflin and Co., 1906.

Broadhead, Sallie M. *The Diary of a Lady of Gettysburg, Pennsylvania, from June 15 to July 15, 1863.* Privately published, n.d.

Bryant, Edwin E. *History of the Third Regiment of Wisconsin Veteran Volunteer Infantry 1861-1865.* Madison, Wis.: Veteran Assoc. of the Reg't., 1891.

Buehler, Fannie J. *Recollections of the Rebel Invasion and One Woman's Experience During the Battle of Gettysburg.* Gettysburg: privately published, 1896.

Burlingame, Michael, ed. *At Lincoln's Side: John Hay's Civil War Correspondence and Selected Writings.* Carbondale: Southern Illinois University Press, 2000.

——. *Lincoln's Journalist: John Hay's Anonymous Writings for the Press, 1860-1864.* Carbondale: Southern Illinois University Press, 1998.

——. *Lincoln Observed: Civil War Dispatches of Noah Brooks.* Baltimore: Johns Hopkins University Press, 1998.

——. *With Lincoln in the White House: Letters, Memoranda, and Other Writings of John G. Nicolay, 1860-1865.* Carbondale: Southern Illinois University Press, 2000.

Burlingame, Michael and John R. Turner Ettlinger, eds. *Inside Lincoln's White House: The Complete Civil War Diary of John Hay.* Carbondale: Southern Illinois University Press, 1997.

Caldwell, J. F. J. *The History of a Brigade of South Carolinians, Known First as "Gregg's" and Subsequently as "McGowan's Brigade."* Philadelphia: King & Baird, 1866.

Calvert, Henry Murray. *Reminiscences of a Boy in Blue.* New York: G. P. Putnam's Sons, 1920.

Campbell, Edward Livingston. *Historical Sketch of the Fifteenth Regiment, New Jersey Volunteers. First Brigade, First Division, Sixth Corps.* Trenton, N.J.: W. S. Sharp, 1880.

Camper, Charles and J. W. Kirkley. *Historical Record of the First Regiment Maryland Infantry.* Washington, D. C.: Gibson Brothers, 1871.

Carter, Robert Goldthwaite. *Four Brothers in Blue; or, Sunshine and Shadows of the War of the Rebellion, A Story of the Great Civil War from Bull Run to Appomattox.* Washington, Press of Gibson Bros., 1913.

Casler, John O. *Four Years in the Stonewall Brigade.* Guthrie, Okla.: n.p., 1893.

Cassedy, Edward K., ed. *Dear Friends at Home: The Civil War Letters and Diaries of Sergeant Charles T. Bowen, Twelfth United States Infantry 1861-1864*. Baltimore: Butternut & Blue, 2001.

Cavada, Frederico F. *Libby Life: Experiences of a Prisoner of War in Richmond, Va., 1863-64*. Philadelphia: J. B. Lippincott & Co., 1865.

Chamberlin, Thomas. *History of the One Hundred and Fiftieth Regiment Pennsylvania Volunteers, Second Regiment, Bucktail Brigade*. Philadelphia: F. McManus, Jr. & Co., 1905.

Cheney, Newell, comp. *History of the Ninth Regiment, New York Volunteer Cavalry, War of 1861 to 1865*. Poland Center, N. Y.: Martin Merz & Son, 1901.

Child, William. *Letters From a Civil War Surgeon: The Letters of William Child of the Fifth New Hampshire Volunteers*. Solon, Maine: Polar Bear & Co, 1995.

Clark, Charles A. *Campaigning with the Sixth Maine*. Des Moines: The Kenyon Press, 1897.

Clark, George. *A Glance Backward, Or, Some Events in the Past History of My Life*. Houston: privately published, 1914.

Collier, John S. and Bonnie B. *Yours for the Union: The Civil War Letters of John W. Chase, First Massachusetts Light Artillery*. New York: Fordham University Press, 2004.

Confederate Reminiscences and Letters 1861-1865. 10 vols. Atlanta: Georgia Division, United Daughters of the Confederacy, 1994-2001.

Cook, Benjamin F. *History of the Twelfth Massachusetts Volunteers (Webster Regiment)*. Boston: Twelfth Regiment Assoc, 1882.

Cooke, John Esten. *Wearing of the Gray: Being Personal Portraits, Scenes, and Adventures of the War*. New York: E. B. Treat & Co., 1867.

Craft, David. *History of the One Hundred Forty-first Regiment, Pennsylvania Volunteers 1862-1865*. Towanda, Pa.: Reporter-Journal Printing Co., 1885.

Crotty, D. G. *Four Years Campaigning in the Army of the Potomac*. Grand Rapids, Mich.: Dygert Bros. & Co., 1874.

Crowninshield, Benjamin W. *A History of the First Regiment of Massachusetts Cavalry Volunteers*. Boston: Houghton-Mifflin & Co., 1891.

Curtis, Orson B. *History of the Twenty-Fourth Michigan of the Iron Brigade, Known as the Detroit and Wayne County Regiment*. Detroit, Mich.: Winn & Hammond, 1891.

Davis, Charles E., Jr. *Three Years in the Army: The Story of the Thirteenth Massachusetts Volunteers from July 16, 1861 to August 1, 1864*. Boston: Estes and Lauriat, 1894.

Davis, Julia. *Mount Up: A True Story of the Civil War*. New York: Harcourt, Brace & World, 1967.

Davis, Sidney Morris. *Common Soldier, Uncommon War: Life as a Civil War Cavalryman*. Charles F. Cooney, ed. Bethesda, Md.: SMD Group, 1994.

Dawes, Rufus R. *Service with the Sixth Wisconsin Volunteers*. Marietta, Ohio: E. R. Alderman & Sons, 1890.

Denison, Frederic. *Sabres and Spurs: The First Rhode Island Cavalry in the Civil War*. Providence: First Rhode Island Cavalry Veteran Assoc., 1876.

Dennett, Tyler, ed. *Lincoln and the Civil War in the Diaries and Letters of John Hay.* New York: Dodd, Mead & Co., 1939.

DePeyster, John Watts. *The Decisive Conflicts of the Late Civil War.* New York: MacDonald & Co., 1867.

de Trobriand, Regis. *Four Years with the Army of the Potomac.* Trans. by George K. Dauchy. Boston: Ticknor and Co., 1889.

Dickert, D. Augustus. *History of Kershaw's Brigade.* Newberry, S.C.: Elbert H. Aull Company, 1899.

Doster, William E. *A Brief History of the Fourth Pennsylvania Cavalry Embracing Organization, Reunions, Dedication of Monument at Gettysburg and Address of General W. E. Doster, Venango County Battalion, Reminiscences, Etc..* Hightstown, N. J.: Longstreet House, 1997.

——. *Lincoln and Episodes of the Civil War.* New York: G. P. Putnam's Sons, 1915.

Doubleday, Abner. *Chancellorsville and Gettysburg.* New York: Charles Scribner's Sons, 1882.

Dowdey, Clifford and Louis H. Manarin, eds. *The Wartime Papers of Robert E. Lee.* 2 vols. Richmond: Commonwealth of Virginia, 1961.

Dunaway, Wayland Fuller. *Reminiscences of a Rebel.* New York: Neale Publishing Co., 1913.

Early, Jubal A. *Autobiographical Sketch and Narrative of the War Between the States.* Philadelphia: J. B. Lippincott, 1912.

Eby, Carl D., Jr. *A Virginia Yankee in the Civil War: The Diaries of David Hunter Strother.* Chapel Hill: University of North Carolina Press, 1961.

Eckert, Edward K. and Nicholas J. Amato, eds. *Ten Years in the Saddle: The Memoir of William Woods Averell, 1851-1862.* San Rafael, Cal.: Presidio Press, 1978.

Ellis, Edward S. *The Camp-Fires of General Lee, from the Peninsula to Appomattox Court House.* Philadelphia: Henry Harrison & Co., 1888.

Elwood, John W. *Elwood's Stories of the Old Ringgold Cavalry 1847-1865.* Coal Center, Pa.: privately published, 1914.

Emerson, Edward W. *Life and Letters of Charles Russell Lowell.* Boston: Houghton, Mifflin & Co., 1907.

Fairchild, C. B. *History of the 27th Regiment N. Y. Vols.* Binghamton, N. Y.: Carl & Matthews, 1888.

Fatout, Paul, ed. *Letters of a Civil War Surgeon.* West Lafayette, Ind.: Purdue University Press, 1996.

Fonerden, C. A. *History of Carpenter's Battery of the Stonewall Brigade 1861-1865.* New Market, Va.: Henkel & Co., 1911.

Ford, Worthington C., ed. *A Cycle of Adams Letters, 1861-1865.* 2 vols. Boston: Houghton-Mifflin, 1920.

Foster, Alonzo. *Reminiscences and Record of the 6th New York V. V. Cavalry.* Privately published, 1892.

Freeman, Warren Hapgood and Eugene Harrison Freeman. *Letters from Two Brothers Serving in the War for the Union to Their Family at Home in West Cambridge, Mass.* Cambridge: privately published, 1871.

Fremantle, Arthur J. L. *Three Months in the Confederate States: April-June, 1863*. New York: John Bradburn, 1864.

Gall, John. *Reminiscences of Four Years as a Private Soldier in the Confederate Army, 1861-1865*. Baltimore: Sun Job Printing Office, 1904.

Gardner, Charles. *Three Years in the Cavalry: The Civil War Remembrances of Charles Garnder.* Tucson, Ariz.: A Plus Printing, 1998.

Garnett, John J. *Gettysburg: A Complete Historical Narrative of the Battle of Gettysburg and the Campaign Preceding It.* New York: J. M. Hill, 1888.

Gibbon, John. *Personal Recollections of the Civil War.* New York: G. P. Putnam's Sons, 1928.

Gilder, Rosamond, ed. *Letters of Richard Watson Gilder.* New York: Constable & Co. Limited, 1916.

Gillespie, Samuel L. *A History of Company A, First Ohio Cavalry, 1861-1865: A Memorial Volume Compiled from Personal Records and Living Witnesses.* Washington, Ohio: Ohio State Register, 1898.

Gilmor, Harry. *Four Years in the Saddle.* New York: Harper & Bros., 1866.

Gilson, J. H. *Concise History of the One Hundred and Twenty-sixth Regiment, Ohio Volunteer Infantry, from the Date of Organization to the End of the Rebellion; With a complete Roster of Each Company, From Date of Muster.* Salem, Ohio: Walton, Steam Job and Label Printer, 1883.

Glazier, Willard. *Battle for the Union: Comprising Descriptions of Many of the Most Stubbornly Contested Battles in the "War of the Great Rebellion."* Hartford, Conn.: Dustin, Gilman & Co., 1875.

——. *Three Years in the Federal Cavalry*. New York: R.H. Ferguson & Co., 1873.

Goldsborough, W. W. *The Maryland Line in the Confederate Army, 1861-1865.* Baltimore: Guggenheimer, Weil & Co., 1900.

Gordon, John B. *Reminiscences of the Civil War.* New York: Charles Scribner's Sons, 1903.

Goss, Warren Lee. *Recollections of a Private. A Story of the Army of the Potomac.* New York: Thomas Y. Crowell & Co., 1890.

Gracey, Samuel L. *Annals of the Sixth Pennsylvania Cavalry*. Philadelphia: E. H. Butler & Co., 1868.

Greenleaf, Margery, ed. *Letters to Eliza from a Union Soldier, 1862-1865.* Chicago: Follett Publishing Co., 1970.

Haden, B. J. *Reminiscences of J. E. B. Stuart's Cavalry*. Charlottesville, Va.: Progress Publishing Co., n. d.

Haines, Alanson A. *History of the Fifteenth Regiment New Jersey Volunteers.* New York: Jenkins & Thomas, 1883.

Hale, Laura Virginia. *History of the Forty-ninth Virginia Infantry, C.S.A., "Extra Billy Smith's Boys": Based on the Unpublished Memoirs of Captain Robert Daniel Funkhouser, "Warren Blues," Company D, 49th Virginia Infantry, C.S.A.* Lanham, Md.: S. S. Phillips, 1981.

Hall, Hillman A., ed. *History of the Sixth New York Cavalry (Second Ira Harris Guard) Second Brigade, First Division, Cavalry Corps, Army of the Potomac, 1861-1865.* Worcester, Mass.: Blanchard Press, 1908.

Hall, Isaac. *History of the Ninety Seventh Regiment New York Volunteers "Conkling Rifles" in the War for the Union.* Utica, N. Y.: Press of L. C. Childs and Son, 1890.

Hall, James E. *The Diary of a Confederate Soldier: James E. Hall.* Edited by Ruth Woods Dayton. Lewisburg, W. V.: privately published, 1961.

Hamlin, Charles, ed. *Maine at Gettysburg.* Portland: Lakeside Press, 1898.

Hampton, Wade. *Address on the Life and Character of Gen. Robert E. Lee, Delivered on the 12th of October, 1871, Before the Society of Confederate Soldiers and Sailors in Maryland.* Baltimore: John Murphy & Co., 1871.

Hard, Abner N. *History of the Eighth Cavalry Regiment, Illinois Volunteers, During the Great Rebellion.* Aurora, Ill.: privately published, 1868.

Harrison, Walter. *Pickett's Men: A Fragment of War History.* New York: D. Van Nostrand, 1870.

Haskell, Frank Aretas. *The Battle of Gettysburg.* Madison, Wis.: Democrat Printing Co., 1908.

Haskin, William Lawrence. *The History of the First Regiment of Artillery, from Its Organization in 1821 to January 1st, 1876.* Portland, Me.: B. Thurston & Co., 1879.

Haupt, Herman. *Reminiscences of General Herman Haupt.* Milwaukee: Wright & Joys Co., 1901.

Haynes, E. M. *A History of the Tenth Regiment, Vermont Volunteers, With Biographical Sketches of the Officers Who Fell in Battle and a Complete Roster of all the Officers and Men Connected With It—Showing All Changes by Promotion, Death or Resignation, During the Military Existence of the Regiment.* Lewiston, Maine: Tenth Vermont Regimental Assoc., 1870.

Haynes, Martin A. *History of the Second Regiment New Hampshire Volunteers: Its Camps, Marches and Battles.* Manchester, N.H.: Charles F. Livingston, 1865.

Hays, Gilbert Adams. *Under the Red Patch: Story of the Sixty Third Regiment Pennsylvania Volunteers 1861-1864.* Pittsburgh: Sixty-third Pa. Vols. Regimental Assoc., 1908.

History of the 121st Regiment Pennsylvania Volunteers. Philadelphia: Press of Burk & McFetridge Co., 1893.

Hodam, James H. *Sketches and Personal Reminiscences of the Civil War as Experienced by a Confederate Soldier Together With Incidents of Boyhood Life of Fifty Years Ago.* Eugene, Ore.: Robert P. Hodam, 1995.

Hoke, Jacob. *The Great Invasion of 1863; or, General Lee in Pennsylvania.* Dayton, Ohio: W. J. Shuey, 1887.

Hood, John Bell. *Advance and Retreat: Personal Experiences in the United States and Confederate States Armies.* New Orleans: Hood Orphan Memorial Fund, 1880.

Hopkins, Luther W. *From Bull Run to Appomattox: A Boy's View*. Baltimore: Fleet-McGinley Co., 1908.

Hotchkiss, Jedediah. *Make Me a Map of the Valley: The Civil War Journal of Stonewall Jackson's Topographer*. Archie P. McDonald, ed. Dallas: Southern Methodist University Press, 1973.

Howard, McHenry. *Recollections of a Maryland Confederate Soldier and Staff Officer Under Johnston, Jackson, and Lee*. Baltimore: Williams & Wilkins Co., 1914.

Howard, Oliver Otis. *Autobiography of Oliver Otis Howard, Major General United States Army*. 2 vols. New York: The Baker & Taylor Co., 1907.

Howard, Wiley C. *Sketch of Cobb Legion Cavalry and Some Incidents and Scenes Remembered.* Atlanta: Camp 159 U. C. V, 1901.

Hubard, Robert T., Jr. *The Civil War Memoirs of a Virginia Cavalryman*. Ed. Thomas P. Nanzig. Tuscaloosa: University of Alabama Press, 2007.

Hubbs, G. Ward, ed. *Voices from Company D: Diaries by the Greensboro Guards, Fifth Alabama Infantry Regiment, Army of Northern Virginia.* Athens, Ga: The University of Georgia Press, 2003.

Hudgins, Garland C., and Richard B. Kleese, eds. *Recollections of an Old Dominion Dragoon*. Orange, Va.: Publisher's Press, 1993.

Hughes, Thomas. *A Boy's Experience in the Civil War 1860-1865*. Privately published, 1904.

Humphreys, Andrew A. *Gettysburg to the Rapidan: The Army of the Potomac, July 1863 to April 1864*. New York: Charles Scribner's Sons, 1883.

Hurst, Samuel H. *Journal History of the Seventy-Third Ohio Volunteer Infantry*. Chillicothe, Ohio: privately published, 1866.

Husby, Karla J. and Eric J. Wittenberg, eds. *Under Custer's Command: The Civil War Journal of James Henry Avery*. Dulles, Va.: Brassey's, Inc., 2000.

Hussey, George A. *History of the Ninth Regiment N.Y.S. M.—N.G.S.N.Y. 1845-1888*. New York: Published by the Veterans of the Regiment, 1889.

Hutchinson, Nelson V. *History of the Seventh Massachusetts Volunteer Infantry in the War of the Rebellion of the Southern States Against Constitutional Authority, 161-1865*. Taunton, Mass.: The Regimental Assoc., 1890.

Hyde, Bill, ed. *The Union Generals Speak: The Meade Hearings on the Battle of Gettysburg*. Baton Rouge: Louisiana State University Press, 2003.

Hyde, Thomas W. *Following the Greek Cross; Or Memories of the Sixth Army Corps*. Boston: Houghton, Mifflin & Co., 1894.

Hyndman, William. *History of a Cavalry Company: A Complete Record of Company "A," 4th Penn'a Cavalry*. Philadelphia: J. B. Rodgers, 1870.

Ide, Horace K. *History of the First Vermont Cavalry Volunteers in the War of the Great Rebellion*. Edited by Elliott W. Hoffman. Baltimore: Butternut & Blue, 2000.

In Memoriam: John Hammond. Chicago: P. F. Pettibone & Co., 1890.

Irby, Richard. *Historical Sketch of the Nottoway Grays, Afterwards Company G, Eighteenth Virginia Regiment, Army of Northern Virginia*. Richmond: J. W. Fergusson & Sons, 1878.

Isham, Asa B. *An Historical Sketch of the Seventh Regiment Michigan Volunteer Cavalry, From its Organization in 1862, to its Muster Out in 1865.* New York: Town Topics Publishing Co., 1893.

Jacobs, Michael. *Notes on the Rebel Invasion of Maryland and Pennsylvania and the Battle of Gettysburg July 1st, 2d and 3d, 1863.* Philadelphia: J. B. Lippincott & Co., 1864.

Johnston, David E. *The Story of a Confederate Boy in the Civil War.* Portland, Ore.: Glass & Prudhomme, 1914.

Jones, John B. *A Rebel War Clerk's Diary at the Confederate States Capital.* 2 vols. Philadelphia: J. B. Lippincott & Co., 1866.

Jones, Terry L., ed. *Campbell Brown's Civil War: With Ewell and the Army of Northern Virginia.* Baton Rouge: Louisiana State University Press, 2001.

Kennedy, Elijah R. *John B. Woodward: An Annotated Memoir.* New York: The De Vinne Press, 1897.

Kent, Charles N. *History of the Seventeenth Regiment, New Hampshire Volunteer Infantry, 1862-1863.* Concord, N.H.: Seventeenth New Hampshire Veteran Assoc., 1898.

Kesterson, Brian Stuart, ed. *The Last Survivor: The Memoirs of George William Watson, A Horse Soldier of the 12th Virginia Cavalry.* Washington, W. V.: Night Hawk Press, 1993.

Kidd, James H. *Personal Recollections of a Cavalryman in Custer's Michigan Brigade.* Ionia, Mich.: Sentinel Printing Co., 1908.

Kiefer, W. R. *History of the 153rd Pennsylvania Volunteer Infantry.* Easton, Pa.: Chemical Publishing Co., 1909.

Klynstra, H, ed. *Letters of Jerome Cutler, Waterville, Vermont, During his Enlistment in the Union Army, 2nd Regiment, Vermont Volunteers, 1861-1864.* Privately published, 1990.

LaBree, Ben. *Camp Fires of the Confederacy.* Louisville: Courier-Journal Job Printing Company, 1898.

Ladd, David L. and Audrey J. *The Bachelder Papers: Gettysburg in Their Own Words.* 3 vols. Dayton, Ohio: Morningside, 1995.

Lee, Fitzhugh. *General Lee.* New York: D. Appleton & Co., 1894.

Lee, William O., comp. *Personal and Historical Sketches and Facial History of and by Members of the Seventh Regiment Michigan Volunteer Cavalry 1862-1865.* Detroit: 7th Michigan Cavalry Assoc., 1902.

Leland, Charles Godfrey. *Memoirs.* London: William Heineman, 1894.

Leon, Louis. *Diary of a Tar Heel Confederate Soldier.* Charlotte, N. C.: Stone Publishing Co., 1913.

Lewis, George. *History of Battery E, First Regiment Rhode Island Light Artillery in the War of 1861 and 1865, to Preserve the Union.* Providence: Snow & Farnham, 1892.

Lincoln, William R. *Life with the Thirty-Fourth Mass. Infantry in the War of the Rebellion.* Worcester, Mass.: Press of Noyes, Snow & Co., 1879.

Lloyd, William P. *History of the First Reg't. Pennsylvania Reserve Cavalry, From Its Organization, August, 1861, to September, 1864, With a List of Names of All Officers and Enlisted Men Who Have Ever Belonged to the Regiment.* Philadelphia: King & Baird, 1864.

Locke, William Henry. *The Story of the Regiment.* Philadelphia: J. B. Lippincott, 1868.

Lockwood, John. *Our Campaign Around Gettysburg: Being a Memorial of What was Endured, Suffered, and Accomplished by the Twenty-third Regiment (N.Y.S.N.G.,) and Other Regiments Associated with them, in their Pennsylvania and Maryland Campaign, During the Rebel Invasion of the Loyal States in June-July, 1863.* Brooklyn, N.Y.: A. H. Rome & Brothers, 1864.

Loehr, Charles T. *War History of the Old First Virginia Infantry Regiment, Army of Northern Virginia.* Richmond: Wm. Ellis Jones, 1884.

Long, Armistead L. *Memoirs of Robert E. Lee: His Military and Personal History Embracing a Large Amount of Information Hitherto Unpublished.* New York: J. M. Stoddart & Co., 1886.

Longstreet, James. *From Manassas to Appomattox: Memoirs of the Civil War in America.* Philadelphia: J. B. Lippincott Co., 1896.

Lyman, Theodore. *Meade's Headquarters, 1863-1865.* Salem, N.H.: Ayer Company Publishing Inc., George R. Agassiz, ed., 1922.

Lynch, Charles H. *The Civil War Diary 1861-1865 of Charles H. Lynch, 18th Conn. Vol's.* Hartford: The Case, Lockwood & Evannard Co., 1915.

Marbaker, Thomas. *History of the Eleventh New Jersey Volunteers.* Trenton: MacCrellish & Quigley, 1898.

Mark, Penrose G. *Red: White: and Blue Badge: Pennsylvania Volunteers. A History of the 93rd Regiment, Known as the "Lebanon Infantry" and "One of the 300 Fighting Regiments" from September 12th, 1861 to June 27th, 1865.* Privately published, 1911.

Marshall, Charles. *An Aide-de-Camp of Lee.* Boston: Little, Brown, 1927.

Marshall, D. Porter. *Company "K" 155th Pennsylvania Volunteer Zouaves.* n.p., 1888.

Matthews, James Mero. *Soldiers in Green: Civil War Diaries of James Mero Matthews, 2nd U.S. Sharpshooters.* Edited by Peter Dalton. Sandy Point, Maine: Richard's Civil War Roundtable, 2002.

McClellan, Henry B. *The Life and Campaigns of Major-General J.E.B. Stuart.* Boston: Houghton-Mifflin Co., 1885.

McClure, Alexander K. *Old Time Notes of Pennsylvania: A Connected and Chronological Record of the Commercial, Industrial and Educational Advancement of Pennsylvania.* Philadelphia: The John C. Winston Company, 1905.

McDaniel, Henry D. *With Unabated Trust: Major Henry McDaniel's Love Letters from Confederate Battlefields as Treasured in Hester McDaniel's Bonnet Box.* Monroe, Ga.: Historical Society of Walton County, 1977.

McDonald, William N. *A History of the Laurel Brigade.* Baltimore: Sun Job Printing Office, 1907.

McKim, Randolph H. *A Soldier's Recollections: Leaves from the Diary of a Confederate.* New York: Longmans & Green, 1910.

McNamara, Daniel G. *History of the Ninth Regiment Massachusetts Volunteer Infantry Second Brigade, First Division, Fifth Army Corps, Army of the Potomac June 1861-June 1864.* Boston: E. B. Stillings & Co., 1899.

McSwain, Eleanor D., ed. *Crumbling Defenses; or Memoirs and Reminiscences of John Logan Black, C. S. A.* Macon, Ga.: The J. W. Burke Co., 1960.

Meade, George Gordon. *The Life and Letters of General George Gordon Meade.* Edited by George Meade. 2 vols. New York: Charles Scribner's Sons, 1913.

Meade, George, Jr. *Did General Meade Desire to Retreat at the Battle of Gettysburg?* Philadelphia: Porter & Coates, 1883.

Meyer, Henry C. *Civil War Experiences Under Bayard, Gregg, Kilpatrick, Custer, Raulston, and Newberry 1862, 1863, 1864.* New York: privately published, 1911.

Michie, Peter S., ed. *The Life and Letters of Emory Upton, Colonel of the Fourth Regiment of Artillery, and Brevet Major-General, U.S. Army.* New York: D. Appleton & Co., 1885.

Mills, George Henry. *History of the 16th North Carolina Regiment (Originally 6th N. C. Regiment) in the Civil War.* Reprint ed. Hamilton, N.Y.: Edmonston Publishing, 1992.

Mitchell, Adele H., ed. *The Letters of Major General James E. B. Stuart.* Richmond: Stuart-Mosby Historical Society, 1990.

Mohr, James C. *The Cormany Diaries: A Northern Family in the Civil War.* Pittsburgh, Pa.: University of Pittsburgh Press, 1982.

Moore, Edward A. *The Story of a Cannoneer Under Stonewall Jackson.* Lynchburg, Va.: J. P. Bell Co., 1910.

Moore, Frank, ed. *The Rebellion Record: A Diary of American Events.* 12 vols. New York: D. Van Nostrand, 1861-1868.

Moore, James, M.D. *Kilpatrick and Our Cavalry.* New York: J. Widdleton, 1865.

Morhous, Henry C. *Reminiscences of the 123rd Regiment, N.Y.S.V., History of Its Three Years Service in the War.* Greenwich, N. Y.: People's Journal Book and Job Office, 1879.

Morrison, James L., Jr., ed. *The Memoirs of Henry Heth.* Westport, Conn.: Greenwood Press, 1974.

Morse, F. W. *Personal Experiences in the War of the Great Rebellion from December 1862 to July 1865.* Albany, N.Y.: privately published, 1866.

Morse, John T., ed. *The Diary of Gideon Welles, Secretary of the Navy Under Lincoln and Johnson.* 3 vols. New York: Houghton-Mifflin, 1911.

Moyer, Henry P. *History of the Seventeenth Regiment Pennsylvania Volunteer Cavalry.* Lebanon, Pa.: Sowers Printing Co., 1911.

Muffly, J. W., ed. *The Story of Our Regiment: A History of the 148th Pennsylvania Vols.* Des Moines: Kenyon Printing & Mfg. Co., 1904.

Mulholland, St. Clair. *The Story of the 116th Regiment Pennsylvania Volunteers in the War of the Rebellion: The Record of a Gallant Command.* Philadelphia: F. McManus, Jr. & Co., 1903.

Murray, R. L., ed. *Letters From Berdan's Sharpshooters.* Wolcott, N.Y.: Benedum Books, 2005.

——. *Letters From Gettysburg: New York Soldiers' Correspondences from the Battlefield.* Wolcott, N.Y.: Benedum Books, 2005.

Myers, Frank M. *The Comanches: A History of White's Battalion, Virginia Cavalry.* Baltimore: Kelly, Piet & Co., 1871.

Nash, Eugene Arus. *A History of the Forty-fourth Regiment New York Volunteer Infantry in the Civil War, 1861-1865*. Chicago: R. R. Donnelley & Sons, 1911.

Neese, George M. *Three Years in the Confederate Horse Artillery*. New York: Neale Publishing Co., 1911.

Nelson, Alanson H. *The Battles of Chancellorsville and Gettysburg*. Minneapolis: privately published, 1899.

Nevins, Allan S., ed. *A Diary of Battle: The Personal Journals of Colonel Charles S. Wainwright, 1861-1865*. New York: Harcourt, Brace & World, 1962.

New York State Monuments Commission for the Battlefields of Gettysburg and Chattanooga, *Final Report on the Battlefield at Gettysburg*. 3 vols. Albany: J. B. Lyon Co., 1900.

Newcomer, C. Armour. *Coles Cavalry; or Three Years in the Saddle in the Shenandoah Valley*. Freeport, N. Y.: Books for Libraries Press, 1970.

Newell, Joseph Keith. *"Ours." Annals of the 10th Regiment, Massachusetts Volunteers in the Rebellion*. Springfield, Mass.: C. A. Nichols & Co., 1875.

Newhall, Frederic C. *Dedication of the Monument of the Sixth Pennsylvania Cavalry on the Battlefield of Gettysburg, October 14, 1888*. Philadelphia: privately published, 1889.

Nicholson, John P., ed. *Pennsylvania at Gettysburg*. 2 vols. Harrisburg: E. K. Meyers, State Printer, 1893.

Norton, Henry. *Deeds of Daring, or, History of the Eighth N.Y. Volunteer Cavalry*. Norwich, N.Y.: Chenango Telegraph Printing House, 1889.

Oates, William C. *The War Between the Union and the Confederacy*. New York: Neale Publishing Co., 1905.

Oeffinger, John C., ed. *A Soldier's General: The Civil War Letters of Major General Lafayette McLaws*. Chapel Hill: University of North Carolina Press, 2002.

Opie, John N. *A Rebel Cavalryman With Lee, Stuart, and Jackson*. Chicago: W. B. Conkey Co., 1899.

Page, Charles D. *History of the Fourteenth Regiment, Connecticut Vol. Infantry*. Meriden, Conn.: Horton Printing Co., 1906.

Parker, Francis J. *The Story of the Thirty-Second Massachusetts Infantry*. Boston: C. W. Calkins & Co., 1880.

Parker, John L. *Henry Wilson's Regiment*. Boston: Press of Rand Avery Co., 1887.

Paver, John M. *What I Saw from 1861 to 1864*. Privately published, n.d.

Peck, Daniel. *Dear Rachel: The Civil War Letters of Daniel Peck*. Martha Gerber Stanford and Eleanor Erskin, eds. Freeman, S.D.: Pine Hill Press, Ltd., 1993.

Peck, Rufus H. *Reminiscences of a Confederate Soldier of Co. C, 2nd Va. Cavalry*. Fincastle, Va.: privately published, 1913.

Penfield, James. *The 1863-1864 Civil War Diary of Captain James Penfield, 5th New York Volunteer Cavalry, Company H*. Crown Point, N. Y.: Penfield Foundation, 1999.

Perry, Bliss. *Life and Letters of Henry Lee Higginson*. Boston: The Atlantic Monthly Press, 1921.

Phisterer, Frederick, comp. *New York in the War of the Rebellion, 1861 to 1865.* 5 vols. Albany: J.B. Lyon Company, 1912.

——. *Statistical Record of the Armies of the United States.* New York: Charles Scribner's Sons, 1881.

Pickerill, W. N. *History of the Third Indiana Cavalry.* Indianapolis: Aetna Printing Co., 1906.

Poague, William Thomas. *Gunner with Stonewall.* Edited by Monroe F. Cockrell. Jackson, Tenn.: McCoway-Mercer Press, Inc., 1957.

Poe, David. *Personal Reminiscences of the Civil War.* Charleston, W. V.: The News-Mail Publishing Co., 1908.

Polley, J. B. *A Soldier's Letters to Charming Nellie.* New York: Neale Publishing Co., 1908.

Pool, S. D., ed. *Our Living and Our Dead: Devoted to North Carolina—Her Past, Her Present, and Her Future.* Vol. 1: September 1874, to February 1875. Raleigh, N. C.: Southern Historical Society, 1897.

Powell, William H. *The Fifth Army Corps (Army of the Potomac): A Record of Operations During the Civil War in the United States of America, 1861-1865.* New York: G. P. Putnam's Sons, 1896.

Powelson, B. F. *History of Company K of the 140th Regiment Pennsylvania Volunteers. 1862-1865.* Steubenville, Ohio: The Carnahan Printing Co., 1906.

Preston, Noble. D. *History of the Tenth Regiment of Cavalry New York State Volunteers, August, 1861, to August, 1865.* New York: D. Appleton & Co., 1892.

Proceedings of the Reunion Society of Vermont Officers, 1864-1884, with Addresses Delivered at Its Meetings. Burlington: Free Press Assoc., 1885.

Public Documents and Extracts from Reports and Papers Relating to Light-Houses, 1789-1871. Washington, D.C.: Government Printing Office, 1890.

Pyne, Henry R. *Ride to War: The History of the First New Jersey Cavalry.* New Brunswick, N.J.: Rutgers University Press, 1961.

Quaife, Milo M., ed. *From the Cannon's Mouth: The Civil War Letters of General Alpheus S. Williams.* Detroit: Wayne State University, 1959.

Rea, D. B. *Sketches from Hampton's Cavalry: Embracing the Principal Exploits of the Cavalry in the Campaigns of 1862 and 1863.* Columbia, S. C.: South Carolinian Steam Press, 1864.

Report of the Adjutant and Inspector General of the State of Vermont for the Year Ending November 1, 1863. Montpelier: Walton's Steam Printing Establishment, 1863.

Report of the Joint Committee on the Conduct of the War at the Second Session, Thirty-Eighth Congress. 2 vols. Washington, D. C.: U. S. Government Printing Office, 1865-66.

Rhodes, Robert Hunt, ed.. *All for the Union: The Civil War Diary of Elisha Hunt Rhodes.* Lincoln, R. I.: Andrew Mowbray, Inc., 1985.

Riley, Franklin L., ed. *Publications of the Mississippi Historical Society.* 14 vols. Oxford, Miss.: Printed by the Society, 1898-1914.

Robertson, Frank. *In the Saddle With Stuart: The Story of Frank Smith Robertson of J. E. B. Stuart's Staff.* Edited by Robert J. Trout. Gettysburg, Pa.: Thomas Publications, 1998.

Robertson, John, comp. *Michigan in the War.* Lansing: W. S. George & Co., 1882.

Rodenbough, Theophilus F., comp. *From Everglade to Canyon With the Second United States Cavalry: An Authentic Account of Service in Florida, Mexico, Virginia, and the Indian Country, 1836-1875.* New York: D. Van Nostrand, 1875.

——. *History of the Eighteenth Regiment of Cavalry Pennsylvania Volunteers 1862-1865.* New York: Regimental Publication Committee, 1909.

Roe, Alfred S. *The Tenth Massachusetts Volunteer Infantry, 1861-1864.* Springfield: 10th Regiment Veterans Assoc., 1909.

——. *The Thirty-Ninth Regiment Massachusetts Volunteers 1862-1865.* Worcester, Mass.: Regimental Veteran Assoc., 1914.

Rohm, Frederic William. *No Braver Man: The Story of Ferdinand F. Rohm, Chief Bugler, 16th Pennsylvania Cavalry.* Fredericksburg, Va.: Sergeant Kirkland's Museum and Historical Society, Inc., 1998.

Rosenblatt, Emil and Ruth, eds. *Hard Marching Every Day: The Civil War Letters of Private Wilbur Fisk.* Lawrence, Kan.: University Press of Kansas, 1992.

Rusling, James F. *Men and Things I Saw in Civil War Days.* New York: Eaton & Mains, 1899.

Sauerburger, Dona Bayard and Thomas Lucas Bayard, eds. *"I Seat Myself to Write You a Few Lines": Civil War and Homestead Letters from Thomas Lucas and Family.* Laurel, Md.: Heritage Books, 2002.

St. Clair, Hugh. *Hugh St. Clair Civil War Diary, 1 Jan. to 31 Dec. 1863.* Hygiene, Col.: Sunshine Press Publications, 2001.

Samito, Christian G. *Commanding Boston's Irish Ninth: The Civil War Letters of Colonel Patrick R. Guiney, Ninth Massachusetts Volunteer Infantry.* New York: Fordham University Press, 1998.

Sawyer, Franklin. *The Eighth Ohio at Gettysburg: Address of General Franklin Sawyer.* Columbus: H. McKay, Printer, 1889.

Scheibert, Justus. *Seven Months in the Rebel States During the North American War, 1863.* Translated by Joseph C. Hayes. Edited by William Stanley Hoole. Tuscaloosa, Ala.: Confederate Publishing Co., 1958.

Scott, Robert Garth, ed. *Fallen Leaves: The Civil War Letters of Major Henry Livermore Abbott.* Kent, Ohio: Kent State University Press, 1991.

SeCheverell, J. Hamp. *Journal History of the Twenty-Ninth Ohio Veteran Volunteers, 1861-1865.* Cleveland: n.p., 1883.

Sessarego, Alan, comp. *Letters Home V: Original Civil War Soldiers &Photographs.* Hanover, Pa.: Americana Souvenirs and Gifts, 2003.

Seville, William P. *History of the First Regiment Delaware Volunteers, from the Commencement of the "Three Months' Service" to the Final Muster-Out at the Close of the Rebellion.* Wilmington: Historical Society of Delaware, 1884.

Sheldon, Winthrop D. *The "Twenty-Seventh." A Regimental History*. New Haven, Ct.: Morris & Benham, 1866.

Sheridan, Philip H. *The Personal Memoirs of P. H. Sheridan*. New York: C. L. Webster, 1888.

Shoemaker, John J. *Shoemaker's Battery, Stuart Horse Artillery, Pelham's Battalion, Army of Northern Virginia*. Memphis, Tenn.: privately published, n. d.

Simons, Ezra D. *A Regimental History. The One Hundred and Twenty-Fifth New York State Volunteers*. New York: privately published, 1888.

Skelly, Daniel Alexander. *A Boy's Experiences During the Battle of Gettysburg*. Gettysburg, Pa.: privately published, 1932.

Small, A. R. *The Sixteenth Maine Regiment in the War of the Rebellion 1861-1865*. Portland, Maine: B. Thurston & Co., 1886.

Smith, A. P. *History of the Seventy-Sixth Regiment New York State Volunteers*. Cortland, N.Y.: Truair, Smith & Miles, 1867.

Smith, John D. *The History of the Nineteenth Regiment of Maine Volunteer Infantry 1862-1865*. Minneapolis: The Great Western Printing Co., 1909.

Smith, John L. *History of the Corn Exchange Regiment 118th Pennsylvania Volunteers, From Their First Engagement at Antietam to Appomattox*. Philadelphia: J. L. Smith, 1886.

Smith, Thomas West. *The Story of a Cavalry Regiment: "Scott's 900", Eleventh New York Cavalry from the St. Lawrence River to the Gulf of Mexico 1861-1865*. New York: Published by the Veteran Association of the Regiment, 1897.

Smith, William F. *Autobiography of Major General William F. Smith 1861-1864*. Edited by Herbert M. Schiller. Dayton, Ohio: Morningside, 1990.

Sorrel, G. Moxley. *Recollections of a Confederate Staff Officer*. New York: Neal Publishing Co., 1905.

Sparks, David S., ed. *Inside Lincoln's Army: The Diary of General Marsena Rudolph Patrick, Provost Marshal General, Army of the Potomac*. New York: Thomas Yoseloff, 1964.

Staats, Richard J., ed. *The Life and Times of Colonel William Stedman of the 6th Ohio Cavalry*. Laurel, Md.: Heritage Books, 2003.

Stanford, Martha Gerber and Eleanor Erskin, eds. *Dear Rachel: The Civil War Letters of Daniel Peck*. Freeman, S. D.: Pine Hill Press, 1993.

Stevens, Charles A. *Berdan's United States Sharpshooters in the Army of the Potomac 1861-1865*. St. Paul: The Price-McGill Company, 1892.

Stevens, George T. *Three Years in the Sixth Corps*. Albany, N. Y.: S. R. Gray, 1866.

Stevenson, James H. *"Boots and Saddles": A History of the First Volunteer Cavalry of the War, Known as the First New York (Lincoln) Cavalry, and also as The Sabre Regiment, Its Organization, Campaigns and Battles*. Harrisburg, Pa.: Patriot Publishing Co., 1879.

Stewart, Robert L. *History of the One Hundred and Fortieth Regiment Pennsylvania Volunteers*. Philadelphia: Published by the authority of the Regimental Association, 1912.

Stiles, Robert. *Four Years Under Marse Robert*. New York: The Neale Publishing Company, 1903.

Stocker, Jeffrey D., ed. *From Huntsville to Appomattox: R. T. Coles's History of the 4th Regiment, Alabama Volunteer Infantry, C.S.A., Army of Northern Virginia.* Knoxville: University of Tennessee Press, 1996.

Stoeckel, Carl and Ellen Battelle, eds. *Correspondence of John Sedgwick, Major General.* 2 vols. Privately published, 1903.

Stone, Edwin W. *Rhode Island in the Rebellion.* Providence: George H. Whitney, 1864.

Stonebraker, J. Clarence. *The Unwritten South: Cause, Progress and Result of the Civil War.* Privately published, 1908.

Stonebraker, Joseph R. *A Rebel of '61.* New York: Wynkoop Hellenbeck Crawford Co., 1899.

Storrs, John W. *The "Twentieth Connecticut": A Regimental History.* Ansonia, Conn.: Press of the Naugatuck Valley Sentinel, 1886.

Styple, William B., ed. *Generals in Bronze: Interviewing the Commanders of the Civil War.* Kearny, N. J.: Belle Grove Publishing Co., 2005.

———. *Writing and Fighting from the Army of Northern Virginia: A Collection of Confederate Soldier Correspondence.* Kearny, N. J.: Belle Grove Publishing Co., 2003.

———. *Writing and Fighting the Civil War: Soldier Correspondence to the New York Sunday Mercury.* Kearny, N. J.: Belle Grove Publishing, 2000.

———. *Writing and Fighting the Confederate War: The Letters of Peter Wellington Alexander, Confederate War Correspondent.* Kearny, N. J.: Belle Grove Publishing Co., 2002.

Summers, Festus P., ed. *A Borderland Confederate.* Pittsburgh: University of Pittsburgh Press, 1962.

Sun-Tzu. *The Art of Warfare.* Trans., Roger T. Ames. New York: Ballantine Books, 1993.

Supplement to the Official Records of the Union and Confederate Armies. 100 vols. Wilmington, N. C.: Broadfoot, 1995.

Swinton, William. *Campaigns of the Army of the Potomac: A Critical History of Operations in Virginia, Maryland and Pennsylvania, from the Commencement to the Close of the War. 1861-5.* New York: C.B. Richardson, 1866.

Taylor, Emerson Gifford, ed. *Gouverneur K. Warren: The Life and Letters of an American Solider 1830-1882.* Boston: Houghton-Mifflin Co., 1932.

Taylor, Dr. Gray Nelson, ed. *Saddle and Saber: The Letters of Civil War Cavalryman Corporal Nelson Taylor.* Bowie, Md: Heritage Books, 1993.

Taylor, Michael W., ed. *The Cry is War, War, War: The Civil War Correspondence of Lts. Burwell Thomas Cotton and George Job Huntley, 34th Regiment North Carolina Troops.* Dayton, Ohio: Morningside, 1994.

Taylor, Walter H. *Four Years with General Lee.* Bloomington: Indiana University Press, 1962.

——. *General Lee: His Campaigns in Virginia 1861-1865 with Personal Reminiscences.* Norfolk, Va.: Nusbaum Book and News Co., 1906.

Terrill, J. Newton. *Campaign of the Fourteenth Regiment New Jersey Volunteers.* New Brunswick: Daily Homes News Press, 1884.

The War of the Rebellion: A Compilation of the Official Records of the Union and Confederate Armies. 127 volumes in four series. Washington, D.C.: Government Printing Office, 1880-1901.

Thomson, O. R. Howard and William H. Rauch. *History of the "Bucktails" Kane Rifle Regiment of the Pennsylvania Reserve Corps (135h Pennsylvania Reserves, 42nd of the Line).* Philadelphia: Electric Printing Co., 1906.

Tilney, Robert. *My Life in the Army: Three Years and a Half with the Fifth Corps Army of the Potomac 1862-1865.* Philadelphia: Ferris & Leach, 1912.

Tobie, Edward P. *History of the First Maine Cavalry 1861-1865.* Boston: Press of Emory & Hughes, 1887.

——. *Service of the Cavalry in the Army of the Potomac.* Providence: N. B. Williams, 1882.

Tomasek, Peter, ed. *Avery Harris Civil War Journal.* Luzerne, Pa.: Luzerne National Bank, 2000.

Toombs, Samuel. *New Jersey Troops in the Gettysburg Campaign from June 5 to July 31, 1863.* Orange, N J.: The Evening Mail Publishing House, 1888.

Trowbridge, John T. *A Picture of the Desolated States; and the Work of Restoration, 1865-1868.* Hartford, CT: L. Stebbins, 1868.

Tower, R. Lockwood, ed. *Lee's Adjutant: The Wartime Letters of Colonel Walter Herron Taylor, 1862-1865.* Columbia: University of South Carolina Press, 1995.

Trout, Robert J. *In the Saddle With Stuart: The Story of Frank Smith Robertson of Jeb Stuart's Staff.* Gettysburg, Pa.: Thomas Publications, 1998.

——. *With Pen and Saber: The Letters and Diaries of J. E. B. Stuart's Staff Officers.* Mechanicsburg, Pa.: Stackpole Books, 1995.

Tyler, Mason Whiting Tyler. *Recollections of the Civil War.* New York: G. P. Putnam's Sons, 1912

Urban, John W. *Battlefield and Prison Pen, or Through the War and Thrice a Prisoner in Rebel Dungeons.* Philadelphia: Hubbard Brothers, 1882.

Vautier, John D. *History of the 88th Pennsylvania Volunteers in the War for the Union, 1861-1865.* Philadelphia: J. B. Lippincott, 1894.

Walker, Francis A. *History of the Second Army Corps in the Army of the Potomac.* New York: Charles Scribner's Sons, 1886.

Ward, Joseph R. C. *History of the One Hundred and Sixth Regiment Pennsylvania Volunteers, 2d Brigade, 2d Division, 2d Corps. 1861-1865.* Philadelphia: Grant, Faires & Rodgers, 1883.

Weaver, Augustus C. *Third Indiana Cavalry: A Brief Account of the Actions in Which They Took Part.* Greenwood, In.: privately published, 1919.

Welch, Spencer Glasgow. *A Confederate Surgeon's Letters to His Wife.* New York: The Neale Publishing Company, 1911.

West, John C. *A Texan in Search of a Fight: Being the Diary and Letters of a Private Soldier in Hood's Texas Brigade.* Waco: J. S. Hill & Co., 1901.

Westbrook, Robert S. *History of the 49th Pennsylvania Volunteers.* Altoona, Pa.: Altoona Times Printing, 1898.

Weygant, Charles H. *History of the 124th Regiment of New York State Volunteers.* Newburgh, N.Y.: Journal Printing House, 1877.

White, Russell C., ed. *The Civil War Diary of Wyman S. White.* Baltimore: Butternut and Blue, 1993.

White, William S. *A Diary of the War, or What I saw of It.* Richmond: Carlton McCarthy & Co., 1883.

Wiley, Ken, ed. *Norfolk Blues: The Civil War Diary of the Norfolk Light Artillery Blues.* Shippensburg, Pa.: Burd Street Press, 1997.

Williams, J. C. *Life in Camp: A History of the Nine Months' Service of the Fourteenth Vermont Regiment, From October 21, 1862, When It was Mustered Into the U. S. Service, to July 21, 1863, Including the Battle of Gettysburg.* Claremont, N.H.: Claremont Manufacturing Co., 1864.

Willson, Arabella M. *Disaster, Struggle, Triumph: The Adventures of 1000 "Boys in Blue" from August, 1862 to June, 1865.* Albany, N. Y.: The Argus Company Printers, 1870.

Winthrop, William Woolsey. *Military Law.* 2 vols. Washington, D. C.: W. H. Morrison, 1886.

Wittenberg, Eric J., ed. *At Custer's Side: The Civil War Writings of James Henry Kidd.* Kent, Ohio: Kent State University Press, 2001.

——. *One of Custer's Wolverines: The Civil War Letters of Bvt. Brig. Gen. James H. Kidd, Sixth Michigan Cavalry.* Kent, Ohio: Kent State University Press, 2000.

——. *"We Have It Damn Hard Out Here": The Civil War Letters of Sergeant Thomas W. Smith, Sixth Pennsylvania Cavalry.* Kent, Ohio: Kent State University Press, 1999.

Wood, James H. *The War; "Stonewall" Jackson, His Campaigns, and Battles, the Regiment as I Saw Them.* Cumberland, Md.: Eddy Press Corporation, 1910.

Woodbury, Augustus. *The Second Rhode Island Regiment: A Narrative of Military Operations.* Providence: Valpey, Angell, & Company, 1875.

Woodward, E. M. *Our Campaigns; The Second Regiment Pennsylvania Reserve Volunteers or, The Marches Bivouacs, Battles, Incidents of Camp Life and History of Our Regiment During Its Three Years of Service.* Philadelphia: John E. Porter, 1865.

Worsham, John H. *One of Jackson's Foot Cavalry: His Experience and What He Saw During the War, 1861-1865.* New York: The Neale Publishing Co., 1912.

Wray, William. *History of the 23rd Pennsylvania Infantry.* Harrisburg: Survivors Assoc. of the 23rd Pennsylvania Volunteer Infantry, 1898.

Wright, Mrs. D. Giraud. *A Southern Girl in '61: The War-Time Memories of a Confederate Senator's Daughter.* New York: Doubleday, Page & Co., 1905.

Wright, Stuart, ed. *Memoirs of Alfred Horatio Belo: Reminiscences of a North Carolina Volunteer.* Gaithersburg, Md.: Olde Soldier Books, n.d.

Websites

An Illustrated History of the Fourth Texas Infantry:
www.pha.jhu.edu/~dag/4thtex/history/history.html

SoldierStudies.org, www.soldierstudies.org
Charles J. C. Hutson letter of July 9, 1863
Nathaniel Rollins diary
Henry E. Shepherd, "Wounded at Gettysburg"

SECONDARY SOURCES

Articles

Alexander, Ted. "Ten Days in July: The Pursuit to the Potomac", *North & South* 2 (August 1999): 10-34.

Bierley, William C. "Battle of Funkstown", *Centennial Observer and C & O Chronicle*, March 1962.

——. "Wounded in Funkstown Placed on Sidewalk", *Centennial Observer and C & O Chronicle*, March 1962.

Brown, Kent Masterson. "A Golden Bridge: Lee's Williamsport Defense Lines and His Escape Across the Potomac", *North & South* 2 (August 1999): 56-65.

Bush, Garry L. "Sixth Michigan Cavalry at Falling Waters: The End of the Gettysburg Campaign", *Gettysburg Magazine* 9 (July 1993): 109-115.

Callihan, David L. "Passing the Test: George G. Meade's Initiation as Army Commander," *Gettysburg Magazine* 30 (January 2004): 30-48.

Campbell, Eric A. "Voices of Gettysburg: How the Army of the Potomac Viewed the Campaign," *North & South* 7 (November 2004): 12-23.

Carter, William H. "The Sixth Regiment of Cavalry", *The First Maine Bugle* (October, 1896): 299.

Cunningham, Steve A. and Beth A. White. "'The Ground Trembled as They Came': The 1st West Virginia Cavalry in the Gettysburg Campaign", *Civil War Regiments* Vol. 6, No. 3 (1999): 59-88.

Dahlgren, Madeleine V. "Colonel Ulric Dahlgren—Service at Gettysburg", *The National Tribune*, February 6, 1896.

Duncan, Richard R. "The College of St. James and the Civil War: A Casualty of the War," *Historical Magazine of the Protestant Episcopal Church* 39 (1970): 265-286.

Elmore, Thomas L. "Independence Day: Military Operations at Gettysburg", *Gettysburg Magazine* 25 (July 2001): 116-128.

French, Steve. "Hurry Was the Order of the Day", *North & South* 2 (August 1999): 35-42.

——. "The Rebels at Williamsport", *Gettysburg Magazine* 27 (July 2002): 85-108.

Giunta, Mary A. "In the Backwater of the Gettysburg Campaign," *America's Civil War* (September 2005): 46-53.

Greene, A. Wilson. "From Gettysburg to Falling Waters: Meade's Pursuit of Lee", included in *The Third Day at Gettysburg and Beyond.* Edited by Gary W. Gallagher. Chapel Hill: University of North Carolina Press, 1994. 161-202.

King, G. Wayne. "General Judson Kilpatrick", *New Jersey History*, Vol. 101, No. 1 (Spring 1973): 35-52.

Klingensmith, Harold A. "A Cavalry Regiment's First Campaign: The 18th Pennsylvania at Gettysburg", *The Gettysburg Magazine* 20 (June 1999): 51-74.

O'Reilly, Frank A. "Introduction," included in Augustus C. Hamlin, *The Attack of Stonewall Jackson at Chancellorsville.* Fredericksburg, Va.: Sgt. Kirkland's, 1997.

Petruzzi, J. David. "Annihilation of a Regiment," *America's Civil War* (July 2007), 26-33.

——. "He Rides Over Everything in Sight," *America's Civil War* (March 2006): 24-30.

——. "The Fleeting Fame of Alfred Pleasonton," *America's Civil War* (March 2005): 22-28.

Poulter, Keith. "Errors that Doomed a Campaign," *North & South* 2 (August 1999): 82-88.

Sears, Stephen W. "General Meade and the Second Battle of Gettysburg," *North & South* 8 (January 2005): 65.

Tap, Bruce. "Bad Faith Somewhere: George Gordon Meade and the Committee on the Conduct of the War", *North & South* 2 (August 1999): 74-81.

Terpeluk, William. "A Lesson in Battle Tempo: The Union Pursuit After Gettysburg", *Parameters* (Autumn 1995): 69-80.

Vermilyea, Peter C. "Maj. Gen. John Sedgwick and the Pursuit of Lee's Army after Gettysburg." *Gettysburg Magazine* 22 (2000): 112-129.

Williams, Frank J. "We Had Only to Stretch Forth Our Hands: Abraham Lincoln and George Gordon Meade", *North & South* 2 (August 1999): 66-72.

Wittenberg, Eric J. "And Everything is Lovely and the Goose Hangs High: John Buford and the Hanging of Confederate Spies During the Gettysburg Campaign", *Gettysburg Magazine* 18 (January 1998): 5-14.

——. "John Buford and the Gettysburg Campaign", *Gettysburg Magazine* 11 (July 1994): 19-55.

——. "This Was a Night Never to be Forgotten: The Midnight Fight in the Monterey Pass, July 4-5, 1863", *North & South* 2 (August 1999): 44-54.

——. "Ulric Dahlgren in the Gettysburg Campaign", *Gettysburg Magazine* 22 (January 2000): 96-111.

Books and Pamphlets

Ackinclose, Timothy R. *Sabres and Pistols: The Civil War Career of Colonel Harry Gilmor, C.S.A.* Gettysburg, Pa.: Stan Clark Military Books, 1997.

Adams, Charles S. *The Civil War in Washington County, Maryland: A Guide to 66 Points of Interest.* Dagsboro, Del.: privately published, 2001.

Alberts, Don E. *Brandy Station to Manila Bay: A Biography of General Wesley Merritt.* Austin, Texas: Presidial Press, 1980.

Armstrong, Richard L. *7th Virginia Cavalry*. Lynchburg, Va.: H.E. Howard Co., 1992.

——. *11th Virginia Cavalry*. Lynchburg, Va.: H. E. Howard Co., 1989.

Anders, Curt. *Injustice on Trial: Second Bull Run, General Fitz-John Porter's Court Martial, and the Schofield Board Investigation That Restored His Good Name.* Cincinnati: Emmis Books, 2002.

Andrews, J. Cutler. *The North Reports the Civil War.* Pittsburgh: University of Pittsburgh Press, 1955.

Arnett, Ethel Stephen. *Mrs. James Madison: The Incomparable Dolly.* Greensboro, N.C.: Piedmont Press, 1972.

Balfour, Daniel T. *13th Virginia Cavalry*. Lynchburg, Va.: H. E. Howard Co., 1986.

Bates, Samuel. P. *History of Pennsylvania Volunteers, 1861-5.* 5 vols. Harrisburg: B. Singerly, 1869-71.

Bell, Herbert C. *History of Leitersburg District Washington County, Md.* Leitersburg, Md.: privately published, 1898.

Benedict, George G. *Vermont in the Civil War.* 2 vols. Burlington, Vt.: Free Press Assoc., 1888.

Bernstein, Iver. *The New York City Draft Riots: Their Significance for American Society and Politics in the Age of the Civil War.* London: Oxford University Press, 1990.

Beyer, Walter F. *Deeds of Valor: How America's Heroes Won the Medal of Honor.* 2 vols. Detroit, Mich.: The Perrien- Keydel Co., 1905.

Blackwell, Samuel, Jr. *In the First Line of Battle: The 12th Illinois Cavalry in the Civil War.* DeKalb, Ill.: Northern Illinois University Press, 2002.

Bridges, David P. *Fighting with Jeb Stuart: Major James Breathed and the Confederate Horse Artillery.* Alexandria, Va.: Breathed-Bridges-Best, 2006.

Brown, J. Willard. *The Signal Corps, U.S.A. in the War of the Rebellion.* Boston: U.S. Veteran Signal Corps Association, 1896.

Brown, Kent Masterson. *Retreat from Gettysburg: Lee, Logistics, and the Pennsylvania Campaign.* Chapel Hill: University of North Carolina Press, 2005.

Burgess, Milton V. *David Gregg: Pennsylvania Cavalryman.* Privately published, 1984.

Busey, John W. and David G. Martin. *Regimental Strengths and Losses at Gettysburg, Fourth Edition.* Hightstown, N. J.: Longstreet House, 2005.

Bushong, Millard K. and Dean M. Bushong. *Fightin' Tom Rosser, C.S.A.* Shippensburg, Pa.: Beidel Printing House, Inc., 1983.

Campbell, Eric A., ed. *"A Grand Terrible Dramma": From Gettysburg to Petersburg: The Civil War Letters of Charles Wellington Reed.* New York: Fordham University Press, 2000.

Carter, Samuel, III. *The Last Cavaliers: Confederate and Union Cavalry in the Civil War.* New York: St. Martin's Press, 1979.

Carter, William H. *From Yorktown to Santiago with the Sixth U.S. Cavalry.* 1900; reprint, Austin, Tx.: State House Press, 1989.

Clark, Walter, ed. *Histories of Several Regiments and Battalions from North Carolina in the Great War, 1861-1865.* 5 vols. Raleigh: E. M. Uzzell, 1901.

Clary, James B. *A History of the 15th South Carolina Infantry, 1861-1864.* Columbia: South Carolina Dept of Archives and History, 2007.

Clemmer, Gregg S. *Old Alleghany: Life and Wars of General Ed Johnson.* Darnestown, Md.: Hearthside Publishing Co., 2004.

Coco, Gregory A. *War Stories: A Collection of 150 Little Known Human Interest Accounts of the Campaign and Battle of Gettysburg.* Gettysburg: Thomas Publications, 1992.

——. *Wasted Valor: The Confederate Dead at Gettysburg.* Gettysburg: Thomas Publications, 1990.

Coddington, Edwin B. *The Gettysburg Campaign: A Study in Command.* New York: Charles Scribner's Sons, 1968.

Coffin, Howard. *Full Duty: Vermonters in the Civil War.* Woodstock, Vt.: The Countryman Press, Inc., 1993.

Cole, Scott C. *34th Battalion Virginia Cavalry.* Lynchburg, Va.: H. E. Howard Co., 1993.

Conrad, William P. *Gloryland: A History of Blacks in Greencastle, Pennsylvania.* Greencastle, Pa.: Beidel Printing House, 1989.

Conrad, W. P. and Ted Alexander. *When War Passed This Way.* Greencastle, Pa.: Beidel Printing House, 1982.

Cook, James F. *The Governors of Georgia, 1754-2004.* 3d ed. Macon, Ga.: Mercer University Press, 2005.

Cooling, Benjamin Franklin. *Symbol, Sword, and Shield: Defending Washington During the Civil War.* Hamden, Conn.: Archon Books, 1975.

Dahlgren, John A. *Memoir of Ulric Dahlgren.* Philadelphia: J. B. Lippincott & Co., 1872.

Davis, Burke. *Jeb Stuart: The Last Cavalier.* New York: Rinehart & Co., 1957.

Davis, Oliver Wilson. *Life of David Bell Birney, Major General United States Volunteers.* Philadelphia: King & Baird, 1867.

Dawson, John Harper. *Wildcat Cavalry: A Synoptic History of the Seventeenth Virginia Cavalry Regiment of the Jenkins-McCausland Brigade in the War Between the States.* Dayton, Ohio: Morningside House, 1982.

Delauter, Roger U., Jr. *18th Virginia Cavalry.* Lynchburg, Va.: H. E. Howard Co., 1985.

——. *62nd Virginia Infantry.* Lynchburg, Va.: H. E. Howard Co., 1988.

Dickinson, Jack L. *16th Virginia Cavalry.* Lynchburg, Va.: H. E. Howard Co., 1989.

Divine, John. *35th Battalion Virginia Cavalry*. Lynchburg, Va.: H. E. Howard Co., 1985.

Driver, Robert J., Jr. *First and Second Maryland Cavalry, C. S. A.* Charlottesville, Va.: Rockbridge Publishing, 1999.

——. *The Staunton Artillery—McClanahan's Battery*. Lynchburg, Va.: H. E. Howard Co., 1988.

——. *1st Virginia Cavalry*. Lynchburg, Va.: H. E. Howard Co., 1991.

——. *10th Virginia Cavalry*. Lynchburg, Va.: H. E. Howard Co., 1992.

——. *14th Virginia Cavalry*. Lynchburg, Va.: H. E. Howard Co., 1988.

Driver, Robert J., Jr. and Harold E. Howard. *2nd Virginia Cavalry*. Lynchburg, Va.: H. E. Howard Co., 1995.

Driver, Robert J., Jr. and Kevin C. Ruffner. *1st Battalion Virginia Infantry, 39th Battalion Virginia Cavalry, 24th Battalion Virginia Partisan Rangers*. Lynchburg, Va.: H. E. Howard Co., 1996.

Dunkelman, Mark H. *Brothers One and All: Esprit de Corps in a Civil War Regiment.* Baton Rouge: Louisiana State University Press, 2004.

Eddy, T.M. *The Patriotism of Illinois.* 2 vols. Chicago: Clarke & Co., 1865.

Eicher, John H. and David J. Eicher. *Civil War High Commands.* Stanford, Cal.: Stanford University Press, 2001.

1886 History of Adams County Pennsylvania. Chicago: Warner, Beers & Co., 1886.

Ellis, William Arba, comp. *Norwich University 1819-1911: Her History, Her Graduates, Her Roll of Honor.* 3 vols. Montpelier, Vt.: The Capital City Press, 1911.

Fishel, Edwin C. *The Secret War for the Union.* New York: Houghton-Mifflin Co., 1996.

Fleming, George T. *Life and Letters of Alexander Hays.* Pittsburgh: n.p., 1919.

Freeman, Douglas Southall. *Lee's Lieutenants: A Study in Command.* 3 vols. New York: Charles Scribner's Sons, 1944.

Frye, Dennis E. *12th Virginia Cavalry*. Lynchburg, Va.: H. E. Howard Co., 1988.

Gettyburg National Military Park. *Mr. Lincoln's Army: The Army of the Potomac in the Gettysburg Campaign (Programs of the Sixth Annual Gettysburg Seminar).* National Park Service, 1998.

Gragg, Rod. *Covered With Glory: The 26th North Carolina Infantry at the Battle of Gettysburg.* New York: HarperCollins Publishers, 2000.

Greater Chambersburg Chamber of Commerce. *Southern Revenge: Civil War History of Chambersburg, Pennsylvania.* Chambersburg, Pa.: Greater Chambersburg Chamber of Commerce, 1989.

Hackley, Woodford B. *The Little Fork Rangers: A Sketch of Company "D" Fourth Virginia Cavalry*. Richmond: Dietz Printing Co., 1927.

Hall, Winfield Scott. *The Captain: An Eighth Illinois Trooper.* Riverside, Ill.: privately published, 1994.

Hamlin, Charles Eugene. *The Life and Times of Hannibal Hamlin.* Cambridge: The Riverside Press, 1899.

Hand, Harold. *One Good Regiment: The 13th Pennsylvania Cavalry in the Civil War, 1861-1865.* Victoria, B. C.: Trafford Publishing, 2000.

Harrell, Roger H. *The 2nd North Carolina Cavalry.* Jefferson, N.C.: McFarland, 2004.

Harris, Nelson. *17th Virginia Cavalry.* Lynchburg, Va.: H. E. Howard Co., 1994.

Harrison, Hall. *Life of the Right Reverend John Barrett Kerfoot.* 2 vols. New York: James Pott & Co., 1886.

Hartley, Chris J. *Stuart's Tarheels: James B. Gordon and His North Carolina Cavalry.* Baltimore: Butternut & Blue, 1996.

Hayes, Lyman Simpson. *History of the Town of Rockingham, Vermont, Including the Villages of Bellows Falls, Saxtons River, Rockingham, Cambridgeport, and Bartonville, 1753-1907, With Family Genealogies.* Bellows Falls, Vt.: Town of Bellows Falls, 1907.

Hays, Helen Ashe. *The Antietam and its Bridges: The Annals of an Historic Stream.* New York: G. P. Putnam's Sons, 1910.

Haywood, Marshall DeLancey. *Lives of the Bishops of North Carolina From the Establishment of the Episcopate in That State Down to the Division of the Diocese.* Raleigh, N. C.: Alfred Williams & Company, 1910.

Helm, Lewis Marshall. *Black Horse Cavalry: Defend Our Beloved Country.* Falls Church, Va.: Higher Education Publications, 2004.

Helman, James A. *Helman's History of Emmitsburg, Maryland.* Privately published, 1906.

Hennessy, John J. *Return to Bull Run: The Campaign and Battle of Second Manassas.* New York: Simon & Schuster, 1993.

Hess, Earl J. *Lee's Tar Heels: The Pettigrew-Kirkland-MacRae Brigade.* Chapel Hill: University of North Carolina Press, 2002.

Hoch, Bradley R. *Thaddeus Stevens in Gettysburg: The Making of an Abolitionist.* Gettysburg: The Adams County Historical Society, 2005.

Holland, Lynwood M. *Pierce M. B. Young: The Warwick of the South.* Athens, Ga: University of Georgia Press, 1964.

Hollingshead, Steve and Jeffrey Whetstone. *From Winchester to Bloody Run: Border Raids and Skirmishes in Western Pennsylvania During the Gettysburg Campaign.* Privately published, 2004.

Hopkins, Donald A. *The Little Jeff: The Jeff Davis Legion, Cavalry, Army of Northern Virginia.* Shippensburg, Pa.: White Mane, 1999.

Hulbert, Archer Butler. *The Cumberland Road.* Cleveland: Arthur H. Clark, 1904.

——. *The Old National Road: A Chapter of American Expansion.* Columbus, Ohio: Press of F. J. Heer, 1901.

Hunt, Roger D. *Colonels in Blue: Union Army Colonels of the Civil War: The New England States: Connecticut, Maine, Massachusetts, New Hampshire, Rhode Island, Vermont.* Atglen, Pa.: Schiffer Military History, 2001.

——. *Colonels in Blue: Union Army Colonels of the Civil War: New York.* Atglen, Pa.: Schiffer Military History, 2003.

—— and Jack R. Brown. *Brevet Brigadier Generals in Blue.* Gaithersburg, Md.: Olde Soldier Books, 1990.

In Memoriam: Henry Warner Slocum 1826-1894. Albany, N. Y.: J. B. Lyon Co., 1904.

Johnson, Rossiter, ed. *The Twentieth Century Biographical Dictionary of Notable Americans.* 10 vols. Boston: The Biographical Society, 1904.

Keller, Roger S. *Events of the Civil War in Washington County, Maryland.* Shippensburg, Pa.: White Mane, 1995.

Kesterson, Brian Stuart. *Campaigning with the 17th Virginia Cavalry Night Hawks at Monocacy.* Washington, W.V.: Night Hawk Press, 2005.

Kirkland, Frazar. *The Pictorial Book of Anecdotes and Incidents of the War of the Rebellion.* Hartford, Conn.: Hartford Publishing Co., 1867.

Krick, Robert E. L. *40th Virginia Infantry.* Lynchburg, Va.: H. E. Howard Co., 1985.

——. *Staff Officers in Gray: A Biographical Register of the Staff Officers in the Army of Northern Virginia.* Chapel Hill: University of North Carolina Press, 2003.

Krick, Robert K. *Lee's Colonels.* Dayton, Ohio: Morningside House, 1991.

——. *13th Virginia Cavalry.* Lynchburg, Va.: H. E. Howard Co., 1982.

"Lee's Retreat from Gettysburg & Meade's Pursuit, 5-14 July 1863: Movements, Actions & Sites", unpublished manuscript in files, Gettysburg National Military Park, Gettysburg, Pennsylvania.

Longacre, Edward G. *The Cavalry at Gettysburg: A Tactical Study of Mounted Operations During the Civil War's Pivotal Campaign, 9 June-14 July 1863.* Rutherford, N.J.: Fairleigh Dickinson University Press, 1986.

——. *Custer and His Wolverines: The Michigan Cavalry Brigade 1861-1865.* Conshohocken, Pa.: Combined Books, 1997.

——. *Fitz Lee: A Military Biography of Major Fitzhugh Lee, C.S.A.* New York: DaCapo, 2004.

——. *General John Buford: A Military Biography.* Conshohocken, Pa.: Combined Books, 1995.

——. *Lee's Cavalrymen: A History of the Mounted Forces of the Army of Northern Virginia.* Mechanicsburg, Pa.: Stackpole Books, 2002.

——. *Lincoln's Cavalrymen: A History of the Mounted Forces of the Army of the Potomac.* Mechanicsburg, Pa.: Stackpole, 2000.

——. *The Man Behind the Guns: A Military Biography of General Henry J. Hunt, Chief of Artillery, Army of the Potomac.* Cambridge, Mass.: Da Capo Press, 2003.

Ludgin, Quentin. *Williamsport, Maryland: Grace Under Fire Project.* Kensington, MD: Forest Glen Commonwealth, n.d.

Mahood, Wayne. *General Wadsworth: The Life and Times of Brevet Major General James S. Wadsworth.* Cambridge, Mass.: Da Capo Press, 2003.

Maier, Larry B. *Leather and Steel: The 12th Pennsylvania Cavalry in the Civil War.* Shippensburg, Pa.: Burd Street Press, 2002.

Martin, Samuel J. *"Kill-Cavalry": Sherman's Merchant of Terror: The Life of Union General Hugh Judson Kilpatrick.* Madison, N. J.: Associated University Presses, 1996.

Meade, Richard Bache. *Life of George Gordon Meade Commander of the Army of the Potomac.* Philadelphia: Henry T. Coates & Co., 1897.

Mingus, Scott L., Sr. *Human Interest Stories of the Gettysburg Campaign.* Orrtanna, Pa.: Colecraft Industries, 2006.

——. *Human Interest Stories of the Gettysburg Campaign, Vol. 2.* Ortanna, Pa.: Colecraft Industries, 2007.

Monaghan, Jay. *Custer: The Life of General George Armstrong Custer.* Lincoln, Neb.: University of Nebraska Press, 1959.

Moore, Robert H. *Chew's, Ashby's, Shoemaker's Lynchburg and the Newtown Artillery.* Lynchburg, Va.: H. E. Howard Co., 1995.

——. *Graham's Petersburg, Jackson's Kanawha, and Lurty's Roanoke Horse Artillery.* Lynchburg, Va.: H. E. Howard Co., 1996.

——. *The 1st and 2nd Stuart Horse Artillery.* Lynchburg, Va.: H. E. Howard Co., 1985.

Morgan, James A., III. *Always Ready, Always Willing: A History of Battery M, Second United States Artillery from Its Organization Through the Civil War.* Gaithersburg, Md.: Olde Soldier, n.d.

Musick, Michael P. *6th Virginia Cavalry.* Lynchburg, Va.: H. E. Howard Co., 1990.

Musselman, Homer D. *47th Virginia Infantry.* Lynchburg, Va.: H. E. Howard Co., 1991.

Nanzig, Thomas P. *3rd Virginia Cavalry.* Lynchburg, Va.: H. E. Howard Co., 1989.

Nichols, James L. *General Fitzhugh Lee: A Biography.* Lynchburg, Va.: H. E. Howard Co., 1989.

Osborne, Charles C. *Jubal: The Life and Times of General Jubal A. Early, CSA.* Chapel Hill: Algonquin Books, 1992.

O'Sullivan, Richard. *55th Virginia Infantry.* Lynchburg, Va.: H. E. Howard Co., 1989.

Owen, Richard and James Owen. *Generals at Rest: The Grave Sites of the 425 Official Confederate Generals.* Shippensburg, Pa: White Mane Publishing Company, Inc., 1997.

Parsons, George W. *Put the Vermonters Ahead: The First Vermont Brigade in the Civil War.* Shippensburg, Pa.: White Mane Books, 2000.

Péladeau, Marius B., comp. *Burnished Rows of Steel: Vermont's Role in the Battle of Gettysburg, July 1-3, 1863.* Newport, Vt.: Vermont Civil War Enterprises, 2002.

Pennypacker, Isaac R. *General Meade.* New York: D. Appleton and Company, 1901.

Petrichick, Gary M. *Pocket Guide to the Civil War on the Chesapeake & Ohio Canal.* Belmont, N.Y.: Dave's Printing, 2003.

Pfanz, Donald C. *Richard S. Ewell: A Soldier's Life.* Chapel Hill: University of North Carolina Press, 1998.

Poirier, Robert G. *"By the Blood of Our Alumni": Norwich University Citizen Soldiers in the Army of the Potomac.* Mason City, Iowa: Savas-Woodbury, 1999.

——. *They Could Not Have Done Better: Thomas O. Seaver and the 3rd Vermont Infantry.* Newport, Vt.: Vermont Civil War Enterprises, 2005.

Rafuse, Ethan S. *George Gordon Meade and the War in the East.* Abilene, Texas: McWhiney Foundation Press, 2003.

Raiford, Neil Hunter. *The 4th North Carolina Cavalry in the Civil War.* Jefferson, N.C.: McFarland, 2003.

Robertson, James I., Jr. *General A. P. Hill.* New York: Random House, 1987.

Rollins, Richard. *The Damned Red Flags of the Rebellion: The Confederate Battle Flag at Gettysburg.* Redondo Beach, Calif.: Rank and File Publications, 1997.

Scharf, J. Thomas. *History of Western Maryland. Being a History of Frederick, Montgomery, Carroll, Washington, Allegany, and Garrett Counties from the Earliest Period to the Present Day; Including Biographical Sketches of Their Representative Men.* 2 vols. Philadelphia: L.H. Everts, 1882.

Schecter, Barnet. *The Devil's Own Work: The Civil War Draft Riots and the Fight to Reconstruct America.* New York: Walker & Co., 2005.

Schenck, John S. *Index of Persons in Ionia County Mentioned in History of Ionia and Montcalm Counties.* Lansing, Mich.: W.P.A. Project, 1940.

Schenck, Martin. *Up Came Hill: The Story of the Light Division and Its Leaders.* Harrisburg, Pa.: Stackpole, 1958.

Schildt, John W. *Roads from Gettysburg.* Shippensburg, Pa.: Burd Street Press, 1998.

Scott, J. L. *36th and 37th Battalions Virginia Cavalry.* Lynchburg, Va.: H. E. Howard Co., 1986.

Searight, Thomas B. *The Old Pike: A History of the National Road, with Incidents, Accidents, and Anecdotes Thereon.* Uniontown, Pa.: privately published, 1894.

Sears, Stephen W. *Gettysburg.* New York: Houghton-Mifflin, 2003.

______________. *Landscape Turned Red: The Battle of Antietam.* New Haven, Conn.: Ticknor & Fields, 1993.

Seilhamer, George O. *Biographical Annals of Franklin County, Pennsylvania: Containing Genealogical Records of Representative Families, Including Many of_the Early Settlers, and Biographical Sketches of Prominent Citizens.* Chicago: Genealogical Pub. Co., 1905.

Slade, A. D. *A. T. A. Torbert: Southern Gentleman in Union Blue.* Dayton, Ohio: Morningside House, 1992.

Smith, Carl. *Gettysburg 1863.* Sterling Heights, Mich.: Osprey, 1999.

Smith, Timothy H. *The Story of Lee's Headquarters, Gettysburg, Pennsylvania.* Gettysburg, Pa.: Thomas Publications, 1995.

Soderberg, Susan Cooke. *A Guide to Civil War Sites in Maryland: Blue and Gray in a Border State.* Shippensburg, Pa: White Mane Books, 1998.

Staats, Richard J. *The History of the Sixth Ohio Volunteer Cavalry 1861-1865: A Journal of Patriotism, Duty, and Bravery.* 2 vols. Westminster, Md.: Heritage Books, 2006.

Starr, Stephen Z. *The Union Cavalry in the Civil War.* 3 vols. Baton Rouge: Louisiana State University, 1975-1979.

Swinfen, David B. *Ruggles' Regiment: The 122nd New York Volunteers in the American Civil War.* Hanover, N.H.: University Press of New England, 1982.

Swisher, James K. *Warrior in Gray: General Robert Rodes of Lee's Army*. Shippensburg, Pa.: White Mane Books, 2000.

Taylor, Frank H. *Philadelphia in the Civil War, 1861-1865*. Philadelphia: published by the city, 1913.

Thomas, Benjamin P. and Harold M. Hyman. *Stanton: The Life and Times of Lincoln's Secretary of War*. New York: Alfred Knopf, 1962.

Thomas, Emory M. *Bold Dragoon: The Life of J.E.B. Stuart*. New York: Harper & Row, 1986.

Thomason, John W. *Jeb Stuart*. New York: Charles Scribner's Sons, 1930.

Trout, Robert J. *Galloping Thunder: The Stuart Horse Artillery Battalion*. Mechanicsburg, Pa.: Stackpole Books, 2002.

——. *The Hoss: Officer Biographies and Rosters of the Stuart Horse Artillery Battalion*. Myerstown, Pa: Jebflo Press, 2003.

——. *They Followed the Plume: The Story of J. E. B. Stuart and His Staff*. Mechanicsburg, Pa.: Stackpole Books, 1993.

Trudeau, Noah Andre. *Gettysburg: A Testing of Courage*. New York: Harper Collins, 2002.

Tucker, Glenn. *High Tide at Gettysburg*. New York: Bobbs-Merrill Co., 1958.

Tucker, Spencer C. *Brigadier General John D. Imboden: Confederate Commander in the Shenandoah*. Lexington: University of Kentucky Press, 2002.

Urwin, Gregory J. W. *Custer Victorious: The Civil War Battles of General George Armstrong Custer*. East Brunswick, N. J.: Associated University Presses, 1983.

Waite, Otis F. R. *Vermont in the Great Rebellion, Containing Historical and Biographical Sketches, Etc*. Claremont, N.H.: Tracy, Chase & Co., 1869.

Warner, Ezra J. *Generals in Gray: The Lives of the Confederate Commanders*. Baton Rouge: Louisiana State University Press, 1994.

Wert, Jeffry D. *Custer: The Controversial Life of George Armstrong Custer*. New York: Simon & Schuster, 1996.

——. *General James Longstreet: The Confederacy's Most Controversial Soldier*. New York: Simon & Schuster, 1993.

——. *The Sword of Lincoln: The Army of the Potomac*. New York: Simon & Schuster, 2005.

Whittaker, Frederick. *A Complete Life of General George A. Custer*. New York: Sheldon, 1876.

Williams, T. Harry. *Lincoln and His Generals*. New York: Alfred A. Knopf, 1952.

Williams, Thomas J. C. *History of Washington County, Maryland, from the Earliest Settlements to the Present Time, Including a History of Hagerstown*, 2 vols. Chambersburg, Pa.: J. M. Runk & L. R. Titsworth, 1906.

Wilson, Clyde N. *The Most Promising Young Man of the South: James Johnston Pettigrew and His Men at Gettysburg*. Abilene, Texas: McWhiney Foundation Press, 1998.

Wilson, James Harrison. *The Life and Services of Brevet Brigadier General Andrew Jonathan Alexander, Untied States Army*. New York: n.p., 1887.

——. *Life and Services of William Farrar Smith, Major General United States Volunteers in the Civil War.* Wilmington, Del.: John M. Rogers Press, 1904.

Winslow, Richard Elliott. *General John Sedgwick: The Story of a Union Corps Commander.* Novato, Calif.: Presidio Press, 1982.

Wittenberg, Eric J. *Gettysburg's Forgotten Cavalry Actions.* Gettysburg, Pa: Thomas Publications, 1998.

——. *Glory Enough for All: The Battle of Trevilian Station and Sheridan's Second Raid.* Dulles, Va.: Brassey's, 2001.

——. *Protecting the Flank: The Battles for Brinkerhoff's Ridge and East Cavalry Field, Battle of Gettysburg, July 2-3, 1863.* Celina, Ohio: Ironclad Publishing, 2002.

—— and J. David Petruzzi. *Plenty of Blame to Go Around: Jeb Stuart's Controversial Ride to Gettysburg.* New York: Savas Beatie LLC, 2006.

——. *Rush's Lancers: The Sixth Pennsylvania Cavalry in the Civil War.* Yardley, Pa.: Westholme Publishing, 2006.

Women's Club of Mercersburg. *Old Mercersburg.* New York: Frank Allaben Genealogical Co., 1912.

Woodward, Harold R., Jr. *Defender of the Valley: Brig. Gen. John D. Imboden, C.S.A.* Berryville, Va.: Rockbridge Publishing Co., 1996.

Zeller, Paul G. *The Second Vermont Volunteer Infantry Regiment, 1861-1865.* Jefferson, N. C.: McFarland, 2002.

Index

About the Authors

Eric J. Wittenberg is an accomplished American Civil War cavalry historian and author. An attorney in Ohio, Eric has authored or edited more than a dozen books on Civil War cavalry subjects, including *The Battle of Monroe's Crossroads and the Civil War's Final Campaign* (Savas Beatie, 2006). His first book, *Gettysburg's Forgotten Cavalry Actions* (Thomas Publications, Gettysburg PA., 1998) won the prestigious 1998 Bachelder-Coddington Literary Award. Eric has also penned dozens of articles in popular magazines such as *North & South*, *Blue & Gray*, *America's Civil War*, and *Gettysburg Magazine.* A favorite speaker at Civil War Roundtables, Eric enjoys conducting tours of cavalry battlefields and related sites. He was instrumental in saving important battlefield land at Trevilian Station, Virginia, and wrote the text for the historical wayside markers located there. Eric lives in Columbus with his wife Susan and their beloved dogs. He is the CEO of Ironclad Publishing Inc.

J. David Petruzzi, an insurance broker in Brockway, Pennsylvania, is a noted American Civil War cavalry historian and author. He wrote the historical text for one of the U.S. Army's recruiting pieces for modern armored and air cavalry and has instructed U.S. soldiers and soldiers of various nations on Civil War-era battlefield tactics and their application to modern maneuvers. His first book (with Eric Wittenberg) was the best-selling *Plenty of Blame to Go Around: Jeb Stuart's Controversial Ride to Gettysburg* (Savas Beatie, 2006). J. D. has also authored many magazine articles on Civil War cavalry topics for *America's Civil War*, *Civil War Times, Illustrated*, *The Gettysburg Magazine*, *Blue & Gray*, and *North & South.* A popular speaker at Civil War Roundtables and related conferences, J.D. also conducts living history programs as a Civil War cavalry officer, gives detailed tours of battlefields and related sites, and has appeared as a main character in two Civil War documentary movies. He is a partner in, and the Marketing Director for, Ironclad Publishing Inc.

A long time student of the Gettysburg Campaign, Michael F. Nugent is a retired US Army Armored Cavalry Officer and the descendant of a Civil War Cavalry soldier. A longtime student of the Civil War and military history, Mike is the author of a wide variety of published articles. *One Continuous Fight* is his first book. Nugent lives in Wells, Maine.